# Understanding Greek Religion

*Understanding Greek Religion* is one of the first attempts to fully examine any religion from a cognitivist perspective, applying methods and findings from the cognitive science of religion to the ancient Greek world. In this book, Jennifer Larson shows that many of the fundamentals of Greek religion, such as anthropomorphic gods, divinatory procedures, purity beliefs, reciprocity and sympathetic magic, arise naturally as by-products of normal human cognition. Drawing on evidence from across the ancient Greek world, Larson provides detailed coverage of Greek theology and local pantheons, rituals including processions, animal sacrifice and choral dance, and afterlife beliefs as they were expressed through hero-worship and mystery cults.

Eighteen in-depth essays illustrate the theoretical discussion with primary sources and include case studies of key cult inscriptions from Kyrene, Kos and Miletos. This volume features maps, tables and over twenty images to support and expand on the text, and provides conceptual tools for understanding the actions and beliefs that constitute a religion. Additionally, Larson offers the first detailed discussion of cognition and memory in the transmission of Greek religious beliefs and rituals, as well as a glossary of terms and a bibliographical essay on the cognitive science of religion.

*Understanding Greek Religion* is an essential resource for both undergraduate and postgraduate students of Greek culture and ancient Mediterranean religions.

**Jennifer Larson** is a professor of classics at Kent State University. Her research interests include Greek poetry, mythology and religion. She is the author of *Ancient Greek Cults: A Guide* (2007) and *Greek Nymphs: Myth, Cult, Lore* (2001).

"*Understanding Greek Religion* is the best possible introduction to ancient Greek religion. There is more to the Greek religion than poetic myths and strange rituals. Jennifer Larson starts from the crucial idea that the ancient Greeks were like us, in that they shared the same mental processes and lived in the same world. Larson shows how this means that there is a lot more that can be said about the role of religion in their lives than simple studies of the ancient texts can reveal. Anyone at all interested in ancient Greek religion should read this book."

Professor Hugh Bowden, *King's College London*

# Understanding Greek Religion

## A cognitive approach

**Jennifer Larson**

LONDON AND NEW YORK

First published 2016
by Routledge
2 Park Square, Milton Park, Abingdon, Oxon OX14 4RN

and by Routledge
711 Third Avenue, New York, NY 10017

*Routledge is an imprint of the Taylor & Francis Group, an informa business*



*British Library Cataloguing-in-Publication Data*
A catalogue record for this book is available from the British Library

*Library of Congress Cataloging-in-Publication Data*
Larson, Jennifer (Jennifer Lynn)
Understanding Greek religion: a cognitive approach / Jennifer Larson.— First [edition].
pages cm.— (Understanding the ancient world)
Includes bibliographical references and index.
1. Greece—Religion. I. Title.
BL783.L38 2016
292.08—dc23
2015032550

ISBN: 978-0-415-68845-1 (hbk)
ISBN: 978-0-415-68846-8 (pbk)
ISBN: 978-1-315-64701-2 (ebk)

Typeset in Times New Roman
by Apex CoVantage, LLC

Printed and bound in the United States of America by Publishers Graphics, LLC on sustainably sourced paper.

**In Memoriam**
**Walter Burkert**

# Contents

# Illustrations, maps and tables

## Illustrations

## Maps



## Tables

# Preface and acknowledgments

The human mind is not, after all, a blank slate upon which culture inscribes patterns of infinite variety. Instead, our minds are equipped from birth with an extensive collection of "software," mental tools which have evolved, just as our hands and teeth have evolved. Like teeth, not all of these tools are fully developed at birth. The best-known example is the universal grammar described by Noam Chomsky, which permits babies to learn their native language quickly and (relative to later second-language acquisition) effortlessly. Even as such tools enhance our cognitive abilities, they shape our cognition: our special ability to recognize human faces, for example, causes us to see them in everything from clouds to emoticons.

"Cognitive science" is the interdisciplinary study of the mind and its software, as opposed to neuroscience, which deals with the hardware of the brain and nervous system. The cognitive science of religion (CSR) is a subfield which studies religion as a set of beliefs and behaviors rooted in the evolutionary development of the mind. I hasten to add that there is no "god gene," and we are not "hardwired" to be religious. Rather, mental tools which have evolved for other purposes produce a tendency to favor and transmit the beliefs and behaviors we call "religious." Despite the variation which has led some theorists to consider religions incommensurable, striking cross-cultural patterns exist in the ways we humans mentally represent gods, spirits and the dead, how we behave toward them, the things we expect from them and how they affect our moral thought. "Religion" is by no means limited to interactions with these superhuman beings, yet such interactions are a hallmark of religion.

This book is the first to apply a wide range of concepts and findings drawn from CSR to ancient Greek religion, and one of the first attempts to fully examine any religion from a cognitivist perspective. As I write in 2015, however, cognitive science is not unknown to Classicists. Its usefulness in the study of oral transmission has been recognized by Homerists, and it has caught the attention of archaeologists. In the area of ancient religion, a few Romanists and scholars of Christianity and Late Antiquity have applied cognitive perspectives. Festinger's famous theory of cognitive dissonance has long informed Henk Versnel's work, and he has taken account of other cognitivist research.[1] Yet CSR has yet to gain much of a foothold among scholars in our discipline. Why make it the foundation for an introductory book, a genre which normally synthesizes familiar and well-established interpretations?

First, "understanding Greek religion" requires that we ask what religion itself is, and why religious beliefs and practices are ubiquitous in human cultures. CSR offers causal explanations of religious concepts and behaviors that recur cross-culturally, such as superhuman agents, divine anthropomorphism, reciprocity, magic, divination and purity practices. While the differences between Greek religion and other religions (say, Christianity or Hinduism) are obvious and undeniable, all religious beliefs and behaviors share the same cognitive foundations, because we all belong to one species equipped with one kind of mind. Individual and cultural diversity do not erase the fact of this unity any more than variable food choices and cuisines erase the fact that we all share the same nutritional requirements and an adaptive (or in many modern contexts, maladaptive) tendency to prefer sweet foods. To moderns, Greek religion can seem alien and bizarre, with its bloody sacrifices, dances and material gods. But the Greeks were not naively credulous people who inexplicably believed in weird things and kept performing "primitive" rituals simply because they were traditional. In fact, their tacit inferences about interaction with the gods had a surprising amount in common with those of other theists, no matter the period or culture.

Second, I expect that cognitive science will soon have a more significant impact upon both Classics and Classical archaeology. CSR, in particular, has generated a plethora of conferences, articles and books, as well as an international association and a number of journals.[2] Unlike standard social science models of religion, CSR consistently produces hypotheses which can be tested experimentally and either falsified or supported by experimental evidence and ethnographic data. For example, many thinkers have suggested that people believe in an afterlife because they are unable to imagine their own annihilation, but Jesse Bering was the first to put this "simulation hypothesis" to the test (see Chapter 5). For students of antiquity, cognitive science is attractive because it offers a new way to study the past. In evolutionary terms, neither our minds nor our bodies have changed much since antiquity. If it is true that the architecture of the mind predisposes us to religious thoughts and behaviors, it follows that studies using modern subjects have much to teach us about how ancient people's minds worked. How their minds worked is certainly not the whole story, but a convincing narrative of religion must begin from the understanding that all cultural constructs rest upon a deep bedrock of cognitive architecture.[3]

Third, multiple strands of recent scholarship in Greek religion mesh well with the findings of cognitivists. Especially pertinent in this regard are Henk Versnel's studies on inconsistency in religion, culminating in his 2011 book *Coping with the Gods: Wayward Readings in Greek Theology*. The new scholarly interest in gods and theology is an important point of contact with the cognitivists, as is the well-established topic of reciprocity. CSR has affinities with both the older study of religious mentalities and the newer interest in ritual dynamics.[4]

Even if it is ultimately predicated on psychological processes, religion is a social phenomenon. Greek religion, in particular, was deeply implicated in most every social institution. One of my readers asked me, "What does this approach tell us about religion and *power*?" Not much, perhaps, since knowledge of general cognitive architecture cannot predict the specifics of time and place.[5] Yet CSR reveals, I think, that the ability of the powerful to shape religious thoughts and behaviors for their own ends is more limited than we once believed. Moreover, our mental tools evolved to help us negotiate a social world of kin, allies and strangers. They affect group interactions in ways we are only just beginning to explore.

Another limitation of CSR is its inability to predict the impact of individual minds. Within our own subfield of Greek religion, I think of Walter Burkert, who remained committed throughout his career to the idea that underlying all religion, there is a biological substrate, shaped by evolution. This idea caught my imagination from the start of my own studies in Classics. Burkert was kind enough to correspond with me as a newly minted Ph.D., and when I met him many years later, I told him that my favorite among his books was *The Creation of the Sacred: Tracks of Biology in Early Religions* (1998). He wryly observed that I was probably unique in that respect. This book is dedicated to his memory.

We will never fully understand ancient Greek religion. Too much evidence has been lost. However clean our hands and however fluent our Greek, we cannot be initiated into the Eleusinian Mysteries. We will never witness a consultation of Apollo at Delphi, a dithyramb for Dionysos or the ox sacrifice for Zeus Polieus on Kos, and we cannot interview women in Kyrene about their adherence to purity laws. But even with these limitations, it is possible to improve on our current knowledge. Archaeological and papyrological discoveries keep adding to our evidence. New ways of organizing and interpreting that evidence continue to yield insights. And now, a new branch of cognitive science promises to help us better understand lost religions, through the study of living minds.

I wish to thank W. R. Connor, Alexander Herda, Anders Lisdorf, Luther H. Martin and Henk Versnel for conversations on topics related to this book and/or comments on chapters in draft form. Their generosity in corresponding with me does not imply their agreement with my views.

Lastly, there would be no book without my beloved husband, Bob, whom I thank with all my heart.

Jennifer Larson
Kent, Ohio
August 2015

## Notes

1 Oral transmission: e.g. Bakker 1990; Minchin 2001. Archaeology: Morgan 1996.45n.15–19 cites several important works by cognitivists in her discussion of transmission and continuity. See also Hodder ed. 2010, and the papers in Issue 1 of the *Journal of Cognitive Historiography* with commentary by Robert Parker (Parker

2014). Romanists: e.g. Beck 2006; Gragg 2004; essays in Martin and Pachis eds. 2009; Martin 2015. Christianity and late antiquity: e.g. Czachesz 2003; Czachesz and Uro 2013. An interesting early application of Dan Sperber's thought to Mithraism is found in Gordon 1980; compare Price 1984.8–9. Cognitive dissonance: Festinger 1957; Versnel 1990.1–38 and *passim*. For Greek religion see also Phillips 1996.284–5; Stowers 2011; Kindt 2012.36–8. Whitehouse's theory of religious modes is briefly discussed in Bowden 2010.15–17 and Stavrianopoulou 2011. I was unable to take account of Johnston 2015a and 2015b, which have several points of contact with my work.

2 Journals: see the bibliographical essay at the end of this volume.

3 Bedrock: see the foreword by John Tooby and Lena Cosmides in Baron-Cohen 1997. xi–xviii.

4 Gods and theology: see the papers in Bremmer and Erskine eds. 2010. Mentalities: e.g. papers in Versnel ed. 1981. Ritual dynamics: e.g. Hüsken ed. 2007; Chaniotis *et al.* eds. 2010; Chaniotis ed. 2011.

5 Religion and power: for a selection of papers on this topic in Greek religion see Hellström and Alroth eds. 1996.

## References


Bakker, Egbert J. 1990. Homeric discourse and enjambment: A cognitive approach. *TAPhA* 120: 1–21.

Baron-Cohen, Simon. 1997. *Mindblindness: An essay on autism and theory of mind*. Cambridge, MA: MIT Press.

Beck, Roger. 2006. *The religion of the Mithras cult in the Roman empire: Mysteries of the unconquered Sun*. Oxford: Oxford University Press.

Bowden, Hugh. 2010. *Mystery cults of the ancient world*. Princeton and Oxford: Princeton University Press.

Bremmer, Jan and Andrew Erskine, eds. 2010. *The gods of ancient Greece: Identities and transformations*. Edinburgh: Edinburgh University Press.

Chaniotis, Angelos, ed. 2011. *Ritual dynamics in the ancient Mediterranean*. Dresden: Franz Steiner Verlag.

Chaniotis, Angelos, Silke Leopold, Hendrik Schulze, Eric Venbrux, Thomas Quartier, Joanna Wojtkowiak, Jan Weinhold and Geoffrey Samuel, eds. 2010. *Ritual dynamics and the science of ritual, Vol. II: Body, performance, agency and experience*. Wiesbaden: Harrassowitz Verlag.

Czachesz, István. 2003. The Gospels and cognitive science. In *Learned antiquity*, ed. MacDonald, Twomey and Reinink, 25–36.

Czachesz, István and Risto Uro, eds. 2013. *Mind, morality and magic: Cognitive science approaches in Biblical studies*. Durham: Acumen.

Festinger, Leon. 1957. *A theory of cognitive dissonance*. Stanford, CA: Stanford University Press.

Gordon, R. L. 1980. Reality, evocation and boundary in the mysteries of Mithras. *Journal of Mithraic Studies* 3: 19–99.

Gragg, Douglas L. 2004. Old and new in Roman religion: A cognitive account. In *Theorizing religions past*, ed. Whitehouse and Martin, 69–86.

Hellström, Pontus and Brita Alroth, eds. 1996. *Religion and power in the ancient Greek world*. Uppsala: Almqvist and Wiksell.

Hodder, Ian, ed. 2010. *Religion in the emergence of civilization: Çatalhöyük as a case study*. Cambridge and New York: Cambridge University Press.

Hüsken, Ute, ed. 2007. *When rituals go wrong: Mistakes, failure and the dynamics of ritual*. Leiden and Boston: Brill.

Johnston, Sarah Iles. 2015a. Narrating myths: Story and belief in ancient Greece. *Arethusa* 48.173–218.

Johnston, Sarah Iles. 2015b. The Greek mythic story world. *Arethusa* 48.283–311.

Kindt, Julia. 2012. *Rethinking Greek religion*. Cambridge and London: Cambridge University Press.

Knust, Jennifer W. and Zsuzsanna Várhelyi, eds. 2011. *Ancient Mediterranean sacrifice*. New York and London: Oxford University Press.

MacDonald, Alasdair A., Michael W. Twomey and Gerrit Jan Reinink. 2003. *Learned antiquity: Scholarship and society in the Near-East, the Greco-Roman world, and the early medieval West*. Leuven: Peeters.

Martin, Luther H. 2015. *The mind of Mithraists: Historical and cognitive studies in the Roman cult of Mithras*. London and New York: Bloomsbury.

Martin, Luther H. and Panayotis Pachis, eds. 2009. *Imagistic traditions in the Graeco-Roman world: A cognitive modeling of history of religious research*. Thessaloniki: Vanias Editions.

Minchin, Elizabeth. 2001. *Homer and the resources of memory: Some applications of cognitive theory to the Iliad and the Odyssey*. Oxford and New York: Oxford University Press.

Morgan, Catherine. 1996. From palace to polis? Religious developments on the Greek Mainland during the Bronze Age/Iron Age transition. In *Religion and power in the ancient Greek world*, ed. Hellström and Alroth, 41–57.

Parker, Robert. 2014. Commentary on journal of cognitive historiography, Issue 1. *Journal of Cognitive Historiography* 1 (2). DOI: 10.1558/jch.v1i2.26007.

Phillips, C. Robert III. 1996. Review of Jan Bremmer. *Greek Religion CP* 91 (3): 281–6.

Price, Simon. 1984. *Rituals and power: The Roman imperial cult in Asia Minor*. Cambridge: Cambridge University Press.

Stavrianopoulou, Eftychia. 2011. The role of tradition in the forming of rituals in ancient Greece. In *Ritual dynamics*, ed. Chaniotis, 85–103.

Stowers, Stanley. 2011. The religion of plant and animal offerings versus the religion of meanings, essences and textual mysteries. In *Ancient Mediterranean sacrifice*, ed. Knust and Várhelyi, 35–56.

Versnel, Henk S., ed. 1981. *Faith, hope, and worship: Aspects of religious mentality in the ancient world*. Leiden: Brill.

Versnel, Henk S. 1990. *Inconsistencies in Greek and Roman religion I. Ter unus: Isis, Dionysos, Hermes. Three studies in henotheism*. Leiden and New York: Brill.

Versnel, Henk S. 2011. *Coping with the gods: Wayward readings in Greek theology*. Leiden: Brill.

Whitehouse, Harvey and Luther H. Martin, eds. 2004. *Theorizing religions past: Archaeology, history, and cognition*. Walnut Creek, CA: Altamira Press.

# Using this book

This book was written for students who are interested in religion studies, Greek religion and/or the cognitive science of religion. I hope that my specialist colleagues in the latter two fields will also find it of interest, for although it is an introductory work, the approach will strike most Classicists as novel, while the culture-specific content will be unfamiliar to most anthropologists and other researchers involved in the interdisciplinary field of CSR.

Each chapter of *Understanding Greek Religion* begins with an introduction to a thematic topic and an explanation of cognitive approaches to the evidence, insofar as I have found it useful to apply them. Each introduction is followed by three essays which delve further into specifics, often with an emphasis on primary sources. Several of the essays are "case studies" of inscriptions or cults, others further illustrate the application of CSR to specific problems, and still others discuss aspects of Greek religion to which CSR is less relevant. The purpose of the essays is to counter the generalizations necessary in an introductory work by letting readers glimpse the complexities of the source material. Given limitations of space, this strategy risks leaving gaps in coverage, but enhances the richness and accuracy of what remains. I trust the gaps are not chasms so wide as to detract from the value of the work as a description of Greek religion.

The chapters are designed to be read in the order they are presented, for successive chapters build on concepts and terms previously introduced. However, readers less familiar with the ancient Greek world may find it useful to consult (together with the introductory material in Chapter 1) the synopsis of historical developments in Greek religion provided in Chapter 6. For an accurate presentation of CSR, it is unfortunately necessary to use a certain amount of jargon, including a few familiar words (representation, relevance, etc.) which have special definitions in this context. Therefore I provide a glossary at the end of the book; I have also included a brief essay describing the origins of CSR as well as key topics, scholars and works.

To keep the bibliography to a feasible size, I have favored works from the 1990s to the present, and I have not attempted to provide full bibliographies of each topic. For convenience, plural festival names are treated as singular.

All dates in this book are BCE unless otherwise specified.

# Abbreviations

For most Greek authors, titles of works and familiar Greek names (Oedipus, Achilles, Crete) I use the conventional English spellings; other Greek words are transliterated. Abbreviations of Classics journals are those used in *L'Année philologique*. The names of non-Classics journals are given in full. Abbreviations of ancient authors conform to the usage of the *Oxford Classical Dictionary* (fourth edition). Other abbreviations are listed here.

| | |
|---|---|
| *BGU* | 1895–1937. *Aegyptische Urkunden aus den koeniglichen Museen zu Berlin. Griechische Urkunden.* Berlin: Weidmann. |
| *CEG* | Peter A. Hansen, ed. 1983. *Carmina epigraphica Graeca saeculorum VIII-V a. Chr. n.* Berlin and New York: Walter de Gruyter. |
| *CEG2* | Peter A. Hansen, ed. 1989. *Carmina epigraphica Graeca saeculi IV a. Chr. n.* Berlin and New York: Walter de Gruyter. |
| *CIE* | Karl Pauli *et al.*, eds. 1893–. *Corpus inscriptionum Etruscarum.* Leipzig: Barth. |
| *CVA* | *Corpus vasorum antiquorum* http://www.cvaonline.org/cva/ |
| *DI* | Albert Rehm and Richard Harder, eds. 1958. *Didyma II: Die Inschriften.* Berlin: von Zabern. |
| *DK* | Hermann Diels and W. Kranz, eds. 1951. *Die Fragmente der Vorsokratiker.* Sixth edition. Zurich: Weidmann. |
| *FGrH* | Felix Jacoby *et al.* 1923–. *Die Fragmente der griechischen Historiker.* Berlin and Leiden. |
| *GJ* | Fritz Graf and Sarah Iles Johnston. 2013. *Ritual texts for the afterlife: Orpheus and the Bacchic gold tablets.* Second edition. London and New York: Routledge. |
| *IG* | 1903-. *Inscriptiones Graecae.* |
| *I.Lindos* | Christian Blinkenberg. 1941. *Lindos: Fouilles et recherches, II. Fouilles de l'Acropole. Inscriptions.* Berlin: Walter de Gruyter. |
| *I.Magn.* | Otto Kern, ed. 1900. *Die Inschriften von Magnesia am Maeander.* Berlin: W. Spemann. |
| *LIMC* | 1981–2009. *Lexicon iconographicum mythologiae classicae.* Zurich: Artemis. |

*LP* Edgar Lobel and Denys Page, eds. 1955. *Poetarum Lesbiorum fragmenta.* Oxford: Clarendon Press.

*LSAM* F. Sokolowski. 1955. *Lois sacrées de l'Asie mineure.* Paris: de Boccard.

*LSCG* F. Sokolowski. 1969. *Lois sacrées des cités grecques.* Paris: de Boccard.

*LSS* F. Sokolowski. 1962. *Lois sacrées des cités grecques.* Supplement. Paris: de Boccard.

*Milet* Theodor Wiegand *et al.*, eds. 1906-. *Milet: Ergebnisse der Ausgrabungen und Untersuchungen seit dem Jahre 1899.* Berlin: G. Reimer.

*ML* Russell Meiggs and David M. Lewis, eds. 1988. *A selection of Greek historical inscriptions to the end of the fifth century BC.* Revised edition. Oxford: Clarendon Press.

*MW* R. Merkelbach and M. L. West, eds. 1967. *Fragmenta Hesiodea.* Oxford: Clarendon Press.

*OF* Bernabé, Alberto, ed. 2004–5. *Poetae epici Graeci II. Orphicorum et Orphicis similium testimonia et fragmenta.* Two fascicles. Munich and Leipzig: Sauer.

*PCG* R. Kassel and C. Austin, eds. 1983–91. *Poetae comici Graeci.* Berlin and New York: Walter de Gruyter.

*PMG* Denys L. Page, ed. 1962. *Poetae melici Graeci.* Oxford: Clarendon Press.

*PSI* G. Vitelli *et al.*, eds. 1912–. *Papyri greci e latini.* Società Italiana per la ricerca dei papyri greci e latini in Egitto. Florence: Le Monnier.

*RE* G. Wissowa *et al.*, eds. 1894–1980. *Paulys Real-encyclopädie der classischen Altertumswissenschaft.* Stuttgart and Munich: Metzler.

*RO* Rhodes, P. J. and Robin Osborne, eds. 2003. *Greek historical inscriptions 404–323 B.C.* Oxford and New York: Oxford University Press.

*SEG* *Supplementum Epigraphicum Graecum.* Leiden: Brill. http://referenceworks.brillonline.com/browse/supplementum-epigraphicum-graecum

*ThesCRA* 2004–14. *Thesaurus cultus et rituum antiquorum.* Los Angeles: J. Paul Getty Museum.

# 1 What is Greek religion?

*Scholars of a relatively new discipline, the cognitive science of religion (CSR), are proposing new approaches to religion which challenge long-standing methodologies in anthropology and sociology as well as Classics. In their view, the human mind is supplied with an array of mental tools which give rise to religious beliefs and practices as by-products of normal cognition. After surveying the geographical and chronological boundaries of our investigation, we turn to the dual-process model, a fundamental cognitive principle which helps to explain why the Greeks were not distressed by what we often perceive as logical inconsistencies in their religion (e.g. between the local and Panhellenic personas of the gods). We then consider the dual-process model in the context of appropriate materials and methods for studying Greek religion, and conclude with the "minimally counter-intuitive concept," another key idea in CSR. The illustrative essays examine strategies for conceptualizing the unlimited Greek pantheon, the interaction between Homer's Hera and the Hera(s) of cult, and the nature of reciprocity, an adaptive feature of human social behavior which is also fundamental to Greek religion.*

## What is religion? A debate in progress

To most people, the proposition that "religion" is mainly about worshiping God or gods is not particularly controversial. They may stipulate in addition that religion is a source of moral instruction, afterlife hopes or emotional support, but higher power(s), however defined, remain at the center of popular perceptions of religion. In the academy, however, a very different attitude has long prevailed, particularly in the social sciences. Definitions of religion have mostly avoided superhuman beings, as if they were an embarrassment. Philosophers of religion have denied that the metaphysical truth claims of religion ("God exists") can be judged as such.[1] Pointing to religious traditions that are supposedly non-theist, scholars of religion have struggled to agree on what constitutes a "religion," and they have favored broadly inclusive definitions.

Anthropologist Clifford Geertz asserted that religions are symbolic systems which people employ both to invest their world with meaning and to operate within that world. Robert N. Bellah, a sociologist, similarly defined religion as "a set of symbolic forms and acts that relate man to the ultimate conditions of his existence."[2] Rather than acknowledging the role of deities, these definitions focus on how people use symbols to answer the big unknowns about life, death and the cosmos, and on how the answers shape their behavior in everyday life.

A very different approach, that of phenomenology, finds the core of religion in the experience of the "sacred" as opposed to the profane; or in the "numinous," that which is wholly alien and therefore frightening, but also possesses a strong power of fascination. From this fundamental experience of something transcendent and unknowable flow our varied cultural understandings of life, death and the cosmos. The phenomenologists include Rudolf Otto and Mircea Eliade. In spite of their mystical bent, they are reluctant to frame religion in terms of gods, preferring impersonal formulations such as "the holy" or "the sacred."[3]

Very few thinkers have concluded that religion is primarily about human relationships with God or gods, and some have denied that gods have anything to do with religion.[4] Émile Durkheim, the father of sociology, defined religion as an "eminently collective thing," a system of beliefs and practices that unites people in a moral community. Sigmund Freud asserted that religion was "an illusion," noted similarities between religion and mental disorders, and traced the roots of religion to childhood fears and desires. Karl Marx described religion as "the sigh of the oppressed creature . . . the opiate of the people," a soothing fantasy which functioned to reconcile the poor to their wretched condition.[5]

More recently, some scholars have concluded that "religion" is not a useful conceptual category for comparative study because the widely varying phenomena we refer to as religions do not have enough in common to justify grouping them together. Jonathan Z. Smith wrote in *Imagining Religion* that religion cannot be distinguished from culture:

> While there is a staggering amount of data, phenomena, of human experiences and expressions that might be characterized in one culture or another, by one criterion or another, as religion – there is no data for religion. It is created for the scholar's analytic purposes by his imaginative acts of comparison and generalization. Religion has no existence apart from the academy.[6]

The theorists of a relatively new discipline, the cognitive science of religion (CSR), are offering surprising new definitions which refocus attention on the role of gods and other superhuman beings in world religions. Already in 1966, Melford Spiro defined religion as "an institution consisting of culturally patterned interaction with culturally postulated super-human beings."[7] Cognitivist scholars such as Todd Tremlin likewise consider superhuman agents, whether they are gods, demons, angels, spirits, ghosts or ancestors, central to the phenomenon of religion:

> While the history of religious studies is marked by an inability to yield a working definition of "religion" – to say nothing of universal agreement that gods are even a necessary component of such a definition – focus on human cognition makes the troublesome task of defining religion easier by showing,

in an empirically testable fashion, that the common variable in discussions of religion at any level – from its slate of beliefs to its system of rituals to its organizational principles – is indeed commitment to superhuman agents.
(Tremlin 2006.164)

Not all cognitivists would agree with Tremlin's absolute formulation, yet a focus on human perceptions of superhuman agency is distinctive of their work. Illka Pyysiäinen offers a less restrictive definition: "Religion is a phenomenon based on the human ability to form counterintuitive ideas, metarepresent them, and treat them symbolically."[8] In this and the following chapters, I will explain the terminology used by Pyysiäinen in more detail. For now it is sufficient to note that the most common "counterintuitive idea" in world religions is an anthropomorphic being with nonhuman superpowers, like invisibility, flight or mind-reading.[9] Dan Sperber, whose ideas have been foundational to CSR, prefers to think of religion as a polythetic or "family resemblance" category under which we can classify a number of related phenomena.[10] This is the best approach for Greek religion, because even if gods or heroes or the dead are central to most of its strands, they cannot account for all.

CSR posits that humans think by applying a variety of mental tools to representational structures (concepts and beliefs). At birth, the mind-brain is not a blank slate, but possesses blueprints for discrete, interlocking systems which govern perception, learning and memory. These systems constrain and shape our perceptions and thoughts to a far greater extent than we realize. A fundamental insight of the cognitive approach to religion is that our mental architecture creates a susceptibility to representations of superhuman agents, a tendency to find them memorable, compelling and plausible.[11] The same is true for magical beliefs, pollution/purity beliefs and certain other widely distributed subsets of religious thought. Together, these beliefs form the bedrock on which ritual, doctrinal and social outcomes are constructed. Religious thought, the cognitivists say, is nowhere near as variable among cultures as social scientists and historians have claimed, but instead manifests itself according to highly predictable patterns. Nor do truly non-theistic religions exist, although religious traditions may develop non-theistic doctrines. Theravada Buddhism is often cited as a non-theistic religion, but interaction with superhuman agents is typical of Theravada traditions in practice.[12] Such contradictions between doctrine and practice often reflect an important distinction between two forms of processing used by the human brain, which I will discuss below: intuitive and reflective cognition.

CSR faces an uphill battle in several sectors of the academy, where it will inevitably be criticized for reducing religion in all its complexity to a set of cognitive biases, and giving short shrift to social dimensions, cultural specificity and complex doctrines.[13] Because it echoes certain Tylorean and Frazerian ideas, it is vulnerable to caricature as "animism plus experiments."[14] Yet a central principle of CSR, that the same cognitive mechanisms underlie all religious experience, refutes the persistent nineteenth-century paradigm of primitivism, of "lower" forms of religion succeeded by "higher" ones. A cognitivist perspective has the potential to enrich our understanding of the role of religion in human experience. It asserts that religion is more than the sum of its political and social functions, a conclusion which challenges common theoretical assumptions in some fields (particularly Classical archaeology and ancient history).[15] Among other things, CSR convincingly explains why religious and paranormal beliefs have not faded away in the modern West for lack of empirical evidence to support them. Instead, such beliefs still thrive because humans continue to possess the same mental architecture that gave rise to religion in the first place. Religious thinking, it would seem, is natural.[16]

Past experience shows that a single theoretical stance or method will never tell us all we wish to know about religions. They must be studied from many disciplinary perspectives, including those of the social sciences and humanities. While CSR may have much to tell us about cross-cultural patterns in religion, it becomes more challenging to apply cognitivist methods as we focus in more detail on specific cultures and traditions.[17] Exactly where the limits lie remains to be seen. In this book, I will show that many aspects of Greek religion (e.g. the anthropomorphism of its gods, its methods of divination and its conceptions of pollution and purity) have a basis in human cognitive architecture. Current cognitive models attempting to map the relations between ritual and society, discussed in Chapter 4, yield mixed results when applied to Greek religion, and yet these models are useful heuristic tools, pointing the way to further research.

Scholars of Greek religion have long focused primarily on its social aspects. By now it is a commonplace to observe that ancient Greek religion was embedded in social and political institutions.[18] We are accustomed to "explaining" religious phenomena in functionalist terms, describing how religious beliefs and behaviors strengthened social cohesion and constructed identity. But heightened group identification and the other social "functions" of religion may be effects rather than causes. That they account for the genesis and transmission of religious ideas and behaviors is more often assumed than demonstrated. Then too, we seldom consider the possibility that religious beliefs and behaviors may have been neutral or even harmful in their effects on the long-term survival of a group. It is difficult to identify a benefit, for example, in the arbitrary Spartan refusal to fight during the festival of Karneia, which caused them to arrive too late at Marathon, and to send a reduced contingent to Thermopylai.[19]

The social aspects of Greek religion are apparent to every student, but religion does not exist solely by virtue of the group. Instead, it exists by virtue of the properties of individual minds. There are no private religions, yet every religious idea begins with an individual mind shaped by human cognitive constraints.[20] Such ideas are then elaborated and transmitted through social interaction to become part of a "religion." In order to understand Greek religion, we need to begin with the mind. The Greeks were confident that their gods and goddesses existed and intervened in the world. For the most part, they gave credence to the content of their myths.[21] They believed that some people were powerful after their deaths, able to affect the world of the living. They thought that oracles revealed the will of the gods. These individual and cultural beliefs had important social consequences. But why would anyone believe these things in the first place?

Classicists who study the Greeks and their gods often observe that the English word "religion" has no equivalent in Greek. That the Greeks lacked an equivalent word or concept does not mean that they lacked religion, but it does present us with a preliminary challenge: we need to identify which aspects of Greek culture are under study in this book, and just what it is that we are attempting to understand.[22] Definitions of religion drawn from sociology and anthropology tend to reflect the distinctive concerns of those disciplines. For our purposes, therefore, I prefer to begin by considering how the word "religion" has typically been used in written English. Fortunately, the lexicographers of the *Oxford English Dictionary* have already performed this descriptive work:

> Religion: Belief in or acknowledgement of some superhuman power or powers (esp. a god or gods) which is typically manifested in obedience, reverence, and worship; such a belief as part of a system defining a code of living, esp. as a means of achieving spiritual or material improvement.[23]

The lexicographical definition, with its heavy emphasis on superhuman powers, overlaps with concepts which were native to Greek culture, such as *eusebeia*, "reverence [toward the gods]" or *ta theia*, "divine matters." The second part, however, is more difficult to align with Greek religion: "such a belief as part of a system defining a code of living, esp. as a means of achieving spiritual or material improvement." This part of the definition has been influenced by the Jewish and Christian traditions, which include detailed codes of personal conduct ordained by a deity. The role of the Greek gods was typically to guarantee and enforce moral conduct rather than to define it. Greek culture, however, had no lack of systems defining a code of living; these were formulated by the poets and philosophers, many of whom were interested in the relationship between the individual and the gods, as well as the relationship between justice and the eschatological fate of the individual. Poets and philosophers also offered alternative answers to another dimension of religion which is omitted from the *OED* definition, but present in other dictionary definitions: explanation of the origin, nature and purpose of human beings, and of the universe.

Surveys of Greek religion often treat mythology, morality, cosmology and eschatology as marginal to the subject, but these are all pertinent to the modern conceptual category of "religion." In worship contexts, Greek religion dealt selectively and sporadically with morality and eschatology, and scarcely at all with cosmology; these matters were instead taken up by the poets and philosophers. The overlap between mythology and worship has been a subject of historical debate and will be treated in Chapter 2.[24] A principal goal of this book is to work toward an understanding of Greek religion in daily practice, with a focus on its ritual component, but reflection on and speculation about the gods, their history and their relationship to humanity are also an important part of what we understand by "religion."

## Everything is full of gods

Every culture produces one or more sets of beliefs about what the world around us is and how it works. Like virtually every other people in the ancient Mediterranean and Near East, the Greeks were polytheists who assumed that the world was full of gods. But the distinction between polytheism, likely the most ancient form of religion, and monotheism, a newer form which defined itself against polytheism, is not necessarily as clear as it seems at first glance. In spite of their claim to exclude all but one god, monotheistic traditions typically posit the existence of multiple superhuman beings (angels, jinn, saints, demons). Polytheistic traditions, for their part, may possess concepts of divine unity. This is the result of theological speculation, but it is not necessarily "late." The *Rig Veda*, one of the oldest canonical texts of Hinduism, describes an original "One" deity who may have been the creator of the cosmos. Later Vedic literature elaborated the concept of the Absolute (Brahman) as the highest reality.[25] The Hellenistic Greek Isis cult developed a theology according to which the goddess encompassed all divine sovereignty within herself.[26] On a far simpler level, a Greek could speak of "the god" or "the divine" rather than a specific deity. Herodotus demonstrated this usage in his account of the Athenian sage Solon's conversation with Kroisos, king of Lydia:

> Kroisos, you ask me about human affairs, I who know that the divine (*to theion*) is utterly grudging and troublesome.
>
> (Hdt. 1.32.1)

Artabanos similarly says to the Persian king Xerxes:

> Life is so wretched that death has become the most elect place of refuge for the human being; the god (*ho theos*) is found to be grudging in this, giving us a mere taste of life's sweetness.
>
> (Hdt. 7.46.4)

In these cases, the speaker is not claiming that only one god exists, but is temporarily conceptualizing the divine as a unity. Herodotus' usage was common among the Greeks.[27] Although the apparent contradiction with "polytheism" in these cases has puzzled scholars, such logical inconsistencies are typical of polytheism and, it should be stated, of religious thought in general. A cognitivist perspective will allow us to understand why. Similarly, polytheists use a variety of strategies to conceptually manage the large number of gods, goddesses, heroes, heroines and other superhuman beings in their cosmologies (Essay 1.1).

During the period we are studying, "belief" and "faith" were not part of the standard discourse about the gods. This was not because the Greeks lacked religious beliefs or were preoccupied with ritual at the expense of belief. That the gods existed and intervened in human affairs was a widely shared inference rather than an article of faith.[28] Confessions of faith happen when adherents to a sect or tradition feel the need to define themselves against others who hold incompatible beliefs. Early Christians, for example, defined themselves against non-Christian Jews by affirming that Jesus was the long-awaited Messiah. In the Gospel of Matthew (16:15–16), Jesus asks Peter, "But who do you say that I am?" and Peter replies, "You are the Christ, the son of the living God." This affirmation of belief in a proposition not accepted by others is a litmus test for membership in the group. Ancient polytheistic religions, and more particularly Greek religion, rarely involved such tests. It was the normal practice in hymns and prayers to affirm the powers, titles and territorial possessions of a particular deity, but the purpose of these affirmations was praise, not confession of belief:

> Oh Lord, you possess both Lykia and lovely Meionia,
> As well as Miletos, a delightful city beside the sea.
> But over sea-girt Delos you mightily rule in person.
> (*Hymn. Hom. Ap.* 179–81)

Generally, the Greeks viewed their myths as accounts of real events in the distant past, but whether one believed a particular story about Apollo among the many told by the poets was a matter of individual opinion, and did not necessarily reflect on one's overall level of piety. Nor was there a competitive marketplace of religions of the kind we observe in the modern West, where individuals choose, maintain and discard religious traditions and beliefs based on personal inclination.[29] Instead, one inherited a set of gods, heroes and rituals belonging to one's family and place of birth. Unless an individual emigrated or lived in a multicultural setting, there was no need to choose a personal pantheon, even if a few cults (notably those involving mysteries) were elective. Nor did the Greeks share the modern perception that there exist distinct religions with more or less incompatible doctrines and customs. Instead of viewing the Egyptian or Babylonian systems as competing or erroneous religions, they typically assumed that these peoples were worshiping the same gods under different names. A Greek who worshiped the Egyptian god Ammon was not an apostate from the cult of Zeus. In fact, he likely assumed that Zeus *was* Ammon. Where there was no clear equivalent, moreover, new and foreign deities could be absorbed into existing local pantheons.

## When and where

The ancient Greeks ranged far beyond Greece. As the Mycenaean civilization was collapsing at the end of the Bronze Age, Greeks of varying ethnicity – Achaians, Aiolians, Dorians – emigrated to Cyprus and Asia Minor. Trade emporia and colonies were established overseas even as a new kind of state, the Greek polis, began to emerge during the eighth century.[30] A map of selected Greek-speaking cities in the Mediterranean and the Black Sea during the Archaic period (ca. 550) reveals how these people blanketed the coastlines and the islands, reaching Phasis (modern Poti, Georgia) in the east, Naukratis on the Egyptian delta and Emporion (Empúries, Spain) in the west. Only in Greece itself did Greeks penetrate and occupy the hinterlands.

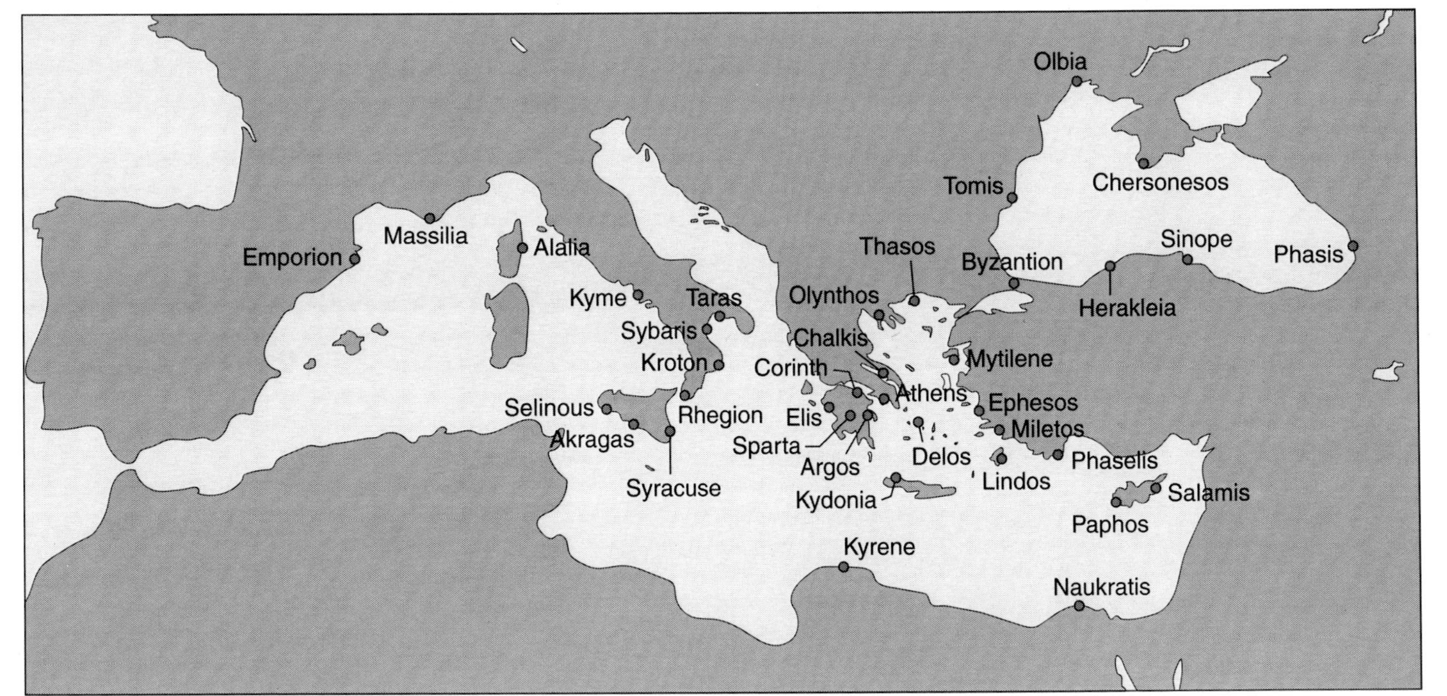


*Map 1.1* Greek-speaking populations in the Mediterranean and Black Sea during the Archaic period.

Given their far-flung settlements, it is no surprise that the Greeks lacked any form of national or political unity before the short-lived empire of Alexander the Great. They often regarded one another with suspicion, as enemies and foreigners. They spread across the Mediterranean and the Black Sea, yet all traced their traditions to ancestral homelands in what we now call Greece. Their poets sang the struggles of great men and women who had lived in the distant but glorious past: battles to the death before seven-gated Thebes, or on the windy plain at Troy. They spoke a common language, albeit in multiple dialects. Many of their gods and rituals too were shared, but (to use the metaphor of language) the morphology and syntax of Greek religion varied from one place to the next. Although its variations were seemingly limitless, they were mutually intelligible, and Greek people shared a remarkably consistent set of inferences about the gods, and how to worship them, over the course of several centuries. This is what allows us to speak of "Greek religion" as a unity, rather than attempting to address a bewildering number of distinct "Greek religions."[31]

Of which centuries are we speaking? Temporally, our investigation will encompass a lengthy period, beginning with the "Greek Renaissance," when the Greek polis first appeared and the Homeric and Hesiodic oral traditions, with their accounts of the gods, were first committed to writing (i.e. the eighth century). The Archaic period, which saw the consolidation of Greek political systems and a growing awareness of Panhellenic culture, is conventionally dated from 800 to 480, the year the Persian king Xerxes invaded Greece. The subsequent Classical period was characterized by a great flowering of Greek poetry, art, philosophy and historiography. These cultural productions brought religion to new heights (as in the refinement of techniques for temple architecture and sculpture), but they also involved critiques of traditional religion (as in the dialogues of Plato and the plays of Euripides). Greek philosophers defined the divine in new ways, and a new culture of philosophical rationalism took root among the educated minority. Political instability in the wake of the Peloponnesian War, and the exigencies of the war itself, damaged the prestige of venerable religious institutions, such as the Delphic oracle.

The dominant political structure, the independent Greek city-state or polis with its priests and festivals of the civic gods, was profoundly changed when the Macedonian Alexander brought a great swath of the ancient Mediterranean and Near East under his sole dominion. Alexander's death in 323 ended the Classical period and ushered in the Hellenistic, a time of ongoing political upheavals, widening disparities between the privileged and the poor, transformative encounters with non-Greek peoples, and new intellectual currents. During this period, the civic structures of many Greek poleis remained in place and the apparatus of traditional religion continued to function, but in a changed environment which inevitably affected its practice and interpretation.[32] Therefore, our discussion will focus on the Archaic and Classical periods, but with glances back to the prehistoric substrate of Greek religion, and forward to the Hellenistic period, particularly the century after Alexander's death.

## Local and Panhellenic religion

In spite of their political fragmentation and their constant wars with one another, the Greeks possessed a shared cultural heritage, and recognized that this was so.[33] Besides their common language, three pillars of this heritage were participation in athletic contests we call "Panhellenic" (most conspicuously those for Zeus at Olympia), consultation of Apollo's oracle at Delphi, and familiarity with the legend of the Trojan War as it was handed down in epic poetry under the name of Homer. Each of these cultural phenomena was in place by the end of the eighth century, and while not every city in the far-flung Greek world could send athletes to Olympia or set its weightiest questions before Apollo at Delphi, all acknowledged the prestige of these institutions. Implicit in these phenomena was a set of theological beliefs: the cosmos was inhabited by a great many gods, of whom the most important lived in a heavenly place, Olympos, in a blessed society of immortals; Zeus was the most powerful of these gods; the gods intervened in human affairs; mortals learned the will of the gods through Apollo's oracular pronouncements.

Beginning in early Archaic times, if not earlier, a constant and dynamic tension existed between Panhellenic ("pertaining to all the Greeks") and distinctively local components of Greek culture. Nowhere was this more true than in respect to the gods. Were a modern student, familiar with the gods as they appear in the *Iliad*, to travel back in time to Classical Sparta, she might be surprised to find that one of the most honored deities there was Orthia, a unique goddess absent from epic poetry. At some point, Spartan Orthia was assimilated to Artemis, but even then, she had little in common with Homer's girlish huntress. Likewise a visitor to ancient Athens would learn that Dionysos and Demeter, two deities barely mentioned in Homer, were central to that city's religious life. The depiction of Hera in the *Iliad* as a shrewish, scheming wife disciplined by her patriarchal husband Zeus is a theological and poetic construct, quite different from the persona of Hera revealed in regional worship (Essay 1.2). This state of affairs resulted from the fact that local pantheons and rituals evolved over centuries with no common yardstick by which to measure their own degree of adherence to or deviation from a cultural norm.

Because epic poetry enjoyed a broad cultural circulation, and was carried far and wide by traveling singers, it formed a counterweight to this particularism. Consider the challenges facing the epic poet whose task was to spin a story about the heroes of old, their interactions with the gods, and deeds of valor enacted in war. Whose gods should be depicted? Zeus as he was worshiped and visualized in Ionian Miletos, or in Dorian Sparta? Over the course of centuries, poets created a synthetic picture of gods and rituals from the mass of local particulars. This synthesis favored elements familiar to all, and avoided those easily recognized as regional and local. Cognitively speaking, local religion was characterized by a heavy reliance on intuitive religious concepts (see the section "Intuitive and reflective cognition"), while Panhellenic religion resulted from attempts to systematize and harmonize this mass of conflicting information. As in the Near Eastern epics that influenced Greek oral poets, the gods of the *Iliad* formed a supra-local pantheon, and were lifted from their earthly abodes in temples (local perspective) to the heavenly city of Olympos (Panhellenic perspective). In Greek cities, relationships among the gods were primarily conceptualized in spatial and functional terms, whereas in the epic, they were familial and hierarchical. Thus in the polis of Athens (local perspective), Athena Polias resided in a fine temple at the city center and concerned herself with civic industries and activities, while Zeus Herkeios, worshiped at individual domestic altars throughout the city, protected the boundaries of each man's home against intruders. Though the father-daughter relationship of Zeus and Athena was not ignored at Athens, it was for the most part irrelevant to these two cults.[34] In epic poetry (Panhellenic perspective) Zeus' relations with other gods, including Athena, are defined by his status as the head of a divine family, and as the supreme ruler of the cosmos.

But if the epic depiction of gods common to all the Greeks is a poetic construct, can we speak of "Panhellenic religion"? We can, because the prestige of epic, and its wide dissemination, also had an impact on ritual practice and material culture. For example, the sons of the tyrant Peisistratos unsuccessfully attempted to build a grandiose Athenian temple to Olympian Zeus, no doubt with the Panhellenic concept of Zeus ruling from Mt. Olympos in mind.[35] Similarly, the sculptor Pheidias was reportedly inspired by lines from Homer when he created the colossal gold and ivory statue of Zeus at Olympia:

> The son of Kronos nodded his dark brow in assent,
> And ambrosial locks flowed in waves from the Lord's
> Immortal head, and he shook great Olympos.
> (Hom. *Il.* 1.528–30)[36]

Even though Panhellenic and local conceptions of a particular deity might vary dramatically in the eyes of moderns, they coexisted in the minds of worshipers, who switched between concepts as needed in different contexts.

## Intuitive and reflective cognition

In order to understand why and how the Greeks so often held contradictory notions about the gods in their minds, we need to return to cognitive science. Concepts and beliefs are processed in the mind through two cognitively distinct pathways. The intuitive pathway is fast, effortless and implicit; the reflective pathway is relatively slow, effortful and explicit. People do not need to expend mental effort learning concepts and beliefs of the first type; they arise naturally from a set of "first-order" mental tools and categories, many of which are established in early childhood as we interact with the environment. Intuitive inferences and the resulting beliefs seem self-evident. Consider the following examples (with the caveat that as intuitive inferences, they would not normally be represented explicitly):

- When I am hungry, I should eat.
- What I throw in the air will come back down.
- Animals move about, but plants do not.

Cognition processed through this first pathway is automatic, experiential, closely tied to the emotions and "inherently highly compelling."[37] It allows us to function in daily life without consciously calculating how to execute every movement and decision.

Concepts and beliefs processed via the reflective pathway include these:

- Eating green vegetables makes me healthy.
- Throwing rocks at other people is against the law.
- Even though barnacles stay put, they are animals.

The second pathway is characterized by analysis, logical connections, abstractions and propositions that do not seem self-evident. It is highly likely to operate through the medium of language. Beliefs processed through this pathway are more easily changed when evidence contradicting them is recognized; indeed, doubting and disbelieving belong to this category of cognition.

Concepts and beliefs processed at these two levels may be held in the mind simultaneously, and they may conflict. For example, most people know that the earth revolves around the sun. But when watching a beautiful sunset, even scientists may remark on the sun's "movement." That the sun moves is understood intuitively; that it is stationary is a conclusion resulting from a more complex process of learning and reflection.[38] Even though we have been taught that the earth is not flat, we tend to visualize the path of an airplane crossing the Atlantic as a straight line rather than an arc. We use "tree" as a taxonomic category, even if we know that an oak is more closely related to a daisy than to a conifer. Dual-process theorists have not settled on a consistent terminology for these two categories or modes of cognition, but Sperber has described the two resulting kinds of beliefs as "intuitive" and "reflective," and this is the terminology I use.[39] Sperber points out that the boundary between intuitive and reflective beliefs is not impermeable. For example, initially reflective beliefs (four is an even number) may enter the intuitive repertoire through repetition and reinforcement, while intuitive beliefs (the earth is flat) may be "unlearned" through reflection.

With respect to religious thought, we can draw a distinction between (1) intuitive mental representations and inferences, particularly as experienced through religion in practice; and (2) reflective propositions, particularly as experienced through myths and other forms of explicit discourse about the gods. Examples of intuitive religious beliefs include these:

- When I pray, Allah understands the language I speak.
- God feels emotions (e.g. anger or gladness).
- Apollo occupies physical space and moves from one location to another.

People are not necessarily conscious of these inferences; they remain unspoken because they seem so obvious. Reflective religious beliefs, on the other hand, are conscious thoughts which we formulate explicitly:

- Allah understands all languages because he knows everything.
- When people have sex outside marriage, God is angry.
- Apollo often carries a bow and arrows.

To a great degree, interactions with superhuman agents are predicated on intuitive cognition. Stanley Stowers refers to this as "the religion of everyday social exchange," by which people interact with gods in ways that reflect very basic human inferences about how other minds work.[40] One such inference is that gods are capable of perceiving what we do. Another is that a god can feel pleasure or displeasure and take action as a result. Thus, intuitive religious thought involves an implicit theology, an unspoken set of assumptions about the properties of gods. People do not need to reason about such matters; intuitive beliefs are the products of our cognitive architecture, which has evolved to help us navigate the physical and social world. In this type of religious thought, a god is perceived as a nearby "interested party" who can enter into a reciprocal relationship with worshipers, interacting with them at a specific time and place (for reciprocity, see Essay 1.3). Another characteristic of the religion of everyday social exchange is "epistemological uncertainty" and an imbalance of knowledge between god and worshiper. That is, the god is presumed to know everything important, but the worshiper has few if any clues to the god's state of mind, or whether the interaction will be successful. This knowledge imbalance distinguishes religious interactions from social interactions.[41]

Reflective cognition produces accounts of the gods and of human interactions with them. These are forms of explicit theology, not necessarily in the sense of systematic study of the divine, but in its original Greek sense of *logoi* (stories, arguments, rationalizations, accountings) concerning the *theoi*, the gods.[42] Religious thought of the reflective type can be expressed orally, visually through painting and sculpture, or in writing.[43] Mythmaking belongs to the reflective form of cognition, as does philosophical speculation concerning the nature of gods and their role in the cosmos. Mythmaking, however, embraces and incorporates intuitive inferences (e.g. the gods' anthropomorphism), while Greek philosophy tends to critique and reject them. Mythmaking also relies far more than philosophy on symbolic thought, which is a special form of reflective cognition (see Chapter 2).

The concept of "superstition" is a product of the reflective religious modality, which may seek to marginalize intuitive beliefs and behaviors as naïve or doctrinally incorrect. But the usefulness of the distinction between reflective and intuitive cognition is not limited to explaining why world religions so consistently exhibit a gap between "theologically correct" doctrine, which is highly reflective, and real-world practice, which favors the intuitive.[44] It also pinpoints, for example, the cognitive mechanism which allowed the Greeks simultaneously to hold mental representations of the gods both as occupants of Olympos and as residents of nearby temples. As students of Greek religion, we too often attempt to explain away such logical inconsistencies, rather than simply allowing them to stand. For example, the Athenians seem to have been quite capable of regarding Zeus Hypatos, Zeus Olympios and Zeus Herkeios as distinct deities. Intuitively, this makes sense, because they were worshiped in separate locations and had differing spheres of interest. Whenever they wished, however, the Athenians could shift to a reflective, mythological mode according to which Zeus was one god who appeared in various places under different cult titles. They generally felt no need to reconcile these contradictory views.[45]

With its temples, festival calendars and mass animal sacrifices, Greek civic religion was a special case of the religion of everyday social exchange, a reciprocal relationship with the local gods writ large and conducted on behalf of the state. It too was primarily predicated on shared intuitive inferences about the gods and their behavior, but it also involved a strong admixture of reflection on religion: priests devised explanations for ritual traditions, the assembly debated how to interact with the gods in crisis situations, poets meditated on the inscrutability of the gods and so on. Additionally, it required a great investment in the curation and oversight of large sanctuaries and their festivals, activities we might call infra-religion. The official who organized a procession, kept temple accounts or purchased a hundred sheep was not directly interacting with a god, but his activities supported the religious life of the city.[46]

## Using the evidence

Because we are studying antiquity, we cannot directly observe a Greek woman praying, or interview a Greek man about his perceptions of what takes place during a sacrifice. We find evidence of historical interactions with the gods in material culture. Sanctuaries, altars and temples formed the physical environment for many interactions. Gifts were left in sanctuaries, sometimes with messages inscribed for the gods. Animal bones and pottery were deposited around altars after ritual feasts. Material culture has the advantage of being firmly moored to historical acts of worship in a specific place and time. Archaeological evidence for religion, however, is difficult to interpret. Even when we can draw firm conclusions about what the worshipers *did*, what they were *thinking* is a different matter.[47] A few, precious inscribed texts record prayers, dedications, hymns, curses and other specific instances of interaction with the divine. For example, two hexameters inscribed on an eight-inch bronze statue (Figure 1.1) read:

> Mantiklos dedicated me to the Far-Shooter of the Silver Bow
> From his tithe. You, Phoibos, give something pleasing in return.
> (*CEG* 326)

This is a record of a message from Mantiklos to (Phoibos) Apollo in the city of Thebes during the first quarter of the seventh century.

Texts like this raise methodological questions of their own. Was this inscription meant for Apollo to "read," or was it intended primarily to impress other people? To what degree does this conventional formula reflect what Mantiklos was thinking when he made the dedication? Did Mantiklos have in mind the local Apollo, Homer's Apollo (who is called "Far-Shooter" and has a silver bow) or both?[48] Still, this type of evidence is the closest we can come to direct observation of ancient religion in practice. It expresses typically intuitive religious beliefs: Apollo is a person with whom Mantiklos can interact; Apollo understands the Greek language; Apollo is pleased by gifts. It also expresses reflective religious

*Figure 1.1* Bronze votive statuette dedicated to Apollo by Mantiklos, ca. 700–675. From Thebes. Photo © 2016 Museum of Fine Arts, Boston

beliefs: Apollo is an archer with a silver bow; when people obtain goods, they ought to share with the gods through the custom of tithing.

The majority of our written evidence for Greek religion comes in the form of texts whose authors are reflecting on religion outside of a ritual context.[49] For example, depictions of gods and/or worshipers in epic poetry form a major category of evidence. Consider the following account of a sacrifice of one hundred cattle in Book 1 of the *Iliad*:

> So he spoke, praying; and Phoibos Apollo heard him.
> But when they had prayed and thrown the barley grains,
> They first drew back the heads of the cattle, cutting their throats, and
> skinned them;
> They removed the thigh-bones, then enveloped them in fat,
> Making two layers, and placed raw meat on top.
> And the old man burned this on firewood, and over it poured
> Bright wine, and the youths with him held five-pronged forks.
> Through the whole day they kept appeasing the god with song,
> The sons of the Achaians, singing the lovely paean,
> And dancing in praise of the Far-Worker, who heard and was glad.
> (Hom. *Il.* 1. 457–63, 472–4)

Although the sacrifice is described with a level of detail which makes it seem realistic, this is not a record of a historical interaction with Apollo, but a fictional description of one, which operates according to somewhat different rules. Notice, for example, that the epic poet suffers from no epistemological uncertainty: he knows what Apollo was thinking and can share this information with his audience. Cognitively speaking, composing a poetic description of a sacrifice is a radically different act from performing the ritual itself. Here, the poet is operating from many of the same inferences as a worshiper, but he is also a creative artist working reflectively within the Panhellenic conventions and traditions of epic.[50]

The distinction between reflective and intuitive cognition is also useful in the analysis of visual culture. Consider a sacrificial scene on a Classical Athenian votive relief (Figure 1.2), a sculpture set up by worshipers in a sanctuary in order to honor a god or hero. Such reliefs commemorate a specific sacrificial occasion, which is represented in a schematized format: the dedicators of the relief (here Panis and Aigirios with their child) approach the deity with hands raised in greeting. They are about to sacrifice to Herakles, who is represented on a larger scale than his worshipers. The god faces them and watches as a slave or a junior member of the family leads forward the animal destined for sacrifice; a female attendant carries a basket with the equipment for the ritual. An inscription identifying both the dedicators and the deity is carved onto the frame.[51]

Compare a Classical Athenian vase painting depicting a sacrificial scene (Figure 1.3): an anonymous adult man, the officiant at a sacrifice, stands at an altar as a younger assistant roasts the viscera of the butchered animal on spits. Because the scene is "post-kill," the species of the sacrificial animal is unclear. The officiant holds a bundle of meat or bones over the altar, as another assistant pours from a jug. To the right, Apollo (represented on the same scale as the humans) observes the activity, apparently unseen by the worshipers. There is a distinct sense of male camaraderie, especially in the eye contact between the older man and his young acolyte.[52]

*Figure 1.2* Herakles leans on his club as a family approaches with a sacrificial ox. Marble votive relief to Herakles, Athens, first half of the fourth century. National Archaeological Museum, Athens, Greece. Photo © Vanni Archive/Art Resource, NY

*Figure 1.3* An adult man and two youths perform a sacrifice to Apollo, who stands on the right. One of the boys holds meat on a spit over the fire while another pours a libation. Attic red figure bell krater by the Pothos painter, ca. 430. Photo: Erich Lessing/Art Resource

Folkert van Straten's study of sacrificial iconography has revealed that almost all Classical Greek votive reliefs with sacrificial scenes show the "pre-kill" phase, while only slightly more than half of vase paintings do. (Of the remaining vase paintings, most, like Figure 1.2, show the handling of meat.) This divergence results from the differing uses of the objects: the votive relief was a memorial of a specific interaction with a god, in which inferences of the intuitive type were dominant. From the perspective of the dedicator, it was important to show the species and age of the sacrificed animal, and thus the value of the gift he was presenting to the god. It was also important that the god be portrayed in the relief, identified by the appropriate attributes and depicted as receptive to the greetings of the worshipers. In artistic contexts that commemorated real-life cult activity or emphasized religious emotion, it was standard to show the god's large size relative to the worshipers, conveying their pious sense of awe before a divine being who was quite literally "superhuman." Once commissioned and completed, the sculpture was set up in the sanctuary as a memorial of a successful sacrifice.[53]

The vase painting, on the other hand, was not a memorial of a specific interaction with a god, but a generic scene designed to attract buyers who would use the vases as household items. On vase paintings of sacrificial scenes, the figures are rarely named, and in scenes of procession to the altar, expensive animals are overrepresented. The recipient deity might or might not be depicted nearby; this was by no means an essential element of the scene, as it was on votive reliefs. In Figure 1.3, Apollo is present, yet the painter does not attempt to represent a direct interaction between god and worshipers, and convention does not require that the god (recognizable by his long hair and laurel staff) be differentiated from the worshipers by size. The two most prevalent "post-kill" scenes on vases show the viscera of the animal roasting on spits, as in this example, or the sacrum and tail burning on the altar.[54] In the standard Classical Athenian procedure for alimentary sacrifice, the main participants tasted the roasted viscera while they burned a variable portion of the animal for the god (the muscle meat was afterwards roasted or boiled, and distributed to guests for feasting). Thus the scenes of roasting innards evoke the fellowship created among the participants as the first taste of meat was consumed. The sacrum and tail were often burned as the god's portion, and the curling of the tail in the fire was considered a favorable sign: the sacrifice had been successful. Such vases offered reflections on the *concept* of sacrifice – especially its social, devotional and culinary pleasures.[55]

The Sanskrit Vedas and the Homeric epics, originally oral compositions, show that explicit theology can thrive in the absence of writing. Systematic theology, however, cannot. Reflection on the gods becomes substantially more complex and sophisticated with the arrival of advanced literacy. Plato's philosophical works, which alternately embraced and critiqued traditional religious beliefs, could not have been composed without the technology of writing. Athenian tragedians problematized the gods as cruel and selfish (Euripides' *Hippolytus*) or explored the ethics of human sacrifice (Aeschylus' *Agamemnon*), even though such sacrifices were not, and likely had never been, a part of the religion of everyday social exchange in their culture.[56]

Although the reflective form of religious cognition typically takes intuitive religious thought as its starting point and either elaborates upon it or reacts against it, we must avoid characterizing the former as "advanced" and the latter as "primitive." The two are parallel cognitive phenomena. Neither cultures nor individuals evolve their way out of the intuitive modality. This explains the substantial gap between the "theologically correct" doctrines of Christianity, Buddhism, Islam and so forth and the actual practices and beliefs of most adherents in their everyday lives. As the product of natural cognition, the religion of everyday social exchange is with us today, in every world tradition, and will likely always be with us. By the same token, theological religion is a product of our human faculties of reason and imagination, which have been with us as long as the gods themselves.

## The Greeks and the counterintuitive

The complex interrelation of intuitive and reflective beliefs in religion is illustrated by the prevalence of minimally counterintuitive concepts (MCIs) in religious thought. To create an MCI, begin with a familiar concept like "pencil," "mountain" or "cat." Each of these belongs to an intuitive ontological category which is established in early childhood. A pencil is an artifact, a mountain is a natural non-living object and a cat is an animal. Now endow each concept with at least one property that violates the intuitive assumptions we hold about its category. Let the pencil grow (a biological property), the mountain listen to what you say (a psychological property) and the cat become invisible (a physical property). Growth in a pencil is counterintuitive, whereas growth in a cat is ordinary. Should a cat grow to weigh forty pounds, this would be bizarre, but not counterintuitive. The counterintuitive need not be impossible or unnatural: tiny, invisible creatures which cause illness are MCIs, yet they exist.[57]

*Table 1.1* Examples of counterintuitive concepts: each concept violates an ontological category by attributing to it contradictory properties from a domain of intuitive knowledge. Adapted from Barrett 2008.410.

| *Ontological Category* | *Folk Psychology* | *Folk Biology* | *Folk Physics* |
|---|---|---|---|
| Person | A person who knows the future | A person born from a tree | A person who exists in two places at once |
| Animal | A horse that talks | A bird with bronze feathers | An invisible cat |
| Plant | A tree that answers questions | A flower that bleeds | An herb that grows in the air |
| Artifact | A ship's prow that gives advice | A statue that walks | A bag that encloses the winds |
| Non-living natural object | An angry mountain | A stone that sheds tears | A spring that is solid in warm weather |

In order to be remembered well and orally transmitted without special memory aids, a concept should be *minimally* counterintuitive. Too many category violations (a pencil that grows, flies, moves through solid objects and solves algebraic equations) will make the concept more difficult to remember. Transferred properties yield good MCIs: the mountain has hearing, a property we intuitively attribute to animals and people, but not to natural objects. If, however, we also stipulate that the mountain hears everything being said anywhere in the world, we have violated our intuitive beliefs about how hearing works. A pan-auditory mountain is a more difficult concept than a simple hearing one, and less readily transmitted.[58]

Greek mythology is full of MCIs: a lion whose hide cannot be pierced; a flying, immortal horse; men with goat's legs and ears; birds who shoot bronze feathers like arrows; a bag that can hold the winds. The metamorphoses so characteristic of Greek myth are counterintuitive because they violate our intuitive inferences that membership in a species and individual personhood are permanent. In 1985, Michael Kelly and Frank Keil tabulated all the transformations in Ovid's *Metamorphoses* and *Grimm's Fairy Tales*. They discovered that metamorphosis follows predictable patterns based on intuitive category assumptions. For example, in the *Metamorphoses*, a conscious being (mortal or god) is much more likely to be transformed into another conscious being (20%) or an animal (51%) than into a plant (10%) or a solid inanimate object (12%). Likewise, an inanimate object is more likely to be transformed into another inanimate object than into a conscious being.[59] Although some transformations may be determined by narrative considerations, these broad patterns reveal cognitive constraints on the concept of metamorphosis. Kelly and Keil recorded zero instances of conscious beings transformed into abstract ideas; such a metamorphosis would be excessively counterintuitive.[60]

Not all MCIs are equally likely to end up as religious concepts. In fact, MCIs are abundant in popular culture: animals talk, crimefighters have super strength and young women start fires with the power of thought alone. These are all examples of MCIs with good inferential potential: they generate stories. Inferentially impoverished MCIs, by contrast, lead nowhere. Which is more interesting, a person who disappears when you speak to him, or a person who grants wishes? Consider an invisible tree. Clearly it is an MCI, but it is far less interesting than a talking or listening tree. This is because having the ability to talk or listen makes the tree an agent. Agentive MCIs are more likely than others to be transmitted as religious concepts. But what distinguishes Superman the comic-book hero from Herakles the god? Why are some MCIs viewed as real-world agents in spite of their counterintuitive properties, while others are just as clearly understood to be fictional?

The answers are contextual. Our ability to mentally represent MCIs may manifest itself reflectively and consciously in creative contexts (as when we read or write fiction), but it may also function in connection with the suite of mental tools we use to recognize and interact with agents in our immediate environment (Chapter 2). For example, suppose that the sound "meow" is heard whenever I visit a certain park. Intuitively, I infer that some agent is making the sound, and that the agent is a cat. If the cat continues to vocalize, yet mysteriously cannot be located, I may reflectively conclude that contrary to my normal expectations, this cat is invisible. When they possess explanatory power and are emotionally compelling, MCIs generated this way may be perceived as "real" rather than fictional, transmitted to other people who find them plausible, and culturally elaborated.[61] For example, many people in the United States interpret coins found in unexpected places as messages (usually of comfort or moral admonition) from deceased loved ones. This concept of "pennies from heaven" explains a minor mystery of everyday life and appeals to deep emotions. It has been disseminated through testimonial letters sent to a widely syndicated newspaper column. According to Pascal Boyer, religious MCIs matter to us in ways that Superman cannot. In cognitive terms, they activate multiple mental systems, "those that govern our most intense emotions, shape our interaction with other people, give us moral feelings, and organize social groups."[62]

In cultures with established traditions of superhuman beings, plausibility is easily achieved, especially if the agent is identified or its existence confirmed by authority figures. The proliferation of cults in Greek polytheism can be attributed in part to intuitive inferences that some superhuman agent needs to be addressed in response to virtually any misfortune, success or unusual event. Consider, for example, the following oracle given to the people of Miletos, who consulted Apollo at Didyma after an earthquake:

> As regards this sign (*sēmeion*), propitiate Steadfast (*Asphaleos*) Poseidon with sacrifices and ask him to come propitiously and to preserve the order of your city unshaken, apart from danger. For he is coming very near you. Him you must guard against and pray to, so that henceforth you may reach old age undaunted by evils.
>
> (*DI* 132.2–7; Fontenrose 1988.190; late second century)

Apollo's oracle advised the citizens to establish a new cult to Poseidon under the name Asphaleos in order to ward off future disasters. The Milesians already worshiped Poseidon, but the earthquake caused them to infer that some dangerous *new* agency was at work. Was Poseidon Asphaleos a different god from the other Poseidons at Miletos? Yes and no. Together with a set of new sacrifices, the use of a new cult title satisfied the need to address this unknown power, while the identification of the dangerous god as Poseidon, a deity "known" to cause earthquakes, situated the new cult within the familiar context of a shared theology.

## Emic and etic approaches

Anthropologists speak of "emic" and "etic" approaches to culture. These terms are derived from the adjectives *phonemic* (referring to the way the sounds of speech are perceived by the speaker) and *phonetic* (referring to the physical production and acoustic properties of the sounds as objects of scientific study). An emic approach to culture, then, represents an insider's point of view or (for ancient historians) an attempt to fully empathize with and grasp that point of view. It reflects the judgments, mental categories and assumptions characteristic of a given culture. An etic approach reflects the broader contextual knowledge of an outsider who is measuring, comparing and analyzing his observations with an entirely different, universalizing frame of reference.

As a practical matter, it is questionable whether moderns have the ability to achieve a truly emic perspective on an ancient culture, yet the emic/etic distinction is useful in thinking through our approaches to the evidence.[63] For example, etic methodology often requires the assumption that those who practice a religion do not understand their own beliefs and behaviors. To see what I mean, imagine that Jack, a modern Classicist, attends a symposium in 425 and has a conversation with an Athenian citizen:

*Jack:* You're from the village of Thorikos, aren't you, Stephanos? Why do you sacrifice twice a year to the hero Thorikos?

*Stephanos:* Thorikos founded the village, and he watches over our affairs.

*Jack:* No, I don't think so. The real reason you sacrifice to Thorikos is because the ritual activity allows you to construct a group identity.

*Stephanos:* No, that's not it. It is ancestral custom to sacrifice to Thorikos at his tomb. My father did so and his father before him.

*Jack:* Yes, your ancestors used that tomb to articulate their territorial claims. And by the way, it's not even a real tomb.

*Stephanos:* (discreetly, to a slave) When you mix the next round, Lydos, more water.

Jack's approach to the ritual is wholly etic; he adopts a functionalist theoretical stance which draws on Émile Durkheim's ideas about religion. Durkheim thought that religion had little to do with gods or the supernatural. Instead, religion was society's way of perpetuating and strengthening itself: God and society were one and the same thing.[64] An emic stance, by contrast, insists on the value of Stephanos' perception that he is dealing with a superhuman being, and that the relationship with this being is important to Stephanos, his family and his village. One of the benefits of a cognitive approach is that it allows us to consider Greek religion etically as an expression of universal human patterns of thought (of which the thinkers themselves may be quite unaware), yet it simultaneously yields insight into emic perspectives. While observing that Stephanos' worship of the hero Thorikos has social consequences, we can also acknowledge and explain his strong intuition that Thorikos is real.

It used to be an axiom of the discipline that Greek religion was about rituals rather than beliefs, and that it was experienced collectively rather than individually. Indeed, rituals and collective experience must dominate any account of Greek religion, because they loom very large in our evidence. Yet Greek religion can be reduced neither to practice nor to group rituals. Epiphanies of the gods in dreaming and waking visions, for example, were not confined to ritual contexts, and gods usually appeared to individuals rather than groups.[65] During the latter half of the twentieth century, the dominance of ritual in scholarly discourse resulted in a marginalization of superhuman powers. Again, etic approaches conflicted with what the Greeks themselves tell us about the importance of the gods and heroes. The first decade of the twenty-first century has seen a resurgence of interest in individual experience, and the gods have been brought back into the equation.[66]

Finally, an emic perspective is that of an insider, but which insider? Cultures are not homogeneous. A well-educated Greek and an illiterate one, a Spartan and an Athenian, a master and a slave, a man and a woman, might have divergent and conflicting ideas about various aspects of religion. Much of the source material for our study of religion consists of writings by intellectuals, highly literate individuals (almost all male) who offered a great many reflections concerning the gods and human relations with them, but whose ideas were not necessarily representative of the population as a whole.

## ESSAY 1.1: TWELVE GODS, AND OTHER WAYS TO LIMIT A PANTHEON

If we counted them all, the total number of Greek gods worshiped in all places and times would reach into the tens if not hundreds of thousands. The Greek cosmos was, as Thales observed, "full of gods." Therefore people needed strategies for limiting this unwieldy, unbounded set of superhuman beings.[67] While nobody attempted to seek out and recognize every god by name, inclusive expressions like "to Athena and the other gods and goddesses" were common in prayers as a means of avoiding offense.[68] Generally, it was understood that an individual honored the deities and heroes whose altars were established in his or her home, neighborhood and state. But not everyone attended to every god. For example, some deities were worshiped electively (Adonis or Sabazios in Classical Athens) or according to one's gender (Herakles often excluded women from his cults). The aggregate of superhuman beings with personal significance and salience for an individual has been called a "meaningful god set."[69] Individuals seem to have intuitively maintained their meaningful god sets without the need to explicitly enumerate them.

If we wish to identify a meaningful god set at the group level, we must first define the group. Is it composed of all the inhabitants of a region, a polis, a village? Male citizens? Their female kin? Aristocratic citizens? The meaningful god set for a given group consists of the superhuman agents who are "significant and salient" for most of its members. When dealing with ancients who are no longer around to be interviewed, we must roughly approximate the criterion of "significant and salient" by equating it to "superhuman agents who were regularly the objects of prayer or other rituals."[70] Beginning in the sixth century, communities sometimes inscribed sacrificial calendars on stone, listing the gods who received sacrifices on behalf of the public; these constituted meaningful god sets for people *in their roles as citizen men and women.*

One of the most complete of these calendars comes from late Classical Erchia, a deme (township) in Attica.[71] It includes sacrifices for eleven (or perhaps twelve) major deities, most of whom had shrines in the deme: Zeus, Hera, Poseidon, Demeter, Leto, Apollo, Artemis (and/or Artemis-Hekate), Athena, Hermes, Dionysos and Ge. If gods with cult titles are counted as separate deities (Apollo Lykeios, Apollo Delphinios, etc.), the number rises to twenty-six. In addition to these, the calendar provides sacrifices for at least fourteen minor figures or collectivities (nymphs, heroines, Herakleidai, Acheloös, Aglauros, etc.), whose offerings are not necessarily lesser in value than those of the "major" gods. Given that the demesmen and women would also have participated in at least some of the cults in the urban center, the number appears astonishingly high, yet people did not hold all of these superhuman figures in their minds at once, nor did everyone attend to every cult. Instead, they focused on different members of the set during each month of the year, and different individuals or families assumed the priestly duties for each god or hero, so that the cognitive burden was spread among many people.[72] Whether at the individual or group level, meaningful god sets were the product of cognitive constraints (the number of significant gods individuals and groups can reasonably attend to), practical constraints (the amount of resources available to devote to them) and contingencies of time, place and culture.

A "local pantheon" consists of the total number of superhuman agents tied to a given geographical area by altars, sanctuaries or other landmarks. Local pantheons were inevitably larger than most individuals' meaningful god sets (i.e. no man or woman of Attica had all the superhuman agents of Attica in his or her meaningful god set). On the other hand, the Greeks had a mental category which corresponds to the local pantheon. They often used expressions like "all the gods, goddesses and heroes who dwell in our city (*polis*) and land (*chōra*)" or "the local gods and heroes" (*theoi kai hērōes enchōrioi*).[73] Local pantheons varied, most obviously in their heroes, river gods and other such figures who were unique to the place. Occasionally they included major deities who were unique, such as the goddess Aphaia on Aigina. In an important sense, deities such as Athena Parthenos in Athens, Artemis Orthia in Sparta and Zeus Ammon in Kyrene were also unique. A deity's cult title or *epiclēsis* ("surname") expressed this individuality.[74] Whether an Athenian citizen thought of Athena as residing on the Athenian Akropolis, its counterpart at Sparta or the heavenly Olympos was a contextual matter. Intuitively speaking, Athena Polias ("of the city") lived in Athens and possessed a unique identity, as did Athena Chalkioikos ("of the Bronze House") at Sparta. Reflectively speaking, Athena was a goddess who lived on Olympos and was worshiped by many cities and peoples.

Certain gods and goddesses, then, were familiar by name and general persona to all the Greeks, even as their functions, titles, rituals, iconography and relative importance varied from one location to the next. Robert Parker proposes (with certain caveats), that from 700 onward virtually all Greek communities worshiped a core group of twelve to thirteen deities: Zeus, Hera, Poseidon, Athena, Apollo,

Artemis, Dionysos, Hermes, Aphrodite, Demeter (normally with Persephone/Kore) and Herakles, as well as Hestia at the level of domestic cult.[75] This assemblage probably matched no one's meaningful god set, yet it reveals a common cultural heritage.

In order to create a narrative or an image representing the concept "all the gods," poets and artists had to be selective. Let us define a "limited pantheon" as any such selection of gods that serves in place of the unbounded, unmanageable whole. In the Homeric poems we observe a limited pantheon which corresponds roughly to Parker's list of gods recognized in cult. But Homer's pantheon is shaped by factors specific to the epic genre and the subject matter of the poems. Zeus, who guides the course of history, and Athena, who watches over Greek heroes, are all-pervasive in the Panhellenic epic. Of sixty-seven deities mentioned in Homer, the most frequently named after Zeus and Athena are Apollo, Ares, Hera, Poseidon, Hephaistos and Aphrodite, in that order. The less commonly worshiped gods Hephaistos, Ares and Hades are significant in the epic, while the universally worshiped Dionysos and Demeter appear but are given short shrift, and Hestia is completely ignored.[76] Homer has many collective expressions for all the gods (*the athanatoi theoi*, "immortal gods"; the *theoi aien eontes*, "gods who are forever"). The Homeric poems refer to a subset of gods who "possess Olympian abodes" (*Olympia dōmat' echontes*), an emic category which was to have a long history.[77]

It is worth pausing to see how Homer handles an episode where most gods are notionally present, but only a selection can be mentioned.[78] Book 20 of the *Iliad*, for example, begins with a divine assembly summoned by Zeus. Homer uses this opportunity to acknowledge the existence of many local gods:

> But Zeus bade Themis[79] call the gods to the meeting place
> From the peak of many-valleyed Olympos, and she journeyed
> Everywhere, calling them to the house of Zeus.
> Not a river was absent, except for Okeanos,
> Nor any nymph, of all that dwell in the fair groves,
> In the sources of the rivers, and the grassy meadows.
>
> (Hom. *Il.* 20.4–9)

Once the gods are assembled, Zeus instructs them to choose sides in the Trojan War and to descend to the battlefield while he himself observes the action from Olympos (22–5). The din of battle disturbs even Aidoneus (61–5), the lord of the dead beneath the earth, who fears that the violence may expose his realm. The fighting gods are arranged in five pairs:

> For there stood opposite Lord Poseidon
> Phoibos Apollo with his winged arrows,
> Against Enyalios [Ares], the goddess grey-eyed Athena;
> Against Hera, Artemis of the golden distaff was pitted,
> The loud-voiced archer, sister of the Far-Shooter;

Against Leto stood the strong, swift runner Hermes
And opposite Hephaistos, the great, deep-eddying river
Whom the gods name Xanthos, and men Skamandros.
(Hom. *Il.* 20.67–74)[80]

Taken as a whole, the episode constructs a theologically coherent pantheon organized by spatial location, with representatives from the earth (rivers and nymphs), the heavens (gods who inhabit Olympos) and the underworld (Aidoneus and the dead). The selection of combatants, on the other hand, is dictated by the requirements of the narrative. Hephaistos, for example, takes the field specifically in order to counter the onslaughts of the river Skamandros with fire.[81] Conspicuously absent from the assembly and the battle are Demeter, Hestia and Dionysos.

Hesiod's *Theogony* (ca. 700) daringly attempted to account for *all* the gods, organizing them by genealogy. This was a remarkable feat of theological classification, and it radically departed from the religion of everyday social exchange, with its sanctuary-based local gods.[82] Like Homer, Hesiod worked within a Panhellenic tradition which stripped most local gods of their individuality and cult titles, replacing them with descriptive epithets suited to the epic meter. In Hesiod's cosmos, as in that of Homer, there was one Zeus, one Athena, one Apollo. The Muses of his local Mt. Helikon were identical to the Muses of Olympos (although it is telling that he allows them both epithets, "Helikonian" and "Olympian").[83] In the proem to the *Theogony*, the Muses hymn (1–21) nineteen members of a limited pantheon:

1 Zeus, who holds the aegis
2 Queenly Argive Hera, who walks on golden sandals
3 Grey-eyed Athena, the daughter of aegis-holding Zeus
4 Phoibos Apollo
5 Artemis, who delights in arrows
6 Poseidon the earth-holder, who shakes the earth
7 Reverend Themis
8 Quick-glancing Aphrodite
9 Gold-crowned Hebe
10 Lovely Dione
11 Leto

Hesiod's theological project is an account of cosmic history and its culmination in Zeus' Olympian regime. This "Olympian" theme reveals that his plan is Panhellenic in scope: it acknowledges geographically unique deities like the rivers and nymphs, but pays them scant attention. The Muses' hymn therefore focuses first and foremost on Zeus' consorts and offspring; only Poseidon falls outside this circle. Hera, whose affiliation with the Argive peninsula ran very deep, is the only major deity to receive a geographical epithet (just as she does in Homer). The absent Demeter and Dionysos, meanwhile, may have been conceptualized as earthly, un-Olympian gods because of their agricultural interests.[84] With the remaining eight deities, Hesiod expands our temporal and physical conception of the cosmos far beyond Homer's tripartite division of earth/sky/underworld:

12 Iapetos
13 Kronos of crooked counsel
14 Eos (Dawn)
15 Great Helios (Sun)
16 Bright Selene (Moon)
17 Gaia (Earth)
18 Great Okeanos
19 Black Night

These are primordial gods, who belong to the generations before Zeus. The Titans Iapetos and Kronos allude to Zeus' struggle for power, and the creation of men through the actions of Iapetos' son Prometheus.[85] Except for Ge and Helios, these divine beings rarely received formal cultic attentions. Yet they were not therefore irrelevant to Greek religion. Okeanos, for example, was an important figure in popular cosmology, while Kronos came to play a significant role in Greek ideas of the afterlife.[86] The Muses' hymn concludes in a prayer-like fashion with the inclusive formula "and the holy race of the other deathless gods."

Next we turn to a limited pantheon in visual form. During the early sixth century, Athenian vase painters grew interested in depicting divine assemblies. The Sophilos dinos (Figures 1.4 and 1.5; ca. 580), for example, illustrates the wedding of Peleus and Thetis, an event attended by "all the gods."[87] Like the Battle of the Gods in *Iliad* 20 and the proem to Hesiod's *Theogony*, it depicted a limited pantheon requiring a process of planning and selection: which gods would be included, and how would they be arranged? Sophilos decided to structure the scene as a real-life wedding procession. He gave Demeter, Hestia and Dionysos important places at the head of the group, in positions which would normally be taken by the bride's relatives. Also on foot in the first cohort are the Olympian goddesses Leto and Hebe, as well as Peleus' friends, the centaur Cheiron and his wife, Chariklo; they are followed by the Olympian Themis with a group of nymphs.[88] The second stage of the procession comprises pairs of deities whose importance is signaled by their mode of travel in chariots. Each is accompanied by an attendant group of minor goddesses:

Zeus and Hera with the Horai (Seasons)
Poseidon and Amphitrite with the Charites (Graces)
Ares and Aphrodite with a group of Muses
Hermes and Apollo with another group of Muses
Athena and Artemis with the Moirai (Fates)

Sophilos' theme is not war but love. Assembling as many erotic and nuptial pairs as possible, he follows Hesiod in pairing Poseidon with Amphitrite, and Ares with Aphrodite. The Seasons, Graces, Muses and Fates, all Olympian daughters

*Figure 1.4* The Sophilos dinos, procession of the gods for the wedding of Peleus and Thetis. From right, Poseidon and Amphitrite in chariot, Ares and Aphrodite in chariot accompanied by the Muses. Lower register: stag and lions. Photo © Trustees of The British Museum

*Figure 1.5* The Sophilos dinos, detail. From right, Athena and Artemis in chariot, Okeanos, Tethys and Eileithyia, Hephaistos. Photo © Trustees of The British Museum

of Zeus, are appropriate to a wedding with its joyful celebration and promise of offspring.[89] At the end of the procession walk Thetis' grandparents, Okeanos (portrayed as a river god) followed by his wife, Tethys, with the Olympian birth goddess Eileithyia, and last of all, Hephaistos on a donkey. Sophilos' limited pantheon is consistent with the Athenian cultic environment, where Demeter, Dionysos and Hephaistos were important, yet it is more attuned to Panhellenic myth than to local cult.[90] He expresses the concept of "all the gods" by uniting a host of Olympian deities with the earth-dwelling guests (Okeanos, Cheiron, Chariklo, nymphs) of Peleus and Thetis. The underworld is ignored, for Hades and the dead would be unwelcome at a wedding.

So far, we have explored the "meaningful god set," which is defined cognitively, and the "local pantheon," which is defined geographically. We compared these with examples of "limited pantheons" in poetry and art, which result from the interaction of local and Panhellenic traditions with narrative and visual constraints. A different way of representing "all the gods," used primarily in cultic contexts, was the "condensed pantheon," an *explicitly* limited selection of gods which could stand for the whole.[91] So far as we know, condensed pantheons did not begin to appear until the late sixth century (522/1), when according to Thucydides (6.54.6), the younger Peisistratos founded an altar dedicated to "The Twelve Gods." The exact composition of these twelve is not known; the site of the altar in the NW agora has been excavated, but no trace of divine iconography from the earliest period was uncovered.[92] Around this time, Athenian vase painters developed an interest in assemblies constructed around the new myth of Herakles' apotheosis and reception on Olympos. Although very few painters aimed for a set of exactly twelve gods, both the "assembly" vases and the altar in the agora suggest new currents of thought about which gods had a claim to a special, exclusive status, whether as "Olympians" or as members of a numerically restricted group.[93]

That the Panhellenic sanctuary of Olympia also organized a condensed pantheon around the number twelve, and did so as early as the sixth century, is suggested by the Homeric *Hymn to Hermes*, which describes Hermes preparing a sacrificial meal with twelve equal portions beside the banks of the Alpheios river.[94] Although the name "Twelve Gods" is not used, Pindar speaks of "six twin altars" at Olympia, and from a fragment of the Greek historian Herodorus, we learn that these were dedicated respectively to Zeus Olympios and Poseidon, Hera and Athena, Hermes and Apollo, the Charites (who apparently counted as one) and Dionysos, Artemis and Alpheios, and Kronos and Rhea.[95] This group is distinctive, reflecting local traditions, such as the myth of Artemis' pursuit by the river god Alpheios, and the rare worship of the Titans Kronos and Rhea. Several "major" gods, including Demeter and Aphrodite, are missing. The three same-sex pairs are complemented by three opposite-sex pairs with erotic or nuptial connotations. Yet in spite of the evident "local" character of this condensed pantheon, only Zeus is supplied with an *epiclēsis* ("Olympios"). The other members of the group are all of Panhellenic renown, and even the local river Alpheios is mentioned by both Homer and Hesiod.[96]

During the sixth century, then, Greek communities began to favor the number twelve as a limiting criterion for condensation of their local pantheons. As noted earlier, Parker's count of indispensable gods also amounts to twelve or thirteen. Thus, the number twelve is large enough to allow coverage of the key gods in the pantheon of a typical Greek city, even as it exerts pressure toward generalization (e.g. the stripping of the *epiclēsis*) and Panhellenization along epic lines. Mesopotamian, Egyptian and Hittite parallels for groups of twelve deities have been suggested, and these may have played a role, yet the number twelve recurs in many Greek cultural contexts.[97] Beyond this, it has the conceptual and iconographic advantage of being divisible by two, three, four and six, so that gods can be broken down into pairs or other combinations; the extant archaeological evidence bears witness to a fascination with these possibilities, and structuralist studies have fruitfully interpreted the resonances thus created.[98] Plato was sensitive to the number twelve, and attracted to the potential for systematization it presented; in the *Laws*, he organized the tribes and monthly festival calendar of his ideal city around the Twelve Gods, but idiosyncratically included Plouton without specifying the composition of the members.[99]

"Twelve Gods" cults came to be associated with the concept of foundation (as at Olympia) and with the heroic expeditions to the boundaries of the known world that established a Hellenic presence overseas. Agamemnon is supposed to have founded an altar to the Twelve at Cape Lekton in the Troad, and Jason at the "Sanctuary" (Hieron), a landmark location on the Bosporos.[100] In contrast to Archaic condensed pantheons occurring in the Greek homeland, such as those of Olympia and Athens, these later references to groups of Twelve express an overtly Panhellenic perspective, where the exact composition of the Twelve is less relevant than the fact that they are a distinctively Greek group of gods.[101] At the height of its empire, Athens promoted the ideology of Panhellenism, presenting itself as an exemplar of what it meant to be a Greek city. Perikles is said to have proposed a Panhellenic congress and spearheaded a Panhellenic colony at Thourioi, while foreigners were encouraged to honor Demeter and Kore at Eleusis, as though the Attic goddesses were universal Greek deities.[102] The east frieze of the Parthenon (completed in 438/7) includes twelve gods seated in two groups of six to witness the Panathenaic procession. Zeus, Hera, Ares, Demeter, Dionysos and Hermes are on the left side of the frieze, and on the right, Athena, Hephaistos, Poseidon, Apollo, Artemis and Aphrodite. The frieze melds a Homeric and Panhellenizing vision of the major gods in the pantheon (Hera and Ares) with the realities of cult and worship (Demeter and Dionysos).[103]

The Hellenistic period saw the spread of the Twelve Gods cult to many Greek cities, where they became guardians of civic harmony and prosperity.[104] Cults of the Twelve resisted standardization and manifested themselves in ways that reflected local priorities. The cult at Delos, for example, is thought to have been organized with four altars of three gods each, an arrangement which would have accommodated the distinctive Delian triad of Apollo, Artemis and Leto.[105] At Magnesia on the Maiandros, a Hellenistic decree (197/6) concerning the cult of Zeus Sosipolis ("Savior of the City") prescribed a procession with individual wooden images of the Twelve Gods, which were brought to a circular area (*tholos*) in the agora near their altar. Three couches (presumably to hold four gods each) and musicians were to be provided. The procession took place in conjunction with separate observances for the key civic deities Zeus Sosipolis, Artemis Leukophryene and Apollo Pythios. In spite of the fact that most localities were able to list "their" Twelve, the lack of specificity in the very concept of "the Twelve" must have facilitated the transmission of the cult from one local context to another. Moreover, the Twelve Gods could be worshiped as a plurality alongside one or more of its individual members.[106]

Given the significant role of Twelve Gods cults in civic ideology, and their relationship to mental representations of the pantheon, it is not surprising that when rulers began to be deified, they attempted to associate themselves with Twelve Gods cults. Beginning in the mid-fourth century, Philip II, Alexander and their successors found alternative solutions to the predicament faced by Herakles, who was said to have refused membership in the Twelve on the grounds that one of the existing members would have to be expelled to make way for him. In a procession at Aigai where images of the Twelve were carried into the theater, Philip had his own statue displayed in such a way that it would be difficult to see him as anything other than the Thirteenth God.[107] At Athens the orator Demades later proposed that Alexander be enrolled as the Thirteenth God, a suggestion which was soundly rejected, although we also hear that Alexander succeeded in having many Greek cities add him to the Twelve. Subsequent rulers attempted to achieve membership by proximity: on Delos, the temple to the Twelve has produced the remains of two colossal statues of Hellenistic kings.[108]

The Twelve Gods were a group of variable composition, and this potential for variation allowed the Twelve to express either a local or Panhellenic identity, depending on the context. The Twelve Gods are therefore to be distinguished from the familiar "Twelve Olympians" of mythology textbooks, a group whose membership seems to have become canonical only in 217, when the Roman Dii Consentes were syncretized with a selection of gods from the Greek pantheon. (The occasion was an attempt to appease the gods after Hannibal's victory at Lake Trasimene.) The Romans held a banquet with food placed before twelve statues, arranged in male-female pairs on six couches.[109] This Graeco-Roman condensed pantheon corresponded to the Parthenon Twelve, but excluded Dionysos/Liber in favor of Hestia/Vesta, presumably because of Vesta's greater importance for the Romans. It still serves us today as a conceptual filter, a Panhellenizing first approach to the Greek gods in all their unmanageable multiplicity.

## ESSAY 1.2: HOMER'S HERA AND THE HERA(S) OF CULT

Next we turn to the dynamic relationship between Panhellenic and local concepts of Hera. The differences outweigh the similarities, yet the portrait of Hera in the *Iliad* reveals knowledge of the Argolic goddess, while local worship of Hera often reflected the influence of epic. Epic poetry aimed to present a coherent picture of Hera by locating her on Olympos and shaping the Olympian pantheon as a patriarchal family ruled by Zeus. Yet epic Hera's special characteristics of partisanship and ferocity reflect her cultic history as the preeminent goddess of the Argolid and the nurturer of its warriors. It is likely that the prestige of the *Iliad* affected the subsequent development of Hera's worship, especially with regard to her role in colonization and perceptions of "Achaian" ethnicity.

In the assembly of gods at the beginning of *Iliad* Book 4, Zeus declares his wish to bring about peace between the warring Achaians and Trojans, and Hera angrily protests. Zeus reproaches Hera for her implacable anger against the Trojans, warning that someday he may see fit to destroy a city dear to her, just as she longs for the ruin of Troy, one of his own favorite cities. Hera replies:

> Indeed three cities are dearest to my heart,
> Argos and Sparta and the broad ways of Mycenae.
> Destroy these, if your heart grows to hate them;
> I neither defend them nor deem them beyond your reach.
> Though I resent and forbid such destruction,
> Resentment is useless against your greater might.
> (Hom. *Il.* 4.51–6)

The idea that a goddess favors certain cities is not a fanciful creation of the poets, but reflects the real-world tendency for each city or region to worship one or more tutelary deities, who overshadowed the other local gods.[110] The same pattern was characteristic of Near Eastern city-states (e.g. Marduk was the patron god of Babylon). Despite the Panhellenizing tendencies of epic, the *Iliad* does not elide the evidence that Hera was a regional goddess, but instead acknowledges it:

> At once the son of Kronos tried to provoke Hera,
> Speaking mockery with malign intent:
> "Twin goddesses are Menelaos' helpers,
> Hera Argeia and Athena Alalkomene."
> (Hom. *Il.* 4.5–8)

The reference to Hera Argeia in this passage clearly alludes to her connection with a city or district called "Argos," just as the epithet Alalkomene is specific to an ancient center of Athena's worship in Boiotia.[111] In the *Iliad*, Hera and Athena are united in their hostility toward the Trojans, yet at the local level, conflicts between individual Greek cities can be expressed in terms of opposition between the two goddesses as civic deities.[112] The idea occurs in a passage from Euripides' *Heracleidae*, when the suppliant Iolaos says to his Athenian host Demophon:

> Gods no lesser
> Than those of the Argives are our allies, my lord.
> For Hera, the wife of Zeus, is their champion,
> But Athena is ours. And I deem this too to be
> Good practice, that we have better gods.
> For Pallas will not suffer herself to be defeated.
> (Eur. *Heracl.* 347–52)

Although he is speaking of the gods in their roles as local deities, Iolaos subtly disparages Hera by invoking the Panhellenic idea that she is the wife of Zeus. The term for "wife" here is *damar*, which is etymologically related to the verb *damazō*, "I overpower, tame, subdue." As a *damar*, Hera was physically and legally subject to her husband, while Athena, famous for her virgin status, was independent and not to be overcome.

Historically, Hera was linked with Zeus as early as the Mycenaean period, when a scribe using Linear B listed "Zeus, Hera, and Drimios" as a cult group in the area of Pylos. The same tablet, however, also mentions the goddesses *Di-wi-ja* and *Po-si-da-e-ja*, whose names are feminine versions of "Zeus" and "Poseidon." They may have been consorts or wives of these gods.[113] The Bronze Age pantheon at Pylos is full of puzzles, and the tablet does not prove that Hera was Zeus' "wife," though it strongly suggests that the pair produced a son called Drimios, whose name was forgotten by the Archaic period. Interestingly, the diction of Homeric Greek preserves the unexpected formula *posis Hērēs* ("husband of Hera") for Zeus, which leaves the impression that Hera is the more important of the two partners.[114] With respect to the religion of everyday social exchange, she was undoubtedly more important to the people in the Argolid peninsula. It was Hera, not Zeus, with whom they interacted most, and on whom they depended for prosperity and victory.

Homer repeatedly makes Hera and the other gods acknowledge the overwhelming power of Zeus, yet cultic arrangements in Greek cities did not reflect his supreme status in myth. Instead, nearly the opposite was the case: although all honored him, relatively few poleis made Zeus their patron deity. His early cults were typically situated in remote rural mountaintops and valleys, and he was also worshiped in domestic contexts.[115] The supreme power of Zeus was recognized at Olympia and Nemea, two Peloponnesian sanctuaries which served during the Geometric period as regional gathering places. In the Argolid itself, however, there is little early evidence for the worship of Zeus in his own right. Instead, he seems to have been regarded as the "husband of Hera": lead plaques depicting Hera and Zeus as a divine couple have been found in three of her eastern Peloponnesian sanctuaries.[116] This state of affairs created a logical conflict between the mythic, Panhellenic understanding of Zeus as ruler of all the gods and the cultic situation in the Argolid, where the preeminent deity was Hera.

Homer and his predecessors were not men of Argos or Mycenae, and they were more concerned with the narrative than the devotional impact of epic song. They responded to the discrepancy between myth and cult by fashioning a theology: Hera, the ferocious partisan of the invading Greeks, comes into constant conflict with Zeus, who sees the bigger picture because he is responsible for the cosmos as a whole. Time and time again, Zeus must bully his deceitful, headstrong wife into submission. He threatens to flog her (Hom. *Il.* 15.16–33), and reminds her how he once hung her from the sky, her feet weighted with anvils, as punishment for her persecution of Herakles. Homer's portrait of Hera as a disobedient, shrewish wife is a poetic construct fashioned in the service of Panhellenic epic, which insists on the primacy of Zeus. Epic depicts the gods as members of an Olympian family with Zeus as a patriarchal husband, a narrative strategy which requires that Hera, like Shakespeare's formidable Katharina, be tamed. The Zeus of the *Iliad*, however, meets with considerably less success than Petruchio in subduing his wife. Even after the death of Hektor, her anger against the Trojans remains undiminished. The unyielding character of Hera in epic is a product of Homeric artistry, but it also reflects certain characteristics of regional "great goddesses," such as Argive Hera and Spartan Orthia, who were by turns nurturing and bloodthirsty.[117] Behind the epic narrative lies an awareness of the power wielded by these preeminent goddesses.

The comic elements in Homer's portrait of Hera do not obscure her special relationship to the Greeks at Troy, and especially to Achilles. The goddess's divine anger seems to fuel the corresponding mortal wrath of Achilles. At Patroklos' funeral, Zeus comments:

> You got your way, ox-eyed Lady Hera;
> You have provoked swift-footed Achilles.
> Truly, the long-haired Achaians sprang from you.
> (Hom. *Il.* 357–9)

Homer's portrait of Hera as a fierce patroness, even a foremother, of Achaian warriors has its origins in her most important regional cult.[118] In the Argolid, Hera seems to have been associated from very early times with the concept of the hero, etymologically, in myth and in worship. A famous and puzzling example is her intimate yet antagonistic relationship with Herakles, the demigod of Tiryns who undertook his labors as a result of her machinations. Hera and Herakles entertained a mutual hostility, yet the name of this native son of Argolis seems to mean "Glory of Hera." On the Tiryns akropolis, where a Bronze Age megaron and altar had fallen to ruins, Hera began to receive archaeologically visible offerings in the eighth century.[119]

The Argive Heraion itself was deliberately juxtaposed to prehistoric ruins, in this case the cemetery of Prosymna, where numerous Geometric offerings were left in Mycenaean tombs. These gifts to the ancient dead were initially interpreted by archaeologists as signs of "hero cult," and later as "tomb cult," the sporadic worship of putative ancestors (Chapter 5). Many of the same gifts (bronze fibulae, pins and rings; bronze offering bowls; terracotta spools and other specific ceramic types) were deposited in both the tombs and the Heraion. The possible role of Prosymna's Mycenaean tombs in the origins of the cult at the Heraion remains the subject of debate.[120] So does the relationship between the Hera cults of the Argolid, which left durable traces by ca. 800, and the *Iliad*, which was first disseminated in writing ca. 750–700, but must have circulated in various oral versions during previous centuries. Did the nobles of Argolis respond to the emergent epic tradition by proudly insisting on their own ties to the goddess, and investing more heavily in her cults?[121]

The *Iliad* indisputably left its mark on Hera's worshipers. One of Homer's epithets for the goddess, *leukōlenos* ("white-armed"), appears on an inscribed gold ring (Figure 1.6; ca. 560), which was probably dedicated in the Argive Heraion: "Ariknidas dedicated it to the goddess, white-armed Hera."[122]

*Figure 1.6* Gold and silver man's ring inscribed with dedication to Hera, probably from the Argive Heraion, ca. 575. J. Paul Getty Museum. Digital image courtesy of the Getty's Open Content Program

The use of Homeric epithets as cult titles was unusual, yet early Archaic inscriptions from Hera's shrine at Perachora also call her "white-armed," suggesting that worshipers in the region were identifying Homeric Hera with the goddess they knew locally.[123]

A similar phenomenon is observable in a fragmentary hymn to Hera by Sappho:

Close by me as I [pray, please show,]
Lady Hera, your [lovely form]
Which Atreus' sons, [the famous] kings
Saw in their prayers.

Having completed [numerous toils,]
First at Troy [then on the sea,]

Setting sail to this place, they were unable
[To reach their destination]

Before they prayed to you and Zeus
And the desirable [son] of Thyone.
So now [have mercy and bring aid]
As you did of old . . .

[Two additional stanzas are mostly lost.]
(Fr. 17 *LP*)[124]

Writing in the early sixth century, Sappho was keenly aware of Hera's identity as the goddess of the "famous kings" Agamemnon and Menelaos, "the sons of Atreus," as they are so often called in the *Iliad*.[125] She also alluded to a tradition that the victorious Greeks stopped at her own island, Lesbos, and prayed to Hera for assistance in reaching home. Sappho had in mind a specific sanctuary at Lesbos, where the goddess was worshiped together with Zeus and Dionysos, "the desirable son of Thyone." Hera was the principal deity here; as in Argolis, Zeus was her spouse but played a secondary role.[126] Sappho blurred the distinction between the epic Hera and the local goddess, using the precedent of help given to Agamemnon and Menelaos as the context for her own, more personal request, which was stated in the lost section of the poem.

Alcaeus, Sappho's contemporary and countryman, took a very different approach in his own hymn to Hera, of which I quote the first three stanzas:

[O Mistress] Hera, to whom the people of Lesbos,
On a conspicuous [mountain], once set up
A large precinct, to be shared by all,
And placed therein altars for the immortals,

Giving Zeus the title "God of Suppliants"
And naming you "Famous goddess of the Aiolians,
Mother of all"; as for the third one here,
They called him "God of the deer,"

"Dionysos who devours them raw." We call on you:
Listen benevolently to our prayers.
Save us from present hardship
And from the sadness of exile.
(Fr. 129 *LP*)[127]

Alcaeus completely ignores the Panhellenic and epic aspects of Hera in order to focus on her local persona. He emphasizes her importance to Lesbos and its people. She is "Mother of all," a title quite foreign to the Homeric conception of Hera. We may interpret it as an indication that Hera of Lesbos was a successor to one of the powerful Bronze Age goddesses who dominated Greek and Anatolian religion. Additionally, she was regarded as a patroness of the Aiolian Greeks on the island. The succeeding sections of the poem deal with Lesbian politics, and Alcaeus prays that Hera and her two divine companions will favor his cause.[128]

Next we turn to Hera's annual festival at the Argive Heraion. The Heraion was a regional cult center, in Classical times under the control of Argos (its earlier status is debated). Although most literary sources on the festival are late, they mention a procession led by shield-bearing youths, girls in white dresses, women's dances, a ritual involving the presentation of a robe to the goddess, and a footrace, again by young men in arms. A shield was the prize in Hera's games.[129] The legend of Kleobis and Biton illustrates Argive piety toward the goddess:

> There was a festival of Hera among the Argives, and it was absolutely necessary for their mother to be brought to the temple by a team of oxen. But the oxen had not returned from the fields, and because they were out of time, the youths took the yoke upon their own shoulders. They drew the wagon, with their mother riding on it, and covered forty-five stades to reach the temple.
>
> (Hdt. 1.31.2)

At the peak of their youth and strength, the brothers lay down in the sanctuary and never woke again, this glorious end being recognized as the reward of Hera. Characteristic is the test of strength which exacts a cruel price from the goddess's male worshipers. In this story, the two strong youths are assimilated to the fine, unblemished cattle, who became pleasing gifts to the goddess in the festival's climactic sacrifice. Hera governed the welfare of cattle herds, the most important index of wealth, as well as the maturation of adolescent boys into warriors, and girls into wives and mothers. Terracotta figurines from the Heraion show the goddess in her maternal role as nurturer of youths (*kourotrophos*), holding a child in her lap. The prominence of cattle in the Argive Hera cult is reflected in a Homeric epithet for the goddess, "ox-eyed" (*boōpis*). Although surprising to modern sensibilities, this title reflects the beauty attributed by pastoral cultures to the animals on which they are economically dependent. In the Argive peninsula, then, Hera gave prosperity, progeny and military victory, each equally crucial to the welfare of the community.

This picture of a goddess who oversaw the most fundamental needs of her people contrasts with that in most other parts of the Greek world, where Hera received far less attention. Homer's testimony of her three favored cities suggests an early cult at Sparta, but she was not a major goddess in the Classical city.[130] Again, if our data were confined strictly to evidence from Athens, we would conclude that Hera was a minor goddess, significant mainly for her role as Zeus' bride, which was celebrated in a festival known as the *Hieros Gamos* (Sacred Marriage), an auspicious time for weddings.[131] The nuptial aspect of Hera's worship is reflected in the most famous Homeric episode involving the goddess, the "Deception of Zeus," in which Hera (after elaborate preparations) uses her sex appeal to distract Zeus while Poseidon helps the Greeks get the upper hand against the Trojans.[132]

> Then the ox-eyed Lady Hera considered
> How to deceive the aigis-bearer Zeus.
> And in her heart this counsel seemed the best,

To adorn herself well and visit the peak of Ida;
If he wished to lie with her, loving her body,
She could shed a harmless, gentle sleep
Over his eyelids and his cunning mind.
(Hom. *Il.* 14.159–65)

In cult, the union of Zeus and Hera was a model for marital sexuality leading to procreation. In the *Iliad,* Zeus lays eyes on Hera and immediately thinks of the first time they made love, not as bride and groom, but in a premarital dalliance, "without the knowledge of their dear parents" (14.296). There follows a negotiation between the amorous husband and his coyly seductive wife about whether to have intercourse outdoors. In the epic context, the Sacred Marriage has been transformed into a titillating narrative device, condemned by Plato because it set a bad example for young people.[133]

Hera appeared as Zeus' consort in many minor cults around the Greek world, but she was worshiped as a preeminent deity in only a few places other than Argolis. According to Furley and Bremer, "There is a remarkable dearth of hymns and prayers to Hera." The only extant examples are the two Lesbian hymns we have examined, and a "very unimaginative" and brief Homeric hymn, which reveals its epic bias by locating the goddess on Olympos and defining her in terms of her relationship to Zeus:[134]

I sing golden-throned Hera whom Rhea bore,
Queen of immortals, of surpassing beauty,
Sister and spouse of loud-resounding Zeus,
Glorious lady, whom all gods on high Olympos
Revere, just as they honor thunder-loving Zeus.
(*Hymn. Hom.* 12)

Second to the Argive Heraion in fame was the goddess's sanctuary on the Ionian island of Samos, founded in the early Geometric period (but not mentioned in the *Iliad*). Conflicting traditions at Samos held on the one hand that the goddess was indigenous, and on the other that her cult was imported from Argos.[135] As in Argolis, Hera was dominant here, a "great goddess." Situated on a well-traveled maritime route, the Heraion at Samos attracted an international clientele of travelers and traders who dedicated rich gifts: Egyptian ivories and scarabs, Phoenician and Babylonian bronzes, and gold jewelry. The luxury of this period is evoked by the epic poet Asius, who described the Ionian men assembling on Samos:

And they used to go with their combed locks
To the precinct of Hera, clad in lovely robes,
Their snow-white tunics skimming the broad earth,
With golden clips like cicadas on them,
And their flowing hair, in gold bands, the breeze lifted,
And they wore intricate ornaments upon their arms
(Asius in Ath. 12.30 [525f])

As in Argolis and Lesbos, Hera's Samian cult helped to shape her people's ethnic and civic identity. Colonists in sixth-century Naukratis, a trading emporium in Egypt, established a sanctuary of Hera, because worship of this goddess was a distinctive sign of their Samian origins.[136]

Unlike Zeus, Archaic Hera was very much a temple deity whose cults used statues as the focus of worship. The Geometric temple at Samos was highly influential, one of the first *hekatompeda* or "hundred-footers," while its Archaic successors were among the largest Greek temples ever built.[137] Another early and extremely rich sanctuary was constructed at Perachora, in the territory of Corinth. Like the Samians, the Corinthians were traders, and Corinth was an important Mediterranean port. Hera's major Aegean sanctuaries (Argos, Samos, Perachora) are notable for Geometric dedications of miniature houses, which have been variously interpreted as models of her earliest temples, or of domestic dwellings. More recently, de Polignac contrasted the house models with a similar series of ship models and actual ships dedicated in Hera sanctuaries (Samos as well as Kroton and Gravisca in Italy), proposing that the houses could have been dedicated by women, and the ships by men. Several other distinctive votive types recur in Hera's Archaic sanctuaries, suggesting consistent themes in her worship. These include metal and terracotta shields, which refer to her ancient role in nurturing warriors.[138]

The ship models in Samos and Italy were probably connected with Hera's sponsorship of maritime trade ventures and colonization, a theme with affinities to her Iliadic role as a patroness of the Greek expedition to Troy. During the eighth and seventh centuries, Greeks emigrated to Italy and Sicily in large numbers. Many were from the northern coast of the Peloponnese, an area which would later be known as Achaia. At the time these colonists left their homeland, the Greek poleis were still in their infancy, and Achaia especially was far from becoming urbanized.[139] There were no major temples or sanctuaries of Hera on the north coast of the Peloponnese to compare with the Argive Heraion. Yet the colonists established important Hera cults at Sybaris, Poseidonia, Kroton and Metapontum and defined themselves as "Achaians." The people of Poseidonia especially seem to have regarded Hera as preeminent, given that two of the city's major sanctuaries were devoted to her, one in the city and one at the extraurban site of Foce del Sele. Like the Hera cult at Samos and numerous others, the sanctuary at Foce del Sele claimed to be an offshoot of the Argive Heraion.[140] Why did the colonists choose Hera as their patron goddess? Homer's catalogue of ships (*Il.* 2.569–80) states that the towns of the northeastern coast (Pellene, Hyperesia, Helike and Aigion) belonged in the holdings of Agamemnon, king of Mycenae. Colonists from this area drew on the epic tradition and expressed a claim to be descendants of Homer's "Achaians" when they installed Hera, protectress of Greek warriors abroad, in the new sanctuaries of the West.[141]

As the case of Hera demonstrates, the relative importance of deities within a local pantheon varied widely, and one god or (more often) goddess might outshine the others in the eyes of a given population. Such preeminent deities helped to shape ethnic, civic and personal identity. The Geometric and early Archaic periods were to some degree an "Age of Hera." Through the medium of Homeric poetry, the whole Greek world heard of Hera's ancient and continuing ties to Argos and Mycenae, and knowledge of her Panhellenic persona stimulated the propagation of her worship in Greek colonies. Yet devotion to Hera was distinctive precisely because it was *not* universal. The regional and ethnic character of Hera's worship ensured that her fortunes rose and fell with those of the peoples who made her their preeminent goddess. Though the prestige of the Mycenaean past clung to her, after the sixth century Hera never again enjoyed the same prominence in the religious landscape of the Greeks.

## ESSAY 1.3: RECIPROCITY IN GREEK RELIGION

Most religions envision superhuman agents who act intentionally in the physical world, and whose actions affect human lives. This in turn opens the way for a human response. When divine actions are beneficial, there may be praise, gifts of thanksgiving and requests for additional blessings. In response to harmful actions, there may be attempts to appease what is felt to be the anger of the deity. When such ongoing relationships are perceived as mutually beneficial, they may be described as reciprocal. Greek religion was predicated on the intuitive inference that the gods were humanlike, in the sense that they were capable of maintaining reciprocal relationships analogous to those cultivated among humans.[142] During the Mycenaean period, for example, rulers and aristocrats maintained relationships of reciprocity with one another by exchanging precious gifts. At the sanctuaries of Olympia, Delphi, Delos and Samos, the aristocrats of the Early Iron Age extended the practice of luxury gift-giving to include the gods.[143]

The nature of this divine-human reciprocity, however, requires further exploration. Traditionally, the Christian West has looked back upon interactions with "pagan" gods as examples of an inferior kind of relationship with the divine. From the viewpoint of Christian theologians, the very nature of pagan worship was suspect because it involved an exchange of one grace or favor (*charis*) for another, whereas the apostle Paul had taught that *charis* was unidirectional rather than reciprocal.[144] This value judgment about the relative inferiority of pagan piety is alive and well in modern scholarship conducted from a Christian perspective. Consider this remark in a 2003 monograph on Paul: "The *do ut des* ("I give that you may give") mentality of Graeco-Roman religion reduced human piety to a mere business transaction."[145]

Even Classicists have maintained that Greek religion was dependent upon a mentality of commercial exchange, citing the Latin formula *do ut des* (which derives not from religion but from Roman contract law) and the supposedly contractual or mechanical nature of the relationship.[146] Indeed, certain practices of Greek religion, such as the vow to provide a gift to a deity should one's goals be achieved, appear at first sight to approximate a commercial transaction. More recent studies of reciprocity influenced by anthropology, however, have drawn a clear distinction between the mentalities of commercial exchange and reciprocity, showing that they are in fact diametrically opposed. Furthermore, while commercial exchange is a relatively recent development in human history, reciprocity is a far more ancient form of human behavior, rooted in moral intuitions which evolved to facilitate social interaction among primates.[147]

## Reciprocity and gift exchange

In gift exchange, which is a form of reciprocity, the presentation of gifts or favors is expected but (crucially) not required. As social relationships shift, there is always the possibility that next time, the giver will find a different, more desirable recipient for his or her largesse. The situation is quite unlike a contractual or commercial one, where it is understood that an agreement can be enforced. If I fail to pay for the earrings I remove from a shop, I engage in theft, just as the shopkeeper commits fraud if she retains my money and fails to produce the goods. Commercial exchanges, moreover, are typically subject to the legal principle of "consideration." That is, they must meet minimum standards of just exchange in order to be valid. According to Roman jurists, a purchase was potentially invalid if the price paid was not at least half the actual value. The presentation of a gift, however, could not be invalidated in this way, because it was not conceptualized as an equitable exchange of goods or services.[148]

In a commercial transaction, then, the value of the goods or services exchanged is ostensibly equal, whereas in gift exchange this is not necessarily the case, especially in the short term. Equivalence is sometimes actively avoided in favor of attempts to place the recipient in one's debt, or for reasons of display, again with no guarantee that the benefit will be returned. Even though they are well aware of the social realities involved, people deliberately "misrecognize" the economic value of gifts in order to emphasize that gifts are *not* commercial transactions ("It's the thought that counts.")[149] People are expected to give according to their means, not necessarily according to what they receive. Furthermore, whereas a commercial transaction does not have the direct goal of maintaining and strengthening the relationship between the parties, this is a key function of gift exchange. Commercial transactions do not depend on trust, and may even erode it, for each party has an inherent interest in taking advantage of the other. In systems of gift exchange, on the other hand, people attempt to build trust by reinforcing a reciprocal relationship over a long period. Commerce can function efficiently even if the parties never expect to meet again, but gift exchange cannot.[150]

Thus a common component in Greek prayer was the reminder to the deity that he or she had been helpful before, or conversely, that the worshiper had a long history of presenting gifts. In Book 1 of the *Iliad*, the priest Chryses prays to Apollo for vengeance against the Greeks. Chryses reminds the god of his previous service in building a "gracious" temple, one that expressed the *charis* (favor or grace) of their reciprocal relationship.[151]

> Hear me, you of the silver bow who guard Chryse,
> Mighty ruler of sacred Killa and of Tenedos,
> If ever I roofed a gracious (*charient'*) temple for you, Smintheus,

Or if ever I burned for you the fat thigh bones
Of bulls and goats, accomplish my desire:
Let the Danaoi pay for (*tiseian*) my tears with your arrows.
(Hom. *Il.* 1.37–42)

Chryses' prayer is sometimes described as a bald assertion that Apollo "owes" him something, but this is a mischaracterization. Chryses does not believe that any gift in particular has bought him an answered prayer, nor is his mentality that of a purchaser who now expects the merchandise to be handed over. It is the *history* of reciprocity between himself and Apollo to which he appeals, as though asking for a favor from a friend. From his perspective, it is not Apollo who has incurred a debt but the Greeks, who must now make "payment" for the wrongs they have committed.

As in human gift exchange, which also worked on the principles of *charis* rather than those of commerce, relationships with the gods did not always turn out as the worshiper hoped, and the omens from sacrifice were not always favorable.[152] Often the gods' rejection of an offering can be traced to moral (or more rarely, ritual) violations by the gift-giver, but other times the reason for the rejection is less clear. Xenophon tells of the Theban Koiratadas, who contracted with a group of mercenaries to become their general, on condition that he supply them with rations. He duly arrived with animals for sacrifice and other supplies, but then things began to go wrong:

> On the first day, Koiratadas did not receive good omens from the sacrifice, nor did he measure out rations to the troops. On the next day, the victims were standing by the altar and Koiratadas, wearing his garland, was about to sacrifice, but Timasion the Dardanian, Neon of Asine, and Kleanor of Orchomenos told him not to sacrifice, for he would not be leading the army unless he gave them what was needed. So he ordered the supplies served out, but when he fell short of supplying each soldier with enough food for a day, he took his victims and left, renouncing his generalship.
>
> (Xen. *An.* 7.1.40–1)

Xenophon refrains from proposing an explicit reason for the rejected sacrifice, but the verdict of the gods seems to have coincided with that of the men, who found Koiratadas unfit to lead the army.

## The limits of the gift exchange model

The form of exchange found in Greek religion more closely approximates gift exchange than commerce, since the parties have no guarantee that past benefits will be rewarded, the value of the exchange is rarely perceived as equivalent, and the goal is to develop long-term amicable relationships which are mutually valued. On the other hand, some aspects of Greek religion fit less comfortably into the model of gift exchange. Although gift exchange systems tend to favor a certain inequality in any given exchange, there is often an expectation that the benefits to parties of similar social standing will, over time, be roughly equivalent. The relationship between humans and gods, however, was highly asymmetrical. Not only were the gods more far more powerful and knowledgeable than human beings, but also the benefits sought from and given by the gods ensured humans' very survival. Even the most elaborate of gifts, the annual sacrifice of hundreds of animals at a time, or the construction of magnificent temples, could scarcely be perceived as equivalent in value.[153]

In order to sustain the analogy with reciprocity in human societies, we must turn to social relations between people of unequal status, where anthropologists have identified reciprocity as a key source of stability. In traditional societies, powerful elites are expected to ensure a minimum standard of living and other periodic benefits in return for the deference they are accorded from the lower social ranks. The *leitourgia* of democratic Athens, a system of redistribution by which wealthy citizens were expected to pay for public benefits enjoyed by all, is an example, but philanthropy by the wealthy was (and is) hardly limited to democracies.[154] Relationships between patrons and clients or landholders and tenants may also involve reciprocity, whereby each side has obligations to the other, though the benefits in each direction are different in kind and in scope.

An important element in reciprocity between humans of different ranks is the deference or respect paid to the powerful. This deference may translate into concrete benefits (as when a Roman patron gathered votes), or the benefit conferred by inferiors may consist of intangible honor and acknowledgment. One of the most consistent themes in Greek myth is the anger of gods when their power is not properly acknowledged, and the consequent application of coercion. Myth offers many examples of "failure to sacrifice" or "failure to tithe" as the reason for the anger of a god or goddess.[155] In Sophocles' *Ajax*, the chorus wonders whether Ajax's madness has come about because he failed to give Artemis her due:

> Was it because of some victory that yielded her no fruit,
> Whether she was cheated of brilliant war spoils,
> Or offered no gifts when a deer was shot?
>
> (Soph. *Aj.* 176–8)

In myth, the most coercive of gods was Dionysos. In Euripides' *Bacchae* (and other "myths of resistance"), he visits madness and gruesome punishments on those who foolishly refuse to acknowledge his divinity. This pattern is related to the special nature of Dionysos as a god who possessed his worshipers; he was not, by and large, an angry god. In worship contexts, however, certain deities were perceived as angry by nature and in need of regular appeasement. Because coercion is inconsistent with reciprocity, a cult based purely on appeasement could not be considered reciprocal. In practice, however, there was always the hope that such gods, once properly provided with honors, would reciprocate by conferring benefits. Angry Poseidon could be transformed into the "steadfast" god who warded off earthquakes, Apollo the plague god could become an averter of plague, and

Ares the war god could give victory. In Aeschylus' *Eumenides* (1006–9), the terrifying Erinyes, who once threatened to blast Athens with plague, are persuaded to "hold back what is baneful to the land, and send what is profitable for the victory of the city." Cult heroes too often began their careers as angry powers in need of appeasement.[156]

Greek deities occasionally solicited worship from humans, in effect asking to begin a reciprocal relationship. As the herald Pheidippides crossed the Arkadian mountains, Pan appeared to him and made his wishes known, using the familiar language of reciprocity: "Crying the name of Pheidippides aloud, Pan bade him ask the Athenians why they paid him no attention, even though he was well disposed toward the Athenians, had often assisted them, and would do so again in the future" (Hdt. 6.105.2).

Whereas the friendly, unassuming Pan presented himself as a gift-giver wondering why he had never received a thank-you note, other gods could be more peremptory. According to the Homeric *Hymn* in her honor, Demeter more or less commanded that the people of Eleusis build a temple for her, and dictated the terms of the reciprocal arrangement:

> But come now, let all the people build me a great temple
> And an altar beneath, below the city and its steep wall
> Upon a rising hill above the Place of Lovely Dances.
> And I myself will instruct you in my mystic rites, that hereafter
> You may perform them in purity and so conciliate me.
>
> (*Hom. Hymn Dem*. 270–74)

In the Homeric *Hymn to Apollo*, the god similarly commanded worship from the bewildered Cretans whom he hijacked and brought to the future sanctuary of Delphi, promising benefits in return:

> I am the son of Zeus, and Apollo is my name;
> I brought you here over the great depth of the sea,
> Meaning you no harm, but here you shall keep my rich temple
> Which is much honored among humans.
> You shall know the plans of the immortals, and by their will
> You shall be honored unceasingly every day, forever.
>
> (*Hymn. Hom. Ap*. 480–85)

Apollo then instructed the Cretans as to the proper forms of his worship, concluding with a dire warning (540–3) that if they were disobedient or unrighteous, he would cause them to be enslaved to other men. Because of myths like these, Greek religion was subject to the charge that its hold over the human mind was predicated on fear of vastly powerful beings and their punishments. This was precisely the criticism of Epicurus. Unlike tyrannical mortals, the gods could not be dislodged from their positions of privilege, except by demolishing a fundamental assumption of Greek religion, that gods acted in the world. Epicurus seems to have been particularly concerned with debunking this notion, as well as the idea of afterlife punishments.[157]

The reciprocal arrangements dictated by Demeter and Apollo resemble the relationship between Yahweh and the Israelites. In Egypt, Yahweh announced to Moses: "I will take you as my own people, and I will be your God. Then you will know that I am the Lord your God, who brought you out from under the yoke of the Egyptians" (*Exod.* 6:7).

Yahweh later informed Moses (*Lev.* 1:1–17) of his requirements for the sacrifice of cattle, sheep, goats and birds. He further established a "covenant" with the Israelites, whereby he made certain specific promises (e.g. freeing them from Egyptian slavery), and in return they were held to a detailed list of specific ritual and ethical requirements. This reciprocal arrangement differs from the Greek examples of Demeter and Apollo in the explicit use of the legalistic, treaty-like format of the covenant.

Each of these narratives is an etiological myth created to explain how an existing relationship with a god began, rather than a description of the relationship in practice. The epistemological uncertainty characteristic of worship contexts is here replaced by a god's unequivocal statement of his or her wishes. The degree of fusion between a theological concept, such as "Apollo brought our ancestors here to tend his sanctuary" or "Yahweh made a detailed covenant with us," and real-time interactions with the deities in question will vary according to the cultural and historical context. In the case of Judaism, the covenantal concept was regularly reinforced through the canonization of the Pentateuch as scripture, encouraging a close correspondence between theology and practice. In the Greek case, it is far less clear what impact the coercive scenarios narrated by the poets of the Homeric *Hymns* had on actual practice and the perceptions of worshipers at Eleusis and Delphi. On the other hand, the widespread practice of tithing in response to the receipt of benefits suggests that certain deities were believed to possess a "right" to material honors in fixed amounts, in return for the good things they gave.[158]

## The theological rejection of reciprocity

In antiquity, reflective critiques of traditional Greek religion questioned the intuitive inference that reciprocity with divine agents was possible. The gods were known to live a blessed life, free of the needs to which humans are subject; therefore, how could they possibly benefit from anything humans had to offer?[159] In Plato's *Euthyphro*, a discussion of piety, Socrates maneuvers his hapless interlocutor into a series of untenable positions:

*Socrates:* Would not the correct way of asking be to ask [the gods] for what we need from them?

*Euthyphro:* What else?

*Socrates:* And would not the correct way of giving be to present them in return with what they need from us? For it would not be skilled giving, to present what someone does not need.

*Euthyphro:* You're right, Socrates.

*Socrates:* Then for humans and gods, piety would be a skill of commercial exchange (*emporikē technē*) with one another?

*Euthyphro:* Yes, commercial, if it pleases you to call it that.

*Socrates:* But it doesn't please me, if it is not true. Tell me, what aid (*ōphelia*) do the gods obtain, from the gifts they get from us? What they give is clear to all, for we have no good which they do not give. But how are they aided, by what they get from us? Or do we get the better of them, in our commerce, to such an extent that we get everything good from them, and they get nothing from us?

*Euthyphro:* But Socrates, you don't suppose, do you, that the gods are aided by the things they get from us?

*Socrates:* But then, Euthyphro, what then would our gifts to the gods be?

*Euthyphro:* Why, what else but honor (*timē*) and perquisites (*gera*) and, as I said before, gratitude (*charis*)?

(Pl. *Euthphr*. 14d-e)

Notice that Socrates deftly blurs the distinction between gifts and commerce, and then suggests that the offering of gifts, in and of itself, impiously implies needs on the part of the gods that can be satisfied with human assistance and resources.[160] Euthyphro rejects Socrates' leading question, because it does not square with his intuitive understanding of worship. For gods as for humans, the getting of *timē* was a matter not of meeting needs but of receiving that which is appropriate to one's status.[161] Surely no worshiper supposed that a god or goddess had need of a piece of armor, or yet another clay figurine. Instead, these gifts demonstrated that the deity was held in honor by the worshiper.

In the religion of everyday social exchange, worshipers saw the gods as desirous of honors (*timai*) and believed that they took pleasure in gifts, prayers, dances and sacrifice. Thus a reciprocal relationship was indeed possible, since humans had something of value to offer. Whereas humans expected *charis* from the gods so that they could survive, reproduce and avoid pain and danger, the *charis* expected by the gods was neither solely nor fundamentally predicated on material gifts. Above all, the gods desired honor and pleasure. Honor was satisfied through material gifts, such as first-fruit offerings and tithes from battle spoils, and through nonmaterial ones, such as hymns.[162] The role of aesthetic pleasure in reciprocal relationships with the Greek gods is often overlooked, but the vocabulary of worship constantly alludes to the pleasure gods experienced from both material (beautiful objects) and nonmaterial forms of worship (dances, athletics).[163] Another passage of the Homeric *Hymn to Apollo* aptly illustrates how the same sights bring pleasure to both humans and gods:

But you, Phoibos, rejoice most in Delos.
Where gather the long-robed Ionians
With their children and modest wives,
They are minded, whenever they set up the contest,

To delight you with boxing and dance and song.
Whoever met them, the Ionians assembled,
Would call them deathless and unaging,
For he would see the grace (*charis*) of all,
And the sight of the men, and the women
With lovely belts, and the swift ships,
And their great wealth would delight his heart.
(*Hymn. Hom. Ap.* 146–155)

Just as we approach powerful people with tokens of respect, requests for favors and thanks for benefits received, the Greeks offered gifts to the gods for the sake of *timē* (honor), *charis* (gratitude) and *chreia* (need), the three reasons for sacrifice suggested by Theophrastus.[164] The view that offerings to the gods were bribes or commercial exchanges is a reflective critique of intuitive belief and practice. Although regularly renewed since ancient times, this critique misrepresents the actual dynamics of worship.

Narratives about the establishment of Greek cults tended to feature a god's outright demand for *timē*. This initial coercion was transformed into a relationship characterized by respectful awe rather than abject fear. Whereas myths often warned of the gods' coercive powers, cult practice almost always attempted to establish or maintain reciprocity. In cases where deities were not perceived as amenable to reciprocity, people dealt with them using magic, a topic to which we will return in Chapter 3.

## Notes

1 Philosophers: this line of reasoning follows Wittgenstein in shifting focus away from truth claims to "forms of life." That is, the significance of religious beliefs lies in how people live, not whether gods exist. See Kishik 2008.113–16.
2 Geertz 1968.4; Bellah 1991.21.
3 Otto 1924 [1917]; Eliade 1959.
4 In this book, I sometimes use "gods" as shorthand for the wide variety of culturally postulated superhuman beings found in polytheistic traditions. With respect to Greek religion, this category includes gods and goddesses; heroes, heroines and other powerful dead; nymphs and other nature spirits; and assorted *daimones*.
5 Marx 1970 [1844].131; Durkheim 1915.47; Freud 1928.39.
6 Smith 1982.xi. For refutation of anthropologists' doubts about the value of "religion" as an etic category see Boyer 1994.29–60, and for the historical use of the term "religion" within the discipline of Classics, see Bremmer 1998b.10–14.
7 Spiro 1987.197, reprinted from a 1966 article entitled "Religion: Problems of Definition and Explanation." Compare Renfrew 2007.113–14. As Burkert notes (1996.7n.23), Spiro's definition insists on culture, but the basic mechanism is extracultural.
8 Pyysiäinen 2003.53. Compare Pyysiäinen 2002a on the problem of defining religion. Barrett (2011.232) declines to give a definition of religion, arguing that cognitive science "does not pretend to exhaustively explain everything that might be called 'religion' (provocative book titles aside)." He is, presumably, referring to Pascal Boyer's *Religion Explained* (2001).
9 Counterintuitive: Atran (2002.13–14), who has proposed a synthesis of cognitive theory with "commitment theory" (focusing on the dynamics of costs and benefits to the

group and individual), defines religion as the "passionate communal display of costly commitment to counterintuitive worlds governed by supernatural agents."

10 Polythetic: Sperber 2004.750.

11 Mental tools: also referred to in the literature as modules (e.g. Sperber 1994) or systems (e.g. Boyer 2001). Sperber and Hirschfeld 2004.41 give a summary of the best-documented mental tools, which include theory of mind, folk biology and face recognition. Susceptibilities: for dispositions (effects which have been positively selected for in biological evolution) versus susceptibilities (side effects of dispositions) see Sperber 1996.67.

12 On the alleged non-theism of Theravada Buddhism, see Spiro 1987.189–97. In my view, Theravada Buddhism is either a religion which includes a set of non-theistic doctrines of varying relevance for practitioners or a non-theistic philosophy which has become (for most practitioners) a religion.

13 See the critique by anthropologist James Laidlaw (2007.213), a specialist in Buddhism and Jainism, who suggests that cognitive scientists successfully explain "what the Enlightenment called 'Natural Religion' and 'superstition,'" but not religion or the specifics of religious traditions.

14 Vulnerable to caricature: as Parker (2014) observes.

15 Political and social: for religion as political ideology see e.g. Knapp 1996. For a history of theoretical perspectives in Greek religion see Morris 1998.

16 Boyer 1994.3: "The content and organization of religious ideas depend, in important ways, on noncultural properties of the human mind-brain." Barrett 2004.21: "Belief in gods arises because of the natural functioning of completely normal mental tools working in common natural and social contexts." It should be noted that scholars sympathetic to theism (e.g. Visala 2011) have been attracted to CSR for this very reason. On the analogy of natural language acquisition see Whitehouse 2004.29.

17 Specifics: For this problem see Whitehouse 2007 (calling for an integration of causal explanation and interpretive methodologies). Compare the caveats of Kindt 2012.44 and Day 2005.86–88 (e.g. the suggestion that the conceptual toolbox of cognitive theory is "infinitely removed from the facts that most scholars of religion want to understand"). Cross-cultural: while I avoid the term "human universal," the evidence suggests that every individual is born with a susceptibility to religion. Furthermore religious beliefs and behaviors are found in every (or nearly every) culture. Whether religion is truly "universal" is a red herring; what requires explanation is its near-ubiquity across cultures. On human universals and cultural relativism see Brown 1991.

18 Embedded: e.g. Price 1999.3: "There is no religious sphere separate from politics and warfare or private life; instead, religion is embedded in all aspects of life, public and private." In spite of this embeddedness, a cognitivist approach suggests that the *causal* factors producing religious beliefs and practices can be distinguished from those driving other aspects of culture.

19 Marathon: Hdt. 6.106.3. Thermopylai: Hdt. 7.206.1. On functionalism see Sperber 1996.47–9.

20 No private religions: Gould 1985.4. Compare Pyysiäinen 2003.233. Most if not all cognitivists would agree with Sørensen (2007.47) that cognitive constraints on the mind are not sufficient to explain cultural phenomena. They are, however, necessary to explain them.

21 Credence: the most educated and skeptical thinkers "purified myth of the marvelous" but did not question the historicity of heroes, the Trojan War and so forth. See Veyne 1988.41–57.

22 No word for religion: the lack of an explicit category of "the religious" in a given culture need not mean that people lack an implicit concept, nor that the category is not useful from an etic perspective. Boyer (1994.31) gives the example of the distinction between an ungrammatical sentence and a meaningless one – everyone intuitively recognizes the difference without having a word for it.

23 Renfrew (2007.113) also discusses this definition.

24 For the categories "religion," "mythology" and "ritual," including the relationship between Greek myth and religion, see Bremmer 1998b.10–24.

25 "One": *Rig Veda* 10.129. For the parallelism between concepts of unity in the *Rig Veda* and the pre-Socratic philosophers, see Mendoza 2011.29–30; Bernabé and Mendoza 2013.

26 Isis: Versnel 1990.39–95, 2011.283–301.

27 For Herodotus' inconsistent use of terminology relating to gods and heroes, and for his concept of divine unity see Harrison 2000.158–81. Common among the Greeks: Harrison 2000.171–5; Versnel 2011.268–80. Sources collected (mostly in French translation) in François 1957.

28 Some historians (e.g. Price 1984.10–11, citing Needham 1972) have denied that "belief as a religious term" was operative in ancient Greek religion, arguing instead that it is a Christian construct. "Belief" was not often articulated as a central component of piety, because assent to the existence of gods who intervene in human affairs was a shared but largely intuitive and tacit inference. See also Price 1999.126–7 and Versnel 2011.292, 539–59 (esp. 540n.6, citing cognitive approaches which affirm, *contra* Needham, that belief is a natural capacity shared by all human beings). Compare Barrett 2004.1–19 on what cognitivists mean by "belief." For interdependency of belief and ritual see Yunis 1988.38–58; Kowalzig 2007.2.

29 For our purposes this reduces the usefulness of rational choice theory, another relatively new approach to religion pioneered by Rodney Stark. For an introduction see the essays in Young 1997.

30 For colonization from pre- and non-polis communities during the eighth century, see Antonaccio 1999.112–13.

31 Unity: Burkert 1985.8. For "Greek religions" see Price 1999.ix, 1–10. As he points out, this terminology usefully foregrounds regional variation. For caveats about "shared" gods and rituals see Polinskaya 2010.48–54.

32 Stressing continuity in the polis against the usual descriptions of civic breakdown: Gruen 1993; Mikalson 1998.288–323.

33 Shared: there is debate over exactly when the majority of Greeks began to think of themselves explicitly as "Hellenes." The current tendency is to place this development quite late and to assign a weightier role in the early Archaic period to family and civic identity: see Konstan 2001.31–6; Hall 2002a.168–220, 2004.50.

34 This is not to suggest that epic poetry utterly neglects cultic understandings of the gods in favor of mythic ones. Homer does in fact mention the cult of Zeus Herkeios (*Od.* 22.333–6), and we know from other sources that this title and function of Zeus were widespread.

35 Temple to Olympian Zeus: Arist. [*Ath. Pol.*] 5.20 (1313b).

36 Pheidias: compare Polyb. 30.10.6, Strabo 8.3.30.

37 Compelling: Epstein and Pacini 1999.463. (Although they refer to the two processes as "experiential" and "rational," intuitive beliefs are not to be regarded as "irrational" but instead merely nonreflective. Most intuitive beliefs are for all practical purposes correct; otherwise we would not be able to function in daily life). For overviews of dual-process approaches, see Chaiken and Trope 1999; Tremlin 2005, 2006.172–182; Evans and Frankish eds. 2009.

38 The sun's movement: Barrett 1999.324.

39 Terminology: Sperber 1997, esp. 78–9, describing how reflective concepts and beliefs arise from the human capacity for metarepresentation (for which see Chapter 2 and the glossary in this volume). See also Mercier and Sperber 2009, reconciling the dual-process model with the cognitivist theory of mental modules specialized for various tasks. Some aspects of the intuitive/reflective distinction were anticipated by Lucien Lévy-Bruhl and Vilfredo Pareto (for a summary see Evans-Pritchard 1965.78–99).

40 I have borrowed Stowers's phrase "the religion of everyday social exchange" and elements of his description (Stowers 2011.37–9) but I differ with his views in other respects.

41 I draw the term "epistemological uncertainty" from Stowers 2011.39. Cf. Burkert 1996.6 on the "knowledge barrier" (*adēlotēs*). For interaction with gods as a fundamentally social activity, but with the difference that unlike human agents, gods always possess "strategic information," see Boyer 2002.77; Tremlin 2006.113–121. On "strategic information" see further Chapter 2.

42 Theology: Henrichs 2010.21 cites the first appearance of the word *theologia* in Pl. *Resp.* 379a6. Arist. *Metaph.* 14.4 (1091a29–b112) refers to "theologians" whom he identifies with the early cosmogonic poets.

43 Epstein and Pacini's model stresses that the "rational" (i.e. reflective) mode is highly verbal and mediated by language. They write (1999.463) that the intuitive/experiential system can be a source of creativity "at its higher reaches, and particularly in interaction with the rational [i.e. reflective] system." For our purposes, I have included the visual arts within the category of "reflection" on religion because they involve metarepresentation. For "visual theology" see Elsner 1996.518.

44 "Theological correctness": Barrett 1999.

45 Inconsistency: Versnel 2011.60–87, 83–6, 517–25. The example of the Zeuses comes from Mikalson 1989.70–3 (cf. Mikalson 1991.3–5), who discusses the paradox that these and several other Zeuses were "treated, particularly in cult, as different, independent, deities." On this topic in relation to cult titles, see Parker 2003.182. As Boyer (1994.41) notes, it is fallacious to assume that the religious representations in a given culture are integrated and logically consistent.

46 Certain duties that we might consider administrative or mundane were, however, sacred in the eyes of Athenians. On a red-figure amphora in the Peiraieus Museum (Inv. 7341), Athena supervises the transport and pouring of her sacred olive oil by two citizen men: Themelis 2007.21–6.

47 On interpreting material culture in terms of specific beliefs see Morris 1998.34–5.

48 Epithets: e.g. Hom. *Il.* 1.14 (Far-Shooter, or perhaps Sure-Shooter), 1.37 (silver bow). Mantiklos' dedication: Day 1994.39–43; Depew 1997.238.

49 Outside a ritual context: for this key distinction see Price 1984.115; Ullucci 2011.60.

50 Using Homer as evidence: for a recent discussion see Whitley 1991.34–9 (concluding that Homer can at best provide "useful suggestions" for interpreting late Dark Age society). Comparison of six sacrificial scenes in Homer: Kirk 1981.64–70. On literary texts as sources for religion, see Harrison 2007, and for tragedy see the differing approaches of Mikalson 1991 and Sourvinou-Inwood 2003.

51 Herakles relief: Robinson 1948; van Straten 1995 fig. 93 (R90). The figure of Herakles on the relief imitates a lost statue sculpted by Lysippos.

52 Vase: Louvre G 496; van Straten 1995 fig. 152 (V200).

53 Van Straten 1995.186–92. For the individual's "different degree of involvement with the sacrifice depicted" on vase and votive relief, see van Straten 2005.27.

54 Victim species: van Straten 1987.161–7, with discussion of methodological issues. Post-kill: van Straten 1995.186–92. On interpreting sacrificial scenes in vase paintings and votive reliefs, cf. Lissarague 2012.565–70.

55 For the god's portion, see Ekroth 2007. For bovids and caprids, the femora (sometimes wrapped in fat) and/or the sacrum and tail were the preferred portion. For adult pigs, different procedures obtained, possibly the burning of bits of meat as in Hom. *Od.* 14.419–38. Preferences of vase buyers: van Straten 1995.24.

56 On the abnormality of human sacrifice in Greek religion see Bonnechere 1994.311–18, 2007.

57 Bizarreness is culturally relative; counterintuitiveness is not. A plant that eats people is counterintuitive because it violates a fundamental inference about the category "plant"; a plant named George is merely strange. Plants that eat people occur regularly

in fantasy books and films precisely because they are minimally counterintuitive. It is unlikely that plants with funny names will ever have the same appeal.

58 My explanation of MCIs is adapted from those of Boyer 2001.51–91 and Barrett 2004.22–30. Cf. Atran 2002.95–107, Pyysiäinen 2002b.

59 Kelly and Keil 1985.408, 413–15 (additionally, conscious beings were more likely to be transformed into mammals or birds than into reptiles, amphibians, fish or insects).

60 The Greeks had a tendency to endow abstract concepts with agency, but not in narratives of metamorphosis. Personifications such as "Justice" and "Grace" seem to arise instead from strongly anthropomorphizing (Chapter 2) habits of thought and corresponding narrative traditions.

61 Barrett 2004.26–7, citing "Chivo Man," a man-goat hybrid believed by some to haunt a citrus ranch in modern-day California. Chivo Man is derived from Mexican folklore.

62 Boyer 2001.135.

63 Truly emic: Evans-Pritchard (1965.24, 43, 47) memorably argued that many scholarly attempts to think emically amount to the "If I were a horse" fallacy. For emic vs. etic approaches to Greek culture see Versnel 1991.184–5; Bremmer 2007.139–43.

64 Durkheim 1915.206. For the need to avoid labeling phenomena as exclusively "social" or "religious" see Morris 1998.32–7. For a critique of Durkheim from a cognitive perspective see Bloch 1989.1–18, 106–36 (against Durkheim's claim that cognitive categories are entirely social in origin); Pyysiäinen 2003.55–75.

65 For a recent formulation of the long-standing scholarly dogma that practice (i.e. ritual) trumps belief in Greek religion see e.g. Price 1999.3. Cf. the statements to this effect by Burkert, Cartledge, Osborne and others, collected in Versnel 2011.544–5.

66 While some Classicists (e.g. van Straten and Versnel) have never lost sight of the gods, increased disciplinary focus on the gods and Greek theology is evident in Bremmer and Erskine eds. 2010 and Naiden 2013. For critique of the view that ritual is primary and fixed while the gods are fluid and variable see Scullion 1994.76–7.

67 Thales 11 A 22 *DK* (= Arist. *De an.* 411a7–8). On managing pantheons see Georgoudi 1996; Parker 2011.70–73; Versnel 2011.1–149, 501–15; Polinskaya 2013.87–115.

68 Avoiding offense: Versnel 1981b.13, 2011.501 with n. 2.

69 Meaningful god set: Polinskaya (2013.92; cf. Levy 1990.273–4) defines a "meaningful god set" as the set of deities that "have common significance and salience for a local community." The scientists (Roberts, Chiao and Pandey 1975) who coined the term, however, were working with individuals. Their Chinese and Hindu informants had meaningful god sets of about fifteen, in spite of their knowledge of 60–100 gods.

70 Agents: but note that a superhuman agent may be salient for an individual or group even if that agent is not, or not regularly, the object of cult (Roberts, Chiao and Pandey 1975.123); the Christian Satan is a good example.

71 Erchia: *LSCG* no. 18 (= *SEG* 21.541). For this calendar see Jameson 1965; Parker 2005.65–71; Mikalson 2010.48–50.

72 The Erchia calendar is divided into five sections labeled alpha through epsilon, each of which represents equal expenses. Most such calendars were inscribed less as ritual *aides-mémoires* than as financial records. The five sections were probably assigned to five "liturgists" or wealthy community members expected to fund the sacrifices. For religion in the Attic demes see Mikalson 1977; Parker 1987, 2005.50–78.

73 Who dwell: *SEG* 19.698 (Kolophon; late fourth century). Local: Thuc. 2.74. For these and other such expressions as a way of ordering the pantheon see Versnel 2011.88–119.

74 On *epiclēseis*: Brulé 1998; Parker 2003.

75 Parker 2011.71.

76 Gods in Homer: Dee 1994. Dowden (2007.45) provides a chart with numerical tabulation.

77 Homeric expressions: e.g. Hom. *Il.* 1.494 (gods who are forever), 2.30 (Olympian abodes), 3.298 (immortal gods). As for the heroes, there is debate over when their worship originated; see Chapter 5.

78 "Homer" is to be understood as shorthand for the collective oral tradition plus one or more individuals who ultimately committed the *Iliad* and *Odyssey* to writing.

79 The name of the Titaness Themis means "divine law." Such personified abstracts were characteristic of Greek theology as far back as we can trace it, and they often appeared in cult. See Stafford 2000.1–44.

80 Aphrodite, we later learn (Hom. *Il.* 21.416–33), attempts to help Ares but is wounded by Athena.

81 Tripartite system: Homer (*Il.* 15.186–93) offers a different tripartite arrangement in the myth of the division of the cosmos between Zeus, Poseidon and Hades. The inclusion of Leto, the mother of Artemis and Apollo, is surprising, yet epic tradition makes her a resident of Olympos, and she is more plausible as a partisan of the Trojans than any of the other major deities.

82 Hesiod's one major concession to cultic matters in the *Theogony* is an embedded "hymn" to the goddess Hekate (*Theog.* 411–52) describing the extensive benefits she confers on mortals.

83 Both epithets: Hes. *Theog.* 1, 25. Cf. Hes. *Op.* 1, "Muses from Pieria" (= Olympos, both the mountain and the heavenly place).

84 For Hera, see Essay 1.2. On the un-Olympian character of Demeter see Shapiro 1989.139. As agricultural deities both she and Dionysos are in some sense earthbound. Hesiod's main narrative describes Aphrodite (*Theog.* 190–8) as an elder goddess born from the severed genitals of Ouranos; however, the appearance of Dione in these lines appears to follow the Homeric tradition (Hom. *Il.* 5.370–84) in which Aphrodite is Zeus' daughter by that goddess. Such inconsistencies result from the techniques of oral composition.

85 Hesiod does not recount Prometheus' creation of man but perhaps assumes it. He attributes the creation of woman to Zeus and Hephaistos (Hes. *Theog.* 560–612, *Op.* 70–82).

86 Okeanos: e.g. Aesch. *PV* 136–43; Hdt. 4.36.2 (skeptical of the popular view); Pl. *Phd.* 112e. Kronos ruled over the Isles of the Blessed: e.g. Hes. *Op.* 166–75; Pind. *Ol.* 2.67–73.

87 Sophilos dinos: Williams 1983. All the gods: Hom. *Il.* 24.59–63. Compare Bremmer (1999.15), who focuses on the depiction of hierarchy in the scene, and Shapiro 2012 for assemblies of gods. Polinskaya (2013.97) is skeptical about the use of visual sources to explore Greek pantheons. The reservations of Laurens (1998.61) apply to a specific type of vase with non-narrative groupings of gods.

88 For our immediate purposes, the "Olympian" gods are not "the major gods" but those regularly described as dwelling on Olympos. By this criterion, Themis, Leto and Hebe are quintessential Olympians, as are the Muses.

89 Poseidon-Amphitrite and Ares-Aphrodite: Hes. *Theog.* 930–7. The group as a whole has strong affinities with Hesiod's description of Zeus' consorts and offspring (*Theog.* 901–23), including Themis, the female pluralities, Leto, Hebe and Eileithyia.

90 Williams (1983.30) interprets the collocation of Demeter and Dionysos in Eleusinian terms.

91 I draw the term "condensed pantheon" from Georgoudi 1998.76: "un mini-panthéon grec, une sorte de panthéon condensé."

92 Altar in Athens: Hdt. 6.108.4; Long 1987.62–6, 159–66; Shapiro 1989.133–41; Georgoudi 1996.43–50. A damaged relief cylinder of unknown function, dating no earlier than the second half of the fourth century, was found near the site (Long 1987.6–7). Of the gods depicted, Poseidon, Demeter with Athena, Zeus with Hera, and Apollo are securely identified.

93 Assemblies and Herakles: Shapiro 1989.133–41.

94 The exact location of Hermes' banquet has been debated and it is not certain that the etiology refers to Olympia. For recent treatments see Georgoudi 1996.66–70; Johnston and Mulroy 2009.8–11; Versnel 2011.309–77.

95 Twin altars: Pind. *Ol.* 5.1–7, ca. 452. Cf. Pind. *Ol.* 10.43–53 (Herakles founds the cult); Long 1987.58–62, 154–7. Herodoros: *FGrH* 31 F 34a-b (ca. 400). Among a profusion of altars in the Altis, Pausanias (5.14.4–10) mentions double altars for Artemis with Alpheios, Apollo with Hermes, and Dionysos with the Charites, as well as an altar of Zeus Laoitas and Poseidon Laoitas, but the theme of twelve gods had been lost by this period.

96 Alpheios: Hom. *Od.* 3.489 (grandfather of Diokles); Hes. *Theog.* 338 (one of the twenty-five sons of Okeanos).

97 Near Eastern parallels: Long 1987.139–52; Rutherford 2010. Number twelve: Weinreich 1924–1937, cols. 767–72.

98 Divisibility: Sissa and Detienne 2000.158. Resonances: e.g. Vernant 1983.127–75 (on Hestia and Hermes).

99 Plat. *Leg.* 745de, 828b-d. Compare Plat. *Phaedr.* 246e-247a, where eleven gods, who are not fully enumerated, drive chariots through the sky, ensuring the order of the cosmos, while Hestia remains "alone in the house of the gods."

100 Agamemnon: Strab. 13.1.48. Jason: Ap. Rhod. *Arg.* 2. 531–4 with scholia; Polyb. 4.39.5–6. The scholiasts supply lists of the twelve at the Bosporos site, where Hades seems to have been included.

101 Foundation and Hellenism: Georgoudi 1996.74–5, 1998.73–7; Rutherford 2010.53–4. A Twelve Gods cult was also attributed to Deukalion, the Greek counterpart of Noah, who founded an altar to the Twelve after the flood. One of Deukalion's sons was Hellen, ancestor of the Hellenes (Hellanicus *FGrH* 4 F 6).

102 Panhellenism: Plut. *Per.* 17 (congress); Diod. Sic. 12.9–11 (Thourioi); Hall 2002a.206–7. Eleusis: Suk Fong Jim 2014.207–19.

103 All the gods of the frieze can be linked to Athenian cults in one way or another (for examples see Long 1987.169–73). Viewers may have perceived them on either the local or the Panhellenic levels, but the presence of Hera and Ares (both relatively insignificant in Attic cult) and the absence of Herakles show that this is not a "meaningful god set" for most Athenians.

104 Civic harmony: Georgoudi 1996.62–4.

105 For Delos see Long 1987.87–90, 182, 198–201; Georgoudi 1996.59–62.

106 Magnesia on the Maiandros: *LSAM* 32 (= *SEG* 46.1467; *IMagn.* 98); Long 1987.53–4. Plurality: Georgoudi 1996.77–8, 1998.82–3; Versnel 2011.270, 510–15.

107 Herakles: Diod. Sic. 4.39.4. Philip: Diod. Sic. 16.92.5, 95.1.

108 Alexander: Ael. *VH* 5.12. Add: Luc. *Dial. mort.* 13.2. Colossal: Long 1987.199–200.

109 For the Dii Consentes and the *lectisternium* of 217 see Long 1987.96–7, 235–9.

110 On this tutelary pattern and its conflict with Panhellenic religion see Parker 2011.86–7.

111 Current scholarly consensus holds that in the Archaic period, Hera was more closely associated with Mycenae and the eastern Argive plain than with Argos itself. Thus the Homeric epithet may refer to the "Argeia" or Argive plain and environs. Discussion: Hall 1995; Auffarth 2006.78–81; Kowalzig 2007.167.

112 Compare the opposing prayers to Hera and Athena in Eur. *Phoen.* 1364–76.

113 Linear B: both goddesses are mentioned in Pylos tablet Tn316. For text and translation see Palaima 2004.120–1.

114 "Husband of Hera": Hom. *Il.* 7.411, 10.5, 10.329, 13.154, 16.88. Compare the name Poseidon, which seems to be composed of *posis* "husband" plus the name of an unknown goddess: O'Brien 1993.121–2. On Hera and Zeus at the Argive Heraion see Pfaff 2013.278n.9.

115 On Zeus see Cook 1914–40 and Farnell 1896–1909, Vol. 1.35–178 (both methodologically out of date but still useful for the collected information); Dowden 2006; Larson 2007.15–28. Linke (2006) suggests that Zeus was avoided as a polis deity precisely because his supremacy was problematic in the context of intra-polis competition, whereas he could safely oversee competition at Panhellenic sanctuaries.

116 Evidence for Zeus: O'Brien 1993.121–2; Aloni-Ronen 1998.14–15. Lead plaques: Mertens-Horn 2002.327 (Argive Heraion, Profitis Elias at Argos, Perachora).

117 For Orthia see Paus. 3.16.9–11; Larson 2007.104–6 with bibliography.

118 Patroness: O'Brien 1993.113–66; Aloni-Ronen 1998.13.

119 For the hypothesis of an etymological connection between the name "Hera" and the word *hērōs*, see Pötscher 1961; O'Brien 1993.117–9 with bibliography, and *contra*, Hall 2002b.94. For a hero cult at the Argive Heraion see Pfaff 2013.279–89. Hall (1997.99–107) discusses the significance of Hera and Herakles for Dorian ethnicity. Hera at Tiryns: de Polignac 1997.120; Baumbach 2004.50–73; Langdon 2008.67–8.

120 Tombs and Heraion: Wright 1982.192–4; Antonaccio 1992.99–100; Pfaff 2013.282–7. As Hall notes (2002b.95–7) there appears to be a strong geographic correlation between Archaic Hera cults in the Argolid (e.g. at Prosymna, Mycenae, Argos, Tiryns) and offerings to the powerful dead, regardless of whether we call them "heroes."

121 First visible cult at the Argive Heraion: Billot 1997.14–15. Impact of epic on Hera's cults: O'Brien 1993.172–5 and *passim*, Aloni-Ronen 1998.15.

122 Ring: Tracy 1986.

123 White-armed: Baumbach 2004.11–49. Compare the Homeric epithet "Far-Shooter" (*wekabolos* in the Boiotian dialect) inscribed on the Mantiklos Apollo, discussed in the introduction to this chapter.

124 Translation adapted from Furley and Bremer 2001.1, no. 4.2.

125 Sons of Atreus: Hom. *Il.* 1.375, 2.249 and so forth.

126 Homer (*Il.* 9.128–30) mentions a raid on Lesbos by Achilles, from which Agamemnon received seven surpassingly beautiful women. The scholiast on these lines says that a women's beauty contest was held in the sanctuary of Hera. Discussion: Furley and Bremer 2001.2.121.

127 Translation adapted from Furley and Bremer 2001.1, no. 4.4.

128 Picard (1946.458–61) sees in Lesbian Hera a pre-Hellenic Anatolian goddess. Discussion: Furley and Bremer 2001.1.172–4. Hera's intimacy here with Dionysos, whom she persecutes in myth, is reminiscent of her connections with Herakles in the Argolid.

129 On the Heraion and the festival: Seaford 1988.122–3; O'Brien 1993.119–36; Billot 1997.46–54; Baumbach 2004.74–104. Shields as prizes: Pind. *Nem.* 10.21–3. Women's dances: Eur. *El.* 171–80. Debate: Hall 1995.

130 Pausanias (3.13.8) mentions a temple of Hera Argeia (said to have been founded by the Argive queen Eurydike) and a sanctuary of Hera Hypercheiria at Sparta. For Hera's major cults see Larson 2007.29–40 with bibliography, and for detailed analysis of votives, Baumbach 2004.

131 Parker 2005.441: in Attica Hera "is reduced to her smallest possible extent" due to the preeminence of Athena. On the sacred marriage in cults of Hera see Jost 1997; Chaniotis 2002.

132 Deception of Zeus: Hom. *Il.* 14.153–353.

133 Pl. *Resp.* 3.390c. The union of Zeus and Hera on Mt. Ida (Hom. *Il.* 14.346–51) causes lush blooms to spring up and cushion them, but is this a hint of the sacred marriage or merely a charming narrative detail, like the golden cloud Zeus spreads about them for privacy?

134 Dearth of hymns: Furley and Bremer 2001.1.166.

135 Samos: Kyrieleis 1993; Baumbach 2004.147–74. Image brought from Argos; goddess born on the island: Paus. 7.4.4. Indigenous worship and Argive influence combine in a legend attached to the principal festival: Menodotus *FGrH* 541 F 1 (cited in Ath. 15.12–15 [671e-74a]). Though they were of varying origin, the Ionians as a group claimed to be "Achaians" (Vanschoonwinkel 2006.115–22, 125) as did later colonists in southern Italy.

136 Naukratis: Hdt 2.178.3.

137 Hera temples: Snodgrass 2006.251–3 (measurements of the first and fourth Samian temples compared with other early temples).

138 Perachora: Tomlinson 1992. Votives at Hera sanctuaries: Brize 1997; de Polignac 1997.116 (houses and ships). Baumbach 2004.89–90 observes that house models are found in sanctuaries of goddesses, not gods. For shields as gifts to goddesses see Larson 2009.

139 Colonists: Parisi Presicce 1985; Antonetti 1998.36–8 (Megara); de Polignac 1997.115, 119 (Euboia, Samos).

140 Poseidonia: Cipriani 1997; Baumbach 2004.105–46. Offshoot: Plin. *HN* 3.70; cf. Paus 3.13.8 (Hera Argeia at Sparta); Paul 2013.59–61 (Hera Argeia on Kos).

141 Achaians: Morgan and Hall 1996.213; Osanna 2002.277; Greco 2006.173. The actual ethnic composition of the colonists in South Italy has been disputed, but they clearly thought of themselves as "Achaians." Giangiulio 2002.294–8 sees ties to the northern Peloponnese more generally, as well as to Achilles. For the impact of other Hera cults (esp. those at Perachora and on Mt. Kithairon) on Western colonies see Parisi Presicce 1985.

142 Reciprocal: Parker 1998.120. For the cognitivist view of reciprocity as a feature of all religions see Barrett 2007.193–4.

143 Early Iron Age: Langdon 1987.

144 Paul: e.g. *Eph.* 2.8–9. Paul typically contrasts divine *charis* with "the works of the law," attacking the form of reciprocity observed by Jews of his day. On *charis* in Greek culture see MacLachlan 1992, and for religion Parker 1998.108–14.

145 Harrison 2003.282.

146 *Do ut des* and Roman contract law: de Villiers 1924.121. Burkert 1979.54 contrasts the mentality of *do ut des* with a "more advanced morality" that attempts to "overcome or sublimate the unabashed selfishness of this act of piety." For Roman religion see Rüpke (2007.148–50), who allows a contractual or judicial component, but with caveats. Critiques of *do ut des* as applied to Greek religion: Patera 2012.57–71; Suk Fong Jim 2014.22–3, 277–9.

147 Reciprocity: van Baal 1976.165–7 (contrasting it with trade); Seaford 1994; van Wees 1998; the classic study is Mauss 1990 [1925]. For Greek religion see Burkert 1987; Yunis 1988.101–10; Parker 1998.118–19; Ullucci 2011.62–4. For reciprocity as an evolutionary adaptation shared with other primates see Flack and de Waal 2000, and for moral intuitions see Chapter 3.

148 de Villiers 1924 citing Justinian *Digest* 23.3.6 and 12.8.1.

149 Misrecognize: Ullucci 2011.62–3, drawing the concept from Bourdieu 1977.5–6.

150 Commerce vs. gift exchange: Seaford 1994.13–25, 1998.2–4.

151 Reminder of a deity's previous help: Hom. *Il.* 16.233–8; Sappho fr. 1.5–7 L-P. For prayers and reciprocity see Pulleyn 1997.16–38.

152 On rejected sacrifice see Naiden 2013.131–82.

153 Asymmetry: Bremmer 1998a.127, 133.

154 Athens: Herman 1998.219–20.

155 Failure: e.g. Menelaos fails to sacrifice and is stranded in Egypt (Hom. *Od.* 4. 4.351–3, 471–80); Oineus fails to offer first fruits, angering Artemis (Hom. *Il.* 9.533–40). On failure to tithe see Suk Fong Jim 2014.83–91.

156 Cult heroes: Johnston 1999.153–5, 2005.

157 Fear: Epicurus' ideas are echoed in Lucr. 3.1018–22, 978–1023. For his views on the gods see also Philodemus' fragmentary work *On Piety* (Obbink 1996).

158 Right to honors: Suk Fong Jim 2014.68–75.

159 Blessed gods: e.g. Xenophanes 21 A32.23–5 *DK*.

160 Moderns (e.g. Vlastos 1991.174) often suppose that this passage demonstrates the "commercial" character of Greek religion in practice.

161 Status: Ullucci 2011.63–4 (the traditional gift of an apple for a teacher does not imply the student's belief that the teacher is hungry). Compare *Hom. Hymn Dem.* 310–13 where the gods fear the loss not of sacrifices but of *timē*.

162 First fruit offerings and battle spoils: Suk Fong Jim 2014.97–116. Hymns as offerings: Day 1994.59.

163 Pleasure: Naiden 2013.117, 131–82 *passim*.
164 Three reasons: Theophr. *On Piety* fr. 2.26–43 Pötscher (= Porph. *Abst*. 2.6.1–4).

## References

Aloni-Ronen, Neta. 1998. Marrying Hera: Incomplete integration in the making of the pantheon. In *Les panthéons des cités*, ed. Pirenne-Delforge, 11–22.

Antes, Peter, Armin W. Geertz and Randi R. Warne, eds. 2008. *New approaches to the study of religion*. 2 Vols. Berlin and New York: Walter de Gruyter.

Antonaccio, Carla M. 1992. Terraces, tombs, and the early Argive Heraion. *Hesperia* 61 (1): 85–105.

Antonaccio, Carla. 1999. Colonization and the origins of hero cult. In *Ancient Greek hero cult*, ed. Hägg, 109–21.

Antonetti, Claudia. 1998. Le développement du panthéon d'une métropole: Mégare. In *Les panthéons des cités*, ed. Pirenne-Delforge, 35–46.

Atran, Scott. 2002. *In gods we trust: The evolutionary landscape of religion*. Oxford and New York: Oxford University Press.

Auffarth, Christoph. 2006. Das Heraion von Argos oder das Heraion der Argolis? In *Kult – Politik – Ethnos*, ed. Freitag, Funke and Haake, 73–87.

Banton, Michael, ed. 1968. *Anthropological approaches to the study of religion*. London: Tavistock.

Barrett, Justin L. 1999. Theological correctness: Cognitive constraint and the study of religion. *Method and Theory in the Study of Religion* 11: 325–39.

Barrett, Justin L. 2004. *Why would anyone believe in God?* Walnut Creek CA: Altamira Press.

Barrett, Justin L. 2007. Gods. In *Religion, anthropology and cognitive science*, ed. Whitehouse and Laidlaw, 179–207.

Barrett, Justin L. 2008. The naturalness of religious concepts. In *New approaches to the study of religion*, ed. Antes, Geertz and Warne, 401–18.

Barrett, Justin L. 2011. Cognitive science of religion: Looking back, looking forward. *Journal for the Scientific Study of Religion* 50 (2): 229–39.

Baumbach, Jens David. 2004. *The significance of votive offerings in selected Hera sanctuaries in the Peloponnese, Ionia, and Western Greece*. Oxford: Archaeopress.

Bellah, Robert. 1991. *Beyond belief: Essays on religion in a post-traditionalist world*. Berkeley and Los Angeles: University of California Press.

Bernabé, Alberto and Julia Mendoza. 2013. Pythagorean cosmogony and vedic cosmogony (RV 10.129). Analogies and differences. *Phronesis* 58 (1): 32–51.

Billot, Marie-Françoise. 1997. Recherches archéologiques récentes à l'Héraion d'Argos. In *Héra*, ed. de la Genière, 11–56.

Bloch, Maurice. 1989. *Ritual, history and power*. London: Athlone Press.

Bonnechere, Pierre. 1994. *Le sacrifice humain en Grèce ancienne*. Athens and Liège: Centre Internationale d'Étude de la Religion Grecque Antique.

Bonnechere, Pierre. 2007. Le sacrifice humain grec entre norme et anormalité. In *La norme en matière religieuse*, ed. Brulé, 189–212.

Bourdieu, Pierre. 1977. *Outline of a theory of practice*. Tr. R. Nice. Cambridge and New York: Cambridge University Press.

Boyer, Pascal. 1994. *The naturalness of religious ideas: A cognitive theory of religion*. Berkeley and Los Angeles: University of California Press.

Boyer, Pascal. 2001. *Religion explained: The evolutionary origins of religious thought*. New York: Basic Books.

Boyer, Pascal. 2002. Why do gods and spirits matter at all? In *Current approaches in the cognitive science of religion*, ed. Pyysiäinen and Anttonen, 68–92.

Bremmer, Jan. 1998a. Giving and thanksgiving in Greek religion. In *Reciprocity in ancient Greece*, ed. Gill, Postlethwaite and Seaford, 127–37.

Bremmer, Jan. 1998b. Religion, ritual, and the opposition sacred vs. profane: Notes towards a terminological genealogy. In *Ansichten griechischer Rituale*, ed. Graf, 9–32.

Bremmer, Jan. 1999. *Greek religion*. With addenda. Oxford: Oxford University Press.

Bremmer, Jan. 2007. Greek normative animal sacrifice. In *A companion to Greek religion*, ed. Ogden, 132–44.

Bremmer, Jan and Andrew Erskine, eds. 2010. *The gods of ancient Greece: Identities and transformations*. Edinburgh: Edinburgh University Press.

Brize, Philippe. 1997. Offrandes de l'époque géométrique et archaïque à l'Héraion de Samos. In *Héra*, ed. de la Genière, 131–9.

Brown, Donald E. 1991. *Human universals*. Philadelphia: Temple University Press.

Brulé, Pierre. 1998. Le langage des épiclèses dans le polythéisme hellénique (l'exemple de quelques divinités féminines). *Kernos* 11: 13–34.

Brulé, Pierre, ed. 2007. *La norme en matière religieuse en Grèce ancienne*. Liège: Centre International d'Étude de la Religion Grecque Antique.

Burkert, Walter. 1979. *Structure and history in Greek mythology and ritual*. Berkeley and Los Angeles: University of California Press.

Burkert, Walter. 1985. *Greek religion*. Cambridge, MA: Harvard University Press.

Burkert, Walter. 1987. Offerings in perspective: Surrender, distribution, exchange. In *Gifts to the gods*, ed. Linders and Nordquist, 43–50.

Burkert, Walter. 1996. *Creation of the sacred: Tracks of biology in early religions*. Cambridge, MA, and London: Harvard University Press.

Chaiken, Shelly and Yaacov Trope, eds. 1999. *Dual process theories in social psychology*. New York and London: Guilford Press.

Chaniotis, Angelos. 2002. Ritual dynamics: The Boiotian festival of the Daidala. In *Kykeon*, ed. Horstmanshoff, Singor, van Straten and Strubbe, 23–48.

Cipriani, M. 1997. Il ruolo di Hera nel santuario meridionale di Poseidonia. In *Héra*, ed. de La Genière, 211–25.

Cook, Arthur Bernard. 1914–40. *Zeus: A study in ancient religion*. 3 Vols. Cambridge: The University Press.

Day, Joseph W. 1994. Interactive offerings: Early Greek dedicatory epigrams and ritual. *HSCP* 96: 37–74.

Day, Matthew. 2005. Rethinking naturalness: Modes of religiosity and religion in the round. In *Mind and religion*, ed. Whitehouse and McCauley, 85–106.

Dee, James H. 1994. *The epithetic phrases for the Homeric gods: A repertory of the descriptive expressions for the divinities of the Iliad and the Odyssey*. New York and London: Garland.

de la Genière, Juliette, ed. 1997. *Héra: images, espaces, cultes: Actes du Colloque international du Centre de recherches archéologiques de l'Université de Lille III et de l'Association P.R.A.C., Lille, 29–30 novembre 1993*. Naples: Centre Jean Bérard.

Depew, Mary. 1997. Reading Greek prayers. *ClAnt* 16 (2): 229–58.

de Polignac, François. 1997. Héra, le navire et la demeure: Offrandes, divinité et société en Grèce archaïque. In *Héra*, ed. de la Genière, 113–22.

de Villiers, Melius. 1924. Consideration in the Roman law of contract. *Journal of Comparative Legislation and International Law* 6 (1): 120–4.

Dougherty, Carol and Leslie Kurke, eds. 1998. *Cultural poetics in archaic Greece: Cult, performance, politics*. Oxford and New York: Oxford University Press.

Dowden, Ken. 2006. *Zeus*. Abingdon and New York: Routledge.

Dowden, Ken. 2007. Olympian gods, Olympian pantheon. In *Companion to Greek religion*, ed. Ogden, 41–55.

Durkheim, Émile. 1915. *The elementary forms of the religious life*. Tr. Joseph Ward Swain. London: Allen and Unwin.

Easterling, P. E. and J. V. Muir, eds. 1985. *Greek religion and society*. Cambridge: Cambridge University Press.

Ekroth, Gunnel. 2007. Thighs or tails? The osteological evidence. In *La norme en matière religieuse*, ed. Brulé, 153–69.

Eliade, Mircea. 1959. *The sacred and the profane: The nature of religion*. Tr. Willard Trask. New York: Harcourt, Brace.

Elsner, Jaś. 1996. Image and ritual: Reflections on the religious appreciation of Classic art. *CQ* 46: 515–31.

Epstein, Seymour and Rosemary Pacini. 1999. Some basic issues regarding dual-process theories from the perspective of cognitive-experiential self theory. In *Dual-process theories in social psychology*, ed. Chaiken and Trope, 462–82.

Evans, Jonathan St. B. T. and Keith Frankish, eds. 2009. *In two minds: Dual processes and beyond*. Oxford and New York: Oxford University Press.

Evans-Pritchard, E. E. 1965. *Theories of primitive religion*. Oxford: Clarendon Press.

Farnell, Lewis Richard. 1896–1909. *Cults of the Greek states*. 5 Vols. Oxford: Clarendon Press.

Flack, Jessica C. and Frans B. M. de Waal. 2000. "Any animal whatever": Darwinian building blocks of morality in monkeys and apes. In *Evolutionary origins of morality*, ed. Katz, 1–29.

Fontenrose, Joseph. 1988. *Didyma: Apollo's oracle, cult and companions*. Berkeley: University of California Press.

François, Gilbert. 1957. *Le polythéisme et l'emploi au singulier des mots ΘΕΟΣ, ΔΑΙΜΩΝ dans la littérature grecque d'Homère à Platon*. Paris: Belles Lettres.

Freitag, Klaus, Peter Funke and Matthias Haake, eds. 2006. *Kult – Politik – Ethnos: Überregionale Heiligtümer im Spannungsfeld von Kult und Politik*. Stuttgart: Franz Steiner Verlag.

Frel, Jiří and Sandra Knudsen Morgan, eds. 1983. *Greek vases in the J. Paul Getty Museum, 1*. Malibu: The J. Paul Getty Museum.

Freud, Sigmund. 1928. *The future of an illusion*. Tr. W. D. Robson-Scott. London: Hogarth Press.

Furley, William D. and Jan Maarten Bremer. 2001. *Greek hymns*. 2 Vols. Tübingen: Mohr Siebeck.

Geertz, Clifford. 1968. Religion as a cultural system. In *Anthropological approaches to the study of religion*, ed. Banton, 1–46.

Georgoudi, Stella. 1996. Les douze dieux des Grecs: Variations sur un thème. In *Mythes grecs au figuré*, ed. Georgoudi and Vernant, 43–80 and 219–21.

Georgoudi, Stella. 1998. Les douze dieux et les autres dans l'espace cultuel grec. *Kernos* 11: 73–83.

Georgoudi, Stella and Jean-Pierre Vernant, eds. 1996. *Mythes grecs au figuré, de l'antiquité au baroque*. Paris: Gallimard.

Georgoudi, Stella, Renée Koch Piettre and Francis Schmidt, eds. 2005. *La cuisine et l'autel: Les sacrifices en questions dans les sociétés de la méditerranée ancienne*. Turnhout: Brepols.

Giangiulio, Maurizio. 2002. I culti delle colonie achee d'Occidente. In *Gli achei e l'identità etnica degli achei d'occidente*, ed. Greco, 283–313.

Gill, Christopher, Norman Postlethwaite and Richard Seaford, eds. 1998. *Reciprocity in ancient Greece*. Oxford and New York: Oxford University Press.

Gould, John. 1985. On making sense of Greek religion. In *Greek religion and society*, ed. Easterling and Muir, 1–33.

Graf, Fritz, ed. 1998. *Ansichten griechischer Rituale: Geburtstags-Symposium für Walter Burkert*. Stuttgart and Leipzig: Teubner.

Greco, Emanuele, ed. 2002. *Gli achei e l'identità etnica degli achei d'occidente: Atti del Convegno Internazionale di Studi Paestum 23–25 febbraio 2001*. Paestum and Athens: Scuola Archeologica Italiana di Atene.

Greco, Emanuele. 2006. Greek colonisation in southern Italy. In *Greek colonisation*, ed. Tsetskhladze, 169–200.

Gruen, Erich S. 1993. The polis in the Hellenistic world. In *Nomodeiktes*, ed. Rosen and Farrell, 339–54.

Hägg, Robin, ed. 1999. *Ancient Greek hero cult*. Stockholm: P. Åströms Förlag.

Hägg, Robin, ed. 2002. *Peloponnesian sanctuaries and cults*. Stockholm: P. Åströms Förlag.

Hall, Jonathan M. 1995. How Argive was the "Argive" Heraion? The political and cultic geography of the Argive plain, 900–400 B.C. *AJA* 99 (4): 577–613.

Hall, Jonathan M. 1997. *Ethnic identity in Greek antiquity*. Cambridge and New York: Cambridge University Press.

Hall, Jonathan M. 2002a. *Hellenicity: Between ethnicity and culture*. Chicago and London: University of Chicago Press.

Hall, Jonathan M. 2002b. Heroes, Hera and Herakleidai in the Argive plain. In *Peloponnesian sanctuaries and cults*, ed. Hägg, 93–8.

Hall, Jonathan M. 2004. How "Greek" were the early Western Greeks? In *Greek identity in the Western Mediterranean*, ed. Shefton and Lomas, 35–54.

Hansen, Mogens Herman, ed. 1996. *Introduction to an inventory of poleis: Symposium August 23–26, 1995*. Copenhagen: Munksgaard.

Harrison, James R. 2003. *Paul's language of grace in its Graeco-Roman context*. Tübingen: Mohr Siebeck.

Harrison, Thomas. 2000. *Divinity and history: The religion of Herodotus*. Oxford: Oxford University Press.

Harrison, Thomas. 2007. Greek religion and literature. In *A companion to Greek religion*, ed. Ogden, 373–84.

Hellström, Pontus and Brita Alroth, eds. 1993. *Religion and power in the ancient Greek world*. Uppsala: Almqvist and Wiksell.

Henrichs, Albert. 2010. What is a Greek god? In *The gods of ancient Greece*, ed. Bremmer and Erskine, 19–39.

Herman, Gabriel. 1998. Reciprocity, altruism, and the prisoner's dilemma: The special case of Classical Athens. In *Reciprocity in ancient Greece*, ed. Gill, Postlethwaite and Seaford, 199–225.

Herrero de Jáuregui, Miguel, Ana Isabel Jiménez San Cristóbal, Eugenio R. Luján Martínez, Raquel Martín Hernández, Marco Antonio Santamaría Álvarez and Sofía Torallas Tovar, eds. 2011. *Tracing Orpheus: Studies of Orphic fragments*. Berlin: De Gruyter.

Hirschfeld, Lawrence A. and Susan Gelman, eds. 1994. *Mapping the mind: Domain specificity in cognition and culture*. Cambridge: Cambridge University Press.

Horstmanshoff, F.H.J., H. W. Singor, F. van Straten and J.H.M. Strubbe, eds. 2002. *Kykeon: Studies in honour of H.S. Versnel*. Leiden: Brill.

Jameson, Michael H. 1965. Notes on the sacrificial calendar from Erchia. *BCH* 89: 154–72.

Johnston, Richard W. and David Mulroy. 2009. The *Hymn to Hermes* and the Athenian altar of the Twelve Gods. *CW* 103 (1): 3–16.

Johnston, Sarah Iles. 1999. *Restless dead: Encounters between the living and the dead in ancient Greece*. Berkeley: University of California Press.

Johnston, Sarah Iles. 2005. Delphi and the dead. In *Mantikē*, ed. Johnston and Struck, 283–306.

Johnston, Sarah Iles and Peter Struck, eds. 2005. *Mantikē: Studies in ancient divination*. Leiden and Boston: Brill.

Jost, Madeleine. 1997. Le theme des disputes entre Héra et Zeus en Arcadie et en Béotie. In *Héra*, ed. de la Genière, 87–92.

Katz, Leonard D., ed. 2000. *Evolutionary origins of morality: Cross-disciplinary perspectives*. Thoverton, UK: Imprint Academic.

Kelly, Michael and Frank C. Keil. 1985. The more things change. . . Metamorphoses and conceptual structure. *Cognitive Science* 9: 403–16.

Kindt, Julia. 2012. *Rethinking Greek religion*. Cambridge and London: Cambridge University Press.

Kirk, G. S. 1981. Pitfalls in the study of Greek sacrifice. In *Le sacrifice dans l'Antiquité*, ed. Rudhardt and Reverdin, 41–90.

Kishik, David. 2008. *Wittgenstein's form of life*. London and New York: Continuum.

Knapp, A. Bernard. 1996. Power and ideology on prehistoric Cyprus. In *Religion and power in the ancient Greek world*, ed. Hellström and Alroth, 9–25.

Knust, Jennifer W. and Zsuzsanna Várhelyi, eds. 2011. *Ancient Mediterranean sacrifice*. New York and London: Oxford University Press.

Konstan, David. 2001. To Hellēnikon ethnos: Ethnicity and the construction of ancient Greek identity. In *Ancient perceptions of Greek ethnicity*, ed. Malkin, 29–50.

Kowalzig, Barbara. 2007. *Singing for the gods: Performances of myth and ritual in Archaic and Classical Greece*. Oxford and New York: Oxford University Press.

Kyriakides, Evangelos, ed. 2007. *The archaeology of ritual*. Los Angeles: Cotsen Institute of Archaeology, University of California.

Kyrieleis, Helmut. 1993. The Heraion at Samos. In *Greek sanctuaries*, ed. Marinatos and Hägg, 125–53.

Laidlaw, James. 2007. A well-disposed social anthropologist's problems with the "cognitive science of religion". In *Religion, anthropology and cognitive science*, ed. Whitehouse and Laidlaw, 211–46.

Langdon, Susan. 1987. Gift exchange in the Geometric sanctuaries. In *Gifts to the gods*, ed. Linders and Nordquist, 107–13.

Langdon, Susan. 2008. *Art and identity in Dark Age Greece, 1100–700 B.C.* Cambridge: Cambridge University Press.

Larson, Jennifer. 2007. *Ancient Greek cults: A guide*. New York and London: Routledge.

Larson, Jennifer. 2009. Votive arms and armor in the sanctuaries of goddesses: An empirical approach. In *Le donateur, l'offrande et la déesse*, ed. Prêtre, 123–33.

Laurens, Annie-France. 1998. Athéna, Apollon, Dionysos et les autres. Panthéons de terre cuite: jeux de poses, jeux de rôles. *Kernos* 11: 35–62.

Levy, Robert. 1990. *Mesocosm, Hinduism and the organization of a traditional Newar city in Nepal*. Berkeley and Los Angeles: University of California Press.

Linders, Tullia and Gullög Nordquist, eds. 1987. *Gifts to the gods: Proceedings of the Uppsala Symposium 1985*. Uppsala: Almqvist and Wiksell.

Linke, Bernhard. 2006. Zeus als Gott der Ordnung. Religiöse Autorität im Spannungsfeld von überregionalen Überzeugungen und lokalen Kulten am Beispiel der Zeuskulte im archaischen Griechenland. In *Kult – Politik – Ethnos*, ed. Freitag, Funke and Haake, 89–120.

Lissarague, François. 2012. Figuring religious ritual. In *A companion to Greek art*, ed. Smith and Plantzos, 564–95.

Long, Charlotte R. 1987. *The Twelve Gods of Greece and Rome*. Leiden and New York: Brill.

MacLachlan, Bonnie. 1992. *The age of Grace: "Charis" in early Greek poetry*. Princeton: Princeton University Press.

Malkin, Irad, ed. 2001. *Ancient perceptions of Greek ethnicity*. Washington, DC: Center for Hellenic Studies.

Marinatos, Nanno and Robin Hägg, eds. 1993. *Greek sanctuaries: New approaches*. London and New York: Routledge.

Marx, Karl. 1970 [1844]. *Critique of Hegel's "Philosophy of right."* Edited by Joseph O'Malley. Tr. Annette Jolin and Joseph O'Malley. Cambridge: University Press.

Mauss, Marcel. 1990 [1925]. *The gift: The form and reason for exchange in archaic societies*. Tr. W. D. Halls. London and New York: Routledge.

Mendoza, Julia. 2011. Ζεὺς Μοῦνος: Philosophical monism and mythological monism. In *Tracing Orpheus*, ed. Herrero de Jáuregui, Jiménez San Cristóbal, Luján Martínez, Martín Hernández, Santamaría Álvarez and Torallas Tovar, 29–33.

Mercier, Hugo and Dan Sperber. 2009. Intuitive and reflective inferences. In *In two minds*, ed. Evans and Frankish, 149–70.

Mertens-Horn, Madeleine. 2002. Il solenne incontro tra Hera e Zeus a Metaponto e in Argolide. In *Gli achei e l'identità etnica degli achei d'occidente*, ed. Greco, 323–30.

Mikalson, Jon. 1977. Religion in the Attic demes. *AJPh* 98 (4): 424–35.

Mikalson, Jon. 1989. *Athenian popular religion*. Chapel Hill: University of North Carolina Press.

Mikalson, Jon. 1991. *Honor thy gods: Popular religion in Greek tragedy*. Chapel Hill and London: University of North Carolina Press.

Mikalson, Jon. 1998. *Religion in Hellenistic Athens*. Berkeley: University of California Press.

Mikalson, Jon. 2010. *Ancient Greek religion*. Second edition. Chichester, UK, and Malden, MA: Wiley-Blackwell.

Morgan, Catherine and Jonathan Hall. 1996. Achaian poleis and Achaian colonisation. In *Introduction to an inventory of poleis*, ed. Hansen, 164–231.

Morris, Ian. 1998. Poetics of power: The interpretation of ritual action in archaic Greece. In *Cultural poetics in archaic Greece*, ed. Dougherty and Kurke, 15–45.

Naiden, F. S. 2013. *Smoke signals for the gods: Ancient Greek sacrifice from the Archaic through Roman periods*. Oxford and New York: Oxford University Press.

Needham, Rodney. 1972. *Belief, language and experience*. Chicago: University of Chicago Press.

Obbink, Dirk, ed. 1996. *Philodemus, On piety: Part 1*. Oxford: Clarendon Press.

O'Brien, Joan V. 1993. *The transformation of Hera: A study of ritual, hero, and the goddess in the Iliad*. Savage, MD: Rowman & Littlefield.

Ogden, Daniel, ed. 2007. *A companion to Greek religion*. Oxford and New York: Oxford University Press.

Osanna, Massimo. 2002. Da Aigialos ad Achaia: Sui culti più antichi della madrepatria delle colonie achee di occidente. In *Gli achei e l'identità etnica degli achei d'occidente*, ed. Greco, 271–81.

Otto, Rudolf. 1924 [1917]. *The idea of the Holy: An inquiry into the non-rational factor in the idea of the divine and its relation to the rational*. Tr. John W. Harvey. London and New York: Oxford University Press and H. Milford.

Palagia, Olga and Alkestis Choremi-Spetsieri, eds. 2007. *The Panathenaic games: Proceedings of an international conference held at the University of Athens, May 11–12, 2004*. Oxford: Oxbow Books.

Palaima, Thomas. 2004. Sacrificial feasting in the Linear B documents. In *The Mycenaean feast*, ed. Wright, 97–126.

Parisi Presicce, Claudio. 1985. L'importanza di Hera nelle spedizioni coloniali e nell'insediamento primitivo delle colonie greche: Alla luce della scoperta di un nuovo santuario periferico di Selinunte. *ArchClass* 37: 44–83, Pl. 5–6.

Parker, Robert. 1987. Festivals of the Attic demes. In *Gifts to the gods*, ed. Linders and Nordquist, 137–47.

Parker, Robert. 1998. Pleasing thighs: Reciprocity in Greek religion. In *Reciprocity in ancient Greece*, ed. Gill, Postlethwaite and Seaford, 105–25.

Parker, Robert. 2003. The problem of the Greek cult epithet. *OpAth* 28: 173–83.

Parker, Robert. 2005. *Polytheism and society at Athens*. Oxford and New York: Oxford University Press.

Parker, Robert. 2011. *On Greek religion*. Ithaca, NY, and London: Cornell University Press.

Parker, Robert. 2014. Commentary on *Journal of Cognitive Historiography*, Issue 1. *Journal of Cognitive Historiography* 1 (2). DOI: 10.1558/jch.v1i2.26007.

Patera, Ioanna. 2012. *Offrir en Grèce ancienne: Gestes et contextes*. Stuttgart: Franz Steiner Verlag.

Paul, Stéphanie. 2013. *Cultes et sanctuaires de l'île de Cos*. Liège: Centre International d'Étude de la Religion Grecque Antique.

Pfaff, Christopher. 2013. Artemis and a hero at the Argive Heraion. *Hesperia* 82: 277–99.

Picard, Charles. 1946. La triade Zeus-Héra-Dionysos dans l'Orient hellénique d'après les nouveaux framents d'Alcée. *BCH* 70: 455–73.

Pirenne-Delforge, Vinciane, ed. 1998. *Les panthéons des cités, des origines à la Périégèse de Pausanias*. Liège: Centre International d'Étude de la Religion Grecque Antique.

Polinskaya, Irene. 2010. Shared sanctuaries and the gods of others: On the meaning of "common" in Herodotus 8.144. In *Valuing others in Classical antiquity*, ed. Rosen and Sluiter, 43–70.

Polinskaya, Irene. 2013. *A local history of Greek polytheism: Gods, people and the land of Aigina, 800–400 BCE*. Leiden and Boston: Brill.

Pötscher, Walter. 1961. Hera und Heros. *RhM* 104: 302–55.

Prêtre, Clarisse, ed. 2009. *Le donateur, l'offrande et la déesse: Systèmes votifs des sanctuaires de déesses dans le monde grec*. Liège: Centre International d'Étude de la Religion Grecque Antique.

Price, Simon. 1984. *Rituals and power: The Roman imperial cult in Asia Minor*. Cambridge: Cambridge University Press.

Price, Simon. 1999. *Religions of the ancient Greeks*. Cambridge and New York: Cambridge University Press.

Pulleyn, Simon. 1997. *Prayer in Greek religion*. Oxford: Clarendon Press.

Pyysiäinen, Illka. 2002a. Introduction: Cognition and culture in the construction of religion. In *Current approaches in the cognitive science of religion*, ed. Pyysiäinen and Anttonen, 1–13.

Pyysiäinen, Illka. 2002b. Religion and the counter-intuitive. In *Current approaches in the cognitive science of religion*, ed. Pyysiäinen and Anttonen, 110–32.

Pyysiäinen, Illka. 2003. *How religion works: Toward a new cognitive science of religion*. Leiden: Brill.

Pyysiäinen, Illka and Veikko Anttonen, eds. 2002. *Current approaches in the cognitive science of religion*. London and New York: Continuum.

Renfrew, Colin. 2007. The archaeology of ritual, of cult, and of religion. In *The archaeology of ritual*, ed. Kyriakides, 109–22.

Roberts, John M., Chien Chiao and Triloki N. Pandey. 1975. Meaningful god sets from a Chinese personal pantheon and a Hindu personal pantheon. *Ethnology* 14 (2): 121–48.

Robinson, David M. 1948. A new Heracles relief. *Hesperia* 17 (2): 137–40.

Roscher, W. H., ed. 1886–. *Ausführliches Lexicon der griechischen und römischen Mythologie*. Leipzig: Teubner.

Rosen, Ralph M. and Joseph Farrell, eds. 1993. *Nomodeiktes: Greek studies in honor of Martin Ostwald*. Ann Arbor: University of Michigan Press.

Rosen, Ralph M. and Ineke Sluiter, eds. 2010. *Valuing others in Classical antiquity*. Leiden and Boston: Brill.

Rudhardt, Jean and Olivier Reverdin, eds. 1981. *Le sacrifice dans l'antiquité: Huit exposés suivis de discussions: Vandœuvres-Genève, 25–30 août 1980*. Geneva: Fondation Hardt.

Rüpke, Jörg. 2007. *The religion of the Romans*. Tr. R. Gordon. Cambridge: Polity.

Rutherford, Ian. 2010. Canonizing the pantheon: The Dodekatheon in ancient Greece and its origins. In *The gods of ancient Greece*, ed. Bremmer and Erskine, 43–54.

Schachter, Albert, ed. 1992. *Le sanctuaire grec*. Geneva: Fondation Hardt.

Scullion, Scott. 1994. Olympian and chthonian. *ClAnt* 13 (1): 75–119.

Seaford, Richard. 1988. The eleventh ode of Bacchylides: Hera, Artemis, and the absence of Dionysos. *JHS* 108: 118–36.

Seaford, Richard. 1994. *Reciprocity and ritual: Homer and tragedy in the developing city-state*. Oxford and New York: Clarendon Press and Oxford University Press.

Seaford, Richard. 1998. Introduction. In *Reciprocity in ancient Greece*, ed. Gill, Postlethwaite and Seaford, 1–11.

Shapiro, H. Alan. 1989. *Art and cult under the tyrants in Athens*. Mainz: Von Zabern.

Shapiro, H. Alan. 2012. Olympian gods at home and abroad. In *A companion to Greek art*, ed. Smith and Plantzos, Vol. 2: 399–413.

Shefton, Brian B. and Kathryn Lomas, eds. 2004. *Greek identity in the Western Mediterranean: Papers in honour of Brian Shefton*. Leiden: Brill.

Sissa, Giulia, and Marcel Detienne. 2000. *The daily life of the Greek gods*. Tr. Janet Lloyd. Stanford: Stanford University Press.

Smith, Jonathan Z. 1982. *Imagining religion: From Babylon to Jonestown*. Chicago: University of Chicago Press.

Smith, Tyler Jo and Dimitris Plantzos, eds. 2012. *A companion to Greek art*. 2 Vols. Malden, MA, and Oxford: Wiley-Blackwell.

Snodgrass, Anthony. 2006. *Archaeology and the emergence of Greece: Collected papers on early Greece and related topics*. Edinburgh: Edinburgh University Press.

Sørensen, Jesper. 2007. *A cognitive theory of magic*. London and New York: Altamira Press.

Sourvinou-Inwood, Christiane. 2003. *Tragedy and Athenian religion*. Lanham, MD: Lexington Books.

Sperber, Dan. 1994. The modularity of thought and the epidemiology of representations. In *Mapping the mind*, ed. Hirschfeld and Gelman, 39–67.

Sperber, Dan. 1996. *Explaining culture: A naturalistic approach*. Oxford: Blackwell.

Sperber, Dan. 1997. Intuitive and reflective beliefs. *Mind and Language* 12: 67–83.

Sperber, Dan. 2004. Agency, religion and magic. *Behavioral and Brain Sciences* 27 (6): 750–1.

Sperber, Dan and Lawrence A. Hirschfeld. 2004. The cognitive foundations of cultural stability and diversity. *Trends in Cognitive Sciences* 8 (1): 40–6.

Spiro, Melford E. 1987. *Culture and human nature: Theoretical papers of Melford E. Spiro*. Edited by Benjamin Kilborne and L. L. Langness. Chicago and London: University of Chicago Press.

Stafford, Emma. 2000. *Worshipping virtues: Personification and the divine in ancient Greece*. London and Swansea: Duckworth and The Classical Press of Wales.

Stowers, Stanley. 2011. The religion of plant and animal offerings versus the religion of meanings, essences and textual mysteries. In *Ancient Mediterranean sacrifice*, ed. Knust and Várhelyi, 35–56.

Suk Fong Jim, Theodora. 2014. *Sharing with the gods: Aparchai and dekatai in ancient Greece*. Oxford: Oxford University Press.

Themelis, Petros. 2007. Panathenaic prizes and dedications. In *The Panathenaic games*, ed. Palagia and Choremi-Spetsieri, 21–32.

Tomlinson, Richard A. 1992. Perachora. In *Le sanctuaire grec*, ed. Schachter, 321–51.

Tracy, Stephen V. 1986. An early inscribed gold ring from the Argolid. *JHS* 106: 196.

Tremlin, Todd. 2005. Divergent religion: A dual-process model of religious thought, behavior and morphology. In *Mind and religion*, ed. Whitehouse and McCauley, 69–83.

Tremlin, Todd. 2006. *Minds and gods: The cognitive foundation of religion*. Oxford and New York: Oxford University Press.

Tsetskhladze, Gocha R., ed. 2006. *Greek colonisation: An account of Greek colonies and other settlements overseas*. 2 Vols. Leiden and Boston: Brill.

Ullucci, Daniel. 2011. Contesting the meaning of animal sacrifice. In *Ancient Mediterranean sacrifice*, ed. Knust and Várhelyi, 57–74.

van Baal, J. 1976. Offering, sacrifice and gift. *Numen* 23 (3): 161–78.

Vanschoonwinkel, Jacques. 2006. Greek migrations to Aegean Anatolia in the early Dark Age. In *Greek colonisation*, ed. Tsetskhladze, 115–41.

van Straten, Folkert T. 1987. Greek sacrificial representations. In *Gifts to the gods*, ed. Linders and Nordquist, 159–70.

van Straten, Folkert T. 1995. *Hiera kala: Images of animal sacrifice in Archaic and Classical Greece*. Leiden and New York: Brill.

van Straten, Folkert T. 2005. Ancient Greek animal sacrifice: Gift, ritual slaughter, communion, food supply, or what? Some thoughts on simple explanations of a complex ritual. In *La cuisine et l'autel*, ed. Georgoudi, Piettre and Schmidt, 15–29.

van Wees, Hans. 1998. The law of gratitude: Reciprocity in anthropological theory. In *Reciprocity in ancient Greece*, ed. Gill, Postlethwaite and Seaford, 13–49.

Vernant, Jean-Pierre. 1983. *Myth and thought among the Greeks*. London: Routledge & Kegan Paul.

Versnel, Henk S., ed. 1981a. *Faith, hope, and worship: Aspects of religious mentality in the ancient world*. Leiden: Brill.

Versnel, Henk S. 1981b. Religious mentality in ancient prayer. In *Faith hope and worship: Aspects of religious mentality in the ancient world*, ed. Versnel, 1–64.

Versnel, Henk S. 1990. *Inconsistencies in Greek and Roman religion I. Ter unus: Isis, Dionysos, Hermes. Three studies in henotheism*. Leiden and New York: Brill.

Versnel, Henk S. 1991. Some reflections on the relationship between magic-religion. *Numen* 38: 177–97.

Versnel, Henk S. 2011. *Coping with the gods: Wayward readings in Greek theology*. Leiden: Brill.

Veyne, Paul. 1988. *Did the Greeks believe in their myths? An essay on the constitutive imagination*. Tr. Paula Wissing. Chicago: University of Chicago Press.

Visala, Aku. 2011. *Naturalism, theism and the cognitive study of religion*. Burlington, VT, and Farnham, UK: Ashgate.

Vlastos, Gregory. 1991. *Socrates, ironist and moral philosopher*. Ithaca, NY: Cornell University Press.

Weinreich, Otto. 1924–1937. Zwölfgötter. In *Ausführliches Lexicon der griechischen und römischen Mythologie*, ed. Roscher, 6: 764–848.

Whitehouse, Harvey. 2004. *Modes of religiosity: A cognitive theory of religious transmission*. Walnut Creek, Lanham and New York: Altamira Press.

Whitehouse, Harvey. 2007. Towards an integration of ethnography, history and the cognitive science of religion. In *Religion, anthropology and cognitive science*, ed. Whitehouse and Laidlaw, 247–80.

Whitehouse, Harvey and James Laidlaw, eds. 2007. *Religion, anthropology and cognitive science*. Durham, NC: Carolina Academic Press.

Whitehouse, Harvey and Robert N. McCauley, eds. 2005. *Mind and religion: Psychological and cognitive foundations of religiosity*. Walnut Creek and Lanham: Altamira Press.

Whitley, James. 1991. *Style and society in Dark Age Greece*. Cambridge and New York: Cambridge University Press.

Williams, Dyfri. 1983. Sophilos in the British Museum. In *Greek vases in the J. Paul Getty Museum*, ed. Frel and Morgan, 9–34.

Wright, James C. 1982. The Old Temple Terrace at the Argive Heraeum and the early cult of Hera in the Argolid. *JHS* 102: 186–201.

Wright, James C., ed. 2004. *The Mycenaean feast*. Princeton, NJ: American School of Classical Studies at Athens.

Young, Lawrence. 1997. *Rational choice theory and religion*. New York: Routledge.

Yunis, Harvey. 1988. *A new creed: Fundamental religious beliefs in the Athenian polis and Euripidean drama*. Göttingen: Vandenhoeck & Rupprecht.

# 2 Implicit theology and the (ir)rational

*From a cognitive perspective, the robust anthropomorphism of the Greek gods is an extreme manifestation of a property all religions have in common. These and other findings give insight into the related phenomena of Greek cult statues and epiphanies. The essential element in anthropomorphism, however, is not physical but mental resemblance. From "What is a god?" we move to the question of how intuitive thought shapes attempts to communicate with the gods. Divination is often considered one of the more irrational aspects of Greek religion. A cognitive model of divination reveals how normal processes of thought give rise to this common human behavior. From a broader perspective, Sperber's theory of symbolic thought shows how "irrational" religious claims arise through fully rational processes. Finally, we consider how Sperber's thought applies to the complex question of the relationship between myth and ritual. The illustrative essays deal with epiphanies of the goddess Athena, the nature of divination at Dodona, and the relationship between myth and ritual in cults of Adonis.*

In Chapter 1, I described a distinction between two forms of cognition, intuitive and reflective. Like most domains of thought, religious thought typically exhibits a mixture of these two modalities. Religion in practice, the immediate experience of people who are interacting with gods, relies more on intuitive cognition, while the poetic, historical, philosophical and visual materials which make up so much of our evidence for Greek religion are the products of reflection, incorporating or rejecting intuitive inferences to various degrees.

Why were the Greeks so certain that their gods existed? To moderns, straightforward belief in Zeus and his thunderbolt or Artemis and her bow may seem irrational. Yet the cognitive mechanisms underlying these beliefs were the same ones supporting the religious faiths of our day. According to cognitivists, the inference that superhuman agents exist results partly from the use of the mental tools that allow us to detect other agents in the environment; we have an innate tendency to over-attribute. Theory of mind, another mental tool, means that we expect other agents to have minds that function like our own, with intentions, beliefs and emotions.[1] As powerful but invisible agents in the environment, "gods," "God" and "the divine" have great inferential potential: they generate stories and provide explanations. The intuition that they exist leads people to think reflectively about how they behave, what changes in the environment might be their doing and how to interact with them.

Every religion involves inferences about the divine which people rarely consider consciously and reflectively ("When I pray, Apollo is aware of it"). This is *implicit theology*. It undergirds a much more extensive body of *explicit theology*, all the representations about God or the gods that are circulated in a given culture. Some of these representations come to be widely distributed because they have properties which make them compelling, relevant and memorable to human minds. Myths are examples of explicit theology to the degree that they set forth the nature, powers and attributes of the gods in relation to one another and to mortals. For example, the Homeric *Hymns* explain that it is Demeter who "increases the life-bearing fruit for humans," that Apollo is concerned with the lyre, the bow and the unfailing will of Zeus, and that Athena, Artemis and Hestia are perpetual virgins. Explicit theology can also be found in statements like this one, placed by Xenophon in the mouth of Kyros' father (*Cyr.* 1.6.46):

> The gods who exist forever know all things, that which has been, and that which is, and that which will be as a result of each of these things, and if people ask the advice of those who are propitious, they foretell what they ought to do, and avoid doing.

Finally there is *systematic theology*, a detailed, logically coherent description of divine matters that is shared, studied and grasped by relatively small groups of people within a culture. Examples of systematic theology include the Stoic Chrysippus' lost book *On the Gods*, the Epicurean Philodemus' *On Piety* and Cicero's great work *On the Nature of the Gods*.[2]

## Anthropomorphism and the Greek gods

Religion in practice tends to draw upon our inferences about the environment around us. From a very early age, we possess an intuitive physics (an apple is a solid object; its juice is a liquid), biology (animals share properties, such as movement and appetite) and theory of mind (minds other than ours possess reason and emotions).[3] When humans interact with gods, or describe gods interacting with us, we are cognitively predisposed to apply these intuitions. Consider a 1996 study in which people were asked to recall a simple recorded story about God interacting with people. The subjects tended to misremember the stories in ways that revealed their anthropomorphic assumptions about God: God moves from one place to another; God performs one task at a time; God needs sensory input (seeing or hearing) in order to perceive phenomena. This was true even though the subjects overwhelmingly professed "theologically correct" beliefs: God knows everything; God can read minds; God is everywhere at once, and so forth.[4]

According to cognitive scientists of religion, widely distributed "god concepts" combine a preponderance of the naturalistic and intuitive properties that we expect other agents to possess (e.g. occupying physical space; feeling emotions) with one or more non-naturalistic and counterintuitive properties (ability to read minds; invisibility). These counterintuitive properties produce a sense of the gods' "otherness" and their incommensurability with humans. Gods may have a wide variety of awe-inspiring superpowers, but they cannot be so counterintuitive that they cease to be good to think with. (In this context, "good to think with" means easily grasped and rich in the potential to generate inferences.) For example, a god who exists only on every other day except Thursdays and Fridays, or a goddess who becomes inactive whenever people pray to her, is unlikely to catch on. The most pervasive religious concepts in daily life (rather than in the writings of systematic theologians) are minimally counterintuitive: familiar enough to grasp and recall easily, but with a few category violations which make them memorable.[5] This is an accurate description of the gods of traditional Greek religion, who are famous for their mental and physical anthropomorphism, but also have properties which are memorably, spectacularly nonhuman.

Anthropomorphism (together with immortality and power) is one of three qualities identified by Albert Henrichs as fundamental to the Greek gods. Immortality itself, as conceived by the Greeks, was a religious concept combining intuitive and counterintuitive properties. The Greek gods were not eternal; each god had a beginning, and most were born from other gods and goddesses in recognizably biological ways. On the other hand (with a few special exceptions) the gods could not die, and once they reached a certain point in their maturation, they did not age.[6] Divine power too had intuitive and counterintuitive manifestations. Zeus ruled the other gods as a king rules his subjects, and according to Homer, his methods included direct physical chastisement of those who disobeyed him:

> Whomever I perceive has a mind to go apart from the gods,
> Wishing to bring aid to either the Trojans or the Danaoi,
> He shall return to Olympos after a shameful pummeling,
> Or I shall seize and hurl him into misty Tartaros,
> Far away, where lies the deepest pit under the earth.
>
> (Hom. *Il.* 8.10–14)

That Zeus might become angry and give another god a beating is a fully intuitive concept, and even that he might hurl another god into a pit, but his unlimited physical strength and his access to otherworldly realms are superhuman. Many counterintuitive divine powers, of course, are precisely those which humans would most like to possess: the ability to control the weather, heal the sick and multiply the flocks.

"Anthropomorphism" is the attribution of human characteristics to whatever is nonhuman. We humans discern faces in the clouds and the moon, assume that our pets can reason as we do, and conclude from environmental disasters that God must be angry. As I mentioned earlier, those of us who have been taught that God is a "spiritual" being may nevertheless intuit that God occupies physical space and is thus in some sense material; typical too among monotheists is the inference that God possesses a gender.[7] The anthropomorphism of traditional Greek religion took such intuitions much further by attributing fully gendered, humanoid, material bodies to the gods. Their physicality was characterized by both naturalistic and non-naturalistic qualities: Demeter's body was shaped like that of a woman, but she was taller and more beautiful. The "default" form assumed by Zeus was a human shape, but he could transform himself at will into a bull or a swan. Physical bodies imply physical appetites: on Olympos the gods feasted, but they did not consume the bread or wine of humans. The gods, and most of the goddesses, felt sexual desire. In their erotic and reproductive capacities, they closely resembled human beings, yet goddesses like Ge (Earth) had the ability to conceive without the participation of a male.[8]

Already at the turn of the sixth century, the philosopher Xenophanes ridiculed the religious anthropomorphism of his contemporaries:

> But if cattle and horses and lions had hands,
> or could draw with their hands and create works as men do,
> then they would draw images of gods or make statues
> each of them exactly as are their own bodies,
> horses' gods like horses, and those of cattle like cattle.
> (21 B 15 *DK*)

Xenophanes seems to have posited instead that the gods were multiple and presumably material, but not morally deficient like the devious, adulterous gods of Homer and Hesiod (B 12).[9] Among them, one god was particularly notable:

> One god, among humans and gods the greatest,
> In no way similar to mortals either in body or in thought.
> (21 B 23 *DK*)

This god "sees, discerns and hears everything," Xenophanes asserted (B 24 *DK*), and relates to the physical world in a way quite different from human beings:

> Always he remains in the same space, not moving at all; nor it is fitting
> for him to go about, now to one place and now to another.
> (21 B 26 *DK*)

Monotheists today typically affirm that God is a "spiritual" being rather than a material one, an idea which we can trace back to Plato's reflective stipulations, developed from predecessors like Xenophanes and Parmenides, about what the divine *must* be like: perfect, rational, good, unchanging and – ultimately – nonmaterial. The philosophers' gods were strikingly un-anthropomorphic and impersonal, little more than lists of absolute properties. Such deities are difficult to worship, and in fact have extremely limited appeal in practice because they are excessively counterintuitive.[10] It is difficult to comprehend exactly what a perfect, transcendent, omniscient, unchanging, eternal deity might be, let alone to interact with "it" (for such an entity certainly could not be gendered). Epicurus took the logical next step of insisting that the perfect gods did not interact with humans or intervene in the world, and that it was therefore useless to pray to or worship them.

Physical anthropomorphism was not a universal rule. Certain gods manifested themselves in animal form (Zeus Meilichios as serpent) or in hybrid form (Pan with goat legs and ears).[11] Deities could be represented in the form of a pillar, plank, boulder or cairn. Physical anthropomorphism was conventional for gods in poetry and art, yet anthropomorphic statues of gods were an important adjunct to worship in specific cults rather than an essential element in all. As Pascal Boyer has observed, "The *only* feature of humans that is *always* projected onto supernatural beings is the mind."[12]

## Cult statue and epiphany

Greek anthropomorphism greatly facilitated interactions with the gods. The inference that the gods were similar to mortals "in body and thought" meant that reciprocal relationships with deities could function in ways analogous to human social interactions. Gods and goddesses, heroines and heroes were provided with housing and invited to attend gatherings in their honor. They enjoyed the same things humans found pleasing: gifts, music, perfumes and poetry. Through appropriate ritual methods, they were presented with food and drink. In turn, they could indicate their acceptance of offerings by means of predetermined signs.

Because the gods had recognizable forms, known to worshipers through statues and paintings, they could appear to people in dreams or waking visions. Scholars have hypothesized a close relationship between the epiphany of gods in anthropomorphic form and the earliest Greek statues of gods, and indeed there is experimental evidence that the use of images and anthropomorphic thinking are mutually reinforcing.[13] Not every religious tradition is reliant on images, but intuitive religious thought tends to be iconophilic and to draw on our innate receptivity to human forms and faces. Depending on the individual and the context, coming face to face with a divine image might itself constitute an epiphany. Beginning with Xenophanes and the Hebrew scriptural ban on "idolatry," however, devotional attachment to statues and icons has been periodically condemned as irrational, naïve and superstitious. The long persistence of religious images in the face of various forms of iconoclasm reveals a historical conflict between intuitive and reflective forms of religious thought.[14]

The concept of the "cult image," a special object designated as the focus of worship in a given Greek cult, has been criticized as an anachronistic modern construct. Scholars have demonstrated that among the numerous terms the Greeks used to denote statues of gods and heroes (*agalma*, *xoanon*, *hedos*, *bretas*, etc.), none was ever used solely to refer to images as objects of veneration.[15] They have also suggested, correctly in my view, that any statue of a god could temporarily become a focus of worship. Yet it is equally clear that some images received more attention than others. Several criteria have been suggested for distinguishing these images from the many others dedicated in temples and sanctuaries. First, they were positioned prominently (e.g. on a base centered in the cella of a temple) so as to command the attention of worshipers. Second, if anthropomorphic, such images were sculpted in conventional, frontal poses which invited interaction with the viewer. (By contrast, narrative depictions of gods, like those regularly found in the pediments of temples, less often afforded a direct line of sight to the god's gaze.) Third, they were incorporated into ritual activities: paraded in procession, covered with fillets of wool, dressed in garments or presented with meals. In some cases, a ritual called *hidrusis* ("seating") was used to inaugurate their special status.[16] Finally, miraculous legends often became attached to them. Images that fit this pattern were venerated.

I use the term "veneration" to suggest that in such cases, the object itself is not merely a focus of worship; it also possesses properties which give rise to feelings of awe. The "minimally counterintuitive concept" (MCI), which I introduced in Chapter 1, is helpful here. Any sculpture or figurine of a deity might evoke feelings of piety or even inspire a prayer, but a "cult image" was an object which possessed attributes of mind or other counterintuitive properties. Such objects were able to sense the presence of worshipers, to hear the prayers of suppliants and to witness sacrifices, choral songs and other offerings. (This is why altars were situated directly opposite temple doors, which were opened during sacrifice to provide a direct line of sight for the cult image.) As Verity Platt has said, "To view a cult image was to encounter a being who looked back."[17] Yet the cult image must be defined more broadly than this, for sometimes the emphasis was on other counterintuitive properties. Some images had miraculous powers of movement and needed to be bound or chained in place. Some had fallen from the sky. Some were talismans which protected the city where they resided. Some were eager consumers of blood. Some caused insanity if viewed or touched by the wrong people.[18]

In a worshiper's reaction to a divine image, either or both of two cognitive processes may be at work. The first is the innate human response to anthropomorphic face and form. The face is most important; it is the face (and especially the eyes) to which infants react almost from birth.[19] Thus, satisfactory images of Dionysos could be constructed from a mask arranged on a draped pole. Similarly abbreviated images called "herms" (with face and genitals only) were used in the worship of Hermes and Dionysos (Figure 2.1).

But anthropomorphic faces alone did not produce veneration, and indeed, many "aniconic" images, unworked stones or roughly carved planks, were venerated.[20] It is the second cognitive principle, minimal counterintuitiveness, which is diagnostic of a cult image, regardless of location, material or appearance. For worshipers, the anthropomorphic statue possesses awareness; it is able to see and hear. Similarly, the unworked stone has fallen from the sky, or confers special powers of protection.

Thinking about divine images in this way helps us to see that aniconic images were not "primitive" versions of anthropomorphic statues (we know that aniconism thrived into late antiquity), but effective MCIs in their own right. A rough boulder with mental attributes is starkly but memorably counterintuitive. A human-shaped statue which can see and hear worshipers is counterintuitive, but

*Figure 2.1* A woman before an altar and a herm (a partially anthropomorphic representation of Hermes with an erect penis). Attic red figure kylix by the Curtius painter, ca. 450. Antikensammlung, Staatliche Museen, Berlin. Photo: Art Resource

it also exploits our intuition that the lineaments of a face, and particularly the eyes, imply an intentional agent. Any individual could experience a momentary intuition concerning any image, but it was the shared perception of counterintuitiveness which gave rise to communal veneration.

Where, then, is the god or goddess? Theologians and philosophers disapprove when worshipers "confuse" a material object with a deity. It may be uncomfortable for us as historians of Greek religion to acknowledge that in many contexts, as epigraphic and other evidence suggests, the statue or stone was for all practical purposes identical to the god.[21] It is not that the Greeks were incapable of distinguishing between a piece of wood and a god. If asked to reflect, a worshiper might well have replied that of course the two were distinct. A fourth-century Athenian vase painter, for example, was happy to depict the "real" Apollo beside his gilded statue, which stands stiffly in a temple (Figure 2.2).[22]

*Figure 2.2* Apollo as a gilded statue in his temple, and sitting beside it with lyre. Fragment of a calyx krater from Taranto, early fourth century. Image courtesy of the Allard Pierson Museum

The intuitive, usually unspoken inference that the statue *is* the god contradicts various reflective beliefs by which worshipers or observers (ancient or modern) have explained the phenomenon: the god is working through the statue; the worshiper uses the statue as a tool to focus his or her attention on the god, and so on.[23] In fact, cognitive theory shows that the same worshiper could hold *both* types of belief, applying them as needed according to the context.

## Cognition, divination and the gods

Multiple forms of divination existed in the ancient Greek world. In addition to well-known oracular sanctuaries, like Delphi, Dodona and Didyma, there were many minor oracles. Nor was the practice of divination limited to specialists in sanctuaries. Every city and every army had its skilled seers, and non-seers divined using simpler methods.[24] In Aeschylus' *Prometheus Bound*, Prometheus claims to have taught numerous divinatory techniques to mortals:

> I marked out many methods of divination (*mantikē*).
> It was I who first judged which dreams would really happen.
> Chance utterances, difficult to interpret, I explained to them,
> And omens of the wayside. The flight of birds with crooked talons
> I delimited, which ones are naturally fortunate and prosperous,
> Which mode of life each has, their enmities, loves and alliances,
> And the smoothness of viscera, what color bile ought to be

> To please the gods, and the well-formed dappled lobe of the liver.
> I led mortals to a difficult art, burning the thigh-bones enveloped
> In fatty savor, and the long tail. And I opened their eyes to signs
> In flame, which before they had seen only dimly.
>
> (Aesch. *PV* 484–495)

These were the skills of the seer (*mantis*): interpreting dreams, chance words or phrases, obstacles or signs met on the road, the flight of birds, the condition of a sacrificed animal's entrails and the behavior of flames.[25] Underlying Greek divination from omens was the intuition that another mind had caused the bird to fly to the right, the lot to fall from the jar or the flame to leap high. When examined reflectively, this intuition of divine agency in rustling leaves or bird flight raised questions. For example, the Stoics (like almost everyone else in antiquity) felt strongly that divination worked, but they also felt a need to explain *how* it worked. They considered and rejected an intuitive explanation: "It is not a Stoic doctrine that the gods concern themselves with individual cracks in the liver or individual bird songs. That is unbecoming, unworthy of the gods, and quite impossible" (Cic. *Div.* 1.118. [Tr. Struck]).

Instead, they proposed a universe of phenomena in which temporal and spatially separated objects and events were interconnected by a divine causal principle, the *pneuma* ("breath"). The interconnectedness of things through the unity of the *pneuma*, which they called *sumpatheia* ("sympathy"), offered an explanation for the otherwise inexplicable link between a well-formed liver and a well-disposed god. In spite of the seeming impersonality of *sumpatheia*, however, the Stoics did not abandon the idea that personal gods were the source of the signs received in divination. One of their arguments for the validity of divination was that the gods make the future known because of their care for humanity.[26]

As Peter Struck points out, divination has been studied primarily with respect to its social effects in building consensus and managing conflict, or as a subset of magic. He observes that both of these approaches have their limitations. Understanding divination as a social tool has been a fruitful approach, yet it sheds light on only one facet of the phenomenon, and "moves all too quickly away from the divinatory moment itself."[27] He goes on to suggest that a key difference between how ancients and moderns have understood divination is "the gap that separates the process of reading signs in an intentional cosmos from reading signs in an unintentional one" (2007.16).

> Divination consistently raises the issue of intentionality. Intention separates two semiotic situations: one in which information is gathered from an unintending source – as in diagnosis or natural observation – and one in which information is gathered from a source that exhibits volition and goal-directed behavior.
>
> (Struck 2007.17)

Struck's observation is consistent with a cognitive approach to divination. It may be that the intuition of an "intentional cosmos" arises naturally from the mental tools with which we are equipped. One of these tools is known as "agent detection," the capacity to recognize intentional behavior from cues in the environment. Overdetection of agency is a better evolutionary strategy than underdetection. If you mistakenly believe that the noise behind you was made by a hungry tiger, there is not much harm done. But if you fail to detect that a tiger is stalking you, the game is over. Therefore, our agent detection tool tends to be hyperactive. Hearing a strange noise in a dark house at night, our first thought is likely to be of intruders, not of an overgrown tree branch scraping the window.[28]

Studies of agent detection, however, suggest that the overattribution of agency occurs especially often when objects in the environment "behave" in unexpected ways. In a classic study, adults who observed geometric shapes "following" or "attacking" each other consistently described the shapes as having beliefs, desires and even genders. Most such experiments have focused on apparently goal-directed movement as the trigger for intuitions of agency, but other triggers include spontaneous sounds from objects that should not be producing noise (as in the case of the "singing" colossus of Memnon), environmental patterns that appear purposeful (crop circles) or other highly unusual phenomena.[29] Hyperactive agent detection, then, might explain the intuition that prodigies such as two-headed calves are "signs," but what about flickering flames, rustling leaves, sneezes and bird flight, all of which are perfectly ordinary phenomena? We will return to this question after considering in more detail the role of agency in the act of divination.

Anders Lisdorf has formulated a cognitive theory of divination based on the existence in the mind-brain of an "action representation system," which enables us to conceive of ourselves and others as intentional agents, as well as other mental tools, such as our capacity for pattern completion.[30] Lisdorf applied his theory to the Roman Republic, distinguishing between two types of divination. In *impetrative* divination, a sign is elicited through a ritual technique, whether it be examining sacrificial entrails, observing flames or scrutinizing the behavior of birds. In *oblative* divination, on the other hand, a sign in the environment is spontaneously encountered and recognized.[31] Lisdorf hypothesized that in impetrative divination, "ritualized action creates an inference of another hidden intentionality, such as a god." He notes that one of the features of ritual is the "displacement of intention," because rituals are regularly characterized by a disconnect between the intent of the performer and the concrete actions performed. Normal intentional action involves a transparent relationship between action and goal (Table 2.1): I unlock and open the front door in order to enter the house. Ritual action, on the

*Table 2.1* Comparison of the action sequence in unlocking a door, a ritual of animal sacrifice and divination by flames. The words in parentheses indicate mental representations supplied by the operator that would not be transparent to an outsider.

| *Agent* | *Action* | *Goal* |
|---|---|---|
| Stephanos | Unlocks door | Entering house |
| Stephanos | Burns thigh bone | (Pleasing Apollo) |
| (Apollo) | Causes flame to leap | Answering Stephanos' question |

other hand, is characterized by nontransparent relationships: I burn a cow's femur on a block of marble in order to . . . please a god. In Lisdorf's theory, the deficient intentional structure of ritualized action causes the mind to search for and supply either another goal or another agent.[32] In the case of impetrative omen divination, the operator is setting up the parameters within which the action will occur and defining a goal, but is displacing his or her own intentionality. The gap is therefore filled by a hidden agent.

Now let us return to our question about the relationship between the cognitive disposition toward "hyperactive agency detection" (HAD) and omens found in ordinary phenomena. The ritualized action of impetrative divination involves defining the conditions and tools through which a sign is to be sought. The diviner may shake a lot from a jar, mark out the portion of the sky where birdflight will be significant, or stipulate that the next word he hears after leaving the house will be the sign. In every case, the necessary condition is that no manifest agent, such as another person, has the ability to affect the outcome. This is what scholars of divination call "randomization."[33] Similarly, HAD cannot function unless the field is cleared of manifest agents. When a football seems to move by itself, the mind searches for a candidate agent. Is the football an animal in disguise? Or did a ghost move it, perhaps? But if we see a person in the bushes who may have attached a string to the ball, that is quite another matter; HAD shuts down.[34] Impetrative techniques, then, work via two mechanisms. First, they artificially create an environment in which HAD can function by excluding other potential agents. Second, in the absence of trigger stimuli, they artificially induce agency detection by setting up an action sequence which is missing one of its key parts. The ritual context, a script which mentally "makes room for the god" as the agent, is what differentiates these forms of divination from games of chance.[35]

Impetrative divination "works" even if we do not have a specific deity in mind as the agent, and people find it very compelling. Even in secular culture, people are attracted to the illusion of hidden agency which is produced when we play with a toy like the "Magic 8-Ball," use a Ouija board or open a fortune cookie. All of these are impetrative techniques in which devices are used to create the necessary conditions for hidden agency to manifest itself. Impetrative divination, then, is a form of self-stimulation which harnesses HAD and other mental tools to evoke hidden agency. In secular contexts, these techniques are used for entertainment, and the hidden agency is mildly intuited but unnamed. In cultural contexts where the existence of gods, spirits, ghosts, heroes or other superhuman agents is taken for granted, divination works equally well whether the hidden agency is attributed to specific deities or the more impersonal "divine" (in Greek, *to theion*). This understanding of the cognitive basis for divination complements theories which describe how it functioned in Greek culture to allay anxiety, manage risk and mediate social conflict.[36]

Lisdorf included inspired prophecy through a medium, as practiced at the oracle of Delphi, in the category of impetrative divination, but there are substantial differences when the "tool" used to obtain a sign is a human being. Apollo's priestess, known as the Pythia, prepared for a prophetic session by bathing, then burning laurel leaves and barley on an altar and drinking special water from a sacred spring. After the sacrifice of a goat by the petitioner, she entered the temple accompanied by priests, and sat on a tripod. She then entered a state of inspiration (*enthousiasmos*), and answered the petitioner's question. Whether she was incoherent and ecstatic or calm and articulate has long been a subject of debate; ecstatic frenzy is suggested in the later sources, though the earlier ones point to coherent speech. Similarly, the question of whether vapors arising from a chasm beneath the tripod induced her altered state of consciousness, as some sources state, has been much discussed.[37] For our current purposes, it is useful to note that the consultation creates an action sequence (Table 2.2) slightly different from that which we observed in impetrative omen divination.

In this situation HAD presumably cannot operate, since there is an obvious candidate agent, the Pythia herself. Oracular mediumship relied instead on the emic concept of *enthousiasmos* to clear the space for the god. In order for the participants to mentally substitute Apollo for the Pythia as the agent of the sign, she had to be "not in her right mind." As Plato observed,

> No one achieves inspired divination (*entheou mantikēs*) or truth when in his right mind (*ennous*), but only when the power of intentional thought (*phronēseōs*) is shackled in sleep, or when it is altered by disease or because of some divine inspiration (*enthousiasmos*).
>
> (Pl. *Ti.* 71e)

This analysis suggests that even though the concept of *enthousiasmos* was familiar in Greek culture, the divinatory, Delphic version needed to be regularly reinforced and elaborated with stories of sacred spring water, chasms, vapors and frenzies in order to support the inference that Apollo, and not the Pythia, was the agent. It also suggests that even if she spoke coherently, the Pythia needed to signal in some fashion (perhaps quite subtle) that she was "not in her right mind."[38]

Inspired divination was held in higher respect among the Greeks than non-inspired, "technical" methods. Given the apparent cognitive obstacle to the inference of divine agency – the presence and potential interference of the medium – we need to explain why this was so.[39] Why did people place credence in the Pythia and other Apolline mediums? The answers appear to be both cultural and cognitive. First, the inspired medium's ability to facilitate two-way *verbal* communication was compelling because it uniquely addressed the "epistemological uncertainty" of relations between humans and gods. Second, processes of oral transmission shaped and reshaped historical responses into brilliant examples of

*Table 2.2* In divination by inspired medium, the participants must mentally represent Apollo as the agent even though an obvious agent is present.

| *Agent* | *Action* | *Goal* |
|---|---|---|
| (Apollo) Pythia | Speaks | Answering question |

Apollo's riddling yet accurate predictions, adding greatly to the credibility of his oracles. No one who has heard the story of how Kroisos of Lydia fulfilled the prophecy that he would "destroy a great kingdom" is likely to forget it.[40] Third, spirit possession itself, the temporary loss of personal agency to a superhuman substitute, appears to be a counterintuitive concept with extremely strong appeal, since it recurs in cultures throughout the world. Other cognitive habits, such as the confirmation bias, also functioned to shore up the credibility of inspired oracles (Essay 2.2).[41]

Much was at stake, given the prestigious role of Delphi and other inspired oracles in advising political authorities. Concern about the possibility of bribery was recurrent.[42] Even in Apolline contexts, where inspired mediums were favored, divination by lots tended to encroach. A fourth-century inscription from Athens reveals that a lot method was used in order to decide whether to rent out some sacred land or leave it untilled. The two alternatives were written on pieces of tin which were rolled up, wrapped in wool to make them indistinguishable and placed in two jugs stored on the Akropolis:

> The people are to choose three men, one from the council and two from all Athenians, to go to Delphi and ask the god according to which of the two written messages the Athenians should act with regard to the sacred land, whether that of the gold water jug or that from the silver water jug.
>
> (*IG* II$^2$ 204.43–7 = *RO* no. 58)

This method ingeniously converted mediumistic divination into a method from which the possibility of human agency had been removed, and presumably increased the Athenians' intuitive certainty that Apollo was the source of the response. Catalogues of Delphic oracles reveal that it was conventional to frame questions in an "either/or" format, which could have allowed the Pythia to use a lot method rather than providing a verbal response.[43]

Now let us turn to oblative divination, in which signs are spontaneously received and therefore *not* elicited through a ritualized consultation process. This type of divination depends on sensitivity to the potential for omens, and a body of widely distributed lore about which types of events are significant. As with impetrative divination, environmental cues selected as oblative signs must be free from human agency, yet they often involve displacement of intention from a god to an animal. For example, Theophrastus disapprovingly describes how a superstitious or "god-fearing" man (*deisidaimōn*) reacts to signs:

> If a weasel crosses his path, he will not proceed until someone else has passed that way, or until he has thrown three stones over the road. Whenever he sees a snake in his house, he invokes Sabazios if it is the red-brown kind, or if it is the sacred kind, he sets up a hero-shrine then and there . . . When he has a dream, he visits not only dream analysts but also seers and bird diviners to ask which god or goddess he should pray to.
>
> (Theophr. *Char*. 16)

*Table 2.3* In oblative divination, the operator mentally represents agent and goal according to a predetermined cultural catalog.

| *Agent* | *Action* | *Goal* |
|---|---|---|
| (Unknown divine agent) Weasel | Crosses path | (Warning of misfortune) |
| (Hero) Sacred snake | Enters house | (Soliciting worship) |

Like black cats in modern Western culture, weasels were considered "bad luck," while snakes were signs of certain deities as well as the powerful dead or heroes. This cultural catalog of potential omens and their meanings supplied both agency and goal in the action sequence, which was constructed after the fact (Table 2.3).

The god-fearing man's problem is not that he believes in signs from the gods, but that his agency detection mechanism is truly hyperactive, and he lacks the judgment to discern which signs are random events. Among the Greeks, oblative divination was often practiced by non-experts because it did not necessarily require specialized knowledge. Theophrastus' account reveals a bias toward expert skills: when a mouse gnaws through the god-fearing man's sack of barley, the expert he consults sensibly advises him to simply have the bag sewn up again. According to Lisdorf, people in all cultures become more receptive to oblative signs when they are in trouble or need to make a decision. In contexts of concern, people may also recognize and interpret oblative signs in personal, idiosyncratic ways.[44]

Theophrastus describes the god-fearing man as one who consults multiple diviners every time he has a dream. As we learned from Prometheus's speech about divination, there is an art to knowing which dreams are messages from the gods and which are not. Again, the god-fearing man overattributes: if he doesn't get the answer he seeks from the dream analyst, he consults someone else. Dreaming could also be used for impetrative divination, as in the ritual of incubation, which typically involved purifying oneself, making an offering and spending the night in a sanctuary. In both cases, the presumption that dreamers lacked intention and were "not in their right mind" allowed their agency to be displaced to a god (Table 2.4).[45]

Another form of non-ritualized divination was the interpretation of spoken or written oracles, the skill practiced by a *chrēsmologos*. Although some chresmologues may have uttered inspired oracles themselves, most seem to have specialized in collecting and interpreting written oracle-books. These were most popular during the sixth and fifth centuries; practitioners included Antichares, who interpreted "oracles of Laios," and Onomakritos, who specialized in "oracles of Musaios." Both Herodotus and the comic poet Aristophanes refer to "oracles of Bakis," and other collections were known.[46] Such oracles differed from

*Table 2.4* In divination from dreams, the dreamer is presumed to lack agency regardless of whether the significant dream is spontaneous or ritually induced.

| *Agent* | *Action* | *Goal* |
|---|---|---|
| (Divine agent) Dreamer | (Causes dream) Dreams | (Sending relevant message) |

those received through consultations at Delphi in that they were not necessarily responses to petitioners' questions. They seem instead to have been poetic texts thought to possess predictive value. For example, Herodotus approvingly quotes the following oracle of Bakis:

> Take care, when a foreign-tongued man casts into the sea
> A yoke of papyrus, to keep bleating goats far from Euboia.
> (Hdt. 8.20.2)

Herodotus thought that Bakis had predicted the invasion by Xerxes, the "foreign-tongued man." Certain oracle collections enjoyed credibility because of their supposed hoary age, and because their authors were thought to have been inspired by gods. Bakis was inspired by the nymphs, and the legendary Musaios perhaps by the Muses themselves, as his name suggests. Musaios was highly respected in Attica and classed together with Orpheus, Homer and Hesiod as an inspired poet.[47] No matter the date of composition, successive generations infer that the contents of "ancient" oracle collections refer to events or concerns of their own day (the same is true of repeated historical attempts to apply apocalyptic texts, such as the Book of Revelation, to current events).[48] To the extent that such oracles are not *post hoc* fabrications, their "accurate predictions" result from cognitive biases toward false-positive pattern detection.[49] In this type of divination, the action sequence involving *enthousiasmos* is projected into the deep past and serves to lend authority and credibility to the oracle. This authority is secondary in cognitive importance to the psychological reinforcement produced when a "confirming" pattern is detected during the process of interpretation.[50]

## Symbolic thinking

From an etic perspective, most religions appear to include irrational or unfounded beliefs together with practices ("rituals") which lack transparent goals and therefore seem irrational. Anthropologists agree that these are cultural manifestations of symbolism, but they do not agree on how symbolism works. Classicists who study religion are familiar with Claude Lévi-Strauss, Victor Turner and Clifford Geertz, all of whom viewed symbolism (and therefore religion) as a system through which meaning is conveyed. Lévi-Strauss thought that symbolism works by expressing relations between categories. Thus when Homer says that the winds carry the savor (*knisē*) of burning sacrificial flesh to heaven, where the gods enjoy it, we might interpret this statement by observing the opposition between mortal and god, earth and heaven, solid meat and insubstantial aroma. The Homeric act of sacrifice defines the spatial and ontological chasm between gods and mortals even as it connects them.[51] Symbols therefore have meaning only in relation to each other, and indeed, their meaning lies in their relationships.

Turner and Geertz, on the other hand, both thought that culture conferred meaning on the symbols themselves. Turner developed a detailed taxonomy of the multiple referents of symbols and how they shifted in different contexts. For Turner, the symbol was "the smallest unit of ritual," and its function was to facilitate social relationships through the sharing of its meaning(s).[52] Geertz thought that culture was transmitted through symbolic systems. He defined a symbol as "any object, act, event, quality or relation which serves as a vehicle for a conception." People use symbols to express "their knowledge about and their attitudes toward life."[53] Both Turner and Geertz employed very broad definitions of symbols and how they function, but they were clear that, like signs, symbols possess referents, relatively stable meanings (or more often, sets of meanings) which can be identified by the anthropologist.[54] It is difficult to suggest a single Turnerian or Geertzian interpretation of Homeric sacrifice, with its *knisē* rising to the gods, but presumably it would express for Turner a wealth of connotations attached to the social relations enacted through sacrificial ritual, and for Geertz, a worldview locating humans in relation to animals, gods and each other.

Each of the foregoing three approaches to symbolic thought allows the anthropologist to avoid confronting what appears to be the irrationality of the statement that smoke from burning fat (*knisē*) goes up to heaven, where the gods sniff it.[55] I suggest that we can understand Greek religion better (or at least as well) by considering another approach formulated by Dan Sperber in 1974. Sperber argued that symbols lack meanings and are always half-understood. It is precisely the lack of meaning in symbolism which makes it useful in religious contexts.

Sperber contrasts symbolic knowledge with empirical knowledge, which he terms encyclopedic.[56] Encyclopedic knowledge is about the world: "Leopards are dangerous." Such propositional statements, described in logic as "synthetic" statements, can be verified or falsified according to evidence in the environment. All of us possess a mental encyclopedia of empirical knowledge, which we constantly adjust based on experience ("Leopards are dangerous, and they can climb trees."). Like encyclopedic knowledge, symbolic knowledge can be expressed by means of synthetic statements. To use an example from Sperber's fieldwork among the Dorze of Ethiopia, "Leopards are Christian animals who observe fast days." Anthropologists who understand symbolism as a code or language, Sperber says, treat this statement as a kind of metaphor. It is part of a symbolic system of cultural categories; therefore its "truth" exists in relation to the logical coherence of the system, not in relation to the empirical world. The Dorze, however, do not make this statement figuratively, but literally. Their attitude seems doubly irrational, for in spite of their stated belief in the Christianity of leopards, they guard their flocks from leopards every day of the week:

> A Dorze is no less careful to guard his animals on Wednesdays and Fridays, fast days, than on the other days of the week. Not because he suspects some leopards of being bad Christians, but because he takes it as true both that leopards fast and that they are always dangerous. These two statements are never compared.[57]

Whereas pieces of encyclopedic knowledge are constantly subjected to checks on their implications and possible contradictions, symbolic knowledge is distinctive precisely because it is not treated this way. Greek worshipers did not ask exactly how the savor of sacrifice was supposed to reach to Olympos, nor how the gods might be able to enjoy blood spattered on altars, or libations poured on the ground.

Sperber asks, "Under what conditions is it logically possible to hold a synthetic statement to be true without comparing it with other synthetic statements which are susceptible of validating or invalidating it?" This turns out to be possible when we metarepresent a concept – that is, when we think about it using our reflective faculty.[58] Compare the following statements:

A. No butterflies have a wingspan larger than three inches.
B. Some butterflies are gynandromorphs.
C. Some butterflies are spirits.

Let us say that a student named Jim hears statement A. He will treat it as encyclopedic knowledge. If and when he sees a butterfly with a wingspan larger than three inches, he will compare the two pieces of information and adjust his encyclopedia accordingly. Hearing statement B, Jim may be puzzled because he does not understand the term "gynandromorph" at all. It matches nothing in his memory. If he has heard the information from what he considers a reliable source, he will mentally represent the statement in this form: "My professor says that some butterflies are gynandromorphs, whatever that means." This metarepresentation is fully rational, and indeed is essential to the process of learning. While he holds this representation in his mind, Jim will not compare it with other statements about butterflies, since he does not have enough information to do so. But having created this placeholder for the concept, Jim may later learn that a gynandromorph is an organism displaying both male and female characteristics, and he may even examine a butterfly specimen which is male on the left side and female on the right. In that case, the statement "Some butterflies are gynandromorphs" will enter his store of encyclopedic knowledge.

Now imagine that Jim is told statement C by his mother, a person he trusts. A similar problem arises. It is not clear exactly what a "spirit" is, or how a butterfly can also be a spirit. Searching his memory, however, he may find a number of associations: Spirits can fly; spirits are related to ghosts, perhaps butterflies have something to do with dead people. Sperber calls this process of memory searching *evocation*. As in the case of statement B, Jim will not subject statement C to comparison and checks for contradiction with his encyclopedic information about butterflies, because the concept of "spirit" remains too vague to allow this. But given that he trusts his mother, he assents to the statement: "[My mother says that] some butterflies are spirits." As in the case of statement B, Jim's assent is fully rational. Sperber points out that most people believe that $e = mc^2$ based on the same reasoning. Unless they are well-versed in physics, they cannot check for contradictions by subjecting $e = mc^2$ to comparison with their other knowledge.[59]

Another option would be for Jim to take his mother's statement figuratively: some butterflies resemble spirits in important ways. This option would also place statement C in a separate category from Jim's encyclopedic knowledge and protect it from comparisons that might falsify it. Metaphor is closer to what we usually think of as "symbolism," but in fact, religious symbolism often involves literal truth claims which are predicated on appeals to authority in combination with the processing of what Sperber calls "information that defies direct conceptual treatment."[60] His model reveals that symbolic thinking is not an aberration of irrational and benighted people, but a mental capacity which we all use extensively in non-religious contexts to help us grasp half-understood concepts. In some cases (as with gynandromorphy and $e = mc^2$), these concepts are susceptible of full explication. In religious thought, the case is precisely the opposite. Successful religious concepts are highly evocative, filling the mind with fertile associations, yet they are characteristically paradoxical and inexplicable. Consider the following synthetic statements:

> God is one, but also three persons, a Father, a Son, and a Holy Spirit.
> Herakles was a man like us, but he died and is now a god.
> The initiated will have a share of the blessings after they die.

One of the implications of Sperber's argument is that different individuals will perform the process of evocation in different ways. That is, the associations evoked during attempts to grasp symbolic concepts will never be identical for every member of a culture. Therefore, Sperber argues, anthropological models which treat symbolic systems as codes or languages to be deciphered are on the wrong track. The essence of a symbol is that it does not correspond to known concepts; it does not pair with the thing signified in the way that signs do. Drivers understand that a red light is, nonnegotiably, a sign meaning "stop." But symbolism is permanently elusive and its meaning is never truly circumscribed. What, precisely, does a Christian cross "mean"? It refers to Christ's crucifixion. But what does *that* mean? The "meanings" of religious symbols may be doctrinally prescribed and taught; there are dictionaries of symbols. But such exegesis must itself be interpreted symbolically in an open-ended process which differs profoundly from the linguistic communication of meaning. Furthermore, even in a carefully taught system of exegesis, the individual process of evocation will function, as the learner attempts to understand statements which are conceptually unfamiliar and not congruent with his or her factual experience.

Sperber's model has explanatory power which other theories of symbolism lack.[61] It explains how people rationally maintain belief in things they do not fully understand – not only logical paradoxes (e.g. the Christian Trinity) and unfalsifiable claims ("God exists") but also many claims that are falsifiable or inconsistent. In religious contexts, the model works in concert with cognitive susceptibilities, such as the tendency to favor and transmit minimally counterintuitive concepts (Christian leopards who fast, or smoke which unerringly travels to the nostrils of the gods). Finally, the model is predicated on the existence of familial or social structures of authority and on verbal communication. Indeed, Mercier and Sperber hypothesized that reflective cognition evolved as human social relationships came increasingly to depend on theory of mind and verbal communication. Symbolic thought, in this view, is a by-product of our ability to think reflectively.[62]

## Religion, myth and ritual

In religious systems with a literate, professional priestly caste and sacred books, such as those of ancient Egypt and the Near East, we can expect to find close ties between myth and ritual. Greek religion, however, possessed no professional priestly caste and no books widely accepted as sacred. Although the gods figured prominently in early Greek poetry, much of the oral tradition was transmitted outside of ritual contexts. Even when writing was introduced, the Greeks did not develop a system of prayerbooks to be used during rituals. Therefore, although the mythic and ritual traditions show many points of contact, they proceeded along parallel but often separate lines. Take, for example, the myth that Zeus incinerated his lover Semele when she insisted that he appear to her in his true form (the thunderbolt). The myth conveys a reflective, theological speculation about Zeus' "true form." Such a tale could be told at a symposium or in any number of contexts which moderns would consider secular, whereas in worship, it might be pertinent or it might not, depending on the local context.[63] This makes Greek religion fundamentally different from religions which favor tight, doctrinally bound ties between myth and ritual (as in the Christian association between the New Testament's Last Supper narratives and rituals of holy communion). Even where ties existed between specific Greek myths and rituals, and where priests could expound on these connections, they did not carry dogmatic weight: there was no religious obligation for the average worshiper to learn them.

Since the mid-twentieth century, scholars of Greek religion have tended to neglect myths in favor of rituals, partly for the reasons stated earlier. Indeed, many myths, such as the Labors of Herakles, appear to have little religious content. On the other hand, Herakles was worshiped from at least the sixth century, so myths of his exploits could have been refashioned for performance in cultic contexts. G. S. Kirk proposed a widely accepted definition of a myth as a "traditional tale," and recognized a subdivision of "sacred myths" while firmly rejecting the notion that myth and religion are two aspects of the same phenomenon.[64] Yet to the degree that the Greeks regarded myths containing counterintuitive representations (immortal people, flying horses, caps of invisibility) as facts rather than fictions, they employed symbolic thinking, just as they did when expressing belief in the efficacy of prayer, divination and sacrifice.[65] In both cases, metarepresentation allowed people to accept as true that which they found compelling but did not fully understand. Thus there is a broad subset of myths which we may legitimately call religious, even if they were not regarded as "sacred" or paired with rituals.

In terms of the dual-process cognitive model explained in Chapter 1, all myths are products of reflective cognition, though they may incorporate inferences of intuitive origin. For example, the myth that Apollo shuttled between Delphi in the spring/summer and the Hyperborean lands in the winter is closely related to, and probably originated in, the idea that Apollo needed to be summoned to undertake his oracular duties; worshipers intuitively inferred that he had to be physically present in order for the oracle to work. Many hymns, including the spring paeans sung at Delphi, had this "cletic" function, and it was a standard part of most Greek sacrificial rituals to "call the god."[66]

When taken as factual, myths with counterintuitive content make up a special subset of "religious myths," and myths about gods and cult heroes are a form of explicit theology. Archaic mythmakers were theologians, credited with an inspired ability to reveal the past mental states and intentions of the gods. Consider this account of Apollo planning the establishment of his sanctuary at Delphi:

> Then Phoibos Apollo pondered in his heart
> About what people he would bring in as priests
> To be his servants in rocky Pytho.
> While he was thinking this over, upon the wine-dark sea
> He noticed a ship . . .
>
> (*Hymn. Hom. Ap.* 388–92)

Mythopoetic knowledge of the gods' past thoughts and intentions stands in stark contrast to the opacity of their mental states in actual worship. Greek ritual was predicated on uncertainty regarding present and future relations with the gods. As we will see in Chapter 4, religious ritual relies to a great degree on intuitive inferences about how to approach the gods, as well as other intuitive beliefs. Of course, it often incorporates reflective elements as well, but people performing rituals are not necessarily pondering the relevant myths at the same time. In fact, what we know about cognition suggests that, other things being equal, the extra mental effort required to do this will be avoided, and that when people do keep myths in mind as they perform rituals, simple narratives will be favored over conceptually complex ones unless written memory aids are available.[67] Greek rituals, therefore, operated within the general conceptual framework of gods and heroes provided by local and Panhellenic myth, but unless a ritual incorporated a myth in some salient fashion, we cannot assume that the participants acted with any myth present to mind.[68]

In order to see how myth and ritual may be interrelated, let us adopt Kirk's definition of a myth as a traditional tale, and provisionally define a religious ritual as a prescribed method of interaction with "the sacred" or a superhuman agent (ritual will be more fully discussed in Chapter 4). As we examine a few of the possibilities, it is useful to consider the degree of fusion and simultaneity between myth and ritual in each case: are the participants keeping a pertinent myth in mind as they carry out the ritual acts? A hymn sung during a ritual typically celebrated the names and attributes of a god, but it might also include narrative content. For example, a traditional paean sung for Asklepios at Erythrai in the fourth century alludes to his father Paian (Apollo) and his mother Koronis:

> Sing, youths, of famous Paian
> Son of Leto, Far-Shooter,
> Ie Paian!

Who brought great relief to mortals
Mingling in love with Koronis
In the land of Phlegyas
Ie Paian, Asklepios!
(Furley and Bremer 2001, no. 6.1.1, lines 1–7)

The paean for Asklepios confines itself to a simple description of the god's family, but many Greek festivals involved skilled performances – dances, hymns, recitations or dramas – featuring far more detailed narratives about the gods.[69] Sometimes these myths had a direct relationship to the ritual occasion and sometimes they did not (thus the myth and ritual were sometimes fused and sometimes not). At Delphi, the Pythian games included a competition in which singers commemorated Apollo's battle with the Python, the founding myth of the sanctuary. Other times, the myths were told for their own sake. Greek tragedies like Sophocles' *Oedipus the King* were performed in the context of festivals for Dionysos and were intended to please an audience both human and divine, but in spite of much discussion about possible Dionysiac and ritual patterns underlying Greek drama, the genres of tragedy and comedy appear to have evolved further away from their ritual roots than their cousin the dithyramb, which was also performed in the theater. The Greeks themselves recognized that comic and tragic subject matter was often "nothing to do with Dionysos."[70]

Next, let us consider cases where the degree of fusion between myth and ritual was very high. Certain rituals involved *reenactment* of a pertinent myth by the ritual participants (as opposed to *skilled performance* before a group of observers without specific ritual roles).[71] In reenactments, the myth was reduced to a very simple form, precisely the opposite of what happened in skilled performance. We have good reason to believe that Dionysiac worship included dances in which worshipers played the roles of mainads and satyrs, celebrating the advent of the god or reenacting the "Return of Hephaistos" to Olympos. Both were easily represented through a simple processional movement, though the dance steps themselves might be complex (see Essay 3.2). During the Eleusinian Mysteries, both priests and worshipers took part in Demeter's search for her abducted daughter Kore, moving through the sanctuary as they did so. In this case, an ancient myth which previously functioned to explain seasonal changes in plant growth was invested with new eschatological meaning, and initiates hoped to achieve a blessed afterlife (Chapter 5). Reenactment of the myth was the essence of the ritual; Demeter's loss and Kore's return from the dead provided a template for the physical movement of participants and supplied the symbolic content pertaining to eschatology. As people participated in the nocturnal rite, the myth was vividly present to their minds, but probably in a simplified, mostly nonverbal form, as current scholarly consensus suggests. I argue in Essay 5.1 that Eleusinian initiates were primed beforehand with more conceptually complex verbal content.[72]

The festival of the Adonia, during which Greek women mourned Aphrodite's dead lover Adonis, provides an example of a simple, "cognitively optimal" myth in fusion with ritual. The festival was inspired by the practices of Near Eastern women who mourned Ishtar's lover Tammuz, but the Greek women who borrowed it had only a vague knowledge of the myth of Tammuz, to judge from their use of his title *Adon* ("Lord") as a personal name. The Adonis lamentations, however, had an emotionally compelling referent quite independent of myth: real-life funerary rituals. The core myth was quite simple: "Aphrodite's beautiful young lover is dead!" The core ritual, meanwhile, seems to have involved the laying out of effigies of Adonis, with plentiful lamentation – a reenactment of Aphrodite's mourning. Myth and ritual in this simple form achieved a high degree of fusion. Elaborate retellings of the Adonis myth, on the other hand, were the province of literate males and were probably transmitted separately (Essay 2.3).

In other cases, the degree of fusion between myth and ritual could be quite low. For example, Hesiod's account of Prometheus and Zeus at Mekone (*Theog.* 535–58) explains why sacrificial meat is typically consumed by the people present at the ritual, while the bones of the animal are burned for the god: Prometheus gave Zeus a choice between two portions, and he selected the one with the bones, thus setting the pattern for future practice. Hesiod's account is highly theological, offering a conceptually complex explanation of Zeus' decision to choose the portion of lesser value (Essay 2.2). This myth was transmitted in the epic tradition, separately from the ritual activity it explains. To my knowledge there is no attested instance of a Greek sacrifice that included an account of Prometheus and Zeus, and it is unlikely that people conducting sacrifices often thought of this myth as they performed the ritual actions. (Compare this lack of fusion with a modern Catholic or Anglican eucharist, in which a complex narrative explaining the origin of the ritual in the Last Supper is recited from a book at every performance of the rite.)

Myths that explain the origin of something (e.g. how the camel got his hump) are called "etiologies," and etiologies of ritual form a common subcategory of myth.[73] The fact that a myth is an etiology, however, does not predict its degree of fusion with ritual. Some etiologies tied to specific cults look like interpretations handed down within a sanctuary's oral tradition, yet outside of a ritual context. For example, Pausanias reports (9.27.6) that the sanctuary of Herakles at Thespiai had a priestess who was required to be a virgin for life. The locals explained this anomaly with the story that Herakles slept with all but one of the fifty daughters of Thestios, condemning to lifelong virginity the one who refused him. Other etiologies of ritual, however, fell into the category of "sacred stories" (*hieroi logoi*), meaning that they were told either during the ritual itself, or beforehand to those about to participate. Such stories were often kept secret (Essay 5.1).[74]

Many further permutations of the myth-ritual relationship are possible. Visual representations of myths, for example, might appear as decorations on vessels or other objects used in ritual. During the Athenian Panathenaia, a robe woven with images of the Gigantomachy (the battle of the gods and giants) was presented to Athena. The weaving of this garment was ritually inaugurated as part of the preparations for the Panathenaia, and the representation of the Gigantomachy drew attention to Athena's martial prowess during a festival which emphasized the might and prestige of the city itself. The Panathenaia did not recapitulate the events of the Gigantomachy, yet the festival was said to have originated in the commemoration of Athena's triumph over one of the giants. The degree of fusion between myth and ritual in such cases must have varied greatly by participant; those involved in the production or presentation of the robe may have had the myth more present to mind than others.[75]

## ESSAY 2.1: EPIPHANIES OF ATHENA

At first, the term "epiphany" seems easy to define: the manifestation of a god to one or more people. Yet complications quickly arise. For the Greeks, a deity's presence could be manifested through miraculous signs, or through visions of him or her in human or animal form. Even "vision" is too narrow a category, for epiphanies may be auditory or visual. And what of the distinction between dreaming and waking visions?[76] Greek epiphanies are surprisingly diverse, yet certain patterns remain consistent across many centuries. We recognize these patterns in the experience of ordinary individuals, but also in literature and art. Epiphanies resulted from the perception of anomalous agency, plus a process of symbolic evocation which drew on cultural conventions about the visual appearance and typical behaviors of the gods.

### Homeric epiphanies of Athena

In the first book of the *Odyssey*, Athena dons winged shoes and descends to Ithaka, where Telemachos welcomes and confides in her, believing that she is a stranger named Mentes, a leader of the Taphians. After advising Telemachos on his next steps with regard to the problem of the suitors, she suddenly drops the Mentes disguise:

> So spoke the goddess, flashing-eyed Athena,
> And went away, flying upward like a bird; and in his heart
> She put strength and courage, making him think of his father
> Even more than before. And in his mind he marked her,
> Marveling, for he deemed that she was a god.
>
> (Hom. *Od.* 1.319–23)

Athena's sudden, uncanny departure amazes Telemachos, who concludes that he has been in the presence of the divine. As Athena intended, the experience renews his determination to resist the suitors, and his hopes for his father's return.

In epic poetry, gods reveal their presence in many ways, through lights, birds, clouds, human disguises and in their own persons.[77] As Odysseus himself says to Athena, "It is difficult, goddess, for a mortal man to know you when he meets you, even a man of understanding, for you make yourself resemble everything" (*Od.* 13.312–13). In a scene from the *Iliad* (4.75–84), Athena is visible to both Trojans and Achaians as she descends from heaven; her appearance is like that of a falling star, and while the men do not recognize her identity, they consider the star a divine portent. These examples are fictional, but they are closely related to oblative divination, and they illustrate cognitive principles pertinent to lived experience. For the Greeks, any unusual phenomenon might trigger agency detection and the process of evocation. Both bird flight and celestial phenomena suggested activity by the gods, understood reflectively as inhabitants of the heavens. But while divine agency could be recognized quite readily, observers faced epistemological uncertainty in identifying the agents themselves, and in understanding their motives and methods.[78]

The gods provide the narrative machinery of epic, manipulating events through various means. Athena often appears in disguise to warn or advise warriors as she advances her own agenda, unbeknownst to them. As Bernard Dietrich noted, in the majority of cases from epic, "So-called epiphanies were nothing more than interventions of one kind or another which did not involve any actual *parousia*, or [sacred] presence."[79] Then again, certain Homeric heroes have a privileged relationship with a deity, especially Athena, as in the cases of Achilles, Diomedes and Odysseus. They knowingly interact with her on more familiar terms than the average person could expect to. Odysseus' theological observations aside, such instances function primarily as narrative devices.[80] In Telemachos' case, however, Athena produced what we might call a partial epiphany by flying upward as a bird, yet stopping short of full self-revelation. Like real-life observers of strange phenomena, he was left to puzzle out the meaning of the event for himself.

In epic, the gods often manifest themselves through dreams. In the fourth book of the *Odyssey* (4.759.67), Penelope weeps in distress for her absent son and makes an offering to Athena, praying for his safety. Then she falls asleep, and Athena speaks to her through a phantom of her sister Iphthime (4.795–841). The phantom tells Penelope that Telemachos is being guarded by Athena, and that Athena herself has sent the dream out of pity for Penelope's sorrow. Penelope wakes and we are told that "her heart was warmed because a clear dream-vision had sped to her from the darkness of night." Her prayer has been answered.[81] As we will see, the dream vision, already frequent in Homer, is one of the most common patterns of epiphany in lived religion.

Dietrich concluded that Homeric epiphanies provide little or no basis for understanding religion in practice, because of their nature as poetic devices and the way their great variety resists classification.[82] He usefully reminds us to evaluate each piece of evidence with an eye to its context; poetic depictions of Greek religion may or may not match the historical experiences of individuals and communities. On the other hand, Homer describes oblative signs and dream visions, both of which were common modes of epiphany in lived experience. Before turning to a more detailed discussion of dreams, let us examine a third possibility, that epiphanies might be induced through symbolic performance.

## Peisistratos and Phye

After his first exile, the Athenian tyrant Peisistratos rode back into Athens in spectacular style. According to Herodotus, he and his ally Megakles dressed a tall and handsome woman named Phye in armor and placed her in a chariot, which the tyrant then mounted:

> Heralds were sent to run before them, and when they came into town urged the people as they had been instructed: "Athenians, give a hearty welcome to Peisistratos. Athena herself has honored him most among men, and she is bringing him back to her own Akropolis." They went about saying this, and right away a rumor spread in the demes that Athena was bringing back Peisistratos, and the people in the town, believing that the woman was the goddess herself, worshiped a human being and received Peisistratos.
>
> (Hdt. 1.60.4–5)

Herodotus (1.60.3) professes himself shocked at the gullibility of the Athenians who were fooled by this "utterly simple-minded" (*euēthestaton*) trick, while Aristotle ([*Ath. Pol.*] 14) describes Peisistratos' method as "old-fashioned and very simple." Modern historians have typically either denied the historicity of this episode, or focused on Peisistratos' "manipulation" of religion, often echoing Herodotus by describing the entry into Athens as a trick, a charade or a ruse. John Boardman famously argued that Peisistratos was capitalizing on the then-current story of Herakles' apotheosis, which vase painters illustrated with scenes of Athena conducting the hero to Olympos in her chariot. Recent commentators have offered more nuanced variations of this explanation, describing Peisistratos' act as symbolic and performative, intended to suggest that he enjoyed the goddess's favor rather than to deceive the Athenians with a fake epiphany. W. R. Connor argues that the crowds were not at all duped, but rather, because they were well-disposed toward Peisistratos, chose to delight in the drama he offered them. The entry thus functioned as "an expression of popular consent" rather than a sign of popular delusion.[83]

Peisistratos was careful to depict himself as the servant of Athena. Although the speech of the heralds reported by Herodotus said that "Athena was bringing back Peisistratos," Aristotle specifies that Peisistratos was the charioteer and Athena the passenger. The performance also hinted that it was the goddess's return as much as the tyrant's, that, in fact, she had been alienated from her city while Peisistratos was in exile. But what of epiphany? Is there any sense in which it would be accurate to describe Peisistratos' entry with Phye as an epiphany? Both Herodotus and Aristotle are quite clear that at least some of the people worshiped Phye as though she was the goddess, and historians have been too quick to dismiss this testimony. Even Connor's interpretation describes their response as knowing and playful rather than fervent. While Herodotus is highly judgmental about the Athenians' reaction, Aristotle is at once more neutral and more descriptive. He says that the people "marveled" at the sight and they responded by "bowing down" as one would to a deity. These are the reactions of people experiencing religious emotions.

The performative scenario is compatible with religious sentiment, yet we need posit neither a uniform response nor a gullible one. In this case we are not dealing with agency detection tools and unexplained phenomena, but with degrees of openness to the symbolic statement, "Athena is bringing back Peisistratos." After hearing the rumor, individuals will have reacted differently according to their backgrounds, personal dispositions and political views (i.e. their personal processes of evocation). A woman in battle armor was simultaneously anomalous and familiar; it would have been clear to any observer that the woman in the chariot resembled artistic depictions of Athena. The display of sacred imagery (e.g. a statue of the Virgin being carried in a Catholic procession) can elicit strong emotions, as well as physical gestures, such as bowing, raising the hands or kneeling. Additionally, there is evidence in some Greek contexts for ritual impersonation of the gods.[84] Therefore, some Athenians may have interpreted the event figuratively, yet found religious meaning in it. Others probably concluded that they had seen the goddess in person (especially in hindsight, as rumors flew). Still others, less receptive to suggestion and to the tyrant himself, will have rejected all symbolic interpretations (whether figurative or literal) of the episode.

## The vision of Meneia

Around the middle of the fourth century, an Athenian woman named Meneia erected a stele, a slim block of stone, on the Akropolis. On it was written "Meneia set this up for Athena after seeing a vision of the goddess's excellence (*aretē*)."[85] We know nothing about Meneia other than the fact that she possessed the resources to have this record of her experience inscribed. Presumably, whatever she experienced had an emotional impact strong enough to motivate the effort and expense involved. Meneia lived in a culture which valued such visible displays of piety, from the smallest clay statues deposited around temples to the most impressive stone monuments topped with specially commissioned sculptures. According to convention, many of these gifts were given either to repay a promise to the deity or in the hope of future benefits.

During the fourth century, the Greeks began to record on stone that their gifts were made in response to epiphanies. Meneia's dedication is one of the first surviving inscription of this kind, but it leaves us wondering about the nature of her experience. The use of the word *aretē* is of special interest. In the Archaic and Classical periods this term had aristocratic connotations, referring to virtues possessed by the well-born. By Meneia's time, when used in a religious context, it had begun to denote a "powerful action" or "manifestation" wrought by a deity. If Meneia saw the goddess herself, it was most likely in a dream. Her formulaic phrase "having seen a vision" (*opsin idousa*) was already used by Herodotus to refer to dream premonitions, and was standard in the dedicatory inscriptions for the dream-healer Asklepios at Epidauros.[86]

Broadly defined, the epiphanic dream (of visitation by a god, spirit, ancestor or dead person) appears to be a well-established cross-cultural phenomenon.[87] While most of the dreams we experience are quickly forgotten, a minority are unusually memorable. This group includes nightmares and other dreams accompanied by vivid imagery, intense emotional arousal, and strong physiological and psychological effects which carry over into the hours or days after the dreamer awakes. Experimental data suggest that dreams with epiphanic content have a distinctive profile: they involve a predominance of positive emotions; low levels of aggression, sexuality and physical contact within the dream; and feelings of well-being upon awakening. As in the case of nightmares (which are often interpreted as warnings), it is not unusual for epiphanic dreams involving the voice or likeness of a god to affect the subsequent behavior of the dreamer. For example, an adolescent American girl who dreamed that a divine voice spoke comfortingly to her reported that afterwards she was moved to give money to homeless people.[88] If a psychological aftereffect proves to be generalizable across cultures and periods, it could provide insight into the development of cultural practices, such as Meneia's votive gift, which allow dreamers to respond to and memorialize epiphanic dreams.

Although records of dream visions in the form of inscriptions left by ordinary Greek people do not begin until the fourth century, there are occasional references to such dreams in earlier periods. In epic, as we saw, gods routinely use dreams to communicate with mortals. While the Homeric examples are poetic constructs rather than case studies from real life, they indicate a cultural familiarity with epiphanic dreams. Reflecting contemporary understandings of how gods functioned through dreams, Pindar (*Ol.* 13.63–82) describes the hero Bellerophon being advised by a seer to sleep beside Athena's altar in order to obtain instructions for the capture of Pegasos. For his part, Herodotus assumes that such phenomena have occurred repeatedly throughout history; his main modification of the Homeric model is to attribute dream visions to unspecified divine agency more often than to named gods.[89]

In Meneia's day, most people took it for granted that the appearance of a god in one's dreams was a divine manifestation rather than, say, a random combination of thought and image. While dream visions commanded a higher level of respect than they do in modern Western culture, they also had the potential to create problems both hermeneutic ("how do I interpret this?") and epistemological ("how do I know this was a god, and how can anyone else share that knowledge?"). Although the Greeks spoke in inscriptions of having "seen a divine vision in a dream," or taken action "according to a [divine] command," dreams were not necessarily straightforward visual manifestations of a god, and they might require consultation with a professional.[90] There must have been a filtering process, performed by both dreamer and interpreter, through which dreams were made to conform to preexisting cultural conventions. Sometimes a dream vision required others to take action, in which case a burden fell on the dreamer to convince them of the dream's validity. But more often, as perhaps in Meneia's case, the dream primarily concerned the dreamer. In the text of Meneia's stele, the specific content of her vision is not considered relevant for the viewer. What is important for the viewer to know is that Meneia experienced a divine manifestation, and that she responded; she and Athena had a personal interaction.

The phenomenon of epiphany was present in Greek religion from the beginning, forming a counterpoint to the group experiences of festival and sacrifice. (Although simultaneous manifestations to groups of people are attested, usually in connection with battles, the vast majority of epiphanies involved the self-revelation of a god to an individual.)[91] Meneia's vision illustrates a growing popular interest during the late Classical period in individual relationships with the gods, and the ways in which the gods' saving power was manifested through healing and other miracles.

## Dream epiphanies at Lindos

Athena's manifestation to Meneia demanded public commemoration, so that the goddess received suitable thanks, but Meneia saw no need to share the details of her experience with the community or persuade onlookers of Athena's great power. Presumably, any benefits she received from the goddess were private in nature, in spite of Athena's role as a civic goddess. Conversely, a famous series of epiphanies recorded centuries later at Rhodes is concerned with Athena's relationship to the community.

The Chronicle of Lindos is a stele erected in 99 at Lindos, where Athena presided as the goddess of the citadel, just as she did in Athens. The monumental stele, almost a meter wide and more than two meters tall, is so large that visitors would have strained to read the writing at the top. It was erected not by an individual but by decree of the Lindians.[92] Their purpose was to create an official record documenting the antiquity and renown of Athena's worship at Lindos:

> Since the sanctuary of Athena the Lindian, both the most ancient and the most venerable in existence, has been adorned with many beautiful offerings from the earliest times on account of the manifestation (*tan epiphaneian*) of the goddess, and since it happens that most of the offerings together with their inscriptions have been destroyed on account of time, it has been resolved with Good Fortune, by the councilors and the Lindians, that by this decree two men be selected. Let those selected set up a stele of stone from Lartos according to what the architect writes, and let them inscribe on it this decree. Let them inscribe from the letters and the public records and the other evidence whatever may be fitting about the offerings and the manifestations (*tas epiphaneias*) of the goddess.
>
> (*I.Lindos* 2, lines 2–8, translation adapted from Higbie 2003.19)

The Lindians understood the relationship between gifts and epiphanies in terms of reciprocity. Donors of beautiful offerings were motivated by the manifestation of the goddess, who was portrayed as a frequent visitor to her shrine at Lindos.[93] Rich gifts to Athena Lindia and her epiphanies were the two aspects of the sanctuary's past which the Lindians considered most important to document. Together, they provided evidence of past glories, the memory of which was in danger of fading. This was a matter of concern to the community as a whole, and while the stele can itself be seen as a kind of offering to Athena, its primary purpose was to burnish and enhance the reputation of Lindos as a city favored by the goddess.

The catalogue of offerings which follows the text of the decree is necessarily selective, focusing on the most famous donors, some of whom are mythical (Kadmos, Helen, Herakles).[94] After the list of offerings come three records of epiphanies, each of which occurred at moments of danger for the community as a whole. The first and oldest tells how the Persian general Datis came to besiege Lindos (probably in 490). The Rhodians on the waterless citadel were ready to submit, when Athena appeared to "one of the rulers" in a dream, saying that she would intercede with Zeus. The Lindians were accordingly saved when rain came, and Datis, who had scoffed at their claims, broke the siege and offered Athena his own garments and carriage. With its rebuke of the unbeliever Datis, the tale emphasizes Athena's power to save her people.

The second epiphany, which can perhaps be dated to the mid-fourth century, involved a different type of crisis. For reasons not explained, an unidentified man was shut into Athena's temple at night. He hanged himself from a beam directly behind the cult statue, causing a ritual pollution by his death within the sanctuary, and in close proximity to the image. Such desecration had the potential to anger and alienate a deity (Chapter 3), and was especially dangerous given that Athena was the patroness of the city. Therefore, the Lindians planned to consult Apollo at Delphi on how to proceed. Far from punishing the Lindians, however, Athena saved them the trip by appearing to her priest in a dream to prescribe the appropriate ritual: the part of the roof directly over the statue was to be removed, that the statue might be washed by rain from Zeus.

The third epiphany records another situation in which Athena offered aid during a civic crisis, this time a siege by Demetrios Poliorketes (305/4). The goddess appeared to a retired priest and advised him to go to the city council and tell them to send to Ptolemy I for assistance. The priest at first discounted the dream, but after having the same dream for several nights, he obeyed, and the city was duly saved. The doubts of the priest may seem surprising, yet the repetition of the dream (regardless of whether it actually happened) can be understood as a device to enhance credibility. It is one thing for an individual to act on a dream, and another for a city to take action based on the claims of an individual. The repetition of an identical dream was a more prodigious event than a single dream, and therefore more likely to be recognized as divine in origin.[95]

In each of these cases, Athena appeared to an individual. In each case, however, the significance of the epiphany did not concern the individual per se, but the welfare of the city as a whole. The compilers of the Chronicle of Lindos were no doubt aware of other epiphanies of Athena, but they chose these examples because they demonstrated the goddess's care for her city. The historicity of these dream epiphanies is arguable. On the one hand, the Chronicle is a synthetic text drawn from historians' accounts and other records of the deep past. It illustrates the Hellenistic interest in "sacred history" and the need to preserve traditions perceived as ancient.[96] The transmission from dream to dreamer's account to written account(s) to inscription on the Lindos stele must have involved interpretation and embellishment. On the other hand, it is quite possible that each of these episodes derives from a historical report of an epiphanic dream.

## ESSAY 2.2: WHAT DO THE GODS KNOW?

"Not all gods can read minds, and few know absolutely everything." Cross-culturally, varying degrees of knowledge are claimed for gods, spirits, ancestors and ghosts. Among the Baining people of Papua New Guinea, ancestor spirits can read minds, but forest spirits cannot.[97] Greek mythology offers many examples of deities who can be deceived. Homer's Zeus, the father of gods and men, was unable to read the mind of his wife Hera when she plotted to distract him from events on the battlefield at Troy. Poseidon and Apollo were tricked by the crafty mortal Laomedon, who refused the reward he had promised them for building the walls of Troy.[98] Although the gods in these examples are represented as superhuman, their access to information is as limited as that of mortals because the narrative contexts demand that the gods be capable of misjudgment.

Not all mythopoetic tales of the gods operate this way, making the gods' knowledge fit the narrative context. Hesiod recounts an old story that Prometheus deceived Zeus on the occasion of the first animal sacrifice, when the portions allotted to humans and gods were to be decided. Prometheus laid out two piles, one with the good meats wrapped in hide and hidden by the stomach, and the other with useless bones wrapped in appetizing fat. Then he bade Zeus make his choice.

> "Zeus, most glorious and greatest of gods who are forever,
> Take whichever of these the heart within you bids."
> He spoke with trickery in mind. But Zeus, knowing imperishable counsels,
> Did not fail to recognize the trick, and in his heart he pictured evils
> For mortal men, which he would bring to pass.
> With both hands he took up the white fat
> And was angry in his mind, and wrath came to his heart
> When he saw the white ox-bones and the crafty trick.
> And because of this the tribes of humans upon earth
> Burn white bones for the immortals upon fragrant altars.
>
> (Hes. *Theog.* 548–58)

In an earlier version, clever Prometheus must have deceived Zeus, who meted out punishment when he discovered his mistake. But according to Hesiod, Zeus *knew* of the deception, yet went along with it anyway, choosing the inferior portion even as he planned his revenge. Outside of the confines of the tale, Hesiod had reflected deeply on what properties the ruler of the cosmos ought to have, and concluded that gullibility was not among them. But Hesiod's theology does not extend to a true declaration of omniscience, that Zeus knows *everything*. Instead, Zeus has *strategic information*. Cognitively speaking, the distinction is important.

In practice, people rarely attribute true omniscience to gods. Even if they have been taught that God knows everything it is possible to know in the past, present and future, they do not suppose that all pieces of information are equally likely to be represented in the mind of God. Boyer gives the following examples:

> God knows the contents of every refrigerator in the world.
> God knows what every single insect is up to.
>
> God knows whom you met yesterday.
> God knows that you are lying.

To most people, the statements in the second pair seem more natural than those in the first. One of the most common characteristics of superhuman agents the world over is their special access to knowledge. But the knowledge they possess is virtually always "strategic information," which Boyer defines as information which "activates the mental systems that regulate social interaction."[99] Strategic information is determined contextually, but includes all information that could affect the way we interact with other people – for example, the knowledge that a friend has told a lie, earns more money than we thought or has a bottle of Scotch in his office. Anything someone prefers to keep secret is likely to be strategic information. The intuitive inference that a god possesses all strategic information is not equivalent to the theological assertion that the god is omniscient.

We have seen that in some mythopoetic accounts, Greek gods have limited access to strategic information, as humans do, and in others they have full access. What about the knowledge gods possess in cultic contexts, particularly oracular contexts? For example, did the Greeks represent their premier oracular god, Apollo, as omniscient? Usually, oracular questions and responses are analyzed in terms of what they tell us about the questioners' concerns. But the extant corpora from Dodona, Delphi, Didyma and other Greek oracles, together with the cultural traditions about these oracles, can tell us much about how Greek worshipers perceived the gods.

The procedure of Greek prophetic oracles reveals the intuitive inference that the gods must hear a question before they can respond. In several cases, Apollo is said to have spoken spontaneously at Delphi, before a question was asked, but this was generally to recognize the petitioner and either to refuse an oracle or to prophesy about a different topic.[100] Only once does the narrative context clearly indicate that he has read the petitioner's mind by answering the contemplated question. Herodotus reports that when Eëtion of Corinth entered the temple to ask about his lack of children, Apollo spoke first: "Eëtion, nobody values you, though you are worthy. Labda conceives and will bear a rolling stone, which will fall among monarchs and set Corinth right" (Hdt. 5.92B.2).

This legend involves a triple demonstration of Apollo's knowledge. First, he knows Eëtion's unspoken question. Second, he possesses the strategic knowledge that Eëtion's wife is pregnant. Third, he has what we might call strategic knowledge of future events, which he conveys in riddling, ambiguous terms.

## Consulting the gods at Dodona

Unfortunately, we do not know the specifics of the oracular procedures at the venerable Panhellenic shrine of Dodona; they seem to have varied substantially over time. Most often we hear of a sacred oak tree which "spoke" (through the noise of rustling leaves or the cooing of doves) and was presumably interpreted by the priestesses.[101] In this case, the priestesses would have functioned like specialized seers, performing impetrative divination on behalf of the petitioners. Dodona has yielded hundreds of small lead tablets containing questions put to the oracle of Zeus and Dione, and in a few cases the responses. The majority of the questions are in a yes-or-no format, like this one:

> God. Good Luck. Archo[nidas?] asks the god whether I should sail into Sicily.[102]

As early as Homer's day, questions at Dodona were framed this way:

> He said that [Odysseus] was going to Dodona,
> That he might hear Zeus' will from the god's high-leafed oak,
> As to how he should return to the rich land of Ithaka,
> Whether openly or in secret, having long been away.
> (Hom. *Od.* 14.327–30)

This convention, together with one piece of testimony from the fourth century, has led scholars to suggest that Dodona normally used a lot oracle. The tablets were folded, which would prevent the priestess or anyone else from reading them. The priestess could select a tablet from one jar and a lot from another jar of bicolored beans or pebbles. By this method, the god is presumed to "read" the tablet, and the petitioner's question remains unspoken.[103] But there are obstacles to accepting this scenario as the principal method of divination during the period when lead tablets were used (ca. 550–167). First, it includes no role for the sacred oak, which was clearly the main source of oracular power. (Tablets were used by both ordinary folk and state petitioners, so it was not a matter of relegating lesser visitors to the lot method.)[104] Second, while a few tablets have an identifying mark or word on the verso, which could have allowed the priestess to match petitioner and response, the majority do not bear such marks.[105] Third, a significant minority of questions are phrased in such a way that they require more than a yes-or-no answer:

> About property, my own, my children's and my wife's, by praying to which god would I fare well?[106]
>
> About the chastity of the girl/my daughter, how could she do these things better and more well?[107]
>
> God. Good Luck. Bokolo and Polymnaste (ask) what they should do for there to be health and offspring like their father and a male child that will survive and security and enjoyment from things to come.[108]

> Gods. Good Luck. Arizelos again asks the god by doing or making what thing it will be better and more beneficial for him, and he will have a good acquisition of property.[109]

These examples, and the nature of certain preserved responses, virtually guarantee that many petitioners spoke their questions aloud to the priestess in addition to writing them.[110] But if this was so, why write on a tablet in the first place? Given the state of our evidence, any explanation must be speculative, but I suggest that in sharing their questions with a priestess, petitioners did not intuitively feel that they were communicating directly with Zeus and his cult partner Dione, who is sometimes addressed in the tablets as well. Zeus and Dione did not possess the priestess, as Apollo did the Pythia. (Indeed, if they had, it would have been difficult to tell which of them was speaking.)[111] Instead, they communicated through the tree and doves. Therefore the lead tablets offered a way to "contact" Zeus and Dione directly. The priestess may have placed the tablet in some natural hole in the tree trunk, or simply held it against the tree, then looked for a yes/no sign in the behavior of the leaves or doves. For more complex questions, additional advice was dispensed in the form of ritual instructions, of the kind that fell within the competence of skilled seers. The intuitive need to bring a written request "closer" to the divine recipient is similarly revealed in the custom of placing curse tablets in tombs or throwing them down wells, where the gods of the underworld could have better access to them.[112]

There is some support for this hypothesis in a fragment from the Hesiodic corpus: "And they dwelt in the trunk of the oak, from which those who live on earth bring back all their oracles" (Hes. fr. 181.8–9 Most = fr. 240 *MW*). The author seems to say that gods live in the trunk of the oak, but also that the trunk itself is the ultimate source of the oracles. Although at some point the divine agents behind the oracle were identified as Zeus and Dione, the oak of Dodona is a minimally counterintuitive concept, a tree that answers questions.[113] Therefore it makes sense that people might have submitted their questions to the oak via a concrete method, just as people in modern times attach written petitions to statues of gods or other holy objects. Why the tablets needed to be folded in most cases is less clear, unless the niche or hole was quite small, but curse tablets were also regularly folded for no obvious reason. Dodona tablets were often reused, so the folding may have signaled that the current question was the one on the "inside."[114] In both the lot scenario and this one, the gods "read" the tablets, but the physical contact between tablet and tree offered petitioners a more intuitively satisfying explanation of how they could do so.

One of the most striking features in the corpus of questions from Dodona is the variation among individual petitioners in the amount of information each deems it necessary to provide as context. Some give plenty of detail: "God. Good Fortune. Did not Archonidas and Archebios, the son of Archonidas, and Sosandros who was then the slave of Archonidas, or of his wife, enslave the son of Aristokles?"[115] Here the petitioner suspects that Archonidas has unlawfully enslaved someone, and he wants Zeus to confirm his hunch. He names the conspirators, explaining for Zeus and Dione's benefit how each is connected with the ringleader

*Figure 2.3* Lead tablet from Dodona. "Hermon (asks) by aligning himself with which of the gods there will be offspring for him from (the woman) Kretaia. . . ." Ioannina Museum. End of sixth/beginning of fifth century. Photo: HIP/Art Resource

Archonidas. Compare this inquiry by a petitioner who phrases his question succinctly, assuming the gods' full knowledge of the situation:

> Did Thopion steal the silver?[116]

Similarly, compare these two questions about marriage:

> [Should Milon accept] Olympias the daughter of Thorakidas for [his son] Thearidas?[117]
>
> Whether he will do better if he takes the woman he has in mind.[118]

One questioner takes care to specify which Olympias he is interested in, while the other neglects to name the woman in question at all. How might we explain these differences? In order to have a successful conversation, we must provide our interlocutors with the information they need in order to make sense of the exchange, and we must make inferences about which pieces of information are unknown to the other party. Petitioners might therefore provide a few details (e.g.

"Olympias the daughter of Thorakidas") in order to ensure that the gods were clear about which Olympias was meant. Once Zeus and Dione understood the question, they could supply the answer from their stock of strategic information. On the theory of the oracular procedure we outlined earlier, however, petitioners spoke their questions aloud to the priestess. If this is true, a significant factor affecting the amount of information supplied must have been the petitioner's desire for privacy. If the petitioner felt the need to formulate her query cryptically, or even to submit it without speaking the question aloud, this created a *new* category of strategic information, to which the gods had equal access.

Some petitioners went so far as to remove all specifics from their questions, trusting that Zeus and Dione knew the pertinent information:

> Should I go?[119]
> To which of the gods must he pray so as to achieve what he has in mind?[120]
> Whether . . . what he has on his mind, you also foretell as an oracle (*kai chrēēi*)?[121]

The third petitioner explicitly asks Zeus to read his mind and to affirm or negate what he is thinking. This type of question is acceptable only because it is framed in a yes-or-no format. To ask "What am I thinking about?" would be viewed as an impious test of the god's knowledge. According to Herodotus, Kroisos ingeniously tested a number of Apolline oracles by sending messengers to ask each of them at the appointed time, "What is King Kroisos of Lydia doing now?"[122] Apollo answered:

> I know the number of the sands and the dimensions of the sea; I hear the dumb and the man who does not speak. I smell a hard-shelled tortoise boiled with lamb meat in a bronze pot, which has a bronze bottom and a bronze lid.
> (Hdt. 1.47.3, 6.125.2 = Fontenrose 1978 Q99)

This legend is clearly designed not only to point out the impiety of Kroisos in daring to ask such a question but also to claim true omniscience for Apollo, who states unequivocally that he has access to *all* information – not just strategic information, like the fact that Kroisos is cooking tortoise and lamb in a bronze pot at this very moment, but also non-strategic information, like the number of grains of sand which exist or how much water is in the sea.

## Divination and conceptual control

McCauley and Lawson use the term "conceptual control" to describe the properties which allow an instrumental ritual to be preserved and transmitted even if specific ritual goals are not achieved: the rain fails to arrive, the plague is not averted or the prophecy fails. According to their analysis, cultures regularly generate rituals with poor conceptual control, but such rituals do not endure. They give the example of a splinter religious group in Papua New Guinea, which devoted itself to rituals designed to make the ancestor spirits return immediately. After their rituals repeatedly failed, the splinter group members returned to their community's mainstream tradition. The transmission of ritual practices is a selective process, and rituals that fail in obvious ways are far less likely to be transmitted than those with good conceptual control (i.e. those which are difficult to falsify). Although the confirmation bias helps to ensure that a failed prophecy or two does not discredit an established authority, repeated falsification will cause ritual activity to be abandoned, modified or focused on a different superhuman agent.[123]

We tend to think of divination as "fortune-telling," a way of predicting the future, and indeed, certain Greek techniques, such as dream interpretation, could be used this way. In practice, however, most people asked about the disposition and inclination of the gods, and how to maximize their chances of success in a planned endeavor. When Xenophon was trying to decide whether to travel to Persia as a mercenary, he did not ask the Delphic oracle, "Will I come back alive and successful?" Instead he asked, "To what god should I sacrifice and pray in order to accomplish my intended journey with good fortune and a safe return?"[124] Formulating his question this way avoided testing the oracle. Responsibility for determining whether Xenophon would return lay not with the oracle but with the specified god, who might or might not choose to fulfill his prayer. A large number of Delphic questions and responses follow this pattern.[125]

In Fontenrose's analysis of question formulas at Delphi, almost all questions were framed as requests for advice: "Shall I do X?" "What shall I do about X?" "To what god shall I sacrifice?" By contrast, very few recorded questions asked Apollo to provide falsifiable information. From a sample of 259 consultations, only seven questioners asked, "Who or what caused X?" and seven asked "Shall I succeed?"[126] A common approach was to present Apollo with a contemplated plan or project – a colonial venture, a piece of legislation, the construction of a temple – and ask for his approval. As many have pointed out, this practice is useful to communities because it confers divine authority on group decisions. Indeed, Delphi's role in setting a divine seal on the enterprises of early Archaic states is well-documented. Yet individuals who had formed plans of action used the same strategy in consulting oracles, even when they had no need to justify their acts to others.[127] Culturally selected conventions about how to consult the oracle, up to and including permissible question formats, were in force. Still, there was always a tension between these conventions and individuals' desire to know the future. Evidence from Dodona reveals that a minority of individuals did ask for falsifiable predictions.[128]

Conceptual control affects oracular responses as well as questions. The Delphic oracle is famous for its riddling answers. Scholarly attitudes toward these have varied. Fontenrose thought that ambiguity, riddling and use of proverbs were clear signs of folkloric origin, and that every response using these devices was therefore inauthentic.[129] Others have observed that such responses had social utility: ambiguous, riddling answers permitted communities to debate until a consensus was reached, thus forcing them to solve their own dilemmas. The best example of this is the debate held by the Athenians when they received the "Wooden Wall" oracle on the eve of the Persian invasion, and decided that it referred to their ships.[130] But the social utility was an effect rather than a cause of oracular ambiguity. States did not consult oracular mediums because they found riddles useful in times of conflict, but because they were convinced that the oracles provided valuable new information if properly interpreted.

Ambiguity is crucial for good conceptual control (and thus for the survival of a given oracle), because it protects oracular pronouncements, even predictions of the future, from falsification. Consider the following oracle, which Fontenrose classified as "not genuine." When Amyris and other men came from Sybaris to ask how long the city's prosperity would last, the Pythia said:

> Fortunate, Sybarite, will you be in your feasts
> Ever, if you honor the race that ever exists.
> But when you worship a mortal before a god,
> Then war and strife of kin will come upon you.
> (Ath. 12.18 [520a-b] = Fontenrose 1978 Q123; if genuine, sixth century)

The Sybarites believed that this response was an accurate prediction of the future. War came after one of the citizens flogged his slave in a god's sanctuary, but relented when the slave fled to the tomb of the man's father. The flexibility of oracular language allowed petitioners to find the "correct" meaning after the fact: one of their citizens had triggered the misfortune through his impious behavior in paying more respect to his father than to the god. Compare the "cold reading" techniques used by modern psychics, including those who sincerely believe in their own powers:

> The best readers always include a statement like, "I only see pieces, as in a jigsaw puzzle. It is up to you to put them together", or, "I may speak of a person being crushed by a house as in *The Wizard of Oz*, but you recognize it as a friend with overdue mortgage payments."[131]

Because this type of ambiguity arises in religious and paranormal contexts as easily as in folklore, Fontenrose was too hasty in excluding ambiguity as a potential characteristic of historical oracular responses. Instead, it was one of the tools used by oracles to increase their conceptual control. Oracles that encouraged non-falsifiable question formats and gave ambiguous responses to questions about the future were more likely to thrive than those that did not.

## ESSAY 2.3: MYTH, RITUAL AND ADONIS

In the early sixth century, Sappho and her female companions lamented Adonis:

> Delicate Adonis is dead, Kythereia, what shall we do?
> Beat yourselves in lamentation, girls, and tear your clothes.
> (Sappho fr. 140a *LP*)[132]

This form of ritual mourning was borrowed from Syro-Phoenician women's annual rooftop laments for Tammuz, the consort of the great goddess Ishtar (their Sumerian equivalents were Dumuzi and Inanna). In its Near Eastern contexts, the myth of Tammuz was connected with the agricultural cycle; Tammuz spent half of the year with Ishtar, and half with the queen of the dead, Ereshkigal. Like the goddess, the women lamented his death and disappearance during the heat of summer.[133]

When Greek women borrowed the custom and mourned Adonis, the beloved of Aphrodite, what myth did they have in mind? "Adonis" likely did not exist before the ritual was borrowed, for his name is simply a Hellenized form of Tammuz's title *Adon* ("Lord"). The most familiar story of Adonis' death, that he perished after being gored by a boar during the hunt, seemingly has nothing to do with Tammuz. It is not attested until ca. 400, and we have no reason to believe that Sappho was aware of it.[134] Could Sappho have known a version in which Adonis spent part of the year with Aphrodite and part with Persephone? A myth along these lines was recounted by the fifth-century epic poet Panyassis: Aphrodite hid the infant Adonis away from the other gods, and gave him to Persephone to nurse; Persephone then refused to give back the beautiful child. Adjudicating the dispute, Zeus awarded "custody" of Adonis to each goddess for a third of the year, with the other third to be spent by Adonis as he chose.[135]

Since this story is most likely Archaic in origin and closer to the time of Sappho, are we then to assume that Sappho and her companions mourned a dead child? This is possible, but seems unlikely in view of an aspect of the myth which recurs over and over, from Sumerian Dumuzi to Babylonian Tammuz to Greek Adonis: each is visualized as a beautiful youth who possesses erotic allure. In the Greek ritual, women allied themselves with the goddess Aphrodite ("Kythereia") to help her lament the loss of her young lover. As Sappho's lament suggests, participants will have understood the ritual as mimetic: they were imitating the actions of Aphrodite and her companions in her grief. From an etic perspective, we may detect additional psychological or social significance. The important role played by women in funerary lamentation was a Pan-Mediterranean cultural constant, such that a festival involving lamentation for a beautiful dead youth would be relatively easy to transmit. A ritual of lamentation also had intrinsic appeal, for the lament allowed women an opportunity to gather in groups, to dress in finery and to share a deeply emotional experience, perhaps calling to mind their own loved ones.[136]

There is a disjunction between the Near Eastern Tammuz/lamentation complex and its counterpart in Greek culture. Tammuz was the name of the month in which the summer solstice begins. The god's dying and reappearance were correlated with the agricultural cycle and embedded in the civic and religious calendars. In transmission, however, the ritual was stripped of both its cultural prestige and its connection to agriculture. Meaning had to be recreated by and for a new audience of Greek worshipers, still primarily women. We have little information about the Adonis myth as worshipers knew it, other than the key idea that Adonis, the young, "delicate" beloved of Aphrodite, perished and must be mourned.[137]

Meanwhile, the Adonis myth evolved on a parallel but separate track. It was developed and recorded by male observers who often viewed the ritual as outsiders, and not particularly sympathetic ones. As Reed observed,

> The early versions of Adonis' life story that have come from the minds and pens of men should not be expected to reflect, nor indeed seem to reflect, the viewpoint of his worshipers, and the two fragmentary accounts by women frustratingly give only the expected sense of grief and tenderness.[138]

The earliest interpretation of the Adonis myth and cult to prevail among modern scholars was that of J. G. Frazer, who wrote that Adonis was one of a group of dying and rising gods, with origins in the Near East, who represented agricultural fertility.[139] Using structuralist methods, Marcel Detienne attacked Frazer's model, arguing that for "the Greeks," Adonis in fact represented not fertility but sterility and illicit sexuality. He drew a contrast between the Thesmophoria, a Greek festival of Demeter celebrated by women to help ensure a bountiful grain harvest, and the Adonia, which he described as a licentious occasion favored by prostitutes, the antithesis of the Thesmophoria. Both involved sexual and plant symbolism, but according to Detienne, the Adonia focused on a type of sexuality whose goal is pleasure rather than procreation.[140] Detienne's interpretation in turn has been criticized on various methodological grounds, but the most cogent objection has been that for the sake of achieving a structuralist symmetry of coded meaning, he made the women worshipers of Adonis gather to draw attention to their own sterility and marginal status by celebrating illicit sexuality.[141] If, however, we are dealing not with a unified cultural system, but with a situation where ritual and myth are, to a great degree, insulated from each other, it becomes possible to recover some of Detienne's insights about the relationship between the myths of Adonis and the "vegetable code" in Greek culture.

Before moving on, let us briefly review some key elements of Detienne's argument, which employs the method established by Claude Lévi-Strauss. The structuralist position is that cultures produce complex but coherent symbolic systems based on binary oppositions, like perfume/stench, cold/hot, impotence/vigor. Among the Greeks, for example, there was a symbolic code pertaining to plants. Myrrh was a sweet-smelling perfume and a heating aphrodisiac; it strongly connoted sexual activity. Lettuce, on the other hand, was a "cold" vegetable, popularly believed to cause sexual impotence. A character in a mid-fourth century Athenian comedy entitled *The Impotent Men* says,

> Wife, don't set lettuce before me
> On the table, or you'll have yourself to blame.
> For in that plant, so the story goes,
> Kypris once laid out the dead Adonis,
> So it is the food of corpses.
>
> (Euboulos fr. 13 *PCG* cited in Ath. 2.80 [69c–d])

This brings us back to Adonis. The interpretive power of Detienne's method lies in his attention to emic, culture-specific details (e.g. the meanings assigned to plants) which are less than transparent to moderns. In most versions of the myth, Adonis is the son of "Myrrha," who has been stricken with an incestuous passion for her own father.[142] Thus the conception of Adonis takes place in a context of extreme, transgressive female desire, represented by the myrrh tree and the perfume made from it. Adonis then becomes Aphrodite's lover, but he is fatally gored while hunting a boar, thus failing the test of manhood.[143] In one version of the myth, he hides in the lettuce to escape the boar, while in another, the lettuce is his funerary bier. Either way, the lettuce can be understood as a sign of Adonis' emasculation and ultimate sterility, the result of his erotic subordination to a goddess. Although sexual, his relationship with Aphrodite was not marital and could produce no legitimate children.[144] When set into its social context, the "vegetable code" turns out to convey a moralizing message which deplores the collocation of female desire, beautiful young men and extramarital sexuality. It is easy to see how literate male mythmakers could have produced these stories and shared similar interpretations of the vegetable code, but far less clear that women worshipers of Adonis had them in mind when celebrating the Adonia.[145]

Our earliest detailed description of how the Adonis festival was celebrated comes from Classical Athens. In Aristophanes' comedy *Lysistrata*, produced in 411, a magistrate tells how the men's deliberations on whether to send a fleet to Sicily were disrupted by the noisy laments of the women on the rooftops.[146]

> Have the women indulged themselves with lamps,
> Drumming, and the crowded Sabazian rites?
> Have they mourned Adonis on the roofs,
> As I heard in the Assembly lately?
> For Demostratos, damn him,
> Was saying we should invade Sicily,
> While a woman kept leaping about
> Crying, "Woe for Adonis!" And Demostratos
> Was saying we should muster men in Zakynthos,
> While the tipsy woman on the roof yelled
> "Beat your breast for Adonis!" He was shut down,
> That goddamned, foul bile-driver,
> By the song of women run amok.
>
> (Ar. *Lys.* 387–98)

The unruly women beat their breasts, danced and cried out, interrupting the serious business of war. In the eyes of the Athenian men, this private ritual, unsanctioned by the state, was an annoying instance of female licentiousness. Nevertheless they permitted it to continue, merely noting among themselves that they needed to keep better control of their wives. Menander's *Samia* (ca. 308) paints a picture of mingling social classes at the Adonia, with both citizen matrons and less respectable women taking part in the uproarious festival.[147]

A second element of the Athenian ritual, mentioned by Socrates in Plato's *Phaedrus* and in the *Samia*, was the "gardens of Adonis," broken pots in which the women sowed fast-germinating seeds, which would sprout by the day of the festival; these pots were then carried up to the rooftops.[148] Socrates describes them dismissively as plantings made for the sake of short-term festivities, in contrast to the farmer's serious sowing of seed grain:

> Now tell me this. Would a sensible farmer, who cared for his seeds and wished them to bear fruit, purposely plant them in summer, in gardens of Adonis, and rejoice at the sight of their lovely sprouts in eight days, or would he do this, when he did it at all, as an amusement and for the sake of the festival? Would he not, when in earnest concerning these things, apply the skills of farming, sow his seeds in fitting ground, and be well pleased when that which he had sowed reached fulfillment in the eighth month?
>
> (Pl. *Phdr*. 276b)

In order to judge the relationship of this element of Adonis ritual to the myth, we must first attempt to understand what range of meanings participants found in the ritual. As Detienne showed, a long subsequent tradition concerning the "gardens of Adonis" made them a byword for whatever is futile, wasted, fruitless; therefore he saw in them symbols of failed agriculture, precisely in opposition to Frazer's fertility model. But did the gardens, as Detienne argued, symbolize not only pleasure but also failure, sterility and impotence, qualities associated with Adonis? The women's attention, like the men's, may have been focused on the inevitable withering of the sprouts, exposed on the roofs to the hot summer sun. But it is also possible that the fresh, moist young shoots evoked the beauty of the youthful Adonis, and that they withered only after the festival was complete.[149]

Another element of the Athenian ritual involved images of Adonis. In his biography of Nikias, Plutarch described the trepidations of the Athenian men about to depart for the ill-fated Sicilian expedition in the summer of 415:

> Many were troubled by the events at the time they sent out the expedition. For the women were celebrating the Adonia then, and in many parts of the city images were laid out, with burial rites and the laments of women round about. As a result, those who held these matters of any account were disgusted, and feared that the mighty armament might quickly wither, even in the peak of its splendidness.
>
> (Plut. *Nic*. 13.7)

Plutarch describes two distinct phenomena: the women's ritual activities and the men's contextual interpretation of their funerary element as a bad omen for the expedition. We do not know whether the Adonis effigies of Classical Athens were doll-sized or life-sized, although Alciphron, an author of the Roman period, refers to miniatures in a fictional letter by a courtesan preparing for the Adonia: "Thettale is preparing the beloved one of Aphrodite. And take care that you are there, bringing a little garden and a little doll (*korallion*), and your own Adonis whom you currently adore, for we will revel with our lovers" (Alciphron 4.14.8, second century CE).

Simms has suggested that the gardens in fact served as miniature funerary biers for these small images of Adonis, which in turn were the focus of the lamentations. When Greek women prepared corpses for laying out, they often placed greenery beneath or around the body; laying the Adonis doll in a bed of greens could be a version of this practice.[150] If this was the case, we can see a direct connection between the planting of the gardens and Adonis' death, the core of the myth. The relation of the two can be expressed simply, with great intuitive resonance: Adonis is dead; mourn for Adonis and prepare his funeral. On the other hand, gardens of Adonis have been positively identified on one Classical vase painting, and in one Hellenistic terracotta sculpture. In neither case does the pot contain a doll, though both contain sprouts and small, unidentified round objects.[151]

Interpreted through the lens of male suspicion of a licentious, emotion-laden women's festival, and male discomfort with the story of a doomed young man who is sexually subservient to a powerful goddess, Adonis with his fruitless garden not surprisingly became a paradigm of frivolous effeminacy, weakness and sterility.[152] Interpreted, on the other hand, through the lens of Greek funerary convention, an arena in which women played important roles, Adonis was *aōros*, emblematic of the youth who dies "out of season," before his promise can be fulfilled, and before he has a chance to beget heirs.[153]

Let us now turn to the Adonis cult as it was practiced in Hellenistic Alexandria under Ptolemy II Philadelphos. Theocritus' *Idyll* 15 is a fictional vignette of two women making their way through a crowd to view effigies of Adonis and Aphrodite at the royal palace. One of the women, Praxinoa, exclaims at the beauty of Adonis:

> And he, lying on his silver couch,
> With the soft down on his cheek! Dearest Adonis,
> Thrice beloved, who even in death is cherished!
> (Theoc. *Id.* 15.84–6)

The women admire the elaborate, costly embroidery of Adonis' robe, and a professional singer performs a hymn addressed to Aphrodite, from which I quote only a few lines:

> Lady of many names and shrines, to please you
> Arsinoë [Berenike's] daughter, a queen lovely as Helen
> Decks Adonis with every exquisite ornament.
> Beside him are fruits in season borne by the trees,
> Tender gardens grown in baskets of silver,
> Golden flasks filled with finest Syrian perfumes
> And molded cakes, the pastry-cook's labors,
> Of flour mingled with every kind of blossom.
> (Theoc. *Id.* 15.109–16)

Unlike the Athenian festival, this celebration of Adonis is sponsored by the state, and presented as part of the cult of Aphrodite. Gone are the raucous private revels and laments on the rooftops (though for all we know, these may also have taken place in private homes). Instead, Theocritus shows us a dignified ritual lavishly funded by Ptolemy's queen Arsinoë. The hymn also suggests that Adonis in his Alexandrian setting evokes seasonal abundance, surrounded as he is by fruits, perfumes, cakes and "tender" potted gardens (*hapaloi kapoi*) which resemble the Athenian gardens of Adonis. The festival seems to have consisted of two phases which loosely corresponded to the phases of a funeral. First, there was the *prothesis* or laying out of the body for visitors to view. At Alexandria, however, this phase was transformed into a sacred marriage, with Aphrodite and Adonis lying on couches side by side:

> One bed holds Aphrodite and one the bridegroom,
> A boy of eighteen or nineteen with pink arms
> And red lips still soft and smooth for her kisses.
> Let Kypris rejoice now in her spouse restored,
> And with the dew of tomorrow's dawn, together
> We'll carry him down to the wave-splashed shore.
> We'll let down our hair and loosen our gowns,
> Baring our breasts as we sing the clear-toned song.
> (Theoc. *Id.* 15.128–35)

The lines allude to Aphrodite's erotic (re)union with her young lover. The celebratory element seems to be predicated upon the idea, first attested in a fifth-century epic by Panyassis, that Adonis alternated between the upper and lower worlds; this feature of the myth is explicitly evoked in the hymn (136–7). But Aphrodite's joy was followed by the sadness of Adonis' return to Persephone: as depicted by Theocritus, he was truly a dying and rising god. The next day of the festival saw the *ekphora*, the funerary procession, when the dead Adonis was carried to the sea.[154] The hymn concludes with a prayer to Adonis:

> Be gracious, Adonis, and smile on the coming year,
> Each time you return, your advent is dear to us.
> (Theoc. *Id.* 15.143–4)

The prayer is a call for blessings in the form of agricultural abundance. If there ever was a "fertility cult," this is it. But are we looking at the Alexandrian cult itself, or Theocritus' interpretation of it?

Recall our earlier observation that reflection on ritual (including myth) can develop along separate lines from the ritual activity itself. Here we have a sophisticated poet purporting to show us an Alexandrian ritual. The hymn within *Idyll* 15 is most likely not a hymn sung at the festival itself, but Theocritus' creative transformation of such a hymn. It is reasonable to assume that the poet accurately depicted the general outlines of the ritual (the laying out of adorned effigies followed by a mourning procession to the sea) and the rich endowment of the festival by queen Arsinoë. What we cannot assume, however, is that participants in the ritual shared the poet's interpretation, which closely aligns the ritual with the myth of Adonis' cyclical travel between the upper and lower worlds. As a court poet, Theocritus also had special reason to dwell upon Adonis' expected role in promoting the welfare of the state as a deity of agricultural plenty. Theocritus' Adonis is a good approximation of Frazer's fertility god, but this understanding of Alexandrian Adonis flows from the poet's own artful deployment of the myth in relation to the Egyptian context (with the model of Isis and Osiris ready to hand) and the Alexandrian ritual. Whether the women who beat their breasts for Adonis by the sea believed that Adonis traveled back and forth between life and death every year, bringing the season's fruits with him, we do not know.

Detienne rightly insisted on the independence of the Athenian Adonia from the Alexandrian.[155] Separated as they are by geography and time, neither festival should be interpreted in terms of the other. The most notable differences are the official patronage at Alexandria, the centralized celebration, and the establishment of formal links to the cult of Aphrodite. Yet the data reveal shared ritual actions and themes between the two festivals: the focus on women celebrants, the funerary analogy, the "gardens" of greenery, the manipulation of Adonis images and the juxtaposition of *erōs* with mourning. This complex of actions and themes could be differently interpreted depending on the social context, and its ties to any specific version of the Adonis myth were fluid.

In place of Theocritus' vignette of the festival, Bion's *Epitaph on Adonis* purports to show us its mythic referent, the actual lament of Aphrodite's companions for the dead Adonis. The speaker begins, and her cry is echoed antiphonally by the Erotes or "Loves" who form part of the goddess's coterie:

> I mourn for Adonis. Fair Adonis is dead!
> "Dead is fair Adonis!" mourn the Loves.
> (Bion *Adonis* 1–2)

This antiphonal call-and-response imitates the traditional practice of women mourners at Greek funerals.[156] From the lament that follows, we learn of Aphrodite's search for Adonis, and her anguished discovery of the corpse, savaged by a boar. Like a mortal woman, Aphrodite disfigures herself in grief, bloodying her hands and chest. Finally the body is returned to the palace for laying out.

> Let Adonis, now a corpse, have your bed, Kythereia.
> Though a corpse, he is lovely, lovely as if asleep.
> Lay him on the soft sheets in which he used to sleep,
> Where he used to toil at sacred sleep by your side,
> Though a hateful sight, lay him in the golden bed.
> Strew him with garlands and blossoms; with him,
> Since this one has died, all flowers have faded away.
> (Bion *Adonis* 70–76)

Bion vividly evokes the demonstrative paroxysms of grief and longing expected at the real-life funeral of a beautiful youth, but he never loses sight of the Adonis myth or ritual. Just as the first lines evoke the cry of the women at the Adonia, the final lines remind us that the festival recurs annually:

> Cease crying for today, Kythereia, and beating your breast.
> You must weep again, and wail again, another year.
>
> (Bion *Adonis* 97–8)

Bion reduces the ritual to its core action of lament over a dead body, shifting the focus away from the gardens and revels of the Adonia, back to the conventions of funerary ritual which made the festival salient and compelling for the women of Archaic Greece. His Aphrodite bemoans her loss of Adonis to Persephone, and far from evoking Adonis' cyclical return, he contradicts (87–96) the theology we observed in *Idyll* 15 by suggesting that Adonis' death is permanent and that there is to be no nuptial reunion. We do not know which historical celebration of the Adonia Bion was familiar with, but like Sappho six centuries before, he makes his narrator address "Kythereia" directly.[157] Both poems dramatically recreate the "original" mythic episode of mourning for Adonis. In both cases, the identity of the initial speaker is ambiguous: is she a nymph mourning alongside Aphrodite in mythic time, or is she a mortal celebrant of the ritual, imitating the goddess and her companions? Sappho's lament was probably used in the communal celebration of her local Adonia. If so, it functioned to temporarily blur the distinction between mythic time and daily life for the female celebrants, so that myth and ritual were fused. Bion's poem, on the other hand, was likely not performed in a ritual context, but read for entertainment, by men. Therefore it represents the opposite dynamic of separation between myth and ritual. Yet by incorporating keenly observed features drawn from real life in his representation of the mourning for Adonis, Bion identified the emotional core of the Adonia, a factor which helped to motivate its transmission over the centuries even as the ritual details varied.[158]

## Notes

1 Agency detection: see Boyer 2001.93–167; Atran 2002.59–63; Barrett 2004, 2007; Tremlin 2006.76–86, and the discussion on pp. 74–5. For theory of mind, a mental tool which is compromised in people with autism, see Baron-Cohen 1997.51–5, 128–30.
2 For these works and their relationships to each other see Thompson 1979–80; Obbink ed. 1996.98, 315–6.
3 Intuitive knowledge: see Chapter 1 and Tremlin 2006.52–86; Barrett 2011.61–8.
4 Theologically correct: Barrett and Keil 1996.226, 229; Barrett 1999; discussion and additional bibliography in Tremlin 2006.96–9. Cf. Versnel 1981b.26–42, 2011.9.
5 Counterintuitive concepts: Boyer 1994.110–19; Sperber 1994.55; Barrett and Keil 1996.222; Barrett 2004.22–30.
6 Henrichs (2010.31) points out that "immortality," strictly speaking, is by definition not a property of cult heroes and heroines, who undergo death. On the powerful dead see further Chapter 5, and for other definitions of the Greek god, Versnel 2011.391–5.
7 For religion as "systematized anthropomorphism" see Guthrie 1993.117, and on the inevitability of anthropomorphism, Versnel 2011.379–83.

8 Metamorphosis: Buxton 2009.189–90 (human shape is, generally speaking, the "representational home base" for Greek gods). On the food and drink of the gods, see Sissa and Detienne 2000.77–81, and on recognizing gods, Gladigow 1990.98–9.
9 Xenophanes as theologian: Henrichs 2010.32; Trépanier 2010.276–81; Versnel 2011.244–66.
10 Barrett and Keil 1996.222: "Too many violations of cognitive intuitions would cause an enormous processing strain." In practice, people have trouble remembering and applying all the "theologically correct" counterintuitive properties of a philosopher's deity.
11 For the special case of Zeus and other gods worshiped in serpent form, see Ogden 2013.271–309.
12 Boyer 2001.144. Mikalson (1983.72) notices the paucity of evidence for anthropomorphic images of the multiple Zeuses of Athenian religion.
13 Epiphany and cult statues: Gordon 1979.9–17; Gladigow 1985–6, 1990; Elsner 1996.525–6; Burkert 2001; Tanner 2006.41–96; Lapatin 2010.142–50; Platt 2011.77–123. Experimental evidence: Barrett and van Orman 1996.
14 Scriptural ban: e.g. *Exod.* 20:4, *Lev.* 26:1. Iconophily should not be viewed as "primitive" or tied to historical stages of development. The Minoans and Mycenaeans, for example, seem to have placed far less value on physical anthropomorphism than did their successors (Blakolmer 2010).
15 Against use of the term "cult statue": Donohue 1997. Cf. Scheer 2000.25–63; Bettinetti 2001.7–10. Discussion: Lapatin 2010.131–5; Mylonopoulos 2010b.4–12.
16 Criteria: Mylonopoulos 2010b.6–12. On the limited evidence for *hidrusis*, which was also used to establish altars, see Pirenne-Delforge 2008, 2010.126–30.
17 Temple doors: Pedley 2005.8. Note that the rule of *minimal* counterintuitiveness is in force: a statue can "see," but it can't see through doors. It can "hear," but you need to be reasonably close when you pray. Statues that look back: Platt 2011.78.
18 Compare Vernant's analysis (1991.154–61) of the supernatural properties of archaic divine images and Bremmer 2013 on the agency of statues. Movement: Hdt. 5.82.1–5.87.1 (falling on the knees). Blood: Artemis Tauropolos in Attica (Eur. *IT* 1456–61), Artemis Orthia at Sparta (Paus. 3.16.7–11; Elsner 1996.524–5). Insanity: Plut. *Arat.* 32.2–3 (the *bretas* of Artemis). For statues as talismans see Faraone 1992.100–6; Tanner 2006.40–44. The intuitive inference in such cases is that physical possession of the talismanic object (statue, heroic bones, etc.) secures its benefits for the owner(s).
19 For the key role of eyes and face in attribution of agency by infants, see Baron-Cohen 1997.31–58; Atran 2002.62–3; Barrett 2011.74–5. As Atran notes, however, infants also have the ability to attribute agency to inanimate, nonhuman-shaped objects.
20 For aniconic images, see Platt 2011.100–5; Gaifman 2012.
21 Theologians and philosophers: for the history of iconoclasm see Besançon 2000. Epigraphic: the statues of Hera at Samos (Ohly 1953.33–4 and appendix 7; Romano 1980.250–62) and Athena Polias at Athens (*IG* II$^2$ 1424a) were referenced in inscriptions as "the goddess."
22 Vase painter: discussion and additional examples: Lapatin 2010.133–4; Platt 2011.120–1. Bremmer (2013.9–10) writes that statues and divinities were not conceptually differentiated until the end of the sixth century, when the first such paintings appear. Yet a statue was never an essential prerequisite for worship, and everyone was familiar with non-statue concepts of deities (as in epic). What was new at the end of the sixth century was an increasing awareness of (and desire to reconcile) the logical contradictions between intuitive and reflective beliefs about the gods.
23 Plato (*Leg.* 931a) offers explicit theology: "When we honor [statues], although they are lifeless, the living gods feel great goodwill and gratitude toward us."
24 Greek divination: Bouché-Leclercq 1963 [1879–82]; Amandry 1950; Parke 1967a, 1967b; Fontenrose 1978, 1988; Vernant 1991.303–17; Johnston 2008; Stoneman 2011.
25 On the *mantis* see Bremmer 1996; Burkert 1983, 1992.41–87; Flower 2008. For the distinction between *mantis* and *chrēsmologos* see Bowden 2003.257–64; Dillery

2005a.168–72. From a cognitive perspective, it is important to distinguish between skill-based divination and inspired mediumship, both of which were called *mantikē*.

26 Stoics: Struck 2007.8–9. Compare Xen. *Cyr.* 1.6.46, *Mem.* 1.4.10–18. Flower's (2008.106–7) discussion of implicit beliefs as the foundation for Greek divination is consistent with a cognitivist view.

27 Struck 2007.3–4. While divination may serve social functions, it is far from intrinsically stabilizing: consider the disruptive potential of apocalyptic prophecy and prophets as rebels. Discussion: Burkert 2005.43–8. For oracular consultation and civic problem-solving see Parker 2000 [1985]. Catherine Morgan (1985, 1990, etc.) has extensively discussed the social functions of the Delphic and other oracles.

28 Evolutionary strategy: Boyer 2001.144–7. Hyperactive agency detection and bumps in the night: Barrett 2004.31–44. Agency detection is rooted in predator-prey relationships: Atran 2002.69–70, 78–9.

29 Adults and geometric shapes: Barrett 2004.32. For a review of these oft-replicated studies see Scholl and Tremoulet 2000. Singing colossus: Strabo 17.1.46. Unusual or fortuitously timed weather patterns could be interpreted as epiphanies: Graf 2004.118–20.

30 Lisdorf 2007a.66n.37. For the action representation system, see the discussion of McCauley and Lawson's ritual form theory in Chapter 4. Pattern completion is a powerful tool known to alter visual perception (Maloney *et al.* 2005). It is a key component of memory and functions across all domains of information processing (Hunsaker and Kesner 2013).

31 From a cognitive perspective, these categories are distinct, first because one involves ritualized action and the other does not, and second because impetrative divination involves initiation of the action by a person, and oblative by a god. Lisdorf (2007a.48n.21) derives the names of his categories from the postclassical Latin terms *signa impetrativa* and *signa oblativa*. Parker (2000.76) translates these respectively as "besought" and "self-offered." For scholarly debate about the modes of Greek prophecy see Ustinova 2013.

32 Hidden agent: Lisdorf 2007a.75–6. Compare Sørensen (2007a.65, 151–69) on displacement of agency; cf. Sørensen 2007b.92–3: the lack of logical connection between proximate and ultimate intentions results in a cognitive search for (a) alternative connections between actions and goal (e.g. in analogical relationships of similarity), or (b) a meaning located in cultural conventions.

33 Lisdorf 2007a.66. With respect to HAD, Lisdorf (2007a.80–9, 2007b) emphasizes intentionality over agency. He suggests (pers. comm. 8/19/14) that HAD results from a combination of distinct mental functions. Attentional bias (we tend to see effects where we are looking for them) may also play a role here: see Houran and Lange 2001.287–96. Randomization: Johnston 2005.15–16.

34 Shuts down: Barrett 2004.32–3, citing Barrett and Johnson 2003, a study within which HAD completely ceased if adult subjects indirectly controlled the timing (but not the direction) of seemingly self-propelled marbles.

35 Compare Graf 2005.61: "[randomization] produces a gap where the hand and mind of the divinity can interfere." For the use of dice and sortition in divination versus selection processes perceived as truly random, such as the selection of jurors, see Johnston 2005.15–16.

36 For anxiety and risk management see e.g. Eidinow 2007, and for mediation of conflict Morgan 1990.153–7.

37 On the Pythia see most recently Maurizio 1995; Johnston 2008.40–60; Stoneman 2011.31–7.

38 For the perceived conflict between "rational" use of signs and the "irrationality" of altered consciousness see Burkert 2005.34–5.

39 Inspired divination more respected: e.g. Pl. *Phdr.* 244b-d. Difficulty of access probably increased its perceived value: Ustinova 2013.33.

40 Kroisos: Hdt. 1.53.2–3, 1.91.4.

41 For spirit possession as a world phenomenon see Maurizio 1995.73–6 with bibliography; and for a cognitive approach, Cohen 2007.11–15, 129–50. Confirmation bias, which takes many forms, is the selection or interpreting of evidence in ways that favor existing beliefs: for an overview, see Nickerson 1998.

42 Bribery: Eidinow 2007.34–5 with n.55. On claims of Delphic partiality see Parker (2000 [1985].82, 106–7) who notes (101–2) that Delphic authority in political matters began a long decline after the Persian Wars.

43 Only a few texts mention lot divination at Delphi, and opinion is divided on the extent to which lots were used. Discussion: Amandry 1950.29–36; Fontenrose 1978.219–23; Johnston 2008.52–5.

44 Idiosyncratic: Lisdorf 2007a.109.

45 For dream divination, see the bibliography in Johnston 2005.4–5.

46 Antichares (Hdt. 5.43.1), Onomakritos (Hdt. 7.6.3), Bakis (Hdt. 8.20.2, 8.77.1–2, 8.96.2, 9.43.1–2, Ar. *Peace* 1070–2, 1119, etc.), Musaios (Hdt. 7.6.3, 8.96.2, 9.43.2, Eur. *Rhes*. 941–7). Discussion and additional sources in Bowden 2003.264–70; Dillery 2005a.178–81, 189–91.

47 Classed with the epic poets: Ar. *Ran.* 1032–5, Pl. *Ap*. 41a and so forth.

48 Their own day: exceptions occur when an oracle is believed to have been fulfilled. For example, Herodotus (9.42–3) cites an oracle interpreted by Mardonios as a reference to Xerxes' invasion, but which he thinks was long ago fulfilled.

49 Pattern detection: "apophenia" is a normal cognitive bias toward seeing connections between unrelated phenomena. In an extreme form it is a symptom suffered by schizophrenics, who tend to interpret such connections as highly pertinent to themselves. Discussion: Brugger 2001.202–13.

50 Confirming patterns: compare the numerous New Testament readings of Jewish prophetic books (especially Isaiah) as oracular references to the life and death of Jesus.

51 Savor (*knisē*): e.g. Hom. *Il.* 1.62–7, 8.545–9, 24.65–70. For more lengthy and nuanced discussions of Lévi-Strauss' structuralism, see Sperber 1985.64–93 (pointing out the non-falsifiable nature of the method but also its interpretive value) and Csapo 2005.217–38.

52 Turner's list of meanings (1967.50–1) includes the exegetical (how it is interpreted emically), the operational (an etic evaluation of how the symbol is used and its affective connotations) and the positional (meaning derived from relationships to other symbols). Smallest unit of ritual: Turner 1967.19.

53 Definition: Geertz 1973.89–91.

54 Critique of Geertz: Pyysiäinen 2003.33–52. Intellectual history of symbols and cognition in anthropology: Bloch 1989.106–36. For Geertz's ideas applied to Greek religion see e.g. Gould 1985.4–6; Kindt 2012.55–89.

55 Naiden 2013.21 elides this problem by saying that the smoke "moved from the scene of the rite to the larger scene, the context in which the god responded." On the centrality of *knisē* to Greek understandings of sacrifice see Detienne 1998.66–74.

56 For reasons of space, I omit Sperber's discussion of semantic knowledge (the knowledge of categories). See Sperber 1974.85–113.

57 Sperber 1974.94. Cf. Sperber 1985.35–63, an essay on "apparently irrational beliefs" in which Sperber describes how a Dorze man asked him to kill a horned golden dragon which had been sighted nearby.

58 Metarepresent: Sperber 1974.99. Differently, Atran 2002.83–113. For approaches to metarepresentation, see the papers in Sperber ed. 2000.

59 Sperber 1974.99–110. Along these lines compare the remarks of Veyne 1988.28–39 (with reference to Sperber's Dorze in the preface).

60 Sperber 1974.148.

61 Explanatory power: Simon Price (1984.8–9) recognized the utility of Sperber's arguments in approaching the thorny question of whether people believed in ruler cults. "People can mean what they say without their statements being fully determinate."

62 On metarepresentations as reflective beliefs, see Sperber 1997 and for the evolution of reflective cognition, Mercier and Sperber 2009. Compare Burkert's (1996.25) observation that "some signs will remain opaque and yet are stored in expectation of later clarification." For the relationship between symbolic thought and counter-intuitive beliefs see Boyer 1994.57–9 (stressing that people are well aware of the difference between symbolic and nonsymbolic beliefs even though both may be held equally true).

63 Semele: compare Paus. 9.12.4 on Thebes, where the *thalamos* ("bridal chamber") of Semele is associated with a piece of wood that fell from heaven rather than (or alongside) the thunderbolt. The thunderbolt in Bacchic-Orphic contexts: *GJ* 125–7.

64 Traditional tale: Kirk 1974.27–8; Cf. Buxton 2004.18 ("a socially powerful traditional story"). Myth and religion: Kirk 1970.8–31 (no necessary relationship). For other definitions of myth see the papers in Dundes ed. 1984. The literature on the complex subject of myth and ritual is voluminous. Versnel (1990b) gives a review of the debate with bibliography.

65 Facts rather than fictions: compare Veyne 1988.52.

66 Spring paeans: Furley and Bremer 2001.1.82–3, citing Pind. fr. 128c and Bacchyl. 16.8–10. "Call the god": Ar. *Ran.* 479 with schol.; Porta 1999.59–61.

67 Cognition: holding multiple things in mind at once creates a cognitive load that is difficult to sustain (Barrett 1999, 2011.69).

68 Present to mind: this circumstance, of course, makes it more difficult to interpret myths in terms of rituals or vice versa. See also Chapter 6, where I argue that verbal content and procedural content in rituals were transmitted via different types of memory with different outcomes for accuracy.

69 Detailed narratives: the best recent account of poetic performances of myth in ritual contexts is Kowalzig 2007. Plato (*Leg.* 887c–e) mentions children's delight in myths told "in prayer" and through "spectacles" at sacrifices.

70 Pythian games: Furley and Bremer 2001.1.92. For the proverb "Nothing to do with Dionysos" and the history of the debate over how "Dionysiac" Greek drama is, see Storm 1998.14–17 with bibliography. Dramas not viewed as "sacred": Scullion 2007.201–3. Discussion of myths and ritual contexts, stressing a division: Parker 2011.20–22. Seaford (e.g. 1994) has written extensively about ritual patterns underlying drama; Calame (2007) argues for strong "ritual dimensions" of tragedy, epinician and other genres. For dithyrambs see Essay 3.2.

71 "Reenactment" and "skilled performance" are two ends of a ritual continuum based on the degree to which all worshipers present actively participate in the performance or passively observe it.

72 Our earliest preserved version of the myth, the Homeric *Hymn to Demeter*, is unlikely to have been used in the rites themselves, but was composed for a wider, Panhellenic audience of potential initiates. On the relationship between the *Hymn* and the Mysteries see Foley ed. 1994.172–8 with bibliography.

73 For the importance of etiological myth see Kowalzig 2007.24–31. Kowalzig stresses the cultic aspect of etiology over the non-cultic and antiquarian (31), but it can be difficult to tease these apart when dealing with late sources.

74 For oral and written etiologies as *hieroi logoi* see Porta 1999.10.

75 Robe and Gigantomachy: Shear 2001.1.31–8.

76 For epiphanies see Lane Fox 1986.102–67; Versnel 1987, 1990a.191 (*epiphaneia* as either miracle or vision); Henrichs 1996, 2010.33–5 (stressing vision); Marinatos and Kyrtatos 2004; Platt 2011. For miracles see Harrison 2000.64–101.

77 Presence: Hom. *Il.* 3.396 (beauty in an old woman), 5.864–7 (dark cloud), 17.333–4 (face of a herald), *Od.* 3.221–2 (Athena in person), 13.287–90 (tall woman), 19.36–43 (lights), 22.239–40 (swallow).

78 Identification as the main challenge: Versnel 2011.38. On Homeric epiphanies see Dietrich 1983; Lane Fox 1986.102–13. On bird epiphanies see Burkert 2004.5–9.

79 Dietrich 1983.62.

80 Narrative devices: Turkeltaub 2007 makes a case that in the *Iliad*, the nature of the epiphany (inherent, visual, auditory and inferred) distinguishes the rank of the hero, with Achilles at the highest level.

81 Penelope's dream: Murnaghan 1995.68–9. On the Homeric dream vision as a literary construct see Morris 1983, Walde 2001.19–72. Bremmer (1983.19–20) suggests that the literary prototype is derived from real-life experience. For other dream visions in Homer see *Il.* 1.605–2.48 (Zeus), 23.58–110 (Patroclus' spirit), 24.673–95 (Hermes); *Od.* 5.481–6.48, 14.518–15.56, 19.600–20.91 (all Athena).

82 Dietrich 1983.67.

83 Peisistratos and Phye: Boardman 1972.61–6, 1989. Popular consent: Connor 1987.44; Forsdyke 2005.114 ("collective ritual"). See also Sinos 1998.84–8 (usefully discussing the symbolic impact of the event); Platt 2011.15, 48 with bibliography.

84 Ritual impersonation and divine epiphany: Burkert 2004.14–18; Clinton 2004; Steinhart 2004.65–100; Pirenne-Delforge 2010.130–2. Cf. Connor 1987.44 on the "epiphany" of Anthia in Xen. Ephes. 1.2.7.

85 *Athēnaai Meneia anethēken opsin idousa aretēn tēs theou*: *IG* II$^2$ 4326 (= Renberg 2003 no. 2). See Platt 2011.38–9.

86 *Opsin idousa*: e.g. Hdt. 1.39.1, 3.30.2, 5.55.1, etc., not necessarily visions of the gods themselves. Discussion and further references see Henrichs 2010.34–5. Compare *SEG* 55.307 (= Renberg 2003 no. 23, ca. 375–50), in which Dionysios the cobbler records that he has seen a divine vision of the hero Kallistephanos in his sleep (*opsin idōn theian en hupnōi*). Epidauros: Renberg 2003.170n.101.

87 Bulkeley 2007.85–90. Harris's (2009.85) statement that epiphany dreams "disappeared" in modern times is too strong; rather, the cultural convention of the epiphany dream was greatly weakened, as he notes, during the early modern period.

88 Subsequent behavior: Bulkeley 2007.86. For the dreamer's private emotional concerns as the most important factor in determining dream content and connections, see Hartmann 2007.18–9. These findings are directly relevant to Greek rituals such as dream incubation for healing.

89 For the Greco-Roman dream epiphany see van Straten 1976, Hanson 1980, Renberg 2003 and Harris 2009.23–122, with discussion of the problems of cultural convention and memory. In Pind. *Ol.* 13, the dream oscillates between sleeping and waking vision, finally resulting in the miraculous apport of a bridle.

90 Not straightforward: a point made by Renberg (2003.17–19 and *passim*).

91 For collective epiphanies, see Graf 2004.115–22.

92 On the Chronicle of Lindos (*I.Lindos* 2; *SEG* 36.747) see Higbie 2003; Platt 2011.161–9.

93 Connection between epiphany, ritual act and mythmaking: Dillery 2005b.516–19.

94 For the catalogue of votives as a "relic of relics" see Koch Piettre 2005.98–103.

95 For the repeated dream as a sign of authenticity, cf. Hdt. 7.12.1–18.4 (Xerxes and Artabanos). Similar stories attached to dream visions of Sarapis (Essay 6.3).

96 Sacred history: Dillery 2005b.

97 "Not all gods can read minds": Barrett 2004.49.

98 Hera: Hom. *Il.* 14.153–353. Laomedon (in varying versions): Hom. *Il.* 7.451–3, 21.442–57; Apollod. *Bibl.* 2.5.9.

99 Boyer 2001.152 (strategic information), 158 ("God knows" examples).

100 Spontaneous: see Fontenrose 1978, Q7, 58, 59, 61, 216, 245 (from a total of 259 extant oracles). Apollo may also have spontaneously addressed the Athenians who came regarding the Persian invasion (Q 146), but at the time, it would not have been difficult to guess the topic of their question.

101 Oak tree: e.g. Soph. *Trach.* 170–1: "He said that the ancient oak once spoke this from the twin doves at Dodona."

102 Lhôte 2006 no. 102; Eidinow 2007.77 no. 9; ca. 375.

103 Lot method at Dodona: Parke 1967b.108–10; Johnston 2008.70; Stoneman 2011.61–4. Discussion: Eidinow 2007.67–71. Testimony: the historian Kallisthenes (*FGrH* 124 F 22 a-b = Cic. *Div.* 1.34.76 and 2.32.69) says that Spartan ambassadors to Dodona set up a vessel in which were lots.

104 For state consultations on the lead tablets, see Lhôte 2006 nos. 1–17.

105 In Lhôte's (2006) corpus of 168 tablets, I count thirteen "verso" inscriptions consistent with the use of an identifying name or mark, twelve inscriptions consistent with a number, eight inscriptions consistent with an abbreviated title or summary of the question, and ten responses. There is also an interesting group of seven tablets with names fully written out, but no question (some are broken, so the recto may have originally contained a question).

106 Parke 1967b.264 no. 3; Lhôte 2006 no. 116; Eidinow 2007.108 no. 1 (fifth century; never folded). Compare Lhôte 2006 nos. 19–22 ("to what god/hero should I pray?").

107 Eidinow 2007.85 no. 11 (ca. 325–300).

108 Eidinow 2007.92 no. 13 (ca. 450–25).

109 Parke 1967b.271 no. 25; Lhôte 2006 no. 107; Eidinow 2007.99 no. 14 (fourth century)

110 Lhôte (2006.427–8) notes that many preserved responses are surprisingly conservative: the oracle advises individuals against going to sea (nos. 92, 127), leaving a wife (no. 35), emigrating (no. 12) and risking capital (nos. 95, 101). Zeus and Dione did not simply rubber-stamp petitioners' plans. Whether this is evidence for or against a lot method is a complex question.

111 Intuitively, only one mind at a time can occupy a body (Cohen 2007.139–41), which would have made it necessary for the agent (Zeus or Dione) to be identified in each session or subsession. Among Archaic and Classical authors, only Plato (*Phdr.* 244a8–b3) says that the priestesses at Dodona, like the Pythia, were "not in their right minds" (*maneisai*, literally "mad") during a consultation. Pausanias (10.12.10) echoes Plato, as do certain Christian authors. Discussion: Eidinow 2007.68–9; Johnston 2008.64–5.

112 For curse tablets see most recently Eidinow 2007.140–55, with full bibliography. Lhôte (2006.xi, 428–9) suggested that the divinatory process at Dodona involved burying the lead tablets near the sacred oak, a procedure in accord with Zeus' "chthonian" nature, but the latter has not been satisfactorily demonstrated.

113 Compare Hes. fr. 270 Most (= fr. 319 *MW*): "He came to Dodona and the oak, seat of the Pelasgians." Parke (1967b.47) insisted that it was "too absurdly undignified" for Hesiod to picture Zeus living in the trunk of an oak tree. Pausanias (7.21.2) speaks of "the doves and the responses from the oak."

114 Lhôte (2006.428) writes that "most" of the tablets were folded. A few were also pierced by nails, an action which also occurred in conjunction with the folding of curse tablets. At Dodona, however, certain tablets may have been pierced for suspension or nailed to trees. It appears that the custom was to leave the tablets in the sanctuary rather than to take them away after use.

115 Parke 1967b.271–2 no. 26; Lhôte 2006 no. 123; Eidinow 2007.116 no. 1 (fifth century).

116 Lhôte 2006 no. 119; Eidinow 2007.117 no. 3 (fourth to third century).

117 Lhôte 2006 no. 38; Eidinow 2007.86 no. 17 (early fifth century).

118 Lhôte 2006 no. 53; Eidinow 2007 85 no. 7.

119 Lhôte 2006 no. 64.

120 Parke 1967b.264 no. 4; Lhôte 2006 no. 67; Eidinow 2007.121 no. 3 (beginning of fifth century).

121 Lhôte 2006 no. 135; Eidinow 2007.121 no. 2 (fifth century).

122 Cf. Fontenrose 1978, L155, Q103 and Xen. *Cyr.* 7.2.17 on the impiety of Kroisos' test. On Apollo's omniscience cf. Pind. *Pyth.* 9.44–9.

123 Abandoned: Barrett 2004.70–72; McCauley and Lawson 2002.98–9, 205–8. At least temporarily, failures function to strengthen bonds within small, tightly knit groups (Festinger 1957.233–59 is the classic discussion), but Flower's point (2008.104) that

this applies doubly to larger communities does not follow. Dawson's (1999) review of failed predictions by small religious groups shows that of thirteen cases studied, there was one immediate dissolution, three later dissolutions, four survivals in a weakened state and five robust survivals. None of the groups studied seems to have sustained repeated failures. On falsification of Greek oracles, cf. Maurizio 2013.66–70.

124 Xen. *An.* 3.1.5–8, 6.1.22; Fontenrose 1978.248 (H11). The consultation took place in 401, and he was told to sacrifice to Zeus Basileus (Zeus the King).

125 The majority of the seventy-five responses that Fontenrose (1978.244–67) deems both historical and genuine follow this pattern, as do many of the responses he classifies as quasi-historical and legendary.

126 Question formulas: Fontenrose 1978.52.

127 For individuals and oracles see Eidinow 2007.42–55. Examples of approval for individual actions already planned include the poet Isyllos' question about inscribing his paean (*IG* IV$^2$ 128 = Fontenrose 1978.252 [H25]) and Xenophon's question about whether he should buy an estate for Artemis (Xen. *An.* 5.3.7 = Fontenrose 1978.248 [H12]).

128 On limitations in the format of questions, see Parker 2000 [1985].78; Morgan 1990.153–6. Requests for falsifiable responses at Dodona include slaves' questions about whether their masters would free them (Eidinow 2007.102 nos. 5–6), Klemedes' question about whether he would be given Olympias as his bride (Eidinow 2007.84 no. 2, differently translated in Lhôte 2006 no. 39) and direct questions about whether specific women would produce children (e.g. Eidinow 2007.89 nos. 2–3).

129 Fontenrose 1978.260.

130 Wooden wall: Hdt. 7.140.1–7.143.3, discussed by Parker 2000 [1985].80; Eidinow 2013.30–2.

131 Earle 1990.6. Cf. Morgan 1990.156–7 (ambiguity as a "protective device"); Parker 2000 [1985].80 (riddling answers "force a client to construct by interpretation his own response").

132 Sappho composed other lines on Adonis, as fr. 168 *LP* shows: "O Adonis!"

133 This essay owes a debt to the innovative work of Joseph Reed (1995, 1996, 1997). Tammuz: Burkert 1979.108–11.

134 Earliest certain attestations in poetry: Lycoph. *Alex.* 831–33 (third century); Glycon 1029 *PMG* (Hellenistic). Possible attestations in red-figure vase painting: *LIMC* I.1 s.v. Adonis, nos. 27–8 (early fourth century).

135 Panyassis fr. 22a Davies, cited in Apollod. *Bibl.* 3.14.4. In later versions (e.g. Ov. *Met.* 10.519–28), Aphrodite disputes the adult Adonis with Persephone.

136 For lamentation and potential "sexual expressiveness" in the ritual see Reed 1995.345–6.

137 For this stripping and reconstruction of meaning when myth and ritual are transmitted across cultures, see also Essay 6.2 on Herakles.

138 Reed 1995.334. The other female witness to the myth is Praxilla (747 *PMG*), who makes Adonis say, "The most beautiful thing I leave behind is the sunlight; secondly the bright stars and the face of the moon and ripe cucumbers and apples and pears."

139 Agricultural fertility: Frazer 1908.3–8.

140 Detienne 1994 [1972].

141 Winkler 1990.188–209; Reed 1995.322; Simms 1997–8.122. Detienne has also been criticized for overly schematizing the participants at the two festivals (matrons at the Thesmophoria vs. prostitutes at the Adonia). Wives celebrating the Athenian Adonia are attested in both Ar. *Lys.* 387–430 and Men. *Sam.* 35–50.

142 Son of Theias and his daughter Smyrna ("Myrrh"): Panyassis fr. 22a Davies. The Hesiodic corpus (fr. 106 Most = fr. 139 *MW*) showed awareness of Adonis' Near-Eastern origins by making him the son of Alphesiboia and Phoinix (apparently not including the incest motif).

143 On hunting as initiation to adulthood see Vidal-Naquet 1981 [1968].158–62; Barringer 1996; Marinatos 2003.132–7. Adonis' wound on the thigh or groin (Lycophr. 831–3; Bion *Adonis* 7, 41; Ov. *Met.* 10.715) suggests emasculation.

144 Several quotations on lettuce are collected and discussed by the ancient food writer Athenaeus (2.80 [69b–70a]) – e.g. Adonis hid from the boar in lettuce (Ath. 2.80 [69b]); Adonis was hidden in lettuce by Aphrodite (Callim. fr. 478 Pfeiffer); lettuce causes impotence (Amphis fr. 20 *PCG*).

145 Reed (1995.322) criticizes the structuralist assumption that a monolithic "meaning" can be extracted from the data, rather than fluid meanings which shift depending on gender, geography and other factors.

146 Earliest: Ar. *Peace* 420 (produced in 421) contains a brief reference: Trygaios promises Hermes that the festivals of Athens will be henceforth be devoted to him: "the Mysteries, the Dipolieia, the Adonia." The contrast between the two venerable civic festivals and the unsanctioned, raucous Adonia must have drawn a laugh. Also late fifth-century is Cratinus fr. 17 *PCG* (a character deprecates the Adonia as a lesser festival worthy only of an inferior chorus).

147 Men. *Sam.* 38–46 (for text with translation see Arnott 2000.21).

148 The seeds are wheat and barley according to Schol. Theoc. 15.113; lettuce and fennel according to Hsch. and *Suda* s.v. *Adōnidos kēpoi*.

149 Reed (1995.324) draws the analogy of the modern Christmas tree.

150 Greens: Simms 1997–8.129–33.

151 Vase: Oakley and Reitzammer 2005, pl. 7a (= *CVA* Karlsruhe 1, Germany 7 pl. 27, nos. 1–4. Terracotta: Oakley and Reitzammer 2005 with plate 6a-b (= Paris Louvre Inv. 233).

152 Subservient to a goddess: Stehle 1990. An effeminate Adonis despised by Athenian men: Ribichini 1981.13–20.

153 On the relationship between the Adonia and women's funerary laments, see Holst-Warhaft 1992.98–101; Alexiou 2002.55–82. In some versions of his myth, Adonis sires children with Aphrodite, but these appear to be post-Classical genealogical elaborations. Sources: Reed 1995.325.n. 35.

154 For *prothesis* and *ekphora* in funerals see Garland 1985.21–37. The deposition of the Adonis effigy in the sea was perhaps a feature borrowed from the Egyptian cult of Osiris: Reed 1997.19–20.

155 Detienne 1994 [1972].135.

156 Antiphonal song: Alexiou 2002.131–50.

157 For Bion's treatment of myth and ritual see Reed 1997.15–26.

158 Likely not performed in a ritual context: Reed 1997.16, 17. For the role of heightened emotion in transmission, see Chapter 4 and Essay 4.3.

## References

Alexiou, Margaret. 2002. *The ritual lament in Greek tradition*. Second edition. Revised by Dimitrios Yatromanolakis and Panagiotis Roilos. Lanham and Boulder: Rowman and Littlefield.

Amandry, Pierre. 1950. *La mantique apollinienne à Delphes: Essai sur le fonctionnement de l'oracle*. Paris: E. de Boccard.

Arnott, W. Geoffrey, ed. 2000. *Menander Volume III*. Cambridge, MA, and London: Harvard University Press.

Atran, Scott. 2002. *In gods we trust: The evolutionary landscape of religion*. Oxford and New York: Oxford University Press.

Baron-Cohen, Simon. 1997. *Mindblindness: An essay on autism and theory of mind*. Cambridge, MA: MIT Press.

Barrett, Deirdre and Patrick McNamara, eds. 2007. *The new science of dreaming. Vol. 3: Cultural and theoretical perspectives*. Westport, CT, and London: Praeger.

Barrett, Justin L. 1999. Theological correctness: Cognitive constraint and the study of religion. *Method and Theory in the Study of Religion* 11: 325–39.

Barrett, Justin L. 2004. *Why would anyone believe in God?* Walnut Creek, CA: Altamira Press.

Barrett, Justin L. 2007. Gods. In *Religion, anthropology and cognitive science*, ed. Whitehouse and Laidlaw, 179–207.

Barrett, Justin L. 2011. *Cognitive science, religion and theology: From human minds to divine minds*. West Conshohocken, PA: Templeton Press.

Barrett, Justin L. and A. H. Johnson. 2003. Research note: The role of control in attributing intentional agency to inanimate objects. *Journal of Cognition and Culture* 3: 208–17.

Barrett, Justin L. and Frank C. Keil. 1996. Conceptualizing a nonnatural entity: Anthropomorphism in God concepts. *Cognitive Psychology* 31: 219–47.

Barrett Justin L. and B. van Orman. 1996. The effects of the use of images in worship on God concepts. *Journal of Psychology and Christianity* 15 (1): 38–45.

Barringer, Judith. 1996. Atalanta as model: The hunter and the hunted. *ClAnt* 15 (1): 48–76.

Besançon, Alain. 2000. *The forbidden image: An intellectual history of iconoclasm*. Tr. Jane Marie Todd. Chicago: University of Chicago Press.

Bettinetti, Simona. 2001. *La statua di culto nella pratica rituale greca*. Bari: Levante.

Blakolmer, Fritz. 2010. A pantheon without attributes? Goddesses and gods in Minoan and Mycenaean iconography. In *Divine images and human imaginations in Greece and Rome*, ed. Mylonopoulos, 21–61.

Bloch, Maurice. 1989. *Ritual, history and power*. London: Athlone Press.

Boardman, John. 1972. Herakles, Peisistratos and sons. *RA* 52–71.

Boardman, John. 1989. Herakles, Peisistratos and the unconvinced. *JHS* 109: 158–9.

Borgeaud, Philippe and Youri Volokhine, eds. 2005. *Les objets de la mémoire: Pour une approache comparatiste des reliques et de leur culte*. Bern: Peter Lang.

Bouché-Leclercq, Auguste. 1963 [1879–82]. *Histoire de la divination dans l'antiquité*. 4 Vols. Reprint. Brussels: Culture Civilisation.

Bowden, Hugh. 2003. Oracles for sale. In *Herodotus and his world*, ed. Derow and Parker, 256–74.

Boyer, Pascal. 1994. *The naturalness of religious ideas: A cognitive theory of religion*. Berkeley and Los Angeles: University of California Press.

Boyer, Pascal. 2001. *Religion explained: The evolutionary origins of religious thought*. New York: Basic Books.

Bremmer, Jan. 1983. *The early Greek concept of the soul*. Princeton, NJ: Princeton University Press.

Bremmer, Jan. 1996. The status and symbolic capital of the seer. In *The role of religion in the early Greek polis*, ed. Hägg, 97–109.

Bremmer, Jan. 2013. The agency of Greek and Roman statues: From Homer to Constantine. *OAth* 6: 7–21.

Bremmer, Jan and Andrew Erskine, eds. 2010. *The gods of ancient Greece: Identities and transformations*. Edinburgh: Edinburgh University Press.

Brugger, Peter. 2001. From haunted brain to haunted science: A cognitive neuroscience view of paranormal and pseudoscientific thought. In *Hauntings and poltergeists*, ed. Houran and Lange, 195–213.

Bulkeley, Kelly. 2007. Sacred sleep: Scientific contributions to the study of religiously significant dreaming. In *The new science of dreaming, Vol. 3*, ed. Barrett and McNamara, 71–94.

Burkert, Walter. 1979. *Structure and history in Greek mythology and ritual*. Berkeley and Los Angeles: University of California Press.

Burkert, Walter. 1983. Itinerant diviners and magicians: A neglected element in cultural contacts. In *The Greek renaissance of the eighth century B.C.*, ed. Hägg, 115–19.

Burkert, Walter. 1992. *The Orientalizing revolution: Near Eastern influence on Greek culture in the early Archaic age*. Cambridge, MA, and London: Harvard University Press.

Burkert, Walter. 1996. *Creation of the sacred: Tracks of biology in early religions*. Cambridge, MA, and London: Harvard University Press.

Burkert, Walter. 2001. From epiphany to cult statue. In *La statua di culto nella pratica rituale greca*, ed. Bettinetti, 118–24.

Burkert, Walter. 2004. Epiphanies and signs of power: Minoan suggestions and comparative evidence. *ICS* 29: 1–23.

Burkert, Walter. 2005. Signs, commands and knowledge: Ancient divination between enigma and epiphany. In *Mantikē*, ed. Johnston and Struck, 29–49.

Buxton, Richard. 2004. *The complete world of Greek mythology*. London: Thames and Hudson.

Buxton, Richard. 2009. *Forms of astonishment: Greek myths of metamorphosis*. Oxford and New York: Oxford University Press.

Calame, Claude. 2007. Greek myth and Greek religion. In *The Cambridge companion to Greek mythology*, ed. Woodard, 259–85.

Clinton, Kevin. 2004. Epiphany in the Eleusinian mysteries. *ICS* 29: 85–109.

Cohen, Beth, ed. 1995. *The distaff side: Representing the female in Homer's Odyssey*. Oxford and New York: Oxford University Press.

Cohen, Emma. 2007. *The mind possessed: The cognition of spirit possession in an Afro-Brazilian religious tradition*. Oxford and New York: Oxford University Press.

Connor, W. R. 1987. Tribes, festivals and processions: Civic ceremonial and political manipulation in Archaic Greece. *JHS* 107: 40–50.

Csapo, Eric. 2005. *Theories of mythology*. Malden, MA, and Oxford: Blackwell.

Curry, Patrick and Angela Voss. 2007. *Seeing with different eyes: Essays in astrology and divination*. Newcastle: Cambridge Scholars Publishing.

Dawson, Lorne. 1999. When prophecy fails and faith persists: A theoretical overview. *Nova Religio: The Journal of Alternative and Emergent Religions* 3 (1): 60–82.

Derow, Peter and Robert Parker, eds. 2003. *Herodotus and his world: Essays from a conference in memory of George Forrest*. Oxford and New York: Oxford University Press.

Detienne, Marcel. 1994 [1972]. *The gardens of Adonis: Spices in Greek mythology*. Tr. Janet Lloyd. Princeton: Princeton University Press.

Detienne, Marcel. 1998. *Apollon le couteau à la main: Une approche expérimentale du polythéisme grec*. [Paris]: Gallimard.

Dietrich, Bernard C. 1983. Divine epiphanies in Homer. *Numen* 30: 53–79.

Dillery, John. 2005a. Chresmologues and manteis: Independent diviners and the problem of authority. In *Mantikē*, ed. Johnston and Struck, 167–231.

Dillery, John. 2005b. Greek sacred history. *AJPh* 126: 505–26.

Dodd, David B. and Christopher Faraone, eds. 2003. *Initiation in ancient Greek rituals and narratives: New critical perspectives*. London and New York: Routledge.

Donohue, Alice A. 1997. The Greek images of the gods: Considerations on terminology and methodology. *Hephaistos* 15: 31–45.

Dougherty, Carol and Leslie Kurke, eds. 1998. *Cultural poetics in archaic Greece: Cult, performance, politics*. Oxford and New York: Oxford University Press.

Dundes, Alan, ed. 1984. *Sacred narrative: Readings in the theory of myth*. Berkeley: University of California Press.

Earle, L. 1990. *The classic cold reading*. USA: Binary Star Publications.

Easterling, P. E. and J. V. Muir. 1985. *Greek religion and society*. Cambridge: Cambridge University Press.

Edmunds, Lowell, ed. 1990. *Approaches to Greek myth*. Baltimore: Johns Hopkins University Press.

Eidinow, Esther. 2007. *Oracles, curses and risk among the ancient Greeks*. Oxford and New York: Oxford University Press.

Eidinow, Esther. 2013. Oracular consultation, fate, and the concept of the individual. In *Divination in the ancient world*, ed. Rosenberger, 21–39.

Elsner, Jaś. 1996. Image and ritual: Reflections on the religious appreciation of Classic art. *CQ* 46: 515–31.

Estienne, Sylvie, Dominique Jaillard, Natacha Lubtchansky and Claude Pouzadoux, eds. 2008. *Image et religion dans l'antiquité gréco-romaine*. Naples: Centre Jean Bérard; Athens: École française d'Athènes.

Evans, Jonathan St. B. T. and Keith Frankish, eds. 2009. *In two minds: Dual processes and beyond*. Oxford and New York: Oxford University Press.

Faraone, Christopher. 1992. *Talismans and Trojan horses: Guardian statues in ancient Greek myth and ritual*. Oxford and New York: Oxford University Press.

Festinger, Leon. 1957. *A theory of cognitive dissonance*. Stanford, CA: Stanford University Press.

Flower, Michael. 2008. *The seer in ancient Greece*. Berkeley: University of California Press.

Foley, Helene P., ed. 1994. *The Homeric Hymn to Demeter: Translation, commentary and interpretive essays*. Princeton: Princeton University Press.

Fontenrose, Joseph. 1978. *The Delphic oracle: Its responses and operations with a catalogue of responses*. Berkeley and Los Angeles: University of California Press.

Fontenrose, Joseph. 1988. *Didyma: Apollo's oracle, cult and companions*. Berkeley: University of California Press.

Forsdyke, Sara. 2005. *Exile, ostracism, and democracy: The politics of exclusion in ancient Greece*. Princeton: Princeton University Press.

Frazer, James George. 1908. *Adonis, Attis, Osiris: Studies in the history of Oriental religion*. London: Macmillan.

Furley, William D. and Jan Maarten Bremer. 2001. *Greek hymns*. 2 Vols. Tübingen: Mohr Siebeck.

Gaifman, Milette. 2012. *Aniconism in Greek antiquity*. Oxford and New York: Oxford University Press.

Garland, Robert. 1985. *The Greek way of death*. Ithaca, NY: Cornell University Press.

Geertz, Clifford. 1973. *The interpretation of cultures*. New York: Basic Books.

Gladigow, Burkhard. 1985–6. Präsenz der Bilder, Präsenz der Götter: Kultbilder und Bilder der Götter in der griechischen Religion. *Visible Religion* 4–5: 114–33.

Gladigow, Burkhard. 1990. Epiphanie, Statuette, Kultbild: Griechische Gottesvorstellungen im Wechsel von Kontext und Medium. *Visible Religion* 7: 98–122.

Gordon, R. L. 1979. The real and the imaginary: Production and religion in the Graeco-Roman world. *Art History* 2 (1): 5–34.

Gordon, R. L. 1981. *Myth, religion and society: Structuralist essays by M. Detienne, L. Gernet, J.-P. Vernant and P. Vidal-Naquet*. Cambridge: Cambridge University Press; Paris: Maison des Sciences de l'Homme.

Gould, John. 1985. On making sense of Greek religion. In *Greek religion and society*, ed. Easterling and Muir, 1–33.

Graf, Fritz. 2004. Trick or treat: On collective epiphanies in antiquity. *ICS* 29: 111–30.

Graf, Fritz. 2005. Rolling the dice for an answer. In *Mantikē*, ed. Johnston and Struck, 51–97.

Guthrie, Stewart E. 1993. *Faces in the clouds: A new theory of religion*. Oxford: Oxford University Press.

Hägg, Robin, ed. 1983. *The Greek renaissance of the eighth century B.C.: Tradition and innovation*. Stockholm: P. Åströms Förlag.

Hägg, Robin, ed. 1996. *The role of religion in the early Greek polis*. Stockholm: P. Åströms Förlag.

Hanson, J. S. 1980. Dreams and visions in the Graeco-Roman world and early Christianity. *Aufstieg und Niedergang der römischen Welt II* 23 (1): 1395–427.

Harris, William V. 2009. *Dreams and experience in Classical antiquity*. Cambridge, MA, and London: Harvard University Press.

Harrison, Thomas. 2000. *Divinity and history: The religion of Herodotus*. Oxford: Oxford University Press.

Hartmann, Ernest. 2007. The nature and functions of dreaming. In *The new science of dreaming, Vol. 3*, ed. Barrett and McNamara, 171–92.

Henrichs, Albert. 1996. Epiphany. In *The Oxford Classical Dictionary*, ed. Hornblower and Spawforth, 546.

Henrichs, Albert. 2010. What is a Greek god? In *The gods of ancient Greece*, ed. Bremmer and Erskine, 19–39.

Higbie, Carolyn. 2003. *The Lindian chronicle and the Greek creation of their past*. Oxford and New York: Oxford University Press.

Hirschfeld, Lawrence A. and Susan Gelman, eds. 1994. *Mapping the mind: Domain specificity in cognition and culture*. Cambridge: Cambridge University Press.

Holst-Warhaft, Gail. 1992. *Dangerous voices: Women's laments and Greek literature*. New York and London: Routledge.

Hornblower, Simon and Anthony Spawforth, eds. 1996. *The Oxford Classical dictionary*. Oxford and New York: Oxford University Press.

Houran, James and Rense Lange. 2001. *Hauntings and poltergeists: Multidisciplinary perspectives*. Jefferson, NC, and London: McFarland.

Hunsaker, Michael R. and Raymond Kesner. 2013. The operation of pattern separation and pattern completion processes associated with different attributes or domains of memory. *Neuroscience and Biobehavioral Reviews* 37 (1): 36–58.

Johnston, Sarah Iles. 2005. Introduction: Divining divination. In *Mantikē*, ed. Johnston and Struck, 1–28.

Johnston, Sarah Iles. 2008. *Ancient Greek divination*. Malden, MA, and Oxford: Wiley-Blackwell.

Johnston, Sarah Iles and Peter Struck, eds. 2005. *Mantikē: Studies in ancient divination*. Leiden and Boston: Brill.

Kindt, Julia. 2012. *Rethinking Greek religion*. Cambridge and London: Cambridge University Press.

Kirk, G. S. 1970. *Myth: Its meaning and functions in ancient and other cultures*. Cambridge: Cambridge University Press; Berkeley: University of California Press.

Kirk, G. S. 1974. *The nature of Greek myths*. Middlesex, UK, and New York: Penguin.

Koch Piettre, Renée. 2005. La chronique de Lindos, ou comment accommoder les restes pour écrire l'Histoire. In *Les objets de la mémoire*, ed. Borgeaud and Volokhine, 95–121.

Kowalzig, Barbara. 2007. *Singing for the gods: Performances of myth and ritual in Archaic and Classical Greece*. Oxford and New York: Oxford University Press.

Lane Fox, Robin. 1986. *Pagans and Christians*. San Francisco: Harper and Row.

Lapatin, Kenneth. 2010. New statues for old gods. In *The gods of ancient Greece*, ed. Bremmer and Erskine, 126–51.

Lhôte, Éric. 2006. *Les lamelles oraculaires de Dodone*. Geneva: Droz.

Lisdorf, Anders. 2007a. *The dissemination of divination in Roman Republican times – A cognitive approach*. PhD Dissertation, University of Copenhagen.

Lisdorf, Anders. 2007b. What's HIDD'n in the HADD? A cognitive conjuring trick? *Journal of Cognition and Culture* 7 (3): 341–53.

Maloney, L. T., M. F. Dal Martello, C. Sahm and L. Spillmann. 2005. Past trials influence perception of ambiguous motion quartets through pattern completion. *Proceedings of the National Academy of Sciences of the United States of America* 102 (8): 3164–9.

Marinatos, Nanno. 2003. Striding across boundaries: Hermes and Aphrodite as gods of initiation. In *Initiation in ancient Greek rituals and narratives*, ed. Dodd and Faraone, 130–51.

Marinatos, Nanno and Dmitris Kyrtatos. 2004. Epiphany: Concept ambiguous, experience elusive. *ICS* 29: 227–34.

Maurizio, Lisa. 1995. Anthropology and spirit possession: A reconsideration of the Pythia's role at Delphi. *JHS* 115: 69–86.

Maurizio, Lisa. 2013. Interpretive strategies for Delphic oracles and kledons: Prophecy falsification and individualism. In *Divination in the ancient world*, ed. Rosenberger, 61–79.

McCauley, Robert N. and E. Thomas Lawson. 2002. *Bringing ritual to mind: Psychological foundations of cultural forms*. Cambridge and New York: Cambridge University Press.

Mercier, Hugo and Dan Sperber. 2009. Intuitive and reflective inferences. In *In two minds*, ed. Evans and Frankish, 149–70.

Mikalson, Jon. 1983. *Athenian popular religion*. Chapel Hill: University of North Carolina Press.

Morgan, Catherine. 1985. Divination and society at Delphi and Didyma. *Hermathena* 147: 17–42.

Morgan, Catherine. 1990. *Athletes and oracles: The transformation of Olympia and Delphi in the eighth century B.C.* Cambridge and New York: University of Cambridge.

Morris, J. F. 1983. Dream scenes in Homer: A study in variation. *TAPhA* 113: 39–54.

Murnaghan, Sheila. 1995. The plan of Athena. In *The Distaff side*, ed. Cohen, 61–80.

Mylonopoulos, Joannis, ed. 2010a. *Divine images and human imaginations in Greece and Rome*. Leiden: Brill.

Mylonopoulos, Joannis. 2010b. Divine images versus cult images. In *Divine images and human imaginations*, ed. Mylonopoulos (2010a), 1–19.

Naiden, F. S. 2013. *Smoke signals for the gods: Ancient Greek sacrifice from the Archaic through Roman periods*. Oxford and New York: Oxford University Press.

Nickerson, Raymond S. 1998. Confirmation bias: A ubiquitous phenomenon in many guises. *Review of General Psychology* 2 (2): 175–220.

Oakley, John and Laurialan Reitzammer. 2005. A Hellenistic terracotta and the gardens of Adonis. *JHS* 125: 142–4, Pl. 6–7.

Obbink, Dirk, ed. 1996. *Philodemus, On piety: Part 1*. Oxford: Clarendon Press.

Ogden, Daniel. 2013. *Drakōn: Dragon myth and serpent cult in the Greek & Roman worlds*. Oxford and New York: Oxford University Press.

Ohly, Dieter. 1953. Die Göttin und ihre Basis. *MDAI(A)* 68: 25–50.

Parke, H. W. 1967a. *Greek oracles*. London: Hutchinson.

Parke, H. W. 1967b. *The oracles of Zeus: Dodona, Olympia, Ammon*. Cambridge: Harvard University Press.

Parker, Robert. 2000 [1985]. Greek states and Greek oracles. In *Oxford readings in Greek religion*, ed. Buxton, 76–108.

Parker, Robert. 2011. *On Greek religion*. Ithaca and London: Cornell University Press.

Pedley, John Griffiths. 2005. *Sanctuaries and the sacred in the ancient Greek world*. New York: Cambridge University Press.

Pirenne-Delforge, Vinciane. 2008. Des marmites pour un méchant petit hermès! Ou comment consacrer un statue. In *Image et religion dans l'antiquité gréco-romaine*, ed. Estienne, Jaillard, Lubtchansky and Pouzadoux, 103–10.

Pirenne-Delforge, Vinciane. 2010. Greek priests and "cult statues": In how far are they necessary? In *Divine images and human imaginations*, ed. Mylonopoulos (2010a), 121–41.

Platt, Verity. 2011. *Facing the gods: Epiphany and representation in Graeco-Roman art, literature and religion*. Cambridge and New York: Cambridge University Press.

Porta, Fred R. 1999. *Greek ritual utterances and the liturgical style*. Dissertation, Harvard University.

Price, Simon. 1984. *Rituals and power: The Roman imperial cult in Asia Minor*. Cambridge: Cambridge University Press.

Pyysiäinen, Illka. 2003. *How religion works: Toward a new cognitive science of religion*. Leiden: Brill.

Reed, Joseph D. 1995. The sexuality of Adonis. *ClAnt* 14 (2): 317–47.

Reed, Joseph D. 1996. Antimachus on Adonis? *Hermes* 124 (3): 381–83.

Reed, Joseph D. 1997. *Bion of Smyrna: The fragments and the Adonis*. Cambridge and New York: Cambridge University Press.

Renberg, Gil. 2003. *Commanded by the gods: An epigraphical study of dreams and visions in Greek and Roman religious life*. Dissertation, Duke University.

Ribichini, Sergio. 1981. *Adonis: Aspetti "orientali" di un mito greco*. Rome: Consiglio nazionale delle ricerche.

Romano, Irene B. 1980. *Early Greek cult images*. Dissertation, University of Pennsylvania.

Rosenberger, Veit, ed. 2013. *Divination in the ancient world: Religious options and the individual*. Stuttgart: Franz Steiner Verlag.

Scheer, Tanja S. 2000. *Die Gottheit und ihr Bild: Untersuchungen zur Funktion griechischer Kultbilder in Religion und Politik*. Munich: Beck.

Scholl, B. J. and P. D. Tremoulet. 2000. Perceptual causality and animacy. *Trends in Cognitive Sciences* 4: 299–308.

Scullion, Scott. 2007. Festivals. In *A companion to Greek religion*, ed. Ogden, 190–203.

Seaford, Richard. 1994. *Reciprocity and ritual: Homer and tragedy in the developing city-state*. Oxford and New York: Clarendon Press and Oxford University Press.

Shear, Julia. 2001. *Polis and Panathenaia: The history and development of Athena's festival*. 2 Vols. Dissertation, University of Pennsylvania.

Simms, Ronda R. 1997–8. Mourning and community at the Athenian Adonia. *CJ* 93 (2): 121–41.

Sinos, Rebecca. 1998. Divine selection: Epiphany and politics in Archaic Greece. In *Cultural poetics in Archaic Greece*, ed. Dougherty and Kurke, 73–91.

Sissa, Giulia and Marcel Detienne. 2000. *The daily life of the Greek gods*. Tr. Janet Lloyd. Stanford: Stanford University Press.

Sørensen, Jesper. 2007a. *A cognitive theory of magic*. London and New York: Altamira Press.

Sørensen, Jesper. 2007b. Malinowski and magical ritual. In *Religion, anthropology and cognitive science*, ed. Whitehouse and Laidlaw, 81–104.

Sperber, Dan 1974. *Rethinking symbolism*. Tr. Alice L. Morton. Cambridge: Cambridge University Press.

Sperber, Dan. 1985. *On anthropological knowledge: Three essays*. Cambridge and London: Cambridge University Press.

Sperber, Dan. 1994. The modularity of thought and the epidemiology of representations. In *Mapping the mind*, ed. Hirschfeld and Gelman, 39–67.

Sperber, Dan. 1997. Intuitive and reflective beliefs. *Mind and Language* 12: 67–83.

Sperber, Dan, ed. 2000. *Metarepresentations: A multidisciplinary perspective*. Oxford and New York: Oxford University Press.

Stehle, Eva. 1990. Sappho's gaze: Fantasies of a goddess and a young man. *Differences* 2 (1): 88–125.

Steinhart, Matthias. 2004. *Die Kunst der Nachahmung: Darstellungen mimetischer Vorführungen in der griechischen Bildkunst archaischer und klassischer Zeit*. Mainz am Rhein: Philipp von Zabern.

Stoneman, Richard. 2011. *The ancient oracles: Making the gods speak*. New Haven and London: Yale University Press.

Storm, William. 1998. *After Dionysus: A theory of the tragic*. Ithaca, NY: Cornell University Press.

Struck, Peter. 2007. A world full of signs: Understanding divination in ancient Stoicism. In *Seeing with different eyes*, ed. Curry and Voss, 3–20.

Tanner, Jeremy. 2006. *The invention of art history in ancient Greece: Religion, society and artistic rationalisation*. Cambridge and New York: Cambridge University Press.

Thompson, Cynthia L. 1979–80. Cicero's editing of mythographic material in the De Natura Deorum. *CJ* 75 (2): 143–52.

Tremlin, Todd. 2006. *Minds and gods: The cognitive foundation of religion*. Oxford and New York: Oxford University Press.

Trépanier, Simon. 2010. Early Greek theology: God as nature and natural gods. In *The gods of ancient Greece*, ed. Bremmer and Erskine, 273–317.

Turkeltaub, Daniel. 2007. Perceiving Iliadic gods. *HSPh* 103: 51–81.

Turner, Victor. 1967. *The forest of symbols*. Ithaca and London: Cornell University Press.

Ustinova, Yulia. 2013. Modes of prophecy, or modern arguments in support of the ancient approach. *Kernos* 26: 25–44.

van der Plas, Dirk, ed. 1987. *Effigies dei: Essays on the history of religions*. Leiden: Brill.

van Straten, Folkert T. 1976. Daikrates' dream: A votive relief from Kos and some other kat' onar dedications. *BABesch* 51: 1–38.

Vernant, Jean-Pierre. 1991. *Mortals and immortals: Collected essays*. Tr. Froma Zeitlin. Princeton, NJ: Princeton University Press.

Versnel, Henk S., ed. 1981a. *Faith, hope, and worship: Aspects of religious mentality in the ancient world*. Leiden: Brill.

Versnel, Henk S. 1981b. Religious mentality in ancient prayer. In *Faith hope and worship: Aspects of religious mentality in the ancient world*, ed. Versnel (1981a), 1–64.

Versnel, Henk S. 1987. What did ancient man see when he saw a god? Reflections on Greco-Roman epiphany. In *Effigies dei*, ed. van der Plas, 42–55.

Versnel, Henk S. 1990a. *Inconsistencies in Greek and Roman religion I. Ter unus: Isis, Dionysos, Hermes. Three studies in henotheism*. Leiden and New York: Brill.

Versnel, Henk S. 1990b. What's sauce for the goose is sauce for the gander: Myth and ritual, old and new. In *Approaches to Greek myth*, ed. Edmunds, 25–90.

Versnel, Henk S. 2011. *Coping with the gods: Wayward readings in Greek theology*. Leiden: Brill.

Veyne, Paul. 1988. *Did the Greeks believe in their myths? An essay on the constitutive imagination*. Tr. Paula Wissing. Chicago: University of Chicago Press.

Vidal-Naquet, Pierre. 1981 [1968]. The Black Hunter and the origin of the Athenian ephebeia. In *Myth, religion and society: Structuralist essays by M. Detienne, L. Gernet, J.-P. Vernant and P. Vidal-Naquet*, ed. Gordon, 147–62.

Walde, Christine. 2001. *Die Traumdarstellungen in der griechisch-römischen Dichtung*. Munich: K. G. Saur.

Whitehouse, Harvey and James Laidlaw, eds. 2007. *Religion, anthropology and cognitive science*. Durham, NC: Carolina Academic Press.

Winkler, John. 1990. *The constraints of desire: The anthropology of sex and gender in ancient Greece*. New York and London: Routledge.

Woodard, Roger, ed. 2007. *The Cambridge companion to Greek mythology*. Cambridge and London: Cambridge University Press.

# 3 Orthopraxy, identity and society

*Greek piety required correct behavior (orthopraxy) in several domains. A pious individual undertook the ritual roles appropriate to his or her age, gender and social status. Most religious activity was organized and supervised by the state, but individuals, families and other groups also exercised religious agency. Piety required the observation of moral precepts ultimately derived from shared intuitions about reciprocity. The Greek gods were concerned with enforcing such behaviors rather than defining them. Greek rituals often incorporated magic, a technique which could be used either to reinforce or to violate moral norms. Although beliefs about magic and divine agency were supported by different cognitive systems, the two often coincided in the same ritual. Magical beliefs underlay another important area of orthopraxy in Greek religion, ritual requirements regarding purity and pollution. A special form of pollution known as* agos *was, in turn, closely intertwined with moral intuition. The illustrative essays examine the inclusiveness of the Panathenaic games and procession, the Greek institution of choral dance for the gods, and an important inscription from fourth-century Kyrene which details the city's purity laws.*

Greek religion was a highly sociable business. While religious thoughts and behaviors originate in the mental processes of individuals, many of these processes themselves evolved to facilitate social behavior and cooperation. Participation in the religious ritual of a given group signals not only membership but also intent to abide by the group's social and moral norms. Group dynamics affect the emotional impact of ritual: one's personal conformity to norms is a source of pride, and the conformity of others draws approval, whereas deviance tends to arouse indignation and to be interpreted as a sign that an individual is not trustworthy, as in the case of early Christians who refused to eat sacrificial meat. Correct religious conduct, or orthopraxy, was not merely a matter of ritual technique. It also required participation in the rituals appropriate to one's social identity, and conformity to certain ethical standards.

Among the Greeks, virtually every conceivable level and variety of familial and social organization had its corresponding worship group. Were modern Americans to become polytheists in this mode, we would honor the gods of (among others) the nuclear family, the extended family, the ethnic group, each grade in primary school, the alma mater, the professional association, the neighborhood, the book club, the sports team, the city, the state and the nation. Each would have its ordained sacrifices. Thus, from a Greek worshiper's point of view, a given ritual instantiated his or her relationship to both the group in question and its guardian deity or hero. This tutelary model was pervasive, but not absolute. Not every religious thought and experience was tied to membership in a group, and certain cults, especially those focused on healing and dispensing oracles, were open to all. The Eleusinian Mysteries of Athens were highly inclusive, and the Panhellenic shrines of Olympia, Nemea, Isthmia and Delphi were predicated on the idea of access for all Greeks (and even a few non-Greeks) with the interest and the means to sacrifice there. Pindar (*Ol.* 3.17–8) describes Olympia as "the grove of Zeus, welcoming to all," while at Delphi Apollo governs the "famous, all-welcoming temple" (*Pyth.* 8.61–2).

## The role of the polis

One of the most influential ideas about Greek religion of the past three decades was Christiane Sourvinou-Inwood's presentation of "polis religion" in two articles published in 1988 and 1990.[1] Her assertion that "the polis anchored, legitimated and mediated" all religious activity, including religious discourse, was consistent with a preexisting consensus in the discipline that Greek religion was communal in nature rather than personal, and that it had to do primarily with ritual action rather than belief. Even prior to the explicit development of this model, scholars such as Anthony Snodgrass had described the relationship between the advent of Greek monumental architecture (nearly always in the form of temples) and the development of the city-state, which organized and funded these efforts.[2] The "polis religion" model is consistent with much – even a majority – of what we know about the religious behaviors of Greeks, and especially Athenians, during the Classical period. A wealth of evidence from inscriptions, orations and other sources reveals, in often numbing detail, the extensive role of the Athenian state and its representatives in organizing, financing and policing the ritual activity of the population.

Yet, as many scholars have noted over the last decade, this model requires qualification. The religious system of each polis was unique, and there are gaps in our knowledge of most poleis compared with Athens. (The archaeological evidence from Classical Olynthos, for example, reveals a puzzling absence of temples, or indeed any identifiable spaces set aside for the conduct of polis religion.)[3] The phenomena we wish to study under the rubric of "Greek religion" extend back in time before the genesis of the polis system, and well after the weakening of the polis that occurred when Hellenistic rulers claimed power.[4] Supra-polis religious activity was conducted in federal states composed of member towns and poleis with a shared ethnicity, in cult-based leagues of multiple states, such as the Delphic amphictyony, in regional institutions of interstate religious pilgrimage (*theoria*) and in Panhellenic institutions, such as the games at Olympia or the Delphic oracle.[5] Finally, overreliance on the polis religion paradigm can lead scholars to

*Figure 3.1* Painted wooden tablet dedicated by three women who performed a private sacrifice to the nymphs in a cave at Pitsa near Sikyon, ca. 540. National Archaeological Museum, Athens. Photo: Nimatallah/Art Resource

neglect and de-emphasize the religious aspects of daily experience that were of little interest to the Greek state, or deliberately performed outside its supervision. These include the personal and private dimensions of religion, conducted in the home or on an individual basis (e.g. vows and their associated offerings); the activities of private religious associations and cult founders; ritual actions performed privately in order to harness divine power for personal benefit ("magic"); and a host of other activities which occurred at a "microscopic" level without state mediation (Figure 3.1).[6]

## Greek piety, social identity and gender

Greek festivals allotted roles to various members of the community, roles which expressed the exclusive or inclusive nature of a given cult as well as differences among the participants in gender, class and other aspects of social status (Essay 3.1). It was normal for foreigners, including Greeks from other cities, to be excluded from direct participation in public rituals. Other social groups, such as slaves or women or men, might also be restricted or entirely barred, depending on the cult and the occasion.[7] Ethnicity, clan affiliation and kinship also formed a common basis for inclusion in and exclusion from worship groups. To give a famous example, Herodotus (5.72.1) tells us that when the Spartan king Kleomenes attempted to enter Athena's shrine on the Akropolis, the priestess told him, "Go back, Lakedaimonian stranger, and do not enter the holy place; it is not lawful for Dorians to be here."[8]

The prominence of the Greek state in matters of religion meant that citizen males controlled most aspects of public relations with the gods, and in particular, the important sacrificial practices upon which public ritual was predicated. It was normally men who performed sacrificial killing; on Attic tombstones, the attribute of the priest is the knife, while that of the priestess is the temple key.[9] Likewise, there was a strong positive correlation between citizen status and access to sacrificial meat. Participation in the athletic and musical contests so characteristic of the gods' festivals was also, for the most part, restricted to males. Although state relations with the gods were primarily administered by men, there were significant exceptions to this rule. Goddesses often required a priestess to serve them rather than a priest, and such women had the same religious authority as their male counterparts (though both were supervised by the state). The all-important ritual of alimentary sacrifice began with a procession led by a virgin girl called a *kanēphoros*, who carried on her head a basket with knife and grain. Certain festivals, notably the Thesmophoria of Demeter and Kore, were the responsibility of a city's married women, and others required the participation of adolescent girls. Finally, a standard element of the Greek festival was the *pannuchis*, a nocturnal celebration characterized by the dances of women.[10]

Rituals involving participation by females at specific stages of life (young girl, adolescent virgin, married woman, woman past childbearing age) were common in Greek religion, more so than equivalent rites for males. Married men, for example, rarely formed a special ritual category, nor did old men. But in Attica alone, at least three festivals were reserved for married women, and two additional rituals, the *arrhēphoria* for Athena Polias and the *arkteia* for Artemis at Brauron, called for the participation of citizen girls aged about six to twelve years. This special focus on female ritual roles is not surprising when we consider that Greek religion was concerned not only with the maintenance of social status and gender norms but also with biological imperatives, such as securing food and producing healthy children. Women's role in reproduction is more complex and fraught with dangers than men's role; therefore their reproductive status was a matter of greater social and ritual import than that of men. Furthermore, females who were not sexually active (because they were either too young or too old to reproduce) were perceived as more ritually pure (see p. 138) and therefore better suited to attend certain goddesses.[11]

## Moral intuition, ethical behavior and the gods

As David Hume recognized in the eighteenth century, people do not derive their moral feelings from religion, or from reason for that matter. Moral reasoning allows us to propose general principles of right behavior, but it does not create the emotions that prompt moral judgments and behaviors: the pride we take in doing good, the shame we feel at doing wrong and the indignation we feel at witnessing injustice. Behind these feelings stand moral intuitions, which arise from our evolutionary history as cooperative, social animals and our capacity to mentally represent the thoughts and feelings of other people. Even very young children of three or four years have sophisticated moral intuitions which derive neither from conscious reasoning nor from authority figures, and in spite of cultural variation, people the world over share similar moral intuitions about the desirability of reciprocity and fairness as well as the wrongness of behaviors like lying, cheating, stealing and killing, particularly when perpetrator and victim belong to the same group.[12]

People disputing the morality of their behavior in a specific situation (say, of lying) rarely defend themselves by suggesting that there is nothing wrong with lying. Instead, they point to the specifics of the case: "I lied to keep from hurting your feelings," or "I lied because you lied to me first." Intuitively, we are moral realists who believe that if we all had full access to the relevant facts and intentions, everyone would come to the same conclusion. Therefore the concept of a superhuman agent who not only possesses all strategic information about a given case but also has the ability to punish wrongdoers is bound to engage our minds and command our attention. This is especially so given that moral intuitions are not processed consciously. We cannot explain why we feel as we do, but we can conceptualize right or wrong behavior by positing that another mind scrutinizes and judges it. For the same reasons, people intuitively believe that atheists are less likely to behave morally.[13]

The semantic range of the Greek term *eusebeia* (piety) included both respectful behavior toward the gods and decent conduct toward other people.[14] Even the rationalist Thucydides (3.82.8) used *eusebeia* as a synonym for morality when he remarked that revolutions inevitably resulted in depravity: "Thus neither side practised reverence (*eusebeia*), but fair words as the pretext for accomplishing anything hateful were well-received." In practice, however, certain behaviors, such as proper treatment of strangers and suppliants, respecting the inviolability of heralds and keeping oaths, were regarded as indicators of a pious and therefore moral disposition. The corresponding transgressions were deemed especially likely to draw divine punishment.[15] Such crimes crucially threatened the shared standards of reciprocity which permitted cooperation among people with no kinship ties. Thus the foreign guest trusted his host not to murder him in his sleep, the parties to an oath trusted each other to abide by its terms, and the generals of opposing armies communicated through heralds who were not to be harmed.

Oversight of human conduct could be conceptualized impersonally as a function of "the divine," but Zeus in particular was regarded as a guarantor of justice. Hesiod stressed that he could be relied on to know when people transgressed:

> Chieftains, see that you pay heed to justice,
> For the immortals coming among men perceive
> Those who wear down others with crooked justice,
> Heedless of the vengeance of the gods.
> Upon the bountiful earth are thrice ten thousand
> Immortal watchers of mortals, from Zeus.
>
> (Hes. *Op.* 248–53)[16]

In Greek religion, this role of moral guarantor was expressed through Zeus' cult titles: Zeus Hikesios protected the suppliant, Zeus Xenios the stranger, and Zeus Horkios the oath.[17] People called upon Zeus in these guises (or alternatively, these Zeuses) to punish non-kin transgressors. Crimes involving kin involved a different form of moral intuition, the feeling that harming blood relations, and especially parents, is an outrage. In myth, the Erinyes were goddesses much concerned with the punishment of the kinslayer, as well as the power of a parental curse. Where they and similar goddesses were invoked, it was typically in contexts related to homicide, ancestors and curses.[18]

The gods themselves were social actors who jealously guarded their own status and honors. The moral category of impiety (*asebeia*) included all offenses that "harmed" a god, such as stealing from a temple, disregarding an obligation to sacrifice, or attacking suppliants claiming asylum in a sanctuary. The interests of gods and humans often coincided; the right of asylum, for example, expressed a god's exclusive control over a sanctuary and everything in it, but it also had social and economic benefits for the community. Occasionally, the interests of humans and gods conflicted, as when the guilty attempted to escape punishment by taking refuge in sanctuaries. In such cases, the rights of the gods took precedence in popular belief, if not always in practice.[19]

As we have seen, the inference that superhuman agents exist tends to reinforce moral intuitions, as well as culture-specific moral standards: when we are under observation, we are more intensely aware of the moral status of our actions. But sometimes the process works in reverse: when they confirm our moral intuitions, random events that appear to be punishments or rewards may be interpreted as the results of invisible agency. So powerful is the urge to attribute agency that in cases of spectacular misfortune, people often suspect the victim of some hidden wrongdoing. Among the Greeks, physical illness was sometimes interpreted as a punishment for offending the gods.[20] But the intuitive inference that a specific individual has been punished is quite a different matter from reflective propositions such as "The gods are always just." Given that the gods themselves were anthropomorphic social actors, the Greeks also attributed misfortune to divine hostility, grudges and indifference.[21]

The highly intuitive nature of the relationship between moral feeling and perceptions of divine punishment generated two significant problems as people approached the topic reflectively. First, experience showed that bad deeds were not always punished. Rather than conclude that the gods were unjust, the Greeks always found alternative explanations (the punishment was delayed, the gods had left the crime to human justice, etc.). Second, moralists objected to "theologically incorrect" descriptions of gods engaging in unethical behaviors, such as adultery and lying. Pindar and Plato alike felt it necessary to "correct" the mythopoetic record.[22]

## Magical thinking, religion and society

What anthropologists describe as "magic" or "magical thinking" was pervasive in Greek religion. By "magic," they typically refer to ritual actions which are viewed by those who perform them as instrumental – that is, capable of bringing about a concrete result, such as making the crops grow well or preventing a plague from entering a city. Scholars of Greek religion tend to use the term "magic" more narrowly, to describe a class of instrumental ritual activities that either pertain primarily to private concerns (e.g. the making and wearing of amulets) or are performed privately because they are considered antisocial by the larger group (e.g. the inscribing and deposition of curse tablets). The latter view of magic more closely reflects the emic categories of *mageia* and *goēteia* in Greek culture.

In the Greek world, however, both civic and private rituals regularly employed what J. G. Frazer called "the laws of sympathetic magic." In practice, gods were often asked to assist in the achievement of the desired goal, but sympathetic magic could be efficacious in and of itself. In any case, magic is not to be construed as a category in opposition to religion.[23] Instead, magic is a ritual technique regularly (but not exclusively) used in religious contexts. Frazer summarized the laws of magic as follows:

> First, that like produces like, or that an effect resembles its cause; and, second, that things which have once been in contact with each other continue to act on each other at a distance after the physical contact has been severed. The former principle may be called the Law of Similarity, the latter the Law of Contact or Contagion.[24]

The Law of Similarity is well illustrated in a fourth-century inscription from Kyrene, which describes an ancient procedure for cursing potential oath-breakers. Wax figures (*kolossoi*) were to be molded, and then burned in the presence of the assembled community, including men, women, boys and girls. The onlookers were to say, "May he who does not abide by these oaths, but transgresses, melt away and dissolve like the *kolossoi*, himself, his offspring and his property." Christopher Faraone has demonstrated that this ritual was borrowed from Near Eastern practices; more common among the Greeks were oath ceremonies in which an animal was killed and cut up, while the oath-takers called down the same fate on themselves if they broke faith. The most solemn form of such an oath involved physical contact with the mutilated animal's body parts or blood.[25] The Law of Similarity was explicitly invoked in an act of self-cursing, while the Law of Contact ensured that the dead animal's fate continued to hold influence over the person swearing the oath. The Greeks were unconcerned with the logical conflict between magical procedures like this and the equally powerful idea that the gods punished oath-breakers. Indeed, oath ceremonies were often conducted in sanctuaries so that the gods might act as witnesses. The role of gods in enforcing oaths was based on their possession of "strategic information" (i.e. they would know if an oath was broken), as well as their power to bring disaster on the guilty.[26] The efficacy of the magical procedure was rooted in quite different yet equally intuitive beliefs.

Psychologists Paul Rozin and Carol Nemeroff, among others, have demonstrated that magical thinking is not a "primitive" stage in cultural evolution, as Tylor and Frazer thought. Instead, the laws of magic operate in the daily cognition of moderns, including educated Western adults.[27] The clearest demonstration of the Law of Similarity occurs in the domain of disgust, where we are likely to react intuitively in ways that confuse appearance with reality. Rozin, Nemeroff and other colleagues found that study participants showed a significant preference for a square piece of fudge over one shaped like dog feces, and were far more willing to hold a clean rubber stopper in their mouths than a clean piece of fake rubber "vomit." In the interpersonal domain, participants were less accurate in aiming darts at pictures of "good" or liked persons (e.g. John F. Kennedy) than at pictures of "evil" or disliked persons (e.g. Adolf Hitler), as though the darts might actually inflict harm on the individuals represented. In another study, educated adult subjects declined to drink sugar water made from sugar labeled "potassium cyanide, poison" although they had watched as ordinary sugar was labeled in this way, and even when they agreed that the beverage was safe. "Nominal realism," the tendency to blur the distinction between a word and its referent, was described by Piaget as a developmental stage of childhood, but it also appears to be present in the normal intuitive cognition of adults, regardless of culture.[28] Much work remains to be done in this area, but the Law of Similarity may be a cognitive by-product of our ability to generalize – that is, to group similar but not identical things into the same mental category. The survival benefits of generalization (e.g. recognizing different-sized potatoes or apples as the same type of object) far outweigh its occasional misfires (real and fake vomit).[29]

The Law of Contact or Contagion is equally powerful for moderns. Rozin and Nemeroff showed that American college students intuitively reject the idea of wearing a clean garment which was previously in contact with a person they consider "creepy," an AIDS patient, a person with an amputated limb or a convicted killer. Germ/residue models were present in the students' thinking about supposed moral "contagion," while the concept of a harmful, non-physical "uncleanness" surfaced in their perceptions of illness and misfortune.[30] Modern people act as though positive essences can rub off ("Let me shake the hand of the person who shook the hand of celebrity X"). The intuition of negative essences is even stronger. A coworker of mine once refused to apply for a desirable job vacated by a person who had died, because she would have to sit in that person's chair. Moderns feel and act on such intuitions even as they readily agree that there is no real danger, but in antiquity, there was a broad cultural consensus, even among educated people, that magic worked. The consensus persisted not because people were foolishly credulous or too "primitive" to understand causal relationships, but because multiple cognitive biases led them to ignore empirical evidence against the efficacy of magic, while the *feeling* that it worked remained as strong as ever.[31]

From the perspective of participants, the ritual performance itself was salient (we will explore this claim further in Chapter 4). Application of the laws of magic made a ritual even more compelling, both cognitively and emotionally. Ludwig Wittgenstein's comments on Frazer capture the impact of this performative effect:

> To burn in effigy. To kiss the picture of the beloved. This is naturally not based upon a belief in a certain effect on the object which the picture represents. It aims at a satisfaction and also obtains it. Or rather it aims at nothing at all; we act in such a way and then feel satisfied.[32]

The deep satisfaction we derive from such actions arises from the same intuition that fuels magic: the effigy and the picture share some essence with the objects they represent. Burning in effigy and kissing a picture are quasi-ritual, quasi-magical acts. But in antiquity, people believed that skilled ritual manipulation of objects and words using magical techniques could produce concrete effects.[33]

Precisely because it worked, magic was dangerous. It could be used to achieve socially approved goals, like healing and oath enforcement, or it could be used illicitly to coerce and do harm. Many public rituals employed magical techniques to benefit the community. During the Thesmophoria, perhaps the most ancient and widespread of Greek festivals, women applied the magical laws when they brought piglets, pine branches and phallic shapes (objects evoking sexuality and fertility) into physical contact with the next year's seed grain. The destructive potential of magic was more likely to be exploited in private, outside the supervision of the Greek state. Anyone could use magic, but the instrumental manipulation of objects and words to cure a malady, harm an enemy, attract a lover or lay a ghost came to be regarded as a specialized skill. Self-proclaimed experts begin to appear in our literary sources by the late fifth century, though there are hints that they existed much earlier. Such men might be called sorcerers (*magoi*), wizards (*goētēs*) or beggar-priests (*agurtai*). It is no coincidence that many of these experts also offered purification, which is a subset of magical belief and practice. They were viewed with suspicion by the educated elites of the fourth century, and in some cities they were outlawed, yet to judge from literary and archaeological evidence, their services were in demand.[34]

Plato found it offensive that the *magoi* claimed to be able to "place the gods at their service" (*Resp.* 364b) and "promised to seduce even the gods, whom they bewitched by sacrifices, prayers and incantations" (*Leg.* 909b). That magical techniques can result in "bewitchment" of gods has caused moralists through the ages to conclude that magic is antithetical to religion. In their view, religion ought to consist of theologically correct, properly reverent requests for aid, rather than attempts to bewitch or coerce deities. From an intuitive perspective, however, the gods were simply another set of social actors, however strange and powerful.[35] Attempts to influence gods, spirits and the dead through public ritual were usually defensive, targeted at those perceived as dangerous. Thus statues of Ares were bound in order to avert bloody warfare, statues of Apollo in his role as a plague god were positioned at gates with bow and arrow pointing away from the city, and *kolossoi* were used to lay ghosts.[36] Yet curse tablets and magical papyri also reveal a widespread belief that the malign powers of the underworld could be co-opted in private to carry out the will of the magician.[37]

## Disgust, pollution and purity

Beliefs about invisible and dangerous "defilements" from which the gods must be insulated exist around the world. They have been interpreted by anthropologists as symbolic systems designed to order human experience (e.g. by marking transitions, such as birth and death) and to reinforce social categories (e.g. belief in female inferiority may be strengthened by assertions of female "impurity"). The best-known anthropological account of purity and pollution is Mary Douglas's *Purity and Danger* (1966), which defined impurity as "matter out of place."[38] Symbolic understandings of purity rules certainly exist, and cultures often correlate purity with social status, yet the symbolic elaboration of the urge to purify does not explain why invisible "dirt" is such a powerful concern in the first place, why pollution fears so often overlap with notions about the gods, or why the cross-cultural parallels in purity matters are as striking as the variations.

A fundamental element of our response to threats of contagion or contamination is the human capacity to feel disgust. Disgust is an emotion elicited by sensory or interpersonal stimuli which causes a desire to avoid, escape or purge the offending stimulus. Disgust has characteristic physiological effects, and a characteristic facial expression, used even by individuals who have been blind from birth.[39] It is a human universal, although the specific objects of disgust vary from culture to culture. For example, whether we find it disgusting to eat dog meat or monkey brains is a matter of culture. In spite of this variation, however, certain stimuli evoke disgust very broadly in cultures across the world. Feces, vomit and putrefying carcasses fall into this category, and to a lesser extent, other bodily fluids and secretions. While differences in food disgust are mostly cultural, true disgust (as opposed to dislike) is almost exclusively associated with foods of animal origin rather than with plant foods. This form of sensory disgust appears to be an evolutionary adaptation to help us avoid food-borne pathogens. It is significant, for example, that the greatest feelings of disgust universally arise at the prospect that an offending object or substance could come into contact with the mouth.[40] In Greek, one of the words for "disgusting" is *apoptustos*, "spat out," and spitting was one of the simplest and oldest methods of magical aversion.[41]

Our intuitions about contaminated objects (whatever these objects may be) are highly predictable and consistent across cultures. We do not need to see the source of contamination to believe it is present. Whatever has been in contact with a contaminated object is to be avoided, even if there are no visible traces of the contact. Finally, even the tiniest amount of contact is enough to result in contamination.[42] These intuitions are not a primitive form of hygienic science. The existence of germs was unknown to the Greeks, and most forms of sickness did not trigger contagion fears unless (like leprosy) they involved visible "dirt," which might be expected to "rub off." Basic contagion beliefs are not reflective beliefs, and for the most part, purity rules do not result from observation and logical deduction.[43]

From a cognitive perspective, rules about purity and pollution are cultural elaborations of an innate disposition to be alert to potential sources of contagion and contamination. This disposition is manifested even in the total absence of knowledge about actual biological sources of contagion. Therefore we can predict that ritual rules will be correlated with bodily functions as well as with putrefaction, but exactly *which* bodily substances and *which* forms of putrefaction are viewed as contaminants in need of cleansing will vary from one culture and period to the next, as will the techniques for dealing with them. Because aversion to contamination has nothing to do with knowledge of actual pathogens, we can expect to find the concept of pollution extended well beyond the core domain of pathogenic substances to a variety of other negative things which might be considered contagious enough to require ritual cleansing or aversion: madness, disfiguring diseases, bad luck and the anger of gods or the dead.[44] Finally, pollution arising from bodily sources is not a matter of morality. Among the Greeks, no shame attached to the woman in childbed, even though she was polluted and her pollution (*miasma*) was contagious. Yet as we will see, moral disapproval and contamination fears were easily conflated.

Purity beliefs and theism are rooted in distinct mental systems. In Greek religion, the connection between them arose in conjunction with two related beliefs about the divine. First, most gods, and particularly the Olympians, were *hagnos*, pure.[45] They did not experience bodily dirtiness (or sickness or age) in the way humans did. Second, involuntary exposure to another person's orifices, bodily products or secretions is a source of insult and offense, and the higher the social standing of the victim in relation to the perpetrator, the greater the offense. Therefore, to confront a god with impurity (e.g. by entering a sanctuary in an impure state) was morally offensive and disrespectful. At its most fundamental level, the relationship between purity and religion is predicated on the intuition that divine agents can feel disgust, just as we do. In *Works and Days*, Hesiod warns of the potential for inadvertent offense:

> Don't pour bright wine after dawn for Zeus
> With unwashed hands, nor for the other immortals,
> Or they will spit back your prayers unheard.
> Don't piss standing upright and facing the sun;
> Remember to do it from sunset to sunrise.
> Don't piss as you walk the road, on it or from it,
> Or expose yourself; the nights are of the blessed ones.
> A godly man with a wise mind squats,
> Or he goes to the wall of a fenced yard.
> Don't expose your private parts bespattered with seed
> Near the hearth in your house, but avoid this.
> (Hes. *Op.* 724–34)

A great deal of energy was expended on ensuring that the gods were insulated from sources of pollution. Sanctuary boundaries were marked, and vessels for washing were placed at the entrances, as were inscriptions recording any special requirements of purity.[46] It seems to have been taken for granted that one did not defecate or urinate in a sanctuary. Few "sacred laws" address the issue, although a fourth-century lease of the Garden of Herakles on Thasos stipulated that the lessee had to keep the area free of *kopros* (feces). If he caught anyone emptying a pot there, he was empowered to confiscate the pot, and to administer a whipping if the offender was a slave.[47] Concern about pollution from human and animal waste was surely one of the reasons for the common stricture against camping in the sacred areas of sanctuaries. In 424, indignant Thebans complained that Athenian invaders were living in the sanctuary at Delion and that "all the things people do on profane ground" were taking place there, including the use of sacred water for unauthorized purposes.[48]

Leaving *kopros* in a sanctuary was offensive, but not high sacrilege. In the ancient city, evidence of mundane and ubiquitous human bodily functions was difficult to escape, even for the gods. Next in order of increasing concern was sexual activity. Herodotus (2.64.1) mentions the widespread belief that it is wrong to "enter shrines without washing after sleeping with a woman." Most purity regulations are likewise written from the male perspective: "[Coming] from a woman, enter on the same day if you have washed."[49] This does not necessarily indicate that the female body was viewed as the source of pollution. "From sex (*aphrodisia*)" and "from intercourse (*sunousia*)" are later functional equivalents to "from a woman," and in fourth-century Kos (Essay 4.1), a man polluted the sacrifice for Zeus Polieus whether he came "from a woman or a man."[50] Inscribed purity regulations addressed men because they were both more likely to be literate and more likely to perform key ritual roles, such as leading a sacrifice. In a rare case of a regulation specifically for women, the reverse terminology was used: the Gerarai, servants of Dionysos at Athens, had to swear that they were pure "from a man's intercourse."[51] As we saw with Hesiod, the offensiveness of sex was linked to sexual secretions, and in particular, the ejaculation of semen. Since this substance was discharged into a woman, the woman was also polluted and needed to wash before approaching the gods.[52] Likewise, having sex in a sanctuary was a double affront to the divine. It showed disrespect by confronting the god with the act, and it stained the sanctuary with bodily fluids. It was the act, not the fact, of sexuality that generated pollution; this explains why representations of genitals could be prominent in the cults of Demeter and Dionysos, even as rituals of these same gods required sexual purity of their participants.[53]

Childbirth and miscarriage were next in the list of bodily matters offensive to the gods. As with sexuality, it was not the concept of birthing that created the problem; goddesses (and even gods, in the special case of Zeus) gave birth, just as they engaged in sexual intercourse. Again, the concern can be traced to the physicality of the event, for human birth is a messy business. Women who had just given birth or miscarried were to stay away from sanctuaries. People visiting a new mother up to three days after a birth typically incurred pollution, while the mothers themselves remained impure for a longer period, usually ten days. Significantly, the rule was not limited to human births: parturient dogs and donkeys could also pollute.[54] The contamination fears aroused by fluids and tissues discharged during birth may have been intensified because of their source in the *aidoia*, the "shameful parts." Menstrual blood may also have been a minor source of pollution concerns, but there are no Greek restrictions to compare with those in Leviticus (15:19–23), where the *niddah* or menstruating woman is a powerful source of contagion.[55]

The most potent physical source of pollution, and the most offensive to the purity of the gods, was the corpse. In Euripides' *Hippolytus*, Artemis declines to witness the death of her favorite, because "It is lawful for me neither to look upon the dead nor to stain my eye with deadly exhalations." Actual physical contact with the dead was most polluting, but as in the case of childbirth, even sharing the same roof with a corpse meant that one was ritually affected.[56] Purification was achieved through washing or bathing at the end of a prescribed period, but in token of grief, mourners might intensify their "dirtiness" by defiling themselves with grime. The period of death pollution came to be coextensive in many cases with a formal period of grieving.[57]

Being confronted with a corpse is a more complex matter, both socially and cognitively, than an encounter with one of the other bodily triggers of contamination fear. The presence of a dead body signals "danger." We feel a need to physically distance ourselves from it, yet our emotions are implicated, especially if the dead person is known to us. Even the corpses of strangers continue to engage our systems for social cognition; we do not perceive them as objects, in the way we do the dead bodies of wild animals. The clash between hazard-precaution (including fears of contamination) and social cognition (including recognition of personhood) produces a dilemma, which funerary rituals help to resolve.[58] Experimental evidence indicates that people intuitively believe it is important to protect an exposed corpse until its proper (i.e. ritual) disposal is assured. Even a stranger's corpse evokes this feeling in normal individuals; psychotic individuals by contrast feel both less disgust and less empathy at the thought of a corpse.[59] In antiquity, the intuition that it was wrong to leave any corpse unburied manifested itself in the idea of divine anger. Thus the shade of Elpenor tells Odysseus (Hom. *Od.* 11.73) that he must return to Kirke's island and bury his body, "lest I become a cause of the gods' wrath against you."[60]

The natural human aversion to leaving the dead unattended, and the offensiveness of the corpse to the gods, are illustrated in Sophocles' *Antigone*. After his command to leave the corpse of Polyneikes unburied, but within the borders of the polis, Kreon learns from Teiresias that the worst possible pollution of the city's altars has occurred: the nightmarish scenario of direct contact with a rotting corpse:

> The city falls sick as a result of your purpose,
> For our altars and hearths, one and all,
> Are filled by dogs and birds with the flesh
> Of Oedipus' ill-fated, fallen offspring.
> So the gods no longer accept from us
> Sacrificial prayer or the fire set to thigh-meat,
> Nor do the birds shrill out clear signs,
> For they ate the slain man's fat and blood.
> (Soph. *Ant.* 1015–22)

Leaving Polyneikes unburied causes a far more serious pollution than his death alone could have done. In real life, the Athenians practiced punitive denial of burial against traitors and temple-robbers, yet their bodies had to be cast out in ways that removed them from sight: in deep pits, in the sea or beyond the borders of

*Figure 3.2* The shade of Elpenor asks Odysseus to bury his corpse. Carcasses of sacrificed rams lie beside the chasm from which Elpenor appears. Attic red figure pelike, fifth century. Museum of Fine Arts, Boston. Photo: Erich Lessing/Art Resource

the polis. Such removal enacted the dead person's expulsion from the community, but it was also consistent with the avoidance of pollution. The punitive display of rotting corpses, on the other hand, was regarded as abhorrent.[61]

The foregoing discussion has focused on examples that illustrate the physical sources of contamination beliefs. The point is not that people always found elimination or sexual acts or childbirth or corpses disgusting, but that the physical residues

The procession was headed by *kanēphoroi* (basket-bearers), girls of high social status and unquestioned virginity who carried baskets containing ritual implements for the sacrifice.[92] Other Athenian women and girls also marched in the procession, as shown on the east side of the Parthenon frieze; their roles probably pertained to traditional elements of the festival which predated the early sixth-century reorganization, such as the preparation of cakes for Athena by *alētrides* ("provisioners") and the weaving by *arrhēphoroi* ("bearers of sacred things") and *ergastinai* ("female workers") of the robe to be presented to the goddess.[93] Just as the priestess of Athena Polias was drawn from the aristocratic clan of the Eteoboutadai, these ritual roles were to be filled by well-born women and girls.

By our lights, the procession already appears more inclusive than the competitions, because both genders participate. Yet this is a conservative element of the festival, reflecting the tendency for goddesses to be served by priestesses and other female attendants. From the perspective of social class, it is highly exclusive. The noble birth and high social status of the *kanēphoroi* were further enhanced by their attendants: the daughters of metics (resident foreigners) carried parasols to shade the *kanēphoroi* from the sun, and stools for them to sit on later in the proceedings. Holding a parasol or carrying belongings for another person was a servile function, and yet metics were free men and women, often wealthy, who made important economic contributions to the city. The metic men themselves wore special purple tunics and served as *skaphēphoroi* ("tray-bearers"), carrying trays of cakes and honeycombs to be offered to the goddess.

Metics' participation in other Athenian civic cults was very limited. On the one hand, their presence in the procession seems inclusive, an attempt by the organizers to recognize the contributions of different segments of society, including non-citizens. But in spite of the fact that they walked in the procession, the metics' roles had no cultic significance. Their presence served mainly to increase the dignity of those who were participating as Athenians. Would the metics and their daughters have viewed holding a parasol for an Athenian girl, or carrying a tray of food up to the Akropolis, as a humiliation or as a privilege? The answer may well have varied with the individual, but there is evidence that their participation was prescribed by law, which suggests that metics were not lining up for the chance to be tray- and stool-bearers.[94]

Although the exact order of all the marchers is not known, those carrying ritual implements or otherwise involved in conducting and supplying the sacrifice probably came after the *kanēphoroi*. These included musicians and water carriers (males on the Parthenon frieze, but daughters of metics in the literary sources). The next large group is likely to have been made up of elected Athenian civic and military officials. Hoplite warriors are notably absent from the Parthenon frieze, where we would expect them to appear if they made up a distinct stage of the parade. However, there are two pieces of evidence for a contingent of hoplites. The first comes from the sixth-century Niarchos band cup, which shows what is probably (but not certainly) an early representation of the Panathenaia, including a group of shield-bearing men. The second is Thucydides' remark that after the assassination of Hipparchos, Hippias went "to the hoplites who were in the procession" and disarmed them. The custom of marching in arms may have been discontinued after the sixth century, but the sources disagree on this point.[95]

Another group included on the Niarchos cup is the *thallophoroi* ("branch-bearers"). According to Xenophon (*Symp.* 4.17), "handsome" old men were chosen for this office.[96] Such branch-bearers are commonly found in religious processions, so these old men were probably part of the Archaic festival. Their inclusion in the procession is interesting because it accounts for an additional segment of Athenian society, the elderly citizens, and gives them a place in the festival where otherwise they would have been marginalized in both the athletic and sacrificial/ritual spheres.

In the 440s, the Athenians legislated a requirement that each of their allies send a cow and a panoply to the procession. These gifts were paraded in the procession and escorted by representatives from the allied cities. Colonists were expected to participate in the same way, although their case was different because colonies normally recognized a religious tie to the mother-city. These levies raise questions similar to those we saw for the metics. It has been suggested that the intent of the decree was inclusive, and that sharing in the sacrifice was a privilege not lightly granted, yet the scholarly consensus is that the allies' contributions, like their tribute payments, were essentially coerced.[97] These forms of inclusiveness, then, provided a public, ritualized opportunity for the citizens in the democracy to set themselves apart from non-citizens. The hereditary nature of citizenship was at issue in the mid-fifth century; Perikles' citizenship decree of 451/50 must have increased the gap in status between citizens on the one hand and metics or allies on the other. The Classical procession was a performance of political unity, but not of equality, under Athens' imperial power.[98]

Victors in the citizen contests perhaps marched somewhere in the middle of the procession, particularly those in the showy *apobatēs* race, featured on the Parthenon frieze. The frieze includes large numbers of cavalry, who close the official procession in grand style. The heavy participation of the cavalry (together with the absence of marching hoplites) seems to link the frieze to the aristocratic warrior ethos on display in the citizen athletic competitions. On the other hand, the south frieze depicts the cavalry in ten ranks, an arrangement which alludes to the ten democratic tribes.[99]

The non-wealthy, non-aristocratic majority of citizens, it seems, had no designated place or special representation in the procession. A mid-fourth-century law regulating the Lesser Panathenaia, however, shows that the general citizenry was allotted a place in this annual version of the festival parade:

> The overseers of the sacred things (*hieropoioi*) along with the cattle-buyers, when they have bought the cows from the 41 minas rent from the New Land and have sent off the procession for the goddess, are to sacrifice all these cows on the great altar of Athena after they have selected one of the most beautiful cows for sacrifice on the altar of Nike, and when they have sacrificed them to Athena Polias and Athena Nike, let them distribute the meat from all the cows bought from the 41 minas to the Athenian people in the Kerameikos as in the other distributions of meat. They are to distribute the portions to each deme according to the numbers of members of the procession that each deme provides.
>
> (*IG* II$^2$ 334 lines 16–27, ca. 335)[100]

Athenian citizens could be organized either by tribes, a political designation, or by demes, a geographical one (the demes were the towns and villages in the territory of Attica). In this case, each demesman who had marched in the parade received meat. Modern calculations suggest that forty-one minas would have purchased about fifty cows, each of which would have yielded 100 kg of meat.[101] This means that the fourth-century procession must have included thousands of citizens, most likely as an informal body of marchers following the cavalry who traditionally closed the procession. We do not know whether this type of parade participation by the general citizenry was a long tradition, or whether (as seems more likely) it began only ca. 335 when this law was passed. Because the law prescribes the use of income from "the New Land" (*Nea*), it suggests that new money was being put toward the annual festival.[102] The other question is whether the provisions in this law reflect similar arrangements for the Greater Panathenaia. During the height of the Athenian empire in the fifth century, more than two hundred cows at a time were sacrificed, which points to a broad distribution of meat to citizens (though not necessarily to their participation in the parade). The ideology of Athenian democracy involved the idea that poor members of the citizen body (*dēmos*) were entitled to sacrificial meat at public expense. The anti-democratic "Old Oligarch," who was opposed to such redistributions of wealth, observes,

> As for sacrifices and sacrificial victims and festivals and sacred lands, the citizen body, knowing each one of the poor is not able to sacrifice and feast and banquet and live in a great and beautiful city, has found a way for these things to be. And so the polis sacrifices many victims at public expense, but it is the members of the citizen body who feast and share the victims.
>
> (Xen. [*Ath. Pol.*] 2.9)

Most citizens, therefore, probably expected to be fed a meat meal during the Greater Panathenaia, either from the Akropolis sacrifice or from tribal banquets subsidized by wealthy citizens. As Victoria Wohl put it, "The *dēmos* got a free meal and a good show."[103]

The Panathenaic procession during the mid-fifth century was certainly not representative of the actual population of Athens, or of "Athenian society" as a whole. The city's numerous slaves were completely excluded, so far as we know.[104] All women except for aristocrats and the wealthy were excluded, and the daughters of rich non-citizens were assigned the "privilege" of attending their social betters. Can the procession be described instead as representative of the democracy, the body of citizen men? As we have seen, officials of the city were featured prominently in the parade. To the degree that they were elected or obtained office by random allotment, these men were representative of the *dēmos*. The cavalry too was marshaled by tribes, so that (as in the athletic events), every tribe and thus every citizen were represented – even if most citizens could not afford to own a horse. Although there may have been a contingent of hoplites, the fifth-century parade seemingly contained no "populist" component specifically designed to recognize the poorer citizens or the citizen body as such. The citizen status of the majority was recognized instead through a different mechanism of the festival, the distribution of sacrificial meat.[105]

Although the Classical Panathenaic festival aimed to increase the pride Athenians felt in their polis, its ritual arrangements reveal only a limited embrace of populist, egalitarian values. The restriction of many athletic events to Athenian citizens, and the introduction of subsidized team events, made athletic victories more accessible to the poor, yet athletics remained primarily the preserve of rich aristocrats. As Athens' imperial power grew, the participation of metics, allies and colonists in the parade emphasized the power of the Athenian *dēmos*, yet hoplites and demesmen as such are conspicuously absent from the Parthenon frieze.[106] Ordinary citizens may not have marched until the mid-fourth century. The emphasis instead was on the political unity of the empire, the corporate power of the Athenian state, and the martial and athletic prowess of its foremost citizens.

The rules for participation in both the Panathenaic games and the festival procession classified people into a complex hierarchy in which status was determined by age, gender, citizenship, wealth and social class. The use of ritual to instantiate these status distinctions was typical of Greek religion. Although it was more elaborate than many other festival processions, the Panathenaic festival also illustrates the general principle that the gods' affairs were embedded in civic life. Over time, the organization of the festival changed in response to political developments. Both games and procession were modified to accommodate the switch to democracy, and later, the growth of empire. Each time changes were made, the ritual arrangements reinforced existing social roles, demonstrating that even in a democracy, some were more equal than others.

## ESSAY 3.2: DANCING FOR THE GODS

To moderns, the centrality of dance in Greek religion is a surprise.[107] Performed by groups of dancers matched in age and gender, choral dances were as ubiquitous at festivals as animal sacrifice and feasting. Together, feasting and dance point to another aspect of Greek religion which is less familiar in the Abrahamic traditions of Judaism, Christianity and Islam: by design, Greek religious activity provided regular opportunities for physical pleasure. Indeed, the creation of a pleasurable experience to be shared with the gods was an essential goal of the festival.[108]

Dance is a human universal. We may define "dance" as any intentionally rhythmical, culturally patterned movement of the body that is distinguished from ordinary motor activities and has aesthetic value. The roots of the human capacity for dance seem to lie in the instinctive rhythmic motor displays of animals, which figure in sexual selection, bonding, territorial marking and social hierarchy.[109] Though human dance often involves similarly basic concerns, it is far more complex and variable. Still, dance is fundamentally a form of display, and its special ability to attract and hold our attention is traceable to its evolutionary origins. Dance produces affect in performer and spectator alike. Both the innate urge to dance and its cognitive salience are factors in its transmission, although its exact forms are constantly changing.[110]

Like ritual behavior, dance is extraordinary: it differs noticeably from mundane movement and is a purposeful activity without a transparent goal.[111] Among the Greeks, dance was a communal activity, usually performed by groups called choruses, accompanied by one or more musicians. Choruses competed during festivals, and dance was regularly incorporated into other ritual actions, such as processions. For the Greeks, dance (together with music and vocal performance) had two principal functions, both of which were related to religion. First, dance was a splendid offering to the gods. Second, dance was a key element in traditional programs of education and socialization.

We tend to equate "education" first and foremost with literacy, but in the mostly oral culture of the Archaic and early Classical Greeks, *paideia* (the training of the child, *pais*) referred primarily to musical education (*mousikē*): learning to sing, dance and play musical instruments. As late as the fourth century, Plato (*Leg.* 654a–b) could still define the uneducated man as one unable to dance and sing in a chorus. Especially for boys, *paideia* included athletic training as well. The physicality of Greek education matched the high cultural value placed on youth, strength and agility, but this should not obscure the cognitive aspects of a rigorous education in dance and athletics. Dance in particular requires significant memory skills.[112] It is also a principal means of instilling gender roles, for traditional dances the world over are characterized by stereotypically masculine and feminine postures and movements.[113] This education in the physical habitus of the ideal man and woman was inseparable from religious education, for knowledge of the local gods, goddesses, heroes and heroines, what Claude Calame has called the community's "mythic patrimony," was transmitted through dances and songs.[114]

Greek dance uniquely engaged both performers and spectators. Research on the "embodied cognition" of dance reveals that observation of dance activates the sensorimotor areas of the brain. We perceive dance by an interior mirroring of the movement not only in the brain but also in the muscles. Learning to dance is cognitively distinct from, say, learning to read, because it involves this embodied imitation of a model, even when we are merely observing. The mirroring effect is stronger when the observer is a trained dancer. Finally, aesthetic pleasure in dance is increased when a test subject has experienced physical training in the steps.[115] Greek festivals therefore involved informed observation of (performing) dancers by (spectator) dancers, high levels of attentional focus on the dance and a high degree of connoisseurship. As expert dancers themselves, the gods were assumed to participate in the distinctive communal bond thus created. The finding that the perception and learning of dance engage the brain/body "mirror system" may also shed light on the special role of *mimēsis* (imitation) in Greek dances. That is, mental and physical imitation is so fundamental to dance that it was conceptualized as reproduction of movement, whether divine, human or animal.[116]

The most detailed description of divine dance occurs in the Homeric *Hymn to Apollo* (3.182–206), where the Muses sing a hymn, after which the Charites (Graces), Horai (Seasons), Harmonia, Hebe (Youth) and Aphrodite perform a ring-dance, with Artemis as the chorus leader. Ares and Hermes "sport" among them, executing acrobatic movements. All the while Apollo plays the lyre, stepping high and gladdening the hearts of his proud parents, Leto and Zeus. Later Apollo uses the same high-stepping movement as he leads a procession of paean-singing Cretans to establish his own worship at Delphi.[117] According to Plato, dance was not merely taught by the gods – it was a pleasurable activity through which gods became present to humans during worship:

> So the gods, pitying the human race born to a weary fate, allotted them the festivals for gods as a restful recompense. And as sharers in the festival, they gave the Muses and Apollo, Leader of the Muses, and Dionysos, in order that humans might set right their upbringing in festivals with the gods. We said that these very gods who were given as our fellows in the chorus, have also been givers of the pleasurable perception of rhythm and harmony, whereby they cause us to move and lead our choruses, connecting us with each other by songs and dances.
>
> (Plat. *Leg.* 653d–54a)

While Artemis, Apollo and Dionysos were closely associated with music and dance, the most consistent dancers in the Greek pantheon were not the Olympian gods but a wide variety of minor deities who functioned as their attendants. The Muses themselves formed a chorus around Apollo, but there were also the Charites, Horai and nymphs, who attended Aphrodite, Artemis and other goddesses. The satyrs, silens and mainads danced around Dionysos, while Pan, the Kouretes and the Korybantes were linked to the figures of Meter, Kybele and Rhea. These collectives were mythic counterparts of choral dancers whose costumes, musical styles and dance movements were appropriate to each deity.[118]

While Greek dances were transmitted via the human cognitive and physiological "mirror system," and were understood to be imitations of divine models, they also involved a third level of *mimēsis* in the specific movements executed by the performers. For example, the Pyrrhic dance imitated movements used in combat, while an entire genre of dance, the *hyporchēma*, was devoted to miming of narratives.[119] In the remainder of this essay, we will first examine the role of dance at Sparta, a city renowned for its devotion to dance and song, especially in the cults of Artemis and Apollo. We will then consider Greek dances for Dionysos, with a focus on a genre of cult song known as the dithyramb.

## Spartan dancers

The Archaic and Classical Spartan state was predicated on the political equality of its male citizens and its iron hold over subject peoples, the Lakonian and Messenian helots. The labor of these serfs left the Spartans free to devote themselves to the interrelated pursuits of military training, physical fitness, musical education and worship.[120] At Sparta, the characteristic Greek love of competition was institutionalized on many levels. Dance was a prime arena for the display of excellence, as well as the assignment of praise and criticism.

According to Plutarch, the Spartan lawgiver Lykourgos ordained that girls, like boys, should receive training in gymnastics. He also accustomed the girls to walk in processions naked, and at certain festivals to dance and sing, making pointed comments about the boys who were present:

> Sometimes they mocked and usefully chided those who had failed, and again they sang the praises of those who were worthy, arousing feelings of ambition and zeal in the youths, for he who was praised for his manliness and brilliance among the maidens went away greatly honored because of their praise, while the sting of their biting jokes was no less sharp than criticism given in earnest, especially because it was delivered in the sight of the kings, the elders and the rest of the citizens.
>
> (Plut. *Lyc.* 14)

The fact that musician-poets like Alcman were hired to compose songs for the girls suggests that the Spartan leadership self-consciously used the institution of the chorus to enforce gender norms and create competitive rivalries in both boys and girls. Although the girls voiced praise and blame, the words they sang were not necessarily their own.[121] An example is preserved in a small fragment of Alcman, which praises the dancing skills of certain youths:

> And you lead the Dymainai, Hagesidamos, a god-beloved chorus-leader, glorious son of Damotimos . . . sons of Tyndareus . . . spear . . .
>
> . . . admirable and desirable chorus leaders; for they are young men of our own age, dear, with neither beard nor mustache.
>
> (Alcman fr. 10 *PMG*)

Rituals involving mockery, however, have an improvisational character, and the Archaic tradition may have developed from a less formal one in which the girls gave voice to their own words.

Girls too were subjected to detailed evaluation of their appearance and skills, framed as competition. Maiden dances (*partheneia*) formed a recognized choral genre, an important function of which was to display the beauty of the dancers to potential suitors and their families.[122] To some degree, however, these contests were rigged, because social rank was an important factor in the calculation of "the most beautiful," the girl who would act as the leader of the chorus (*chorēgos*). This convention is already apparent in the *Odyssey*, when the poet compares the princess Nausikaa, the most beautiful of her age-mates, to Artemis among her nymphs:

> When she and her handmaids had enjoyed food,
> They threw off their veils and played with a ball,
> And white-armed Nausikaa was leader of the dance.
> Just as the archer Artemis runs over the mountains,
> Along towering Taygetos or Erymanthos,

Taking delight in boars and swift deer,
And with her play the daughters of aigis-bearing Zeus
The nymphs of the wild – and Leto is glad at heart,
For Artemis holds her head above them all,
Easy to recognize, though all are beautiful—
So did the unwed maiden outshine her servants.

(Hom. *Od.* 99–109)

An early example of a maiden song is the Louvre *Partheneion*, composed by Alcman in the seventh century for a chorus of Spartan girls, and dedicated to an unknown goddess.[123] In it, the dancers praise their two most beautiful members, Agido and Hagesichora, whose names evoke the idea of the chorus leader. In an allusion to their fine breeding, both are compared to prize racehorses, and their dance may have been choreographed to match these images:

Don't you see?
The racehorse is Venetic: and the mane
Of my cousin
Hagesichora blooms
Like imperishable gold
And her face is silver.
Why do I tell you openly?
This is Hagesichora.
But whoever is second to Agido in beauty
Will run like a Kolaxian horse against an Ibenian.

(Alcman fr. 1.50–9 *PMG*)

Given that the girls sang these complex songs as they danced, their movements are unlikely to have been highly energetic. There are scattered hints, however, that some Spartan girls' and women's dances, particularly certain dances for Artemis, were fast-paced and wild, performed with cymbals or tambourines. The ancient lexicographers list these and describe them as "Bacchic" in character, but of these dances, their contexts, and the age and social class of the performers, we know very little.[124]

In his travelogue of Greece, Pausanias mentions traditional maiden dances for Artemis at Karyai, which were still being performed in the Roman period:

> From the straight road, the third branch on the right leads to Karyai ("The Nut Trees") and to the sanctuary of Artemis. Karyai belongs to Artemis and the nymphs, and in the open air stands an image of Artemis Karyatis. Here the Lakedaimonian maidens set up choruses every year, and they have a local style of dance.
>
> (Paus. 3.10.7)

At Karyai, the mimetic character of the dance was apparent in Artemis' association with the nymphs, goddesses of the wild places who formed the divine counterpart to the human chorus. As in the passage from the *Odyssey*, Artemis herself must have been visualized in the role of divine *chorēgos*. So famous was this dance that it became emblematic of Spartan culture.[125] In Sparta, as in most parts of the Greek world, Artemis presided over the maturation of girls. Above all, the period ruled by Artemis was one of uncertainty and danger, encompassing the introduction of the *parthenos* to the community, her first experience of sex, and the pregnancy which followed. Interestingly, the spatial arrangement of Artemis' sanctuaries also expresses this concept of "dangerous passage," for they were typically situated in remote areas, on borderlands, at mountain passes or overlooking narrow straits. Dancing for Artemis required travel to one of these sanctuaries, many of which were linked to legendary or historical instances of violent conflict. Legends of the abduction of *parthenoi* from choruses by enemy Messenians were attached to the Spartan cults of Artemis at Karyai (near the border with Arkadia) and Limnai (on the border with Messenia). As early as Homer, Greek myths told of girls abducted as they danced for Artemis. Even the young Helen, it was said, had been abducted from Sparta itself as she danced for Artemis Orthia. A girl's performance in the goddess's chorus was a rite of passage of concern to all citizens, for the safety of its most vulnerable members was an index of the Spartan state's security.[126]

Once a Spartan girl married, her opportunities to dance were fewer. Males, on the other hand, danced regularly from childhood and throughout their adult lives. The themes of competition and social control recur in Plutarch's description of Spartan music, which he says involved praise of those who had died for Sparta, censure of cowards, and "summons and boasts of valor":

> At their festivals they set up three choruses according to the three ages, and the chorus of old men sang first:
> *We were stout-hearted youths once!*
> Then the chorus of men in their prime sang in response:
> *We are now, look and see if you like!*
> And the third chorus, composed of boys, sang:
> *We will be better by far!*
>
> (Plut. *Lyc*. 21)[127]

Spartan male choruses were organized around three great summer festivals associated with Apollo, the god who governed male maturation and citizenship. At the festival of the Hyakinthia, Apollo of Amyklai, a colossal bronze god portrayed as a helmeted warrior, was celebrated in traditional dance: "Numerous choruses of youths came to sing the poetry of their hometowns (*poiēmatōn epichōriōn*), and dancers mingling among them performed steps in the ancient fashion to the double flute and the song" (Polykrates in Athen. *Deip*. 5.17 [139e]). Despite the ideology of homogeneity adopted by the Spartan state, the "epichoric" or distinctively local nature of each dance was a matter of pride. Such songs celebrated the heroes and heroines native to each region of the polis.[128]

With regard to dancing, perhaps the most famous of the Spartan festivals was the Gymnopaidiai, named for the characteristic choral dance which was performed in the nude, in a dedicated part of the agora called the "dance floor" (*choros*). This may have been the festival (mentioned earlier) with three choruses of different ages. Athenaeus (14.30 [631b]) tells us that the movements of the *gumnopaidikē* imitated those of wrestlers. The display of the dancers' bodies advertised their masculinity and fitness for battle as well as their citizen status. The festival was tied to legends of Sparta's struggle with Argos over a disputed border area called Thyrea. The chorus leaders wore "Thyreatic" wreaths commemorating the city's victory. Pausanias' comment (3.11.9) that the Spartans "took this festival seriously" is supported by the story that when news arrived during the Gymnopaidiai of their crushing defeat by the Thebans at Leuktra, the Spartan ephors did not stop the performance of the men's chorus but, on the contrary, allowed it to continue.[129]

Finally, the festival of Karneia, focusing on Apollo as an archetypal leader in the domains of warfare and colonization, was widespread among Dorian Greeks. At Sparta, it included a famed musical competition. This was an honor appropriate for Apollo, and although specifics are lacking, there must have been dancing. Together with the tests and challenges of Spartan military training (known as the *agōgē*), male participation in these festivals formed a program leading to adulthood, marriage and citizen status.[130]

## Dancing for Dionysos

Dionysos' boisterous mythical retinue consisted of female mainads and male satyrs or silens, whose intoxicated revels, danced to the stimulating music of the double flute (*aulos*), were complementary to the choruses ordered by Apollo's harmonious lyre. In ritual, the worshipers of Dionysos imitated his disorderly divine companions. Similarly disruptive behavior is attested in Carnival traditions around the world, which are interpreted by some scholars as a ritual means of reaffirming existing norms through a temporary enactment of deviance and license, and by others as actual drivers of social change.[131] Ritually and in myth, Dionysos was represented as an "arriving" god, a deity whose periodic advent, ostensibly from "outside" the community, brought both disruption and renewal.[132] The most characteristic and indispensable feature of his rituals was dance.

In myth, females who resisted the worship of Dionysos were driven raving into the mountains, "madwomen" (*mainades*) who rejected the social role of the wife, murdered their own children and tore animals limb from limb to eat their flesh raw. Historical mainadism was, in contrast, a controlled, periodic and far milder ritual expression of the deviant impulse, represented as an "imitation" of the mainads of old. Many Greek cities held festivals every other year in which married women led privately organized groups in revelry for the god.[133] In the opening lines of Euripides' *Bacchae*, Dionysos explains why he has come to Thebes after traveling through Lydia, Phrygia, Persia and the rest of the world:

> After causing those peoples to dance (*choreusas*), and establishing
> My secret rites (*teletas*), I have come to this city first among the Greeks,
> That I might be manifest as a god to mortals.
>
> (Eur. *Bacch.* 20–22)

Dionysos characterizes the two key elements of his worship as dance and a ritual "accomplishment" or "fulfillment" known as *teletē*. Originally this special element must have been possession by the god: in a ritual pattern well known to anthropologists, a trance state (what the Greeks called *mania*) was achieved through the rhythmic stimulation of music and dance.[134] By the end of the sixth century, however, *teletē* might also refer, as it did in the Eleusinian Mysteries (Essay 5.1), to a ritual transformation which brought the initiate a blessed afterlife.

Dionysiac revelry, trance and transformation were not restricted to women. The private Bacchic worship group (*thiasos*) could be mixed-gender, though most civic rituals for the god were assigned either to males of varying age or to married women.[135] Men had their own distinctive modes of worshiping Dionysos, which involved wine consumption, dance and the temporary rejection of their normal social identities. In particular, males costumed as satyrs or silens, with mask, prominent phallos and tail, are attested in several interrelated Archaic genres of performance dedicated to Dionysos: *kōmos* (revel-song), *dithurambos*, satyr play and early comedy. (The first two are in some contexts synonymous.)[136] In its first and simplest form, the dithyramb was likely a processional hymn, sung as a drunken party of men led a sacrificial ox or goat to the altar of Dionysos. The earliest evidence is a fragment by the seventh-century poet and mercenary Archilochus, who sang,

> I know how to lead the beautiful song of Lord Dionysos,
> The dithyramb, while my wits are thunderstruck with wine.
> (Fr. 120 West)

These dances were performed in a rowdy fashion with plenty of sexual humor. What may be fragments of another dithyramb by Archilochus refer to female breasts and genitals as "unripe grapes" and "sweet figs," and mention someone called "the Screwer," possibly the god himself.[137] Masking and mumming were important components in early dithyrambs, and animal costumes were especially popular. According to a dithyramb of Pindar (fr. 70b, 22–3 Maehler), Dionysos "is charmed even by dancing herds of beasts."[138] Mummery in the guise of animals or animal-human hybrids enabled men to temporarily assume a "bestial" identity through disorderly behavior, hedonism and hypersexuality, yet this license was balanced by the discipline of the choral performance itself. What pleased Dionysos was not mere bestiality but beasts who danced in synchrony.[139]

By the early sixth century, some Dionysiac dances seem to have involved a narrative component to be mimed and sung by the dancers. A favorite subject in Athens was the return to Olympos of a drunken Hephaistos, escorted by Dionysos and his companions. Another early theme may have been the celebration of Dionysos' wedding to Ariadne.[140] The traditional subject of the dithyramb itself was the birth of Dionysos, an event laden with symbolic evocations of divine epiphany and triumph over death. Such performances were predecessors of the later theatrical genres of satyr play, tragedy and early comedy. Dance was integral to each of these, and each, like the dithyramb, took place in the theater, which originated as a public dancing space dedicated to Dionysos. At Athens, the god's altar stood at the center of the dance floor, and his statue was brought to the theater at festival time to view the performances staged for his pleasure.

Like the other theatrical genres, the dithyramb sustained many changes over time. The first major development took place ca. 600, when the musician Arion is supposed to have introduced a circular dance around the altar as part of the dithyrambic procession in Corinth. According to legend, Arion was rescued from pirates by a friendly dolphin, and his innovation was associated with the movement of dolphins, who swim in a straight line, and then stop to "dance" by leaping in a circular motion. The dancing dolphin motif was widely disseminated, together with the dithyramb, in Greek cities throughout the Mediterranean. Arion's legend reveals that the dithyramb was conceptually aligned with the new maritime mobility, connectivity and prosperity of the Greek states in the Archaic period, phenomena which weakened the power of the land-based nobility. Dancing and singing the dithyramb for Dionysos, a god whose popularity burgeoned during the sixth century, became an activity emblematic of the Hellenic identity and citizen status.[141]

During the Classical period, Greek hymns, like other poetic genres, were increasingly treated as commodities. Dionysiac festivals especially, with their characteristic competitions, created an insatiable hunger for new material, while the technology of writing permitted poets a creative license they had never before enjoyed. In Athens alone, the newly formed democracy (ca. 508) recruited a thousand citizen men and boys every year to dance in twenty dithyrambic choruses organized by tribe. The economic impact of the Athenian *chorēgia*, the civic duty to costume and train choruses, must have rivaled that of the sacrificial economy.[142] The intensive citizen participation in dance, meanwhile, created a culture of expert performers and spectators.

To ask how "religious" their experience was, as opposed to patriotic or educational or aesthetic, is anachronistic, yet it is worth noting that when the dithyramb, like the other theatrical genres, became a vehicle of intense creativity during the fifth century, its subject matter did not remain limited to Dionysos. Of Bacchylides' six extant dithyrambs, only one (Bacch. 19) explicitly mentions the god; instead they focus on the adventures of heroes (Theseus, Herakles) and heroines (Io, Marpessa). On the other hand, Pindar's Theban dithyramb evokes the awe-inspiring spectacle of the gods themselves dancing in heaven to honor Dionysos.[143] The dithyrambs of the late Classical period were characterized by a new musical style and a fervent, devotional focus on Dionysos, with elaborate invocations. This "new music" drew condemnation from critics both ancient and modern – and was wildly popular in its time. The religious zeal of these hymns, together with their popularity, points to the continued vibrancy of the genre in the worship of Dionysos.[144]

## ESSAY 3.3: THE KYRENE CATHARTIC LAW

An inscription on two sides of a marble stele, the Kyrene cathartic law was discovered in present-day Libya in the ruins of one of the most prosperous Greek poleis of the ancient Mediterranean.[145] Kyrene was founded in the seventh century by Dorian colonists from the Aegean island of Thera, and the dialect of the law reflects their distinctive speech. The inscription itself dates to the late fourth century – that is, the beginning of the Hellenistic period, after the death of Alexander the Great. Although many aspects of the text remain enigmatic, the law is one of our earliest and most detailed examples of a written code addressing purity and pollution. In the following translation, material in square brackets indicates restored text or gaps where the inscription is damaged, and material in parentheses has been added for explanatory purposes.

> A.1–3: APOLLO DECREED that (the Kyrenaians) should live in Libya [forever (?)] observing methods of purification and states of purity and [supplication (?)].

Unlike many other sacred "laws," this text has a good claim to be regarded as a set of rules promulgated by the state. Toward the end of the fourth century, the Kyrenaians seem to have decided to gather a group of regulations that existed in written form in various sanctuaries, and to combine them into a standard code. Once composed, this code was presented to Apollo at Delphi for approval. Side A begins by stating that the code deals with *katharmoi*, "methods of purification," and *hagnēiai*, "pure states" as well as another unknown topic, perhaps concerning the "visitants" who appear at the end of the code.

> A.4–7: If disease [or famine(?)] or death should come against the country or the city, sacrifice in front of the gates [in front of] the shrine of aversion (?) to Apollo the Averter a red billy goat.

The instructions for averting harm from the city combined sympathetic magic with an appeal to divine agency. On the one hand, Apollo Apotropaios (Averter) belonged to a class of gods whose images were placed at the city gates, facing outward. Thus he stood squarely in the path of any noxious powers attempting to enter. Apollo himself was a plague god, but his arrows could be positioned to point away from the city, and his favor could be sought by means of a sacrifice.[146] This prescription illustrates the conceptual overlap between the aversion of danger or sickness and the cleansing of pollution. A similar overlap appears later in the text of the inscription (B.29–39), where magic is used to expel a hostile spirit from a house.

> A.8–10: Wood growing in a sanctuary. If you pay the god the price, you can use the wood for sacred, profane, and polluted purposes.

Many cult regulations included prohibitions on using the wood from trees in sanctuaries, or other natural resources, such as water from springs. Everything within the boundaries of a sanctuary belonged to the god(s) of the place, and its unauthorized use or removal was a religious offense. In this case (probably pertaining specifically to Apollo's sanctuary), wood was available for any use. The parties to the transaction were not the user and the priest but the user and Apollo. The law distinguished between sacred (*hiara*), profane (*babala*) and polluted (*miara*) uses. Sacred use would have included lighting a fire on an altar for sacrifice, profane uses meant ordinary activities like crafting or cooking, and polluted use probably meant the burning of corpses or anything unclean. Thus the categories of "sacred" (or pure) and "polluted" were two extremes, each set apart from the mundane, neutral category of the profane.[147]

> A.11–15: Coming from a woman a man, if he has slept with her by night, can sacrifice [whatever/wherever] he wishes. If he has slept with her by day, he can, after washing [. . .] go wherever he wishes, except to [(two lines missing)].

Again, this probably has to do with the sanctuary of Apollo. A man who wished to sacrifice might do so even if he had recently had sex, so long as the act had taken place at night. Presumably the standard ritual lustration with water from a basin outside the sanctuary (Figure 3.3) was sufficient purification in such cases; this consisted of sprinkling water in a circle around oneself.[148]

Having sex during the daytime was more polluting, perhaps because it was more visible. As we have seen, Hesiod (*Op.* 727–8) similarly gave instructions not to urinate during the daytime, and especially not facing the sun.

> A.16–20: The woman in childbed shall pollute the roof. She shall [pollute the person under the roof, but] she shall not pollute the person outside the roof, unless he comes under it. Any person who is inside shall be polluted for three days, but shall not pollute another, no matter where the person goes.

The regulation carefully defined exactly who was affected by childbirth pollution. The source was the mother. All who lived in the house (family members, slaves and any other residents) and all who visited it were polluted for the next three days, though they were not "contagious." Pollution was not tied to kinship, but physical proximity to the source. In regulations from other cities, we read that a priest or priestess might be prohibited from visiting at all, until the end of a prescribed period. Tokens were hung on the door (in Attica, an olive wreath for a boy and a piece of wool for a girl) to announce the event. People who were particularly scrupulous or anxious about pollution, such as the "god-fearing man" described by Theophrastus, might avoid houses where a birth or death had recently occurred, in order not to expose themselves to the taint.[149]

> A.21–5: There is permission for everyone, both profane and pure, with respect to the Untiring Ones. There is not permission for one who is pure, coming from any place where a man died, except from the man Battos the Leader, and the Tritopateres and from Onymastos the Delphian. With respect to the shrines, there is permission for everyone.

*Figure 3.3* Stone *perirrhantērion* (water basin for purification) from the sanctuary of Poseidon at Isthmia, ca. 660. The basin is supported by female figures who hold the tails of lions (mostly missing). Heads of sacrificed rams are placed between the figures. Archaeological Museum, Corinth. Photo: Gianni Dagli Orti/Art Resource

This difficult passage addresses whether it was religiously permissible (*hosiā [esti]*) for people of two ritual statuses, the pure (*hagnoi*) and the profane (*babaloi*), to visit certain sanctuaries. The "pure" were perhaps members of priesthoods subject to special purity requirements, while the "profane" likely included everyone other than murderers, who would have been excluded from all shrines. Although the syntax of the regulation is perplexing, it seems to have prohibited "the pure" from visiting places associated with death, such as graveyards or houses where people had died. If they visited such places anyway, their pure status was compromised.

There were several exceptions to this rule. The pure could freely visit the tomb of Battos the Leader, the heroized founder of the colony (for more on Battos, see Essay 5.3). Likewise, they could visit the shrine of the Tritopateres, who were ancestral spirits and thus connected with the dead, as well as the tomb of another local hero, Onymastos. Greek cities normally required that all dead be buried outside the city limits, but special exceptions were made for the tombs of heroes and heroines.

The Akamantes ("Untiring Ones" or perhaps "Undying Ones") mentioned in line 21 are probably either heroes or ancestral spirits like the Tritopateres. Which shrines or rites are meant in the final line (25) is unknown, but the author may have intended a contrast between heroes/ancestors and gods.[150]

> A.26–31: If he sacrifices on an altar a victim which it is not customary to sacrifice, let him remove the fatty residue (?) from the altar and wash it off and remove the other filth from the shrine and take away the ashes from the altar and take away the fire to a pure spot. And then let him wash himself, purify the shrine, sacrifice a full-grown animal as a penalty, and then let him sacrifice as is customary.

Gods often required certain sacrificial animals and prohibited others from their altars. The species most often rejected were pig and goat (perhaps because these animals had a reputation for eating anything, including dung), but the Greeks lacked any consistent rules of this sort.[151]

At Kyrene, it was a religious offense to attempt to sacrifice the wrong species or an animal unfit in some other way. In this rule, the remains of the offending animal were conceptualized as the source of the pollution and described as "filth" (*luma*). All the remains, including the ashes of any burned portions, were to be removed and the shrine thoroughly cleaned, while the fire was kept alight elsewhere. The erring worshiper also had to wash himself because he had been in contact with the filth. "Purifying the shrine" probably meant fumigation, a common cathartic technique in which the purifier used smoke, often fortified with acrid-smelling sulphur, to drive out the pollution.[152]

> A.32: A man is bound as far as his brother's children.

This rule defined the relationship between religious obligation and kinship. In other words, in the event that an individual was unable to pay his debt to a god, his father or paternal uncles could be required to do so on his behalf.

> A.33–42: If a grown man is subject to a tenth, having purified himself with blood he shall purify the shrine (of Apollo). After being sold in the marketplace for the most that he is worth, he shall make a preliminary sacrifice, before the tenth, of a full-grown animal, not from the tenth, and then he shall sacrifice the tenth and carry it away to a pure spot. (If the procedure is) otherwise, the same measures will still be necessary. Everyone who sacrifices shall bring a vessel.

If a boy is polluted involuntarily, it is sufficient for him to purify himself and a penalty is not necessary. If he is polluted voluntarily, he shall purify the shrine and, as a penalty, make a preliminary sacrifice of a full-grown animal.

The custom of the "tenth" (*dekatē*) involved tithing a portion of one's gains (conventionally but not universally a tenth) to a god as a thank offering. At Kyrene, as elsewhere, the practice was especially connected with Apollo, and inscriptions record tithes of military spoils and other profits.[153] In this law, however, tithing pertains not to voluntary offerings but to penalties incurred for offenses specific to males. The nature of these offenses is unclear, but given that "grown men" are contrasted with "boys" as potential offenders, they may have had to do with misconduct related to the festivals over which Apollo presided; these were much concerned with the socialization of youths and the admission of adult males to citizen status. If a man became *dekatos*, subject to a tenth, a humiliating mock sale was held to determine his "worth."[154] Presumably he was then required to pay a tenth of this amount to the god in the form of sacrifices, but not until he had made a preliminary sacrifice as well. The law was far more lenient on boys who incurred pollution, regardless of whether it was voluntarily. The juxtaposition of the grown man with the boy (*anēbos*) in this rule, taken together with the fact that boys could be voluntarily or involuntarily polluted, suggests a sexual offense, perhaps unauthorized sexual contact with a citizen youth.[155]

Whatever the nature of the offense, it was serious enough to require a stronger method of purification than simple washing: the offender was to cut the throat of a piglet and trace a circle around himself with the dripping body. As with water lustration, the demarcation of this line (regardless of the amount of actual blood) functioned magically to separate him from the impurity. The carcass of the piglet was then disposed of by burning or deposition. This was a standard method of purification among the Greeks, used to cleanse meeting spaces, sanctuaries and people of a wide variety of pollutions.[156]

Lines A.43–72, omitted here, provide more details on the custom of tenths. Property could also become subject to a tenth, perhaps in the case of some lesser offense. No one was to make funerary offerings from such property until Apollo's tithe had been paid; this procedure insulated the god's presumptive property from contact with death pollution. The law then returns to the topic of the man designated as *dekatos*: if such a man died before paying his tenth, his lineal heirs had to fulfill the same requirement.[157] This is another sign that the offense of the *dekatos* was a serious insult to Apollo; it created a heritable *agos* which persisted until appropriate atonement was made. Lines A.73–82 are too fragmentary to restore with confidence; they deal with sacrificial procedures and purification. The entire section of the law on tenths (lines 33–82) can be broken down into discrete sections of ten lines, an arrangement which was surely deliberate. It may have been intended to endow the law of "tenths" with magical force.

B.2–8: A bride, [before going to the sleeping chamber (?) must go down] to Artemis. But she herself shall not be under the same roof as her husband nor

> shall she incur pollution until she comes to Artemis. Any woman who, without doing this, is voluntarily polluted, after purifying the temple of Artemis shall sacrifice in addition as penalty a full-grown animal, and then shall go to the sleeping chamber. But if she is polluted involuntarily, she shall purify the shrine.

Side B begins with a lengthy section involving female purity in relation to Artemis, a goddess who was offended by loss of virginity, by sexual intercourse and by pregnancy, the visible evidence of sexual activity. The Kyrenaian rules were designed to guide a young woman through her first experience of these dangerous events. The law addressed the betrothed woman, the bride and the pregnant wife. Young women were to refrain from sexual intercourse with their future husbands. If they had premarital sex, they were to purify the temple (again, fumigation was likely the method used), sacrifice an animal in payment of the penalty and visit the "sleeping chamber" (*koitatērion*). The specific object of this visit is unknown, but it probably involved spending the night in the temple of Artemis, which lay within the sanctuary of Apollo. Before marriage, Greek girls often served Artemis for a time, living in her sanctuary as a sign of their consecration to the goddess.[158]

Like Apollo, Artemis was lenient toward the young person who became polluted involuntarily. The same passive form of the verb *miainō* is used whenever the law contemplates the situation of the legal minor (boy or wife) who incurs pollution through prohibited sex with an adult male. This usage is consistent with the Greek conceptualization of boys and women as passive sexual partners penetrated by an active male. While insisting on the rights of Apollo and Artemis, the law recognized the social reality that boys and women did not have control over their own bodies.[159]

> B.9–14: A bride must go down to the bride-place to Artemis, whenever she wishes at the Artemisia, but the sooner the better. Any woman who does not go down [shall offer in sacrifice (?)] to Artemis [what she wishes (?)] at the Artemisia. Because she has not gone down, [she shall purify the Artemision] and sacrifice in addition a full-grown animal as penalty.

The gaps in this section make it difficult to interpret, but the rule seems to have required a postnuptial propitiation of Artemis by newly married women who had lost their virginity. Brides were to perform the necessary (purificatory?) ritual at the "bride-place" (*numphēion*) during Artemis' annual festival, and then sacrifice to the goddess. The congregation of brides at the festival would have made the ritual a public rite of passage. If a woman failed to go to the bride-place beforehand, she had to atone for the omission.[160]

> B.15–23: [A pregnant woman before giving birth] shall go down to the bride-place to Artemis. [. . .] she shall give to the Bear the feet and head and skin. If she does not go down before giving birth, she shall go down with a full-grown animal. She who goes down shall observe purity on the seventh and

> eighth and ninth, and she who has not gone down shall observe purity on those days. But if she is polluted, she shall purify herself, purify the shrine and sacrifice in addition as penalty a full-grown animal.

Pregnancy required further sacrificial propitiation of Artemis, who had the power to give or withhold safe childbirth. The pregnant woman owed a perquisite from the sacrifice to the priestess of Artemis, who was known as "the Bear."[161] Even if she successfully gave birth without the sacrifice, she was still required to offer it after the fact. Additionally, the pregnant woman was to abstain from sex three days of each month.[162] Those who did not remain abstinent faced a penalty comparable to that for presenting an unfit victim (A.26–31). No penalty was levied directly on the husband responsible for the polluting act, though both the extra expense of the penalty victim and the fear of a difficult labor could have acted as deterrents. It is notable that this complex system of ritual atonements depended on the acknowledgment, before the goddess and fellow worshipers, of activities performed in private.

> B.24–7: If a woman miscarries, if it is distinguishable, they are polluted as from one who has died, but if it is not distinguishable, the house itself is polluted as from a woman in childbed.

The ritual impact of miscarriage at Kyrene, equal to that of death or childbirth, was significant. This does not necessarily mean that a fetus was mourned or buried in the same way as a child. What we know of ancient Greek attitudes toward fetuses and newborns suggests that perceptions of full personhood were delayed until the naming of an infant, which took place several days after its birth.[163] Instead, the law suggests that the physical realities of a miscarriage could not be ignored, and that they had non-trivial consequences for the ritual purity of people under the same roof. Although the Kyrene law omits a detailed discussion of death pollution, the period of exclusion from sanctuaries after a death in the household was probably comparable to that after childbirth.[164]

> B. 28: OF VISITANTS/SUPPLIANTS.

The next section of the law begins with a heading in large letters: *Hikesiōn*. The adjective *hikesios* is here used as a noun. It is related to the noun *hiketēs*, "suppliant," and literally means "one who comes." Three types of foreign visitants are envisaged. The first is a hostile superhuman agent, the second is a human suppliant whose situation is unclear and the third is a more recognizable figure, an exiled killer who has supplicated a private citizen in order to seek purification. To us, it seems odd that the same terminology (*hikesios*) could denote both an angry spirit and a human killer, but one was a surrogate for the dead, while the other was the dead person's target. The state of pollution, of being tainted with the anger of the dead, was intrinsic to a killer's identity until his purification and integration into a new community.

The Greek ritual of supplication was used by people in situations of extreme danger or helplessness, who threw themselves on the mercy of a more powerful person, using gestures (touching the knees or chin) and signs (carrying a branch) to indicate their ritual intent. The person supplicated could accept or reject the request, but if the request was granted, it created a binding obligation to aid the suppliant, one enforced by Zeus Hikesios ("Zeus of Suppliants"). In many cases, the suppliant was an outcast seeking a new home, and the reason for his exile was a killing. If his supplication was successful, the stranger was purified and accepted into the new social group. We begin, however, with the superhuman visitant:

> B.29–39: Visitant from afar. If a visitant is sent against the house, if he (the householder) knows from whom it came to him, he shall name him/her by proclamation for three days. If he/she (the sender of the visitant) has died in the land or perished anywhere else, if he (the householder) knows the name, he shall make proclamation by name, but if he does not know, (in the form) "O person, whether you are a man or a woman." Having made male and female figures either of wood or of earth, he shall entertain them and offer them a portion of everything. When you have done what is customary, take the figurines and portions to an unworked wood and deposit them there.

Here the visitant is a spirit sent by an angry dead person who possessed intention and emotion, but not the ability to act directly in the world of the living.[165] Those who had died young (*aōroi*), unburied (*ataphoi*) or by violence (*biaiothanatoi*) were all thought to be restless. Each was capable of causing a disruptive, dangerous pollution.[166] Anger, pollution and spirit were three modalities of the same phenomenon. Therefore, affliction caused by the dead might be "purified" through a ritual of propitiation and soothing. The Kyrene law prescribed a magical cure by which a householder could rid himself of a hostile spirit. First, he needed to get the attention of the dead person by repeating his or her name. If he did not know the name, he was to use an inclusive formula, recognizing that the dead person might be either male or female. Next, he employed a magical technique, entertaining male and female figures (*kolossoi*) to a pleasing meal, just as he would do for an honored guest. The propitiated spirit was then expelled from the house through the physical removal of the figures to "an unworked wood" – that is, the opposite of an inhabited place.

> B.40–49: Second suppliant, assessed or not assessed, having taken his seat at the public shrine. If an (oracular) injunction is made, let him be assessed at whatever price is enjoined. If an injunction is not made, let him sacrifice fruits of the earth and a libation annually forever. But if he omits it, twice as much next year. If a child forgets and omits it, and an injunction is made to him, he shall pay to the god whatever is told him when he consults the oracle, and sacrifice, if he knows (where it is), on the ancestral tomb, and if not, consult the oracle.

Very little is understood about this provision of the law. It seems to deal with a request by a foreigner to be accepted as a member of a worship group at Kyrene. It could (simultaneously or alternatively) represent the ritual aspect of conferring citizenship on a foreigner. The words referring to "assessment" are related to the verb *teleō*, which was used to describe liability to taxation and tithing; it also connoted membership in a group by virtue of such payments.[167] The "injunctions" are instructions from a (local?) oracular god, most likely Apollo. On this interpretation, individuals seeking citizenship (?) were "assessed" at a price which represented their obligation to the god. The obligation was passed down to their children. If the children failed to fulfill it, they were required not only to make it up to the god but also to propitiate the founder of their line by sacrificing at his tomb.

> B.50–55: Third suppliant, a killer with his own hand (or, of his own kin). He shall present the suppliant to the [. . .] cities (?) and the three tribes. When he announces that (the killer) has arrived as a suppliant, he shall seat him on the threshold on a white fleece, [wash] and anoint him, and they shall go out into the public road, and all shall keep silent while they are outside, obeying the announcer [. . .] cause to go beside him the one who is no longer a suppliant [. . .] and those following [. . .] sacrifices, and those following [up to 20 lines missing]

This provision transferred the old, private rite of purifying a killer to a new civic context. By tradition, a killer seeking purification knelt silently at the hearth of the person he was supplicating. If the host accepted the suppliant, he performed a ritual of purification which employed a magical technique. The "blood on the hands" of the killer was reproduced using the blood of a piglet, and then washed away. In Apollonius of Rhodes's epic *Argonautica*, Kirke purified Jason and Medeia of a murder using this method, and poured "soothing libations," invoking Zeus of Purification. Kirke's maidservants then removed the dirty washwater and the carcass of the piglet, and she made additional offerings to the Erinyes.[168]

Our real-life parallel apparently breaks off before the all-important ritual of blood purification, but it includes the seating of the killer on a sheep's fleece, which functioned to absorb his impurity (or perhaps to insulate the surface where he sat or stood from the taint). Zeus, the god of suppliants, presided over the purification of killers, and this fleece is recognizable in other sources as the *Dios kōidion*, or "Fleece of Zeus."[169]

The killer had been expelled from his home because of the pollution he bore and the new antipathy of his victim's kin. Only in another community could he start life anew. The Kyrene law shows that the purification of an individual stained by lethal bloodshed was not a trivial event but a solemn one to be witnessed by the citizens. Socially, it was a rite of passage which made him fit to interact with his new neighbors.

To conclude, the law illustrates the three principal classes of pollution. The first class included the simple bodily pollutions of sex, birth and death, incurred through contact or proximity. The second class was incurred through acts that angered the gods or the dead. These could be minor (as in the case of cutting wood without paying the god) or major (as in the offense of the *dekatos*). A third class comprised pollutions incurred through attack from an external source, like the plague described at the beginning of the law. The "supplication" section of the law deals with three types of foreign "visitants," each of whom represented an actual or potential pollution, and the proper ritual procedures by which the safety and integrity of the community were to be secured.

## Notes

1 Polis religion: Sourvinou-Inwood 2000a, 2000b.
2 Monumental architecture: Snodgrass 2006.212–13 (a chapter originally published in 1977).
3 Olynthos: Morgan 2010.35–7, 2011.459–61.
4 "There is religion without the polis, even if there is no polis without religion": Burkert 1995.203. For a recent evaluations see Bremmer 2010; Eidinow 2011; Kindt 2012.12–35; Polinskaya 2013.24–5; Jameson 2014.232–7 (a chapter originally published in 1998); and compare Parker 2011.57–61.
5 Supra-polis religion: Kindt 2012.32–4. *Theoria*: see Kowalzig 2007.56–128 and the papers in Part I of Elsner and Rutherford eds. 2005. Delphic amphictyony: Lefèvre 1998. Religion and federal states: see the extensive discussion of Mackil 2012.147–236 and the papers in Funke and Haake eds. 2013.
6 Independence of domestic religion from public cult: Faraone 2012.6–7; Boedeker 2012.229–30. Private religion: Versnel ed. 1981; Purvis 2003; Versnel 2011.119–37. On ancient religion and the individual see also Rüpke 2013b.4–6. For my definition of magic see p. 133.
7 Gender and festival participation: Parker 2005.154–77. Exclusion of foreigners and women: Cole 1992.105.
8 Dorians: An epigraphic parallel in *IG* XII 5.225 + *IG* XII Suppl. p. 206 (= *LSCG* 110) (ca. 450): Dorian strangers and slaves are barred from the Parians' rites for Kore.
9 Men and sacrifice: Detienne, Vernant *et al.* 1989.131–3. Keys and knives: Connelly 2007.14–15, plates 20–21, fig. 1.1; Dillon 2002.80–83, 245–6.
10 Women in the *pannuchis*: Bravo 1997.25–9, 123–31. For Athens see the list in Parker 2005.165 with n. 42.
11 Girls vs. boys in Athenian ritual: Parker 2005.218–52. On virgin priestesses and priestly roles for women past menopause see Cole 1992.112. Old women: Bremmer 1987.197–9 (suggesting that old women more often encountered impurity due to their roles as midwives). The "initiation" explanation for the role of girls in these rituals (e.g. Burkert 2001 [1990].37–63 on the *arrhēphoroi*) is problematic, in part because most were too young for rituals of "maturation" to be meaningful.
12 Reason and moral feeling: Hume 1998 [1777].83–4. The literature on moral intuition and its evolution as an adaptive human trait is immense. For an introduction see Katz ed. 2000. Children's moral intuitions: Turiel 1998.
13 Moral realism, strategic information and superhuman agents: Boyer 2001.169–91; Barrett 2004.45–51; cf. Griffin 1978 (on divine watchers and morality in the *Iliad*). "Because we have social minds, we also have social gods": Tremlin 2006.117–20. Acknowledgment of gods is associated with moral behavior: e.g. Hom. *Od.* 6.119–21 (people who "love strangers" are "god-fearing," *theoudēs*). Suspicions about ancient atheists: Kearns 2010.141–50.
14 For the social dimensions of *eusebeia* see Zaidman 2001.109 ("respect des dieux et justice entre les hommes"). Among other people, those with the greatest right to respect were one's parents and the dead: see e.g. Lycurg. *Leoc.* 94–7.

15 Strangers and suppliants: Hes. *Op*. 327; Thgn. 143–4. Heralds: Hdt. 7.133.1–7.137.3. Oaths: Hdt. 6.86C.1–2. For divine punishment of those who break their compact with a suppliant see Naiden 2006.122–9 and on all these crimes Parker 1983.180–90.

16 On Zeus' role in justice see Lloyd-Jones 1983.3–8, 29–30; Burkert 1985.249. Cf. Hom. *Il*. 16.385–92 (Zeus punishes the unjust with damaging rainstorms). Mikalson 1983.30 distinguishes sharply between popular and literary or philosophical positions on theodicy.

17 Zeus rarely had state cults under these *epiclēseis*. This does not mean that they were irrelevant in lived religion, but rather that they were invoked on an ad hoc basis. Zeus Hikesios: Thuc. 3.14 1 (Mytilene). Compare Hdt. 1.44.2, where Kroisos tailors Zeus' titles to the immediate circumstances.

18 On the Erinyes see Parker 1983.107; Johnston 1999.250–87.

19 Social benefits of asylum: Sinn 1993. Religious significance of *asulia* and conflict with human law: Chaniotis 1996.

20 Under observation: Shariff and Norenzayan 2007 with cited literature. Wrongdoing by victim: Bering 2006.460–1. Physical illness: Chaniotis 1997.152–4, 2012.129–30.

21 On the motives of the gods, see Harrison 2000.158–81 and on *phthonos* (envy or spite) Whitehead 2009. Belief in the "spite" of the gods against mortals' good fortune is likely the result of a cognitive bias known as "the gambler's fallacy" (Ayton and Fischer 2004), which causes people to infer that bad luck will inevitably follow a run of good luck. Compare the reputed saying of Philip (Plut. *Mor*. 177c): "Oh Lady Luck, give me a small amount of bad to offset my many goods."

22 Alternatives: Harrison 2007.377–9. Corrections: e.g. Pind. *Ol*. 1.36–53 (cannibalism); Pl. *Resp*. 377d-78e (Hesiod and battles of gods), 386a–394b (detailed critique of Homer).

23 Frazer (1922.48–60) described a "radical conflict of principle" between magic (the universe acts according to impersonal laws) and religion (the universe is overseen by divine agency). Use of magic and appeal to divine agency regularly occur together without perception of a conflict, because the logical conflict is perceived only when we think reflectively in terms of universal principles. Perceptions of magical efficacy and of divine agency are rooted in different cognitive systems. Within Greek religion, a distinction has often been drawn between public, communal, sanctioned activity and private, unsanctioned activity, yet both used magical techniques. On the more recent scholarly integration of magic and religion see Parker 2005.116–35 (magic is unsanctioned religion); Collins 2008.25; Kindt 2012.90–122. For critique of Frazer and his predecessor Edward Tylor, see Tambiah 1990.42–64.

24 Frazer 1922.11. While these two laws cover most instances of magical thinking, my intent in quoting them is not to limit the definition of magic. Nemeroff and Rozin (2000.5, 24) speak in broader terms of patterns of thought that collapse the boundaries between appearance and reality, or between the mind and the external world. For example, the widespread belief in "the evil eye" attributes causal efficacy to another person's envy or hostile intent. On extensions of Frazer's laws see Collins 2008.14–24, and for a nuanced exploration of "analogical relations" in magic see Tambiah 1985.60–86.

25 Kyrene law: *ML* no. 5, lines 44–9; Faraone 1993; Berti 2006.183–200. The fate envisioned for the oath-breakers is not literally to melt but rather to be somehow destroyed, and so the homology between the act and the desired result is not exact (cf. Graf 1997.145).

26 On strategic information, see Chapter 2. Oaths in sanctuaries: Berti 2006.207.

27 Moderns: whereas Tylor (1874.1.112–13) attributed magic to "the lowest known stages of civilization," Nemeroff and Rozin (2000.19–20, 23) note that magical thinking arises "as a natural by-product of the adaptive functioning of the mind." Discussion: Pyysiäinen 2004.101–5.

28 Feces, vomit and darts: Rozin, Millman and Nemeroff 1986. Nominal realism: Rozin, Markwith and Ross 1990. For the role of language in magic see Tambiah's seminal paper (1985.17–59, originally published in 1968).

29 Generalization: Nemeroff and Rozin 2000.7, 20–21 (the "representativeness heuristic"). For discussion of Nemeroff and Rozin's findings in relation to perceptions of causality, see Sørensen 2007.95–170.

30 Polluted garment: Nemeroff and Rozin 1994; Rozin, Markwith and McCauley 1994; Nemeroff and Rozin 2000.11, 16.

31 The same factors, including the confirmation bias and fallacies such as *post hoc ergo propter hoc*, help to explain the robust persistence of paranormal and pseudoscientific beliefs today. In antiquity, magic was "not susceptible to discursive reflection" (Collins 2008.19; compare Pyysiäinen 2004.108–11). The reasons for this were not primarily social but cognitive.

32 Wittgenstein's comments on Frazer are translated and discussed by Tambiah (1990.54–63). Wittgenstein correctly argued against Frazer that magical actions are not based on reasoned beliefs; instead they are "actions of instinct" (56).

33 Concrete effects: Collins 2008.18–19.

34 On the terminology and social status of the sorcerer, which was still fluid until the end of the fifth century, see Graf 1997.20–35. Most evidence is Attic. A key literary text is Oedipus' defamation of Teiresias as *magos* and *agurtēs* (Soph. *OT* 387–9). Plato (*Symp*. 202e) expresses disapproval of "wizardry" (*goēteia*) and of the unethical activities of *agurtai* and *manteis* (*Resp*. 364b). Archaeological evidence: Gager 1992; Wilburn 2012 (Roman period). For the legality of magic see Pl. *Meno* 89b; Gager 1992.23–4. On purifiers and their Archaic antecedents see Parker 1983.207–34.

35 Social actors: cf. the comments of Collins 2008.7–11 on the "social context" of Greek magic, which includes the dead and the gods.

36 On binding and other defensive manipulation of images see Faraone 1992.54–93, 118–22.

37 Gods, spirits and magical technique: Gager 1992.12–21; Graf 1997.148–51. The extant magical papyri date from the Hellenistic period and later; they draw eclectically from Greek, Egyptian, Jewish and other traditions (Betz 1996).

38 Matter out of place: Douglas 1984 [1966].40. Characteristic of Douglas's approach is the following (115): "We cannot possibly interpret rituals concerning excreta, breast milk, saliva and the rest unless we are prepared to see in the body a symbol of society. . ." For Greek pollution and purity see Moulinier 1975 [1952]; Parker 1983 (indispensable); Vernant 1980 [1974].121–42; Cole 2004.92–145.

39 Facial expression: Rozin, Haidt and McCauley 1999.430.

40 Animal foods and sensitivity regarding the mouth: Rozin and Fallon 1987; Rozin *et al.* 1995.321; Rozin, Haidt and McCauley 1999.431–3. These facts also help to explain the common preoccupation in world religions with dietary taboos, particularly in regard to foods of animal origin, and the widely distributed belief (e.g. in Greek Orphism) that a vegetarian diet is "pure."

41 For *apoptustos* used of sexual secretions coming in contact with the mouth, see Ar. *Eq*. 1285. Compare Eur. *Hec*. 1276, of "spitting out" an undesirable prophecy and the murderer's attempt to avert anger by spitting out the victim's blood: Ap. Rhod. *Argon*. 4.478. Gods offended by uncleanliness spit out (reject) human prayers: Hes. *Op*. 726. Bad luck and spitting: Parker 1983.219. Eating at the same table as a polluted person was of special concern: Antiph. *Tetralogies* 1.1.10. Pathogens: Bloom 2004.171–2.

42 Intuitions: Boyer 2001.118–20. In many cases, we feel the need to avoid even coming close to the source of contamination. Experimental evidence identifies physical contact as a fundamental principle of contagion (Nemeroff and Rozin 2000.14), but to my knowledge proximity models (e.g. visiting a home containing a corpse) and kinship models (pollution through shared "essence") have not yet been explored.

43 On attempts to explain pollution beliefs as hygienic measures, see Parker 1983.57–8.

44 Contagiousness of bad luck: Parker 1983.219. The madness of Orestes was potentially contagious: Eur. *Or*. 792–4. The presence of a polluted man could cause a ship to sink or ruin a sacrifice: Antiph. *Herodes* 5.82.

45 Purity attributed to the gods: Moulinier 1975 [1952].271. Certain deities strongly associated with death and pollution (Hekate, Erinyes) were considered impure. Heroes and ancestral deities, such as the Tritopateres, could be classified as either pure or impure for ritual purposes (Essay 3.3).

46 The chronological development of Greek purity rules is unclear. Purity concerns are clearly present in Homer, yet limited (Vernant 1980 [1974].122–3; Parker 1983.66–9, 130–4). Purity beliefs may have intensified with the development of organized sacred space in the Archaic period. The oldest extant *perirrhantēria* (purification basins) belong to the seventh century: Dillon 2002.54–5 with fig. 2.11; cf. the example from Olympia in this volume (Figure 3.3).

47 The Greek "sacred laws" or *leges sacrae* are inscriptions setting forth a wide variety of rules and regulations involving cult practice. Many of them are not the result of legislation. On this term and the corpus of "laws" see Lupu 2005.3–112; Carbon and Pirenne-Delforge 2012. Garden of Herakles: *LSCG* 115.4–6 (fourth century). Compare *SEG* 42.785: no *kopros* is to be thrown into streets leading to the sanctuary of Herakles and the Charites (Thasos, ca. 470–60; cf. *IG* II$^2$ 380, a fourth-century regulation protecting streets in the Peiraieus at Athens). The dumping of *kopros* is specifically prohibited in several inscriptions – e.g. *LSCG* 57.6 (Argos); *LSCG* 116.4–5, 14–17 (Chios; fourth century); *LSS* 53.7–8 (Delos; third century) – although some, like the Chian law, are probably aimed at discouraging illicit use of sanctuary land for cultivation. Where cultivation was desired, however, *kopros* was used in the normal way as fertilizer (*LSCG* 78.21 [Delphi, fourth century]). See Dillon 1997.118, 125–6 with note 123.

48 Delion: Thuc. 4.97. Camping: Dillon 1997.112–3. Cf. Parker 1983.62. *Onthos*, the semi-fecal contents of animal intestines, was also cause for concern: *LSCG* 3.11 (Athens Akropolis, fifth century), 9.3–4 (Vari cave, fifth century). Compare the washing of the piglet intestines before burning in the ritual for Zeus Polieus on Kos (Essay 4.1).

49 "Coming from a woman": *LSS* 115 A 11 (Kyrene, fourth century = *SEG* 9.72); see also Essay 3.3. Pollution and the "dirtiness" of sex: Parker 1983.74–103. The fact of intercourse, not the gender of the partner, is the source of pollution. Compare another part of the Kyrene law (A 40–2), where a youth may "incur pollution" willingly or unwillingly (perhaps referring to masturbation and wet dream, or to pederastic contact).

50 *Aphrodisia*: e.g. *LSS* 108.1 (Rhodes, first century CE). *Sunousia*: e.g. *LSCG* 139.14 (Lindos, second century CE), *LSS* 91.17 (Lindos, third century CE). Additional examples: Parker 1983.74–5 with n.4. Cole (1992.108–9) and Carson (1990) maintain that the female body was popularly viewed as more polluted than the male, a view which has perhaps been overstated. Assertions of female inferiority (e.g. Arist. *Gen. an.* 728a on menstrual blood as a less "pure" form of semen) borrow the language of purity, but the purity concept itself was not predicated on gender. For ritual purposes, women's "dirtiness" was a function not of femaleness but of sexually active status.

51 Pseudo-Demosthenes 59.78 (*ap'andros sunousias*).

52 Ejaculation as "polluting oneself": Ar. *Ran.* 753 with schol. Plutarch (*Quaestiones Naturales* 36) says that bees, thought to be very "pure" insects, hate the smell of people who have had sex. For the woman's need to wash after sex, see Ar. *Lys.* 912–14. Oral sex could pollute the man who performed it (Ar. *Eq.* 1280–9; Polyb. 12.13.7; cf. Parker 1983.97, 99) but the gender of the partner is not specified. The trigger was direct contact of the mouth with "dirty" parts of the body, whether male or female.

53 Sex in a sanctuary: Hdt. 2.64.1; Burkert 1983 [1972].59–60 with n. 11 (collecting mythic violations); Cole 1992.107. Purity before (and at) the Thesmophoria: Parker 1983.81–3 with n. 33. Purity of the women attending the wife of the *archōn basileus* at the Anthesteria: Pseudo-Demosthenes 59.78.

54 Childbirth, miscarriage and abortion: Parker 1983.48–55; Cole 1992.109–11; Lupu 2005.210–13. Dogs and donkeys: *LSAM* 51.6–9; *LSS* 91.11.

55 For examples of menstruation in Greek cult regulations (mostly Hellenistic and pertaining to cults of non-Greek origin) see Parker 1983.100–103; Cole 1992.111; Lupu

2005.210 with n. 36. The lack of explicit restrictions regarding menstruation is paralleled by the lack of concern with lochial bleeding, which continued well past the point when ritual purity was restored: Cole 1992.119 n.65. Popular (but not ritual) beliefs: Hes. *Op.* 753–4 (avoid bathing in water used by a menstruating woman); Ar. *De somno et vigilia* 459b-60a (a menstruating woman can cloud a mirror); Ach. Tat. 4.7.7 (avoid intercourse with a menstruating woman).

56 Deadly exhalations: Eur. *Hipp.* 1437–8. Touching of a woman in childbed or a corpse: Eur. *IT* 380–4. Bathing or washing after the funeral and before the feast: Parker 1983.34–6, with discussion of *IG* XII 5.593 (= *LSCG* 97, fifth century, from Keos) and other sources.

57 Fouling oneself with dirt as a sign of mourning: Hom. *Il.* 18.23–5 (Achilles), 22.414 (Priam), etc. On the question of "the primacy of the physical," Parker (1983.39–40) notes that kin were typically polluted for a longer period than acquaintances and that in other cultures pollution can occur by kinship alone without contact. For limits on ostentatious grieving expressed as limits on pollution see the fifth-century law from Ioulis on Keos: *LSCG* 97; Kearns 2010.110–12.

58 Confrontation with a corpse: Boyer 2001.212–24. Resolve: McCorkle 2010. My discussion is not intended to minimize the well-documented ways in which Greek funerary rituals advertised social status and reinforced gender roles (for the interplay of pollution belief and social factors see e.g. Frisone 2011). Rather I suggest that the universality of funerary rituals cannot be adequately explained without reference to cognitive factors. For "hazard precaution" as a specialized mental tool, see Chapter 4.

59 Experimental evidence: McCorkle 2010.141. Casual disposal of infant corpses in antiquity (Lindenlauf 2001.91–2) may be related to perceptions of incomplete personhood.

60 Necessity to bury even strangers: Parker 1983.44. Laws of the gods: e.g. Soph. *Aj.* 1130, 1335; Eur. *Suppl.* 563. The Athenians pronounced curses on anyone who committed this crime of omission: Soph. *Ant.* 255 with schol. Cf. Hor. *Carm.* 1.28, where a corpse on the beach threatens vengeance if the passerby fails to provide at least token burial.

61 On denial of burial see Parker 1983.41–8; Lindenlauf 2001.88–93. Denial of burial within Attica: Lycurg. *Leoc.* 113; Xen. *Hell.* 1.7.22. Public display of corpses: Soph. *Ant.* 198–206 is a mythic exploration, as is Achilles' treatment of Hektor's corpse in Hom. *Il.* 24.12–21 (but with prevention of decay by divine action). Possible historical examples include Hdt. 5.113.1–5.115.1 (Onesilos' head); Plut. *Nic.* 28.4 (Demosthenes and Nikias); Diod. Sic. 17.118.4 (Olympias). Token burial even in extreme conditions of war or plague: Lindenlauf 2001.93. The archaeological invisibility of burials of the poor during the Dark Age (Morris 1989.97–110) does not necessarily imply lack of ritualization.

62 Weddings: Parker (1983.63–4) notes that weddings differ from births and deaths in that the latter two events are not within human control. Hence their ritualization can be seen as an attempt to reassert order.

63 Contact with the mother was the usual concern (Parker 1983.49–50, 352–6), but mother and process were often conceptually blurred: Eur. *IT* 380–4 (*locheia*, childbirth, is polluting); Cole 2004.107. Only (?) *LSAM* 84.3–4 mentions the newborn infant, who was perhaps polluted by contact with bodily fluids during birth.

64 Impurities and disease: Jouanna 1998.156–7, 192–3 on Hippocratic thought. Tragic catharsis: Arist. *Poet.* 1449b.

65 *Miaros*: e.g. Dem. 21.19, Ar *Eq.* 831. Compare Hdt. 2.47.1: Egyptians consider the pig an unclean (*miaros*) animal. In Dem. 25.28, the superlative *miarōtatos* ("most vile") simultaneously expresses the moral and ritual pollution of Aristogeiton. For the modern period see Bloom 2004.176–8.

66 Illicit sex: e.g. *LSCG* 139.14–17 specifies "lawful intercourse." Such distinctions are characteristic of the late Hellenistic period, although awareness of conflicts between ritual and moral purity begins in the late fifth century. Discussion: Parker 1983.74–5 with n. 4; Cole 1992.108–9; Chaniotis 1997, 2012.128. Book 9 of Plato's *Laws*

(865a–874c) contains an extensive homicide code designed to reconcile pollution and moral beliefs.

67 Pseudo-Demosthenes 59.85–7. Adultery: Mikalson 1983.87–8.

68 *Agos* results from "a material act that attacks a god": Moulinier 1975 [1952].249. For the etymological relationship of *hagneia*, "purity," and *agos*, "accursedness," see Vernant 1980 [1974].128, 135–6; Parker 1983.6–10.

69 *Agos*: Parker 1983.5–12, 104–206. Material nature of homicide pollution: Vernant 1983.122. Heritability of the accursed state: Gagné 2013, esp. Chapters 3–5.

70 Ambiguity of blood: Vernant 1980 [1974].129. Human blood as offering: e.g. Eur. *IT* 1449–61 (Artemis Tauropolos). Meatless/bloodless offerings: some cultic contexts required *hagna thumata*, "pure sacrifices" (e.g. the Diasia for Zeus Meilichios in Athens: Thuc. 1.126). Shared vocabulary of pollution (e.g. *prostropaios, palamnaios*) for victim, victim's blood, victim's avenging spirits and killer: Hatch 1908; Parker 1983.108–9.

71 The classic example is Kreon's error in thinking that he could avoid polluting the city and maintain "clean hands" by burying Antigone alive: Soph. *Ant.* 773–80, 889–90, 1339–46.

72 Crop failure, infertility and plague are mentioned in Soph. *OT* 25–30, admittedly an extreme and mythic case. Dangers of associating with a killer: Antiph. *Herodes* 5.82–3. Avenging spirits: Johnston 1999.127–60.

73 Anger of the victim: Pl. *Leg.* 865d-e; Xen. *Cyr.* 8.7.18–19; Parker 1983.107–8, 124–5.

74 Killing in self-defense or killing an accursed person does not create impurity: *LSCG* no. 56 (Kleonai; first half of the sixth century). Chaniotis (1997.148–51, 2012.127–8) describes this as a historical development in homicide pollution connected to the rise of secular law.

75 Homicide pollution thus represents a largely intuitive, circumstantial moral response to killing rather than a reflective response based on reasoning about universal rules of justice. It may have conferred a survival advantage on communities, for the polluted killer's exile prevented destructive blood feuds (Parker 1983.125). Powerless: Antiphon (6.4) attests that in Athenian custom, a man who killed his slave could purify himself (i.e. he did not need to leave the city). Cf. Dem. 47.55, 68–73 (failure to seek justice for a freedwoman); Pl. *Leg.* 865c–d (killing a slave requires the same purifications as involuntary manslaughter), and the Spartan practice of making a *pro forma* declaration of war against the helots so that killing them was free from defilement (*euagēs*): Arist. fr. 538 Rose (= Plut. *Lyc.* 28.4).

76 Attributing mental states to the dead: Whitehouse 2013.72–3. Experimental research: Bering 2002, 2006; Bering and Bjorklund 2004. See also Boyer 2001.216–17; Barrett 2004.56–9.

77 Avenging spirits: Johnston 1999.139–48, esp. 140. Unambiguous cases of "ordinary" victims acting directly on their killers are few. Rohde (1987 [1925].211n.48) argues for an evolution from direct action to substitute avenger. Extraordinary victims might join the ranks of the counterintuitive, powerful dead (Chapter 5).

78 This essay is based on the innovative work of Miller 1992 and Maurizio 1998 on the Panathenaic procession (see also Wohl 1996). In order to provide a broader perspective on the festival, I have added discussion of the competitions. Populist: Figueira 1984.469. Inclusive and participatory: Neils 1992b.23–4, 27; Osborne 1994.145; Shear 2001.1.166. De Polignac (1995 [1984].84) writes that "the whole society" marched in the procession.

79 Reorganized: Kyle 1992.80.

80 Ethnocentric and international: Kyle 1992.80. Tracy (2007.53) describes the Greater Panathenaia as "a bit chauvinistic."

81 Inscription: *IG* II$^2$ 2311. For a translation see Neils 1992b.16. Rhapsodic competitions were introduced by the sixth century (Pl. [*Hipp.*] 228b4-c3). On musical and rhapsodic competitions at the Panathenaia see Shapiro 1996.

82 List of open gymnastic and hippic events: Shear 2001.1.242–96.

83 *Apobatēs* race: there is debate over whether it was a holdover from the Dark Age (similar races are depicted on Geometric vases) or was added when the Greater Panathenaic festival was organized ca. 566. Discussion: Schultz 2007.

84 Pyrrhic choruses and *euandria*: Kyle 1992.94–6; Neils 1994.154–9; Boegehold 1996; Wilson 2000.37–8. List of tribal events, including dithyrambic choruses and a mock cavalry battle (not mentioned in *IG* II² 2311): Shear 2001.1.296–350.

85 Torch race: Bentz 2007.

86 Hoplites: The *hoplitēs*, a men's race in armor, is attested as early as the mid-sixth century from prize amphoras (Shear 2001.1.271–2), but this was one of the open competitions.

87 Maidens: Eur. *Her.* 780–3 suggests noncompetitive choruses during the all-night celebration (*pannuchis*), but this is the only evidence for female dance. During the Hellenistic period, wealthy non-Athenian women were permitted to compete as sponsors of horses and chariot teams: Tracy and Habicht 1991.202.

88 Aristocratic: Kyle 1992.97–8: "Despite public gymnasia and civic rewards, no revolutionary popularization of athletic competition took place at Athens." Compare the prosopographical study in Kyle 1993.102–23. Shapiro (1996.219) suggests broader participation by citizens in the less expensive events.

89 The program of competition evolved over time (often through the addition of new events). We do not know whether the ship race existed in the fifth century. For liturgies at the Panathenaia see Wilson 2000.36–43.

90 Ionic frieze: there have been attempts (e.g. Connelly 1996) to dissociate the Parthenon frieze from the procession, but the connection is generally accepted.

91 Lists of marchers: Maurizio 1998.298–304; Parker 2005.258–64. Discussion: Shear 2001.1.155–67, 2.742–61.

92 *Kanēphoroi*: Thuc. 6.56, Arist. [*Ath. Pol.*] 18.2; Shear 2001.1.130–2; Dillon 2002.37–42.

93 On women's roles in the festival see Lefkowitz 1996; Shear 2001.1.88–9; Dillon 2002.57–60.

94 On the servile function of the metics, see Miller 1992.304; Maurizio 1998.305; Parker 2005.258–261. Aelian *VH* 6.1 says that the Athenians "compelled the daughters of metics to carry parasols for their own daughters in the processions, and the wives of metics for their own wives; and the men (they compelled) to carry trays." Shear 2001.1.138: the inclusion of metics and their daughters "publicly recognized them as members of the community."

95 Armed men in the procession: Thuc. 6.56.2, 6.58.2 (in the time of Peisistratos); Arist. [*Ath. Pol.*] 18.4 (introduced under the democracy); Robertson 1992.114–19; Shear 2001.1.128, 2.758–0; Parker 2005.260. Niarchos band cup (ca. 560): *LIMC* Athena no. 574; Neils 1996a.181–3, 2007.45.

96 *Thallophoroi*: Shear 2001.1.132–3. Schol. Ar. *Vesp.* 544b says that old women once served as *thallophoroi* but if true, this appears to have been an anomaly.

97 Allies and colonists: Shear 2001.1.139–43. Jameson 2014.127: the cow and panoply were both "Athenian muscle flexing" and "a privilege not lightly granted." For the requirement see *ML* no. 46, lines 41–2 (= *IG* I³ 34), no. 69, lines 57–8 (= *IG* I³ 71.55–8).

98 Perikles' citizenship decree: (Ar. [*Ath. Pol.*] 26.3; Plut. *Per.* 37.3). On the balance between democracy and imperialism in the festival see Shapiro 1996.219, 221.

99 Cavalry: Shear 2001.2.747–8.

100 Translation adapted from *RO* no. 81 B. See also Tracy 2007.

101 Calculations: Jameson 1988.93–8; *RO* 401.

102 New money: Rosivach 1991.436–42; Shear 2001.1.73–83. Alternatively, the law may simply change the funding source for the (preexisting) meat distribution by assigning the income from the Nea.

103 Free meal: Wohl 1996.61; Parker 2005.267. On public sacrifice, democracy and access to meat in Athens, see Schmitt-Pantel 1992.121–43; Rosivach 1994.64–6.

104 One ancient source (*Anecd. Bekk.* 1.242.3–6) states that "freedmen and other barbarians" carried oak branches through the Agora in the Panathenaic festival. It is likely that the freedmen's participation was a phenomenon of a later period, when the ideology of the procession had shifted from its Classical focus on citizenship.

105 The full citizen body could be not accommodated in the procession itself, nor could every citizen be fed. At the height of its empire under Perikles, Athens is thought to have sacrificed more than 220 cattle during the Panathenaia. Even this number, however, would not have been sufficient to feed the entire male citizenry of Athens, which has been estimated at somewhere between twenty thousand and thirty thousand (Rosivach 1994.6, citing Hansen 1986.68–9).

106 Hoplites and demesmen: Maurizio 1998.301.

107 Dance: *ThesCRA* 2.300–36 (Shapiro *et al.*) with bibliography; Lonsdale 1993; Calame 1997 [1977]; Naerebout 1997, 2006; Kowalzig 2007.1–12. Ancient discussions of dance include Pl. *Leg.* Books 2 and 7; Luc. *Salt.*; Ath. 14.25–30 (628c–31e). For dance and world religions see Gundlach 2008.

108 On festivals and divine pleasure see Connor 1996.84–5.

109 Definition adapted from Hanna 1987.19. Discussion: Naerebout 1997.159–66. Human and nonhuman dance compared: Hanna 1987.76–7.

110 Folk dances change more over time than scholars have assumed: Hanna 1987.179; Naerebout 1997.202. Novelty was desirable in Greek festival music (Pl. *Leg.* 665c; Burkert 1985.103) but some songs became traditional. Affect: Hanna 1987.67–9.

111 Extraordinary: Hanna 1987.74–5; compare Burkert 1985.102 on ritual.

112 Memory skills: Bläsing *et al.* 2012.303.

113 The gendered quality of dance: Luc. *Salt.* 12; Ath. 14.25 (628d).

114 Patrimony: Calame 1997.230. Mythic content was also transmitted to children by nurses and mothers, outside of ritual contexts: Pl. *Resp.* 2.377c.

115 Embodied cognition and dance: Sevdalis and Keller 2011 (esp. 232–3); Bläsing *et al.* 2012 (esp. 303–4 on memory). Aesthetic pleasure and training: Kirsch, Drommelschmidt and Cross 2013. For the relationship between motor function and music perception, see Leman and Maes 2014.84–6.

116 The Greek understanding of dance as *mimēsis* of the gods is well documented: *ThesCRA* 2.303–8 (Shapiro *et al.*); Lonsdale 1993.48–68; Naerebout 1997.185–6 with n. 401; Steinhart 2004.1–7; Kolotourou 2011.176–8. On *mimēsis* specifically as reenactment of myth, see Nagy 1990.42–5.

117 Hymn to Apollo: Lonsdale 1993.52–62. "High-stepping" (*hupsi bibas*): *Hymn. Hom. Ap.* 516.

118 Mythic counterparts: Pl. *Leg.* 7.815c; Burkert 1985.173.

119 Pyrrhic dance: Pl. *Leg.* 7.815a. *Hyporchēma*: Pind. fr. 107 Race (imitation of hunting dogs); Luc. *Salt.* 16; Ath. 1.27 (15d-e), 14.25 (631c). On imitation of gods, animals and everyday activities (rowing, threshing, weaving) in Greek dances, see Lonsdale 1993.30–32.

120 Helots: Cartledge 2002.4–5, 52–3; Luraghi 2008.101–5, 137–40.

121 Spartan leaders and gender norms: Stehle 1997.30–58, 71–107.

122 Maiden dances: a full list by geographical location: *ThesCRA* 2.325–30 (Shapiro *et al.*).

123 *Partheneion*: the divine recipient was a goddess of dawn, titled both Orthria and Aotis. Whether she was Artemis, Aphrodite or some other deity is unknown and much debated.

124 Wild dances for Artemis: Calame 1997.148, 171–4. Dithyrambs, a genre usually performed by males for Dionysos, executed by Spartan women: D'Alessio 2013.123–32. Dionysiac elements in Spartan dances: Constantinidou 1998.

125 Dancers of Karyai: Calame 1997.149–56; D'Alessio 2013.127–8. Emblematic by the late fifth century: Plut. *Artax.* 18.1. The use of the term "Caryatid" to refer to columns shaped like dancing women is due to the fame of this Spartan dance.

126 Abduction: already in Hom. *Il.* 16.182–3; *Hymn. Hom. Ven.* 117–21. Sanctuaries of Artemis, girls' rites of passage, and security: Cole 2004.178–230. Messenians and Karyai: Paus. 4.16.9–10. Limnai: Strabo 6.1.6; Paus. 4.4.2–3. Helen: Plut. *Thes.* 31. On these cults see Calame 1997.142–74; Leitao 1999.

127 Plato drew on the three Spartan choruses for his ideal state in *Laws* 664b–665e. Mature rather than old men: Robertson 1992.158–61.

128 On the Hyakinthia see Xen. *Hell.* 4.5.11; Richer 2012.352–82.

129 Gymnopaidiai: Robertson 1992.147–65; Petterson 1992.42–56; Richer 2012.383–422. Ephors: Xen. *Hell.* 6.4.6. The religious aspect of the festival has been questioned, but in the time of Pausanias (3.11.19) it was clearly Apolline.

130 Karneia: Petterson 1992.50–71; Richer 2012.423–56. Dancing at the Karneia in Kyrene: Callim. *Hymn* 2, 85–7; Ceccarelli and Milanezi 2007.195–204 (on epigraphic evidence of the fourth century). On Spartan military training see Cartledge 2001.79–90.

131 Social change: Turner 1969; Cohen 1993.4 (Carnival is "always political"). The reinforcement of social norms is the more prevalent view of Dionysiac ritual among Classicists (e.g. Dillon 2002.148), but compare Kowalzig's views (e.g. 2007.8–9, 37–40, 43–55) on cult song as a "medium" for social change along the lines of Turner's *communitas*.

132 On Dionysos as the "arriving god" see Otto 1965 [1933].79–85 with Henrichs 2011. On epiphanies of Dionysos cf. Henrichs 1993.19–22.

133 Imitation: Diod. Sic. 4.3.3. Ritual mainadism probably had Archaic roots, but our first unambiguous evidence belongs to the mid-fourth century: Plut. *De mul. vir.* 13, 249e–f (Thyiads at Amphissa). Other key texts include Paus. 10.4.3 (the Delphic-Attic Thyiads) and *I.Magn.* 215 (= *SEG* 60.1255, an oracle text of Hellenistic origin commanding the Magnesians to fetch mainads from Thebes). Discussion: Henrichs 1978, 1982.143–7; Bremmer 1984; Versnel 1990.131–57 with bibliography.

134 Trance: the terms "ecstasy" and "trance" are often used interchangeably. For the sake of precision, I have adopted Rouget's (1985.3–12) terminology, which places trance (characterized by movement, sensory stimulation, group activity and lack of hallucination) and ecstasy (characterized by immobility, sensory deprivation, solitude and hallucination) on opposite ends of a spectrum. Trance was far more prevalent among the Greeks. For trance and ecstasy see Bremmer 1984.278; Goodman 1992.35–43; Lewis 2003; Graf 2010. For a cognitivist approach to spirit possession see Cohen 2007. The physiological role of percussive stimulation in trance is clear (Vaitl *et al.* 2013.15–17), but it must be facilitated by cultural conventions (Rouget 1985.315–26).

135 Mixed-gender *thiasoi*: Henrichs 1982.147; Jaccottet 2003.1.69–71 (such groups grew ubiquitous during the Hellenistic period). The earliest evidence is the initiation of Skyles at Olbia: Hdt. 4.79–80; cf. Eur. *Bacch.* 170–90 for male revelry in a mainadic context (old men dancing for the god). Festivals involving (female only) mainadism included the Boiotian Agrionia and perhaps the Attic/Ionian Lenaia: Larson 2007.134–5, 138–9.

136 Satyrs, silens and genres: Hedreen 2007; Shaw 2014.30–77. Male transvestism is also well attested in Dionysiac contexts: Henrichs 1982.58–9; Csapo 1997; Parker 2005.321–4.

137 Archilochus: in Mnesiepes inscription, Gerber 1999 T 3 (= *SEG* 15.517). On the early dithyramb see Lonsdale 1993.89–99; Csapo 2003; Hedreen 2007.185–7, 2013; Steinhart 2007.209–16; D'Alessio 2013.114–18; Kowalzig 2013; Shaw 2014.30–43.

138 Masking and mumming: Steinhart 2004.8–31; Hedreen 2013.178–87. An early alternative to satyr or animal costumes was grotesque buttock and stomach padding, worn by "komasts" depicted on sixth-century Corinthian vases: Steinhart 2004.32–64; Csapo and Miller eds. 2007.13–21 (cf. the essays in Part I of their edited volume); Shaw 2014.33–7. Komastic activity was less differentiated than that of the satyrs and could be performed in honor of other deities.

139 On the combination of libidinal impulse and orderly performance inherent in Dionysiac choral dancing see Hedreen 2007.172–3, 181–3.

140 Narrative component: Hedreen 2007.169–81 (wedding of Dionysos and Ariadne on Attic vases); Steinhart 2007, esp. 198–208 (return of Hephaistos and hunting scenes on Corinthian komast vases).

141 Circular chorus and Arion: Hellanicus *FGrH* 4 F 86. Herodotus (1.23) credited Arion with the "invention" of the dithyramb. Connectivity and Hellenic identity: Kowalzig 2013.

142 Economy and dithyramb in Athens: Kowalzig and Wilson eds. 2013.17–18. For the financing of these elaborate spectacles by wealthy citizens, see Wilson 2000.65–7, 93–5.

143 Pindar's Theban dithyramb: fr. 70 b Maehler. For this song as "Olympian Dionysia" see Hedreen 2013.195–6.

144 The "new music": Csapo 2004; Franklin 2013.

145 *LSS* 115 (= *SEG* 9.72). The translation here is adapted from that of Parker 1983.332–56. I have also profited from the discussions of Dobias-Lalou 2000; *RO* 494–505, no. 97; Kearns 2010.101–7 and Robertson 2010.259–374.

146 On warding off plagues, see Parker 1983.275–6; Faraone 1992.125–31.

147 Sacred, profane and polluted uses for wood: Parker 1983.335. Dobias-Lalou (2000.205) contrasts *hiaros* and *babalos* with *miaros* as an extreme case of the category *babalos*. For *bebēloi* as the uninitiated see Porta 1999.50–53.

148 Sprinkling water around oneself (*perirrhainesthai*): Cole 2004.43–6.

149 Priesthoods: Parker 1983.54. Tokens: Hsch. s.v. *stephanon ekpherein*. God-fearing man: Theophr. 16.9.

150 Ancestral: cf. the sacrifice to Akamantes with Tritopatores in an Attic calendar: Lambert 2000.46, line B.32. Discussion: *RO* 502–3. On the Tritopateres (multiple spellings are attested), see Jameson, Jordan and Kotansky 1993.107–14; Clinton 1996.170–2; Johnston 1999.51–3; Scullion 2000.

151 Dung: Parker 1983.360. For pig and goat see also von Ehrenheim 2011.28–31.

152 Fumigation: Parker 1983.227.

153 For tithing to Apollo at Kyrene see Dobias-Lalou 2000.110–11, 208–9; Suk Fong Jim 2014.131 with n. 6.

154 Compare this ritual sale to the "sale" of an ox in the sacrificial ritual for Zeus Polieus on Kos (*LSCG* 151 A, lines 22–6), discussed in Essay 4.1. The purpose is to arrive at a public proclamation of value. The Lygdamis decree (*ML* no. 32; Carawan 2008, ca. 460) specifies forfeiture of property to Apollo and/or sale as a slave for those who abrogate its terms. In fourth-century Athens, disenfranchisement for political offenses could result in confiscation of property with a tenth allotted to Athena: Andoc. 1.96–8; Suk Fong Jim 2014.264–6.

155 Like its mother cities Sparta and Thera, Kyrene may well have had a system of male socialization which included pederasty. In the Spartan system, pederastic relationships ideally excluded physical gratification (Xen. *Cons. Lac.* 2.13). Exile and suicide are mentioned as the fates of offenders (Ael. *VH* 3.12). Discussion: Cartledge 2001.91–105; Hubbard ed. 2003.7–10. Robertson (2010.302, 305) suggests a pederastic interpretation, yet views the activity as "mischief" which is "irrelevant" to the situation of the *dekatos*. Compare B.2–8, where young women incur pollution either voluntarily or involuntarily, but almost certainly through sexual intercourse with their future husbands.

156 Piglet: for this procedure see Cole 2004.48–9, 138–9; Clinton 2005.168–74. The key factor here is the demarcation with a purifying object or substance. As noted earlier, blood was unambiguously polluting only in the context of homicide (*contra* Parker 1983.373 and Cole 2004.140). Neither was the pig an unambiguously impure animal, since it was offered in normative sacrifices (Clinton 2005.168).

157 Compare the secularized provision in Dem. 43.58, an Athenian law making heirs responsible for debts owed to the gods and heroes. Instead of pollution, they inherited his *atimia* (disenfranchisement) until they paid up. At Kyrene, a non-lineal heir could fulfill the requirement by having the dead man's worth assessed (lines 53–62), but all lineal heirs, even those deceased, were themselves subject to assessment (lines 63–72 with the comments of Parker 1983.342; Robertson 2010.306).

158 On the sleeping chamber (probably in the temple) and the "bride-place" in the next section, see Robertson 2010.321–3.

159 For the legal equivalence of *anēbos* and woman, cf. the Gortyn law code, Col. XI.18–9 (Willetts 1967.49).

160 On this provision see Calhoun 1934 (with suggestion that the bride is prohibited from sacrificing); Dillon 1999. Rhodes and Osborne (*RO* 499) read 93–4 as "Any bride who fails to go down is to make an additional sacrifice to Artemis as ordained at the Artemisia."

161 On the significance of the bear in Artemis' cults: Perlman 1989.

162 The meaning of "the seventh, eighth and ninth" is debated. Parker (1983.51, 346) suggests that these could be the three days before the naming ceremony on the tenth day after child's birth (hence a one-time obligation rather than a monthly one), but this seems rather soon after birth for the resumption of sex to be an issue: Kearns 2010.107.

163 On attitudes toward children in Classical Athens, Golden 1990.82–101, and on the naming ceremony (*amphidromia*), Golden 1990.23; Demand 1994.8–9, 62.

164 The temporal extent of pollution from death varied widely. Extant inscriptions note periods ranging from three to forty days, with most on the lower end of the scale: Parker 1983.37n.17.

165 Numerous interpretations of this difficult text have been proposed, but the current consensus (e.g. *RO* 505) holds that the first *hikesios* is not a human visitor. A close parallel has been recognized in a law from Selinous: Jameson, Jordan and Kotansky 1993.55, 76; Clinton 1996.179 (distinguishing between "ghost" and supernatural avenger); Johnston 1999.46–63.

166 For these emic categories of the angry dead see Johnston 1999.127–60. For the similar figure of the *elasteros* in the law from Selinous, see Jameson, Jordan and Kotansky 1993.116–20.

167 The word I have translated as "assessed" appears in other translations of the law as "initiated," but it is unlikely that the references here are to a mystery cult. Compare Hdt. 2.168; Arist. *Ath.* 55.3; Lys. 32.24, etc., where the verb *teleō* refers to taxation; Robertson 2010.362–3 ("paid or not paid"); and Dobias-Lalou 2000.210–11.

168 Kirke: Ap. Rhod. *Arg.* 4.685–717. Purification by blood: Burkert 1985.80–2; Parker 1983.370–92 with appendix of mythic examples of suppliant killers purified. Washing off the blood is emphasized in an expounder's tradition from Athens: *FGrH* 356 F 1.

169 Fleece of Zeus: references (from the lexicographers) listed in Jameson, Jordan and Kotansky 1993.83.

## References

Adrados, Francisco and M. V. Sakellariou, eds. 1996. *Colloque international Démocratie athénienne et culture*. Athens: [Académie d'Athènes].

Antes, Peter, Armin W. Geertz and Randi R. Warne, eds. 2008. *New approaches to the study of religion*. 2 Vols. Berlin and New York: Walter de Gruyter.

Assmann, Jan, Henning Wrogemann and Theo Sunndermeier, eds. 1997. *Schuld, Gewissen und Person: Studien zur Geschichte des inneren Menschen*. Gütersloh: Gütersloher Verlagshaus.

Ayton, Peter and Ilan Fischer. 2004. The hot hand fallacy and the gambler's fallacy: Two faces of subjective randomness? *Memory & Cognition* 32 (8): 1369–78.

Barrett, Justin L. 2004. *Why would anyone believe in God?* Walnut Creek, CA: Altamira Press.

Bentz, Martin. 2007. Torch race and vase painting. In *The Panathenaic games*, ed. Palagia and Choremi-Spetsieri, 73–80.

Bering, Jesse M. 2002. Intuitive conceptions of dead agents' minds: The natural foundations of afterlife beliefs as phenomenological boundary. *Journal of Cognition and Culture* 2 (4): 263–308.

Bering, Jesse M. 2006. The folk psychology of souls. *Behavioral and Brain Sciences* 29 (5): 453–62.

Bering, Jesse M. and D. F. Bjorklund. 2004. The natural emergence of reasoning about the afterlife as a developmental regularity. *Developmental Psychology* 40 (2): 217–33.

Berti, Irene. 2006. Now let Earth be my witness and the broad heaven above, and the down flowing water of the Styx (Homer, Ilias VX, 36–7): Greek oath rituals. In *Ritual and communication*, ed. Stavrianopoulou, 181–209.

Betz, Hans Dieter, ed. 1996. *The Greek magical papyri in translation including the Demotic spells*. Second edition. Chicago: University of Chicago Press.

Bläsing, Bettina, Beatriz Calvo-Merino, Emily S. Cross, Corinne Jola, Juliane Honisch and Catherine Joanna Stevens. 2012. Neurocognitive control in dance perception and performance. *Acta Psychologica* 139: 300–308.

Blok, Josine and P. Mason, eds. 1987. *Sexual asymmetry: Studies in ancient society*. Amsterdam: J. C. Gieben.

Bloom, Paul. 2004. *Descartes' baby: How the science of child development explains what makes us human*. New York: Basic Books.

Bodel, John and Saul M. Olyan, eds. 2012. *Household and family religion in antiquity*. Oxford and Malden, MA: Blackwell.

Boedeker, Deborah. 2012. Family matters: Domestic religion in classical Greece. In *Household and family religion*, ed. Bodel and Olyan, 229–47.

Boedeker, Deborah and Kurt Raaflaub, eds. 1998. *Democracy, empire and the arts in fifth-century Athens*. Cambridge, MA: Harvard University Press.

Boegehold, Alan. 1996. Group and single competitions at the Panathenaia. In *Worshiping Athena*, ed. Neils (1996b), 95–105.

Boyer, Pascal. 2001. *Religion explained: The evolutionary origins of religious thought*. New York: Basic Books.

Bravo, Benedetto. 1997. *Pannychis e simposio: Feste private notturne di donne e uomini nei testi letterari e nel culto*. Pisa and Rome: Istitituti Editoriali e Poligrafici Internazionali.

Bremmer, Jan. 1984. Greek maenadism reconsidered. *ZPE* 55: 267–86.

Bremmer, Jan. 1987. The old women of ancient Greece. In *Sexual asymmetry*, ed. Blok and Mason, 191–215.

Bremmer, Jan. 2010. Manteis, magic, mysteries and mythography: Messy margins of polis religion? *Kernos* 23: 13–35.

Burkert, Walter. 1983 [1972]. *Homo Necans: The anthropology of ancient Greek sacrificial ritual and myth*. Tr. Peter Bing. Berkeley, Los Angeles and London: University of California Press.

Burkert, Walter. 1985. *Greek religion*. Cambridge, MA: Harvard University Press.

Burkert, Walter. 1995. Greek poleis and civic cults. In *Studies in the ancient Greek polis*, ed. Hansen and Raaflaub, 201–10.

Burkert, Walter. 2001 [1990]. *Savage energies: Lessons of myth and ritual in ancient Greece*. Tr. Peter Bing. Chicago and London: University of Chicago Press.

Buxton, Richard, ed. 2000. *Oxford readings in Greek religion.* Oxford and New York: Oxford University Press.

Calame, Claude. 1997 [1977]. *Choruses of young women in ancient Greece: Their morphology, religious role, and social function.* Tr. Derek Collins and Janice Orion. Lanham, MD, and Boulder, CO: Rowman and Littlefield.

Calhoun, George M. 1934. Lex sacra Cyrenaica. *CP* 29 (4): 345–6.

Carawan, Edwin. 2008. What the *MNEMONES* know. In *Orality, literacy, memory*, ed. Mackay, 163–84.

Carbon, Jean-Mathieu and Vinciane Pirenne-Delforge. 2012. Beyond Greek "sacred laws." *Kernos* 25: 163–82.

Carpenter, Thomas H. and Christopher Faraone, eds. 1993. *Masks of Dionysus*. Ithaca and London: Cornell University Press.

Carson, Anne. 1990. Putting her in her place: Women, dirt, and desire. In *Before sexuality*, ed. Halperin, Winkler and Zeitlin, 135–69.

Cartledge, Paul. 2001. *Spartan reflections*. Berkeley and Los Angeles: University of California Press.

Cartledge, Paul. 2002. *The Spartans: An epic history*. London: Macmillan.

Ceccarelli, Paola and Silvia Milanezi. 2007. Dithyramb, tragedy – and Cyrene. In *The Greek theatre and festivals*, ed. Wilson, 185–214.

Chaniotis, Angelos. 1996. Conflicting authorities: Asylia between secular and divine law in the Classical and Hellenistic poleis. *Kernos* 9: 65–86.

Chaniotis, Angelos. 1997. Reinheit des Körper – Reinheit der Seele in den griechischen Kultusgesetzen. In *Schuld, Gewissen und Person*, ed. Assmann, Wrogemann and Sunndermeier, 142–79.

Chaniotis, Angelos, ed. 2011. *Ritual dynamics in the ancient Mediterranean.* Dresden: Franz Steiner Verlag.

Chaniotis, Angelos. 2012. Greek ritual purity from automatisms to moral distinctions. In *How purity is made*, ed. Rösch and Simon, 123–39.

Clinton, Kevin. 1996. A new lex sacra from Selinus. *CP* 91: 159–79.

Clinton, Kevin. 2005. Pigs in Greek rituals. In *Greek sacrificial ritual, Olympian and chthonian*, ed. Hägg and Alroth, 167–79.

Cohen, Abner. 1993. *Masquerade politics: Explorations in the structure of urban cultural movements*. Berkeley: University of California Press.

Cohen, Emma. 2007. *The mind possessed: The cognition of spirit possession in an Afro-Brazilian religious tradition.* Oxford and New York: Oxford University Press.

Cole, Susan G. 1992. Gynaiki ou themis: Gender differences in the Greek leges sacrae. *Helios* 19: 104–22.

Cole, Susan G. 2004. *Landscapes, gender and ritual space: The ancient Greek experience.* Berkeley and Los Angeles: University of California Press.

Collins, Derek. 2008. *Magic in the ancient Greek world.* Malden, MA, and Oxford: Blackwell.

Connelly, Joan. B. 1996. Parthenon and parthenoi: A mythological interpretation of the Parthenon frieze. *AJA* 100: 53–84.

Connelly, Joan B. 2007. *Portrait of a priestess: Women and ritual in ancient Greece.* Princeton and Oxford: Princeton University Press.

Connor, W. R. 1996. Festival and democracy. In *Démocratie athénienne*, ed. Adrados and Sakellariou, 79–89.

Constantinidou, Soteroula. 1998. Dionysiac elements in Spartan cult dances. *Phoenix* 52 (1–2): 15–30.

Coulson, William D. E., O. Palagia, T. L. Shear Jr., H. A. Shapiro and F. J. Frost, eds. 1994. *The archaeology of Athens and Attica under the democracy*. Oxford: Oxbow Books.

Csapo, Eric. 1997. Riding the phallus for Dionysus: Iconology, ritual and gender role deconstruction. *Phoenix* 51: 253–95.

Csapo, Eric. 2003. The dolphins of Dionysus. In *Poetry, theory, praxis*, ed. Csapo and Miller, 69–98.

Csapo, Eric. 2004. The politics of the new music. In *Music and the Muses*, ed. Murray and Wilson, 207–48.

Csapo, Eric and Margaret C. Miller, eds. 2003. *Poetry, theory, praxis: The social life of myth, word and image in ancient Greece. Essays in honor of William J. Slater*. Oxford and New York: Oxford University Press.

Csapo, Eric and Margaret C. Miller, eds. 2007. *The origins of theater in ancient Greece and beyond: From ritual to drama*. Cambridge and New York: Cambridge University Press.

D'Alessio, Giambatista. 2013. The name of the dithyramb: Diachronic and diatopic variations. In *Dithyramb in context*, ed. Kowalzig and Wilson, 113–32.

Dalgleish, Tim and Mick J. Power, eds. 1999. *Handbook of cognition and emotion*. Chichester and New York: John Wiley and Sons.

Damon, William, ed. 1998. *Handbook of child psychology*. Fifth edition. 4 Vols. New York: Wiley.

Demand, Nancy. 1994. *Birth, death and motherhood in Classical Greece*. Baltimore: Johns Hopkins University Press.

de Polignac, François. 1995 [1984]. *Cults, territory, and the origins of the Greek city-state*. Tr. Janet Lloyd. Chicago: University of Chicago Press.

Detienne, Marcel, Jean Pierre Vernant, Jean-Louis Durand, Stella Georgoudi, François Hartog and Jesper Svenbro. 1989 [1979]. *The cuisine of sacrifice among the Greeks*. Tr. Paula Wissig. Chicago and London: University of Chicago Press.

Dillon, Matthew. 1997. The ecology of the Greek sanctuary. *ZPE* 118: 113–27.

Dillon, Matthew. 1999. Post-nuptial sacrifices on Kos (Segre, "*ED*" 178) and ancient Greek marriage Rites. *ZPE* 124: 63–80.

Dillon, Matthew. 2002. *Girls and women in Classical Greek religion*. Abingdon and New York: Routledge.

Dobias-Lalou, Catherine. 2000. *Le dialecte des inscriptions grecques de Cyrène*. Paris: C. E. A.M. Institut d'Art et d'Archéologie.

Douglas, Mary. 1984 [1966]. *Purity and danger: An analysis of the concepts of pollution and taboo*. Reprint. London and Boston: Ark Paperbacks.

Eidinow, Esther. 2011. Networks and narratives: A model for ancient Greek religion. *Kernos* 24: 9–38.

Elsner, Jaś and Ian Rutherford, eds. 2005. *Pilgrimage in Graeco-Roman and early Christian antiquity*. Oxford and New York: Oxford University Press.

Faraone, Christopher. 1992. *Talismans and Trojan horses: Guardian statues in ancient Greek myth and ritual*. Oxford and New York: Oxford University Press.

Faraone, Christopher. 1993. Molten wax, spilt wine and mutilated animals: Sympathetic magic in Near Eastern and early Greek oath ceremonies. *JHS* 113: 60–80.

Faraone, Christopher. 2012. Household religion in ancient Greece. In *Household and family religion in antiquity*, ed. Bodel and Olyan, 210–28.

Figueira, Thomas J. 1984. The Ten Archontes of 579/8 at Athens. *Hesperia* 53 (4): 447–73.

Franklin, John Curtis. 2013. Songbenders of circular choruses: Dithyramb and the "demise of music." In *Dithyramb in context*, ed. Kowalzig and Wilson, 213–36.

Frazer, James George. 1922. *The golden bough: A study in magic and religion*. Abridged edition. London: Macmillan.

Frisone, Flavia. 2011. Construction of consensus: Norms and change in Greek funerary rituals. In *Ritual dynamics*, ed. Chaniotis, 179–201.

Funke, Peter and Matthias Haake, eds. 2013. *Greek federal states and their sanctuaries: Identity and integration*. Stuttgart: Franz Steiner Verlag.

Gager, John. 1992. *Curse tablets and binding spells from the ancient world*. New York: Oxford University Press.

Gagné, Renaud. 2013. *Ancestral fault in ancient Greece*. Cambridge and London: Cambridge University Press.

Gerber, Douglas. 1999. *Greek iambic poetry: From the seventh to the fifth centuries BC*. Cambridge, MA: Harvard University Press.

Golden, Mark. 1990. *Children and childhood in Classical Athens*. Baltimore: Johns Hopkins University Press.

Goodman, Felicitas. 1992. *Ecstasy, ritual and alternate reality: Religion in a pluralistic world*. Bloomington and Indianapolis: Indiana University Press.

Graf, Fritz. 1997. *Magic in the ancient world*. Tr. Franklin Philip. Cambridge, MA, and London: Harvard University Press.

Graf, Fritz. 2010. The blessings of madness. *ARG* 12: 167–180.

Griffin, Jasper. 1978. The divine audience and the religion of the Iliad. *CQ* 28 (1): 1–22.

Gundlach, Helga Barbara. 2008. New approaches to the study of religious dance. In *New approaches to the study of religion*, ed. Antes, Geertz and Warne, 139–63.

Hägg, Robin and Brita Alroth, eds. 2005. *Greek sacrificial ritual, Olympian and chthonian*. Stockholm: P. Åströms Förlag.

Halperin, David, John J. Winkler and Froma Zeitlin, eds. 1990. *Before sexuality: The construction of erotic experience in the ancient Greek world*. Princeton: Princeton University Press.

Hanna, Judith Lynne. 1987. *To dance is human: A theory of nonverbal communication*. Chicago and London: University of Chicago Press.

Hansen, Mogens Herman. 1986. *Demography and democracy*: *The number of Athenian citizens in the fourth century B.C.* Herning: Systime.

Hansen, Mogens Herman and Kurt A. Raaflaub, eds. 1995. *Studies in the ancient Greek polis*. Stuttgart: Steiner.

Harrison, Thomas. 2000. *Divinity and history: The religion of Herodotus*. Oxford: Oxford University Press.

Harrison, Thomas. 2007. Greek religion and literature. In *A companion to Greek religion*, ed. Ogden, 373–84.

Hatch, William Henry Paine. 1908. The use of αλιτηριος, αλιτρος, αραιος, εναγης, ενθυμιος, παλαμναιος, and προστροπαιος: A study in Greek lexicography. *HSPh* 19: 157–86.

Haysom, Matthew and Jenny Wallensten, eds. 2011. *Current approaches to religion in ancient Greece*. Stockholm: Swedish Institute at Athens.

Hedreen, Guy. 2007. Myths of ritual in Athenian vase-paintings of silens. In *The origins of theater*, ed. Csapo and Miller, 150–95.

Hedreen, Guy. 2013. The semantics of processional dithyramb: Pindar's *Second Dithyramb* and Archaic Athenian vase-painting. In *Dithyramb in context*, ed. Kowalzig and Wilson, 171–97.

Henrichs, Albert. 1978. Greek maenadism from Olympias to Messalina. *HSPh* 82: 121–60.

Henrichs, Albert. 1982. Changing Dionysiac identities. In *Jewish and Christian self-definition*, ed. Meyer and Sanders, 137–60.

Henrichs, Albert. 1993. He has a god in him: Human and divine in the modern perception of Dionysus. In *Masks of Dionysus*, ed. Carpenter and Faraone, 13–43.

Henrichs, Albert. 2011. Göttliche Präsenz als Differenz: Dionysos als epiphanischer Gött. In *A different god?* ed. Schlesier, 105–16.

Hubbard, Thomas K. ed. 2003. *Homosexuality in Greece and Rome: A sourcebook of basic documents*. Berkeley and Los Angeles: University of California Press.

Hume, David. 1998 [1777]. *Enquiry concerning the principles of morals*. Edited by Tom L. Beauchamp. Oxford and New York: Oxford University Press.

Jaccottet, Ann-Françoise. 2003. *Choisir Dionysos: Les associations dionysiaques, ou la face cachée du dionysisme*. 2 Vols. Zurich: Akanthus.

Jameson, Michael H. 1988. Sacrifice and animal husbandry in Classical Greece. In *Pastoral economies in Classical antiquity*, ed. Whittaker, 87–119.

Jameson, Michael H. 2014. *Cults and rites in ancient Greece: Essays on religion and society*. Cambridge: Cambridge University Press.

Jameson, Michael H., David R. Jordan and Roy D. Kotansky. 1993. *A lex sacra from Selinous*. Durham, NC: Duke University.

Johnston, Sarah Iles. 1999. *Restless dead: Encounters between the living and the dead in ancient Greece*. Berkeley: University of California Press.

Jouanna, Jacques. 1998. *Hippocrates*. Tr. M. B. DeBevoise. Baltimore, MD: Johns Hopkins University Press.

Katz, Leonard D., ed. 2000. *Evolutionary origins of morality: Cross-disciplinary perspectives*. Thoverton, UK: Imprint Academic.

Kearns, Emily. 2010. *Ancient Greek religion: A sourcebook*. Malden, MA, and Oxford: Wiley-Blackwell.

Kindt, Julia. 2012. *Rethinking Greek religion*. Cambridge and London: Cambridge University Press.

Kirsch, Louise P., Kim A. Drommelschmidt and Emily S. Cross. 2013. The impact of sensorimotor experience on affective evaluation of dance. *Frontiers in Human Neuroscience* 7, Article 521.

Kolotourou, Katerina. 2011. Musical rhythms from the cradle to the grave. In *Current approaches to religion in ancient Greece*, ed. Haysom and Wallensten, 169–87.

Kowalzig, Barbara. 2007. *Singing for the gods: Performances of myth and ritual in Archaic and Classical Greece*. Oxford and New York: Oxford University Press.

Kowalzig, Barbara. 2013. Dancing dolphins on the wine-dark sea: Dithyramb and social change in the Archaic Mediterranean. In *Dithyramb in context*, ed. Kowalzig and Wilson, 31–58.

Kowalzig, Barbara and Peter Wilson, eds. 2013. *Dithyramb in context*. Oxford and New York: Oxford University Press.

Kyle, Donald G. 1992. The Panathenaic games: Sacred and civic athletics. In *Goddess and polis*, ed. Neils (1992a), 77–101, 203–8.

Kyle, Donald G. 1993. *Athletics in ancient Athens*. Second revised edition. Leiden and New York: Brill.

Lambert, Stephen D. 2000. The sacrificial calendar of the Marathonian Tetrapolis: A revised text. *ZPE* 130: 43–70.

Larson, Jennifer. 2007. *Ancient Greek cults: A guide*. New York and London: Routledge.

Lefèvre, François. 1998. *L'amphictyonie pyléo-delphique: Histoire et institutions*. Athens: École Française d'Athènes.

Lefkowitz, Mary. 1996. Women in the Panathenaic and other festivals. In *Worshipping Athena*, ed. Neils (1996b), 78–91.

Leitao, David. 1999. Solon on the beach: Some pragmatic functions of the limen in initiatory myth and ritual. In *Rites of passage in ancient Greece*, ed. Padilla, 247–77.

Leman, Marc and Pieter-Jan Maes. 2014. Music perception and embodied music cognition. In *The Routledge handbook of embodied cognition*, ed. Shapiro, 81–9.

Lewis, I. M. 2003. *Ecstatic religion: A study of shamanism and spirit possession*. Third edition. London and New York: Routledge.

Lindenlauf, Astrid. 2001. Thrown away like rubbish – Disposal of the dead in ancient Greece. *Papers from the Institute of Archaeology* 12: 86–99.

Lloyd-Jones, Hugh. 1983. *The justice of Zeus*. Second edition. Berkeley and Los Angeles: University of California Press.

Lonsdale, Steven. 1993. *Dance and ritual play in Greek religion*. Baltimore: Johns Hopkins University Press.

Lupu, Eran. 2005. *Greek sacred law: A collection of new documents*. Leiden and Boston: Brill.

Luraghi, Nino. 2008. *The ancient Messenians: Constructions of ethnicity and memory*. New York: Cambridge University Press.

Mackay, Anne, ed. 2008. *Orality, literacy, memory in the ancient Greek and Roman world*. Leiden and Boston: Brill.

Mackil, Emily. 2012. *Creating a common polity: Religion, economy and politics in the making of the Greek koinon*. Berkeley and Los Angeles: University of California Press.

Marinatos, Nanno and Robin Hägg, eds. 1993. *Greek sanctuaries: New approaches*. London and New York: Routledge.

Maurizio, Lisa. 1998. The Panathenaic procession: Athens' participatory democracy on display? In *Democracy, empire and the arts in fifth-century Athens*, ed. Boedeker and Raaflaub, 297–317, 415–21.

McCorkle, William W. 2010. *Ritualizing the disposal of the deceased: From corpse to concept*. New York and London: Peter Lang.

Meyer, B. F. and E. P. Sanders, eds. 1982. *Jewish and Christian self-definition III: Self-definition in the Graeco-Roman world*. London: SCM Press.

Mikalson, Jon. 1983. *Athenian popular religion*. Chapel Hill: University of North Carolina Press.

Miller, Margaret C. 1992. The parasol: An Oriental status-symbol in late Archaic and Classical Athens. *JHS* 112: 91–105.

Morgan, Janett. 2010. *The Classical Greek house*. Exeter: Bristol Phoenix Press.

Morgan, Janett. 2011. Families and religion in Classical Greece. In *A companion to families in the Greek and Roman worlds*, ed. Rawson, 447–64.

Morris, Ian. 1989. *Burial and ancient society: The rise of the Greek city-state*. Cambridge and New York: Cambridge University Press.

Moulinier, Louis. 1975 [1952]. *Le pur et l'impur dans la pensée des Grecs d'Homère à Aristote*. Reprint. New York: Arno Press.

Murray, Penelope and Peter Wilson, eds. 2004. *Music and the Muses: The culture of "mousikē" in the Classical Athenian city*. Oxford and New York: Oxford University Press.

Naerebout, F. G. 1997. *Attractive performances. Ancient Greek dance: Three preliminary studies*. Amsterdam: J. C. Gieben.

Naerebout, Frederick G. 2006. Moving events. Dance at public events in the ancient Greek world: Thinking through its implications. In *Ritual and communication*, ed. Stavrianopoulou, 37–67.

Nagy, Gregory. 1990. *Pindar's Homer: The lyric possession of an epic past*. Baltimore and London: Johns Hopkins University.

Naiden, F. S. 2006. *Ancient supplication*. Oxford and New York: Oxford University Press.

Neils, Jenifer, ed. 1992a. *Goddess and polis: The Panathenaic festival in ancient Athens*. Princeton: Princeton University Press.

Neils, Jenifer. 1992b. The Panathenaia: An introduction. In *Goddess and polis*, ed. Neils (1992a), 13–27.

Neils, Jenifer. 1994. The Panathenaia and Kleisthenic ideology. In *The archaeology of Athens and Attica under the democracy*, ed. Coulson, Palagia, Shear Jr., Shapiro and Frost, 151–60.

Neils, Jenifer. 1996a. Pride, pomp and circumstance: The iconography of procession. In *Worshipping Athena*, ed. Neils (1996b), 177–97.

Neils, Jenifer, ed. 1996b. *Worshipping Athena: Panathenaia and Parthenon*. Madison: University of Wisconsin Press.

Neils, Jenifer. 2007. Replicating tradition: The first celebrations of the Greater Panathenaia. In *The Panathenaic games*, ed. Palagia and Choremi-Spetsieri, 41–51.

Nemeroff, Carol and Paul Rozin. 1994. The contagion concept in adult thinking in the United States: Transmission of germs and interpersonal influence. *Ethos* 22 (2): 158–86.

Nemeroff, Carol and Paul Rozin. 2000. The makings of the magical mind: The nature and function of sympathetic magical thinking. In *Imagining the impossible*, ed. Rosengren, Johnson and Harris, 1–34.

Ogden, Daniel, ed. 2007. *A companion to Greek religion*. Oxford and New York: Oxford University Press.

Osborne, Robin. 1994. Democracy and imperialism in the Panathenaic procession: The Parthenon frieze in its context. In *The archaeology of Athens and Attica under the democracy*, ed. Coulson, Palagia, Shear Jr., Shapiro and Frost, 143–50.

Otto, Walter Friedrich. 1965 [1933]. *Dionysus, myth and cult*. Tr. Robert Palmer. Bloomington: Indiana University Press.

Padilla, Mark, ed. 1999. *Rites of passage in ancient Greece: Literature, religion, society*. Lewisburg: Bucknell University Press.

Palagia, Olga and Alkestis Choremi-Spetsieri, eds. 2007. *The Panathenaic games*. Oxford: Oxbow Books.

Parker, Robert. 1983. *Miasma: Pollution and purification in early Greek religion*. Oxford: Clarendon Press.

Parker, Robert. 2005. *Polytheism and society at Athens*. Oxford and New York: Oxford University Press.

Parker, Robert. 2011. *On Greek religion*. Ithaca and London: Cornell University Press.

Perlman, Paula. 1989. Acting the she-bear for Artemis. *Arethusa* 22: 111–33.

Petterson, Michael. 1992. *Cults of Apollo at Sparta: The Hyakinthia, the Gymnopaidiai and the Karneia*. Stockholm: The Swedish Institute at Athens.

Polinskaya, Irene. 2013. *A local history of Greek polytheism: Gods, people and the land of Aigina, 800–400 BCE*. Leiden and Boston: Brill.

Porta, Fred R. 1999. *Greek ritual utterances and the liturgical style*. Dissertation, Harvard University.

Purvis, Andrea. 2003. *Singular dedications: Founders and innovators of private cults in Classical Greece*. New York and London: Routledge.

Pyysiäinen, Illka. 2004. *Magic, miracles and religion: A scientist's perspective*. Walnut Creek, CA, and Lanham, MD: Altamira Press.

Rawson, Beryl, ed. 2011. *A companion to families in the Greek and Roman worlds*. West Sussex, UK, and Malden, MA: Wiley-Blackwell.

Richer, Nicolas. 2012. The religious system at Sparta. In *A companion to Greek religion*, ed. Ogden, 236–52.

Robertson, Noel. 1992. *Festivals and legends: The formation of Greek cities in the light of public ritual*. Toronto and Buffalo: University of Toronto Press.

Robertson, Noel. 2010. *Religion and reconciliation in Greek cities: The sacred laws of Selinus and Cyrene*. Oxford and New York: Oxford University Press.

Rohde, Erwin. 1987 [1925]. *Psyche: The cult of souls and belief in immortality among the ancient Greeks*. Tr. W. B. Hillis. Reprint. Chicago: Ares Publishers.

Rösch, Petra and Udo Simon, eds. 2012. *How purity is made*. Wiesbaden: Harrassowitz Verlag.

Rosengren, Karl S., Carl N. Johnson and Paul L. Harris, eds. 2000. *Imagining the impossible: Magical, scientific and religious thinking in children*. Cambridge and New York: Cambridge University Press.

Rosivach, Vincent J. 1991. IG $2^2$ 334 and the Panathenaic hekatomb. *PP* 46: 430–42.

Rosivach, Vincent J. 1994. *The system of public sacrifice in fourth-century Athens*. Atlanta: Scholars Press.

Rouget, Gilbert. 1985. *Music and trance: A theory of the relations between music and possession*. Chicago and London: University of Chicago Press.

Rozin, Paul and April Fallon. 1987. A perspective on disgust. *Psychological Review* 94 (1): 23–41.

Rozin, Paul, Jonathan Haidt and Clark R. McCauley. 1999. Disgust: The body and soul emotion. In *Handbook of cognition and emotion*, ed. Dalgleish and Power, 429–45.

Rozin, Paul, Maureen Markwith and C. R. McCauley. 1994. The nature of aversion to indirect contact with another person: AIDS aversion as a composite of aversion to strangers, infection, moral taint and misfortune. *Journal of Abnormal Psychology* 103: 495–504.

Rozin, Paul, Maureen Markwith and Bonnie Ross. 1990. The sympathetic magical law of similarity, nominal realism and neglect of negatives in response to negative labels. *Psychological Science* 1 (6): 383–4.

Rozin, Paul, L. Millman and Carol Nemeroff. 1986. Operation of the laws of sympathetic magic in disgust and other domains. *Journal of Personality and Social Psychology* 50: 703–12.

Rozin, Paul, Carol J. Nemeroff, Matthew Horowitz, Bonnie Gordon and Wendy Voet. 1995. The borders of the self: Contamination sensitivity and potency of the body apertures and other body parts. *Journal of Research in Personality* 29: 318–40.

Rüpke, Jörg, ed. 2013a. *The individual in the religions of the ancient Mediterranean*. Oxford and New York: Oxford University Press.

Rüpke, Jörg. 2013b. Individualization and individuation as concepts for historical research. In *The individual in the religions of the ancient Mediterranean*, ed. Rüpke (2013a), 3–28.

Schlesier, Renate, ed. 2011. *A different god? Dionysos and ancient polytheism*. Berlin: De Gruyter.

Schmitt-Pantel, Pauline. 1992. *La cité au banquet: Histoire des repas publics dans les cités grecques*. Rome: École Française de Rome.

Schultz, Peter. 2007. The iconography of the Athenian ἀποβάτης race: Origins, meanings, transformations. In *The Panathenaic games*, ed. Palagia and Choremi-Spetsieri, 59–72.

Scullion, Scott. 2000. Heroic and chthonian sacrifice: New evidence from Selinous. *ZPE* 132: 163–71.

Sevdalis, Vassilis and Peter E. Keller 2011. Captured by motion: Dance, action understanding, and social cognition. *Brain and Cognition* 77: 231–6.

Shapiro, H. Alan. 1996. Democracy and imperialism: The Panathenaia in the age of Perikles. In *Worshipping Athena*, ed. Neils (1996b), 215–25.

Shapiro, Lawrence, ed. 2014. *The Routledge handbook of embodied cognition*. London and New York: Routledge.

Shariff, Azim F. and Ara Norenzayan. 2007. God is watching you: Priming god concepts increases prosocial behavior in an anonymous economic game. *Psychological Science* 18 (9): 803–9.

Shaw, Carl. 2014. *Satyric play: The evolution of Greek comedy and satyr drama*. Oxford and New York: Oxford University Press.

Shear, Julia. 2001. *Polis and Panathenaia: The history and development of Athena's festival*. 2 Vols. Dissertation, University of Pennsylvania.

Sinn, Ulrich. 1993. Greek sanctuaries as places of refuge. In *Greek sanctuaries*, ed. Marinatos and Hägg, 88–109.

Snodgrass, Anthony. 2006. *Archaeology and the emergence of Greece: Collected papers on early Greece and related topics*. Edinburgh: Edinburgh University Press.

Sørensen, Jesper. 2007. *A cognitive theory of magic*. London and New York: Altamira Press.

Sourvinou-Inwood, Christiane. 2000a [1988]. Further aspects of polis religion. In *Oxford readings in Greek religion*, ed. Buxton, 38–55.

Sourvinou-Inwood, Christiane. 2000b [1990]. What is polis religion? In *Oxford readings in Greek religion*, ed. Buxton, 13–37.

Stavrianapoulou, Eftychia, ed. 2006. *Ritual and communication in the Graeco-Roman world*. Liège: Centre International d'Étude de la Religion Grecque Antique.

Stehle, Eva. 1997. *Performance and gender in ancient Greece: Nondramatic poetry in its setting*. Princeton: Princeton University Press.

Steinhart, Matthias. 2004. *Die Kunst der Nachahmung: Darstellungen mimetischer Vorführungen in der griechischen Bildkunst archaischer und klassischer Zeit*. Mainz am Rhein: Philipp von Zabern.

Steinhart, Matthias. 2007. From ritual to narrative. In *The origins of theater*, ed. Csapo and Miller, 196–220.

Suk Fong Jim, Theodora. 2014. *Sharing with the gods: Aparchai and dekatai in ancient Greece*. Oxford: Oxford University Press.

Tambiah, Stanley J. 1985. *Culture, thought and social action: An anthropological perspective*. Cambridge, MA, and London: Harvard University Press.

Tambiah, Stanley J. 1990. *Magic, science, religion and the scope of rationality*. Cambridge and New York: Cambridge University Press.

Tracy, Stephen V. 2007. Games at the lesser Panathenaia? In *The Panathenaic games*, ed. Palagia and Choremi-Spetsieri, 53–7.

Tracy, Stephen V. and Christian Habicht. 1991. New and old Panathenaic victor lists. *Hesperia* 60: 187–236.

Tremlin, Todd. 2006. *Minds and gods: The cognitive foundation of religion*. Oxford and New York: Oxford University Press.

Turiel, E. 1998. The development of morality. In *Handbook of child psychology*, ed. Damon, Vol. 3: 863–932.

Turner, Victor. 1969. *The ritual process: Structure and anti-structure*. Chicago: Aldine Publishing.

Tylor, Edward B. 1874. *Primitive culture: Researches into the development of mythology, philosophy, religion, language, art and custom*. 2 Vols. Boston: Estes and Lauriat.

Vaitl, Dieter, Niels Birbaumer, John Gruzelier, Graham A. Jamieson, Boris Kotchoubey, Andrea Kübler, Ute Strehl, Dietrich Lehmann, Wolfgang H. R. Miltner, Thomas Weiss, Ulrich Ott, Gebhard Sammer, Peter Pütz, Jiri Wackermann and Inge Strauch. 2013. Psychobiology of altered states of consciousness. *Psychology of Consciousness: Theory, Research and Practice* 1: 2–47.

Vernant, Jean-Pierre. 1980 [1974]. *Myth and society in ancient Greece*. Tr. Janet Lloyd. Reprint. New York: Zone Books.

Vernant, Jean-Pierre. 1983. *Myth and thought among the Greeks*. London: Routledge & Kegan Paul.

Versnel, Henk S., ed. 1981. *Faith, hope, and worship: Aspects of religious mentality in the ancient world*. Leiden: Brill.

Versnel, Henk S. 1990. *Inconsistencies in Greek and Roman religion I. Ter unus: Isis, Dionysos, Hermes. Three studies in henotheism*. Leiden and New York: Brill.

Versnel, Henk S. 2011. *Coping with the gods: Wayward readings in Greek theology*. Leiden: Brill.

von Ehrenheim, Hedvig. 2011. *Greek incubation rituals in Classical and Hellenistic times*. Dissertation, Stockholm University.

Whitehead, David. 2009. Spiteful heaven: Residual belief in divine phthonos in post fifth-century Athens? *AAntHung* 49 (3): 327–33.

Whitehouse, Harvey. 2013. Immortality, creation and regulation: Updating Durkheim's theory of the sacred. In *Mental culture*, ed. Xygalatas and McCorkle, 66–79.

Whittaker, C. R., ed. 1988. *Pastoral economies in Classical antiquity*. Cambridge: Cambridge Philological Society.

Wilburn, Andrew T. 2012. *Materia magica: The archaeology of magic in Roman Egypt, Cyprus and Spain*. Ann Arbor: University of Michigan Press.

Willetts, Ronald F. 1967. *The law code of Gortyn*. Berlin: Walter de Gruyter.

Wilson, Peter. 2000. *The Athenian institution of the khoregia: The chorus, the city and the stage*. Cambridge: Cambridge University Press.

Wilson, Peter, ed. 2007. *The Greek theatre and festivals: Documentary studies*. Oxford and New York: Oxford University Press.

Wohl, Victoria. 1996. Eusebeias heneka kai philotimias: Hegemony and democracy at the Panathenaia. *C&M* 47: 25–88.

Xygalatas, Dimitris and William W. McCorkle, Jr., eds. 2013. *Mental culture: Classical social theory and the cognitive science of religion*. Durham, UK, and Bristol, CT: Acumen.

Zaidman, Louise Bruit. 2001. *Le commerce des dieux: Eusebeia, essai sur la piété en Grèce ancienne*. Paris: La Découverte.

# 4 Ritual, festival and sacrifice

*The principal scholarly models of ritual explain it in functionalist terms as a behavior which increases group cohesion, or as a symbolic language by which people communicate meaning between and within social groups. Actual participants in religious rituals, meanwhile, often describe them as efficacious methods for achieving desired goals or for communicating with gods. Cognitive approaches to ritual trace its characteristic features to intuitive processes, including those which have evolved to help us identify threats in the environment. Whitehouse's modes theory asks how certain features of a given ritual system, such as frequency and emotional intensity, correlate with its social context and the types of memory activated in its transmission. McCauley and Lawson's ritual form theory proposes that ritual features are tied to the relative agency of gods and worshipers in a given ritual. Greek rituals were located in time by the festival calendar, and in space by the sanctuary and the procession. Animal sacrifice, the most important Greek ritual, has generated a long history of interpretation. The illustrative essays examine sacrifice in the Koan festival for Zeus Polieus, trace the growth of Theseus' cult in Athens and apply ritual form theory to a sample of Greek rituals.*

## Theories of ritual

*In response to fears of disease and war, an assembled community dances around a set of urns, completing a circular motion three times, and comes to a stop. An ox is led counterclockwise three times around this group. Those who supplied the ox approach it and rub themselves against its forehead. The ox is cut open at the upper abdomen; its stomach is removed and it is killed with two blows of an axe, and then bisected. In an order determined by age, gender and marital status, participants walk from east to west between the two parts of the ox, being sure to step on a puddle of chyme from its stomach, in which the axe has been placed. The participants return to the dance area and are splashed with water from the urns, after which a seer prescribes a list of activities which will now be prohibited for a time. All run frantically toward the east, arms raised, yelling "Sky, help us!" Finally, a second ox is killed, and its meat is distributed among the elder males.*

This is a simplified description of part of a multi-day ritual performed among the Turkana of modern-day Kenya.[1] It is easy to imagine a similar sequence of activities taking place in ancient Greece. Why people all over the world engage in elaborately scripted behaviors like this, particularly in the context of religion, is a question which has generated diverse answers from social scientists. Using Bronislaw Malinowski's approach, we might suggest that the Turkana perform these acts in order to alleviate their anxiety about disease and war.[2] Theorists following Émile Durkheim and Roy Rappaport would point to the role of this ritual in promoting group solidarity (all members of the community must participate, and all must step in the chyme). It also reinforces existing social categories (older men walk through the two halves of the ox first, followed by unmarried girls and women, married women with children, and finally, unmarried youths) and statuses (only the elder men receive meat, but they may give some to the younger men).[3] Students of Victor Turner or Mary Douglas might emphasize the ways in which the ritual generates and communicates meaning through symbolic oppositions (water/chyme; ox renounced/ox eaten) and patterns (passing from east to west through a "gate" and returning). Then, too, the ritual helps to regulate individual behavior (prohibitions enjoined by the seer include no big-game hunting for the next month). Applying principles set forth by Clifford Geertz and Jonathan Z. Smith, one could conclude that the ritual allows the Turkana to conceptually structure the environment in which they live (the cardinal directions; sky and earth; relations among animal, human and divine) and to reconcile ideal and actual mental representations of their world (safety, plenty and certainty versus danger, disease and doubt). Theorists of ritual as performance or practice-based could point to the special gestures, movements and instances of physical contact (rubbing against the ox, stepping in chyme, dancing) that mark off this sequence of actions from everyday activities. For participants, the meanings of the ritual are internalized through physical experience in ways that are distinct and more direct than any verbal explanation.[4]

As varied as they are, these theoretical approaches propose that people perform and transmit ritual behaviors *primarily* because the behaviors confer psychological and social benefits, or in order to "communicate" something to each other. (The goal of communicating with superhuman agents, such as "Sky" in the Turkana example, is usually downplayed.) Yet given how differently individual members of a culture may interpret the same ritual, nonverbal ritual behavior appears to be an inefficient method of communication with other people.[5] To be sure, ritual can transmit cultural values, reinforce social hierarchies and strengthen group bonds, but these processes also happen through other avenues, independent of ritual, and a religious ritual does not always require a group, or even an audience.[6] What, then, accounts for the unique characteristics of ritual behavior itself? Most scholars agree that ritual behavior involves distinctive features. These include acts without transparent goals (rubbing against the ox); repetition (circling three times); rigid adherence to a prescribed procedure (circling no more and no fewer than three times); defined spatial boundaries and physical order (dancing in a line, alignment to cardinal directions); and specific concerns such as protection against invisible danger (omens of disease).[7]

## The cognitive roots of ritualized behavior

If ritualized behavior is a human universal, we ought to be able to locate not only its origins but also an element of ongoing motivation in human evolutionary psychology. Because human ritual shares many characteristics with the "ritual" behavior of animals, Walter Burkert proposed that the "tracks of biology" are discernable in certain Greek ritual behaviors, such as finger sacrifice. Yet the phylogenetic gap between any specific animal ritual and putatively analogous human behavior is great, and he acknowledged the difficulties in tracing such connections.[8] It is possible that certain human rituals send intraspecies signals in ways comparable to the ritual behavior of animals. War dances, for example, communicate a simple, intelligible message of physical prowess and they occur cross-culturally; in certain contexts they may confer a survival or reproductive advantage upon the performers.[9]

A related approach draws on evolutionary biology and economic theory to posit that the point of religious ritual is its costliness: it sends "hard to fake signals of commitment," thus increasing trust and cooperation among members of the worship group.[10] But like the anthropological and sociological theories outlined earlier, theories describing complex ritualized human behavior as evolutionary adaptations fail to account for many of its defining characteristics. We now turn to the suggestion that ritualized human behavior is not itself an evolutionary adaptation but a by-product of mental tools which have evolved for other uses.[11]

Cognitive science has revived Freud's observation that there exist striking similarities between religious rituals and psychological disorders characterized by obsessive-compulsive behavior. The urge to engage in ritualized behavior, however, is common among normal individuals as well, particularly at certain stages of life (e.g. early childhood and new parenthood). Alan Fiske and his colleagues compared a large, culturally diverse sample of ritual sequences with clinical descriptions of individuals suffering from obsessive-compulsive disorder, and showed that both data sets consistently exhibit the same themes. Particularly common in both religious ritual and obsessive-compulsive disorder (OCD) is a concern with purity and cleansing from invisible contaminants (e.g. repeated hand-washing in individuals with OCD, and lustration with water when entering a sacred place in religious ritual). Fiske and Haslam proposed that the disposition to perform rituals is a human universal, one which becomes overactive in individuals with OCD.[12] Further work has resulted in a theory that human cognitive architecture includes a "hazard-precaution system" focused on perceived threats of predation, stranger intrusion, contamination and contagion. This system produces active or latent predispositions to repetitive behaviors like washing, contact avoidance, marking or observing boundaries, and checking one's surroundings. Individuals in whom this system is overactive experience intrusive, anxious thoughts which can be soothed through the performance of tightly scripted, detailed actions adapted from activities of everyday life.[13]

Liénard and Boyer, in turn, have integrated these findings into the cognitive study of religion. They do not propose, as Freud did, that human ritual behavior is individual compulsion writ large, but instead that human beings find collective ritual compelling (and therefore remember and transmit it) because it "activates" intuitive mental tools, including the hazard-precaution system. Significantly, most rituals also engage intuitive beliefs about social relations, and religious rituals in particular engage intuitive beliefs about superhuman agents.[14] In other words, religious ritual has an intrinsic ability to engage our minds through multiple, highly compelling avenues. This engagement increases the likelihood that ritual behavior will be attended to and transmitted. Liénard and Boyer, however, draw attention to an important distinction between individual neurosis and collective ritual. Whereas individuals always experience their private rituals as compelling, in most group rituals there is a combination of true *ritualized behavior* (high control, attentional focus, explicit emphasis on proper performance) and *routinized behavior* (possible automaticity, low attentional demands, less emphasis on proper performance). In other words, participants in the same religious ritual may experience it in different ways, depending on their levels of habituation.[15]

Liénard and Boyer's theory convincingly explains several features of the Turkana *ariwo* ritual, such as repetitive actions, a concern for spatial demarcation and fear of disease as a triggering event. It offers clues as to why transparent goals are so often absent from ritual behavior, and why people are unable to explain many of their ritual behaviors.[16] It has room for the social aspects of ritual: for example, group rituals may be more compelling than individual ones because they engage the mental mechanisms we use to gauge trustworthiness in our fellows. Crucially, the theory also allows us to address the issue of superhuman agency: ritual behavior involving gods, spirits or ghosts may be the most compelling of all, for reasons we have explored in the previous chapters. But what of the details of individual rituals in specific cultural contexts? Why do the Turkana, after all, rub against the ox's forehead and step in the chyme from its stomach? Even culture-specific details such as these may have been influenced by cognitive factors. For example, Liénard has proposed that such details of the Turkana *ariwo* sacrifice are salient (and therefore remembered and reproduced) because they involve the counterintuitive representation of a living thing as an artifact (rubbing against the live ox) and of artifacts (chyme from the dead animal) as retaining the essence of the living animal. Indeed, the *transformation* of a member of one ontological category (animal) into another category so far removed (artifact) may be particularly salient. On this hypothesis we would expect the conversion of animals into artifacts (food, clothing, tools) to generate more attention (and to be incorporated in ritual more often) than analogous transformations of plants or non-living objects.[17]

Do ritual details such as stepping in chyme have meaning? Standard anthropological theory encourages us to approach religious rituals as repositories of coded information, which can always be deciphered given sufficient cultural knowledge (Chapter 2). Pointing to the fact that many people do not even attempt to grasp the "meaning" in the details of their own rituals, and that if explanations are solicited, they vary widely, cognitivists have suggested that these actions possess intrinsic salience for the human mind, but no meanings. Of course, meanings can be attributed to ritual objects or actions by participants or institutions on the one hand, and by scholarly observers on the other. But such attributions are not likely to be consistently shared within a culture unless they are *explicitly* taught and reinforced. On this view, "reading" a ritual as a chain of symbols endowed with stable meanings is always an act of interpretation rather than one of causal explanation. Yet both methods are necessary in order to understand a ritual in its cultural context.[18]

Some religious rituals, however, include mimetic behaviors which tend to evoke similar interpretations regardless of the observer's culture. For example, setting food or drink before an anthropomorphic figurine on the one hand and repeatedly piercing the same figurine with a sharp object on the other are likely to activate intuitions of friendliness and hostility. (Despite the intelligibility of this type of ritual action, it may be performed not to communicate a meaning but rather to effect a concrete result using sympathetic magic.) A dance in which a warrior brandishes his weapon and simulates the movements of fighting could equally function (among other things) as sympathetic magic or as a signal to an observer of the dancer's fitness and willingness to engage in aggression. To the degree that ritual actions are both intuitive and intelligible, then, it seems reasonable to conclude that they possess intrinsic meaning and communicative potential.

From an emic point of view, and also from the ethnographer's point of view, many ritual details which seem random to outsiders are salient to insiders because their meanings have been taught (e.g. the reason why unleavened bread is consumed during the Jewish holiday of Passover), or simply because of their roles in long-established orthopraxy ("We have always done it this way"). When the Turkana ritually kill an ox, they manipulate its stomach contents. Greeks would be more likely to interest themselves in the animal's blood and its *splanchna*, the upper viscera including the heart and liver. The use of these materials in ritual is privileged by their respective cultures and has symbolic value in the ritual context.[19] Many ritual details, therefore, persist because they have been taught, implicitly or explicitly. Where there is intercultural contact, distinctive procedures may become further entrenched and elaborated, because they allow individuals to self-identify as Greeks or Jews or Turkana people. In Essay 4.1, we will examine a specific case of Greek ox sacrifice with a view to how extracultural, intuitive factors and culture-specific, contingent factors have been blended in a ritual context.

## Whitehouse's modes of religiosity

The theoretical model of "modes of religiosity" proposed by Harvey Whitehouse has been among the most productive concepts in the cognitive science of religion over the last decade, giving rise to multiple conferences and a flurry of new research designed to test its predictions.[20] As Whitehouse notes, anthropologists have long observed dichotomies in world religious practices between infrequent, emotionally intense, highly stimulating rituals (e.g. a tribal rite of passage in Papua New Guinea which involves isolation, tongue-piercing and masked dances) and those that are repetitive, routinized and performed in a relatively calm atmosphere (e.g. weekly attendance at a Presbyterian church service).[21] These psychological features seem to correlate with sociopolitical features: emotionally intense rituals are associated with small, cohesive groups and their interpretation is not controlled by central authorities, whereas repetitive, routinized rituals are associated with larger, more diffuse and inclusive groups, and their interpretation is policed by highly organized, centralized systems with strong leadership. Highly intense rituals produce "identity fusion" strong enough to motivate self-sacrifice for the sake of the group's goals (as in the initiations and hazings of warrior bands and military subcultures), while routinized rituals produce a more conventional "group identification." Finally, emotionally intense rituals are less frequently performed, and they are associated with internally generated reflection on their meaning, while repetitive, routinized rituals are performed regularly and associated with explicitly taught doctrines.

Whitehouse calls these sets of correlations the "imagistic" and "doctrinal" modes (summarized in Table 4.1). As he emphasizes, the modalities are not strictly delineated typologies of societies nor of individual rituals, but "attractor positions" toward which religious systems and subsystems tend to migrate. Features of the modalities may coexist within religious systems.[22]

The imagistic and doctrinal modes of religiosity activate long-term memory in distinctive ways. Human long-term memory can be divided into the procedural (memory for skills, such as how to drive a car or braid hair) and the declarative (memory for concepts, facts and verbal content, such as what happened at our tenth

*Table 4.1* Whitehouse's modes of religiosity compared (Whitehouse 2000, 2004a; Whitehouse and Lanman 2014).

| *Imagistic Mode* | *Doctrinal Mode* |
|---|---|
| Rituals produce high sensory stimulation and arousal, often dysphoric | Rituals produce low sensory stimulation and low arousal |
| Rituals are infrequent (e.g. seven-year intervals) | Rituals are frequent (e.g. weekly, monthly) and routinized |
| Verbalization less important than sensory stimulation and imagery | Verbal doctrines and narratives important |
| Activates episodic memory and (within expert group) semantic memory | Activates semantic and procedural memory; often supported by writing |
| Interpreted through spontaneous exegetical reflection by individuals plus "expert" knowledge within a restricted group | Interpreted through explicit teaching of conceptually complex exegesis, often supported by writing |
| Diversity of interpretation; non-centralized | Standardized teachings; centralization and policing for uniformity |
| Leadership is diffuse, passive or absent | "Dynamic" religious leaders have authoritative knowledge |
| Creates group "identity fusion" | Creates "group identification" |
| Paleolithic origins; characteristic of tribal social organization and small, cohesive groups | Origins in past six thousand years; characteristic of states based on agriculture and larger, diffuse groups |

birthday party, or the significance of the date 1066). Declarative memories in turn are either episodic or semantic. Episodic memory is the capacity to reexperience events and circumstances of the past. It is arguably unique to humans and dependent on our awareness of ourselves as beings in subjective time. Episodic memories are likely to be encoded when an experience is accompanied by heightened emotions like fear or joy. Semantic memory, which we share with nonhuman animals, is the ability to store and retrieve a knowledge base about the world. In humans, semantic memory is encoded when we are repeatedly exposed to information, or when we consciously attempt to memorize. At the core of Whitehouse's theory is the proposition that religious systems evolve toward "attractor positions" which help ensure their transmission using different types of memory.[23]

Rituals of the imagistic type include terrifying or otherwise emotionally arousing rites of passage as well as various forms of ecstatic or trance-inducing rituals that activate episodic memory. Because of their infrequent performance, the verbal content of such rituals is not retained, but the vividness of the memories ensures the transmission of ritual details. Because the meanings of these events are not taught, people who undergo and administer imagistic rituals engage in "spontaneous exegetical reflection," leading to a diversity of rich, complex interpretations.[24] In the doctrinal mode, on the other hand, ritual procedures and their associated doctrines tend to be repeated frequently, so that they become routinized. Sequences of actions enter procedural memory, while much verbal content enters semantic memory.[25] Fixed interpretations are taught, and policed, by authorities. The advent of literacy contributes to the "mnemonic support" typically required to sustain the doctrinal mode.

Whitehouse identified a third, default "attractor position" in addition to the imagistic and doctrinal modes. This is the cognitively optimal position, applicable to systems in which most religious activity is intuitive, consisting of relatively simple interactions with superhuman agents whose properties are easily remembered and grasped. Rituals characteristic of this mode will be intuitively understood (e.g. offering food or drink as to a guest). Narratives attached to the rituals will be simple and memorable; complex interpretations and fixed doctrines will be absent. Cognitively optimal religiosity is not an evolutionary stage, an original state superseded by more complex forms of religion; rather, it is an ever-present default mode which is less dependent on explicit long-term memory than the other modes.[26] Although it assumes familiar patterns everywhere (e.g. superhuman beings, simple forms of divination, purity measures), its cultural specifics are subject to constant, incremental change. Whitehouse contrasts this "natural" religion with the cognitively costly religion of the imagistic and doctrinal modes, both of which carry a heavier conceptual load, and both of which are more likely to produce fanatical and/or violent commitment. Practitioners of the other two modes often criticize cognitively optimal beliefs and practices as false, shallow or misleading.[27]

Modes theory raises some important questions for Greek religion, which conforms well to neither of the "costly" modes. To what degree was it a cognitively optimal, "natural" religion? Which forms of memory were activated in its transmission? After the Bronze Age but before the rise of the polis, when Greek society was organized along kinship and tribal lines, did it follow a more "imagistic" pattern, with characteristically dysphoric rites of passage? A few such rites existed in later centuries and have generated long-running debates about whether they are survivals of a period when "initiation rituals" were prevalent. For example, the ritual performed for Zeus every nine years on Mt. Lykaion, in which young men ate from a kettle supposedly containing both animal and human flesh, clearly belongs to the imagistic mode. The youths were told that whoever ate the human flesh would be transformed into a werewolf, and they were threatened with death if they revealed the secret.[28] Cannibalism and homicide are common themes in imagistic rituals. According to modes theory, however, we need not tie imagistic rituals to earlier or more "primitive" stages of culture. They can arise in any circumstances, ancient or modern, where relatively small social groups seek "hard to fake signals of commitment" from their members.

In its civic manifestations, Greek religion involved centrally supervised, high-frequency, routinized rituals which relied for their transmission on semantic memory, procedural memory and (in some cases) writing. It is uncontroversial that these rituals produced "group identification."[29] Yet at every level of social organization, Greek religion lacked the orthodoxies, authoritative leaders and scriptures of the doctrinal mode in its ideal form. "Doctrines" in the loose sense of widely known teachings and narratives about the gods were plentiful (e.g. in Panhellenic poetry), but these were not consistently and firmly tied to corresponding rituals, nor were specific interpretations of rituals enshrined as the only acceptable ones. Indeed, diversity of interpretation was the rule. For example, the Karneia, the most important festival of the Dorian Greeks, generated multiple and contradictory explanations of its name and origin: Apollo Karneios took his name from a sacred cornel-tree (*kraneia*); the name is derived from a word for "ram" (*karnos*); the Karneian festival was founded to atone for the murder of a seer named Karnos; Karneios Oiketas ("of the household") was a pre-Dorian divinity of Sparta.[30]

While poetry was ubiquitous in Greek ritual contexts, writing and literacy were only sporadically deployed in the service of standardization, in part because of a preference for oral tradition, and in part because of the local nature of Greek religion: there was little need to coordinate practice and belief among states, since each place had its own myths and rituals.[31] Common festivals developed along divergent lines in different geographical locations, as in the case of the Karneia (celebrated in Sparta, exported to Thera, and later still to Kyrene). Each priest's knowledge and authority were limited to, but also inherent in, his or her own localized cult (itinerant religious specialists, on the other hand, were more likely to make use of books to bolster memory and authority). The unifying phenomena of Panhellenic poetry, festivals and oracles emerged as the Greeks recognized their shared cultural heritage, but never with the goal of homogenizing or "reforming" local practices and beliefs.

Greek religion included quite a few low-frequency, high-arousal rituals sure to be encoded in the episodic memory of those who experienced them: sleeping in the temple of Asklepios for healing, consulting the terrifying underground oracle of Trophonios or witnessing the light-filled Mysteries at Eleusis (Chapter 5). Yet while these rituals used imagistic elements, very few of them fit the full profile of an imagistic ritual. Some (like the Bacchic mysteries) were transmitted within small cohesive groups, as in Whitehouse's model, but many were administered to all comers by specialist initiators, did not depend for transmission on episodic memory and involved large numbers of initiates. At the height of their popularity, for example, Eleusis and other major mystery sanctuaries initiated thousands of people at a time, many of whom were strangers who would not meet again. While rites of passage were ubiquitous in Greek culture, only a very few involved experiences potent enough to create "identity fusion." The Spartan polis is known to have used imagistic-type hazings and ordeals to train warriors (precisely in order to replace family ties with identity fusion), but the brutality of their system was unusual.[32]

In many respects, Greek *ritual* systems leaned toward the cognitively optimal position, while other aspects of Greek religious experience were conceptually complex and/or dependent on writing for transmission. Although the corpus of Greek rituals appears extremely detailed to us, the labor of performing and transmitting them was divided among innumerable local experts, and the procedures themselves were shaped more by intuitive than by reflective processes. The greatest cognitive load lay not with priests but with poets and philosophers, who increasingly relied upon writing as their explorations of the divine became more reflective and sophisticated. Consider Hesiod's insistence on the justice of Zeus in *Works and Days*, Pindar's esoteric teachings about reincarnation (Chapter 5), the cruelty of Aphrodite and Artemis in Euripides' *Hippolytus* and Plato's criticism of traditional piety in the *Euthyphro* (Essay 1.3). Works such as these were seldom used in ritual contexts directly relevant to their subject matter. Only in religious subcultures, such as Pythagoreanism and Orphism, were complex doctrines consistently tied to ritual practice and daily life. Notably, the fanaticism found in both the doctrinal and imagistic modes was virtually absent from Greek religion.

## McCauley and Lawson's ritual form theory

McCauley and Lawson proposed an alternative theory with attractor positions based on the perceived roles of agent, act and "patient" (that which is acted upon) in ritual. These three roles are basic components in the mind's "action representation system," which enables awareness of our own intentional agency in performing actions ("I decided to pick up this pencil"). Action representation is essential to theory of mind, the attribution of mind and intention to other beings ("He picked up the pencil because he decided to").[33] McCauley and Lawson define religious rituals narrowly, as those predicated on (a) the pattern of agent, act, patient and (b) the direct or indirect involvement of counterintuitive agents, such as gods, demons, ancestors or saints.[34] (For convenience, I will use "god" or "gods" in what follows as shorthand for "counterintuitive agent.") These features distinguish religious ritual from other types of ritual, such as the changing of the guard at Buckingham Palace.

For McCauley and Lawson, the position at which a god is inserted into the ritual determines everything else. The god may himself be the agent, or may invest the agent (often a priest) with the ability to act. The god may, alternatively, be most closely associated with the instrument through which the ritual act is accomplished, making it "special" (e.g. holy water). Finally, the god may be the patient who is acted upon. McCauley and Lawson developed a complex method for determining the god's "distance" from a given action role within the full structural description of a ritual.[35] They propose that the form of the ritual, as determined by these factors, predicts a number of other variables, such as the frequency of performance, the levels of sensory pageantry and emotional arousal, the reversibility of the ritual, and the degree to which substitutions are permitted (Table 4.2).[36] Although individual rituals will correspond to one of the two attractor positions, enduring religious *systems* will include rituals of both types.

How does the ritual form hypothesis apply to Greek religion? Examples of special agent rituals include certain rites of passage, mystery cult initiations, trance rituals and incubation for healing (Figure 4.1), all situations of relatively low frequency and high arousal in which gods were presumed to be acting upon humans. Special patient rituals include all the oft-repeated ceremonies that aimed to affect the disposition of a god through animal sacrifice, first-fruit offerings and so forth. Notably, these were the rituals which most often permitted substitutions, such as the offering of animal sacrifice by a non-priest, or the presentation of a clay ox figurine in place of an ox sacrifice.[37] The effects of these offering rituals were presumed to be temporary, whereas the effects of certain special agent rituals (e.g. initiation into the Eleusinian Mysteries) were considered permanent.

Experimental research designed to test McCauley and Lawson's theory supports the hypothesis that ritual form influences people's intuitive judgments about the repeatability, reversibility and emotionality of rituals involving gods.[38] Additionally, people's intuitive judgments about the relative importance of action and agency for ritual efficacy vary depending on whether a god is involved. That is,

*Table 4.2* McCauley and Lawson's ritual forms compared (McCauley and Lawson 2002).

| *Special Agent Ritual* | *Special Patient (or Instrument) Ritual* |
|---|---|
| Gods are responsible for what happens | People are responsible for what happens |
| Gods act directly, OR their most direct connection to the ritual is through a priest | Gods are acted upon OR have their most direct connection with a ritual instrument |
| Low performance frequency per individual patient | High performance frequency per individual agent |
| Consequences lasting | Consequences temporary |
| Ritual substitutions rare or disallowed | Ritual substitutions common |
| More sensory pageantry and emotional arousal (relative within a specific religious community) | Less sensory pageantry and emotional arousal (relative within a specific religious community) |
| Encoded in episodic memory | Encoded in semantic and procedural memory |

*Figure 4.1* Asklepios heals a sleeping woman during incubation. To the right is Asklepios' wife Hygieia (Health) and to the left, a group of worshipers. Marble votive relief, ca. 350. Peiraieus Museum. Photo: Foto Marburg/Art Resource

people have different intuitions about what is most important for ritual success if they believe that action X will automatically lead to result Y without the involvement of a god. In the latter case, it matters only that action X takes place, whereas the involvement of a god generates the intuition that the action must be performed intentionally (i.e. by a person). This research plausibly suggests that in rituals involving gods, people will favor a mental model of social causation over one of mechanistic causation.[39] In my view, however, it is still necessary to take account of the use of mechanistic techniques (i.e. sympathetic magic) alongside social ones in a given ritual.

Additionally, McCauley and Lawson describe religious systems as "balanced" or "unbalanced" depending on whether they include a mix of special agent and special patient/instrument rituals. They predict that systems in which special patient rituals dominate will give rise to the sporadic efflorescence of special agent rituals which revitalize the system as a whole:

> Ritual systems in which special patient rituals receive the overwhelming (if not exclusive) emphasis involve the uninterrupted repetition of rituals that have unremarkable levels of sensory pageantry and involve participants doing things to satisfy the CPS agents time and time again. Although they may enjoy long periods of stability, as we have seen, tedium is inevitable.
>
> (McCauley and Lawson 2002.193)

The ritual form hypothesis, therefore, has the potential to shed light on the historical dynamics that produced trance, incubation and other "special agent" cults within the larger context of state religion dominated by rituals in which the gods received routinized human attentions. Indeed, McCauley and Lawson predict that the transmission of religious *systems* will be dependent on the motivating effects of special agent rituals.[40] If they are correct, this means that despite its fundamental role, the principle of reciprocity (Chapter 1.3) is not sufficient to sustain a system in the long term. The gods must not only provide good things; they must be felt and seen to act *within ritual contexts* upon a significant number of individuals in ways that produce emotional arousal and reinforce confidence in the system as a whole. The ritual form hypothesis, however, is not without its flaws. Crucially, it does not take account of the role of magic in shaping ritual form (Essay 4.3). More work is needed in order to pinpoint how ritual form is related to sensory arousal, individual experience and emotionality, and how these factors are affected by participation versus observation.[41] Finally, as we have seen (Essay 2.1; cf. Essays 4.3, 6.3), dream epiphanies and other divine manifestations sometimes happened spontaneously, apparently outside of formal ritual contexts, yet they were highly motivating.

## Constructing the Greek festival in time and space

To provide context for the specifics we will encounter in the essays below, we now turn to the methods by which the Greeks located their public rituals in time (by means of festival calendars) and space (by marking off sanctuaries and conducting processions), concluding with a detailed look at alimentary sacrifice, the most frequently performed public ritual in Greek religion. Organization of time by days (one period of light plus one period of dark, or the reverse) and by lunar months makes intuitive sense, for the units of time involved are not large, and the phases of the moon are easily observed.[42] Predictable changes in sunlight, temperature and plant growth also produce an intuitive concept of "year," although the vexatious problem of exactly how many days and months belong in a year received no definitive answer during the period of our study, for the lunar and solar years were reconciled only on an ad hoc basis. Important markers within a year could be established by observation of stars and constellations. Hesiod, for example, makes the cyclical behavior of Orion and the Pleiades (*Op.* 383–4, 609–17) his indicators for the appropriate times to plow fields and to harvest crops.

Greek religious festivals (*heortai*) took place on fixed dates each year; they both interrupted and articulated everyday life.[43] Calendars varied by city, but all were based on a cycle of twelve lunar months. The first day of the month was the new moon, and different cities began their year in different months, though many marked the start of the year in autumn. Most month names were drawn from the names of festivals or associated gods, suggesting that religion was implicated in the development of Greek systems for measuring time. Systematic calendars were developed and overseen by the Greek states, though certain month names appear to predate the period of state formation in the eighth century, just as many regional festivals must also have predated the formation of the Classical *polis* (city state) and *ethnos* (federal state). Ethnicity was signaled by one's calendar: Ionians and

Athenians celebrated the Anthesteria during Anthesterion, while several Dorian calendars included the month Karneios and its corresponding festival, the Karneia. Retrospective timekeeping was managed by naming years according to the then-holder of an important office or priesthood. Thus Argos based its chronology on successive priestesses of Hera, and Athens on its annually elected archons.[44]

A typical civic festival consisted of procession to a sanctuary plus activities performed within the sacred space (usually sacrifice, feasting and choral song). The sanctuary (*temenos*, "cut-off area") was a space "owned" by a god, just as an individual might own a plot of land. The only essential features of a sanctuary were a boundary and an altar, though many also included temples, dining houses and other cult buildings. As we have seen, spatial demarcation is a fundamental feature of ritualized behavior. The marking and elaboration of boundaries to define intrusion by strangers (whether the protected space is a house, a sacred area or a political territory) often become a ritual which directly engages the "hazard-precaution system" posited by Boyer and Liénard. Thus, while territorial marking has important social functions, it also possesses intrinsic salience to human minds.

The placement of sanctuaries has been a fertile area of study over the past three decades. Greek sanctuaries were regularly located in urban areas, but also immediately outside them ("suburban" or "extramural" sanctuaries) and, quite often, miles away on borderlands ("extraurban" sanctuaries). What could account for such variation? François de Polignac's study *Cults, Territory and the Origins of the Greek City-State* proposed that extraurban sanctuaries played a fundamental role in the development of the Greek polis as markers of the territory belonging to a nascent city-state.[45] He further proposed a "bipolar" model according to which cities demonstrated their territorial sovereignty by holding civic processions from a major urban sanctuary to a distant one. Subsequent comparison of his hypotheses with the data have yielded mixed results. While it is clear that many sanctuaries sat at boundaries between civic territories, and that possession of them was often contested, it is difficult to show that emergent poleis purposely founded sanctuaries in order to mark their borders. Growth and change over time meant that what originally counted as a "border" sanctuary could eventually be transformed into an extramural or even an urban sanctuary. Various processes were in play: once-communal sanctuaries often fell under the control of expanding states (as when Corinth took over Isthmia), and the work of politically unifying several towns resulted in the incorporation of their sanctuaries, wherever these might be in relation to a new urban center (as Eleusis and Brauron were absorbed into the emergent state of Athens).[46]

A neglected aspect of sanctuary placement has to do with the economic role of the sanctuary in facilitating trade and festival markets. Travelers engaged in interstate trade relied on the sacred inviolability of sanctuaries (*asulia*, "prohibition on robbery") for protection. The sanctuary of Artemis at Ephesos was able to function as a bank because of this guarantee of security. Thus while some sanctuaries became markets because of their fortuitous placement near borders, states may have chosen the sites of others with an eye to the economic advantages of secure places to trade with their neighbors.[47] Still other sanctuary sites appear to have been determined by the personas of their resident gods: particularly in the Archaic period, Zeus was worshiped on mountaintops and Athena on citadels, while Artemis had an affinity for low-lying, marshy places.[48]

Most festivals began with a parade or procession (*pompē*, "sending"). Processions normally involved the transport and/or display of sacrificial animals, cult statues or sacred objects. Like the sacrifice, the chorus and the competition, processions were considered pleasing offerings to the gods.[49] As de Polignac pointed out, major Greek processions also had a significant political dimension. They operated on multiple levels corresponding to participation, topography and occasion. First, people march (or cause others to march) in a parade in order to be seen. Inclusion or exclusion and one's position in the lineup reveal nuances of status and power (Essay 3.1). Second, the route of the procession marks places of importance: not only the two endpoints but also points between. Cognitively, there is a relationship between linear space and memory, such that physical travel along a route, or even mental rehearsal of such travel, strengthens the semantic memory for information associated with various stops. Greek processions often paused at points along a "sacred way" to perform dances and hymns, and it is possible that the processional practice aided in the transmission of these rituals (Essay 6.1).[50]

## Greek sacrifice: Shifting paradigms

"Sacrifice," broadly defined, refers to the process by which anything consumable (e.g. food, drink or incense) is offered to a god or set apart as sacred. Etymologically, the word is from Latin, and in the Roman context, it indicated that something had been made *sacer*, set apart from everyday life. Animal sacrifice is a special subset, because the process always involves the death of the animal (with all the practical and cognitive consequences of this event) and because it often overlaps with the dining practices of a given culture, in themselves a complicated subject of study. For clarity's sake, the term "sacrifice" in this book refers to animal sacrifice unless otherwise specified.

Ritual slaughter of animals (usually "for" an invisible but powerful entity) occurs in cultures all over the world, but it is not necessarily invested with the same meaning, nor even understood as a distinct rite. For example, in ancient Egypt animals were killed and burned for gods or dedicated to them as mummies, but the slaughter itself was not perceived as the central act of the ritual.[51] Depending on the perspective of the participants and/or the scholarly observer, sacrifice may be conceptualized as a single act (of ritual killing), a process with several stages (preparation, serving and consumption of a meal) or a stage in a lengthier ritual (a festival with multiple ritual components). Sacrificial atonement for disobedient acts was important in ancient Judaism, but far less so among the Greeks. Some Greek sacrifices were performed primarily for purification, and some for divination. Most were alimentary sacrifices which resulted in a meat meal for participants, but some were predicated on the renunciation of the animal's body as food. Even if we confine ourselves to ancient Greek culture, sacrifice is difficult to define.[52]

Most modern approaches to sacrifice have either sought meaning in its origins or rejected the quest for origins as irrelevant. The late nineteenth century was dominated by origins-based approaches which posited stages of cultural development. In *Primitive Culture*, E. B. Tylor wrote that very "primitive" peoples considered sacrifice a gift to the deity, while "higher" cultures viewed sacrifice as a form of self-abnegation, the giving up of something precious.[53] Robertson Smith's *Lectures on the Religion of the Semites* inaugurated a long tradition of scholarship in which sacrifice was analyzed as a social and alimentary activity. For Smith, the original function of sacrifice was to establish group bonds through consumption of a totem animal identified with the god; this function was later supplemented by others, such as gift-giving and expiation.[54] Henri Hubert and Marcel Mauss, on the other hand, rejected the notion that the origins of sacrifice shed light on its meaning. Instead, they favored a synchronic approach. In their view, every form of sacrifice can be explained by the need to mediate between the sacred and profane worlds. Such mediation, whether for gift-giving, purification, expiation or other purposes, requires the destruction of all or part of a victim. Since they viewed the sacred/profane distinction as a symbolic representation of the relationship between group and individual, Hubert and Mauss argued (like their mentor Durkheim) that sacrifice functions to build social cohesion through a group experience.[55]

Each of the accounts I have described so far is universalizing: each views sacrifice as a distinct ritual which occurs across cultures and has the same meaning. Evans-Pritchard's detailed study of the Nuer people is an unusual example of a non-universalizing, contextual approach to sacrifice. He insisted that sacrifice be understood in its cultural context, and objected to the sociologist's habit of treating sacrifice as "a mechanical rite without reference to religious thought and practice as a whole, without regard to what men conceive their own nature and the nature of the gods to be."[56]

During the twentieth century, an important trend located the origin and meaning of sacrifice in violence and aggression. Sigmund Freud opined that sacrifice gave expression to repressed violent impulses, while simultaneously alleviating the guilt associated with them.[57] In *Violence and the Sacred*, René Girard proposed that sacrifice was a fundamental element of human culture, ritually displacing homicidal impulses and primordial guilt through the slaughter of animals.[58] Pinpointing the origin of Greek sacrifice in Paleolithic hunting ritual, Karl Meuli argued that it arose as a means of allaying the guilt aroused by the killing of a hunted animal; the ritual was then transferred to domesticated animals during the Neolithic period.[59] Meuli's interest in the relationship between hunting and sacrifice was taken up by Walter Burkert, who eclectically combined research on human evolution (especially the role of hunting in the development of human social behavior) with Durkheimian functionalism and a structuralist's attention to symbolic oppositions. Drawing on Konrad Lorenz's studies of animal aggression, he posited that as a ritualized hunt, sacrifice offers a redirection of aggressive human urges which might otherwise rend the community, and permits a resolution of the paradox that humans inflict death in order to live: "The ritual betrays

*Figure 4.2* A sacrificial pig is held up to an altar so that blood will spill there as its throat is cut (blood from a previous sacrifice is visible). Attic red figure cup by the Epidromios Painter, ca. 510–500. Photo: RMN-Grand Palais/Art Resource

an underlying anxiety about the continuation of life in the face of death."[60] Freud, Girard and Burkert all assumed that the origins of sacrifice were pertinent to its later manifestations, and all offered universalizing explanations which placed sacrifice at the center of religion.

A different approach was developed in Paris by Jean-Pierre Vernant and his colleagues, who focused not on killing but on serving and eating as key aspects of sacrifice among the Greeks.[61] The Paris school rejected origins-based, universalizing analyses in favor of a structuralist, synchronic approach, and limited the scope of its inquiry to ancient Greek sacrifice, which Vernant (like his predecessors Hubert and Mauss) described as a technology for mediation between the human and divine worlds, but also as a symbolic system which defined the human being's place between god and beast and articulated his social relations. In turn,

Marcel Detienne argued that all consumable meat came from ritually slaughtered animals, which implied a "cuisine of sacrifice" and a significant overlap between the realms of the culinary and the sacred.[62] The Paris school further emphasized the relationship between meat-eating and citizenship, for a Greek individual's civic status was marked by inclusion (or exclusion) from the distribution of meat, and by the cuts and portions to which he or she was entitled.[63] Despite the differences between Burkert and the Paris school, they shared the conclusion that the meaning of sacrifice was to be located in its regulation of social behavior. And while Vernant emphasized *la cuisine* over *la violence*, he did not discount the conceptual force of the fact that human beings must kill in order to eat; both theories asserted that the sacrificial rite involved a self-conscious concealment of the preparations for slaughter.[64]

With the turn of the century, a paradigm shift began, as scholars increasingly questioned the influential views of Girard, Burkert and, to a lesser extent, the Paris school.[65] Burkert based his analysis on the "Man the Hunter" anthropological paradigm first proposed in the 1940s, which envisioned killer apes evolving into aggressive humans. This version of human prehistory has been questioned, as have Meuli's data on prehistoric hunting rituals.[66] The twentieth-century concept of an essential link between violence and sacrifice, as well as the notion that participants in a sacrifice feel guilt, has been criticized on the grounds that, empirically speaking, there is little evidence to support these claims, or even the idea that witnessing the death of an animal inevitably causes emotional arousal. (Cognitive theory, which posits an inverse relationship between frequency and arousal, predicts that arousal will be high for people unaccustomed to slaughter, but low for those who regularly witness it.)[67] The visual evidence of vase paintings and votive reliefs similarly weighs against the idea that animal sacrifice was an occasion for guilt over the shedding of blood, even if Greek myth plentifully demonstrates a preoccupation with the possibility of human sacrifice.[68] Far less attention has been paid to Burkert's interpretation of the role of sacrifice in expressing and reconciling the conceptual opposition between death and life, although Jay McInerney recently offered a neo-Burkertian interpretation in which sacrifice ritualizes the paradox perceived by pastoral peoples in relation to the necessity of both nurturing and killing their animals.[69]

As the weakening of the existing paradigms created opportunities to test new approaches, recent years have seen a plethora of conferences and new volumes on sacrifice.[70] A key element of the Vernant-Detienne formulation for Greece has been falsified by Gunnel Ekroth, who used osteological evidence to show that even in sanctuaries, not all meat consumed had to come from sacrificed animals – a finding which weakens the picture of a social and political system primarily regulated through the cuisine of sacrifice.[71] Additionally, the concept of equal distribution as the sign of citizen status has been questioned on the grounds that the meat yield from sacrifice was distributed to elites rather than the general citizenry.[72] Although the special relevance of community to sacrifice cannot be denied, a renewed interest in the role of the gods in Greek religion stimulated F. S. Naiden's criticism of functionalist analyses that "preserve the human aspects of sacrifice at the expense of the divine aspects."[73] Although there is as yet no full analysis of Greek sacrifice from a cognitive perspective, Naiden's approach is consistent with an understanding of alimentary sacrifice as an activity through which people maintain reciprocity with superhuman agents, while McInerney's work suggests that, however routine it may be, the slaughter of domesticated mammals in a subsistence culture tends to trigger ritualization.

## ESSAY 4.1: SACRIFICING TO ZEUS POLIEUS ON KOS

Greek alimentary sacrifice usually followed a familiar pattern: procession to the altar; purification and prayer; slaughter of the animal and burning of select parts for the god; division of meat and consumption by the participants. Within this normative model, however, myriad procedural variations were possible, including groupings of multiple sacrifices.[74] A second category of Greek sacrifice was non-alimentary or "renunciatory": ritual killing that did not result in consumption of the animal. Again the procedures varied widely, but might include a holocaust (burning the flayed carcass of the entire animal) or special manipulations of its blood; sometimes the animal's body functioned primarily as a tool for divination or purification. A third category consisted of hybrid cases: alimentary sacrifice with partial meat consumption, or a sequence in which a non-alimentary phase with one animal was followed by a consumption phase with a second animal.[75]

To what degree such details were influenced by the identity of the god receiving the sacrifice has long been the subject of debate, but it is clear that the traditional scholarly assignment of alimentary procedures to celestial "Olympian" gods and renunciatory procedures to earthly "chthonian" gods (together with these labels themselves) is too rigid to be useful. Correlations, but not rigid requirements, existed between individual deities and the species, age, sex and color of animals presented to them. For example, piglets were given to Demeter and, surprisingly often, to Zeus; female animals were more likely to be preferentially assigned to goddesses, and uncastrated male animals to gods.[76] Other determining factors have been suggested, including the nature of the occasion rather than the identity of the god. Nock wrote that solemn actions, such as ceremonies to ward off evil, to purify or to "exercise direct and efficacious influence," required special renunciatory procedures exemplified by holocaust sacrifice.[77] Following van Baal, Ekroth has suggested that sacrificial rites be divided into "low intensity" (normative procedures representing the ideal relationship between humans and gods) and "high intensity" (unusual procedures, such as large animal holocaust, which were employed in crisis situations), with a spectrum of hybrid rituals in between.[78] Pragmatic considerations could be expected to produce a bias toward alimentary sacrifice or hybrid procedures that permitted humans to consume some of the meat, and toward the use of less expensive, more widely available animals for renunciatory sacrifice (e.g. a piglet versus an ox).[79]

In order to explore these questions further, let us turn to a ritual calendar of the mid-fourth century from the island of Kos.[80] Inscribed on four stone slabs set up in the sanctuary of the Twelve Gods, the calendar is incomplete. Among the preserved parts are directions for the conduct of a major civic and religious event, the annual festival of Zeus Polieus ("Zeus of the City") during the month of Batromios.[81] This calendar provides an unusual wealth of ritual detail, probably because the political unification of Kos in 366 required multiple changes to existing procedures; the disruption to oral tradition in such cases often stimulated the creation of a written record. The festival for Zeus Polieus includes a procession, heralds who perform various auxiliary roles, a preliminary sacrifice to Hestia, purification, libations, non-meat food offerings and carefully calculated distribution of meat. All these are widely attested, normative sacrificial activities. Other features, such as the method of selection for the victims, are unusual. In the following translation, content in parentheses is added for explanatory purposes.

> Lines 1–9: . . . and pray to the gods brought in to the other tribes just as to the other gods. Let the priest and the guardians of sacred things and the magistrates proclaim the yearly seasonable things as a festival; and let the overseers of the sacred rites and the heralds go to each tribal division. Let them drive nine oxen, an ox from each Ninth, from A – and First Pasthemidai, and from Nostidai. Let the Pamphyloi drive (their oxen) to the agora first, and in the agora they (i.e. the oxen) mix together. Let the priest sit at the table wearing the sacred garment, and the overseers of the sacred rites on each side of the table.

Side A of the inscription begins with an incomplete sentence, perhaps a reference to the unification of Kos, which must have required certain gods to be "brought in" where they had not been worshiped before. The festival for Zeus requires the participation of many officials, each of whom has a distinct role to play; some (the "guardians of sacred things" and the "overseers of the sacred rites") have primarily religious roles. The most important of these officials is the priest of Zeus Polieus, Athena Polias and the Twelve Gods, whose full title is known from other inscriptions.[82] Others, like the "chief magistrates," are concerned with the broader affairs of the city. (In lines 22–9 we also hear of "presidents" who take an oath, perhaps their oath of office for the year). Although we do not know in which season the month Batromios occurred, "the yearly seasonable things" (*eniautia hōraia*) sounds like a reference either to sowing or harvest time. The preparations involve a proclamation of the festival to the citizens of Kos, who begin the process by driving nine oxen into the agora, the city center, where the officials are waiting.

> Lines 9–18: Let the Pamphyloi drive up the three finest oxen, on the chance that one of these may be chosen. If (one is) not (chosen), let the Hylleis drive three, on the chance that one of these may be chosen. And if (one is) not (chosen), let the Dymanes drive the remaining three, on the chance that one of these may be chosen. And if (one is) not (chosen), let them drive others into the agora, and drive them past in the same way to see if one of them may be chosen. If not, let them drive a third (group) in for selection according to the same procedures. If none of those is chosen, let them select an additional

> ox from each tribal division. When they have driven these, they mix (them) with the others, and make a selection straightaway and pray and make the proclamation.

The new polis of Kos was made up of members of three old Dorian tribes, the Pamphyloi, Hylleis and Dymanes. Each of these tribes was further divided into three groups for a total of nine subsets, each of which brings its finest oxen to the agora. The elaborate procedure for selecting the sacrificial ox reflects the union of the three tribes into one polis, though it is clear that a hierarchy of some kind exists, in which the Pamphyloi have the first shot at providing the ox for Zeus. Although the method of choosing the victim is not explicitly stated, most scholars think that the ox must have self-selected in some way, either by lowering its head or by tasting grain placed on the table. If it were merely a matter of determining which animal was "best" in terms of physical condition, there would be no need for the labor-intensive procedure of bringing so many oxen to the agora, or of driving each group of oxen forward in turn.

The selection procedure is a form of impetrative divination, an attempt to displace agency in the matter of choice to the god, who causes the animal to perform a predetermined act (hence the wording "to see if one may be chosen"). But why was the special procedure used for this festival, and not for others? First, let us recall Liénard's proposal that the interplay between the intuitive ontological categories of "living kind" and "artifact" in the transformation from animal to useful object makes certain aspects of sacrifice salient phenomena across cultures. This would be true for virtually any form of animal sacrifice, but the Koan practice elaborates and intensifies the "puzzle" of the transformation by adding an element of risk. The Koans slaughtered an ox, the animal on which they depended for their ability to plow the fields. Because agriculture was an important theme of the festival, the killing of the ox revealed a conflict between its value as a living draft animal on the one hand and, on the other, as a collection of non-living artifacts – prestigious cuts of meat, valuable hide and so on.[83] Similar concerns were at work, together with similar oddities of ritual, in the Athenian Bouphonia, another ox sacrifice for Zeus Polieus.[84] The festival of Bouphonia ("Ox-killing") involved not only the "self-selection" of the ox but also a disclaimer of responsibility by the man who wielded the knife, and the symbolic restoration of the animal by stuffing its hide and yoking it to a plow. In the context of a cult concerned with grain agriculture and the welfare of the city, the risk involved in killing and consuming draft animals could be addressed through a ritual in which the sacrifice was endorsed through divine selection of the victim.[85]

Unfortunately, the inscription does not specify the content of the prayer, but we can compare a prayer delivered to Zeus Sosipolis (Savior of the City) at Magnesia on the Maiandros. The Magnesians pray

> for the salvation of the city and the land and the citizens and women and children and others staying in the city and country, for peace and wealth and the fruitfulness of the grain, and of all the other fruits of the earth and of the herds.
> (*LSAM* 32.7, lines 10–14, 26–31 = *SEG* 46.1467)

At Kos, Athens and Magnesia, the citizens did not make lavish gifts of multiple oxen, in spite of the importance of these civic cults of Zeus. Instead, they sacrificed a single ox, the archetypal draft animal.[86] Although pairs of oxen were commonly used, one could do the job, as Hesiod says (*Op.* 405): "First of all, get a house and a woman and an ox for the plough."

> Lines 18–22: Thereafter they drive up (oxen) again according to the same procedures. And (an ox) is sacrificed if it bows to Hestia. The Bearer of the Privileges of the Kings performs the sacrifice, both supplying the (customary) offerings and an additional half-measure. He receives as perquisites the hide and a leg, the overseers of the sacred rites (receive) a leg, (and) the rest of the meat (belongs to) the city.

The same method is used to select an ox for Hestia, and again the agency in the choice of victim is displaced by interpreting the ox's behavior as a sign. Hestia, the hearth goddess, looked after both domestic and civic security.[87] It was standard protocol to inaugurate a sacrificial ritual, particularly a major state festival, with offerings to Hestia, although less common to present her with an expensive ox. The ox for Hestia, it has been suggested, is a practical measure augmenting the amount of meat available to feed "the city" at this important festival.[88] The additional ox is not assigned to Zeus, perhaps because the core ritual assumes a *single* ox as the god's choice. For a larger-scale sacrifice, the elaborate divinatory method would have been extremely cumbersome, yet it could not be abandoned.

The ox for Hestia is slaughtered and butchered according to standard procedures which are left unspecified because they were considered common knowledge (i.e. there is no need for the special procedures we will encounter below with regard to the ox of Zeus). The calendar does specify, however, the shares to be given to the overseers and to the one who performs the sacrifice, an official called the "Bearer of the Privileges of Kings." His office seems to be a relic from the time when the Koans were ruled by kings, and he is required to supply some of the usual non-meat offerings (typically cakes or grain) himself.

> Lines 22–9: The heralds lead the (ox) chosen for Zeus to the agora. When they are in the agora, he who owns the ox, or another, favorably inclined on behalf of that one, proclaims, "I supply the ox for the Koans, let the Koans pay the price to Hestia." Let the presidents, once they have taken the oath, immediately determine the value (of the ox). When the valuation has been made, let the herald publicly proclaim how much the valuation was. Then they drive up the ox beside Hestia Phamia and sacrifice. The priest places a wool fillet on the ox and pours out a cup of mixed wine before it.

In the next stage of the ritual, the ox's owner or his representative has the privilege of publicly announcing his contribution. The value of the ox is formally established. The transaction is framed as a "sale" in order to make clear that the ox is being presented to Zeus not by an individual but by the Koans as a people.

Instead of accepting payment for the ox, however, the owner asks that the price be given to Hestia (i.e. added to the public funds). From the agora, the participants gather at the altar of Hestia, where she receives a small preliminary offering (unspecified, but perhaps incense).[89] The ox for Zeus is then marked as his possession with a wool fillet (used as a garland) and libation.

> Lines 29–38: Then they bring the ox and the (piglet to be used as) burnt offering and seven cakes and honey and a wool fillet. As they go, they call for holy silence. There, having tied the ox, they begin the rite with olive and laurel branches. The heralds burn the piglet and the innards upon the altar, making a libation of honey and milk on them; having thoroughly washed the intestines, they burn them beside the altar. After they have been burned without wine, let him (the priest) pour a libation of honey and milk on them. Let the herald proclaim that they are celebrating the yearly seasonable things of Zeus Polieus as a festival. Let the priest sacrifice, in addition to the intestines, incense and cakes and (wine) libations, both mixed and unmixed, and a garland.

From the altar of Hestia, there is a solemn procession to another altar (of Zeus Polieus?), during which participants and onlookers are to keep silence, as is normal during the most sacred stages of a ritual. Here, after purification with water sprinkled from sweet-smelling branches, they slaughter a piglet and remove its internal organs. The piglet is placed on the altar together with its upper viscera; over these is poured *melikraton*, a mixture of honey and milk. The intestines are carefully washed and burned; then honey and milk are poured out again. *Melikraton* belongs to a special category of "wineless" libations. It marks this portion of the ritual as different from the norms of alimentary sacrifice. The piglet is a holocaust ("entirely burned"), meaning that nobody will eat its flesh; this too departs from the norm. Scholars debate the meaning of these "marked" features. Should we interpret them as elements in the self-contained logic of the ritual procedure itself, signaling successive phases which give the ritual its formal structure? This is the view shared by Burkert and by Graf, who notes that after the piglet sacrifice and proclamation, the return to normalcy is signaled by the array of cakes, garland and incense burned with a libation of mixed wine, plus a shot of strong, unmixed wine, which is the opposite of the mild *melikraton*.[90]

Scullion, however, has defended the older idea that there is an independent reason for the marked features: they are found in connection with gods of a "chthonian" character, those conceptually associated with the earth (*chthōn*) or the underworld. Such gods and goddesses gave agricultural bounty, but they also required propitiation. Thus sober, soothing milk and honey were preferred to a stimulating libation of wine for the appeasement stage of the ritual, and the god received the entire piglet, rather than sharing it with his human worshipers. On this view, Zeus Polieus, an agricultural deity, was given distinctive ritual treatment because his local identity included a chthonian element, despite the Panhellenic concept of Zeus as a sky god. (Whether it is useful to describe Zeus Polieus and other gods of similarly "mixed" nature as "chthonian" remains a matter of debate.)[91] A third alternative is to identify the marked features as indicators that the Koans consider their appeal to Zeus for another year of prosperity a particularly "high-intensity," solemn occasion.

> Lines 38–44: Then let the priest and herald go to the overseers of the sacred rites at the public building; the overseers of the sacred rites entertain the priest and heralds as guests on this night. When they have made libations, let the priest choose from among the overseers of the sacred rites a slaughterer of the ox which is to be sacrificed to Zeus Polieus, and let him (the priest) publicly order that he (the slaughterer) keep himself pure from woman and man during the night. Let the heralds choose whomever they wish among themselves as a slaughterer of the ox, and let him, whoever is willing, publicly order the one who has been chosen (to act) according to the same regulations.

Instead of proceeding immediately to the sacrifice of the ox, the participants pause and the animal is given a reprieve of one night, during which the men expected to participate most directly in the sacrifice are entertained. The two who will wield the knife are chosen, one from the overseers and one from the heralds. Each is publicly commanded to abstain from sexual activity, in order to maintain an especially pure state in advance of the sacrifice. Presumably, a similar level of abstention was expected of the priest, but it is significant that the participants enjoined to purity are precisely those who will be the direct agents of the slaughter. The special selection process for the ox-slayers is another marked feature; normally the killing would be performed without much of a fuss by one person only, either the priest or a hired butcher/cook.[92]

> Lines 46–55: On the twentieth day: the chosen ox is sacrificed to Zeus Polieus. The things to be wrapped are wrapped in hide. Upon the hearth, a measure of barley meal is sacrificed, two half-measure loaves of wheat bread, one of which contains cheese, and the things wrapped in hide. The priest pours a libation over these, three mixing bowls of wine. The hide of the ox and the leg are the priest's as perquisites – the priest supplies the offerings – and half of the breast and half of the belly. From the leg belonging to the overseers of the sacred rites, the end of the hip is given to the incense-bearer. A double portion of meat, from the shoulder, (and) a three-pronged spit of blood pudding to the heralds, a double portion of meat from the back to the Sons of Nestor, meat to the physicians, meat to the flute player, (portions of) the brain to each of the smiths and potters; the rest of the meat (belongs to) the city. All of these things are not to be carried outside of the city.

At last the principal act of the festival is undertaken, the sacrifice of the chosen ox. The "things wrapped in hide" may be the *splanchna*, the ox's viscera; if so, they are burned rather than being consumed by participants as in a normative alimentary sacrifice. They are accompanied by offerings of wheat bread, barley and cheese, further accentuating the concept of Zeus Polieus as a god concerned with agricultural bounty. Note that there is no terminological distinction between the "sacrifice" of the ox and the "sacrifice" of barley or loaves of bread. The verb *thuō*, "I sacrifice," means "I burn all or part of something for a deity." A hearth (*hestia*), rather than an altar, is unexpectedly specified as the place where the offerings are burned. Perhaps this is actually the civic hearth in the "public building" (*to oikēma to damosion*) where the previous night's festivities had occurred, but this is only a guess; certainly the hearth reinforces the close link between Hestia and Zeus in this festival.[93]

As in any major animal sacrifice, there is a careful sharing out of the meat according to a social and cultic hierarchy. Some of the designated recipients are participants in the sacrificial action (the heralds and flute player); others appear to be professions singled out for favor during this festival (physicians, smiths, potters). The role of the Sons of Nestor is unknown, though they appear to be a Koan family group, and they receive a very choice portion. The restriction on removing the meat from the city is another marked feature pointing to the special status of this sacrifice.[94]

> Lines 55–7: On the same day: to Athena Polias (sacrifice) a pregnant ewe. The priest performs the sacrifice and supplies the offerings. He receives as perquisites the skin and a leg.

The festival is rounded out with the sacrifice of a pregnant ewe to Zeus Polieus' cult partner, Athena Polias. Zeus and Athena are paired in several other cults on Kos (as elsewhere) and the connection here underlines their joint care for the city.[95] The receipt of a pregnant animal by Athena reflects her interest in agriculture, as pregnant victims were most often given to goddesses in contexts where vegetable fertility was at issue.[96]

To summarize, multiple factors shaped the complex procedures for the sacrifice to Zeus Polieus on Kos. Intuitively, Zeus was represented primarily as a local deity who resided at the center of the city, not as a faraway god on Olympos; yet there was a potentially Panhellenic dimension in the joint cult of Zeus and Athena with the Twelve Gods. The priest, identified by a sacred garment, was designated to interact with Zeus on behalf of the city, and the points of contact were the god's altar and (possibly) the civic hearth. The concrete device of the "sale" made the conversion of the ox from individual to communal offering intuitively plausible. As a deity concerned with grain agriculture, a business fraught with uncertainty and risk, Zeus Polieus had to be approached using special measures. Because of the recipient and the occasion (perhaps the start of a new agricultural cycle), purity beyond the norm was deemed necessary for efficacy; the role of purification in the ritual was a highly intuitive element. To grain-farming peoples, the conflict between the value of a living draft animal and that of a collection of inert artifacts (hide, cuts of meat, blood puddings) may be a locus of anxiety. Therefore in this context of risk, selection of the victim was displaced to the gods, and the ox-slaughterers themselves received special attention, both on Kos and in other civic Zeus cults. Many ritual details, such as the use of grain, bread, *melikraton* and wine, were specific to the Koan way of life and symbolically evocative for Koans in ways which non-agricultural, non-Mediterranean peoples would not recognize. Turning to social aspects, the sacrifice was but one element within a festival for Zeus as the main "poliad" or civic deity. The civic element of the festival was manifest in the extra attention paid to Hestia, goddess of the state's common hearth, and the ritual emphasized the roles of all the city's most important officials, priestly or otherwise. The ritual also reflected the unification of Kos (the cattle presented by the three Dorian tribes), while recognizing the superior social status of certain groups (the Pamphyloi and the Sons of Nestor) through privileges such as the distribution of meat.

## ESSAY 4.2 THESEUS AND THE ATHENIAN CALENDAR

The mythic and cultic profiles of the hero Theseus changed radically during the century spanning the transition from the Archaic to the Classical period. At first portrayed primarily as an ephebe (youth), he gained a mature kingly dignity. At first an adventurer of questionable moral status, he became a model of gentlemanly probity, justice and compassion. Where he originally had few cults at Athens, he became an important figure in Athenian religion, and his exploits were etiologically tied to a raft of new and preexisting rituals. As far as we can tell, these transformations began after the middle of the sixth century and were completed by the end of the Classical period in the mid-fourth century.[97] In this essay we will examine Theseus' relationship to the Athenian festival calendar.

Theseus was known to Homer as a daring but slightly disreputable character. The *Iliad* (3.144) alludes to the taking of his mother, Aithra, as a hostage by the Dioskouroi, as payback for Theseus' abduction of the young Helen. The story was popular in Greek art and poetry during the seventh century. In the *Odyssey* (11.321–5), we hear that Artemis was responsible for the death of Ariadne after Theseus brought her to the island of Dia; though the slaying of the Minotaur is not mentioned, we can assume knowledge of the story. The Minotaur and Helen's abduction are also the two earliest-attested exploits of Theseus in Greek art, both belonging to the seventh century. Their first appearances occur not in Athens but in Boiotia and the Peloponnese. The Athenian iconographic tradition begins with the François Vase (Figure 4.3; ca. 570), which includes a scene of Theseus leading the Athenian youths and maidens as they are greeted by Ariadne and her nurse, and another of him battling the Centaurs at Peirithous' wedding.[98]

That Theseus was an Athenian gave him a crucial advantage over Herakles, previously the single most popular heroic figure in Attica. As the sixth century yielded to the fifth amidst great social and political change, the time was right for a hero who could personify Athens, embodying the virtues of justice and compassion which the Athenians attributed to their city. In the time of Peisistratos, Theseus may already have possessed a shrine in the city. From the second half of the sixth century, his growing popularity among Athenian vase painters paralleled the development of the new democracy under Kleisthenes. He seems to have been

*Figure 4.3* Theseus and the Athenian youths and maidens arrive in Crete. Theseus greets Ariadne while one of the youths lifts his hands in anguished prayer. On the lower register, a battle scene of Lapiths and Centaurs. Detail on the François Vase, by Ergotimos and Kleitias, ca. 570. Museo Archeologico, Florence. Photo: Scala/Art Resource

the subject of a new epic poem, the *Theseis*, around this time, but it was the clever general Kimon who sparked the final stage in the revolution by which Theseus was to become symbolic of Athens itself.[99]

Theseus, it was said, had appeared at Marathon to lend his aid when the Athenian general Miltiades led the Greek forces against the Persian invaders. Miltiades' son Kimon was a political rival of Themistokles, who had masterminded the equally important naval victory at Salamis. In 476, when he captured the island of Skyros, where Theseus was supposed to have died, Kimon achieved a public relations coup by "discovering" the hero's bones and returning them to Athens.[100]

> For the Athenians had received an oracle telling them to bring back the remains of Theseus to the city, and to honor him as a hero. But they did not know where he lay, for the Skyrians disagreed with the story and would not allow a search. But now Kimon with great ostentation and after some difficulty discovered the tomb, and placing the bones in his own trireme conveyed them with all honor and magnificence to the hero's own land, after nearly four hundred years. And for this, in particular, the people were pleased with him.
>
> (Plut. *Cim.* 8.5–6)[101]

Although political manipulation by Kimon, and by Kleisthenes before him, unquestionably played its part, the Athenian embrace of Theseus as a popular hero, national founder and cult figure was so thorough and enthusiastic that it cannot be explained simply as the result of propaganda. Nor do contemporary Athenians seem to have noticed the artificiality of Theseus' prominent new role in Athenian religion. Instead, as we will see, even educated citizens like Thucydides were quite ready to accept the historicity of the "new" Theseus and his contributions to Athens. It must have seemed appropriate to establish honors for Theseus in celebration of his "homecoming." Meanwhile, a number of local traditions concerning the hero were expanded and elaborated, and he was grafted onto festivals which originally had little or nothing to do with him. To understand the process, we need to recognize that in the early fifth century, Athenian culture was more oral than literate, and there were no authoritative histories to consult. Instead, there was speculation, popular enthusiasm and mythmaking.

Yet Theseus' emergence in the Classical festival calendar was neither random nor entirely fanciful, but shaped by a new dynamic between preexisting myths and preexisting rituals. The principal traditions concerning Theseus appear to be tied to three days of the month: the sixth, seventh and eighth, governed respectively by Artemis, Apollo and Poseidon.[102] Throughout the year, festivals with Thesean connections occurred on these days of the month and were connected with these gods. Interestingly, it was not the mature statesman of the Athenian tragedians who dominated the calendar, but the youthful hero of the François Vase, undergoing the ordeal of the Minotaur with his age-mates.

The most detailed ancient account of Theseus' role in Athenian religion is found in Plutarch's life of the hero; his primary sources of information were late Classical Attic historians, such as Philochorus and Demon, which makes his *Theseus* a valuable window on local tradition.[103] Another important witness, though a late one, is Pausanias, who describes the Theseion, a sanctuary located on the southern edge of the agora. It was decorated with fifth-century paintings of Theseus battling the Amazons and defending the Lapiths against the Centaurs, as well as a scene from Theseus' confrontation with Minos during the crossing to Crete with the twice-seven youths and maidens.[104] The first two subjects, with their references to the routing of foreign and barbaric enemies, were favorites in Athens after the Persian Wars and were also used on the metopes of the Parthenon. As we will see, the crossing to Crete had special resonance in Athenian religion.

Athenian traditions repeatedly tie Theseus to Apollo Delphinios, a god concerned with political life and the maturation of youths into adult citizens.[105] Although his importance in Athens was diminished by the Classical period, Apollo Delphinios represented a shared heritage dating to the Dark Age and linking Athens, the Ionian cities (including their religious center at Delos) and Crete. Miletos, for example, had historical and legendary ties to Crete, and Apollo Delphinios was the key civic deity of the Milesians (Essay 6.1). Of Theseus' arrival in Athens on the eighth day of the first month of the year, Pausanias reports that men constructing a temple for Apollo Delphinios jeered at the young man's effeminate costume (apparently the long Ionian robe also worn by Apollo), and that he demonstrated his masculinity by throwing a yoke of oxen higher than the roof of the temple. It was also in the Delphinion that Aigeus, about to poison the stranger at the behest of Medeia, recognized his own sword in Theseus' hands and immediately acknowledged him as his son and successor. Before leaving for Crete, Theseus made vows and prayers to Apollo Delphinios, dedicating a suppliant's olive branch. Plutarch mentions a girls' procession to the Delphinion to supplicate Apollo, held annually on 6 Mounichion, the date of Theseus' departure.[106]

Legend located the departure for Crete at the port of Phaleron. The Kybernesia ("Festival of the Pilot") took place on 8 Boedromion; it honored Poseidon (Theseus' divine father) and heroes who had tombs in the vicinity. One of the heroes was said to be Theseus' pilot Nausithoös (or Nauseiros), and another his lookout Phaiax. According to Plutarch, these were sailors from Salamis whom Theseus recruited for the mission. Not coincidentally, this festival was given special attention by the Salaminioi, an Athenian *genos* (plural *genē*, a hereditary cult association) whose name connotes the island of Salamis, and sacrifices to Poseidon and the heroes are noted in their festival calendar.[107] The Salaminioi seem to have wielded a fair amount of influence in Athenian religious affairs, and may have been instrumental in the mythmaking that tied Theseus to the Kybernesia. (The names Nauseiros and Phaiax, reminiscent of the seagoing Phaiakians in the *Odyssey*, suggest that a far different etiology prevailed before the Thesean version was created.) The establishment of these hero shrines was, of course, credited to Theseus. The attraction of local heroes like those at Phaleron into the orbit of Theseus was a recurrent phenomenon throughout Attica. Many of these developments must have taken place in the late sixth century, when the political geography of Athens was reorganized with the advent of democracy.[108]

The major Thesean celebrations of the year came early in Pyanopsion (October/November), which was the month of the autumn sowing as well as the vintage. The Oschophoria ("carrying of grape-laden vine branches") most likely took place on the sixth.[109] Administered by the Salaminioi, it featured a procession from a shrine of Dionysos in Athens to the shrine of Athena Skiras in Phaleron, followed by a sacrifice, a feast and a footrace of youths organized by tribes. Clearly a pre-existing festival related to the vintage, the Oschophoria included an unusual ritual feature: the procession was led by the *oschophoroi*, two boys dressed as women and carrying vine branches. Plutarch explains that this was because Theseus had hit upon the strategem of substituting a pair of comely young men for two of the maidens destined to be the Minotaur's victims. Other distinctive features of the Oschophoria were also given Thesean etiologies: the cry prescribed for the onlookers seemed to express both joy (at Theseus' return) and sorrow (at the death of Aigeus); the female *deipnophoroi* ("meal-bearers") at the feast were included in memory of the mothers of the youths and maidens, who brought food for the children selected to journey to Crete. Finally, tales were told at the festival in imitation of the tales these mothers told "to comfort and encourage their children."[110]

With its procession from Athens to Phaleron, the Oschophoria connected the port and the city center, a ritual feature equally appropriate for commemorating Theseus' departure and his homecoming. Indeed, some Oschophoric traditions collected by Plutarch focus on Theseus' departure (the mothers who supply food and comforting tales), while others refer to his joyous return (the procession). Thus the myth of Theseus intruded itself on an existing ritual of Dionysos and/or Athena Skiras, obscuring and replacing any older myths about these deities and their connection to the festival. Meanwhile, the dress of the young *oschophoroi* and other details of the ritual provided the inspiration for new mythmaking about the hero and his companions.[111] In his analysis of the Oschophoria, Scullion suggests that while etiological myth was a highly productive and dynamic form of mythmaking, it may also have been more a preoccupation of poets and historians than of the actual participants in the cults. Certainly Theseus' role in the activities at Phaleron appears post hoc and artificial, and we must consider the possibility that there was a very low degree of fusion between myth and ritual – that some of the etiologies are the educated guesses of antiquarians, accessible only to the literate. On the other hand, Theseus' growing popularity during the fifth century may have stimulated this mythmaking, in tandem with systematic efforts by various interested groups (the Salaminioi) and individuals (Kimon) to guide the process.[112]

The Apolline festival of Pyanopsia ("Bean-Boiling"), held on 7 Pyanopsion, involved the consumption of a variety of seeds and beans cooked together in a pot; at this time boys also carried olive branches hung with figs and other autumn produce from house to house. The Theseus myth was grafted to the Pyanopsia, and the seventh of the month was identified as the date of his joyous return from the adventure of the Minotaur. Plutarch says that the hero and his companions disembarked at the port of Phaleron, where he fulfilled the sacrifices and libations vowed upon his departure. The stew of varied beans and pulses, perhaps originally a consecration of the seeds soon to be planted, was explained as a homecoming meal, thrown together from the chance ingredients the newly returned youths and maidens had on hand, while the branches carried by the boys recalled Theseus' supplication of Apollo Delphinios.[113]

Theseus' encroachment on the Pyanopsia and Oschophoria must have resulted from the selection of 8 Pyanopsion as the date for his own festival, the Theseia.[114] This was administered by another of the old Athenian *genē*, the Phytalidai. Certain families involved in funding the Theseia traced their descent to the twice-seven youths and maidens. They owed this privilege to the fact that they had been the first to welcome Theseus to Athens when he arrived from Troizen on 8 Hekatombaion, the first month of the year. The Phytalidai had provided hospitality and purified Theseus from the blood pollution incurred when he slew his cousin Skiron. The participation of an aristocratic *genos* in the cult of Theseus seems to afford it a venerable pedigree, but it is probably no coincidence that Kimon hailed from the same deme as the Phytalidai. Again, it is plausible that a number of Athenian families traced their descent to the twice-seven youths and maidens. For them, myth and ritual would have been well integrated in the celebration of the Theseia.[115]

Our earliest reference to the Theseia indicates that it included an element of food distribution to the poor, a typically Thesean (and Kimonean) feature: "Oh! You old fellows, who used to soak up soup at the festival of Theseus with the tiniest pieces of bread, how fortunate are you!" (Ar. *Plut.* 627–8).[116] The scholia on this passage indicate that not only 8 Pyanopsion but also the eighth day of every month was sacred to Theseus, together with Poseidon. This special monthly form of observance was normally reserved for the gods; the only other hero to be so honored was the deified Herakles, who shared the fourth day of the month with Hermes and Aphrodite. During the next hundred years, the festival of Theseus grew in size and importance. By the 330s, it cost more to conduct than the Lesser Panathenaia. This expansion continued through the Hellenistic period to include a more elaborate quadrennial version, with a full range of athletic events imitating those of the Panathenaia.[117]

Delos too, an island of great religious and strategic importance, was implicated in Thesean mythmaking.[118] According to tradition, the Athenians had vowed that if the youths and maidens were saved from the Minotaur, they would send a sacred delegation (*theoria*) to Apollo's Delian shrine every year. Until the ship returned, the city must be maintained in a state of purity, and no executions could take place. In 399, Socrates' execution was delayed due to the departure of the *theoria* to Delos. The ship used to convey the *theoria* was believed to be the vessel used by Theseus himself, so oft-repaired that philosophers debated the question of whether it was the same ship.[119] Scholars often associate the *theoria* with the great pan-Ionian festival of the Delia, when similar delegations with choruses were sent to compete in the games. (The dates of both rites are uncertain, though they are plausibly assigned to 6 and 7 Thargelion.)[120] Indeed, Plutarch says that Theseus stopped at Delos on the way home, where he dedicated a statue of Aphrodite, performed the "Crane" dance around Apollo's altar with the youths and maidens and instituted games. Although the *theoria* for Theseus seem to be distinct from the choruses sent to the Delia, the two were closely related. The choristers were called *ēitheoi*, the same poetic and cultic term used for the youths of Minos' tribute.[121]

Most Thesean calendar dates pertain to the Cretan voyage, and therefore are elaborations of the early Archaic myth illustrated on the François Vase. Another layer of Thesean mythmaking, however, seems to have originated during the Persian Wars. The Battle of Marathon was commemorated on 6 Boedromion even though this was not the actual anniversary but a festival for Artemis Agrotera, who had aided the Athenians in the battle and whose sacred day was the sixth.[122] Theseus' epiphany on the battlefield was depicted on the famous "Painted Stoa," a building tied, like the Theseion, to Kimon's propagandizing activities.[123] The Stoa also featured a painting of Theseus battling the Amazon invaders of Attica, an event tied to Apollo's festival of Boedromia on the seventh of the month. One day prior to the Theseia, a corresponding ritual with sacrifices for the Amazons took place on the seventh at the Horkomosion ("Place of the Oath"), where the treaty with the Amazons had been concluded. The Amazon invasion myth, therefore, allowed Theseus to prefigure the leadership of Miltiades in warding off barbarian attackers.[124]

Theseus' most notable achievement as king was the unification of the towns and villages of Attica into one state. On 16 Hekatombaion, the Athenians celebrated a minor but ancient festival called the Synoikia, with sacrifices to Athena Phratria and Zeus Phratrios, deities of citizenship.[125] According to Thucydides,

> Theseus' rule was characterized by both intelligence and strength. Among other reforms, he organized the country by merging the councils and magistracies of the other cities into one, creating the council and town hall of the present capital. He caused them to live together, all enjoying their own property, just as they did before he compelled them to be part of this one city, which he left as his legacy to them, now that it had become great by virtue of its inclusion of all the citizens. And the Synoikia, which to this day the Athenians celebrate for the goddess at public expense, dates from that period.
>
> (Thuc. 2.15.2; cf. Plut. *Thes*. 24.1–4)

Euripides went so far as to attribute democracy itself to Theseus, even though everyone knew that Theseus had been a king. Aristotle was more circumspect, allowing only a "slight deviation from monarchy," but observing that Theseus had been the first leader to "lean toward the mob."[126] These traditions demonstrate the conceptual ties between Theseus' unification of Attica and the real-life establishment of the Kleisthenic democracy. Theseus himself did not (so far as we know) receive sacrifices at the Synoikia, but the institution of the festival was attributed to him. His career as warrior and ruler generated a parallel career as a founder of cults, which in turn enhanced his reputation as a just and pious king. So powerful was his mythic persona that he began to encroach on the earlier and well-established tradition that Erichthonios had founded the Panathenaia.[127]

Numerous Athenian festivals, then, were refashioned to commemorate the deeds of Theseus. Furthermore, the hero himself was said to have instituted the rituals, prescribing the details of his own worship just as the gods often did.[128] Several Thesean etiologies focus on the return of the Athenian youths and maidens, whose actions could be ritually recapitulated by latter-day counterparts. The prominence in all these matters of Apollo, god of maturing youths, suggests that Theseus the triumphant ephebe was presented as a model for Athenian boys, and it has been suggested that Theseus was a patron of the institution known as the *ephebeia*, the period of training for youths prior to the achievement of hoplite status.[129] Only one votive relief inscribed to Theseus is extant; it belongs to the early fourth century and depicts a beardless but muscular Theseus greeted by an adult man and his son. Similar iconography was used for reliefs commemorating the "introduction" of youths to Herakles.[130] Thus the image of Theseus the ephebe persisted in religious contexts, simultaneously with the very different visualizations of the mature king that became standard in Athenian tragedy.

How did the Athenians decide where to add Theseus to the calendar? Thesean dates cluster in the calendar on the sixth, seventh and eighth of the month (Table 4.3). The eighth was the day of Theseus and Poseidon, marking the hero's initial arrival in Athens, the Kybernesia festival of seafaring and the Theseia itself. Therefore, we may choose to interpret the etiologies of the sixth and seventh

*Table 4.3* Theseus in the Athenian calendar. Mythic events are shown in bold.

| | *6 (Artemis)* | *7 (Apollo)* | *8 (Poseidon)* | *16* |
|---|---|---|---|---|
| Hekatombaion (July/Aug) | | | **Theseus first arrives in Athens** | Synoikia |
| Boedromion (Sept/Oct) | Battle of Marathon commemorated<br>**Theseus epiphany**<br>Sacrifice for Artemis Agrotera fulfills vow made at Marathon | **Theseus battles Amazon invaders**<br>Boedromia for Apollo | Kybernesia for Poseidon and Theseus' crewmen at Phaleron | |
| Pyanopsion (Oct/Nov) | Oschophoria?<br>Salaminioi sacrifice a pig to Theseus | **Return of Theseus from Crete**<br>Pyanopsia for Apollo<br>Sacrifices to the Amazons<br>Sacrifice of a ram for Theseus' tutor | Theseia | |
| Mounichion (Apr/May) | **Departure of Theseus for Crete**<br>Girls' procession to Delphinion | | | |
| Thargelion (May/June) | These dates are sometimes assigned to the Delia for Apollo and associated with the sacred delegation (*theoria*) commemorating Theseus | | | |

Unknown date: The Hekalesia in the deme of Hekale, commemorating **Hekale's hospitality to Theseus**

(including the Oschophoria and the Amazon-related events) as secondary, the result of "spillover" from the original day of celebration. Still, Theseus' ties to Apollo Delphinios, whose day is the seventh, seem ancient, and the inclusion of day six (Artemis) in the Theseus complex reflects the Archaic "youths and maidens" theme. Therefore it was convenient that the eighth allowed proximity to Apolline festivals. Only the old festival of Synoikia, falling on 16 Hekatombaion, is clearly an outlier in the Thesean calendar. The date of the Synoikia must have been firmly set before the intensification of Theseus' myth and cult throughout Attica. The same was probably true of the Hekalesia, a festival held on an unknown date in the deme of Hekale. It commemorated the elderly heroine Hekale's hospitality toward young Theseus when he mastered the Bull of Marathon, but the presence of Zeus Hekaleios in the tradition indicates that it originally had nothing to do with Theseus.[131]

The rise of Theseus as an Athenian hero reveals that, under the right circumstances, Greek myth and cult were highly receptive to change. In this case, pre-existing traditions about Theseus were developed and augmented in response to political events, yet the political aspects of Theseus' cult in no way conflicted with pious belief in his powers as an Athenian cult hero. Already under Peisistratos, as vase painting and sculpture reveal, Theseus' popularity was growing. The advent of democracy and the Persian Wars created another opportunity for change which was embraced by individuals like Kimon, by interested groups in Attica, such as the Salaminioi and the Phytalidai, and by the Athenian people as a whole. Kimon had a significant hand in reshaping Theseus as a mature warrior and democratic statesman like himself, and it was this Theseus who appeared to such advantage in Greek tragedy. Yet the persistence of the youthful Theseus in the religious consciousness of the Athenians suggests that in the family and local traditions of the Attic demes, there existed an old substrate of lore about the hero as son of Aigeus and protégé of Apollo Delphinios, ready to be incorporated into the state calendar when the time was right.

## ESSAY 4.3: RITUAL FORM AND THE GREEK EVIDENCE

In this essay, we explore McCauley and Lawson's hypothesis that ritual form (as determined by the active or passive role of the god) is correlated with frequency of performance per individual, levels of sensory and emotional arousal, and other variables.[132] Our use of the ritual form theory will adapt rather than reproduce the method of McCauley and Lawson. First, our analysis will consider the possibility that the use of magic affects ritual form. (As we saw in Chapter 3, magic is a ritual technique often, but not exclusively, used in concert with appeals to superhuman agents.) Second, for the purposes of this essay, we will define a "religious ritual" as a transitive action sequence (agent, act, patient) involving a god.[133] Third, we will take an interest in the *degree* of activeness or passivity of the gods in the action sequence.

Let us begin by considering sensory and emotional arousal. As McCauley and Lawson have pointed out, this must be defined relative to a cultural baseline. Because Greeks in general were accustomed to noisy crowds, processions, costumes, music, dances, the use of torches at night to light festivals, the slaughter of sacrificial animals and the like, the baseline must have been relatively high for the average adult citizen (many women and most children, however, will have had a lower baseline due to their more limited observation of, and participation in, civic cults and festivals). Therefore, for a given ritual or festival to meet the criterion of "high sensory arousal," it must include sensory experiences less common or more intense than the standard ones. "Emotional arousal" too is relative to a cultural baseline. Because of the effects of habituation, it is reasonable to assume that frequent participation (in the same or a similar role) in any ritual will decrease its emotional impact. The occasion of the ritual (e.g. whether it is routine or in response to a crisis) may also affect its emotional intensity.

What does "frequent" mean? For this purpose it is necessary to distinguish between common ritual components or subrituals which were performed as part of most festivals (e.g. processions, dedication of gifts and alimentary sacrifice) and the festivals themselves, which were usually annual. Commonly performed components were encoded in semantic and procedural memory through repetition. Consider the festival for Zeus Polieus on Kos (Essay 4.1). Koan citizens will have been familiar with basic procedures for sacrifice, since these were performed often throughout the year. The ritual for Zeus Polieus, however, included actions which were undertaken only once per year, such as the cumbersome driving of oxen by tribes to the agora and the selection of two slaughterers from the overseers and heralds. It also included nonstandard sacrificial techniques, such as the immolation of a piglet with libations of honey and milk. Before the cult inscription provided a memory aid, it was the responsibility of the priest and "overseers" to remember all such details. Because annual festivals were the norm in Greek religion, let us count annual participation in the same role (e.g. priest, herald, overseer) as the minimum criterion for experience of a ritual to be considered "frequent," with the understanding that some components of these rituals were likely to be repeated far more often.

While maintaining McCauley and Lawson's distinction between special agent (active god) and special patient (passive god), we can posit degrees of activeness or passivity in the god's role, so that special patient rituals and special agent rituals form a spectrum (the midpoint, with a god present but neither acted upon nor acting, will be empty or very thinly populated). Also, complex rituals may involve a combination of special patient and special agent action sequences. For example, during an animal sacrifice, Greek gods could actively indicate through divination whether they had accepted or rejected the offering (we will return to this question in the discussion of divination on p. 223).[134]

The majority of Greek rituals were special patient rituals in which gods, goddesses, heroes and heroines became the recipients of prayers, hymns, dances or material offerings, as Zeus and Hestia did in the Koan festival for Zeus Polieus. Such rituals belong to the model of reciprocity we explored in Chapter 1; they are performed either in the hope that at a future time, *outside the ritual context*, the god will bestow benefits, or in thanks for benefits already received. Allied to these rituals, but less concerned with mutual *charis*, were the special patient rituals designed to appease an angry deity and convince him or her not to cause harm. A good example is the advice of the oracle at Didyma regarding Poseidon Asphaleos, who had caused an earthquake: "Propitiate Steadfast (*Asphaleos*) Poseidon with sacrifices . . . Him you must guard against and pray to, so that henceforth you may reach old age undaunted by evils." Similarly, the people of Phigaleia in Arkadia used to bring libations and offerings to Demeter in order to prevent the crop failures she would cause unless she was properly honored.[135]

Special patient rituals have an affinity with magic because the goal of such rituals is to bring about a specific effect in the god toward whom the ritual is directed. Magic is instrumental, and easily accommodated in the special patient template of "agent (human), act, patient (god)." Yet magic operates in tension with reciprocity, for we do not coerce those with whom we wish to maintain relations of *charis*. Therefore special patient rituals may mix techniques aiming at appeasement, reciprocity and/or mechanistic coercion. An example of a coercive special patient ritual is the procedure recommended by the oracle of Apollo at Klaros when the citizens of Pamphylia were threatened by pirates:

> Set up an image of Ares, the blood-stained slayer of men, in the midst of your town and perform sacrifices beside it, while Hermes holds him [Ares] in iron bonds. On the other side let Dike [Justice] giving sentence judge him; let him be like one who is pleading. For thus he will be peacefully disposed to you; after he has driven out the unholy mob far from your native land, he will raise up much-prayed-for prosperity.[136]

The ritual uses sympathetic magic to "bind" Ares, who often personifies the negative aspects of armed violence, and subject him to the power of "Justice." Notably, however, the ritual also employs sacrifice as a propitiating measure, and there is an expectation that the pacified Ares will be able to enter into a relationship of reciprocity with the Pamphylians. Similarly coercive procedures were used in other cults of Ares/Enyalios, and to deal with harmful ghosts.[137] Contrary to the predictions of McCauley and Lawson, examples like this suggest that at the extreme end of the spectrum, some special patient rituals may be performed only infrequently, in response to a crisis. Once the immediate danger is warded off, a reciprocal relationship can be encouraged through less coercive means.[138]

Magic, therefore, appears to have a significant impact on the variables of ritual form. McCauley and Lawson predict that substitutions will be more common in special patient than in special agent rituals. In Greek religion, for example, we find many non-priests successfully conducting private and even public sacrifices, but if an uninitiated person were to perform a mystery initiation, it would certainly be regarded as invalid. However, the acceptability of substitutions is to a great degree a function of the magical content in a given ritual. For example, if the efficacy of a ritual depends on magical factors such as the gender similarity and purity of a performer (see below), a less pure person or a person of the wrong gender cannot take his or her place. Magic itself may also function to permit substitutes: when the people of Orneai were unable to fulfill an extravagant vow to conduct daily sacrifices at Delphi, they hit on the solution of dedicating bronze statues of a sacrificial procession.[139] The use of this type of magic in gifts to the gods (e.g. a miniature vase in place of a full-size one) was very common.

There is nothing inherently group-oriented in special patient rituals, for individuals can use the same basic procedures to develop appeasement, reciprocal or even coercive relationships with gods. Yet in the Greek cultural context, special patient rituals were often conducted on behalf of groups, and particularly on behalf of the citizens of a state. The ability to supervise and control relations with the gods is a corollary of power, and Greek leaders of every period displayed their power through lavish offerings which required progressively greater levels of group organization to achieve. Gift exchange systems recognize the value of the "widow's mite" (value is relative to the resources of the giver), but this also means that a powerful, wealthy person or state is expected to give more. Then too, virtually all aspects of special patient rituals are under the control of the human partners in the relationship. Therefore, special patient rituals are the preferred ritual modality for the maintenance of a sociopolitical status quo.

In Greek special patient rituals, we often see tension between the desire for the presiding individual to possess political authority (i.e. to be a king, noble, civic magistrate or head of a family) and the need for that person to enhance ritual efficacy (i.e. to be an appropriate ritual actor, usually a priest or priestess). There was no universal rule that rituals must be conducted by a *hiereus* (m.) or *hiereia* (f.), the word we usually translate as "priest/priestess."[140] On the other hand, many rituals required that the performers meet stipulated requirements of gender, age, bodily wholeness and/or purity, but not necessarily of authority, knowledge or skill (though they had to be competent enough to perform to community standards). Requirements might apply not only to the priestess or priest but also to other ritual performers: a *kanēphoros* (basket bearer) must be a female virgin, and the Daphnephoria procession at Thebes must be accompanied by a boy with both parents living.[141] Such stipulations were rooted in implicit magical beliefs, especially the belief that like attracts like (Chapter 3). When served in cult or made the object of a request, gods would respond more favorably to those like themselves in gender, beauty and purity. Intuitions about this aspect of ritual efficacy were most likely to surface when individuals were chosen to act on behalf of a group, and were less evident in domestic religion, where scope for choice was narrowed. Stipulations varied by cult, and plenty of exceptions (e.g. priestesses serving male deities) can be identified. Yet no man in Athens, whatever his degree of power or expertise, could successfully have performed the ritual roles of the priestess of Athena Polias or her young female assistants, the *arrhēphoroi*. Similarly, when the Eleusinian cult for Demeter and Kore developed mysteries, male ritual actors such as the Hierophant and other cult officials supplemented but did not replace the priestess.[142]

Let us turn to special agent rituals. McCauley and Lawson predict that special agent rituals will be less frequently experienced per individual "patient," and more arousing with respect to both senses and emotions. Furthermore, the consequences of such rituals will be lasting. In Greek examples of these rituals, the role of priests and other ritual performers was to create conditions favorable to superhuman action: although humans set up the ritual parameters, the gods were responsible for what happened. Since the behavior of the active god could not be controlled, nor the impact on worshipers, such rituals were potentially antithetical to the maintenance of a status quo. The more active the deity's role, and the more people he or she affected, the less likely the ritual was to be welcomed by those in power, and the more likely it was to be maintained and spread through popular enthusiasm rather than official sanction. Greek states tamed gods who tended to manifest as "special agents" by immobilizing them in sanctuaries, hedging them round with special patient rituals and exercising supervision over the selection of priests.

As we have seen, special patient rituals often required that ritual actors establish a magical affinity with the "patient" deity through stipulations of gender, age, bodily wholeness and purity. If these conditions were not met, the ritual would not be efficacious. This close symmetry between agent and patient is not found in special agent rituals (Table 4.4).[143] Like all sanctuaries, oracles and healing shrines imposed basic purity requirements on visitors (Chapter 3), but ritual efficacy did not require that "patients" be healthy individuals, virgins, people with no amputations, children with both parents living or women past the age of childbearing. Special agent rituals were more likely to be inclusive, elective and open to non-citizens, people of either gender and slaves. Special patient rituals, by contrast, tended to be exclusive affairs, with participation off-limits to anyone who was not a member of a specific social group, yet expected or required of those who were.

Before proceeding to the more dramatic forms of special agent ritual, however, we must consider two anomalous types: impetrative divination (Chapter 2) and religious vows, which have an important structural affinity.[144] According to our interpretation of the action sequence in Greek impetrative divination, the ritual performer set up the parameters within which the action would occur and defined a goal, but displaced his or her own intentionality; the gap was therefore filled by a hidden agent. Rituals such as entrail-reading and bird augury created opportunities for a god to become active, and are therefore best understood as special agent rituals, yet they were also frequently performed, involved relatively low arousal and welcomed by those in power. A clue to the anomaly may lie in the fact that impetrative divination strictly limited the god's action. In many cases, the god could communicate only a yes or no. Omens from sacrifice, for example, were typically favorable or unfavorable, and there was a bias toward positive results. When used as the god's portion, the curving of the victim's tail in the fire was interpreted as a positive sign, but experiments have shown that such curvature normally results from high temperatures. When faced with negative omens, battlefield commanders felt free to sacrifice repeatedly in an attempt to elicit the results they wanted.[145]

*Table 4.4* Ritual form and ritual efficacy. Words in bold indicate the action sequence. Words in parentheses indicate mental representations supplied by the ritual performers which would not be transparent to an outsider.

| | *Agent* | *Act* | *Patient* |
|---|---|---|---|
| Special Patient Ritual | **Ritual performer(s)** Rigid stipulations for efficacy common | **Present offering/ Make request** | **(Deity)** |
| Special Agent Ritual | **(Deity)** Non-agent ritual performer(s); stipulations for efficacy vary | **(Advise/Command/ Heal /Transform/ Possess/etc.)** | **Ritual performer(s)** Few stipulations for efficacy other than simple purity measures |

Next let us consider the second anomalous category: the religious vow. The cultural institution of the vow, whereby a thank offering was promised to a specific deity should a specific goal be realized, was compelling because it allowed people to identify the agency at work by the same cognitive strategy used in impetrative divination, but with a greater time lag. The petitioner specified the god concerned and the action to be performed. If the desired outcome took place, there was no uncertainty about the agent responsible, and the promised thank offering was due. Therefore while a vow appears at first sight to be a special patient ritual, it has important similarities to special agent ritual.[146] Arguably, vows were more likely to be made in situations of fear or crisis, and were therefore correlated with greater emotional intensity and lower frequency.

Returning to the topic of divination, oracular mediums potentially presented a greater element of uncertainty for those in power, since the scope of the god's possible responses was wider. Yet the authority of oracular pronouncements helped leaders justify a planned course of action. Cultural selection of oracular techniques resulted in a preference for yes-or-no questions (thus limiting the scope of the god's answer) and for ambiguous responses (Essay 2.2). The Pythia at Delphi is the best known of the Greek mediums, but there were many others, such as the prophet of Apollo at Klaros and the *mantis* (seer) at Didyma. Consultation of an inspired medium fits the action sequence of a special agent ritual.[147] From an emic perspective, Apollo acted directly to command or advise petitioners, substituting his own agency for that of the medium. The ritual of consultation both created and limited Apollo's opportunities to speak. Generally, he did not speak unless spoken to, although a few legends say that he piped up before even hearing the question (i.e. he became more active and more unpredictable than usual). Frequency of performance per individual "patient" must have been low, since access to inspired mediums was limited (at Delphi, for example, consultation was available only one day a month, and not in winter). Of course, in cases of state consultation, the impact of the god's response extended far beyond the individual petitioner.[148]

Incubation, an oracular ritual usually performed for healing, required that petitioners purify themselves, pay a fee and/or sacrifice and then sleep in the sanctuary. During the night, the owner of the shrine (e.g. the hero-god Asklepios) would appear in their dreams to give advice or administer treatment. Clearly, such experiences had a powerful emotional impact. Because of fees, frequency of use per "patient" must have been relatively low, although people could perform the ritual more than once. In spite of the fees, the earliest testimonia show that women and slaves had access to incubation in the cult of Asklepios.[149] The sensory environment of a prosperous incubation shrine would have been unfamiliar, architecturally imposing and perhaps disturbing because of the close proximity of many ill and suffering people. The phenomenal rise in popularity of the healer-god Asklepios' cults from the late fifth century onward may have resulted in part from the introduction of the new special agent ritual, with its emotionally compelling experience, although petitioners in healing sanctuaries continued to exercise a choice between incubation and the alternative format of the vow.[150]

An interesting variation on incubation was performed for oracular purposes at the shrine of Trophonios in Lebadeia. There, after extensive sacrifices and purification, a lone petitioner entered an artificial chasm in the earth:

> The one going down lies with his back on the foundation, holding barley-cakes kneaded with honey, thrusts his feet into the hole and himself follows, striving to get his knees into the hole. After his knees, the rest of his body is at once drawn in, just as the largest and swiftest river will catch a person in its eddy and carry him under. After this, those who have entered the innermost place learn the future, not in one and the same way, but one perhaps sees and another hears. The return upwards is by the same opening, and the feet dart out first.
>
> (Paus. 9.39.11)[151]

The experience of "going down to Trophonios" was so terrifying that immediately after emerging, the petitioner was "possessed by fear and unware of both himself and his surroundings." Tradition had it that he was also unable to laugh, and it is unlikely that most petitioners undertook the ritual more than once.[152]

Mystery initiations were highly inclusive, although like the oracle of Trophonios, they might require significant investments of time and money by prospective initiates.[153] During a mystery initiation, people experienced a transformation under divine auspices. Depending on the cult, initiates might thereafter be safe from drowning at sea, or freed of malaise, or confident of a better fate after death. Mysteries attached to specific locations (Eleusis, Samothrace, Lykosoura) provide clear-cut examples of both heightened emotions and sensory arousal.[154] Initiates experienced sensory and emotional stimuli associated with the presence of the divine: reenactments of myth, dramatic alternations of darkness and light, spectacular imagery, music, dance and the revelation of sacred objects. Dysphoric elements (fear, but not pain so far as we know) might be used in order to heighten subsequent euphoric emotions of relief and joy.[155] Eleusinian initiates were described as passive absorbers of stimuli, "imprinted" by the sights and sounds of the ritual (Chapter 5). Once this type of initiation was complete, the effects were permanent and irreversible. An individual could undergo the principal transformation only once, although some mystery cults offered higher grades of initiation, presumably with corresponding levels of benefit.

The other main form of mystery initiation was private, not bound to sanctuaries, and associated with the concepts of *mania*, "madness," and divine possession.[156] In this type of ritual, gods were highly active, and people highly receptive. Small groups called *thiasoi* (sing. *thiasos*) came together under the guidance of a leader (an individual less likely to be given the title "priest" or "priestess") in order to experience the god or goddess directly.[157] In Classical Athens the deities to whom manic *thiasoi* were devoted included Meter ("Mother"), a goddess of Phrygian origin who was also known as Kybele; Meter's attendants, the youthful male Korybantes; Sabazios, another Phrygian god; and perhaps Dionysos.[158] Trance and divine possession were ritually induced through rhythmic music and vigorous dancing. At some point after trance was achieved, sacred objects called *orgia* were displayed to the participants. Depending on the cult, purifications, wine drinking and snake handling might also be elements of the ritual. The Ferrara krater (Figures 4.4 and 4.5) illustrates such a scene, probably celebrated for Meter (the identities of the enthroned goddess and god on the vase are debated).[159] The leaders who organized these private *thiasoi* were apparently in many cases self-appointed, and ritual efficacy was (I hypothesize) less likely than in civic contexts to depend on stipulations concerning their gender, age, sexual status or bodily perfection.[160]

The existence of a *thiasos* implies recurrent performance of its ritual, but an individual could experience initiation only once. Ethnographic parallels indicate that the behavioral patterns of initiates and adepts in trance cults are different. The initial experience "irreversibly modifies" an individual's relations with herself, the deity and society, while subsequent participation involves a refinement of skills. In cases where the Greek rituals produced purification and healing, they seem to have been repeated as needed. Theophrastus' "god-fearing man" went to the Orphic ritual expert with his family every month, a habit which contemporaries regarded as excessive. Korybantic initiations were fairly elaborate, involving bathing, sacrifice, "kraterizing" (presumably a component involving wine) and a

*Figure 4.4* A god and goddess enthroned in a temple observe the processional dance of their worshipers. An altar sits before them. To the right, a worshiper carries an object hidden by a cloth, while a musician plays the *aulos*. Attic red figure krater. Museo Archeologico, Ferrara. Photo: Scala/Art Resource

*Figure 4.5* Dancers experiencing trance during worship of a god and goddess. The musical instruments include the *aulos* (double flute) and the *tumpanon* (drum). Detail of the Ferrara krater. Photo: Scala/Art Resource

ceremony of "enthronement" during which dancers leaped about the seated initiate. The enthronement itself probably happened only once; thereafter, however, the initiate experienced an altered state when administering the rites to others.[161]

According to the ritual form hypothesis, too-frequent performance of these rituals by initiates will have caused them to lose emotional intensity. Some Dionysiac trance cults, for example, may have relaxed into special patient formats in which cult associations met to dance and feast in honor of the god, with few or no manifestations of *mania*. There is a related distinction between established (state-sponsored) and non-established private forms of these cults. The established worship of Meter-Kybele in fifth-century Athens, for example, was stripped of its trance elements, and the goddess was transformed from a special agent to a special patient.[162] The same phenomenon probably happened in the ancient mainadic festivals of Dionysos, which were celebrated only every other year. In its established form, mainadic ritual at Athens seems to have been reduced to a vestigial state by the Classical period, and elsewhere too it lost much of its trance character, becoming more dignified and sanctuary-bound, with priestesses and public *thiasoi*.[163] The Bacchic-Orphic initiations which spread through the Greek world from the fifth century on represented a resurgence of the "special agent" element in Dionysiac religion.

Greek women were drawn to special agent rituals with trance elements.[164] The usual explanation is that such rituals provided women with opportunities for emotional and physical expression otherwise unavailable to them. We can take the argument further. In the context of Classical Greek gender norms, passive and receptive ritual roles were consistent with femininity, and thus could be safely undertaken by women, but they were potentially problematic for men. Greek masculinity was tied to agency, citizenship and self-control.[165] Special patient rituals were consistent with masculinity because the ritual performers were intuitively understood to be agents rather than patients. Furthermore, conducting a relationship of mutual *charis* with someone more powerful than oneself (a king, a tyrant, a god) did not compromise masculinity, and might even enhance it.

Both ancient and modern commentators have stigmatized trance-based special agent rituals as vulgar, effeminate and foreign. Lynn Roller's work on Meter, however, demonstrates that although the goddess originated in Phrygia, the trance elements in the cult, including the use of the *tumpanon* (a kind of drum) for rhythmic stimulation, were most likely of Greek origin. Dionysos too was visualized as a stranger from the exotic East. (Even Apollo, the god of oracular trance, was described as a Lykian, a partisan of the Trojans.)[166] Trance rituals were in no way foreign to Greek religion, nor were the assimilated gods who presided over them truly "foreign." Rather, trance was attributed to deities perceived to have foreign origins because demonstrative emotion and loss of control over oneself were difficult to reconcile with Greek notions of citizenship, political power and masculinity. The youthful participation of the Athenian orator Aeschines in such rites, complete with snake handling, gave his enemy Demosthenes an opportunity to sneer:

> When you became a man, you read the books for your mother when she conducted initiations and you organized the other things, clothing the initiates in fawnskins, performing the krater ritual, and purifying them, wiping them with mud and bran, then standing them up and bidding them say, "I have fled evil, I have found a better way," exulting in the fact that nobody ever gave the women's cry so loudly as you . . . In the daytime, you led lovely *thiasoi* through the streets, crowned with fennel and poplar leaves, squeezing the snakes and lifting them over your heads.
>
> (Dem. 8.259, 260)

In contrast, non-citizens (women, slaves and foreigners) had far less to lose by participating, and something to gain.[167] Because the rites were private, they enjoyed an access which was denied them in the case of most major civic rituals. Women organizers of *thiasoi* had an opportunity to exercise leadership without transgressing gender norms. Finally, to switch to Whitehouse's terms, trance rituals included imagistic elements, which strengthen the cohesion of small groups. For disenfranchised segments of the population, they must have offered not so much the appeal of the exotic as a satisfying sense of belonging.

Developed as a pan-cultural model of ritual dynamics, McCauley and Lawson's distinction between special patient and special agent rituals seems consistent with the Greek evidence.[168] We have noted correlations between ritual form and social aspects of ritual, such as the gender and political status of participants, and the preferential use of special patient rituals by those in power. Most Greek rituals clustered around the special patient attractor position, which enhanced transmission via the frequency effect (encoding in procedural and semantic memory). The transmission of special agent rituals too benefited from the frequency effect, because their organizers performed them often (even if many "patients" experienced the ritual only once). Yet because of their retention in episodic memory, and because of the god's active role, special agent rituals produced heightened motivation, including a "multiplier effect" whereby these cults were propagated across Greek states.

## Notes

1 Liénard 2006.349–51. In the following description of ritual and cognitive science, I have summarized Liénard and Boyer 2006.815–22.

2 Anxiety: e.g. Malinowski 1948.90.

3 Social categories: e.g. Durkheim (1915.218–9) sees the origin of religion in the "effervescence" produced by human social groups. Rappaport 1979.197, 1999.27–8: ritual contains a "consummation" or "sealing" of the social contract and has a significant moral element. Rappaport disavows the functionalist label, asserting that ritual does not have the "purpose" of strengthening the social contract (final cause) but that it nevertheless always creates this result (formal cause). Compare Atran's (2002.173, 268–9) approach: ritual enhances cooperation and displays commitment to shared values.

4 Performance: see e.g. Tambiah 1979; for practice compare Bell 2009, esp. 30–46, 74–117. For a summary of ritual theories, see Bell 2006 and for full discussion and bibliographies of this vast literature, Kreinath, Snoek and Stausberg eds. 2006. Of particular interest are Durkheim 1915; Malinowski 1948; Turner 1967; Geertz 1973; Smith 1987b; Bell 1997, 2009 (originally published in 1992); Rappaport 1999.

5 In order to argue that ritual functions *primarily* as a form of communication, theorists are forced to redefine communication less as "transmission of information" than as an event with "interactions" and "processual value." See e.g. Stavrianopoulou ed. 2006.9, 18 (citing "norms of behaviour, the demonstration of intentions, the assignment of tasks and roles, the inclusion or exclusion of individuals" as types of information communicated). Burkert (2006.23) defines ritual as "a schematised action functioning as a message," but adds that a "message" is to be taken to mean that the action is "something perceived [and] demonstrative." Cognitivists, on the other hand, have been known to argue that ritual is designed to *reduce* the amount of information conveyed: Boyer 2001.232–3 citing Bloch 1974.

6 Individual ritual: A Greek example is the presentation of a votive gift. For rituals performed in private, Rappaport (1999.47) speaks of "auto-communication."

7 For these elements see Liénard and Boyer 2006.816–17. Compare the list in Rappaport 1999.32–50 (conforming to previous encoding, decorum, invariance, performance, lack of physical efficacy). For the historical development of "ritual" as a conceptual category see Bremmer 1998.14–24.

8 Finger sacrifice: Burkert 1996.34–47. Burkert's link between religion and biology is discussed from a cognitive perspective by Boyer 1998; Guthrie 2002.

9 For the Greek *purrhikē* or dance in armor see Pl. *Leg.* 7.815a (imitation of defensive and aggressive moves); Wheeler 1982.231–2; Kyle 1992.94. For the debate over whether human ritualized behaviors can be considered adaptive (as opposed to side effects of an adaptation) see Liénard and Boyer 2006.824–5. Ethology and human behaviors of dominance and submission: Burkert 2006.30–5. Warrior dances in Africa and cross-culturally: Hanna 1987.136–7, 179–98.

10 Hard to fake signals of commitment: e.g. Sosis 2006.

11 Evolutionary byproducts with no adaptive value per se play important roles in both physiology and behavior, and are known as "spandrels" in the term coined by Stephen Jay Gould. In the cognitive domain, Sperber (1996.66–7) calls them "susceptibilities."

12 Freud 1963 [1907]. OCD: Dulaney and Fiske 1994; Fiske and Haslam 1997.

13 "Hazard-precaution system": Liénard and Boyer 2006.820 with bibliography. Cf. Boyer 2001.119–20, 212–15, 238–41. These findings cohere with Malinowski's description of rituals as anxiety-reducing (earlier, note 2).

14 Intuitive beliefs: Boyer 2001.240–63 identifies the contagion system, social relations and supernatural agents as three domains that make ritual behavior salient and compelling to human minds.

15 Habituation: Liénard and Boyer 2006.819, 824. This "tedium effect" can reduce the likelihood of transmission (see the discussion of ritual form theory, pp. 227–8).

16 Transparent goals: for complementary theories about this key characteristic of ritual, see the discussion of divination in Chapter 2 and Humphrey and Laidlaw 1994.2, 94 (ritualization "severs the link" between intentional meaning and act).

17 Liénard 2006.355–6. That humans form universal, intuitive ontological categories (living kind, artifact, etc.) has a firm experimental basis: see e.g. Medin and Atran 2004; Barrett 2011.61–9 with bibliography; Chapter 1 (this volume) on counterintuitive concepts.

18 On the inherent "meaninglessness" of ritual cf. Staal 1989.208 and *passim*; Humphrey and Laidlaw 1994.168–226. However, cognitivists such as Whitehouse, who are experienced ethnographers, insist on the value of interpretation (i.e. the attribution of meaning by participants, institutions or researchers) as a complement to causal explanation: Whitehouse 2007. For a Classicist's perspective see Graf 2002.114–16 (rituals are "chains of symbols" whose meaning is based on group consensus, but unless it has an ethological dimension, meaning is arbitrary because it is culturally constructed).

19 The symbolic value of blood or stomach chyme in this example should be understood in relation to the arguments of Sperber (Chapter 2); why blood (or milk or wine) needs to be poured on an altar is always a half-understood concept. As Whitehouse (2004a.7, 22–4) notes, the selection of religious representations is driven ("filtered") both by properties located in minds, and by the cultural and physical environment in which mental processes unfold.

20 Of special interest is the volume arising from a 2002 symposium in Vermont which included Classicists: Whitehouse and Martin eds. 2004.

21 Dichotomies: Whitehouse 1995.193–202, citing e.g. Lewis's (2003.26–31) distinction between "central" (mainstream) and "peripheral" (ecstatic or trance) cults. Routinization: Whitehouse 1995.83–8. Versnel (1990.182–3) traces the distinction between "institutional, routinized" and "charismatic, deviant" forms of religion to Max Weber.

22 On the potential for interaction between modes in religious systems see Whitehouse 2004a.75–7.

23 For these theoretical models of memory, see Tulving and Craik eds. 2000, ch. 34–9; Whitehouse 2004a.87–118 with bibliography. Episodic memory: Tulving 1983, 2002. The two declarative systems are rooted in distinct brain structures (episodic memory being closely associated with the hippocampus), develop at different ages (episodic memory becoming active around age four, but semantic memory much earlier) and can function independently, as studies of amnesiacs reveal.

24 Imagistic rituals: Whitehouse 2004a.70. Groups of people who are responsible for performing imagistic rituals may over time develop a body of expert knowledge held in *semantic* memory. The "profoundly complex" and "philosophically challenging" nature of this knowledge is emphasized by ethnographers (Whitehouse 2004a.80–1, 115). Unless memory aids (e.g. poetic meter) are used to transmit this information, however, it would appear that such bodies of knowledge are in constant flux and differ greatly among individual experts. Martin and Pachis (2009) collect papers on the imagistic mode in "Graeco-Roman" (mostly Roman period) religion.

25 In Chapter 6, I discuss writing, semantic memory and procedural memory in the transmission of Greek rituals.

26 Cognitively optimal religion: Boyer 1994.99–100 (on "representation without transmission"), 121–2; Norenzayan and Atran 2004.152–60; Whitehouse 2004a.29–47, 58, 2004b.188–99, 2009.1–4.

27 Whitehouse 2004a.29, 2005.216–17 (default mode); 2004a.119–36 (fanaticism); 2004a.46 (false, shallow, misleading).

28 Zeus Lykaios: Pl. *Resp.* 565d–e; Bonnechere 1994.85–96 with bibliography.

29 Centrally supervised: here, "centrally" means "by civic leadership" and implies no Panhellenic centralization. Frequency: Greek festivals and specific sacrifices were usually annual, biennial or quadrennial, falling squarely between the typical frequencies of the doctrinal and imagistic attractors (i.e. daily/weekly/monthly versus every 7–9 years). However, many components of festivals were repeated far more often (see the discussion of ritual form theory, p. 220, and Chapter 6). Unlike Stavrianopoulou (2011.91), I classify most state-sponsored festivals focused on sacrifice and other common procedures as high-frequency, low-arousal rituals. Numerous such rituals occurred every year, even if the divine recipients differed. Sacrifices were pleasurable events, but not necessarily highly arousing in and of themselves, or likely to persist in episodic memory.

30 Paus. 3.13.3–5 (cornel tree, the seer Karnos, Karnos Oiketas); Hsch. s.v. *karnos* (ram). Discussion and additional sources in Burkert 1985.234–6. Compare the diversity of meanings attributed to Jain *puja* rituals: Humphrey and Laidlaw 1994.16–63 with Whitehouse 2004a.96–7.

31 Preference for oral tradition: e.g. Pausanias (5.15.10) is reluctant to record the words spoken during libations and the traditional hymns at Olympia, even though many people witnessed these and they were hardly "secret."

32 By "rites of passage" I mean rituals marking a transition from one state or stage of life to another, such as the Athenian Apatouria, which marked the induction of a boy into his phratry (Parker 2005.458–61). For Sparta see Levy 1988 (collecting primary sources on the *krupteia*); Cartledge 2001.79–90. For scary maturation rituals with masked dancers see Langdon 2007.174–80.

33 For the sense of agency in the mind-brain, see David, Newen and Vogeley 2008. Action representation system: McCauley and Lawson 2002.10–13, 2007.220–30; Sørensen 2007.91–3. The "system" is composed of a number of mental tools, including agent detection and the ability to represent causal relations between actions and results.

34 For more on their definition of "religious ritual" see Essay 4.3. Counterintuitive agents: McCauley and Lawson 2007.220 (this term replacing "culturally postulated superhuman agents," which was used in their 2002 book).

35 The "full structural description" of a ritual requires the inclusion of any "embedded" rituals that guarantee the effectiveness of the ritual under study. For example, unless performed by an ordained priest, a Roman Catholic marriage ritual is invalid; therefore the priest's ordination is embedded in the full structural description. Ordination invests the priest with his authority from God, the superhuman agent pertinent to the marriage ritual. Evidence for prior consecration of Greek ritual performers is sparse; for an example from Hellenistic Kos see Paul 2013b.254–6 (*teleta* consisting of purification and sacrifice). Cf. Theon of Smyrna (p. 22 Hiller), who describes garlanding as a ritual for Hierophants and Torchbearers at Eleusis.

36 Variables: McCauley and Lawson 2002.8–37; compare the earlier formulation in McCauley and Lawson 1990.84–136.

37 For votive substitutions and animal sacrifice see e.g. Naiden 2013.122–8.

38 Experimental research: Malley and Barrett 2003; Whitehouse 2004a.39–40.

39 Action and agency: Barrett and Lawson 2001. Whitehouse (2004a.142) correctly points out that McCauley and Lawson's theory, unlike his own, is inapplicable to rituals from which gods are absent. Greek religion incorporated both automatic and agent-based concepts of efficacy, often in the same ritual: see Chapter 3 on the curse against oath-breakers at Kyrene.

40 McCauley and Lawson 2002.199. Compare Versnel (1990.184) on the "need for charismatic experiences" even in a Weberian "institutional religion."

41 The role of "sensory pageantry" is problematic, because the perception of sensory pageantry is relative to baselines within a ritual system (acknowledged in McCauley and Lawson 2002.101–103, 118–9 and *passim*) and may differ among individuals. Cf. the criticisms by Whitehouse (2004a.142–3, 151–3). On participation vs. observation see McCauley and Lawson 2002.127–8.

42 Time: Samuel 1972.13–18.

43 Interrupted and articulated: the phrase is from Burkert 1985.225. Because they counted inclusively, the Greeks called biennial festivals "trieteric" and quadrennial ones "penteteric." The most common intervals (every 1, 2, 4, 8 years) were based on the periods of intercalation used to reconcile the lunar and solar year (Samuel 1972.11–13, 33–42, 189–94). Quadrennial festivals, such as the Olympics, were grander affairs than annual ones, though this is not necessarily true for festivals at intervals longer or shorter than four years.

44 Month names: Trümpy 1997 includes an index of month names and cities. Argos: the historian Hellanicus (*FGrH* 4 F 74–84) used the Argive priestesses as the basis for one of his works. Statues of the priestesses outside the Heraion (Paus. 2.17.3) must have served as a memory aid. Athenian archons: Samuel 1972.195–237.

45 de Polignac 1995 [1984].

46 Borders: Malkin (1996) points out that de Polignac's thesis works well if applied to the late development of colonial poleis, as in Kyrene's use of sanctuaries to mark the limits of its territory.

47 On sanctuaries and *asulia* see Sinn 1993 and especially 1996 (citing the large number of border sanctuaries in Arkadia). Bank at Ephesos: e.g. Xen. *An.* 5.3.6.

48 For sanctuary placement and specific gods, see Schachter 1992b.36–54.

49 *Pompē*: *ThesCRA* 1.1–20 (True *et al.*); Burkert 1985.99–101; Connor 1987; Graf 1996 (distinguishing between centripetal and centrifugal movement). Offerings: Kavoulaki 2011.146.

50 Linear space and memory: Barrett 2011.59–61. Thyiads of Athens hold dances along the road to Delphi: Paus. 10.4.3. Dionysiac procession at Athens with multiple stops: Sourvinou-Inwood 2003.70 citing Xen. *Eq. mag.* 3.2. On sacred ways in Archaic Ionia, see Greaves 2010.180–93.

51 Egypt: Frankfurter 2011.75–93.

52 For objection to "sacrifice" as a category of study, see e.g. Naiden 2013.276–330.

53 Tylor 1874.2.376–410, with a theory of progression from gift to homage to abnegation.
54 Smith 1889.247–9 (social and alimentary aspects linked with morality), 294–5 (victim as totem), 328–31 (evolution to gift and atonement).
55 Hubert and Mauss 1964 [1899].97 (mediation). For discussion of the relationship with Durkheim's thought see Allen 2013.
56 Evans-Pritchard 2003 [1954].198. See also Evans-Pritchard 1956.197–230, 272–86.
57 Freud 1918.219–55, adapting Robertson Smith's totemism to his own Oedipal theory.
58 Girard 1977.302 (scapegoating, including sacrifice, as "the very basis of cultural unification").
59 Meuli 1975 [1946]. On the strengths and weaknesses of Meuli's analysis see Kirk 1981.70–2.
60 Burkert 1983 [1972].16.
61 Vernant 1981a, 1991.290–302 (English translation of Vernant 1981b); Detienne, Vernant *et al.* 1989 [1979].
62 Mediation; rejection of universalizing/origins approaches: Vernant 1991.290–91, 297. All consumable meat: Detienne, Vernant *et al.* 1989 [1979].3.
63 Inclusion and exclusion: Detienne, Vernant *et al.* 1989 [1979].3–5, 13; Detienne 1988; Lissarrague and Schmitt-Pantel 1988; Schmitt-Pantel 1992.126–30.
64 Killing to eat and concealment: Vernant 1991.294, 301. Evaluation of the Paris school's findings by one of its members, twenty years later: Georgoudi 2010.92–7.
65 State of the paradigm: Knust and Várhelyi eds. 2011.3–18; Graf 2012; Naiden 2013.9–15.
66 Critique of "Man the Hunter": Hart and Sussman 2008.11–32. For the development of theories about the relationship between evolution and hunting, see Pickering 2013, esp. 71–2. Meuli's prehistoric data: Smith 1987a. Other recent perspectives on the relationship between hunting and domestication: McInerney 2010.35–7; Graf 2012.48–50.
67 Inverse relationship: for the "tedium effect" see Whitehouse 2000.44–6; McCauley and Lawson 2002.49–50, 179–90. Greek women often ululated (*ololuzein*) during a sacrifice, but also in other ritual contexts; unfortunately we do not have enough evidence about this custom to draw firm conclusions about its relationship to sacrifice. See e.g. Hom. *Od.* 3.450 (at moment of death), 4.767 (during prayer); Aesch. *Ag.* 595 (offering of incense), 1118 (metaphor for slain victim), *Sept.* 269 ("sacrificial scream"); Hdt 4.189 (origin in Libya); Eur. *Bacch.* 689 (signal); Burkert 1983 [1972].5; Clark 2009.10.
68 Refuting the scholarly orthodoxy of a "comedy of innocence" and concealment of violence: Georgoudi 2005; Naiden 2013.83–99. Visual evidence: Peirce 1993. Van Straten (1995.103–14, 188) does not take a position in opposition to Burkert but emphasizes the festive aspects of sacrifice. Human sacrifice: Henrichs 1981.234; Bonnechere 1994. Oath sacrifice is the one sacrificial situation where the animal's suffering is the undeniable focus, because it requires magical transfer of the suffering animal's fate to the oath-breaker: Faraone 1993; Berti 2006.187.
69 McInerney 2010.36–40. Compare my discussion of the Koan ox-sacrifice for Zeus in Essay 4.1.
70 Volumes resulting from recent conferences on sacrifice include Georgoudi, Piettre and Schmidt eds. 2005; Hägg and Alroth eds. 2005; Mehl and Brulé eds. 2008; Stavrianopolou, Michaels and Ambos eds. 2008; Knust and Várhelyi eds. 2011; Faraone and Naiden eds. 2012; Hitch and Rutherford eds., forthcoming.
71 Ekroth 2007a.251–2, 2007b.140–1. Cf. Naiden 2013.35, 232–58. The strongest arguments in favor of regular, non-sacrificial consumption involve pigs. Berthiaume 1982 is the fundamental work on butchering; see also Rosivach's arguments (1994.84–88) that butchers sold meat left over from sacrifice, with 84n 56 on pigs.
72 Meat yield: Naiden 2012, 2013.183–231. A clear example of meat distribution to the general citizenry is *IG* $II^2$ 334 (ca. 335; see Essay 3.1) The sacrificial rules for Zeus

Polieus at Kos (Essay 4.1) specify meat "for the city" as well as for specific groups of citizens, such as physicians and potters, but the total amount from the two oxen was far too small to feed all the citizen males.

73 Naiden (2013.13) polemically questions most of the fundamental assumptions of the late twentieth-century paradigm, including the social and communal nature of sacrifice, and even its centrality to Greek religion.

74 For the variety of procedures in alimentary sacrifice, see van Straten 1995; Bremmer 2007.132–8.

75 Divination: as before a battle, e.g. Xen. *An.* 1.8.15, 4.3.17–9 (favorable omens before battle, but also offerings to gods); Burkert 1985.60. Purification: see the discussion of purification with piglet blood in Essay 3.3. On hybrid sacrificial procedures see especially Ekroth 2000, 2002; Georgoudi 2010. Flaying appears to have been standard for large animal holocausts, and piglets may have been cut up: Scullion 2007b.

76 Piglets for Zeus: Georgoudi 2010.101–4.

77 Nock 1972.2.590; I substitute the English "solemn actions" for his "*heilige Handlungen.*" For this term see discussion in Scullion 1994.78–9, 98 and *passim.*

78 van Baal 1976.168–78; Ekroth 2008.90–91.

79 Holocausts were relatively rare, and most involved small animals, such as piglets or lambs: Ekroth 2002.217–28, 2008.89–90.

80 Kos calendar: *RO* no. 62 (= *LSCG* 151 A). My translation is adapted from *RO* plus Kaestner 1976. The most recent discussion of the sacrificial procedures is Paul 2013a.30–44, 266–82.

81 Month: Rhodes and Osborne (*RO* 308) suggest that Batromios is roughly equivalent to our January, but note uncertainties about the season in Scullion 1994.86.

82 Priest of Zeus Polieus, Athena Polias and the Twelve Gods: see Paul 2013b.248, 255–6.

83 Liénard 2006.356 (on the "puzzle" created by the moment of transformation); cf. Bloch 1993.118–20.

84 On the Bouphonia, the main event at the Athenian Dipolieia: Nilsson 1995 [1906].14–6; Burkert 1983 [1972].136–43; Vernant 1991.299–302; Scullion 1994.84–7; Parker 2005.187–91. The most important primary sources are Paus. 1.24.4 and Porph. *Abst.* 2.28.4–2.30.

85 Draft animals: According to Aelian (*VH* 5.14), an Athenian tradition prohibited the sacrifice of a plow ox. Rosivach (1994.161–3) concludes that such oxen were nevertheless sacrificed at the end of their working lives. On cross-cultural reluctance to slaughter domesticated animals see McInerney 2010.34–8. The Koan procedure contains a fail-safe option in case an ox is not "chosen" but details are not specified. The "mixing" of oxen suggests a random element.

86 The Magnesian bull was consecrated to Zeus at sowing time and sacrificed at harvest time. For the similarity of these cults see Nilsson 1995 [1906].14–27; Scullion 1994.82–88.

87 Security: Larson 2007.161; Detienne 1988.180–4. Burkert (1983 [1972].138n.10) understood the text to refer to one ox sacrifice only; I agree with Scullion (1994.84n. 20) and Paul (2010.67n.5) that a second ox was given to Hestia.

88 The oddity of sacrificing only one animal to Zeus at such an important civic event has been noted, most recently by Paul 2013a.266–7. Rhodes and Osborne write (*RO* 309), "If there was a separate sacrifice to Hestia, its practical function will have been to feed those already gathered for the festival of Zeus. . ." They observe that even two oxen (about 200 kg of meat) would not have fed the entire male citizenry of Kos, which was something less than nine thousand. For the amount of meat per animal see Jameson 1988.95.

89 Hestia's cult title Phamia ("She who speaks") is rare, and may be related to an oracular function. Other suggestions have been offered (*RO* 308–9; Scullion 1994.83) but Phamia is elsewhere attested on Kos: Paul 2013a.36, 228–30.

90 Graf 1980.219; Burkert 1983 [1972].9n.41 ("we are dealing with antithesis within the ritual").

91 Zeus as chthonian: Scullion 1994. *Contra*: Paul 2010.73. For the debate see Parker 2011.80–84.

92 I have omitted the portions of lines 44–46 that prescribe the sacrifice of a piglet and kid for Dionysos Skyllitas on the same day as the preliminaries for Zeus Polieus. Because Dionysos receives the same offerings at least three times during the month of Batromios (on the 19th, the 21st and the 24th), the juxtaposition with the festival of Zeus Polieus appears to be coincidental. The same is not true for the sacrifice to Athena, the regular cult partner of Zeus (lines 55–7).

93 On the "intercalation" of procedures for Hestia and Zeus: Paul 2010.68.

94 Sons of Nestor: Paul 2013a.39. Removal of meat: in a normative situation, participants would have the option of taking the meat home, or even of selling it.

95 Zeus and Athena: Paul 2010.

96 Pregnant victims: for a summary of the evidence see Bremmer 2005 (arguing against the standard fertility interpretation). Demeter is the most common recipient (Clinton 2005.178–9).

97 Transformations: Kearns 1989.117 (last quarter of the sixth century); Parker 2005.375 (fifth to fourth centuries). For Theseus' obscurity prior to the sixth century see Connor 1970.143–4. Theseus' moral transformation: Mills 1997.1–42. Robertson (1992.3–9) dates the myth of Theseus' arrival to the Dark Age.

98 Youths and maidens on the François vase: Shapiro 1989.146–7; von den Hoff 2013.

99 Shrine: Arist. [*Ath. Pol.*] 15.4 says Peisistratos called a meeting in the Theseion; he is contradicted by Polyaenus *Strat.* 1.21.2 and Pausanias 1.17.6. Role of Solon and Peisistratos: Shapiro 1989.145–9. Role of Kleisthenes: Schefold 1946.65–6, Kearns 1989.117–18. Role of Kimon: Shapiro 1992. On evidence for one or more poems called *Theseis*, see Arist. *Poet.* 8.1451a19; Plut. *Thes.* 28; Neils 1987.11–12.

100 Theseus and Marathon: Plut *Thes.* 35.5; Paus 1.15.3. Theseus' bones: Osborne 2006.56–61.

101 On Kimon see also Plut. *Thes.* 36.1–2; Paus 1.17.6.

102 For the monthly festival days as "birthdays" of specific gods (common to many Greek cities), see Mikalson 1975.13–24. The eighth as Poseidon's day: Plut. *Thes.* 36.3.

103 For Theseus and the Atthidographers see Harding 2008.52–72.

104 Theseion: Paus. 1.17.2–3. Paintings: Barron 1972.

105 Apollo Delphinios: Graf 2009.109–11; see also Essay 6.1 in this volume. Robertson 1992.4–9 connects Hekatombaion 8 with a lapsed festival during which Athenian youths were enrolled as citizens.

106 Jeering: Paus. 1.19.1. Recognition: Plut. *Thes.* 12. Procession: Plut. *Thes.* 18.1, Mikalson 1975.140; Calame 1996.143.

107 For the *genos* (plural *genē*) see Bourriot 1976; Parker 1996.5–66, 284–327. Most evidence is from Athens.

108 As a festival of Poseidon, the Kybernesia likely fell on the eighth, and the Salaminioi sacrificed to the associated heroes on 8 Boedromion. For the calendar, *RO* no. 37 lines 90–2 (including a sacrifice to Teukros, a hero of Salamis). See Calame 1996.127, 148–50; Parker 1996.315. Recruited: Plut. *Thes.* 17.6 citing Philochorus (*FGrH* 328 F 111). For the Phaleron heroes, see Paus. 1.1.4; Kearns 1989.38–41. Theseus and local heroes: Kearns 1989.96–7, 120–124.

109 While we do not know with certainty that the Oschophoria fell on 6 Pyanopsion, the festival is usually placed hereabouts because of the sacrifice of a pig to Theseus by the Salaminioi on the sixth, and because Plutarch associates the Oschophoria with the activities of Theseus' return on the seventh. I follow the sequence established by Ferguson 1938. See the cautions of Mikalson 1975.68–9; Robertson 1992.124–5; Parker 1996.315–16.

110 Oschophoria: Plut. *Thes*. 23.3 citing Demon (*FGrH* 327 F 6).

111 The Oschophoria is oft-discussed as an initiation ritual for youths: e.g. Vidal-Naquet 1981 [1968]; Leitao 1995. On this festival see also Rutherford and Irvine 1988 (Pindar's oschophoric song); Calame 1996.128–9, 143–8; Pilz 2011.

112 Etiology and the Oschophoria: Scullion 2007a.196–201. Salaminioi: Parker 1996.315.

113 Disembarkation: Plut. *Thes*. 22.1–5. Pyanopsia: Simon 1983.19–21; Calame 1996.126–7, 150–3. Plutarch (*Thes*. 4.1) places a sacrifice of a ram to Theseus' tutor on this day, preliminary to the Theseia.

114 Encroachment: a similar argument in Calame 1996.447–8.

115 Phytalidai: Plut. *Thes*. 12.1, 23.3 (descendants of youths and maidens fund Theseus' festival); Parker 1996.318. Deme (Lakiadai): Plut. *Cim*. 4.2; Parker 1996.168–70. For the names of the youths and maidens on the François Vase and their relationships to Athenian *genē* see von den Hoff 2013.1.137–9.

116 Kimon's distributions to the poor: Plut. *Cim*. 10.1–4.

117 The epigraphic record for the Theseia is rich: see Bugh 1990, and for the program of athletic events Kyle 1993.40–1.

118 Strategic value of Delos and Thesean mythmaking: Connor 1970.148.

119 Socrates: Pl. *Phd* 58a-c; Xen. *Mem*. 4.8.2. Same ship: Plut. *Thes*. 23.1.

120 Pherekydes (*FGrH* 3 F 149) says Theseus himself vowed the yearly *theoria* to Delos in honor of Apollo and Artemis. The most likely date for the Delia is the purificatory Spring month of Thargelion, which falls immediately after Mounichion. For the ship of Theseus, the Delia and calendar matters, see Chankowski 2008.86–118.

121 *Ēitheoi:* Parker 2005.81.

122 Marathon: *Thes*. 35.5; Paus. 1.15.4; Francis and Vickers 1985.100; Mills 1997.40–2. Artemis Agrotera (to whom the Athenians made a vow of sacrifices should they win the battle): Plut. *De malignitate Herodoti* 26 (*Mor*. 862a); Mikalson 1975.50.

123 Painted Stoa and Kimon's family: Plut. *Cim*. 4.5; Shapiro 1992.30–1.

124 Amazons: Plut. *Thes*. 27.3, 5 citing Kleidemos (*FGrHist* 323 F 18).

125 Synoikia: Mikalson 1975.30; Robertson 1992.32–89.

126 Democracy: Eur. *Suppl*. 353, 404–8, 433–41; Plut. *Thes*. 25.2 citing Aristotle, with Ar. [*Ath. Pol*.] 41.2; cf. Plut. *Thes*. 24.2. For Theseus the democratic king see Davie 1982.

127 Panathenaia: Plut. *Thes*. 24.3; other sources collected by Shear 2001.1.60–6. Theseus as cult founder: Calame 1996.141–84.

128 Theseus and associated heroes: Kearns 1989.117–24.

129 Theseus and Apollo: Graf 2009.86–9.

130 Votive relief: Flashar, von den Hoff and Kreuzer 2003.34 with fig. 33; Ekroth 2010.

131 For Hekale and the Hekalesia see Plut. *Thes*. 14 citing Philochorus (*FGrH* 328 F 109); Kearns 1989.121, 157–8; Hollis ed. 2009.265–9.

132 I have avoided McCauley and Lawson's term "sensory pageantry" in favor of "sensory arousal" in order to make clear that I am focusing on experience of stimuli rather than efforts at stimulation.

133 McCauley and Lawson 2002.13–6, 2007.223–5 exclude "religious actions" such as prayer from the definition of "religious ritual." For them, a "ritual" is an action sequence involving a superhuman agent which (a) brings about a change in the religious world, where (b) that change is confirmable based solely on what can be observed by a coreligionist. They exclude an action like public prayer, which can be simulated (and therefore is not confirmable by the observer). However, I question whether the distinction applies to Greek public prayer. Intuitively, words spoken aloud would be heard by gods as by humans, regardless of the intent of the speaker. Compare the myth of Cydippe and Acontius in Ovid. *Her*. 20–1.

134 Compare McCauley and Lawson 2002.74 on the embedding of special patient rituals in special agent rituals.

135 Poseidon: *DI* 132.2–7; see Chapter 1. Demeter of Phigaleia: Paus. 8.42.1–12 (including a Delphic oracle in verse); Larson 2007.79–81 with bibliography.

136 Oracle: *SEG* 41.1411; Parke 1985.157–8; Faraone 1992.75–8. Translation of this excerpt adapted from Chaniotis 2007.93–4 (with complete text).

137 Faraone (1992.118–9) speaks of a spectrum of ritual "rhetorical strategies" from suggestion to persuasion to manipulation.

138 Less coercive: see Faraone 1993.84–5 on the frequency of such rituals and the pattern according to which bound images were provided with annual sacrifices. Compare the distinction between low-intensity and high-intensity sacrifices proposed by van Baal (1976), where the occasion determines the level of intensity.

139 Orneai: Paus. 10.18.5. If historical, the story probably belongs to the early sixth century.

140 No universal rule: Pirenne-Delforge 2010.121–2. The English translation "priest" is problematic (Henrichs 2008) but no better alternative has been proposed, especially given the long-standing lack of clarity about the exact definition of *hiereus/hiereia*. For the purposes of this book, I define a Greek "priest" or "priestess" as a person (a) designated to represent a group in ritual interaction with gods (b) whose presence was believed to increase ritual efficacy. Other ritual performers might meet criterion (b) but not be the single individual designated as the representative. Still other people were "cult officials" whose roles were important for practical or social reasons, but who met neither criterion.

141 *Kanēphoros*: Dillon 2002.37–42. *Amphithalēs* (child with both parents living) at Daphnephoria and elsewhere: Nilsson 1967.1.117–18, 126 with sources. The *amphithaleis* was both more fortunate (in not being orphaned) and less tainted by death than other children. On a "symbolic link" between priest and deity, see Pirenne-Delforge 2010.122, 130–9. Stavrianopolou (2007.194, 2009.214) ties "ritual competence" to authority and knowledge. Although ritual efficacy and priestly knowledge might coincide (Chaniotis 2008), whether a Greek ritual performer possessed authority or knowledge was not relevant to the success of a ritual provided that correct procedures were followed.

142 Exceptions: e.g. the priestess of Herakles at Thespiai (Paus. 9.27.6–8) inverts the common prohibition of women from his cults. Eleusis: compare Pseudo-Dem. 59.116, which describes the punishment of the Eleusinian Hierophant for performing a sacrifice reserved by ancestral custom to the priestess of Demeter.

143 With regard to non-agent ritual performers (see Figure 4.4) I suspect that stipulations for efficacy correlate inversely with the god's degree of activeness (e.g. priests or priestesses in trance cults should have fewer stipulations).

144 McCauley and Lawson (2002.17, 29; 2007.229) describe "rituals of divination" as special instrument rituals, which are closely allied to special patient rituals. In a special instrument ritual (e.g. the sprinkling of holy water in a Christian blessing performed by a layperson), the god's most direct connection to the ritual is through a "special instrument" which has been ritually enabled (e.g. holy water has been blessed by a priest, and a Zulu diviner uses ritually selected bones). But the success of a Greek divinatory ritual did not necessarily depend on previous ritual treatment of sacrificial goats or birds or firewood; these items might be in no way "special" until they came to play a role in the divinatory ritual itself. In my opinion magical inferences are at work in many of McCauley and Lawson's "special instrument" rituals (e.g. aspersion with holy water).

145 Curling tail: van Straten 1995.118–33, 190–1. Repeated sacrifice: Xen. *An.* 6.4.12–5.2. Battlefield divination represented a real element of uncertainty: Hdt. 9.36–7; Xen. *Hell.* 3.4.15.

146 The crux of the matter is how to define the boundaries of the ritual(s) involved; yet setting aside this puzzle, it is clear that the vow differs from standard special patient

ritual in that it eliminates epistemological uncertainty by confirming the intentional agency of a specific god.

147 Didyma: Fontenrose 1988.45. The gender of the *mantis* at Didyma is unknown. The legend of Mopsos suggests a male prophet at Klaros: Parke 1985.112–24. Some of Apollo's prophets were male and some female, but each sanctuary had its own custom: Fontenrose 1978.228. The process of artistic inspiration, governed by Apollo and the Muses, was likewise represented using the metaphor of special agent ritual, but I know of no actual rituals carried out for this purpose. Plato (e.g. *Phdr*. 244c–45c) was fascinated by poetic inspiration and other states of receptivity to the divine, which he classified as forms of *mania* (madness).

148 Speaking before the question: Fontenrose 1978, Q7, 58, 59, 61, 216, 245. Limited: Morgan 1990.159–60, 177 (on Delphi).

149 Purification, fees, sacrifice: von Ehrenheim 2011.20–74; for incubation as a "high-intensity" ritual, see 147–56 and for women and slaves, 98, 174, 184–8. I thank Hedvig von Ehrenheim for allowing me to read her revised dissertation, a much-needed study of incubation which is forthcoming as a *Kernos* supplement. It is not known in what proportions women and men used incubation. The cure records from Asklepios' shrine at Epidauros list thirty-three men cured and thirteen women; however, the male priests of the sanctuary may have found men's cures more interesting (King 1998.108–10).

150 Rise in popularity: von Ehrenheim 2011.157–93 (tracing the increasing tendency for incubation to focus on healing). Vow: von Ehrenheim 2011.11, 95–7.

151 On Trophonios see Bonnechere 2003a, 2003b. The procedure of going down into the cave (or ascending) is mentioned as early as Hdt. 8.134.1. Cf. Eur. *Ion* 300–2; Diod. Sic. 15.53; Ath. 14.2 (614a) (inability to laugh).

152 Possessed by fear (*katochon eti tōi deimati*): Paus. 9.39.13. The sensory deprivation, solitary nature and apparent hallucinatory potential of the consultation suggest (in Rouget's terminology, 1985.3–12) an ecstatic rather than a trance experience.

153 Bremmer (2014.3–4) notes that the fees at Eleusis were considerable.

154 Eleusis: see Chapter 5 and Essay 5.1. Samothrace: for what is known of the rite see Clinton 2003.67–70 (suggesting a blindfolded search). Lykosoura: Jost 2003.157–64; Bremmer 2014.82–5. The ritual included dances by people masked as animals.

155 Dysphoria in Greek mysteries: Bremmer 2014.13–4.

156 *Mania*: e.g. Hdt. 4.79.3–4 where Bacchic trance is described as "going mad" and "being taken by the god" (*mainesthai*; *hēmeas ho theos lambanei*). For an ethnographer's view of *mania* and possession among the Greeks see Rouget 1985.187–226. Cross-culturally, the music used in such cults "belongs" to the possessing deity, and recognizing it helps to trigger the trance state: Rouget 1985.322–4.

157 Less likely: leaders of *thiasoi* are usually termed "those who initiate" using the verb *teleō*, or simply "those who organize *thiasoi*." However, Dem. 19.281 refers to two women leaders of *thiasoi* for Sabazios as *hiereiai* (priestesses).

158 Bacchos: Parker 1996.161–2, 191–4, 2005.325. *Thiasōtai* of "Iacchos" (Eleusinian Bacchos) in a mystery context: Ar. *Ran*. 327. Meter/Kybele: Roller 1999.149–61; Bowden 2010.86–91. On Bacchic *thiasoi* see also Bowden 2010.110–24; Jaccottet 2003.1.123–46.

159 Ferrara krater (early fifth century): Roller 1999.152–3, figs. 43–4. The term *orgia* refers to a wide variety of secret, sacred objects, and also to their associated rituals. *Orgia* were used in most mystery rites, including the Eleusinian: see Motte and Pirenne-Delforge 1992; Jaccottet 2003.1.133–6. Snake handling: fear of snakes is universal to primates, including humans (Barrett 2011.38, 39, 49); snake handling can therefore be understood as a way to heighten arousal in ritual contexts.

160 Private *thiasoi*: *LSAM* 48 (Miletos, third century) distinguishes between the public priestess (*hiereia*) who administers public *thiasoi* and "women who wish to initiate" in private *thiasoi*.

161 Ethnographic parallels: Rouget 1985.32. Korybantic initiation: Plato *Euthyd.* 277d–e; Edmonds 2006; Bremmer 2014.48–53.

162 Meter at Athens: Roller 1999.162–9. Compare the difference in emotional intensity between the private (Classical Athenian) and public (Alexandrian) rituals for Adonis (Essay 2.3). While the Alexandrian public ritual belongs to the special patient category, the close conceptual ties attested in Ar. *Lys.* 387–98 between Adonis and trance cults like that of Sabazios (with dance and drumming) suggest that in some contexts the Adonia went beyond demonstrations of mourning to include trance (Kearns 2010.127).

163 Vestigial: the Athenian festival of Lenaia may once have been mainadic, but Parker (2005.324–6) is skeptical. Sanctuary-bound: Jaccottet 2003.1.78–9 (with primary sources on the Delphic Thyiads, Athenian Gerarai, etc.). Dignified: e.g. Jaccottet 2003.2.244–7, no. 146 (Magnesia on the Maiandros), 250–3, nos. 149–50 (= *LSAM* 48, Miletos), all Hellenistic.

164 Women: for a summary see Dillon 2002.107–82.

165 Masculinity: for descriptions of gender norms see e.g. Csapo 1997 and the essays in Foxhall and Salmon eds. 1998; Rosen and Sluiter eds. 2003. A selection of primary sources in translation is provided in Larson 2012.

166 Negative perceptions of trance ritual: e.g. Dem. 8.260. Discussion: Roller 1999.161–9. Dionysos: e.g. Eur. *Bacch.* 13–22. "Lykian-born Apollo": e.g. Hom. *Il.* 4.101, 119. One advantage of the term "special agent ritual" is that it helps us avoid the misleading category of the "foreign" cult as well as the Christian-derived Weberian terminology of "charismatic" ritual.

167 Less to lose: exceptionally, during the fourth century certain organizers of private *thiasoi* in Athens were tried for impiety under complex political circumstances. See Versnel 1990.115–31.

168 McCauley and Lawson's theory specifically addresses ritual contexts, but gods also acted spontaneously outside of rituals to cause miracles, unsolicited dream apparitions and possession. Dream epiphanies were usually regarded as benign, and often interpreted as a request by the deity to begin relations of mutual *charis* (Essay 2.1). "Seizure" by a god or goddess could be interpreted either positively, as the beginning of mutual *charis*, or negatively as a hostile attack (e.g. phenomena described in Hipp. *Morb. sacr.* 4). See Connor 1988; Borgeaud 1988.107–9; Larson 2001.11–20.

## References

Allen, Nick. 2013. Using Hubert and Mauss to think about sacrifice. In *Sacrifice and modern thought*, ed. Meszaros and Zachhuber, 147–62.

Atran, Scott. 2002. *In gods we trust: The evolutionary landscape of religion.* Oxford and New York: Oxford University Press.

Barrett, Justin L. 2011. *Cognitive science, religion and theology: From human minds to divine minds.* West Conshohocken, PA: Templeton Press.

Barrett, Justin L. and E. Thomas Lawson. 2001. Ritual intuitions: Cognitive contributions to judgments of ritual efficacy. *Journal of Cognition and Culture* 1 (2): 183–201.

Barron, J. P. 1972. New light on old walls: The murals of the Theseion. *JHS* 92: 20–45.

Bell, Catherine. 1997. *Ritual: Perspectives and dimensions.* Oxford and New York: Oxford University Press.

Bell, Catherine. 2006. Ritual. In *The Blackwell companion to the study of religion*, ed. Segal, 397–411.

Bell, Catherine. 2009. *Ritual theory, ritual practice.* New York and London: Oxford University Press.

Berthiaume, Guy. 1982. *Les rôles du mágeiros: Étude sur la boucherie, la cuisine et le sacrifice dans la Grèce ancienne*. Leiden: Brill.

Berti, Irene. 2006. Now let Earth be my witness and the broad heaven above, and the down flowing water of the Styx (Homer, Ilias VX, 36–7): Greek oath rituals. In *Ritual and communication*, ed. Stavrianopoulou, 181–209.

Bloch, Maurice. 1974. Symbols, song, dance, and features of articulation: Is religion an extreme form of traditional authority? *European Journal of Sociology* 15: 55–81.

Bloch, Maurice. 1993. Domain-specificity, living kinds and symbolism. In *Cognitive aspects of religious symbolism*, ed. Boyer, 111–20.

Bonnechere, Pierre. 1994. *Le sacrifice humain en Grèce ancienne*. Athens and Liège: Centre Internationale d'Étude de la Religion Grecque Antique.

Bonnechere, Pierre. 2003a. *Trophonios de Lébadée: Cultes et mythes d'une cité béotienne au miroir de la mentalité antique*. Leiden: Brill.

Bonnechere, Pierre. 2003b. Trophonius of Lebadea: Mystery aspects of an oracular cult in Boeotia. In *Greek mysteries*, ed. Cosmopoulos, 169–92.

Borgeaud, Philippe, ed. 1988. *The cult of Pan in ancient Greece*. Tr. Kathleen Atlass and James Redfield. Chicago: University of Chicago Press.

Bourriot, Félix. 1976. *Recherches sur la nature du genos: Étude d'histoire sociale athénienne*. 2 Vols. Lille: Université Lille III; Paris: Librairie Honoré Champion.

Bowden, Hugh. 2010. *Mystery cults of the ancient world*. Princeton and Oxford: Princeton University Press.

Boyer, Pascal, ed. 1993. *Cognitive aspects of religious symbolism*. Cambridge and New York: Cambridge University Press.

Boyer, Pascal. 1994. *The naturalness of religious ideas: A cognitive theory of religion*. Berkeley and Los Angeles: University of California Press.

Boyer, Pascal. 1998. Creation of the sacred: A cognitivist view. *Method and Theory in the Study of Religion* 10: 88–92.

Boyer, Pascal. 2001. *Religion explained: The evolutionary origins of religious thought*. New York: Basic Books.

Bremmer, Jan. 1998. Religion, ritual, and the opposition sacred vs. profane: Notes towards a terminological genealogy. In *Ansichten griechischer Rituale*, ed. Graf, 9–32.

Bremmer, Jan. 2005. The sacrifice of pregnant animals. In *Greek sacrificial ritual*, ed. Hägg and Alroth, 155–65.

Bremmer, Jan. 2007. Greek normative animal sacrifice. In *A companion to Greek religion*, ed. Ogden, 132–44.

Bremmer, Jan. 2014. *Initiation into the mysteries of the ancient world*. Berlin and Boston: De Gruyter.

Bremmer, Jan and Andrew Erskine, eds. 2010. *The gods of ancient Greece: Identities and transformations*. Edinburgh: Edinburgh University Press.

Brulé, Pierre, ed. 2007. *La norme en matière religieuse en Grèce ancienne*. Liège: Centre International d'Étude de la Religion Grecque Antique.

Bugh, Glenn R. 1990. The Theseia in Late Hellenistic Athens. *ZPE* 83: 20–37.

Burkert, Walter. 1983 [1972]. *Homo Necans: The anthropology of ancient Greek sacrificial ritual and myth*. Tr. Peter Bing. Berkeley, Los Angeles and London: University of California Press.

Burkert, Walter. 1985. *Greek religion*. Cambridge, MA: Harvard University Press.

Burkert, Walter. 1996. *Creation of the sacred: Tracks of biology in early religions*. Cambridge, MA, and London: Harvard University Press.

Burkert, Walter. 2006. Ritual between ethology and post-modern aspects: Philological-historical notes. In *Ritual and communication*, ed. Stavrianopoulou, 23–35.

Calame, Claude. 1996. *Thesée et l'imaginaire athénien: Légende et culte en Grèce antique*. Second edition. Lausanne: Editions Payot Lausanne.

Carter, Jeffrey, ed. 2003. *Understanding religious sacrifice: A reader*. London and New York: Continuum.

Cartledge, Paul. 2001. *Spartan reflections*. Berkeley and Los Angeles: University of California Press.

Chaniotis, Angelos. 2007. The dynamics of ritual norms in Greek cult. In *La norme en matière religieuse*, ed. Brulé, 91–105.

Chaniotis, Angelos. 2008. Priests as ritual experts in the Greek world. In *Practitioners of the divine*, ed. Dignas and Trampedach, 17–34.

Chaniotis, Angelos, ed. 2011. *Ritual dynamics in the ancient Mediterranean*. Dresden: Franz Steiner Verlag.

Chankowski, Véronique. 2008. *Athènes et Délos à l'époque classique: Recherches sur l'administration du sanctuaire d'Apollon délien*. Athens and Paris: École française d'Athènes.

Clark, Christina. 2009. To kneel or not to kneel: Gendered nonverbal behavior in Greek ritual. *Journal of Religion and Society*, Supplement Series 5: 6–20.

Clinton, Kevin. 2003. Stages of initiation in the Eleusinian and Samothracian mysteries. In *Greek mysteries*, ed. Cosmopoulos, 50–78.

Clinton, Kevin. 2005. Pigs in Greek rituals. In *Greek sacrificial ritual*, ed. Hägg and Alroth, 167–79.

Cohen, Ada and Jeremy B. Rutter, eds. 2007. *Constructions of childhood in ancient Greece and Italy*. *Hesperia*, Supplement 41. Princeton, NJ: American School of Classical Studies.

Connor, W. R. 1970. Theseus in Classical Athens. In *The quest for Theseus*, ed. Ward *et al.*, 143–74.

Connor, W. R. 1987. Tribes, festivals and processions: Civic ceremonial and political manipulation in Archaic Greece. *JHS* 107: 40–50.

Connor, W. R. 1988. Seized by the nymphs: Nympholepsy and symbolic expression in Classical Greece. *ClAnt* 7 (2): 155–89.

Cosmopoulos, Michael B., ed. 2003. *Greek mysteries: The archaeology of ancient Greek secret cults*. London: Routledge.

Csapo, Eric. 1997. Riding the phallus for Dionysus: Iconology, ritual and gender role deconstruction. *Phoenix* 51: 253–95.

David, Nicole, Albert Newen and Kai Vogeley. 2008. The sense of agency and its underlying cognitive and neural mechanisms. *Consciousness and Cognition* 17 (2): 523–34.

Davie, John N. 1982. Theseus the king in fifth-century Athens. *G&R* 29 (1): 25–34.

de Polignac, François. 1995 [1984]. *Cults, territory, and the origins of the Greek city-state*. Tr. Janet Lloyd. Chicago: University of Chicago Press.

Detienne, Marcel. 1988. I limiti della spartizione in Grecia. In *Sacrificio e società nel mondo antico*, ed. Grottanelli and Parise, 177–91.

Detienne, Marcel, Jean-Pierre Vernant, Jean-Louis Durand, Stella Georgoudi, François Hartog and Jesper Svenbro. 1989 [1979]. *The cuisine of sacrifice among the Greeks*. Tr. Paula Wissig. Chicago and London: University of Chicago Press.

Dignas, Beate and Kai Trampedach, eds. 2008. *Practitioners of the divine: Greek priests and religious officials from Homer to Heliodorus*. Cambridge, MA: Harvard University Press.

Dillon, Matthew. 2002. *Girls and women in Classical Greek religion*. Abingdon and New York: Routledge.

Dulaney, Siri and Alan Page Fiske. 1994. Cultural rituals and obsessive-compulsive disorder: Is there a common psychological mechanism? *Ethos* 22 (3): 243–83.

Durkheim, Émile. 1915. *The elementary forms of the religious life*. Tr. Joseph Ward Swain. London: Allen and Unwin.

Edmonds, Radcliffe G. III. 2006. To sit in solemn silence? θρόνωσις in ritual, myth, and iconography. *AJPh* 127 (3): 347–66.

Ekroth, Gunnel. 2000. Offerings of blood in Greek hero cults. In *Héros et héroïnes*, ed. Pirenne-Delforge and Suárez de la Torre, 263–80.

Ekroth, Gunnel. 2002. *The sacrificial rituals of Greek hero cults*. Liège: Centre International d'Étude de la Religion Grecque Antique.

Ekroth, Gunnel. 2007a. Meat in ancient Greece: Sacrificial, sacred or secular? *Food and History* 5 (1): 249–72.

Ekroth, Gunnel. 2007b. Thighs or tails? The osteological evidence. In *La norme en matière religieuse*, ed. Brulé, 153–69.

Ekroth, Gunnel. 2008. Burnt, cooked or raw? Divine and human culinary desires at Greek animal sacrifice. In *Transformations in sacrificial practices*, ed. Stavrianapoulou, Michaels and Ambos, 87–111.

Ekroth, Gunnel. 2010. Theseus and the stone: The iconographic and ritual contexts of a Greek votive relief in the Louvre. In *Divine images and human imaginations*, ed. Mylonopoulos, 143–69.

Evans-Pritchard, E. E. 1956. *Nuer religion*. Oxford: Clarendon Press.

Evans-Pritchard, E. E. 2003 [1954]. The meaning of sacrifice among the Nuer. In *Understanding religious sacrifice*, ed. Carter, 189–209.

Faraone, Christopher. 1992. *Talismans and Trojan horses: Guardian statues in ancient Greek myth and ritual*. Oxford and New York: Oxford University Press.

Faraone, Christopher. 1993. Molten wax, spilt wine and mutilated animals: Sympathetic magic in Near Eastern and early Greek oath ceremonies. *JHS* 113: 60–80.

Faraone, Christopher and F. S. Naiden, eds. 2012. *Greek and Roman animal sacrifice: Ancient victims, modern observers*. Cambridge and New York: Cambridge University Press.

Ferguson, W. S. 1938. The Salaminioi of Heptaphylai and Sounion. *Hesperia* 7: 1–74.

Fiske, Alan P. and Nick Haslam. 1997. Is obsessive-compulsive disorder a pathology of the human disposition to perform socially meaningful rituals? Evidence of similar content. *Journal of Nervous and Mental Disease* 185: 211–22.

Flashar, Martin, Ralf von den Hoff and Bettina Kreuzer. 2003. *Theseus: Der Held der Athener*. Munich: Biering and Brinkmann.

Fontenrose, Joseph. 1978. *The Delphic oracle: Its responses and operations with a catalogue of responses*. Berkeley and Los Angeles: University of California Press.

Fontenrose, Joseph. 1988. *Didyma: Apollo's oracle, cult and companions*. Berkeley: University of California Press.

Foxhall, Lin and John Salmon, eds. 1998. *When men were men: Masculinity, power and identity in Classical antiquity*. London and New York: Routledge.

Francis, E. D. and Michael Vickers. 1985. The Oenoe painting in the Stoa Poikile, and Herodotus' account of Marathon. *ABSA* 80: 99–113.

Frankfurter, David. 2011. Egyptian religion and the problem of the category "sacrifice." In *Ancient Mediterranean religion*, ed. Knust and Várhelyi, 75–93.

Freud, Sigmund. 1918. *Totem and taboo: Resemblances between the psychic lives of savages and neurotics*. Tr. A. A. Brill. New York: Moffatt, Yard.

Freud, Sigmund. 1963 [1907]. Obsessive acts and religious practices. In *Character and culture*, ed. Rieff, 17–26.

Geertz, Clifford. 1973. *The interpretation of cultures*. New York: Basic Books.

Gelzer, Thomas, ed. 1975. *Karl Meuli: Gesammelte Schriften*. 2 Vols. Basel: Schwabe.

Georgoudi, Stella. 2005. L' "occultation de la violence" dans le sacrifice grec: Données anciennes, discours modernes. In *La cuisine et l'autel*, ed. Georgoudi, Koch Piettre and Schmidt, 115–47.

Georgoudi, Stella. 2010. Sacrificing to the gods: Ancient evidence and modern interpretations. In *The gods of ancient Greece*, ed. Bremmer and Erskine, 92–105.

Georgoudi, Stella, Renée Koch Piettre and Francis Schmidt, eds. 2005. *La cuisine et l'autel: Les sacrifices en questions dans les sociétés de la méditerranée ancienne*. Turnhout: Brepols.

Girard, René. 1977. *Violence and the sacred*. Tr. Patrick Gregory. Baltimore: Johns Hopkins University Press.

Gordon, R. L., ed. 1981. *Myth, religion and society: Structuralist essays by M. Detienne, L. Gernet, J.-P. Vernant and P. Vidal-Naquet*. Cambridge: Cambridge University Press; Paris: Maison des Sciences de l'Homme.

Graf, Fritz. 1980. Milch, Honig und Wein. In [n. a.] *Perennitas: Studi in onore di Angelo Brelich*, 209–21.

Graf, Fritz. 1996. Pompai in Greece. In *The role of religion in the early Greek polis*, ed. Hägg, 55–65.

Graf, Fritz, ed. 1998. *Ansichten griechischer Rituale: Geburtstags-Symposium für Walter Burkert*. Stuttgart and Leipzig: Teubner.

Graf, Fritz. 2002. What is new about Greek sacrifice? In *Kykeon*, ed. Horstmanshoff, Singor, van Straten and Strubbe, 113–25.

Graf, Fritz. 2009. *Apollo*. London and New York: Routledge.

Graf, Fritz. 2012. One generation after Burkert and Girard: Where are the great theories? In *Greek and Roman animal sacrifice*, ed. Faraone and Naiden, 32–51.

Greaves, Alan M. 2010. *The land of Ionia: Society and economy in the Archaic period*. Chichester, UK, and Malden, MA: Wiley-Blackwell.

Grottanelli, Cristiano and Nicola F. Parise, eds. 1988. *Sacrificio e società nel mondo antico*. Rome: Laterza.

Guthrie, Stewart E. 2002. Animal animism: Evolutionary roots of religious cognition. In *Current approaches in the cognitive science of religion*, ed. Pyysiäinen and Anttonen, 38–67.

Hägg, Robin, ed. 1996. *The role of religion in the early Greek polis*. Stockholm: P. Åströms Förlag.

Hägg, Robin and Brita Alroth, eds. 2005. *Greek sacrificial ritual, Olympian and chthonian*. Stockholm: P. Åströms Förlag.

Hamerton-Kelly, Robert G., ed. 1987. *Violent origins: Walter Burkert, René Girard & Jonathan Z. Smith on ritual killing and cultural formation*. Stanford: Stanford University Press.

Hanna, Judith Lynne. 1987. *To dance is human: A theory of nonverbal communication*. Chicago and London: University of Chicago Press.

Harding, Phillip. 2008. *The story of Athens: The fragments of the local chronicles of Attika*. London and New York: Routledge.

Hart, Donna and Robert W. Sussman. 2008. *Man the hunted: Primates, predators and human evolution*. Expanded edition. Boulder, CO: Westview Press.

Haysom, Matthew and Jenny Wallensten, eds. 2011. *Current approaches to religion in ancient Greece*. Stockholm: Swedish Institute at Athens.

Hellström, Pontus and Brita Alroth, eds. 1996. *Religion and power in the ancient Greek world*. Uppsala: Almqvist and Wiksell.

Henrichs, Albert. 1981. Human sacrifice in Greek religion. In *Le sacrifice dans l'antiquité*, ed. Rudhardt and Reverdin, 195–242.

Henrichs, Albert. 2008. What is a Greek priest? In *Practitioners of the divine*, ed. Dignas and Trampedach, 1–14.

Hitch, Sarah and Ian Rutherford, eds. (Forthcoming) *Animal sacrifice in the ancient Greek world*. Cambridge and New York: Cambridge University Press.

Hollis, Adrian S., ed. 2009. *Callimachus: Hecale*. Second edition. Oxford and New York: Oxford University Press.

Horster, Marietta and Anja Klöckner, eds. 2013. *Cities and priests: Cult personnel in Asia Minor and the Aegean Islands from the Hellenistic to the Imperial period*. Boston: De Gruyter.

Horstmanshoff, F. H. J., H. W. Singor, F. van Straten and J. H. M. Strubbe, eds. 2002. *Kykeon: Studies in honour of H.S. Versnel*. Leiden: Brill.

Hubert, Henri and Marcel Mauss. 1964 [1899]. *Sacrifice: Its nature and functions*. Tr. W. D. Halls. London: Cohen and West.

Humphrey, Caroline and James Laidlaw. 1994. *The archetypal actions of ritual: A theory of ritual illustrated by the Jain rite of worship*. Oxford: Clarendon Press.

Jaccottet, Ann-Françoise. 2003. *Choisir Dionysos: Les associations dionysiaques, ou la face cachée du dionysisme*. 2 Vols. Zurich: Akanthus.

Jameson, Michael H. 1988. Sacrifice and animal husbandry in Classical Greece. In *Pastoral economies in Classical antiquity*, ed. Whittaker, 87–119.

Jost, Madeleine. 2003. Mystery cults in Arcadia. In *Greek mysteries*, ed. Cosmopoulos, 143–68.

Kaestner, Deborah. 1976. The Coan festival of Zeus Polieus. *CJ* 71 (4): 344–8.

Kavoulaki, Athena. 2011. Observations on the meaning and practice of Greek *pompe* (procession). In *Current approaches to religion in ancient Greece*, ed. Haysom and Wallensten, 134–50.

Kearns, Emily. 1989. *The heroes of Attica*. *BICS* Supplement 57. London: Institute of Classical Studies.

Kearns, Emily. 2010. *Ancient Greek religion: A sourcebook*. Malden, MA, and Oxford: Wiley-Blackwell.

King, Helen. 1998. *Hippocrates' woman: Reading the female body in ancient Greece*. London and New York: Routledge.

Kirk, G. S. 1981. Pitfalls in the study of Greek sacrifice. In *Le sacrifice dans l'Antiquité*, ed. Rudhardt and Reverdin, 41–90.

Knust, Jennifer W. and Zsuzsanna Várhelyi, eds. 2011. *Ancient Mediterranean sacrifice*. New York and London: Oxford University Press.

Kreinath, Jens, Jan Snoek and Michael Stausberg, eds. 2006. *Theorizing rituals*. 2 Vols. Leiden: Brill.

Kyle, Donald G. 1992. The Panathenaic games: Sacred and civic athletics. In *Goddess and polis*, ed. Neils, 77–101, 203–8.

Kyle, Donald G. 1993. *Athletics in ancient Athens*. Second revised edition. Leiden and New York: Brill.

Kyriakidis, Evangelos, ed. 2007. *The archaeology of ritual*. Los Angeles: Cotsen Institute of Archaeology, University of California, Los Angeles.

Langdon, Susan. 2007. The awkward age: Art and maturation in early Greece. In *Constructions of childhood*, ed. Cohen and Rutter, 173–91.

Larson, Jennifer. 2001. *Greek nymphs: Myth, cult, lore*. Oxford and New York: Oxford University Press.

Larson, Jennifer. 2007. *Ancient Greek cults: A guide*. New York and London: Routledge.

Larson, Jennifer. 2012. *Greek and Roman sexualities: A sourcebook*. London and New York: Bloomsbury.

Leitao, David. 1995. The perils of Leukippos: Initiatory transvestism and male gender ideology in the Ekdusia at Phaistos. *ClAnt* 14 (1): 130–63.

Levy, Edmond. 1988. La kryptie et ses contradictions. *Ktema* 13: 245–52.

Lewis, I. M. 2003. *Ecstatic religion: A study of shamanism and spirit possession*. Third edition. London and New York: Routledge.

Liénard, Pierre. 2006. The making of peculiar artifacts. Living kind, artifact and social order in the Turkana sacrifice. *Journal of Cognition and Culture* 6 (3–4): 343–73.

Liénard, Pierre and Pascal Boyer. 2006. Whence collective rituals? A cultural selection model of ritualized behavior. *American Anthropologist* 108 (4): 814–27.

Lissarrague, François and Pauline Schmitt-Pantel. 1988. Spartizione e comunità nei banchetti greci. In *Sacrificio e società nel mondo antico*, ed. Grottanelli and Parise, 211–29.

Malinowski, Bronislaw. 1948. *Magic, science and religion, and other essays*. Selected and with an introduction by Robert Redfield. Boston: Beacon Press.

Malkin, Irad. 1996. Territorial domination and the Greek sanctuary. In *Religion and power in the ancient Greek world*, ed. Hellström and Alroth, 75–81.

Malley, Brian and Justin Barrett. 2003. Can ritual form be predicted from religious belief? A test of the Lawson-McCauley hypotheses. *Journal of Ritual Studies* 17 (2): 1–14.

Marinatos, Nanno and Robin Hägg, eds. 1993. *Greek sanctuaries: New approaches*. London and New York: Routledge.

Martin, Luther H. and Panayotis Pachis, eds. 2009. *Imagistic traditions in the Graeco-Roman world: A cognitive modeling of history of religious research*. Thessaloniki: Vanias Editions.

McCauley, Robert N. and E. Thomas Lawson. 1990. *Rethinking religion: Connecting cognition and culture*. Cambridge and New York: Cambridge University Press.

McCauley, Robert N. and E. Thomas Lawson. 2002. *Bringing ritual to mind: Psychological foundations of cultural forms*. Cambridge and New York: Cambridge University Press.

McCauley, Robert N. and E. Thomas Lawson. 2007. Cognition, religious ritual and archaeology. In *The archaeology of ritual*, ed. Kyriakidis, 209–54.

McInerney, Jay. 2010. *The cattle of the sun: Cows and culture in the world of the ancient Greeks*. Princeton: Princeton University Press.

McNamara, Patrick, ed. 2006. *Where God and science meet: How brain and evolutionary studies alter our understanding of religion*. 3 Vols. Westport, CT: Praeger Publishers.

Medin, Douglas L. and Scott Atran. 2004. The native mind: Biological categorization and reasoning in development and across cultures. *Psychological Review* 111 (4): 960–83.

Mehl, Véronique and Pierre Brulé, eds. 2008. *Le sacrifice antique: Vestiges, procedures et strategies*. Rennes: Presses Universitaires de Rennes.

Meszaros, Julia and Johannes Zachhuber, eds. 2013. *Sacrifice and modern thought*. Oxford and New York: Oxford University Press.

Meuli, Karl. 1975 [1946]. Griechische Opferbräuche. In *Karl Meuli: Gesammelte Schriften*, ed. Gelzer, 2: 907–1021.

Mikalson, Jon. 1975. *The sacred and civil calendar of the Athenian year*. Princeton: Princeton University Press.

Mills, Sophie. 1997. *Theseus, tragedy and the Athenian empire*. Oxford: Clarendon Press.

Morgan, Catherine. 1990. *Athletes and oracles: The transformation of Olympia and Delphi in the eighth century B.C.* Cambridge and New York: University of Cambridge.

Motte, André and Vinciane Pirenne-Delforge. 1992. Le mot et les rites: Aperçu des significations de ὄργια et de quelques dérivés. *Kernos* 1992: 119–40.

Mylonopoulos, Joannis, ed. 2010. *Divine images and human imaginations in Greece and Rome*. Leiden: Brill.

Naiden, F. S. 2012. Blessèd are the parasites. In *Greek and Roman animal sacrifice*, ed. Faraone and Naiden, 55–83.

Naiden, F. S. 2013. *Smoke signals for the gods: Ancient Greek sacrifice from the Archaic through Roman periods*. Oxford and New York: Oxford University Press.

Neils, Jenifer. 1987. *The youthful deeds of Theseus*. Rome: Bretschneider.

Neils, Jenifer, ed. 1992. *Goddess and polis: The Panathenaic festival in ancient Athens*. Princeton: Princeton University Press.

Nilsson, Martin Persson. 1967. *Geschichte der griechischen Religion*. Third edition. 2 Vols. Munich: Beck.

Nilsson, Martin Persson. 1995 [1906]. *Griechische Feste von religiöser Bedeutung*. Second edition. Stuttgart and Leipzig: Teubner.

Nock, Arthur Darby. 1972. *Essays on religion and the ancient world*. 2 Vols. Oxford: Oxford University Press.

Norenzayan, Ara and Scott Atran. 2004. Cognitive and emotional processes in the cultural transmission of natural and nonnatural beliefs. In *The psychological foundations of culture*, ed. Schaller and Crandall, 149–69.

Ogden, Daniel, ed. 2007. *A companion to Greek religion*. Oxford and New York: Oxford University Press.

Osborne, Robin. 2006. Relics and remains in an ancient Greek world full of anthropomorphic gods. *P&P* 206 Suppl. 5: 56–72.

Parke, H. W. 1985. *The oracles of Apollo in Asia Minor*. London and Sydney: Croom Helm.

Parker, Robert. 1996. *Athenian religion: A history*. Oxford and New York: Oxford University Press.

Parker, Robert. 2005. *Polytheism and society at Athens*. Oxford and New York: Oxford University Press.

Parker, Robert. 2011. *On Greek religion*. Ithaca and London: Cornell University Press.

Paul, Stéphanie. 2010. À propos d'épiclèses "trans-divines": Le cas de Zeus et d'Athéna à Cos. *ARG* 12: 65–81.

Paul, Stéphanie. 2013a. *Cultes et sanctuaires de l'île de Cos*. Liège: Centre International d'Étude de la Religion Grecque Antique.

Paul, Stéphanie. 2013b. Roles of civic priests in Hellenistic Cos. In *Cities and priests*, ed. Horster and Klöckner, 247–78.

Peirce, Sarah. 1993. Death, revelry and thysia. *ClAnt* 12 (2): 219–60.

[n. a.] 1980. *Perennitas: Studi in onore di Angelo Brelich*. Rome: Edizioni dell'Ateneo.

Pickering, Travis Rayne. 2013. *Rough and tumble: Aggression, hunting, and human evolution*. Berkeley: University of California Press.

Pilz, Oliver. 2011. The performative aspect of Greek ritual. In *Current approaches to religion in ancient Greece*, ed. Haysom and Wallensten, 151–67.

Pirenne-Delforge, Vinciane. 2010. Greek priests and "cult statues": In how far are they necessary? In *Divine images and human imaginations*, ed. Mylonopoulos, 121–41.

Pirenne-Delforge, Vinciane and Emilio Suárez de la Torre, eds. 2000. *Héros et héroïnes dans les mythes et les cultes grecs*. Liège: Centre International d'Étude de la Religion Grecque Antique.

Pyysiäinen, Illka and Veikko Anttonen, eds. 2002. *Current approaches in the cognitive science of religion*. London and New York: Continuum.

Rappaport, Roy. 1979. *Ecology, meaning and religion*. Richmond, CA: North Atlantic Books.

Rappaport, Roy. 1999. *Ritual and religion in the making of humanity*. Cambridge and London: Cambridge University Press.

Rieff, Philip, ed. 1963. *The collected papers of Sigmund Freud: Volume 1: Character and culture*. New York: Collier Books.

Robertson, Noel. 1992. *Festivals and legends: The formation of Greek cities in the light of public ritual*. Toronto and Buffalo: University of Toronto Press.

Roller, Lynn. 1999. *In search of god the mother: The cult of Anatolian Cybele*. Berkeley and Los Angeles: University of California Press.

Rosen, Ralph M. and Ineke Sluiter, eds. 2003. *Andreia: Studies in manliness and courage in Classical antiquity*. Leiden and Boston: Brill.

Rosivach, Vincent J. 1994. *The system of public sacrifice in fourth-century Athens*. Atlanta: Scholars Press.

Rouget, Gilbert. 1985. *Music and trance: A theory of the relations between music and possession*. Chicago and London: University of Chicago Press.

Rudhardt, Jean and Olivier Reverdin, eds. 1981. *Le sacrifice dans l'antiquité: Huit exposés suivis de discussions: Vandœuvres-Genève, 25–30 août 1980*. Geneva: Fondation Hardt.

Rutherford, Ian and James Irvine. 1988. The Race in the Athenian Oschophoria and an Oschophoricon by Pindar. *ZPE* 72: 43–51.

Samuel, Alan E. 1972. *Greek and Roman chronology: Calendars and years in Classical antiquity*. Munich: C. H. Beck.

Schachter, Albert, ed. 1992a. *Le sanctuaire grec*. Geneva: Fondation Hardt.

Schachter, Albert. 1992b. Policy, cult and the placing of Greek sanctuaries. In *Le sanctuaire grec*, ed. Schachter, 1–64.

Schaller, Mark and Christian S. Crandall, eds. 2004. *The psychological foundations of culture*. Mahwah, NJ, and London: Lawrence Erlbaum.

Schefold, Karl. 1946. Kleisthenes. *MH* 3: 59–93.

Schmitt-Pantel, Pauline. 1992. *La cité au banquet: Histoire des repas publics dans les cités grecques*. Rome: École Française de Rome.

Scullion, Scott. 1994. Olympian and chthonian. *ClAnt* 13 (1): 75–119.

Scullion, Scott. 2007a. Festivals. In *A companion to Greek Religion*, ed. Ogden, 190–203.

Scullion, Scott. 2007b. Holocausts and hides in a sacred law of Aixone. In *La norme en matière religieuse*, ed. Brulé, 153–69.

Segal, Robert A., ed. 2006. *The Blackwell companion to the study of religion*. Malden, MA, and Oxford: Blackwell.

Shapiro, H. A. 1989. *Art and cult under the tyrants in Athens*. Mainz: Von Zabern.

Shapiro, H. Alan. 1992. Theseus in Kimonian Athens: The iconography of empire. *MHR* 7 (1): 29–49.

Shapiro, H. Alan, Mario Iozzo and Adrienne Lezzi-Hafter, eds. 2013. *The François Vase: New perspectives*. 2 Vols. Zürich: Akanthus.

Shear, Julia. 2001. *Polis and Panathenaia: The history and development of Athena's festival*. 2 Vols. Dissertation, University of Pennsylvania.

Simon, Erika. 1983. *Festivals of Attica: An archaeological commentary*. Madison: University of Wisconsin Press.

Sinn, Ulrich. 1993. Greek sanctuaries as places of refuge. In *Greek sanctuaries*, ed. Marinatos and Hägg, 88–109.

Sinn, Ulrich. 1996. The influence of Greek sanctuaries on the consolidation of economic power. In *Religion and power in the ancient Greek world*, ed. Hellström and Alroth, 67–74.

Smith, Jonathan Z. 1987a. The domestication of sacrifice. In *Violent origins*, ed. Hamerton-Kelly, 191–205.

Smith, Jonathan Z. 1987b. *To take place: Toward theory in ritual*. Chicago: University of Chicago Press.

Smith, W. Robertson. 1889. *Lectures on the religion of the Semites. First series: The fundamental institutions*. New York: Appleton.

Sørensen, Jesper. 2007. *A cognitive theory of magic*. London and New York: Altamira Press.

Sosis, Richard. 2006. Religious behaviors, badges and bans: Signaling theory and the evolution of religion. In *Where God and science meet*, ed. McNamara, Vol. 1: 61–86.

Sourvinou-Inwood, Christiane. 2003. *Tragedy and Athenian religion*. Lanham, MD: Lexington Books.

Sperber, Dan. 1996. *Explaining culture: A naturalistic approach*. Oxford: Blackwell.

Staal, Frits. 1989. *Rules without meaning: Ritual, mantras and the human sciences*. New York and Bern: Peter Lang.

Stavrianapoulou, Eftychia, ed. 2006. *Ritual and communication in the Graeco-Roman world*. Liège: Centre International d'Étude de la Religion Grecque Antique.

Stavrianopoulou, Eftychia. 2007. Norms of public behavior towards priests. In *La norme en matière religieuse*, ed. Brulé, 213–29.

Stavrianopoulou, Eftychia. 2009. Norms of behaviour towards priests: Some insights from the leges sacrae. In: *La norme en matière religieuse*, ed. Brulé, 213–29.

Stavrianopoulou, Eftychia. 2011. The role of tradition in the forming of rituals in ancient Greece. In *Ritual dynamics in the ancient Mediterranean*, ed. Chaniotis, 85–103.

Stavrianopoulou, Eftychia, Axel Michaels and Claus Ambos, eds. 2008. *Transformations in sacrificial practices: From antiquity to modern times*. Berlin and Piscataway, NJ: Transaction Publishers.

Tambiah, Stanley J. 1979. A performative approach to ritual. *Proceedings of the British Academy* 65.113–69.

Trümpy, Catherine. 1997. *Untersuchungen zu den altgriechischen Monatsnamen und Monatsfolgen*. Heidelberg: C. Winter.

Tulving, Endel. 1983. *Elements of episodic memory*. Oxford: Clarendon Press.

Tulving, Endel. 2002. Episodic memory: From mind to brain. *Annual Review of Psychology* 53: 1–25.

Tulving, Endel and Fergus I. M. Craik, eds. 2000. *The Oxford handbook of memory*. Oxford and New York: Oxford University Press.

Turner, Victor. 1967. *The forest of symbols*. Ithaca and London: Cornell University Press.

Tylor, Edward B. 1874. *Primitive culture: Researches into the development of mythology, philosophy, religion, language, art and custom*. 2 Vols. Boston: Estes and Lauriat.

van Baal, J. 1976. Offering, sacrifice and gift. *Numen* 23 (3): 161–78.

van Straten, Folkert T. 1995. *Hiera Kala: Images of animal sacrifice in Archaic and classical Greece*. Leiden and New York: Brill.

Vernant, Jean-Pierre. 1981a. Sacrificial and alimentary codes in Hesiod's myth of Prometheus. In *Myth, religion and society*, ed. Gordon, 57–79.

Vernant, Jean-Pierre. 1981b. Théorie generale du sacrifice et mise à mort dans la θυσία grecque. In *Le sacrifice dans l'antiquité*, ed. Rudhardt and Reverdin, 1–39.

Vernant, Jean-Pierre. 1991. *Mortals and immortals: Collected essays*. Tr. Froma Zeitlin. Princeton, NJ: Princeton University Press.

Versnel, Henk S. 1990. *Inconsistencies in Greek and Roman religion I. Ter unus: Isis, Dionysos, Hermes: Three studies in henotheism*. Leiden and New York: Brill.

Vidal-Naquet, Pierre. 1981 [1968]. The Black Hunter and the origin of the Athenian ephebeia. In *Myth, religion and society*, ed. Gordon, 147–62.

von den Hoff, Ralf. 2013. Theseus, the François Vase and Athens in the sixth century B.C. In *The François Vase*, ed. Shapiro, Iozzo and Lezzi-Hafter, 132–51.

von Ehrenheim, Hedvig. 2011. *Greek incubation rituals in Classical and Hellenistic times*. Dissertation, Stockholm University.

Ward, Anne G., W. R. Connor, Ruth B. Edwards and Simon Tidworth. 1970. *The quest for Theseus*. New York: Praeger.

Wheeler, E. L. 1982. Hoplomachia and Greek dances in arms. *GRBS* 23: 223–33.

Whitehouse, Harvey 1995. *Inside the cult: Religious innovation and transmission in Papua New Guinea*. Oxford: Clarendon Press.

Whitehouse, Harvey. 2000. *Arguments and icons: Divergent modes of religiosity*. Oxford: Clarendon Press.

Whitehouse, Harvey. 2004a. *Modes of religiosity: A cognitive theory of religious transmission*. Walnut Creek, CA, Lanham, MD, and New York: Altamira Press.

Whitehouse, Harvey. 2004b. Toward a comparative anthropology of religion. In *Ritual and memory*, ed. Whitehouse and Laidlaw, 187–205.

Whitehouse, Harvey. 2005. The cognitive foundations of religiosity. In *Mind and religion*, ed. Whitehouse and McCauley, 207–32.

Whitehouse, Harvey. 2007. Towards an integration of ethnography, history and the cognitive science of religion. In *Religion, anthropology and cognitive science*, ed. Whitehouse and Laidlaw, 247–80.

Whitehouse, Harvey. 2009. Graeco-Roman religions and the cognitive science of religion. In *Imagistic traditions in the Graeco-Roman world*, ed. Martin and Pachis, 1–11.

Whitehouse, Harvey and James Laidlaw, eds. 2004. *Ritual and memory: Toward a comparative anthropology of religion*. Walnut Creek, CA: Altamira Press.

Whitehouse, Harvey and James Laidlaw, eds. 2007. *Religion, anthropology and cognitive science*. Durham, NC: Carolina Academic Press.

Whitehouse, Harvey and Jonathan A. Lanman. 2014. The ties that bind us: Ritual, fusion and identification. *Current Anthropology* 55 (6): 674–95.

Whitehouse, Harvey and Luther H. Martin, eds. 2004. *Theorizing religions past: Archaeology, history, and cognition*. Walnut Creek, CA: AltaMira Press.

Whitehouse, Harvey and Robert N. McCauley, eds. 2005. *Mind and religion: Psychological and cognitive foundations of religiosity*. Walnut Creek, CA, and Lanham, MD: Altamira Press.

Whittaker, C. R., ed. 1988. *Pastoral economies in Classical antiquity*. Cambridge: Cambridge Philological Society.

# 5 Eschatology, mysteries and hero cults

*Among cognitivists, there is debate over whether the widely distributed belief in the persistence of psychological states after death has an intuitive basis or is solely the result of learning. Greek representations of death varied widely, but at all periods, afterlife beliefs were more common than the belief that death is the annihilation of the individual. Counterintuitive concepts of exceptional dead people with superhuman agency were also widespread. No later than the sixth century, belief in the powerful dead led to the distinctively Greek institution of hero cult. During the same period, the Eleusinian and Bacchic-Orphic mysteries promised "life" after death: unlike the majority of humanity, the privileged initiate would retain full mental and sensory capacities in pleasant surroundings. Popular eschatologies of punishment and reward also appeared. By the fourth century if not earlier, many individuals aspired not only to a "better" afterlife but also to one in which they would enjoy hero-like or even godlike status. The illustrative essays examine the role of doctrine in the Eleusinian Mysteries, compare fourth-century tomb inscriptions with the Bacchic-Orphic gold tablet texts and detail three cases in which individuals were worshiped in hero cults soon after their deaths.*

## Intuition and reflection in afterlife beliefs

Throughout the world, at every period of history, people have entertained afterlife beliefs. Why is the concept of some form of continued existence after death so widespread and persistent? Sociological explanations focus on the symbolic dimension of the afterlife. According to Durkheim, for example, the soul of a human being represents the transcendence of society itself: profane bodies die, but the sacred soul, like society and its moral imperatives, continues to exist. Standard psychological explanations, meanwhile, attribute afterlife beliefs to wish fulfillment, or posit that they address a universal fear of death.[1]

For their part, cognitivists have offered two principal models to explain the ubiquity of afterlife beliefs. The first holds that afterlife beliefs are rooted in naturally developing intuitions. Although it is easy to grasp the concept that bodily functions come to an end when death occurs, it is more difficult to envision the utter cessation of all mental processes, since we cannot easily imagine ourselves losing them. According to this "simulation hypothesis," a person operating from a purely intuitive understanding of death will expect the loss of bodily faculties, such as locomotion, vision and hearing, but the persistence of mental faculties, like thinking, desiring and feeling emotions. In Jesse Bering's experiments, adults and children were more likely to attribute to the dead easy-to-simulate losses (e.g. loss of vision or hearing) than difficult-to-simulate losses (e.g. having no thoughts). Very young children showed a tendency to attribute psychobiological states, such as hunger, to a dead mouse in a puppet show. Older children did not, yet they still inferred that the mouse felt emotions. Even some adults who agreed that "the conscious personality . . . ceases permanently when the body dies" nevertheless inferred that a dead individual can *know* he is dead.[2]

On the other hand, an experiment with Vezo children in Madagascar, who were regularly exposed to both animal and human corpses, found that young children were more likely than their older peers to infer that a dead person lacks all mental activity. Vezo adults applied a contextual approach, with many saying that a newly dead person has no mental activity, while a person in a tomb (the site of extensive rituals addressed to ancestors) possesses emotions and intentional agency. It may be the case, then, that intuitive inferences about death depend on one's environment. From early childhood onward, a Vezo person's familiarity with human and animal corpses may foster the intuitive inference that the dead are inert, regardless of his or her reflective beliefs about the ancestors, which are acquired through socialization.[3] As we have seen, such contradictions between intuitive and reflective beliefs often go unexamined.

The second cognitivist approach, therefore, holds that the representation of the dead as persons who continue to possess self-awareness and agency can be fruitfully understood as a minimally counterintuitive concept. On this view, humans have an intuitive, "folk biological" understanding of death as the cessation of both physical and mental processes, an event which renders even the strongest man (or ox or horse) completely helpless and inert. People may reflectively represent the dead, however, as violating these expectations by continuing to think, remember, feel emotions, perceive events and move about (with or without a body). Such concepts of the dead cogently appeal to our systems for social cognition (including our moral intuition, since the dead often monitor the behavior of the living) and to our emotions. Even more riveting is the idea of individuals or collectivities who exert a decisive influence on events despite their deadness. According to this hypothesis, afterlife beliefs do not arise directly from natural intuition, but when they occur as reflective beliefs, they are liable to be culturally propagated and elaborated because of their salience and memorableness.[4]

The disagreement boils down to a question about whether humans possess a *natively* intuitive understanding of death, and if so, whether it involves the persistence or cessation of mental processes. The question, however, is more complex than this. "Death" may not be a fully intuitive concept which develops early through interaction with the environment, as "animal," "tool" or "liquid" do. An individual's level of exposure to death, dead bodies and culturally sanctioned interpretations of death varies widely by culture. Further, an individual's intuitive representation of death is unlikely to be unitary, for our systems of social cognition inevitably affect our experience. The deaths of an ant, a sheep, a stranger and a parent may be represented quite differently, and envisioning one's own death may be different again to these.[5] For our purposes in this chapter, I wish to propose a cognitive distinction between the weak and the powerful dead. Regardless of whether a dead person's consciousness persists in some form, it is consistent with current research to describe as "intuitive" the inference that death compromises his mental and physical capabilities. Likewise, the idea that he continues to possess normal human mentation and agency (or even superagency) is clearly counterintuitive. In the Greek context, this category of the powerful dead includes both beneficial heroes and harmful ghosts.[6]

Even though afterlife beliefs are ubiquitous, they are also highly variable by individual, regardless of whether a culturally sanctioned set of doctrines exists.[7] As we have seen, the intuitive components will vary depending on direct experience. In practice, all (or virtually all) afterlife beliefs include reflective components and require the application of symbolic thought (Chapter 2). How does someone in the grave know when we visit? How does someone in Hell feel pain? According to Sperber, the associations evoked during the attempt to grasp such half-understood concepts will necessarily differ by individual. Among the ancient Greeks this variability, together with the lack of authoritative eschatological doctrines, led to a marvelous chaos of contradictory afterlife beliefs. Although we can point to certain trends, such as the "moralization" of eschatology during the Classical period, it is best to avoid notions of chronological development from one prevailing form of belief to the next. In any given century, Greek ideas on the afterlife were probably no more consistent than our own.

## Death, Hades and the afterlife

In Homeric poetry, our earliest Greek source for explicit beliefs about the dead, the cessation of life results from the separation and departure of the *psuchē* (literally, "breath") from the rest of the body. Although the word *psuchē* is conventionally translated "soul," it is not conceived of in epic as an eternal, spiritual entity. Rather, the *psuchē* is the component of the person that enables life. It can leave the body temporarily, as in a swoon, and then return.[8] Funerary rites, and the consequent passage of the *psuchē* into Hades, serve as the confirmation of a full and permanent separation. The *psuchē* possesses the shape of its original owner, yet it is insubstantial, like a shadow. It lacks the psychological attributes of the living, including *thumos* and *mēnos*, which manifest the emotions and will, and *noos*, which corresponds to reason or understanding.[9] When sundered from the body, the *psuchē* possesses no intentional agency.

How consistent is Homer's viewpoint with the hypothesis of native intuition about death? Surely it reflects concrete, real-world observation (the apparent cessation of all processes once the "breath" or "life" leaves the body), yet behind it stands a reflective theory of the individual personality's constituent parts, complete with names and anatomical anchors (e.g. the *thumos* resides in the chest).

Whatever its origins, this view of death serves a sophisticated poetic goal, confirming that the only "immortality" to which a human being can aspire is glorious renown, celebrated in epic song.[10] Moreover, the Homeric "Hades" is a Panhellenic construct standing in contrast to the more intuitive idea that the dead reside at their gravesites – just as the idea of Olympos contradicts the intuitive understanding of gods residing in sanctuaries.

The *Odyssey* includes an apt illustration of the dismal fate awaiting the general population, and a counterintuitive exception. Advising Odysseus on how to return home, Kirke tells him,

> You must first complete another journey, and reach the house of Hades and dread Persephone, to consult the *psuchē* of Theban Teiresias, the blind seer, whose wits (*phrenes*) are steadfast. Even though he is dead, Persephone gave him reason (*noos*), and he alone is conscious (*pepnusthai*); but the others flit about as shadows.
>
> (Hom. *Od.* 10.490–5)[11]

The poem emphasizes that the dead as a group are pitiful and impotent.[12] Yet it also hints that they are not completely insensible. When he arrives at the land of the dead, Odysseus pours libations of honey-sweetened milk, wine and water, and vows gifts and offerings in the event of his safe return home. He discovers that "the powerless heads of the dead" (*Od.* 10.536) are attracted to the blood of the ram and ewe he sacrifices. Those permitted to drink the blood temporarily regain consciousness and memory. The episode is shaped to fit the needs of the narrative (it makes for a better story if Odysseus can talk to his dead mother), but the ritual resembles historical rites intended to appease and honor the dead. These were characterized above all by the pouring of liquids, in keeping with the widespread belief that the dead were "dry" or "thirsty." An intuitive component of this belief is illustrated by the custom of pouring libations onto the ground, or even into tubes extending into a tomb, so that the soothing fluids could make contact with the desiccated physical remains.[13]

The Homeric poems suggest that Greeks of the Dark Age had low expectations for the continuation of consciousness after death, but we do not know to what degree the depiction of Hades in epic reflects the beliefs of ordinary people. Even Homer endows the *psuchē* (in the strictly limited period before burial) with awareness of whether it has received proper funeral rites; thus Patroklos calls on Achilles for help, and Elpenor on Odysseus.[14] In Chapter 3, we noted that Classical funerary ritual helped the living to deal with the cognitive and social impact of the changes wrought by death. Certain circumstances, such as murder, yielded representations of a dead person whose mental activity was reduced to deep anger and narrowly circumscribed memories. In spite of his dangerous anger, the murder victim's personal agency was limited. He had to rely either on kin or on substitute avengers like the Erinyes to exact justice from a killer.

Archaic and Classical evidence for attitudes toward funerary ritual shows that people were far from indifferent to how their remains were treated after death, behaving as though they would be able to perceive abuse or neglect (though not necessarily to punish it). Above all, people expected their kin not only to conduct a decent funeral with observances on the third and ninth day after death, but also to tend the tomb itself and visit it annually to pour libations (typically on the birthday of the deceased). It was the duty of a son or daughter to provide these attentions, and the plight of the childless person, facing afterlife neglect, was to be pitied.[15] Intuitively speaking, this "afterlife" was intimately tied to kinship and, in particular, to the parent-child bond. The mental activity of the ordinary dead in their tombs was narrowly focused on what was due to them from their own kin. They possessed desire, but little or no agency.[16]

## The nature of mystery cults

From the Archaic period onward, new eschatological ideas evolved to address hopes for a different kind of afterlife, one in which people might fully retain their personal identities, together with the capacity for reason, memory, emotion and sensory pleasures analogous to those enjoyed by the living. These ideas were disseminated through mystery cults and philosophical sects. Mystery cults varied widely, but had in common three defining characteristics. First, they involved a ritual of initiation. In McCauley and Lawson's terms (Chapter 4 and Essay 4.3), this was a "special agent ritual," during which gods acted upon people. Second, mysteries were elective, and individuals must choose to join the group of initiates. Third, initiates were bound to secrecy concerning the details of the ritual.[17]

Greek mysteries typically followed one of two organizational models established no later than the sixth century.[18] The first is the model of the Eleusinian Mysteries, state-sanctioned rites which were made available only in one place, and timed according to a local festival calendar. The Andanian mysteries of Demeter and Kore, the mysteries of Demeter and Despoina at Lykosoura, and the Samothracian mysteries of the Great Gods followed this pattern.[19] The second model is that of the Bacchic mysteries, private rites administered on demand to individuals or groups by itinerant initiators. This category includes the Korybantic mysteries as well as certain rites of Meter/Kybele. By the Hellenistic period, there were hybrid models, such as the mystery initiations offered by the priests of Isis. These were tied to fixed sanctuaries, but administered on an ad hoc basis to individuals (e.g. Lucius in Apuleius' *Metamorphoses*) who had the time and money to devote to them.[20]

Not every mystery cult was concerned with the afterlife, though this was the dominant theme in both the Eleusinian and Bacchic rites. The Samothracian gods are known to have specialized in protecting initiates from death at sea. Other mysteries aimed to address mental or physical illnesses. Aristotle identified the "something extra" offered by these cults as a form of therapy:

> An emotion which strongly affects some souls (*psuchai*) is found in all, though to a greater or lesser degree – for example pity and fear, and also religious excitement (*enthousiasmos*); for some persons become possessed

> under the influence of this passion, and we see that as a result of sacred songs, these people, whenever they make use of songs that excite the soul to a mystic frenzy, are restored as if they had received medical treatment and taken a cleansing (*katharsis*).
>
> (Arist. *Pol.* 1342a)

As in Aristotle's *Poetics* (1449b), the heightening of emotion through a dramatic, musical and/or ritual performance brings about a therapeutic purgation, and a consequent feeling of relief.[21] Aristotle had in mind trance-inducing dancing like that performed by Bacchic or Korybantic initiates, but to some degree his analysis is applicable to all types of mysteries, because these rituals evoked powerful emotions, including pity, fear, awe and joy.

## An innovative cult

The earliest of the new eschatologies was offered through an Attic cult of Demeter and Persephone, the famous Eleusinian Mysteries. The theology and eschatology of the Mysteries were rooted in a very old myth related in the Homeric *Hymn to Demeter*, the abduction of the Grain-Mother's child by the King of the Underworld. The anger of the mother resulted in a famine which could be ended only through a compromise: the annual transit of the daughter, now the queen of the dead, to the upper world, and her cyclical return to her spouse for a third of the year. As the daughter of Demeter, Kore ("Girl") represented the annual scything and rebirth of the crops themselves. Kore died but rose to the upper world again; thus she herself divinely modeled a paradox of death in life and life in death. Such, at any rate, is a modern reading of the myth; ancient initiates did not discuss their interpretations so explicitly.[22] The singer of the *Hymn* merely observes that Kore's travels are tied to the seasons:

> But when earth blooms with fragrant spring flowers
> Of all kinds, then from the murky nether darkness
> You rise, a great wonder to gods and mortal men.
>
> (*Hom. Hymn Dem.* 401–3)

The Archaic sanctuary at Eleusis was active by the eighth century, if not earlier, although scholars are divided on whether the Bronze Age remains are pertinent to the Demeter cult, and when the mystery aspect was instituted. Certainly the Mysteries were in place by the time the Homeric *Hymn to Demeter* was composed in the late seventh or early sixth century, and the first recognizable Telesterion (initiation hall) at Eleusis belongs to the same period, roughly contemporary with Solon.[23] The Mysteries may have arisen as a local innovation on the widespread and ancient festival of Demeter and Kore/Persephone known as the Thesmophoria, during which women gathered, apart from men, to perform a holy rite: the mixing of seed grain with a sort of sacred compost formed of soil and various offerings, including the remains of sacrificial piglets.[24] The Thesmophoria and the

Eleusinian Mysteries shared the sacred myth of Kore's abduction, and both were concerned with grain agriculture. Regardless of whether the mystery element at Eleusis grew from the Thesmophoria, it may have been precipitated by a period of famine or other crisis.[25]

Whatever the historical genesis of the Mysteries, by the Classical period they possessed, in addition to the priestess of Demeter and Kore, a number of male cult officials, among them the Hierophant ("Revealer of the sacred things"), Dadouchos ("Torchbearer") and Keryx ("Herald").[26] In the Mysteries, the agricultural concerns of the Thesmophoria were expanded to include eschatology, with an emphasis on the ultimate fate of the individual, which was new in Greek religion. Probably the Mysteries began as an exclusive affair, restricted to a few local kinship groups, yet the trend was always toward a greater inclusivity which developed in tandem with, and finally surpassed, the leveling effects of the Athenian democracy.[27] Perhaps for the first time, the average citizen (and eventually the slave and the foreigner) was offered the chance to experience a blessed afterlife, which had previously been reserved, in the ideology of epic, for a privileged few.[28]

The exact content of the promises made to initiates at Eleusis is unknown, but many ancient authors provide clues (Essay 5.1). Often mentioned is the goal of changing one's lot in the afterlife, so as to be counted among "the blessed" (*olbioi*) rather than the unfortunate masses of the uninitiated. Missing from the Archaic and Classical discourse about the blessings of Eleusis (so far as we know) was an explicit doctrine of the soul's immortality or a strong opposition between body and soul. Instead, the teachings seem to have been consistent with Homeric ideas of the dead in Hades, with the difference that the initiated would enjoy "life" there.[29] Although the Eleusinian Mysteries were very popular in Attica, there is no sign that they significantly affected Athenian funerary practices or released children from the obligation to attend to their dead parents in the tomb. In fact, funerary inscriptions alluding to the Mysteries are rare (Essay 5.2). Tomb tendance was more intuitive and concrete, while mystery initiation was more reflective and myth-dependent. Logical conflicts between the two were left unexamined.

The Eleusinian Mysteries were of fundamental importance to the state. According to mythic accounts, Eleusis had once been an independent town conquered by Athens; modern opinion holds instead that it was part of the Athenian polis from the start.[30] In any case, Athens invested significant resources in supervising, maintaining and publicizing the Eleusinian cult of the Two Goddesses, which possessed sanctuaries at Eleusis, at Phaleron and in Athens itself.[31] Both Peisistratos and Perikles presided over extensive, costly remodeling of the Telesterion so that it could accommodate more initiates. During the sixth century, Eleusis became a centerpiece for Athenian propaganda: the city, it was said, had disseminated the civilizing knowledge of grain agriculture to the rest of the world. Other Greeks were invited to send first-fruit offerings to Eleusis in thanks for this gift, and the Delphic oracle supported Athens' claim.[32]

Meanwhile, popular eschatology included a newly moralizing emphasis on reward and punishment. Like the Eleusinian teachings, these traditions drew on epic depictions of Hades, where according to a late stratum of the *Odyssey*

(11.570–600) sinners such as Tantalos and Sisyphos who had outraged the gods were punished. In the mid-fifth century, Polygnotos painted a mural of Hades which showed mythic heroes and heroines in Hades alongside an ordinary man being punished for maltreating his father, and another man paying the penalty for sacrilege.

Minos, already a judge of the dead in the *Odyssey*, was joined by Rhadamanthos and Aiakos. Plato wrote that stories (*muthoi*) were told in his day about Hades and the punishment of the wicked after death; those conscious of wrongdoing lived with "bad expectation" while "sweet hope" was near as a support in old age for those who had been virtuous.[33] His contemporaries held a wide range of beliefs about divine rewards and punishments:

> Musaios and his son have a more exuberant song than these, of the good things the gods give to the just, for in their tale, they bring them to the house of Hades, and have them henceforth setting up a drinking-party of the righteous, reclining with wreaths on their heads, deeming it the finest reward of virtue to be everlastingly drunk. And some extend the reward of the gods even further than these, for they say that the children's children and the posterity of the righteous and oath-keeping man will never die out. Such are their praises of justice. But the unrighteous and unjust they bury in the house of Hades in mud, and force them to carry water in a sieve.
>
> (Pl. *Resp.* 2.363c-d)

According to Plato's narrator Adeimantos, those who spread such notions made them sound legitimate by attributing them to legendary poets like Musaios. As we will see, this was a common strategy for promulgating new religious ideas.

## Bacchic-Orphic mysteries

Ionia was the point of origin for Greek speculation about an immortal (but not necessarily personalized) soul, composed of a material distinct in nature from the clay of the body.[34] In the mid-sixth century, the Ionian philosopher Pythagoras founded a philosophical sect in Kroton, a Greek city of southern Italy, where the members were taught a variety of unconventional ideas. These included a doctrine of metempsychosis, the belief that the immortal soul transmigrates many times into different bodies, including those of animals. Pythagoras' followers developed an elaborate system of purifications and ascetic practices which were designed to allow the soul, trapped in the impure physical world, to escape from the endless cycle of rebirths. His philosophical system, with its sharp division between low-value body and high-value soul, had a powerful impact on Plato.[35] By the mid-fifth century, the Sicilian philosopher Empedokles developed a related worldview. His poem *Katharmoi* ("Purifications") described the cycle of metempsychosis and the soul's alternating fate of life and death. He himself claimed to have become "a god, no longer a mortal."[36] The set of beliefs and practices we call "Orphism" had much in common with these teachings. Plato associates with followers of Orpheus the teaching that "the body is a tomb" (*sōma sēma*) in which the soul is imprisoned.[37] Distinctive of Orphism, however, was the attribution of release from this prison to eschatological deities, especially Dionysos.

Although Dionysos Lysios, the Releaser, is less familiar to moderns than Dionysos the wine god, his impact on Greek religion was deep and lasting.[38] It is surely no coincidence that the principal eschatological deities, Demeter (with Kore/Persephone) and Dionysos, were agricultural gods, given the potent metaphor of the seasonal cycle by which plants grow, wither and are reborn. Furthermore, Dionysos was notable as a "special agent," a transformative god whose most characteristic rituals directly altered the mental state of individual worshipers. To experience Dionysiac madness was both "to be initiated" and "to be fulfilled" (*telesthēnai*), the same terminology used at Eleusis. Perhaps these circumstances led to an early eschatological role for Dionysos independently of Orphism. In practice, however, it is difficult to identify a purely Dionysiac ("Bacchic") mystery tradition.[39] In Euripides' *Bacchae* (72–7), for example, the chorus calls blessed (*makar*) the one who "makes his life pure and joins his soul with the *thiasos*, performing Bacchos' rites on the mountains with hallowed cleansings." Purity as the path to "blessedness" sounds characteristically Orphic.

The Bacchic-Orphic mysteries can be traced back to the late sixth and early fifth centuries. During this early period they seem to have been popular in the eastern and western reaches of the Greek Mediterranean, rather than the Greek mainland. One of the "hot spots" was southern Italy, the home of Pythagoras' community. The exact relationship between the Pythagoreans and the innovators who fashioned the new Dionysiac mystery cult(s) is unclear, although purity practices (especially food and clothing taboos), metempsychosis and secrecy are found in both systems of thought. The resemblance was noted already in the fifth century: Herodotus (2.81) thought that certain rites (*orgia*) called "Orphic and Bacchic" were actually Egyptian and Pythagorean, and Ion of Chios alleged that Pythagoras was the author of certain poems attributed to the hero Orpheus, whom the Bacchic innovators claimed as originator and prophet.[40]

The Bacchic-Orphic mysteries were disseminated on a very different model from those at Eleusis. Whereas the Eleusinian rites were tied to the town of Eleusis itself, the Bacchic mysteries moved freely throughout the Greek world with the itinerant initiators who offered them.[41] Eleusinian initiates did not continue to meet after undergoing the rites, but the *thiasos* or cult group was a regular feature of Dionysiac worship. While the Eleusinian Mysteries were closely supervised by the Athenian state, the Bacchic mysteries were most often independent, privately organized and difficult to regulate. In the case of Eleusis, continuity of location, hereditary cult officials and state oversight permitted the formation of a relatively stable (but not static) set of doctrines and rituals. In contrast, the absence of centralized authority and the wide geographical distribution of the Bacchic mysteries seem to have led to greater doctrinal and ritual diversity. Still, the itinerant Bacchic initiators often inherited their profession, and unlike the Eleusinian authorities, they used written texts, an innovation in Greek ritual practice.[42]

By the fifth century, groups who called themselves "Orphics" were representing Dionysos as an eschatological deity. A bone tablet from the Black Sea town of Olbia, inscribed "Life death life/ truth/ Dio(nysos)/ Orphics" is one of the earliest pieces of evidence for the connection between Orphism and Dionysos.[43] The Orphics taught a myth which explained why Dionysos could secure a better afterlife for them, a myth they attributed to the primordial poet-hero Orpheus. Unfortunately, the best ancient testimony comes from a very late author, the sixth-century CE Neoplatonist Olympiodorus. In a commentary on Plato's *Phaedo*, he wrote that "according to Orpheus," four cosmic reigns have existed. The first was that of Ouranos (Heaven), who was succeeded by Kronos, who himself was overthrown by Zeus. Up to this point, the story closely resembles the familiar cosmogonic myth in Hesiod's *Theogony*, which ends with the permanent rule of Zeus. But then, continues Olympiodorus,

> Dionysos succeeded Zeus. Through the plotting of Hera, they say, the Titans who were around him tore him to pieces and ate his flesh. Angered by the deed, Zeus blasted them with his thunderbolts, and out of the sublimate of the vapors that rose from them came the matter from which humans were created.
>
> (Olympiodorus *Commentary on Plato's Phaedo* 1.3)[44]

A great innovation here is the elevation of Dionysos, son of Zeus, to the position of ultimate power in the cosmos. The wicked Titans abruptly cut short his reign, and were duly punished by Zeus. Olympiodorus' terminology ("sublimate of vapors") reveals his Neoplatonist, alchemical background and cautions us that he may be adapting or interpreting the story for his own ends. Although he is the only ancient author to link the myth of Dionysos' dismemberment to the creation of humans, far earlier sources attest a tradition that human beings were descended in some way from the Titans. That Dionysos' body was reconstituted from the torn pieces after the assault, and that he was restored to life, is a strand we can trace back to the Hellenistic period.[45]

Orpheus' adventures included a descent to the underworld, making him a plausible authority on afterlife matters, and a body of poetry attributed to the hero-musician (but actually composed from the late sixth century on by persons concerned with advancing new religious ideas) recounted an alternative cosmogony, with Dionysos as the central deity. By the Hellenistic period, and probably much earlier, the Orphic tradition held that Dionysos' mother was the queen of the dead, Persephone. This teaching contradicted Homer and Hesiod, both of whom identified Semele, the daughter of Kadmos, as the god's mother. On the other hand, it plausibly explained why Dionysos had the power to grant a blessed afterlife.[46] In order to be convincing as eschatological deities, both Demeter and Dionysos needed to be close kin to Persephone.

The "Orphic myth" must be reconstructed by scholars from many bits and pieces belonging to different times and places, and it is important to recognize that there never existed a widely recognized Panhellenic version. Rather, multiple and contradictory versions of the myth were in circulation, and (like all myths) could be interpreted in differing ways. Additionally, we must distinguish between Orphic poetry, which seems to have been a not-so-secret genre dealing with cosmogonic and eschatological matters, and the "Orphic and Bacchic" observances mentioned by Herodotus, which involved private initiation and secret information. Beginning no later than the fourth century, some of these rituals included deposition of gold tablets inscribed with special formulas in the tombs of initiates (Essay 5.2). The public Orphic poetry and the secret rituals are related in no systematic way.[47] Yet the story that Dionysos, son of Persephone, was heir to the cosmos, died violently and was reborn or resurrected is clearly a mythic justification of his eschatological role.

A final element of "the" Orphic myth is more speculative, and continues to be controversial. This is the idea that humans carry a collective stain of guilt because of the crime of Dionysos' murder, and that initiation into the Bacchic mysteries permitted individuals to expiate this guilt.[48] Even if this doctrine was developed early, we cannot assume that it was always imparted to prospective initiates, or that it was a central to all forms of the mysteries. The itinerant practitioners who offered Bacchic initiations were too diffuse a group to have shared a consistent set of myths and doctrines. In this sense they are comparable to the earliest Christians, whose decentralized activities during their first two hundred years produced substantial mythic and doctrinal variation among local congregations, despite a growing reliance on written texts.[49]

Early scholarly discussions of these mysteries postulated a "church" of Orphic initiates who believed that a resurrected god offered them salvation from the stain of an original sin; in reaction to this apparent retrojection of Christian doctrine back to the Classical period, the next generation of scholars maintained a rigorous skepticism about the existence of Orphism. Today, there is little doubt that an Orphic movement existed, even if no single feature of "Orphism" is necessary or sufficient to define it.[50] Most scholars would agree that it was characterized by unusual purity practices, the use of written texts, and a Dionysian eschatology. There is continuing debate about whether we can reconstruct shared Orphic doctrines, and whether early Orphic thought included a myth about the origin of humans and a concept of original sin.

## Plato and Pindar on *teletai* and eschatology

The Bacchic-Orphic initiators were not universally accepted as legitimate, and they were part of a larger group of itinerant religious specialists who offered their services for a fee, citing the authority of "ancient" oracles and legendary poets like Musaios and Orpheus. In the *Republic*, Adeimantos complains that many contemporary afterlife beliefs lack an acceptable moral foundation:

> Begging-priests (*agurtai*) and seers go to the doors of the rich and convince them that through sacrifices and charms, the gods have furnished them a power to cure with pleasant festivities any wrongful deed by the individual

himself or his ancestors. And if a man wishes to ruin an enemy, for a trifling expense he will harm the just and the unjust alike with incantations and binding spells, persuading the gods, so they say, to become their servants . . . [Adeimantos describes how these itinerant hawkers of religion quote Homer and Hesiod to suit their purposes.] And they produce a hubbub of books by Musaios and Orpheus, children of the Moon and of the Muses, so they claim, which they employ ritually, convincing not only private citizens but states that indeed there exist releases (*luseis*) and purifications from bad deeds by means of sacrifices and pleasant pastimes for the living. For the dead also there are rites they call initiations (*teletas*), which provide us release from the evils in that other place, but terrible things await those who do not sacrifice.

(Pl. *Resp.* 2.364b–65a)

In this passage, Plato lumps together the sellers of magical binding spells, used to harm enemies, with the initiators who promise to "release" people from their own sins or those of their forebears through mystery rites, *teletai*. While modern scholarship usually considers these activities separately, we have no way of knowing how much overlap there was in actual practice. Besides the mention of Orpheus, two other features of the description point to Bacchic mysteries. First, the initiators target "the doors of the rich." Because of their access to gold, we can be certain that the owners of the Bacchic-Orphic tablets were relatively affluent. Second, the begging-priests and seers emphasize the need for "release" from past misdeeds and their attendant afterlife punishments, terminology which also appears in connection with Bacchic initiation. While the ancient murder of Dionysos could be invoked in this context, many people must have sought "release" from bad deeds of their own, or from imagined family curses.[51]

Plato's Socrates (*Meno* 81a–d) holds a far more approving opinion of certain "wise men and women," priests and priestesses, who have studied "so as to be able to give an account of what they are pursuing," unlike the door-to-door peddlers of afterlife services. These learned individuals, who we may speculate are Pythagoreans, teach that the soul (*psuchē*) is immortal, and comes to an end – an event we know as death – but that it is reborn and never utterly perishes. Therefore one ought to live "the holiest (*hosiōtata*) life possible" in hopes of earning the ultimate reward. Socrates goes on to quote lines by Pindar which allude to a similar doctrine:

Persephone shall accept the penalty paid for ancient grief,
And to the upper sunlight in the ninth year
She restores these people's souls again.
From them arise glorious kings,
And men who are swift in strength and greatest in wisdom.
For all remaining time they are called pure heroes (*hērōes hagnoi*)
Among humankind.

(Pl. *Meno* 81b = Pindar fr. 133 Maehler)

Pindar flourished in the first half of the fifth century, when the new Bacchic initiations were gaining in popularity. He accepted commissions from patrons deeply interested in Bacchic cult and eschatology. Pindar's work hints at the nature of afterlife beliefs among the Greek aristocrats of Italy and Sicily, but, as a poet, he may have adapted his source material in many ways. His mention of an "ancient grief" for which Persephone accepts payment may (or may not) allude to the crime of Dionysos' murder. He describes a process of metempsychosis, by which souls are reborn after a period in the underworld. Only those who have "paid the penalty" (perhaps Bacchic initiates) can look forward to an ultimate, blessed fate, first as mortals of superior achievement and then as "heroes" in the eschatological sense.

In an ode composed for the Sicilian tyrant Theron of Akragas in 476, Pindar paints a vivid picture of afterlife rewards and punishments:

> The reckless minds of those who have died in this world
> Immediately pay the penalty. Sins committed here in Zeus' realm
> Someone under the earth judges, pronouncing the sentence
> With hateful necessity.
>
> But having the Sun always in equal nights
> And equal days, the good receive a life free from toil,
> Troubling neither the land nor the seawater
> With the strength of their arms, for the sake of a living.
>
> Before the honored gods, those who rejoiced in oath-keeping
> Graze a tearless age, and the rest endure suffering unbearable to see.
> Those who have had the courage, three times on either side,
> To stand fast in their souls from all unjust deeds,
> Accomplish the Road of Zeus, by the Bastion of Kronos.
> There about the Isle of the Blessed
> Ocean's breezes blow and golden flowers blaze,
> Some from splendid trees on dry land, while water nourishes others.
>
> (Pind. *Ol.* 2.56–74)

In this afterlife, there is leisure for the good (with oath-keeping, as in Homer, the litmus test of goodness) and frightful punishment for the wicked. But only those who have been good for three full lifetimes (as well as three "deathtime" intervals) achieve the final reward of a blessed existence with heroes, such as Kadmos, Peleus and Achilles.

Pindar does not set forth a consistent eschatology in his works. Here he draws on the *Odyssey*'s description of the Elysian plain with its Oceanic breezes, populated by a few privileged heroes who never experience death at all.[52] In his moralizing revision, everyone who dies faces the threat of punishment for sins (*alitra*) and the promise of rewards for virtue. In the afterlife, all the dead retain some form of self-awareness, as well as sensory capacities. As we have seen, these ideas were current in the fifth century, and not uniquely tied to Bacchic/Orphic eschatologies. The allusion to metempsychosis, however, is more specific to the contemporary brew of Pythagorean, Empedoklean and Bacchic-Orphic beliefs. Still, Pindar avoids giving this ode a strongly Bacchic flavor, and names neither Dionysos nor Persephone.

## Heroization and eschatology

> Fate is the same for the man who holds back and the one who fights hard.
> We are all held in a single honor, the brave with the weaklings.
> The man who has done nothing dies, just like the one who has done much.
> (Achilles in Hom. *Il.* 9.318–320)

A fundamental theme in the *Iliad* is the idea that its antagonists Hektor and Achilles, like all other men, must die and lose self-awareness in Hades. Although he wishes for eternal life, Hektor cannot become a god, and Achilles will die even though he is the best of the Achaians. The immortality they achieve will not be eschatological but poetic.[53] As we have seen, however, many of Pindar's contemporaries not only hoped for a fully conscious afterlife but also aspired to the blessed fate popularly attributed to "the heroes," an existence free from suffering, devoted to the enjoyment of beautiful things. In this version of the afterlife, the dead retained mental and at least some physical faculties, but their agency was limited to stereotypical activities in the otherworld; they had no impact on the world of the living.

From an early date, however, the Greeks recognized and honored powerful dead people who exercised agency among the living. The joint cult of beautiful Helen and her husband Menelaos, who was promised immortality in the Elysian plain, flourished at Sparta from the seventh century. Erechtheus, the legendary king of Athens, seems to have been worshiped on the Akropolis by the eighth century. Perseus, Theseus, Oedipus and Agamemnon all became recipients of cults.[54] The worship of deceased contemporaries, likewise, began no later than the seventh century and continued, consistently if sporadically, through the Roman period. By the late sixth century, powerful dead men and women who conducted relations of reciprocity with the living were called "heroes" and "heroines" regardless of whether they had lived in the age of heroes or later.[55] At their tombs, whether real or putative, they received sacrifices, choral entertainments and votive gifts. At first such honors were limited to individuals perceived by their communities as extraordinary. During the early Hellenistic period, the expectation of community consensus fell away, as individuals and families began to call themselves "heroes" and to provide for their own postmortem cults.

As recipients of worship, Greek heroes and heroines form a notoriously heterogeneous group upon which generations of Classicists have labored to impose order. L. R. Farnell divided them into faded gods (Ariadne), sacral heroes and heroines (priestly figures or seers like Melampous), functional heroes or *Sondergötter* (Muiagros, whose name means "Fly-Catcher," or Kyamites, the "Bean-Man"), divinized heroes (Herakles, Asklepios), epic heroes (Achilles, Agamemnon), ancestors (usually unnamed and corporate) and real persons of the historical period (e.g. lawgivers or famous athletes).[56] Where Farnell documented the variations among loosely related groups, like heroes, ancestors and ghosts, Angelo Brelich attempted to locate a coherent pattern in the apparent chaos. Applying a more restrictive definition of the hero than Farnell had used, he argued that every hero cult (and indeed, every heroic myth) was built on a group of nine fundamental themes: death, warfare, athletics, prophecy, healing, mysteries, rites of passage, the founding of cities and kinship. Of fly-catching, he has little to say.[57] Gregory Nagy's treatment of the problem made a clear distinction between the epic/mythic and cultic spheres, associating the former with Panhellenic song and the latter with local tradition, but firmly maintaining the heroes' link to poetry and the past.[58]

Most recently, Robert Parker proposed that the heroes of cult form a coherent group, and offered a succinct definition: biographically, a hero or heroine was a dead mortal, but functionally, a minor god.[59] Quite a few heroes and heroines seem to have functioned as nameless powers attached to specific places ("Hero at the Salt Flat," "Hero at the Tower"), or carrying out specific functions ("Gate-holder," "Save-ship").[60] Parker suggests that even these apparent *Sondergötter* would have been understood as "dead mortals who retain power" under the influence of the broader Classical conception of heroes as *hēmitheoi*, the great "demigods" of a past age.[61] But how did such heroes come to exist in the first place? Surely nobody would have begun to sacrifice to a fly-catcher hero on the assumption that he was one of the great *hēmitheoi* described in epic poetry. But was the fly-catcher then, originally a (very) minor god, only later identified as a "hero"? There is a third possibility: our fly-catcher may have originated not as a god but as a powerful dead man with no particular ties to the demigods of the glorious past.

A related problem of definition is the significant overlap between heroines and minor goddesses, especially nymphs. Whether anonymous ("the Heroines of Thorikos") or named (Pandrosos, Aglauros and Herse, the daughters of Kekrops), Attic heroines had a tendency to manifest themselves as pluralities. In Aristophanes' *Clouds*, Strepsiades meets a comic chorus of Clouds, invoked by the crackpot Socrates as great goddesses. Puzzled, he asks, "They aren't heroines, are they?" Strepsiades knows he probably doesn't have the answer right (and indeed Socrates corrects him), but it leaps to mind when he sees an undifferentiated group of females whom he understands to be *polutimētoi*, "highly honored."[62] The Greeks did not always use the terms "hero" and "heroine" as precisely as we could wish, but the notion of a *powerful dead individual, able to enter into a relationship of reciprocity with worshipers*, describes how most Greeks perceived most of these figures during the period under study in this book.

The question of origins is a related conundrum. The old theory that cults of the powerful dead were primarily inspired by the spread of Homeric epic is untenable, for had this been the case, Homeric heroes ought to dominate the list of cult recipients; instead, they are a tiny minority. Archaeologists have downdated the worship of epic heroes like Agamemnon and Odysseus to the sixth century or later.

Arguably, however, the Homeric poems themselves already contain evidence of the worship of powerful dead.[63] Hesiod's myth of the five races of men attests a belief in the powerful dead of the past, though he fails to explicitly attribute continuing agency to the heroes of epic. Then, too, fascination with the heroic past may have been stimulated by the presence of monumental tomb architecture, particularly in areas where burial customs had radically shifted so that the tombs seemed anomalous.[64] Evidence of offerings brought to prehistoric tombs (particularly those of Mycenaean date) goes back to the eleventh century and peaked in the late eighth century. Such offerings were usually sporadic, and the votives so sparse as to suggest only a few visits by worshipers; Christopher Pfaff has therefore suggested that they were made to propitiate the dead when tombs were disturbed. At Prosymna, Argos and Mycenae, people feasted near prehistoric tombs, making food offerings on special circular platforms, which points to a more sustained practice. Carla Antonaccio has rightly cautioned against the conflation of this "tomb cult" with the familiar "hero cult" of the Archaic and Classical periods.[65]

Most scholars, nevertheless, view tomb cult as a phenomenon related to hero cult, and attribute its origin to social and political developments in the Early Iron Age. Offerings at Mycenaean tombs have been interpreted as local attempts to stake claims on land through appeal to the ancestral inhabitants.[66] Other theories link tomb cults to the development of the polis: the worship of ancestors by noble chieftains was replaced by worship of mythic figures who functioned as communal "ancestors" of the city.[67] De Polignac sees sporadic tomb cult as a transitional activity performed by noble individuals or families, while sustained cults were a manifestation of organized effort, the hallmark of newly established "aristocratic solidarities" and civic order. In both cases the intent was to appropriate the prestige of the glorious past, and the social context was one of intense rivalry and competition.[68]

Interpretations focusing on the sociopolitical role of hero cult in creating group identity have long dominated the scholarly discussion, and these are essential for certain types of heroes, such as the ancestor of a lineage or the founder of a colony. "Eponymous" heroes like Eumolpos, mythic ancestor of the Athenian Eumolpidai, were common enough.[69] Institutional founders of all kinds were numerous among the powerful dead, and they were not limited to figures of the legendary past. Numerous examples of Early Iron Age tomb cult seem to have addressed the *recently* deceased in ways that are distinct from ordinary funerary practice. These are generally explained as cases of aristocratic families promoting their own members as powerful dead – but why some and not others?[70] The honored individuals may have been perceived as founders of important lineages. A similar phenomenon was perhaps at work in the Archaic Lakonian veneration of certain dead couples or individuals (Figure 5.1), whose power is indicated by their huge size relative to their worshipers.[71]

Colony founders too were given cult honors upon their deaths, perhaps as the metaphorical fathers of their cities. Irad Malkin has proposed that these cults, which began as early as the seventh century, influenced the hero cult in mainland

*Figure 5.1* A heroized man and woman sit on thrones; the man holds a wine cup and the woman pulls back her veil. A snake rears up behind the thrones. At bottom right, tiny worshipers bring gifts. Lakonian gravestone from Chrysapha, ca. 550–40. Photo: Art Resource

Greece, as developing poleis were stimulated to identify and memorialize their own mythic founders.[72]

That the Greeks, throughout antiquity, recognized cases in which contemporaries retained agency and power after their deaths should perhaps be our baseline for understanding the phenomenon of "hero cult," rather than the more common idea that it was founded upon the numinous prestige of glorious mythic figures and their ancient monuments. Both concepts were at work, but for the latter to emerge, an understanding that "the powerful dead happen" must first have been present. Sarah Johnston has observed that among the recorded oracular responses from Delphi, more are concerned with the powerful dead than with any other single topic, including colonization. In most cases, the responses mandated the establishment of honors for individuals recently dead who had retained an ability to affect the living.[73] These powerful dead were often recognized through "hyperactive agency detection." After displaying the head of their fallen enemy Onesilos on the city gates, for example, the people of Amathous in Cyprus observed that a swarm of bees had settled in it. Their transgressive treatment of his corpse, followed by the unusual activity of the bees (creatures noted for their purity), produced the inference of superhuman agency. Consulting an oracle, they were told to offer Onesilos cult honors.[74]

People who possessed extraordinary qualities in life (charisma, power, talent, noble birth or beauty) were more likely to be perceived as blessed and powerful in death. For example, the Greeks heroized many athletes, one of whom was Philip of Kroton, "the most beautiful Greek of his day." Like many eschatological beliefs, this one is based on exclusivity, and it brings us back to the idea of the heroic age, when men were far mightier than their descendants.[75] The epic poets' Elysion and Isles of the Blessed were likewise reserved for a fortunate few. Mystery cults represent a democratization of access to the blessed beyond, yet such cults encouraged initiates to believe that they were among the privileged few, and even that they would gain special powers in the afterlife and join the ranks of the powerful dead. The gold tablets of the Bacchic-Orphic cults reveal that some initiates laid claim to divine ancestry, while others expected to "rule with the other heroes." Centuries later, the apostle Paul would ask his small band of converts, "Do you not know that we are to sit in judgement over angels?"[76]

It used to be thought that the sacrificial worship of heroes was nearly identical to certain types of funeral offerings made for the dead, and that both heroes and the dead received libations of blood as well as *enagismos/enagisma*, a form of sacrifice which excluded living participants from sharing the offerings. Indeed, some of the best-known hero cults can be cited in support of this view. Pindar says that the hero Pelops received *haimakouriai*, blood offerings, at Olympia, while Aristotle notes that the putative tyrant-slayers Harmodios and Aristogeiton were offered *enagismata* at Athens.[77] The work of A. D. Nock and, more recently, Gunnel Ekroth has refuted this long-standing scholarly orthodoxy. Ekroth demonstrated that prior to the Roman period, the worship of both gods and heroes typically involved *thusia*, the normative form of alimentary sacrifice. The status of the hero as a dead person, however, was not forgotten but acknowledged through the use of special techniques derived from the funerary sphere.[78] Blood from the sacrificed animal could be collected and poured on the hero's tomb prior to the banquet, or the hero's portion of the animal victim could be burned on the altar and put off limits to the diners. On the other hand, heroes and heroines were often given a couch and invited to dine at a table laden with food, a ritual also used to entertain gods. Certain hero cults involved the singing of laments, while others featured the periodic repetition of "funeral games." Contact with some heroes and heroines caused their worshipers to incur pollution (as at a funeral), while contact with others did not.[79] The variation and hybridity in ritual practice were a response to the paradox created by the category of "hero": the hero was dead, yet counterintuitively possessed agency and power among the living.[80]

## ESSAY 5.1: HOW MYSTICAL WERE THE ELEUSINIAN MYSTERIES?

Our word "mysticism" derives from Greek terminology pertaining to mystery initiations, which (so far as we know) were first conducted at Eleusis. Although the Eleusinian "mystic" experience is not to be equated with the forms of mysticism that have succeeded it in the Western tradition, all can be said to value direct experience over doctrines, and extraordinary experience over daily practice. In this essay, we will examine the roles of the direct and the extraordinary relative to the doctrinal and the mundane in the rites at Eleusis.

The secrecy attached to the Mysteries at Eleusis means that we lack coherent descriptions of the rituals carried out there, but it is clear that initiation did not depend on the teaching of text-based doctrines. Instead, we hear repeatedly that the core experience was induced visually, that it was emotional rather than intellectual and that it produced a feeling of joy and consolation in the face of death. Moreover, initiation brought about a change in the state of the individual, so that he or she joined the ranks of the "happy" or "blessed" (*olbioi*). Parallel to these traditions are occasional hints, often overlooked in modern descriptions of the Eleusinian Mysteries, that initiation also involved learning. Indeed, the dogma that one does not "learn" the mysteries but "sees" or "experiences" them was explicitly propounded in antiquity and has been accepted by most modern scholars. But this may be as much a prescriptive statement about the Mysteries as an accurate description.

The earliest text to allude to the rites is the *Homeric Hymn to Demeter* (ca. 600), which includes a *makarismos* or formulaic assertion of the initiate's blessed state.[81] The experience of initiation is described as a visual event which transforms an individual's fate:

> Blessed (*olbios*) is the earth-dwelling human who has seen these things
> But the uninitiate (*atelēs*), with no share in the sacred things, never
> Has the same lot (*aisa*), once deceased in the murky darkness below.
> (*Hom. Hymn Dem.* 480–82)

In a funeral dirge for an initiate, Pindar too describes the experience of Eleusinian initiation as a visual one:

> Blessed (*olbios*) is he who goes beneath the earth having seen those things.
> He knows (*oide*) the end (*teleutan*) of life,
> He knows (*oiden*) the Zeus-given beginning.
> (Pindar fr. 137 Maehler)

Pindar adds something new to the formulation in the *Hymn*: seeing the Mysteries results in knowledge. The initiate now "knows" death, a knowledge which contributes to his or her blessed state. Even more intriguingly, the initiate also possesses knowledge of the beginning of life, and specifically that it is heaven-sent, a gift of Zeus.[82]

Sophocles uses a *makarismos* formula in a fragment of his *Triptolemus*, a play about the Eleusinian culture hero who spread knowledge of grain agriculture: "Since thrice-blessed (*trisolbioi*) are those among mortals who go to Hades having viewed the rites; for they alone have life there, while others have every kind of evil" (Soph. fr. 837 Radt).

Once again, a blessed state is attributed to visual experience. Seeing the rites does not exempt an individual from death; he or she must still go to Hades, as must everyone. Yet "those who have seen" will paradoxically enjoy life after death. Sophocles' formulation departs subtly from that of the *Hymn*, however, by suggesting that the uninitiated will not only fail to share in the happiness of the blessed but also endure sufferings.

In Aristophanes' *Frogs*, the chorus of Eleusinian initiates greets Dionysos and Xanthias with a song that equates their ritual experience with the eternal happiness of the afterlife:[83]

> Dance now the sacred circle-dance of the goddess up the flowery grove, with those who share in the festival dear to the goddess . . . Let us dance up to the flowery meadows of many roses, taking our playful turn in the loveliest of dances, which the blessed Fates (*olbiai Moirai*) organize.
>
> (Ar. *Ran.* 444–6, 449–54)

As initiates, the chorus is led by "blessed Fates," in contrast to the other dead. Yet they attribute their blessed state not only to the ritual experience of the Mysteries but also to their own ethical disposition and practices while alive: "For ours alone is the sun and the cheerful light, we who have been initiated and have maintained pious habits toward strangers and citizens" (Ar. *Ran.* 455–9).

In the afterlife of the *Frogs*, the initiated are equated with the morally good, while those who have committed wicked deeds (and presumably skipped initiation) are condemned to lie in a slough of "mud and ever-flowing shit." In Aristophanes' day, popular eschatology called for afterlife rewards and punishments, a fact of which the organizers of the Mysteries had to take account.[84] Previously there had been few if any conceptual links between the rite and the moral behavior of the initiate. Now initiation was regarded as a prerequisite even for the good, while initiates were perceived as more likely to behave ethically. Already in the fifth century, Polygnotos' famous painting of the underworld showed two women condemned to carry water in broken pitchers, and labeled them "uninitiate."[85]

How did the transformation of the initiate to a blessed state take place? The Christian bishop Synesius, a Neoplatonist, wrote an essay in which he argued that even Christian ascetics, who claimed to experience God directly, required some previous exercise of reason to properly prepare them. Synesius admitted that ultimate revelation is not a rational experience:

> On the contrary, to compare small with greater, it is just as Aristotle thought: initiates are not supposed to learn anything (*mathein ti*) but rather

> to experience (*pathein*) and to be disposed in a certain way (*diatethēnai*), becoming manifestly fit (*epitēdeious*).
>
> (Arist. fr. 15 Rose, quoted by Synesius *Dion* 8.48a = Scarpi 2002.1.172, e26a)

Yet this state of "fitness" for revelation, Synesius believed, is irrational without a scaffolding of knowledge to support it. Synesius' argument echoes Plato, who understood both extensive instruction and aptitude as necessary preludes to mystic experience. In the *Symposium* (210a), Socrates' teacher Diotima tells him, "Even you, Socrates, might become an initiate into matters of love, but I do not know whether you could compass the reason they exist, the ultimate rites and revelations for those who properly pursue the question." She goes on to describe how a series of more advanced "lessons" (*mathēmata*) progressively leads the lover/initiate to "behold the marvelous" – that is, Beauty itself rather than its earthly manifestations. This gradual acquisition of virtue (*aretē*) makes a man beloved of the gods and secures his immortality.[86] Plato effectively offers a philosopher's alternative to Eleusis in which the role of the senses, and especially vision, is important, for the lover is led toward mystic experience by the sight of the beloved. Yet vision is merely a means to the ultimate goal of knowledge, which cannot be acquired without mental preparation.[87]

In a discussion of differences between the instructional and ritual modes of revelation, a Byzantine philosopher gave another version of Aristotle's observation:

> The first comes to people by listening, and the second when the mind itself experiences enlightenment, which Aristotle called mystery-like, and similar to the events at Eleusis, for in these the initiate was imprinted with the sight, but not taught.
>
> (Michael Psellus, *Scholia on John Climacus* 6.171 = Scarpi 2002.1.172, e26b)

Aristotle apparently described Eleusinian initiates as being passively transformed (*pathein*) rather than actively learning something (*mathein*).[88] The source of this central doctrine that "seeing the rites" led directly to a blessed state was surely the Eleusinian authorities, a group whose prestige was based on perceptions of their ritual expertise and the transformative power of the Two Goddesses. This doctrine logically conflicts with the idea, so dear to the philosophers, that blessedness required moral goodness (therefore a daily practice) and knowledge (to which there was no royal road). Indeed, "knowledge" was not presented as a goal of the rite, however much Platonists (and Pindar, who similarly favored the esoteric) may have insisted upon that point. The Eleusinian authorities were not philosophers.[89]

The doctrine "*pathein* not *mathein*" meshed well with the surprisingly egalitarian practices of Eleusis in accepting slave, women and non-citizen candidates for initiation. A better afterlife was not to be achieved through knowledge, least of all through reading books or listening to teachers, and required neither literacy nor elaborate, lifelong purity practices. Instead, it was achieved through a profound, one-time transformation which could be brought about only by a ritual encounter with the Two Goddesses under the supervision of the ritual adepts at Eleusis. There is a clear contrast here with what we know of the Bacchic-Orphic mysteries, which seem to have been more elitist, more focused on knowledge as the key to a blessed afterlife, far more demanding in terms of daily practice, and more text-based. In Euripides' *Hippolytus*, Theseus famously ridiculed his son as an Orphic: "Show off your vegetarian diet; with Orpheus as your master be a Bacchant, and honor the smoke of many books!" The author of the Derveni papyrus, a document which comments on the Bacchic-Orphic tradition, assumed that knowledge was the goal of mysteries, even if initiations, whether private or public, often failed to produce it.[90]

What did the Eleusinian initiates experience? Setting aside the theory, popular on the Internet but scarcely so among Classicists, that the Eleusinian authorities administered hallucinogenic ergot to unwitting initiates, we can point to a number of ritual components conducive to altered states of consciousness: fasting, music, visual stimulation and crowd dynamics.[91] Yet surprisingly few of the sources say or even hint that initiates experienced *enthousiasmos* or possession, and there is no reason to think that the climactic ritual induced a trance state.[92] Eleusinian initiation has been described in terms of the imagistic ritual mode described by Harvey Whitehouse (Chapter 4).[93] At first glance, the fit is plausible because the ritual clearly included imagistic elements, such as heightened emotions (especially fear) and secrecy, but the dysphoric aspects of the ritual clearly did not rise to the level of a searingly painful ordeal (Whitehouse's "rites of terror"). Further, Eleusis does not fit the social profile of the imagistic mode. Hundreds or even thousands of aristocrats and slaves, men and women, foreigners and Athenians were initiated simultaneously. The ritual produced only a very limited group identity among them, and no identity fusion of the type to be found, say, among Spartan warriors or cells of Islamic extremists. Finally, rituals of the imagistic mode lack doctrinal scaffolding, forcing participants to interpret the experience for themselves. But as we will see, despite the prescription of "*pathein* not *mathein*," there is reason to believe that Eleusinian initiates received a significant amount of instruction prior to the climactic ritual. Such teachings, however, were conceptualized as peripheral and incidental, in keeping with the doctrine that blessedness was attained through direct experience.

Before we plunge into the evidence, however, we need to note that we will be juxtaposing data from different centuries in our examination of the Mysteries.[94] True, the rites were performed in one place more or less continuously, and their custodians will have been predisposed to conservatism. But over a span of a thousand years, or even five hundred, the unwritten Eleusinian rituals, and especially the accompanying exegesis, could scarcely have remained unchanged (see Chapter 6). As Walter Burkert observed, the problem is not that we are told too little about the Mysteries. It is that we are told too much, and the information fails to cohere.[95] Some of our evidence comes from hostile Christian sources, and some may simply be guesswork by people who were not initiated; above all, discrepancies may result from change over time. Therefore all reconstructions of the Mysteries, including the one I present here, are speculative.

The Classical festival of the Mysteria lasted several days, and we can glimpse a general outline of events: the *mustēs* (candidate for initiation) attended an opening proclamation in the agora on Boedromion 15 (= the end of September); he or she took a purifying bath in the sea at Phaleron and sacrificed a piglet on the sixteenth. The activities of the *mustai* during the next two days are unknown to us, except that on the seventeenth, they stayed home; perhaps they fasted then. On the nineteenth or twentieth there was a great procession of *mustai* from Athens to Eleusis, where the climactic ritual took place after dark within the walls of the sanctuary; and on the last day, the festivities concluded with libations poured on the earth.[96] In developing their analogy between the Mysteries and philosophic enlightenment, Plato's successors referred to a three-stage process consisting of purification, learning (*paradosis*) and mystic vision. Although there is plenty of evidence for purification, it has never been clear exactly when (or if) a distinct stage of *paradosis* took place.[97]

A festival called the Lesser Mysteries, conducted at Agrai seven months before the Greater Mysteries, may have involved preliminary instruction. Plato says that this was a mandatory first step, and Agrai was associated with the prototypical foreign initiate Herakles. Very little is known about the Lesser Mysteries; one late source describes them as "an imitation of things to do with Dionysos," while others refer to purification.[98] Neither of these scenarios seems pedagogical in nature. Despite Plato's testimony, it is unlikely that the Lesser Mysteries were required in the case of foreign candidates, given the lengthy gap between the two festivals. Epigraphic evidence for fees collected in 407/6 indicates that a far greater number of people were initiated at the Greater Mysteries than at the Lesser. In all probability, the Lesser Mysteries were set forth as part of an ideal sequence, but they were inessential to the experience of the Greater.[99]

An inscription from the Athenian Eleusinion attests another preliminary rite: any member of the *genē* of the Eumolpidai or the Kerykes had the right to conduct *muēsis*, a term usually understood to denote "initiation." This rite could take place either in the court of the sanctuary at Eleusis, or in the Athenian Eleusinion, so it seems to have involved the sharing of secret information in preparation for the main event, and candidates were charged a fee. Only after receiving this preliminary *muēsis* was an individual permitted to enter the sanctuary at Eleusis.[100] A few sources speak of *mustagōgoi* ("leaders of *mustai*"), who acted as escorts or sponsors of candidates for initiation. It is reasonable to suppose that this activity was also the province of the Eumolpidai and Kerykes, who would have found it a handy source of income. *Mustagōgia* specifically in connection with Eleusis is not attested until the first century, though the fourth-century comic poet Menander knew the term. Whether *mustagōgia* and pre-initiation were identical is another difficult question. Kevin Clinton argues that the two were "inseparably connected" but not "coterminous." In his opinion, pre-initiation could be conducted at any time of year, usually in the two weeks before the Lesser and Greater Mysteries respectively, while the role of the mystagogue was to accompany the candidate into the sanctuary during the climactic ritual.[101]

In spite of the doctrine of "*pathein* not *mathein*," then, candidates for initiation were required to receive secret information before undergoing the *teletē*, the nocturnal rite in the sanctuary at Eleusis. At least some initiates, at some periods, also used a knowledgeable escort who could assist them during the ritual. This is significant, because it contradicts the prevailing ancient and modern depiction of initiation as a transformation predicated solely on a singular visual experience. Clinton downplays the contradiction, reassuring us that such instruction would have been "limited."[102] Indeed, the ancient commentators have little to say about preliminary *muēsis* or *mustagōgia*, as though they were relatively insignificant. But as we will see, the list of things that initiates had the motive and the opportunity to learn is surprisingly lengthy and detailed.

What was the climactic ritual like? Dio Chrysostom, a Greek orator of the first century CE, alluded to the Mysteries as a ritual in which one would "see many mystic sights (*mustika theamata*) and hear many such voices, where light and darkness would appear to him alternately, and a thousand other things would occur." Plutarch compared the ritual experience with that of the dead initiate, who wanders confusedly in terror on dark paths, to be met at the end of the journey by bright lights, holy words and dances in a meadow with the other privileged souls.[103] From sources like these, scholars have concluded that the large crowd of *mustai* wandered through a predetermined path in the dark, encountering scary apparitions suggestive of the afterlife punishments awaiting the uninitiated, but also witnessing a ritual drama enacting Demeter's wandering, Kore's emergence from the underworld and the joyous reunion of mother and daughter.[104] The *mustai* eventually arrived at an outdoor space where dances took place. Finally, the doors of the brilliantly torchlit Telesterion were opened, and there the Hierophant revealed certain objects and spoke certain words.[105] At this point, or perhaps on the following night, the *epoptai* ("watchers"), those undergoing the ritual for a second time, were permitted to see something off-limits to the *mustai*.

These descriptions, vague as they are, confirm that the most memorable aspects of initiation were the sense-experience (primarily visual, but also auditory and kinetic) and the emotionally resonant drama. The experience seems to have been one part dramatic performance with audience participation, one part divine epiphany and one part "Hell House." Clinton is skeptical that the ritual drama was detailed enough to present the myth in full, or that narration took place. He stresses the simplicity of the revelations during the Mysteries and their emotional impact.[106] If he is correct, it seems probable that *mustai* were primed in advance with doctrines and narratives. They then used this information to interpret the sense-experience.

The preliminary meeting of the *mustai* with their instructors must have been conducted at a relatively calm emotional level, and the information provided, at least in its general outlines, would have been committed to memory. What did they learn? First, they surely had questions about what to expect after death. After all, the Bacchic-Orphic mysteries (Essay 5.2) offered a high level of specificity on this subject. The *makarismos* formulas in the Homeric *Hymn to Demeter* and other sources are vague by design; in the Mysteries themselves, further details could be revealed. According to Plato's *Apology*, popular belief at Athens held that there were judges in the afterlife, and that one of these was the Eleusinian hero Triptolemos. This points to a specifically Eleusinian version of the afterlife, with a special fate reserved for those whom Triptolemos recognized. As Jan Bremmer has suggested, the preliminary teachings about afterlife expectations must have shifted and developed with the intellectual currents over the centuries.[107]

The *mustai* also needed to learn the basics of Eleusinian theology and topography. The Mysteries involved deities specific to the local rites (e.g. Iacchos and Euboulos) and special ritual names for familiar gods. According to the church father Hippolytus, the Hierophant proclaimed during the secret part of the ritual, "The Lady Brimo has given birth to a holy son, Brimos." Many scholars believe that Brimo is Demeter and Brimos is her son Ploutos, the personification of wealth and abundance. At Eleusis, Hades/Plouton and Persephone/Kore were referred to as Theos and Thea, "God and Goddess."[108] Initiates need hardly have been experts in Eleusinian theology and nomenclature, but in order for the ritual to be intelligible, especially to Greeks from other cities, a minimal level of exposition was required. The point is illustrated by an anecdote about strangers in Eleusis:

> On the day of the rites, two uninitiated Acarnanian youths inadvertently entered the sanctuary together with the crowd, unware of the stricture against it. Their words easily gave them away, for they asked particularly incongruous questions, and they were brought before the overseers of the sanctuary. Although it was clear that they had entered by mistake, they were put to death as though they had committed a heinous crime.
>
> (Livy 31.14.7–8)

The young men's questions quickly revealed a lack of knowledge which, as legitimate initiates, they ought to have possessed by this point. They may have been ignorant of special terminology, or more likely, of sacred structures and topography in the sanctuary (Figure 5.2).[109]

*Hieroi logoi* ("sacred stories") were a recognized part of most mysteries, typically understood to be part of the secret content of which the initiate was not permitted to speak. According to Isocrates, initiates were privy to a narrative concerning Demeter's visit to Attica:

> When Demeter came to our land, wandering after the rape of Kore, and kindly disposed toward our ancestors because of services which can be heard by no one other than her initiates, she gave these two greatest gifts: the fruits of the land, thanks to which we need not live like beasts, and the secret rite (*teletē*), those who partake of which have sweeter hopes concerning the end of life and eternity.
>
> (Isoc. *Paneg.* 28)

Isocrates makes clear that initiates were given specific details about the hospitality provided to Demeter, and these were orally transmitted. Hearing, the normal avenue of instruction in ancient times, was essential for the experience of the

*Figure 5.2* The "Ploutoneion" or cave of Plouton/Hades in the sanctuary of Demeter and Kore at Eleusis was used during the ritual drama of the Mysteries. Photo: Album/Art Resource

Mysteries. Perhaps this explains why all initiates were required to know Greek: they needed to comprehend the *hieroi logoi*.[110] If sacred *logoi* were shared before the *mustai* entered the sanctuary, their transmission depended on an informal system of oral instruction by members of the Athenian *genē* eligible to collect fees for this service. This hypothesis helps to explain the wide variety of attested Eleusinian *logoi*. Without the use of writing, it would have been quite difficult to exercise control over the teachings.[111]

Many scholars think that initiates were required to speak a mystic *sunthēma* ("password"), such as the one reported by the church father Clement of Alexandria: "I fasted, I drank the *kukeōn*, I took from the box (*kistē*), and after working I deposited in the basket (*kalathos*), and from the basket to the box."[112] This ritual formula asserts that the initiate has completed (either literally or metaphorically) the necessary preparations to progress to the final stage of initiation. The first two elements, fasting and drinking the *kukeōn* (a beverage served to the goddess in the Homeric *Hymn*), involve imitations of Demeter's actions while in mourning for Kore. As a practical matter, initiates must have had an opportunity, either before or during the ritual, to learn this riddling *sunthēma* and any actions associated with it. The password was then to be committed to memory.

Finally, what it meant to keep the Mysteries secret is far from self-evident. In order to avoid divine and temporal penalties, initiates needed to form some idea of which pieces of information belonged to the category of *aporrhēta* ("things not to be spoken") and which could be mentioned openly. We saw earlier that Isocrates alluded to services provided by the Athenians to Demeter, though he identified their exact nature as part of the *aporrhēta*. Even the ultra-cautious Pausanias (1.37.4) felt safe revealing that there existed a secret concerning beans. "Whoever has been initiated at Eleusis, or has read the so-called Orphica, will know what I mean," he says. These authors seem to have believed that allusions to certain *hieroi logoi* were acceptable, so long as one did not connect the dots. But how did an individual initiate make such distinctions, since absolute silence was not required, yet the penalty for violating the secrecy of the Mysteries was death?[113]

Eschatological promises, cult terminology, *hieroi logoi* tied to the landscape of the sanctuary, the significance behind a riddling "password," and rules of secrecy: each category of information helped an initiate participate in the ritual, grasp its import and successfully assume his or her new status after the festival. The total represents a surprisingly large amount to be learned by each *mustēs*, especially when considered in relation to the norms of Greek religion. State religious festivals usually involved collective experience, and for this reason, grasping a shared exegesis was not necessary for a given participant in most Greek cults. At Eleusis, by contrast, the situation was different, in that both myth and ritual had a direct bearing on the destiny of each individual.

Initiation at Eleusis seems to have blended elements from Whitehouse's imagistic and doctrinal modes, which clearly correspond to different forms of memory (episodic and semantic). Significantly, however, the two modes were kept ritually distinct. The imagistic elements of the climactic ritual could have formed the initial basis for transmission (perhaps at intervals less frequent than annually) within the *genē* of the Eumolpidai and Kerykes. The doctrinal elements, requiring prior orientation to essential Eleusinian matters, would have become more important as access was broadened to all the citizens of Athens. The Mysteries were opened to foreigners and became (at least to some degree) "moralized" during the fifth century, increasing the trend toward doctrinalization. With the passage of time, the cult generated a significant body of exegetical knowledge, which was transmitted via semantic memory through the *genē* of the Eumolpidai and Kerykes. Everyone involved would have perceived this knowledge as fixed and ancestral, even though it changed significantly over the centuries.

## ESSAY 5.2: TEXTS TO ACCOMPANY THE DEAD

In ancient tombs from several areas of the Greek-speaking world (including Italy, Thessaly, Crete, Macedonia and Rome), excavators have found certain of the dead buried with tiny golden tablets. The tablets were placed in various positions: in the hand of the deceased, on the chest or on the mouth; they might be folded before deposition, or dropped into a vessel used as a grave gift. Although fashioned from the most precious metal, the tablets were not inscribed by highly educated people. While the texts are intended to be poetic, they may alternate between prose and verse, or fall short of "proper" dactylic hexameter, the meter used in poetry attributed to Orpheus. Most of them date to the late Classical and early Hellenistic periods; the earliest was inscribed ca. 400. New examples continue to turn up.[114]

As the number of gold tablets has grown, it has become possible to classify them according to the content of the texts. Certain tablets refer directly to Dionysos/Bacchos as an eschatological deity, while others do not, but the texts as a whole can be interpreted in relation to the Bacchic-Orphic model of mystery initiation. By the fourth century, it was customary among at least some groups of Bacchic initiates to be buried with such a tablet. We also possess another, much larger corpus of "texts to accompany the dead," verse epitaphs which were inscribed on tombstones by the general public, who may or may not have been initiates of one or another mystery cult. By studying epitaphs closely contemporary with the gold tablets, we can form an idea of the very broad spectrum of eschatological ideas current during the late Classical and early Hellenistic periods (with due recognition that some of these ideas were conventions, not necessarily reflecting the personal views of the deceased).[115]

The gold tablets fall into three main groups, with a few outliers. The first group consists of very brief texts with nothing more than the name of the initiate (presumably an identifying token for the underworld powers) or a short message like "Philiste greets Persephone." The second and third groups comprise what Sarah Iles Johnston calls the "geographic" and "purity" tablets. [116] The geographic tablets (Figure 5.3) provide a guide or mnemonic for the newly dead person who is entering the underworld realm. They assume that secret knowledge gained

*Figure 5.3* "This is the work of Memory, when you are about to die . . ." Bacchic-Orphic gold "geographical" tablet from Hipponion, Italy. Found on the upper chest of a female skeleton in its tomb, ca. 400. Archeological Museum of Vibo Valentia. Photo: Gianni Dagli Orti/Art Resource

through initiation is essential for a blessed afterlife. For example, a geographic tablet from Pharsalos in Thessaly, inscribed for a man, reads:

> In the House of Hades you will find to the right a spring,
> And standing beside it, a white cypress.
> Do not even draw near to this spring.
> Further on you will find, from the lake of Memory,
> Cold water pouring forth, and there are guardians thereupon.
> These will ask by what necessity you have come.
> And you, recount to them the whole truth.
> Say, "I am a child of Earth and Starry Heaven.
> My name is Starry, and I am dry with thirst. But give me
> To drink from the spring."
>
> (*OF* no. 477 [= *GJ* no. 25], ca. 350–300)

In this tablet, the initiate's knowledge is of two kinds. The first is practical knowledge: immediately after death he will encounter a specific topography, and a password to be recited to the guardians of the spring of Mnemosyne (Memory).[117] But the initiate also possesses a more esoteric form of knowledge concerning his true identity. He lays claim to divine ancestry as a child of the Titans Ge (Earth) and Asterios Ouranos (Starry Heaven). This self-knowledge gives him the right to a new name (Asterios/Starry) and a special status after death. Unlike the souls in the Homeric underworld, who lack self-awareness, the initiate will remember who he is. One of the concepts traditionally associated with the underworld was oblivion (*lēthē*). By drinking the waters of Memory, the initiate could set himself apart from the crowd.[118] His adoption of the title Asterios may indicate an expectation that his soul will ultimately reside in heaven rather than under the earth. In some tablets, the dead man or woman is told to expect heroization (corresponding to an abode at the end of the earth or beneath it), while in others, the expectation is apotheosis (corresponding to a heavenly abode).[119]

The Bacchic-Orphic form of mystery initiation created lasting relationships among small groups of initiates. At Thourioi in Italy, a group of fourth-century burials included gold tablets. One of the dead was a man cremated in a wooden coffin, with two tablets, one folded into another, beside his head. After the cremation a white cloth was spread over the remains, and a massive tumulus, known as the Timpone Grande, was constructed atop the grave. Thereafter, people visited the spot repeatedly to conduct sacrifices and libations, resulting in eight strata of ashes and pottery fragments, each covered with a layer of earth, clay and pebbles. Nearby, a smaller tumulus contained three gold tablet recipients who were inhumed rather than cremated, as was the usual practice. The tablet belonging to the occupant of the large tumulus includes the declaration "You have become a god instead of a mortal." One of the dead from the small tumulus received a tablet with a similar formula. Some form of personal apotheosis seems to have been the expectation of all the initiates in this Bacchic-Orphic *thiasos*, but the occupant of the Timpone Grande was clearly regarded as one of the powerful dead, an individual capable of entering a reciprocal cultic relationship with the living. Given the presence of a hymnic text on one of his tablets, he may have been the group's leader.[120]

In the "purity" tablets, on the other hand, the key to a better afterlife is not primarily knowledge but the purity attained as a result of initiation, together with adherence to the group's rules of behavior. An example of a "purity" text is this tablet from Macedonia, inscribed for a woman:

> Pure and sacred, of Dionysos
> Bacchios am I,
> Archeboule
> (Daughter) of Antidoros.
> (*OF* no. 496n [= *GJ* no. 30], late fourth to early third century)

Like a letter of recommendation, the tablet affirms that Archeboule is in the correct ritual state to enter into a blissful afterlife, and that in fact she is "of" Dionysus Bacchios, having been initiated into the *thiasos*.

Another purity text adds to our understanding of Dionysos' role in the eschatology of Bacchic mysteries. It comes from a tablet found in a woman's grave at Pelinna, a town in Thessaly. The woman was laid in a sarcophagus with two tablets shaped like leaves of ivy (a plant with Dionysiac associations), one on each side of her chest. The twin tablets are similar, though one is missing some of the lines. The fuller text reads:

> Now you have died and now you have been born, thrice-blessed, on this same day.
> Tell Persephone that the Bacchic one himself released you.
> Bull, you leaped into milk,
> Quickly you leaped into milk,
> Ram, you fell into milk.
> You have wine as your fortunate honor,
> And under the earth, the same attainments (*telea*) as the other blessed ones are in store for you.
> (*OF* no. 485 [= *GJ* no. 26a], late fourth century)[121]

This tablet gives us a sense of the ritual formulas spoken, at the time of initiation, the time of burial or both. The motif of rebirth is common to both these rites of passage.[122] The formula declares that the initiate has attained a "thrice-blessed" state and will be a member of an exclusive group after death. Such *makarismos* formulas, familiar to us from similar claims made about the Eleusinian Mysteries (Essay 5.1), are common in the tablets. The references to animals leaping into milk are cryptic, but they must have symbolic value in connection with the initiation event (just as Christians may speak of being "washed in the blood of the lamb").[123] Finally, the text contains a password: "Tell Persephone that the Bacchic one himself has released (*eluse*) you." Conventionally, the intoxication of wine was a release from sorrow and pain, but eschatologically, Dionysus Lyseus or Lysios ("The Releaser") freed the initiate from the cycle of rebirths, or from the stain of pollution, so that he or she could exist eternally in a community of the pure and blessed.[124]

While the gold tablets served as amulets with secret messages that assisted and protected the individual, epitaphs had a different function, to publicly identify the dead person and perpetuate his memory. The gold tablets addressed an individual's hopes for her own fate, while the epitaphs focused on how others – family, friends, community – responded to a death. Both attempted to express ideas about death in hexametric verse, with the goal of creating a dignified and elevated effect, and both drew upon a pool of traditional ideas, such as the role of Persephone as queen of the dead. As we will see, the gold tablets come at the beginning of a slow-growing trend toward the expression of afterlife hopes on funerary monuments. Yet allusions to eschatology on inscribed gravestones remained rare during our period of study. Scholars disagree on whether the relatively few stones that allude to a blessed afterlife are to be attributed, in the main, to members of philosophical or mystery circles, or whether they represent a broader evolution of popular beliefs.[125]

Many of our early epitaphs come from graves in Attica, the part of Greece that has been most extensively excavated. No gold tablets have been found in Attic tombs; perhaps there the Eleusinian Mysteries were favored more than the Bacchic-Orphic mysteries.[126] Yet even in Attica, where a sizable percentage of the population must have been Eleusinian initiates, epitaphs of the fourth century (i.e. contemporary with most of the gold tablets) send a message which reverses the mysteric emphasis on a privileged or blessed existence after death. These epitaphs often assert that all the dead share a common fate, a sentiment which is both traditional and appropriate for public expression in the context of Athenian democracy.[127] They also focus far more explicitly than the gold tablets on the moral virtues of the deceased, praising his or her *sōphrosunē* (moderation) and *aretē* (excellence), as in this epitaph from Eleusis:

> Dear to all during my seventy years of life, having caused pain to no one,
> Having partaken of moderation, excellence and justice
> I have my share of the fate common to all.
>
> (*CEG2*, no. 554, ca. 350)

In this conventional view, which reflects the outlook of the *Iliad*, the only immortality the dead can expect is in the memory of the living, yet this "afterlife" is desirable, especially when the memory is lasting and communal.[128] Around the year 392, the orator Lysias (2.80) said of the Athenian war dead, "Because of their nature (*phusis*) they are mourned as mortal, but they are praised as immortal because of their excellence (*aretē*)." Thus memory plays a key role in mainstream epitaphs, just as in the gold tablets, but the perspectives are contrasting. The inscribers of the epitaphs have an "exterior" perspective. They envision that the living members of the community, aided by an inscribed public monument, will perpetuate the memory of the deceased regardless of his or her individual fate. The inscribers of the gold tablets work from the "interior" perspective of the dead person, who expects to enjoy a blessed afterlife, and specifically to retain her memory and personal identity, with the aid of the tablet. The "purity" tablets function as tokens of recognition for the underworld gods, while the "geographical" tablets are memory aids for the dead.

Another dominant theme in epitaphs is the sorrow suffered by the living, as in the following epitaph by a husband for his wife. The husband's allusion to the inevitability of departure from the "light" of life into darkness notably contrasts with the Eleusinian imagery of initiates eternally dancing in the light:

> While alive, you had the greatest praise for your ways,
> Archestrate, granddaughter of Lysandros son of Pittheus, and now
> You leave great yearning (*pothos*) to your friends, and especially
> To your own husband, you who have left the light for a fated death.
> (*CEG2*, no. 543.1–4, ca. 350?)

The importance of mourning and grief in epitaphs reflects their social function. The gold tablets, on the other hand, take no account of family or the city, only (on occasion) the fellow initiates. Presumably, the funerary rituals of Bacchic initiates functioned to some extent as a consolation to grieving relatives. Although some cemeteries or plots seem to have been reserved for Bacchic initiates, we know very little about family patterns of Bacchic initiation, especially during the Classical period.[129] Euripides' vignette of the Bacchic-Orphic initiate Hippolytos in conflict with his father Theseus suggests that family members may not always have been willing to observe special funerary practices, such as deposition of gold tablets, or burial in linen rather than wool.[130] Unlike the Eleusinian Mysteries, Bacchic-Orphic initiations had the potential to divide loyalties because of the initiate's ongoing relationship to a *thiasos*. This potential and the high level of investment sometimes expected of initiates (e.g. vegetarianism) are points of comparison with early Christianity. Both systems promised a correspondingly high level of reward.

Whereas the gold tablets express great expectations for the initiate's privileges after death, the few contemporary epitaphs which allude to an afterlife take a more cautious approach:

> Melitta, daughter of Apollodoros, a favored resident (*isotelēs*).
> The earth here below covers the good nurse
> Of Hippostrate, and now she longs for you.
> In life I loved you, nurse, and now too I still honor you,
> Though you are beneath the earth, and I shall honor you as long as I live.
> I know that for you, even beneath the earth, if indeed there is a privilege
> (*geras*) for the good,
> The first honors fall to you, nurse, with Persephone and Plouton.
> (*CEG2*, no. 571; ca. 350)

In this heartfelt tribute, Hippostrate has no doubts that her nurse Melitta deserves a privilege (*geras*), but she does not know whether goodness is in fact rewarded when a person dies.[131] On the other hand, Hippostrate's reference to "Persephone and Plouton" as paired eschatological figures is very rare in epitaphs before the third century. This pairing is found in both Eleusinian and Bacchic contexts and could indicate familiarity with a mystery-based eschatology.[132]

Expression of doubt about the afterlife state is combined with certainty about a loved one's virtue in this memorial for a dead spouse:

> Nikoptoleme, time will never destroy the immortal memory
> Of your excellence (*aretē*), which you left to your husband.
> If there is gratitude (*charis*) for piety in the house of Persephone,
> Fortune also gave you a share of this when you died.
>
> (*CEG2*, no. 603, fourth century)

The content of epitaphs changed over time and was to some extent ruled by fashion, just as it is today. While Hades (both god and place) was regularly mentioned in Attic verse epitaphs before the fourth century, during that century it was Persephone who dominated the convention.[133] Persephone was the deity most often credited with direct power over the fate of the dead, whether in mainstream funerary epitaphs, the Eleusinian Mysteries or the Bacchic-Orphic initiations.[134]

Agnosticism on the question of whether the dead are aware of events among the living is so common among Athenian orators and tragedians as to form a "cultural cliché."[135] Some people certainly entertained the possibility of final annihilation, as Kebes notes in the *Phaedo*: "But in regard to the soul, many people are prone to disbelief, fearing that when it departs from the body, it no longer exists anywhere, but on the day a person dies, it is destroyed and perishes . . ." (Pl. *Phd.* 70a).

During the Hellenistic centuries, by far the most common form of afterlife hope expressed on epitaphs was a popular belief, ultimately derived from pre-Socratic cosmology, that departed souls rose to the aether after death, because souls and the upper air were of the same substance.[136] This idea had already been expressed in an epitaph for the Athenians who died at Poteidaia in 432: "The aether received the souls (*psuchas*) and the earth the bodies (*somata*) of these [men] . . ." (*CEG* no. 10.iii 5–6). A fourth-century epigram from Peiraieus echoes this sentiment, while insisting that the dead man retains his personal identity: "The moist aether holds the soul (*psuchēn*) and the powerful intelligence (*hyperphialous dianoias*) of Eurymachos, but this tomb holds his body" (*CEG2* no. 535; before 350?).

Euripides several times mentions aether as the abode of souls. In the *Suppliants*, Theseus urges: "Let now the dead be covered in earth, and each element return to the place whence it entered the light: the breath (*pneuma*) to the aether, the body (*sōma*) to the earth" (Eur. *Suppl.* 531–4). As a popular eschatology, the aetheric afterlife permitted varied opinions about the continued existence of the individual after death.[137] In the Euripidean formulation, the "breath" is indestructible, yet it does not possess individuality, and joins the generalized aether after death. In either case, however, the implication is that the dead share a common fate. The aetheric hypothesis was a simple materialistic explanation of the soul's fate, openly voiced. It stands in contrast to the metaphysical and mythopoeic teachings of the mystery cults and the Pythagoreans, which were secret and exclusivist.

Related to the aetheric eschatology is the idea that the dead become stars in the heavens. Aristophanes gave it a comic treatment in his play *Peace*, well before it was first expressed in extant epitaphs:

*Servant:* Strolling about in the sky (*aera*), did you see anyone besides yourself?
*Trygaios:* No, only two or three souls (*psuchas*) of dithyrambic poets.
*Servant:* What were they doing?
*Trygaios:* They were flying back and forth, trying to gather some preludes floating on the midday breeze.
*Servant:* So it's not wrong, what they say, that we become stars in the sky when someone dies?
*Trygaios:* Quite right.

(Ar. *Peace* 828–31)

Proponents of exclusivist eschatologies were attracted to this concept, which preserves each individual as a distinct entity in the afterlife. The followers of Pythagoras developed an eschatology assigning each soul a star in heaven, to which it could return only if its behavior was flawlessly righteous during its most recent lifetime.[138] The mystic/philosophic identification of souls with stars followed a sixth-century development in Greek mythmaking according to which mortals were translated to the sky as semidivine beings. Among the earliest of these star myths, for example, were those of the Pleiades and Orion.[139] A related strand of thought is present in the Bacchic-Orphic tablets, where initiates are instructed to claim kinship with Starry Heaven, meaning that that the dead soul partakes of Heaven's immortality. These developments anticipated the popularity of astral eschatology in epitaphs of the later Hellenistic period, and the notion that rulers were destined for the stars.[140]

## ESSAY 5.3: THREE HEROIC FOUNDERS

The Greek habit of transforming certain dead contemporaries into objects of worship is strange to modern sensibilities. Most often the criterion for heroization was exceptional achievement in politics, war, poetry or athletics, but a variety of uncanny circumstances could also trigger a cult.[141] In the Archaic and Classical periods, the average individual did not expect to receive hero-worship after death, because new hero cults were established only in response to the genuinely exceptional, whether splendid or terrifying. During the fourth century, the term *hērōs* began to lose its exclusivity. As we have seen, Bacchic-Orphic groups drew on the concepts of heroization and apotheosis in order to express the initiate's hopes of a life after death in which it was possible to retain not only personal identity but also agency. This century also saw a seismic shift in popular eschatology, whereby people began to apply the hero-concept to themselves, as they hoped or expected to exist in the afterlife, and to incorporate concepts, rituals and terminology drawn from hero cult into funerary practices. The theme of exclusivity did not disappear, however, because funerary heroization was practiced especially by affluent families and individuals attempting to draw attention to their own elite status.[142]

Broader application of the hero-concept proceeded by fits and starts in different geographical regions. Already in late Classical Boiotia, tombstones of the ordinary dead used the word "hero" as an honorific. The term occurs on a relatively small proportion of stones, and seems especially to be applied to children and young people, who belonged to a group of restless dead known as the "untimely ones" (*aōroi*). Missing from the Boiotian phenomenon, so far as we can tell, was a relationship of reciprocity between hero and worshipers; the dead were not represented as agents with the ability to act in the world of the living. In many parts of the Greek world, meanwhile, iconography which had previously been reserved for gods and heroes (Figure 5.4) came to be applied to the ordinary dead in the form of the so-called *Totenmahl* reliefs, sculptures which (arguably) showed the blessed enjoying a banquet in the afterlife.[143]

*Figure 5.4* A hero or god reclines holding a rhyton (horn-shaped drinking vessel) while his consort sits beside him and an attendant serves wine. On the left, a family of worshipers brings a sheep and pig for sacrifice. Marble votive relief, Megara, fourth century. Athens, National Museum. Photo © Vanni Archive/ Art Resource

By the late fourth century, some Greeks were using their wills to found and endow private cult associations devoted to perpetuating the memory of themselves and their families.[144] The development of this type of funerary cult has been linked to the widening socioeconomic gap between elites and the rest of the population in Hellenistic cities. It differed from traditional forms of ancestor worship in the way specific individuals were singled out by name from the corporate ancestral dead and given elaborate honors in association with deities – at their own behest. Usually the worshipers were limited to the family of the deceased, but sometimes testamentary provision was made for public feasting and games.[145] Like today's endowments of hospital wings or charitable trusts, funerary cults offered people a way to perpetuate their names in memory, but these cults also expressed personal eschatological hopes. In the rest of this essay, we will examine three examples of heroized contemporaries – each in some sense a "founder" – and their relationship to concepts of the afterlife.

## Battos of Kyrene

Battos founded the colony of Kyrene in Libya around 630 and was worshiped after his death by its citizens. We have an unusually rich store of information about the circumstances under which Battos became one of the powerful dead, information which is doubly precious because his is such an early case of worship paid to a deceased contemporary.[146] Battos' colonizing venture seems to have arisen out of necessity, when the island of Thera could not sustain its population. In Herodotus' account (4.150–159), the Therans were plagued by a seven-year drought. More than once they consulted Delphi, and the Pythia repeatedly urged them to send a colony to Libya, naming Battos as the intended founder.

> At this the Therans sent out Battos with two fifty-oared ships. But once they had sailed to Libya, not knowing what else to do, the men came back to Thera. The Therans shot missiles at them as they put in, and would not allow them to reach the shore, ordering the men to sail back.
>
> (Hdt. 4.156.3)

Like Aeneas, the long-suffering Battos faced a series of failures and struggles before finally achieving his goal; he first settled on Platea, an island offshore from Libya, but finding little success there after two years, he moved to the mainland. After another six years, the Libyans eventually led the colonists to the site they named Kyrene. The "Oath of the Settlers" from Kyrene preserves a description of the conditions under which the original colonists left, and hints that the colonization effort was the result of civil strife and overpopulation:

> Oath of the Settlers. The assembly decided: since Apollo spontaneously told Battos and the Therans to colonize Kyrene, the Therans resolve to send out Battos to Libya as founder (*archāgetās*) and king (*basileus*), with Therans

> to sail as his companions. They are to sail on fair and equal terms, according to households, one son to be chosen (from every family?) from those who are adults; and from the rest of Therans, those free men (who are willing?) may sail.
>
> (*ML* no. 5.23–30)[147]

The inscription further specifies that, although the settlers could return after a trial period of five years, any man who balked at being chosen was to suffer the death penalty. In a sense, Battos and his men were being exiled from the city, yet Battos was to be "founder and king" (the inclusion of these titles in the inscription may be anachronistic, but Battos probably possessed them by the time of his death). The title *archāgetās*, "founder/first leader," was shared with Pythian Apollo, who acted as a divine founder and patron of colonies; it referred to the establishment of both the settlement and its cults. A founder embodied the colony's ties to its mother-city and cultural traditions, even as the colony maintained its political independence.[148]

It is Pindar who informs us that Battos became the object of a cult. In an ode for Battos' kingly descendant Arkesilas, who had won the chariot race in the Pythian games of 462, he refers to Battos' role in laying out the sanctuaries of the gods, and to his ultimate reward:

> He founded greater groves of the gods,
> And he established, for the processions of Apollo,
> Protector of mortals, a straight-cut, level, paved road
> Sounding with horses' hooves, where at the edge of the marketplace he lies
> Apart in death. Blessed (*makar*) among men
> He dwelt, and afterwards as a hero, worshipped by the people.
>
> (Pind. *Pyth*. 5.89–95)

For Pindar, there was continuity between Battos' existence before and after death: already in life he was *makar*, a term used of the gods as well as the heroic inhabitants of the *makarōn nēsoi*, the Isles of the Blessed.[149] Herodotus emphasizes Battos' uncertain early steps, while Pindar focuses on his ultimate glory, yet both make clear that the founding of Kyrene was part of a divine plan, which Battos was chosen to carry to fruition. His heroization is conceptualized less as a reflection of his personal superiority (Herodotus mentions that he was illegitimate and a stutterer) than as a manifestation of his blessed fate as a founder.[150] Excavation at Kyrene revealed a seventh-century house or temple associated with a mound-covered tomb on the southeastern edge of the marketplace. The tomb, constructed in the first quarter of the sixth century, contained a cremated skeleton as well as a substantial ash altar.[151] As Malkin has shown, the intimate link between the occupant of a tomb (perhaps only later to be styled "the hero") and the land meant that tombs of the powerful dead served as symbols of colonial territorial claims. After all, the heroes themselves occupied the land in the most concrete way imaginable.[152]

## Brasidas the Spartan

In 422, the Spartan general Brasidas won a resounding victory at Amphipolis, striking a heavy blow against Athens and bringing about the death of his Athenian opponent Kleon, yet losing his own life in the process. A seasoned commander with almost a decade of experience, Brasidas had marched to Chalkidike in the northern Aegean in order to destabilize Athens' control over its subject cities in Thrace.

Events at Amphipolis were of personal interest to Thucydides, a veteran of the Peloponnesian War and the historian to whom we owe most of our information about Brasidas. In 424/3, when Brasidas initially captured the city, its Athenian defenders called upon Thucydides for aid, but he arrived too late to change the outcome. For this failure, he was eventually recalled to Athens, tried and exiled for twenty years.[153] Meanwhile, the fall of Amphipolis forced the Athenians to negotiate with Sparta, and an armistice of one year was arranged for 423. When the armistice ended, Kleon sailed from Athens to confront Brasidas. Thucydides says (5.10.11) that in the ensuing battle, Brasidas took a mortal wound and was carried off the field by his men. He lived long enough to hear of his victory.

> After this all the allies attended Brasidas in arms, and buried him at public expense in the city, in front of what is now the marketplace. The Amphipolitans enclosed his tomb, and ever afterwards they have sacrificed (*entemnousi*) to him as a hero and have given him honors, contests and annual offerings. They attributed to him the founding of their city, and pulled down the buildings pertaining to Hagnon (*Hagnōneia oikodomēmata*) and destroyed everything that was likely to remind them of his having founded the place; for they deemed that Brasidas had been their savior (*sōtēra*) and they courted an alliance with the Lakedaimonians [i.e. the Spartans] for fear of the Athenians, while due to their hostile relations with the latter, Hagnon likewise could not receive his honors in a fashion either useful for them or pleasurable to himself.
>
> (Thuc. 5.11.1)

Fifteen years before the climactic battle, the Athenian Hagnon had founded Amphipholis, but once Athenian claims to the territory were repudiated, it was necessary for both political and religious reasons to erase the memory of Hagnon and to replace him with a new hero. The "buildings pertaining to Hagnon" were probably Hagnon's house as well as his hero shrine, constructed within the city walls to serve as his final resting place.[154]

Thucydides recognizes that political motivations drove the Amphipolitans to raze Hagnon's buildings, and to seek favor with the Spartans by installing Brasidas as their new "founder." Yet far from considering these motives mutually exclusive with religion, he also acknowledges that the citizens could not, after they had rebelled from Athens, engage in a normative cultic relationship with the heroized Hagnon. Such relationships involved reciprocity, whereby the citizens sought to give the hero pleasure through sacrifices and other honors, while he looked after the city in return. With their change in loyalties, the Amphipolitans had created for themselves a serious dilemma. The death in battle of the brilliant Spartan who had liberated them from Athens suggested an ideal solution, and his military prowess must have made the prospect of a new cult even more attractive. In death, Brasidas would continue to be a powerful ally, whereas the still-living Hagnon had neglected the city and did not even reside there. Thus, in establishing the cult of Brasidas, the Amphipolitans were preoccupied with concerns about the present and the future, and uninterested in cementing ties to the past, except insofar as Brasidas evoked the glories of epic heroes. So glorious was Brasidas' reputation that a few decades after his death, Plato (*Symp*. 221c) found nothing odd in likening him to Achilles.

The case of Brasidas demonstrates the Classical emphasis on extraordinary achievement or unusual personal qualities as the basis for heroization of the recent dead. At this point in the Classical period, the heroization of dead contemporaries was still exceptional, although it had become customary in certain situations. The Sicilian tyrants of the Classical period were heroized upon their deaths, and the heroization of founders was taken for granted, Hagnon's case excepted. Brasidas had been crowned and garlanded "like an athlete" by the people of Skione, who hailed him as "liberator of Hellas," while the Amphipolitans described him as a savior (*sōtēr*). His cult anticipated the (mostly divine) honors paid to the living generals of the fourth century under similar circumstances of political upheaval, yet it was distinct from them to the degree that it recapitulated traditional features of hero cult.[155] His tomb was constructed beside the marketplace, like that of Battos, and his honors (*timai*) were extensive: animal sacrifice with blood libations (indicated by the verb *entemnein*), and funeral games as well as annual feasting. Excavation at Amphipolis revealed a cist tomb within the city walls, which may have belonged to Brasidas. Within the tomb were a wood and silver box containing the cremated remains of a man in the prime of life, and a simple wreath of golden olive leaves. Nearby, a second cist contained pottery of the fifth and fourth centuries, probably dedications to the hero.[156]

In life, Brasidas had already earned extraordinary praise. He was an exceptional man whose violent and glorious death triggered a spontaneous response, both political and devotional, in the Amphipolitans. As in the case of Battos, his status as a hero symbolized a claim to the land. Yet it was not the claim of independent Amphipolitans; rather, it was mediated through the power of Sparta. Where Battos had been a traditional founder, the very concept of "founding the city" had to be modified in order to accommodate Brasidas' cult. Finally, his heroization was not, so far as we know, decreed by the gods or even approved by the Delphic oracle, a normal step when establishing a founder's cult. His cult was perceived less as the outcome of divinely allotted destiny than as a recognition of Brasidas' extraordinary personal qualities and achievements, which set him apart from other men in both life and death. His eschatological status is not explicitly discussed in the sources (except indirectly in Thucydides' discussion of Hagnon), but implicit in the honors (*timai*) assigned to him was the concept of an ongoing reciprocal relationship between Brasidas the "savior," as one of the powerful dead, and the citizens of Amphipolis.[157]

## Epikteta of Thera

Epikteta was an elite woman of Thera who founded a hero cult for her family ca. 200. In the inscription known as her "testament," there are both radical departures from tradition and significant areas of continuity.[158] The concept of a private hero cult was not new: private associations which met for the purpose of sacrifice and worship went back to the early sixth century, at least in Attica, where groups of "sacrificial associates" known as *orgeōnes* worshiped minor heroes, heroines and gods. Epikteta's cult association (*koinon*), like its Athenian counterparts, was hereditary, and its charter document was modeled on civic decrees.[159] Like all such private sacrificial clubs (*thiasoi, koina*, etc.), Epikteta's association possessed detailed rules for membership and participation. What makes Epikteta's cult different and new is that she herself, together with her husband and sons, was the intended recipient of heroic honors. Her testament reflects a third-century trend toward family cults and private heroization in the southeastern Aegean.[160]

The sociopolitical transformations of the Hellenistic period allowed property to be concentrated in the hands of women, a phenomenon often found among endogamous aristocratic families. As wealthy benefactors and founders, women were able to participate in civic life alongside men, even though they could not vote or serve in political office.[161] Although Epikteta's testament specifies no explicit gift to the community, her act of foundation must be understood within this broader context of euergetism ("doing good works" or philanthropy), since she and her husband Phoinix may well have been benefactors to their fellow Therans during their lifetimes. In the Hellenistic city, public and private endowments were complementary strategies for self-memorialization.[162]

The "testament," so called because it takes the form of a will, is a document of 288 lines. Its four panels were once attached to a statue base designed to hold images of Epikteta flanked by her two sons. According to the wishes of her husband, Epikteta completed the construction of a shrine:

> I leave (this will) according to the instruction given to me by my husband Phoinix, who had the Mouseion built for our deceased son Kratesilochos, and had the lifelike sculptures (*ta zōia*) and the statues of himself and Kratesilochos and the heroic monuments (*ta hērōia*) brought there, and had asked me to finish the construction of the Mouseion and to erect the Muses and the statues (*andriantas*) and the heroic monuments.
>
> (*IG* XII 3.330, 7–15)[163]

Two years after the death of her husband, Epikteta lost her other son, Andragoras, who asked that he too might receive the honors given to his father and brother, and that "the association (*koinon*) of the men's club of relatives" be endowed (16–23). The premature death of both Epikteta's sons seems to have been a factor in the decision to establish the *koinon*. In the absence of male heirs, the *koinon* would perform the essential function of honoring the memory of the dead. The most obvious continuity with Classical hero cult is the use of the terminology *hērōs* for the cult recipients, and *hērōia* for monuments associated with them (in this case, the *hērōia* were probably the tombs of the heroized family members, constructed inside the Mouseion). The "lifelike sculptures" mentioned in the testament may well have been of the *Totenmahl* type, depicting family members dining in eternity, though of this we cannot be certain.

With her husband Phoinix and their two deceased sons, Epikteta was to be honored in a shrine of the Muses. Whereas the cult of the Muses was ancient, the Mouseion itself was a relatively new, high-status cultural institution associated with poetry, philosophy and education; the Mouseion at Alexandria, of which the renowned Library was a part, had been founded in the early third century.[164] Famous intellectuals were commemorated through the erection of their statues alongside those of the Muses, as Plato was in the Academy, and Aristotle in the Lyceum. The cultic and quasi-cultic commemorations of these philosophers were based in turn on the tradition that Pythagoras had died in a Mouseion and on the continuing honors he received.[165] Thus, the cult of the Muses came to connote eschatological beliefs concerning the immortality of the soul, in addition to the preexisting role of the Muses, daughters of Mnemosyne, in ensuring remembrance of the deceased. By constructing the Mouseion, Epikteta's family were drawing attention to themselves as members of a cultural elite, symbolically completing the education (*paideia*) of their deceased sons, and expressing belief in a blessed afterlife.[166] In the monument as realized by Epikteta, all these ideas were blended with the inferences supporting hero cult.

As a Greek woman, Epikteta was careful to attribute the agency in founding the Mouseion to her husband and sons, and she acted "with" her legal guardian Hypereides, probably her son-in-law. Yet there can be little doubt that Epikteta regarded herself as a founder, given her instrumental role in completing the construction of the family sanctuary, funding the *koinon* and establishing its rules: "So that the association will gather in the Mouseion, I give three thousand drachmas to the aforementioned association, so that they are owed on the land I possess and acquired myself in the Melainai . . ." (*IG* XII 3.330, 29–33).

Epikteta organized the *koinon* as a hereditary cult association, established on the principle of male primogeniture, with twenty-five male relatives serving as priests in order of seniority. But she also stipulated that these men's wives and children were to be members of the *koinon*, and even added a list of seven additional women (presumably her personal friends) who were to be admitted, along with their husbands and children. Epikteta's foundation, therefore, was not strictly a family cult.[167]

It is unclear whether Phoinix originally envisioned that Epikteta herself would be numbered among the heroes, but significantly, her name (and not that of Phoinix) appears on the statue base, between the names of her two sons; Phoinix's statue must have stood on a separate plinth. No provision was made for Epiteleia, the daughter of Phoinix and Epikteta, to join the heroes upon her death, perhaps because she was married (therefore part of a separate household) and had a living son who could see to her obsequies. This same grandson of Epikteta, however, was to serve as the first priest of the Muses and Heroes.

Epikteta left her estate and the Mouseion to Epiteleia, who was instructed to make regular payments to the association (35–40). Its purpose was to hold an annual three-day festival during the month of Delphinios:

> The one who serves on the first day as sacrificial priest shall sacrifice to the Muses a victim and sacred offerings, cakes (*ellutas*) made from five *choinikes* of grain and one *statēr* of dried cheese. He shall provide crowns for the goddesses and all the other things for the sacrifice. Of these he shall burn for the goddesses the parts of the victim that are considered sacred, and a cake.
>
> The one who serves on the second day as sacrificial priest (shall sacrifice) to the heroes Phoinix and Epikteta a victim and sacred offerings, cakes made of five *choinikes* of grain and one *statēr* of dried cheese. He shall also provide crowns for the heroes and all the other things for the sacrifice, and he shall burn the parts of the victim that are considered sacred, and one cake and a loaf of bread (*arton*) and a cake-bread (*paraka*) and three small fish.
>
> The one who serves on the third day shall sacrifice to the heroes Kratesilochos and Andragoras following the same rules that are written down for offering to Phoinix and Epikteta.
>
> (*IG* XII 3.330, 177–94)

Epikteta's instructions called for *thusia*, the type of participatory animal sacrifice regularly found in the cults of gods and heroes, supplemented with food offerings (cakes and cheese). However, the loaves, cake-breads and fish, common funerary offerings, signaled a category distinction between Epikteta's family, who were heroes, and the Muses, who were goddesses. The finances, assemblies and governance of the association were spelled out in great detail in the rest of the testament, which included a provision for the will to be inscribed on the statue base and copied onto wooden tablets (thus ensuring accuracy in the transmission of the ritual procedures). Epikteta's testament did not make her eschatological assumptions explicit, but her unusual arrangements for perpetual sacrifice leave open the possibility of a reciprocal relationship between the newly heroized dead and their worshipers. By this act of foundation, Epikteta's family laid claim to an exceptional status in death which matched their privileged position in life.

## Notes

1 Durkheim 1915.262–4; discussion in Whitehouse 2013.67–72. Psychological approaches: Hood, Hill and Spilka 2009.184–94.

2 Bering and Bjorklund 2004; Bering 2006.454–5. Many other psychologists too have concluded that mind-body dualism is a feature of normal development in children and could contribute to afterlife beliefs: see e.g. Bloom 2004.173–83 and D. Estes's comments in Bering 2006.470.

3 Vezo: Astuti 2007a, 2007b; Astuti and Harris 2008. For methodological issues involved in comparing these studies see Bering 2006.491.

4 Minimally counterintuitive: Astuti and Harris 2008.735 citing Boyer 2001.

5 Different: e.g. theory of mind continues to generate inferences about the feelings and preferences of people we know well even after they have died, but this is less the case with people we do not know: Barrett 2011.104. On the multiplicity of mental tools activated by encounters with death (leading to inevitable contradictions), see Boyer 2001.210–28.

6 Heroes and heroines are discussed on pp. 263–7. Harmful ghosts include the female child-killing demons (Johnston 1999.161–99) and the murderous *daimōn* known as the Hero of Temesa (Paus. 6.6.7–11).

7 Variable: e.g. Astuti 2007a.169, 2007b.242–3. This variability places obstacles in the way of "reading" funerary rituals as culturally determined symbolic systems.

8 Swoon: Hom. *Il.* 22.467 (Andromache).

9 Shadow: Bremmer 1983.78–82. When visible by others, the *psuchē* is often described as an *eidōlon* or "simulacrum" of the dead (e.g. Hom. *Od.* 11.83, 20.355). Psychological attributes: Bremmer 1983.84–5. The exact nature of Homeric *thumos*, *mēnos*, *noos* and other components of the individual is much debated; see Onians 1951.13–89 and *passim*.

10 Homer does not necessarily tell us what his audience believed: Edmonds 2013.251. Homer's "stagecraft": Vermeule 1979.29.

11 The *Odyssey* also contemplates yet another possibility: the avoidance of death altogether. This is the fate of the heroes who are "translated" to Elysion (Hom. *Od.* 5.561–9; cf. Hes. *Op.* 167–73), while Odysseus himself refuses the gift of immortality from Kalypso (Hom. *Od.* 5.208–10, 23.333–6).

12 On the weakness and mental lethargy of the ordinary dead, see Vermeule 1979.1–41; Garland 1985.1–12.

13 For the dryness of the dead and the life-giving properties of fluids, see Onians 1951.202–23, 271–8. The thirsty dead: Vermeule 1979.57–8. On the ground: e.g. Aesch. *Cho.* 97, 164 ("My father now has the *choai* imbibed by earth"), *Pers.* 621–4. Tubes: Garland 1985.114.

14 Hom. *Il.* 23.69–92 (Patroklos), *Od.* 11.71–8 (Elpenor).

15 Duty of the son and kin: Rohde 1987 [1925].162–71; Garland 1985.104–18.

16 Not full agency: or not consistently so. There is some evidence for reciprocity and prayers to the dead to "send up" good things (Rohde 1987 [1925].203n.120), but the cultural emphasis is overwhelmingly on giving to the dead rather than receiving from them. Attic funerary vases suggest the continuing presence of the dead at their tombs: Vermeule 1979.31–2.

17 On secrecy and mysteries see Blakely 2012.

18 Two models: Nock 1972.2.792–6.

19 Andanian mysteries: Bowden 2010.68–71; Gawlinski 2012; Bremmer 2014.86–96. Lykosoura: Jost 2003.157–64; Bowden 2010.73–4. Samothrace: Cole 1984; Bowden 2010.49–67; Blakely 2012; Bremmer 2014.22–36. For the many lesser-known mystery sanctuaries see also Graf 2003; Bowden 2010.68–82.

20 Bacchic: Bremmer (2014.70–9, 100–9) distinguishes between the "Orphic-Bacchic" mysteries of the Classical and Hellenistic periods and the "Dionysiac" mysteries of Imperial date. Korybantes: Bremmer 2014.48–53 (including a publicly sponsored cult in Hellenistic Erythrai). Meter/Kybele: Roller 1999.149–61, 227; Bowden 2010.83–104. Isis: Bowden 2010.156–80; Bremmer 2014.110–25.

21 Relief: Burkert 1987.19 and *passim* follows Aristotle in emphasizing the therapeutic value of mysteries. Cf. Ar. *Vesp.* 114–24 (Korybantes); Pl. *Phdr.* 244d-45a.

22 Paradox: Paul used a similar idea to explain Christian resurrection (1 Cor 15.36–8): "Fool; that which you sow does not come alive unless it dies." Cf. John 12.24. For Christianity and the mysteries see Bremmer 2014.147–54 with bibliography.

23 Early Eleusis: Mylonas 1961.55–76. Cosmopoulos 2003b.16–8 argues for cult activity of unknown nature in the Bronze Age Megaron B; the eschatological element was instituted in the sixth century according to Sourvinou-Inwood 1997.136–41 (Solonian Telesterion), 2003.27–8.

24 On the Thesmophoria see Larson 2007.70–2 with bibliography, and for Athens, Parker 2005.270–83. Discussion of the relationship between Thesmophoria and Mysteries: Clinton 1992.28–37, 60–63; Stehle 2007.

25 Crisis: Sourvinou-Inwood (1997.153–9, 2003.26–8) suggests the Kylonian pollution as the precipitating event.

26 Personnel at Eleusis: Clinton 1974; Connelly 2007.64–8. In Clinton's reconstruction there were three important female ritual actors: the Priestess of Demeter and Kore plus two *hierophantides*, who handled the sacred objects and may have impersonated the goddesses during the ritual drama. See Clinton 2004.85–8; sources in Scarpi 2002.1.82–103.

27 The mysteries of the Athenian *genos* of the Lykomidai, to which Themistokles belonged, may offer an analogy for early Eleusis: Graf 2003.246.

28 On the egalitarianism of the Mysteries see Foley ed. 1994.86. Non-Athenian Greeks admitted by the early fifth century: Hdt. 8.65.4.

29 Life: Soph. fr. 837 Radt (for this passage see Essay 5.1).

30 Athenian from the start: e.g. Sourvinou-Inwood 2003.26–7 (citing the early presence of the Eleusinion at Athens).

31 On Eleusis and Athens see Foley ed. 1994.169–75; Parker 1996.25; Sourvinou-Inwood 1997, 2003.25–8. On other elements of the Eleusinian cult of Demeter and Kore see Parker 2005.326–45. The city Eleusinion was established by the seventh century.

32 Remodeling: Parker 1996.68, 72 (Peisistratos); Shear 1982 (Perikles). Propaganda: *IG* $I^3$ 78 = *ML* 73 (the "First Fruits Decree"); Isoc. *Paneg.* 31; Parker 2005.330–2.

33 Mural: Paus 10.28.2. Judges of the dead: Pl. *Grg.* 523a–27a. Sweet hope: Pl. *Resp.* 330e–331a. Minos is already a judge in Hom. *Od.* 567–71. Less specific are Pind. *Ol.* 2.57–60 and Aesch. *Suppl.* 273–4, *Eum.* 230–1. Punishments from "the gods in Hades": Dem. 25.52–3. On the variety of popular beliefs (most evidence is from Athens) see Garland 1985.60–76; Edmonds 2013.258–9.

34 Ionian speculation on the soul as partaking in the totality of cosmic life: Rohde 1987 [1925].364–74. Depending on the period and author, the *psuchē* may be represented as mortal or immortal, material or immaterial, and personal or impersonal.

35 Compare Pl. *Phd.* 66a–67a. For Pythagoras see Burkert 1972.97–120; Kahn 2001.5–23; Bremmer 2002.11–15. In contrast to Homer, Plato and Aristotle located the intellectual and moral faculties in the soul: Richardson 1985.65–6.

36 For Empedokles and his eschatology see Zuntz 1971.181–274; Kingsley 1995.217–32.

37 *Sōma sēma*: Pl. *Cra.* 400b–c, *Grg.* 493a.

38 Releaser: *GJ* no. 26 ("the Bacchic one has released you"), and in civic cult Paus. 2.2.6, 2.7.5, 9.16.6. Exactly what evils Dionysos releases people from is always usefully vague: pollution, curses, death, madness, daily cares. On this question: Graf 2010.176–9.

39 To be fulfilled/initiated: e.g. Hdt. 4.79 (Skyles). Bremmer (2014.77–8) suggests that the private mysteries conducted by the Lykomidai of Athens were Orphic but non-Bacchic, and that many Bacchic mysteries lacked Orphic elements.

40 Resemblances: the Pythagoreans were less interested in Dionysos than in Apollo, a god much concerned with purification: Ael. *VH* 2.26. Orphics and Pythagoreans: Boyancé 1937.93–99; Kingsley 1995.260–61. West (1983.7–15, 18) suggests that the two systems were parallel and drew on a common "field of origin" in sixth-century Ionia. Bremmer 2002.24 describes Orphism as "the product of Pythagorean influence on Bacchic mysteries." Ion of Chios: Diog. Laert. 8.1.8.

41 Itinerant initiators: Burkert 1982; *GJ* 144–6, 191–2.

42 Written texts: Henrichs 2003.223–31 with discussion of Dem. 18.259 (texts used in a trance ritual at Athens) and of *BGU* 6.1211, a Ptolemaic decree commanding that

"persons who perform initiation rites for Dionysos" hand in a sealed copy of their sacred text (*hieron logon*).

43 Bone tablet: Dubois 1996 no. 94a (= *OF* no. 463). For accessible texts with translation and illustrations of the Olbian Bacchic materials see *GJ* 214–17. The tablets may have functioned as amulets or as tokens demonstrating initiate status.

44 Olympiodorus goes on to say that "our bodies are Dionysiac" because of the portion of the god's flesh eaten by the Titans. However, he is the only extant source for this idea.

45 Neoplatonist: Brisson 1995.493–4. Plato (*Leg.* 710b–c = *OF* no. 9) mentions the "so-called ancient Titanic nature" which inclines people toward evil deeds but he does not link this idea with Dionysos' murder. The earliest extant account of Dionysos' dismemberment is given by the Epicurean philosopher Philodemus, who says that the poet Euphorion (third century) agrees with his version; see Henrichs 2011.63. Philodemus' version says that the god was restored to life when his body was reassembled by Rhea; compare Diod. Sic. 3.62.1–8.

46 Semele: Hom. *Il.* 14.325; Hes. *Theog.* 940–2. Persephone in Orphic poetry: Bremmer 2014.62–3. Diodorus Siculus (3.63.3–64.5) mentions four distinct figures called Dionysos, whose mothers included Persephone and Semele.

47 Orphic myth: for a recent reconstruction see *GJ* 66–93. The many interlocking pieces of evidence are collected in *OF*. Orphic poetry and rituals: West 1983.2–3.

48 Guilt: the most detailed source for this idea is Plut. *De esu carnium* 1.7 (996b); other sources in *OF* nos. 318, 320. For anthropogony in Orphic myth, see Bernabé 2002, 2012; *GJ* 67 with 225n.7; 193n.7. For the skeptical view see Brisson 1995; Edmonds 1999, 2009, 2013.296–391.

49 Bremmer 2014.76: it is "almost certain" that the penalties mentioned in the gold tablets refer to the guilt of the Titans' crime. Edmonds (2013.95–138) argues against the prevailing view that use of texts was central to Orphism.

50 Skepticism: e.g. Linforth 1941; Zuntz 1971. Edmonds (2013.71–6) proposes a polythetic definition (i.e. one based on "family resemblances").

51 Misdeeds: cf. Pl. *Phdr.* 244d. The destructive power of ancestral pollution caused concern through the fifth century and beyond. See Gagné 2013, esp. 451–60.

52 Breezes: cf. Hom. *Od.* 4.563–8. For Pindar's statements on death see Currie 2005.31–5.

53 Hektor's wish to become a god: Hom. *Il.* 8.538–541; Nagy 1999.151–73.

54 Promise: Hom. *Od.* 4.563. Helen and Menelaos at Therapne: Antonaccio 1995.155–66. A dedication to "Helen wife of Menelaos" was inscribed ca. 675–50; the first dedication inscribed to Menelaos alone belongs to the early fifth century. Erechtheus: Hom. *Il.* 2.547–51. For other mythic heroes in cult see Farnell 1921.280–342; Larson 2007.197–200.

55 Bremmer (2006.18) notes that the religious meaning of "hero" is not attested until the late sixth century. On the use of *hērōs* see also Currie 2005.62–70.

56 Farnell 1921.vii–xv.

57 Brelich stresses (1958.153–5) that anonymous and functional heroes were "assolutamente sporadici" compared to the mass of named heroes. The epigraphic record, however, suggests that they were numerous at the local level.

58 Nagy 1999.118–210.

59 Parker 2011.110, citing the fundamental work of Kearns 1989.1–2, 125–9; cf. Parker 1996.33–39. For the hero's relationship to death see Brelich 1958.80–90; Nagy 1999.9–10; Henrichs 2010.31.

60 Heroes of the Salt Flat and of the Tower: from the calendar of the Salaminioi (*RO* no. 37, lines 37–8, 53–4, 86, 87). Gate-holder and Save-ship: from the Thorikos deme calendar: *SEG* 26.136. Discussion and further examples: Parker 2011.111–14. On the functional and anonymous heroes, cf. Foucart 1918.52–8; Farnell 1921.71–94.

61 *Hēmitheoi*: Hom. *Il.* 12.23; Hes. *Op.* 160; Parker 2011.107. On the *hēmitheoi* see also Nagy 1999.159–61.

62 Strepsiades: Ar. *Nub*. 315. On defining the hero, see the important discussion of Kearns 1989.1–4. For the special case of heroines, Ferguson and Nock 1944.165 and *passim*; Kearns 1989.22; Larson 1995.18–19, 31.

63 Direct influence of Homeric poetry: Coldstream 1976; Burkert 1985.204; the thesis already rejected by Foucart (1918.58). Downdating of cults for Agamemnon (Mycenae) and Odysseus (Polis bay, Ithaka): Morgan and Whitelaw 1991.89; Antonaccio 1995.147–55. Cults mentioned in Homer: Hadzisteliou Price 1973; Kearns 1989.49–50, 128–31.

64 Races: Hes. *Op*. 106–201. But see Nagy 1999.151–9 for analysis of all four past races as representatives of the class of heroes, with the first two generations perceived as the cultic aspect and the second two as the epic. Monumental tombs: *ThesCRA* 2.132 (Mazarakis-Ainian).

65 Propitiation: Pfaff 2013.285. Tomb cult: Antonaccio 1994.402 (only two tomb cults exhibit long-term use), 1995.5–9, 1998.50 (platforms). See also Hägg 1987; Whitley 1995.54; Boehringer 2001; Kyrieleis 2006.72. Deoudi (1999.12–15) divides early sites for "hero cult" into houses, stone platforms used for ritual meals, Bronze Age tombs, and sanctuaries.

66 Claims: e.g. Snodgrass 1980.39 ("attempts to consolidate the ownership of land"), 1982.117 (correlation with free peasantry). Compare Whitley 1988, 1995 (emphasizing regional differences).

67 Ancestors: Nagy 1999.115–16 following Rohde 1987 [1925].117–20. "Ancestor worship" in the form of extraordinary cult provisions for long-dead kin is not attested for the Archaic and Classical periods; instead the veneration of ancestors took place through mediating gods (Apollo Patroios), generic spirits (the Tritopateres, apparently patrilineal ancestors of the third generation past) or in general festivals of the dead. Nevertheless, ancestor worship or the need to "appropriate ancestors" is commonly invoked to explain the varied phenomena of tomb cult (e.g. Antonaccio 1995.199–243, 1998.47–8). Discussion: Whitley 2002.124.

68 New civic order: de Polignac 1995 [1984].142–3. For Bérard (1982.101–2), warrior princes were converted upon their deaths into "heroes" and thus incorporated into the emergent polis.

69 Eumolpos: Kearns 1989.68–9, 114–15, 163.

70 Geometric tomb or hero cults of the recently dead: *ThesCRA* 2.135–8 (Mazarakis-Ainian). For "heroic burials" giving rise to cults: Bérard 1982; de Polignac 1995 [1984].129–38.

71 For Lakonian reliefs depicting the powerful dead, see Salapata 2006 with bibliography.

72 Malkin 1987.263, 1993.232. Antonaccio 1999.120 cautions that archaeological evidence for very early founder cult is weak.

73 Delphi: Johnston 2005, with appendix of the relevant oracles.

74 Onesilos: Hdt. 5.113.2–14; Visser 1982.405–6. Beheading, mutilation and exposure of an enemy corpse were not commonly practiced.

75 Philip: Hdt. 5.47.1–2. Hero-athletes: Fontenrose 1968; Lunt 2010. Mightier: Hom. *Il*. 1.259–74 (Nestor's speech on the men of old).

76 "Rule with the other heroes": fourth-century Bacchic gold tablet from Petelia: *GJ* no. 2. Paul: 1 Cor 6:3.

77 Pelops: Pind. *Ol*. 1.90–93. Tyrant-slayers: Ar. [*Ath. Pol.*] 58.

78 Orthodoxy refuted: Ferguson and Nock 1944.141–66 [= Nock 1972.575–605]; Ekroth 2002.303–341. Special techniques: Ekroth 2000. Although prominent in epic and tragedy, animal sacrifice and blood offerings for the dead were probably no longer the norm by the Classical period: Ekroth 2002.228–33.

79 Cult tables and *theoxenia*: Ekroth 2002.136–40, 276–86. Funeral games and laments: Seaford 1994.120–3, 139n.151. Pollution: *LSS* 115.21–5 = *SEG* 9.72 (for this inscription see Essay 3.3); Plut. *Arat*. 53.1–3 (Aratos' tomb at Sikyon not polluting); Parker 1983.39 (examples of priests excluded from hero cult).

80 Paradox: by contrast, gods were intentional agents with counterintuitive properties of invisibility, immortality, etc., but these properties do not, like deadness, conflict with the exercise of agency which is almost always attributed to superhuman beings.

81 *Makarismos*: Gladigow 1967; Porta 1999.343–9.

82 Compare Cic. *Leg.* 2.36: *ita re uera principia uitae cognouimus, neque solum cum laetitia uiuendi rationem accepimus, sed etiam cum spe meliore moriendi.* "[Through the Mysteries] we thus truly come to know the principles [or beginnings] of life, and we perceive not only the way to live with happiness, but also the way to die with better hope."

83 There is general scholarly agreement that the chorus in *Frogs* is to be understood as a group of Eleusinian initiates; for Eleusinian references in the first half of the play see Graf 1974.40–50.

84 Slough: Ar. *Ran.* 145–59. On the ethical element in the Mysteries see Graf 1974.79–126 (attributed to influence from Orphism); Edmonds 2004.142n94, 198–215. Diogenes the Cynic (Diog. Laert. 6.39) observed that it would be ludicrous if the uninitiated Spartans Agesilaus and Epaminondas lay in the mud while less worthy men went to the Isles of the Blessed, merely because they were initiated. See also Pl. *Phd.* 69c, *Resp.* 363d (popular belief that the uninitiated will lie in mud).

85 Uninitiate (*ou memuēmenōn*): Paus. 10.31.9.

86 On mystery-derived metaphor and terminology in the philosophical tradition see Riedweg 1987, especially 2–29 on the *Symposium*.

87 Knowledge (*epistēmē*): Pl. *Symp.* 210d. Compare Pl. *Phd.* 69c–d, where *teletai* (in this case probably of the Bacchic kind) are metaphorically congruent with philosophy.

88 Contrast the Greek wisdom tradition, in which one "learns by experience" (*pathei mathos*: Aesch. *Ag.* 177). For the Mysteries as "un-mystical" and communal see Burkert 1983 [1972].248. Scarpi (2002.1.534) sees an opposition between active and passive learning.

89 The Eumolpidai were recognized as "expounders" of (unwritten) sacred matters, including but not limited to those pertaining to Eleusis: Pseudo-Lysias 6.10; Parker 1996.295–7. To what degree the Eumolpidai formulated a detailed or systematic theology of the Mysteries is unknown.

90 Theseus: Eur. *Hipp.* 952–54. Derveni Papyrus: Col. XX.10. According to Papadopoulou (2014.xvii), the Derveni author "insists upon the importance of *manthanein*, of comprehending tradition and science, both mystic, both demanding knowledge and teaching." *Contra*: Rusten 2014.127–9. For the papyrus see Laks and Most eds. 1997; Betegh 2004; Papadopoulou and Muellner eds. 2014.

91 Ergot: the "entheogen" hypothesis cannot be discounted without careful consideration, given the occasional pharmacological properties and therapeutic uses (Rosen 1987.416–23) of the beverage called *kukeōn*, which was drunk by initiates. However, ergoline alkaloids are dangerous and difficult to dose, with multiple risks of side effects, especially uterine contractions and miscarriage (van Dongen and de Groot 1995). It strains credulity to suppose that the Eleusinian authorities were able to deliver a safe yet hallucinogenic dose of infected barley meal to each initiate, or that the properties of ergot could have been kept secret for centuries, or that if they were known, ergot would not have been used by physicians. Furthermore, I know of no anthropological parallel for the administering of entheogens to large groups of people unaware that they are using a mind-altering substance. Typically, entheogens other than alcohol are used by individuals (e.g. shamans) or in small groups, and their properties are well recognized by users (as they were in the case of the Vedic *soma*).

92 *Enthousiasmos*: The most promising source in this regard is Proclus, *Commentary on the Republic* 2.108.17–30, but Proclus was a Neoplatonist philosopher of the fifth century CE.

93 Imagistic: Martin 2005.351–2; Bowden 2010.15–17. For application of modes theory to Hellenistic and Roman mystery cults see Martin 2006; Martin and Pachis eds. 2009.

94 Primary sources are gathered in Scarpi 2002 Vol. 1 (with Italian translation).

95 Burkert 1983 [1972].275. Bremmer (2014.9–16) reconstructs a two-night sequence of revelations, one for the new initiates and one for the *epoptai* (repeat initiates). If he is correct, the two rituals could account for some of the variety in our evidence. On conservatism and change in Greek ritual over centuries see Cole 2008, and on changes in Eleusinian belief and practice, Sourvinou-Inwood 2003.28–9; Patera 2011.

96 General outline: Mylonas 1961.247–85; Parke 1977.59–72; Simon 1983.24–35; Parker 2005.347–50; Bowden 2010.33–8.

97 *Paradosis teletēs* is mentioned by Theon of Smyrna (p. 14 Hiller = Scarpi 2002.1.160, E7) as a stage in initiation, but this may refer to the climactic rite itself, as it is followed in order by contemplation, *epopteia*. Clement of Alexandria (*Stromata* 5.11.70.7–71.1 = Scarpi 2002.1.78, B10) proposes three stages: purification, Lesser Mysteries (instruction) and Greater Mysteries (contemplation).

98 Mandatory: Pl. *Grg*. 497c with schol. Preparation: Clement of Alexandria *Stromata* 5.11.70.7–71.1 (= Scarpi 2002.1.78, B10). Purification: Diod. Sic. 4.14.3 (Herakles); Polyaen. *Strat*. 5.17.1 (= Scarpi 2002.1.78, B8); Schol. Ar. *Plut*. 845f (= Scarpi 2002.1.78, B9). Imitation concerning Dionysos: Steph. Byz. s.v. *agra kai agrai*. On the Lesser Mysteries, see Clinton 2003.59–60; Parker 2005.344–6. On the preparatory ritual called *thronōsis*, which may have been used in the Lesser Mysteries: Burkert 1983 [1972].266–8, to be read with Edmonds 2006.

99 Collection of fees: *IG* I$^3$ 386.144–6; Parker 2005.344 with n. 74.

100 Preliminary: there is epigraphic evidence for *muēsis* administered to slave workers in the sanctuary, and to stonecutters delivering stone there (*IG* I$^3$ 6.23–31). Clinton (2008a.8–11, 2008b) marshals the evidence for a definitive argument that "pre-initiation" was a regular requirement at Eleusis. On "pre-initiation" cf. Roussel 1930; Simms 1990; Clinton 2003.60; Parker 2005.345.

101 Clinton 2008b.32 n.19. An assembly of mystagogues at Eleusis: *LSS* 15, first century; text also in Clinton 2003.57. Menander (*PCG* fr. 500 = fr. 714 Körte-Thierfelder) refers to guardian spirits assigned to individuals as "mystagogues of life." On *mystagōgoi* see Plut. *Alc*. 34.5; Foucart 1914.281–4; Bremmer 2014.3.

102 Clinton 2008a.11.

103 Dio Chrys. *Or*. 12.33 (= Scarpi 2002.1.179, E33); Plutarch fr. 168 Sandbach (= Scarpi 2002.1.177, E32).

104 Ritual drama as *mimēsis* of the myth: e.g. Tert. *Ad nat*. 2.7 (a priestess is abducted); Lactant. *Div. Inst. Epitome* 18.7 ("Proserpina is sought with lighted torches"). More sources and discussion in Foucart 1914.457–85 (double drama of abduction and Demeter's union with Zeus), Mylonas 1961.261–9, 310–11; Clinton 1992.84–90; Sourvinou-Inwood 2003.29–35. Empousa or other underworld terrors as *phasmata* in the Mysteries: Brown 1991; Johnston 1999.130–35; Parker 2005.354–5; Clark 2009.

105 Hierophant: Hippol. *Haer*. 5.8.39–40 says (in a much-disputed passage) that the Hierophant revealed a freshly reaped ear of grain. See Sourvinou-Inwood 2003.35–6. Christian fathers also report that the content of the Mysteries included sexual relations between Demeter and a partner (perhaps Keleus), acted out by the Hierophant and a priestess. See Burkert 1983 [1972].284; Parker 2005.356–7. On the "mime" of the hierophant, apparently involving sacred dance (but not completely silent), see Parker 2005.352–3.

106 Hell House: "Hell Houses" are events staged at Halloween by evangelical Christian churches in the United States during which people are escorted through frightening tableaux of afterlife punishments (Pellegrini 2007). Simplicity: Clinton 2007.344, 354–5. Bowden (2010.45–6) suggests that each initiate had to independently develop an understanding of the ritual's meaning.

107 Triptolemos: Pl. *Ap*. 41a. Intellectual currents: Bremmer 2014.19.

108 Euboulos and Iacchos: Parker 2005:337–9, 349–50. Brimo and Brimos: Hippol. *Haer*. 5.8.40; Clinton 1992.91–4. Theos and Thea: Parker 2005.335–6 with fig. 24.

109 Lack of knowledge: Parker 2005.346 makes the same point about this story. The episode took place in 200 during Athens' war with Philip V of Macedon. Sacred topography included the "Mirthless rock" where Demeter sat to lament her daughter: Clinton 1992.14–25. Pausanias (1.38.7) wrote that a dream forbade him to reveal the topography of the sanctuary.

110 On *hieroi logoi* in mysteries see Burkert 1987.69–70; Henrichs 2003; *GJ* 177–85. Exclusion of non-Greek speakers: Isoc. *Paneg.* 157 (= Scarpi 2002.1.194, F19), Theon of Smyrna p. 14 Hiller (= Scarpi 2002.1.192, F18).

111 Some initiates knew a story explaining why the discovery of bean horticulture was not to be attributed to Demeter (Paus. 1.37.4), and others knew why some parts of sacrificial animals were not to be consumed (Clement of Alexandria *Stromata* 2.20.106.1, 171.2–5).

112 Clement of Alexandria *Protreptikos* 2.21.2. On passwords see Burkert 1983 [1972].269–70; Porta 1999.87–128 (with corpus); Parker 2005.354; Bremmer 2014.3 (attributing the activities mentioned by Clement to the pre-initiation period). Some (e.g. Mylonas 1961.294–300) are skeptical, noting that Clement's saying may apply to rites practiced in Alexandria rather than Eleusis.

113 On secrecy see Arist. *Eth. Nich.* 1111a (the trial of Aeschylus); Burkert 1983 [1972].252–3.

114 Physical and textual characteristics of the tablets: Bernabé and Jiménez San Cristóbal 2008.2–8.

115 Chaniotis (2000.162–3) proposes that grave epigrams should not be taken to reflect the beliefs of the deceased unless they explicitly refer to cultic or philosophical eschatologies.

116 Philiste: *OF* no. 496k (Hellenistic); *GJ* no. 37. For the "geographic" and "purity" tablets see *GJ* 96–131. Only the geographic tablets are treated as a discrete category in Bernabé and Jiménez San Cristóbal 2008.9–59.

117 His identity: the grammatical gender used in this tablet is masculine and the initiate is assumed to be male; however, there are "gender hesitations" in the formulaic texts of the tablets: Bernabé and Jiménez San Cristóbal 2008.59.

118 Oblivion: Simonides (Ep. 67 Campbell = *Anth. Pal.* 7.25) is first to mention "the halls of Lethe." Cf. Ar. *Ran.* 186; Pl. *Resp.* 621a (both speak of the "plain of Lethe"). Plato emphasized the role of memory (e.g. *Meno* 81d) in the cycle of life and death. For him, reborn souls who were able to remember "all they knew before" about virtue had an eschatological advantage. For Mnemosyne (Memory) in the tablets: Bernabé and Jiménez San Cristóbal 2008.15–19.

119 Heroization: e.g. *OF* no. 476 (= *GJ* no. 2), from Petelia in the "toe" of Italy: "You will rule among the other heroes." For apotheosis see pp. 278–9 and *GJ* 123–7.

120 Timpone Grande: *OF* no. 487, fourth century (= *GJ* no. 3). The tablet is of the geographic type and was enclosed within a second tablet (*OF* no. 492 = *GJ* no. 4; Bernabé and Jiménez San Crístobal 2008.137–50) containing a hymn-like poem periodically interspersed with untranslatable letters. The poem addresses numerous deities and includes the word *hērōs* (line 9). The three occupants of the Timpone Piccolo were interred with tablets alluding to their being struck by lightning (either literally or in reference to the punishment of the Titans by Zeus): *OF* nos. 488–90 (= *GJ* nos. 5–7). For the archaeological details see Cavallari 1878–9; Zuntz 1971.288–93.

121 For detailed commentary see Bernabé and Jiménez San Cristóbal 2008.61–94.

122 On the relationship between the poetry of the tablets and their ritual context see Obbink 2011.

123 According to Plato (*Ion* 534a), Bacchic worshipers under the influence of the god drew "honey and milk" from the rivers, while Euripides (*Bacch.* 695–710) describes the madwomen of Dionysos nursing wild animals and scratching the earth so that milk welled from the ground. On milk and the motifs of rushing and leaping in the tablets see Faraone 2011.318–26.

124 Dionysos the Releaser: Bernabé and Jiménez San Cristóbal 2008.72.

125 A few Hellenistic epigrams refer to mysteries, but it is not clear whether these were used on actual tombstones: see Mirto 2012.114–15; Austin and Bastianini eds. 2002, nos. 43 (Eleusis), 44 (Dionysiac dance in the mountains). Scholarly disagreement: Wypustek 2013.6–9.

126 Eleusinian vs. Bacchic mysteries in Attica: Parker 2005.368.

127 See Tsagalis 2008.121–5 on the pervasiveness of this theme in fourth-century Attica. Sourvinou-Inwood (1995.199–207) argues for hopes of heroization from the fifth century on.

128 For the vocabulary of praise in Classical epitaphs see Clairmont 1970.52. Praise of the dead and fear of the dead, both cross-culturally prevalent, may be two sides of the same coin: Bering, McLeod and Shackelford 2005.

129 Reserved: *LSS* 120, mid-fifth century: "It is unlawful to lie here unless one is a Bacchic initiate."

130 Theseus: Eur. *Hipp.* 948–54. Prohibition on wool: Hdt. 2.81.

131 Compare the conditional formulations in Lattimore 1942.56.

132 Tsagalis 2008.100–10 emphasizes connections between this inscription and the cults of Demeter and Kore. For Persephone and Plouton in the gold tablets: *GJ* nos. 15, 17 (= *OF* nos. 494, 495, both from Crete). Presumably these resulted from Bacchic initiations but the texts are too brief to confirm this.

133 Tsagalis 2008.87, 95. The "chamber of Persephone" is used in preference to "Hades." Compare Aesch. *Pers.* 624 ("chambers beneath the earth") and Eur. *Suppl.* 1022 ("chambers of Persephone"). The term *thalamos* has feminine and nuptial connotations.

134 For Hades and Persephone in epitaphs, see the examples in Lattimore 1942.88. Persephone in the western colonies: Zuntz 1971.70–173.

135 Parker 2005.364, citing e.g. Isoc. 9.2 "If the dead have any perception . . ."

136 Only a few exceptional epitaphs of Classical date refer to the distinction between body (*sōma*) and soul (*psuchē*). Clairmont 1970.52 lists three in his corpus of inscribed Archaic and Classical monuments. For early views on apotheosis in the aether, Rohde 1987 [1925].435–7, 460–62; Wypustek 2013.39–53. That Euripides (*El.* 59; *Suppl.* 531–6, 1140) mentioned aether in his works suggests a fairly widespread knowledge of the concept in Athens.

137 Varied opinions: Parker 2005.366; Wypustek 2013.45.

138 Star myths gained traction in the sixth and fifth centuries with the Hesiodic corpus. Pythagoreans: Pl. *Tim.* 42b (the speaker Timaios being a follower of Pythagoras).

139 The Pleiades, Orion and other star names are recorded as early as Homer (e.g. *Il.* 18.486–8), but the earliest known myths of "catasterism" seem to belong to the Hesiodic corpus. For the Pleiades in Pseudo-Hesiod see Thomas 2007.20.

140 Astral eschatology: Wypustek 2013.48–64, with discussion of its appeal across the social spectrum. Possible early attestations in epitaphs: *Anth. Pal.* 7.64 (Diogenes the Cynic), 7.670 (attributed to Plato). For the conflation of celestial and underworld abodes cf. Eur. *Suppl.* 1141–4 (souls "achieve Hades on wings") and Orion's presence in the underworld in Hom. *Od.* 572–5. Hellenistic and Roman examples: Le Bris 2001.113–20.

141 Uncanny: Johnston 1999.153–5. For malignant and harmful heroes, see also Boehringer 1996.37–8, 41–4; García Teijeiro and Molinos Tejada 2000.

142 Funerary: epitaphs referring to the heroization of the deceased did not become popular until the first century, though most originate in the second and third centuries CE (Le Bris 2001.97–112). In some cases the attribution of "heroic" status was a simple convention, while in other cases the epitaphs reveal that heroic cult honors were paid to the deceased. See Wypustek 2013.71–95 for an overview of the scholarly debates.

143 Early use of "hero" on tombstones in Thessaly and Boiotia: Plato Comicus *PCG* fr. 77 ("Why don't you hang yourself and become a hero in Thebes?"), Lattimore 1942.97n.

77, 99; Rohde 1987 [1925].208n.134. "Heroization" by inscription caught on less quickly in Attica (Kearns 1989.5) and Rhodes (Fraser 1977.76–81) but was popular through most of the southeastern Aegean and Asia Minor (Graf 1985.127–35; Hughes 1999.170). *Totenmahl* reliefs: Thönges-Stringaris 1965.64–7; Dentzer 1982.301–63; Closterman 2014.6–7 (the latter two authors arguing against eschatological interpretations of the banquet scenes).

144 Wills: compare the cults of Diomedon of Kos and Poseidonios of Halikarnassos. Laum 1914. I.68–74; Kamps 1937.150–55 (Diomedon), 155–8 (Poseidonios); Hughes 1999.168–70; Carbon and Pirenne-Deforge 2013; Paul 2013.108–17 (Diomedon). The philosopher Epicurus founded a successful cult to himself and other family members: Kamps 1937.169–70; Obbink 1996.10; Clay 1998.75–102. On the relationship between eschatology and heroization, Kearns 1989.5–6.

145 Public feasting and games: Kamps 1937.172–9; Humphreys 1980.122.

146 Earliest: possible earlier cases include the warrior hero at the West Gate in Eretria (Bérard 1970, 1982) and the legendary Spartan lawgiver Lykourgos (Hdt. 1.66, Plut. *Lyc*. 31.3), who was referred to as a god. Some historians have been skeptical about the evidential value of Herodotus' account; for discussion see Malkin 2003.

147 Oath of the Settlers: *ML* no. 5 (= *SEG* 9.3; Graham 1964.224–6). In spite of the late date of the fourth-century inscription, the Oath is thought to reflect the sense of an Archaic original: Graham 1960.109 ("a genuine document edited in the fourth century"); Jeffrey 1961.

148 *Archāgetās*: Jeffrey 1961.144. Herodotus (4.153) gives Battos the related title of *hēgemōn* ("Leader"). On Battos as legendary founder: Malkin 1987.204–214; Dougherty 1993.103–19; Calame 2003.106–8.

149 "The Blessed Ones": Hom. *Il*. 1.339, *Od*. 10.299 (of gods); Hes. *Op*. 141 (the second race of men). Isles of the Blessed: e.g. Hes. *Op*. 171.

150 Illegitimacy and stuttering: Hdt. 4.155. These flaws viewed as "heroic" characteristics: Boehringer 1996.39–40.

151 Tomb and remains: Stucchi 1965.58–98; Büsing 1978.66–79; Malkin 1987.215–16. On the earliest structures (modified in the fifth century) see Parisi Presicce 2007.251–6. The house may have been Battos' residence.

152 Territorial claims: Malkin 1993.230–31.

153 Thucydides as general: Thuc. 4.108.1–7, 5.26.5.

154 Hagnon was still alive in 422, but we need not conclude (with Currie 2005.164–6) that he was already being worshiped.

155 Cults of the tyrants: Diod. Sic. 11.38.5 (Gelon), 11.49.2, 11.66.4 (Hieron), 11.53.2 (Theron). Brasidas at Skione: Thuc. 4.121. Cults of living generals: e.g. Lysander and Demetrios Poliorketes. See Currie 2005.158–200; Mitchell 2013.61–79.

156 Excavation: Koukouli-Chrysanthaki 2002 (with appendix by A. Agelarakis on the cremated bones). Gold wreath: Thuc. 4.121. The identification is tentative because the relationship between the tomb and the classical agora is unclear.

157 Praise in Brasidas' lifetime: Xen. *Hell*. 2.3.9–10 (eponymous ephor at Sparta). Cenotaph at Sparta: Paus. 3.14.1. His superiority: Diod. Sic. 12.43.2, 12.74.1–4 (he died *hērōikōs* and was "best of the Lakedaimonians"), etc. On Brasidas' prowess and his heroization see Hoffman 2000.367.

158 Epikteta: *IG* XII 3.330; Laum 1914 II, no. 43; Boyancé 1937.330–344; Kamps 1937.159–68; Wittenburg 1990; Hughes 1999.168–9; Clay 2004.72–4; Carbon and Pirenne-Delforge 2013.71–4.

159 *Orgeōnes*: Ferguson and Nock 1944.68–76; Kearns 1989.73–5. Epikteta's testament expressed as a decree of the *koinon*: *IG* XII 3.330, lines 109–131; Carbon and Pirenne-Delforge 2013.98. For the imitation of civic decrees and organization by private associations see Foucart 1873.51. Voluntary associations, including cultic associations, expanded greatly during the Hellenistic and Roman periods: Kloppenborg 1996.17.

160 For private cults in general see Laum 1914.I.61–87; Purvis 2003.1–13. For Thera see Wittenburg 1990.128; Hughes 1999.172n.31. Postmortem hero cults were particularly common among Dorians: Laum 1914.I.68–9; Mannzmann 1962.143–7.
161 Benefactors: Kron 1996; Dignas 2006.
162 Self-memorialization: Schmitt-Pantel 1982.
163 My translations are adapted from Wittenburg 1990.
164 Library: Bagnall 2002.
165 Plato's statue in a Mouseion in the Academy: Diog. Laert. 3.25. Aristotle: Diog. Laert. 5.51. Pythagoras' death in a Mouseion: Diog. Laert. 8.40 (citing Dikaiarchos); Pythagoras honored by the Italians: Arist. *Rh.* 2.23.11 (= 1398b). For the cults of Pythagoras, Plato and Epicurus see Boyancé 1937.231–327.
166 Hardie (2005) argues for the eschatological significance of the Muses as early as Sappho.
167 Not strictly family: Laum 1914.I.243; Mannzmann 1962.142.

## References


Antonaccio, Carla. 1994. Contesting the past: Hero cult, tomb cult, and epic in early Greece. *AJA* 98 (3): 389–410.

Antonaccio, Carla. 1995. *An archaeology of ancestors: Tomb cult and hero cult in early Greece*. Lanham, MD: Rowman and Littlefield.

Antonaccio, Carla. 1998. The archaeology of ancestors. In *Cultural poetics in archaic Greece*, ed. Dougherty and Kurke, 46–70.

Antonaccio, Carla. 1999. Colonization and the origins of hero cult. In *Ancient Greek hero cult*, ed. Hägg, 109–21.

Astuti, Rita. 2007a. Ancestors and the afterlife. In *Religion, anthropology and cognitive science*, ed. Whitehouse and Laidlaw, 161–78.

Astuti, Rita. 2007b. What happens after death? In *Questions of anthropology*, ed. Astuti, Parry and Stafford, 227–48.

Astuti, Rita and Paul Harris. 2008. Understanding mortality and the life of the ancestors in rural Madagascar. *Cognitive Science* 32: 713–40.

Astuti, Rita, J. P. Parry and C. Stafford, eds. 2007. *Questions of anthropology*. New York: Berg.

Austin, C. and G. Bastianini, eds. 2002. *Posidippi Pellaei quae supersunt omnia*. Milan: Edizioni Universitarie di Lettere Economia Diritto.

Bagnall, Roger S. 2002. Alexandria: Library of dreams. *PAPhS* 146 (4): 348–62.

Barrett, Justin L. 2011. *Cognitive science, religion and theology: From human minds to divine minds*. West Conshohocken, PA: Templeton Press.

Bérard, Claude. 1970. *L'Hérôon à la porte de l'ouest*. Berne: Francke.

Bérard, Claude. 1982. Récupérer la mort du prince. In *La mort, les morts dans les sociétés anciennes*, ed. Gnoli and Vernant, 89–105.

Bering, Jesse M. 2006. The folk psychology of souls. *Behavioral and Brain Sciences* 29 (5): 453–62.

Bering, Jesse M. and D. F. Bjorklund. 2004. The natural emergence of reasoning about the afterlife as a developmental regularity. *Developmental Psychology* 40 (2): 217–33.

Bering, Jesse M., Katrina McLeod and Todd K. Shackelford. 2005. Reasoning about dead agents reveals possible adaptive trends. *Human Nature* 16 (4): 360–81.

Bernabé, Alberto. 2002. La toile de Pénélope: A-t-il existé un mythe orphique sur Dionysos et les Titans? *RHR* 219: 401–33.

Bernabé, Alberto. 2012. A brave netherworld: The Orphic Hades as utopia. In *Demeter, Isis, Vesta and Cybele*, ed. Mastrocinque and Scibona, 11–23.

Bernabé, Alberto and Ana Isabel Jiménez San Cristóbal. 2008. *Instructions for the netherworld: The Orphic gold tablets*. Tr. Michael Chase. Leiden and Boston: Brill.
Betegh, Gábor. 2004. *The Derveni Papyrus: Cosmology, theology, and interpretation*. Cambridge and London: Cambridge University Press.
Blakely, Sandra. 2012. Toward an archaeology of secrecy: Power, paradox, and the Great Gods of Samothrace. *Archaeological Papers of the American Anthropology Association* 21 (1): 49–71.
Bloom, Paul. 2004. *Descartes' baby: How the science of child development explains what makes us human*. New York: Basic Books.
Boehringer, David. 1996. Zur heroisierung historischer Persönlichkeiten bei den Griechen. In *Retrospektive: Konzepte von Vergangenheit in der griechisch-römischen Antike*, ed. Flashar, Gehrke and Heinrich, 37–61.
Boehringer, David. 2001. *Heroenkulte in Griechenland von der geometrischen bis zur klassischen Zeit: Attika, Argolis, Messenien*. Berlin: Akademie Verlag.
Bowden, Hugh. 2010. *Mystery cults of the ancient world*. Princeton and Oxford: Princeton University Press.
Boyancé, Pierre. 1937. *Le culte des Muses chez les philosophes grecs*. Paris: E. de Boccard.
Boyer, Pascal. 2001. *Religion explained: The evolutionary origins of religious thought*. New York: Basic Books.
Brelich, Angelo. 1958. *Gli eroi greci: Um problema storico-religioso*. Rome: Ediziono dell'Ateneo.
Bremmer, Jan. 1983. *The early Greek concept of the soul*. Princeton, NJ: Princeton University Press.
Bremmer, Jan. 2002. *The rise and fall of the afterlife*. London and New York: Routledge.
Bremmer, Jan. 2006. The rise of the hero cult and the new Simonides. *ZPE* 158: 15–26.
Bremmer, Jan. 2014. *Initiation into the mysteries of the ancient world*. Berlin and Boston: De Gruyter.
Bremmer, Jan and Andrew Erskine, eds. 2010. *The gods of ancient Greece: Identities and transformations*. Edinburgh: Edinburgh University Press.
Brisson, Luc. 1995. *Orphée et l'orphisme dans l'antiquité gréco-romaine*. Aldershot, UK, and Brookfield, VT: Variorum.
Brown, Christopher. 1991. Empousa, Dionysus and the Mysteries: Aristophanes, Frogs 285ff. *CQ* 41 (1): 41–50.
Burkert, Walter. 1972. *Lore and science in ancient Pythagoreanism*. Tr. Edwin L. Minar, Jr. Cambridge, MA: Harvard University Press.
Burkert, Walter. 1982. Craft versus Sect: The Problem of Orphics and Pythagoreans. In *Self-definition in the Graeco-Roman world*, ed. Meyer and Sanders, 1–22.
Burkert, Walter. 1983 [1972]. *Homo Necans: The anthropology of ancient Greek sacrificial ritual and myth*. Tr. Peter Bing. Berkeley, Los Angeles and London: University of California Press.
Burkert, Walter. 1985. *Greek religion*. Cambridge, MA: Harvard University Press.
Burkert, Walter. 1987. *Ancient mystery cults*. Cambridge, MA: Harvard University Press.
Büsing, H. 1978. Battos. In *Thiasos: Sieben archäologische Arbeiten*, ed. Lorenz, 51–79.
Calame, Claude. 2003. *Myth and history in ancient Greece: The symbolic creation of a colony*. Princeton and Oxford: Princeton University Press.
Carbon, Jean-Mathieu and Vinciane Pirenne-Delforge. 2013. Priests and cult personnel in three Hellenistic families. In *Cities and priests*, ed. Horster and Klöckner, 65–120.
Casadio, Giovanni and Patricia A. Johnston, eds. 2009. *Mystic cults in Magna Graecia*. Austin: University of Texas Press.

Cavallari, F. S. 1878–9. Sibari. *NSA* 3: 245–53.

Chaniotis, Angelos. 2000. Das Jenseits – Ein Gegenwelt? In *Gegenwelten: Zu den Kulturen Griechenlands und Roms in der Antike*, ed. Hölscher, 159–81.

Chaniotis, Angelos, ed. 2011. *Ritual dynamics in the ancient Mediterranean*. Dresden: Franz Steiner Verlag.

Clairmont, Christoph W. 1970. *Gravestone and epigram: Greek memorials from the archaic and classical period*. Mainz: Philip von Zabern.

Clark, Raymond J. 2009. The Eleusinian Mysteries and Vergil's "appearance-of-a-terrifying-female-apparition-in-the-underworld" motif in Aeneid 6. In *Mystic cults in Magna Graecia*, ed. Casadio and Johnston, 190–203.

Clay, Diskin. 1998. *Paradosis and survival: Three chapters in the history of Epicurean philosophy*. Ann Arbor: University of Michigan Press.

Clay, Diskin. 2004. *Archilochos heros: The cult of poets in the Greek polis*. Washington, DC: Center for Hellenic Studies.

Clinton, Kevin. 1974. *The sacred officials of the Eleusinian mysteries*. Philadelphia: American Philosophical Society.

Clinton, Kevin. 1992. *Myth and cult: The iconography of the Eleusinian mysteries*. Göteborg: P. Åströms Förlag; Stockholm: Acta Instituti Atheniensis Regni Sueciae.

Clinton, Kevin. 2003. Stages of initiation in the Eleusinian and Samothracian mysteries. In *Greek mysteries*, ed. Cosmopoulos (2003a), 50–78.

Clinton, Kevin. 2004. Epiphany in the Eleusinian mysteries. *ICS* 29: 85–109.

Clinton, Kevin. 2007. The mysteries of Demeter and Kore. In *A companion to Greek religion*, ed. Ogden, 342–56.

Clinton, Kevin. 2008a. *Eleusis: The inscriptions on stone. Documents of the sanctuary of the Two Goddesses and public documents of the deme. Volume 2: Commentary*. Athens: Archaeological Society at Athens.

Clinton, Kevin. 2008b. Preliminary initiation in the Eleusinian Mysteria. In *Mikros hieromnēmōn*, ed. Matthaiou and Polinskaya, 25–34.

Closterman, Wendy. 2014. Family meals: Banquet imagery on Classical Athenian funerary reliefs. In *Cities called Athens*, ed. Daly and Riccardi, 1–22.

Coldstream, J. N. 1976. Hero cults in the age of Homer. *JHS* 96: 8–17.

Cole, Susan G. 1984. *Theoi megaloi: The cult of the great gods at Samothrace*. Leiden: Brill.

Cole, Susan G. 2008. Professionals, volunteers and amateurs: Serving the gods kata ta patria. In *Practitioners of the divine*, ed. Dignas and Trampedach, 55–72.

Connelly, Joan B. 2007. *Portrait of a priestess: Women and ritual in ancient Greece*. Princeton and Oxford: Princeton University Press.

Cosmopoulos, Michael B., ed. 2003a. *Greek mysteries: The archaeology of ancient Greek secret cults*. London: Routledge.

Cosmopoulos, Michael B. 2003b. Mycenaean religion at Eleusis: The architecture and stratigraphy of Megaron B. In *Greek mysteries*, ed. Cosmopoulos (2003a), 1–24.

Currie, Bruno. 2005. *Pindar and the cult of heroes*. Oxford and New York: Oxford University Press.

Daly, Kevin F. and Lee Ann Riccardi, eds. 2014. *Cities called Athens: Studies honoring John McK. Camp II*. Lewisburg: Bucknell University Press.

Dentzer, Jean-Marie. 1982. *Le motif du banquet couché dans le Proche-Orient et le monde grec du VIIe au IVe siècle avant J.-C*. Rome: Bibliothèque des Écoles françaises d'Athènes et de Rome.

Deoudi, Maria. 1999. *Heroenkulte in homerischer Zeit*. Oxford: Archaeopress.

de Polignac, François. 1995 [1984]. *Cults, territory, and the origins of the Greek city-state*. Tr. Janet Lloyd.. Chicago: University of Chicago Press.

Derow, Peter and Robert Parker, eds. 2003. *Herodotus and his world: Essays from a conference in memory of George Forrest*. Oxford and New York: Oxford University Press.

Dignas, Beate. 2006. Benefitting benefactors: Greek priests and euergetism. *AC* 75: 71–84.

Dignas, Beate and Kai Trampedach, eds. 2008. *Practitioners of the divine: Greek priests and religious officials from Homer to Heliodorus*. Cambridge, MA: Harvard University Press.

Dougherty, Carol. 1993. *The poetics of colonization: From city to text in Archaic Greece*. Oxford and New York: Oxford University Press.

Dougherty, Carol and Leslie Kurke, eds. 1998. *Cultural poetics in archaic Greece: Cult, performance, politics*. Oxford and New York: Oxford University Press.

Dubois, Laurent. 1996. *Inscriptions grecques dialectales d'Olbia du Pont*. Droz: Geneva.

Durkheim, Émile. 1915. *The elementary forms of the religious life*. Tr. Joseph Ward Swain. London: Allen and Unwin.

Easterling, P. E. and J. V. Muir, eds. 1985. *Greek religion and society*. Cambridge: Cambridge University Press.

Edmonds, Radcliffe G., III. 1999. Tearing apart the Zagreus myth: A few disparaging remarks on Orphism and original sin. *ClAnt* 18 (1): 35–73.

Edmonds, Radcliffe G., III. 2004. *Myths of the underworld journey in Plato, Aristophanes, and the "Orphic" gold tablets*. Cambridge and New York: Cambridge University Press.

Edmonds, Radcliffe G., III. 2006. To sit in solemn silence? θρόνωσις in ritual, myth, and iconography. *AJPh* 127 (3): 347–66.

Edmonds, Radcliffe G., III. 2009. A curious concoction: Tradition and innovation in Olympiodorus' "Orphic" creation of mankind. *AJPh* 130: 511–32.

Edmonds, Radcliffe G., III, ed. 2011. *The "Orphic" gold tablets and Greek religion: Further along the path*. Cambridge and New York: Cambridge University Press.

Edmonds, Radcliffe G., III. 2013. *Redefining ancient Orphism: A study in Greek religion*. Cambridge and London: Cambridge University Press.

Ekroth, Gunnel. 2000. Offerings of blood in Greek hero cults. In *Héros et héroïnes*, ed. Pirenne-Delforge and Suárez de la Torre, 263–280.

Ekroth, Gunnel. 2002. *The sacrificial rituals of Greek hero cults*. Liège: Centre International d'Étude de la Religion Grecque Antique.

Faraone, Christopher. 2011. Rushing into milk: New perspectives on the gold tablets. In *The Orphic gold tablets and Greek religion*, ed. Edmonds, 310–30.

Farnell, Lewis Richard. 1921. *Greek hero cults and ideas of immortality*. Oxford: Clarendon Press.

Ferguson, W. S. and A. D. Nock. 1944. The Attic orgeones and the cult of heroes. *HThR* 37 (2): i–iv, 61–174.

Flashar, M., H.-J. Gehrke, and E. Heinrich, eds. 1996. *Retrospektive: Konzepte von Vergangenheit in der griechisch-römischen Antike*. Munich: Biering & Brinkmann.

Foley, Helene P., ed. 1994. *The Homeric Hymn to Demeter: Translation, commentary and interpretive essays*. Princeton: Princeton University Press.

Fontenrose, Joseph. 1968. The hero as athlete. *California Studies in Classical Antiquity* (= *ClAnt*) 1: 73–104.

Foucart, Paul. 1873. *Des associations religieuses chez les Grecs: Thiases, éranes, orgéons, avec le texte des incriptions relatives à ces associations*. Paris: Klincksieck.

Foucart, Paul. 1914. *Les mystères d'Éleusis*. Paris: Picard.

Foucart, Paul. 1918. *Le culte des héros chez les grecs*. Paris: Imprimerie Nationale.

Fraser, P. M. 1977. *Rhodian funerary monuments*. Oxford: Clarendon Press.

Gagné, Renaud. 2013. *Ancestral fault in ancient Greece*. Cambridge and London: Cambridge University Press.

García Teijeiro, M. and M. T. Molinos Tejada. 2000. Les héros méchants. In *Héros et héroïnes*, ed. Pirenne-Delforge and Suárez de la Torre, 111–123.

Garland, Robert. 1985. *The Greek way of death*. Ithaca, NY: Cornell University Press.

Gawlinski, Laura. 2012. *The sacred law of Andania: A new text with commentary*. Berlin and Boston: De Gruyter.

Gladigow, Burkhard. 1967. Zum Makarismos des Weisen. *Hermes* 95 (4): 404–33.

Gnoli, Gherardo and J. P. Vernant, eds. 1982. *La mort, les morts dans les sociétés anciennes*. Cambridge: Cambridge University Press; Paris: Maison des Sciences de l'Homme.

Golden, Mark and Peter Toohey, eds. 1997. *Inventing ancient culture: Historicism, periodization and the ancient world*. London: Routledge.

Graf, Fritz. 1974. *Eleusis und die orphische Dichtung: Athens in vorhellenistischer Zeit*. Berlin: de Gruyter.

Graf, Fritz. 1985. *Nordionische Kulte: Religionsgeschichtliche und epigraphische Untersuchungen zu den Kulten von Chios, Erythrai, Klazomenai und Phokaia*. Rome: Schweizerisches Institut in Rom.

Graf, Fritz. 2003. Lesser mysteries: Not less mysterious. In *Greek mysteries*, ed. Cosmopoulos (2003a), 241–62.

Graf, Fritz. 2010. The blessings of madness. *ARG* 12: 167–80.

Graham, A. J. 1960. The authenticity of the ΟΡΚΙΟΝ ΤΩΝ ΟΙΚΙΣΤΗΡΩΝ of Cyrene. *JHS* 80: 95–111.

Graham, A. J. 1964. *Colony and mother-city in ancient Greece*. Oxford: Manchester University Press.

Hadzisteliou Price, Theodora. 1973. Hero-cult and homer. *Historia* 22 (2): 129–44.

Hägg, Robin. 1987. Gifts to the heroes in Geometric and Archaic Greece. In *Gifts to the gods*, ed. Linders and Nordquist, 93–9.

Hägg, Robin, ed. 1999. *Ancient Greek hero cult*. Stockholm: Paul Åströms Förlag.

Hardie, Alex. 2005. Sappho, the Muses, and life after death. *ZPE* 154: 13–32.

Hellström, Pontus and Brita Alroth, eds. 1996. *Religion and power in the ancient Greek world*. Uppsala: Almqvist and Wiksell.

Henrichs, Albert. 2003. Hieroi logoi and hieroi biblioi: The (un)written margins of the sacred in ancient Greece. *HSPh* 101: 207–66.

Henrichs, Albert. 2010. What is a Greek god? In *The gods of ancient Greece*, ed. Bremmer and Erskine, 19–39.

Henrichs, Albert. 2011. Dionysos dismembered and restored to life: The earliest evidence (OF 59 I-II). In *Tracing Orpheus*, ed. Herrero de Jáuregui, Jiménez San Cristóbal, Luján Martínez, Martín Hernández, Santamaría Álvarez and Torallas Tovar, 61–8.

Herrero de Jáuregui, Miguel, Ana Isabel Jiménez San Cristóbal, Eugenio R. Luján Martínez, Raquel Martín Hernández, Marco Antonio Santamaría Álvarez and Sofía Torallas Tovar, eds. 2011. *Tracing Orpheus: Studies of Orphic fragments*. Berlin: De Gruyter.

Hoffman, Geneviève. 2000. Brasidas ou le fait d'armes comme source d'héroïsation dans la Grèce classique. In *Héros et héroïnes*, ed. Pirenne-Delforge and Suárez de la Torre, 365–75.

Hölscher, Tonio, ed. 2000. *Gegenwelten: Zu den Kulturen Griechenlands und Roms in der Antike*. Munich and Leipzig: Saur.

Hood, Ralph W., Peter C. Hill and Bernard Spilka. 2009. *The psychology of religion: An empirical approach*. Fourth edition. New York: Guilford Press.

Horster, Marietta and Anja Klöckner, eds. 2013. *Cities and priests: Cult personnel in Asia Minor and the Aegean Islands from the Hellenistic to the Imperial period*. Boston: Walter de Gruyter.

Hughes, Dennis D. 1999. Hero cult, heroic honors, heroic dead: Some developments in the Hellenistic and Roman periods. In *Ancient Greek hero cult*, ed. Hägg, 167–75.

Humphreys, Sally C. 1980. Family tombs and tomb cult in ancient Athens: Tradition or traditionalism? *JHS* 100: 96–126.

Jeffrey, Lilian H. 1961. The pact of the first settlers at Cyrene. *Historia* 10 (2): 139–47.

Johnston, Sarah Iles. 1999. *Restless dead: Encounters between the living and the dead in ancient Greece*. Berkeley: University of California Press.

Johnston, Sarah Iles. 2005. Delphi and the dead. In *Mantikē*, ed. Johnston and Struck, 283–306.

Johnston, Sarah Iles and Peter Struck, eds. 2005. *Mantikē: Studies in ancient divination*. Leiden and Boston: Brill.

Jost, Madeleine. 2003. Mystery cults in Arcadia. In *Greek mysteries*, ed. Cosmopoulos (2003a), 143–68.

Kahn, Charles H. 2001. *Pythagoras and the Pythagoreans: A brief history*. Indianapolis, IN: Hackett Publishing.

Kamps, Werner. 1937. Les origines de la fondation cultuelle dans la Grèce ancienne. *Archives d'histoire du droit oriental* 1: 145–79.

Kearns, Emily. 1989. *The heroes of Attica*. *BICS* Supplement 57. London: Institute of Classical Studies.

Kingsley, Peter. 1995. *Ancient philosophy, mystery, and magic: Empedocles and Pythagorean tradition*. Oxford and New York: Clarendon Press and Oxford University Press.

Kloppenborg, John. 1996. Collegia and thiasoi: Issues in function, taxonomy and membership. In *Voluntary associations*, ed. Kloppenborg and Wilson, 16–30.

Kloppenborg, John and Stephen G. Wilson, eds. 1996. *Voluntary associations in the Graeco-Roman world*. New York and London: Routledge.

Koukouli-Chrysanthaki, Chaido. 2002. Excavating Classical Amphipolis. In *Excavating Classical culture*, ed. Stamatopolou and Yeroulanou, 57–73.

Kron, Ute. 1996. Priesthoods, dedications and euergetism: What part did religion play in the political and social status of Greek women? In *Religion and power*, ed. Hellström and Alroth, 139–82.

Kyrieleis, Helmut. 2006. *Anfänge und Frühzeit des Heiligtums von Olympia: Die Ausgrabungen am Pelopion 1987–1996*. (= *OlForsch* 31) Berlin: de Gruyter.

Laks, André and Glenn W. Most, eds. 1997. *Studies on the Derveni Papyrus*. Oxford and New York: Clarendon Press.

Larson, Jennifer. 1995. *Greek heroine cults*. Madison, WI: University of Wisconsin Press.

Larson, Jennifer 2007. *Ancient Greek cults: A guide*. New York and London: Routledge.

Lattimore, Richmond. 1942. *Themes in Greek and Latin epitaphs*. Urbana: University of Illinois Press.

Laum, B. 1914. *Stiftungen in der griechischen und römischen Antike*. Leipzig and Berlin: Teubner.

Le Bris, Anne. 2001. *La mort et les conceptions de l'au-delà en Grèce anciènne à travers les epigrammes funeraires: Étude d'epigrammes d'Asie mineure de l'époque hellénistique et romaine*. Paris: L'Harmattan.

Linders, Tullia and Gullög Nordquist, eds. 1987. *Gifts to the gods: Proceedings of the Uppsala Symposium 1985*. Uppsala: Almqvist and Wiksell.

Linforth, Ivan M. 1941. *The arts of Orpheus*. Berkeley and Los Angeles: University of California Press.

Lorenz, Thuri, ed. 1978. *Thiasos: Sieben archäologische Arbeiten*. Amsterdam: Castrum Peregrini Presse.

Lunt, David J. 2010. *Athletes, heroes and the quest for immortality in ancient Greece*. Dissertation, Pennsylvania State University.

Malkin, Irad. 1987. *Religion and colonization in ancient Greece*. Leiden and New York: Brill.

Malkin, Irad. 1993. Land ownership, territorial possession, hero cults, and scholarly theory. In *Nomodeiktes*, ed. Rosen and Farrell, 225–34.

Malkin, Irad. 2003. Tradition in Herodotus: The foundation of Cyrene. In *Herodotus and his world*, ed. Derow and Parker, 153–70.

Mannzmann, Anneliese. 1962. *Griechische Stiftungsurkunden*. Münster: Aschendorff.

Martin, Luther H. 2005. Aspects of "religious experience" among the Hellenistic mystery religions. *Religion and Theology* 12 (3): 349–69.

Martin, Luther H. 2006. Cognitive science, ritual and the Hellenistic mystery religions. *Religion and Theology* 13 (3–4): 383–95.

Martin, Luther H. and Panayotis Pachis, eds. 2009. *Imagistic traditions in the Graeco-Roman world: A cognitive modeling of history of religious research*. Thessaloniki: Vanias Editions.

Mastrocinque, Attilio and C. G. Scibona, eds. 2012. *Demeter, Isis, Vesta and Cybele*. Stuttgart: Franz Steiner Verlag.

Matthaiou, Angelos P. and Irene Polinskaya, eds. 2008. *Mikros hieromnēmōn: Meletes eis mnēmēn Michael H. Jameson*. Athens: Hellēnikē Epigraphikē Hetaireia.

Meyer, B. F. and E. P. Sanders, eds. 1982. *Jewish and Christian self-definition III: Self-definition in the Graeco-Roman world*. London: SCM Press.

Mirto, Maria Serena. 2012. *Death in the Greek world: From Homer to the Classical Age*. Tr. A. M. Osborne. Norman: University of Oklahoma Press.

Mitchell, Lynette. 2013. *The heroic rulers of Archaic and Classical Greece*. London and New York: Bloomsbury.

Morgan, Catherine and Todd Whitelaw. 1991. Pots and politics: Ceramic evidence for the rise of the Argive state. *AJA* 95 (1): 79–108.

Mylonas, George E. 1961. *Eleusis and the Eleusinian Mysteries*. Princeton, NJ: Princeton University Press.

Nagy, Gregory. 1999. *The best of the Achaeans: Concepts of the hero in archaic Greek poetry*. Second edition. Baltimore and London: Johns Hopkins University Press.

Nock, Arthur Darby. 1972. *Essays on religion and the ancient world*. 2 Vols. Oxford: Oxford University Press.

Obbink, Dirk, ed. 1996. *Philodemus, On piety part 1*. Oxford: Clarendon Press.

Obbink, Dirk. 2011. Poetry and Performance in the Orphic gold leaves. In *The "Orphic" gold tablets and Greek religion*, ed. Edmonds, 291–309.

Ogden, Daniel, ed. 2007. *A companion to Greek religion*. Oxford and New York: Oxford University Press.

Onians, Richard Broxton. 1951. *The origins of European thought about the body, the mind, the soul, the world, time, and fate*. Cambridge and New York: Cambridge University Press.

Papadopoulou, Ioanna. 2014. Introduction: Testing our tools: Open questions on the Derveni papyrus. In *Poetry as initiation*, ed. Papadopoulou and Muellner, ix–xxiv.

Papadopoulou, Ioanna and Leonard Muellner, eds. 2014. *Poetry as initiation: The center for Hellenic studies symposium on the Derveni papyrus*. Washington, DC and Cambridge, MA: Harvard University Press.

Parca, Maryline and Angeliki Tzanetou, eds. 2007. *Finding Persephone: Women's rituals in the ancient Mediterranean*. Bloomington: Indiana University Press.

Parisi Presicce, Claudio. 2007. La casa di Batto, il culto del'eroe fondatore e il regime democratico a Cirene. *Karthago* 27: 245–64.

Parke, H. W. 1977. *Festivals of the Athenians*. Ithaca and New York: Cornell University Press.

Parker, Robert. 1983. *Miasma: Pollution and purification in early Greek religion*. Oxford: Clarendon Press.

Parker, Robert. 1996. *Athenian religion: A history*. Oxford and New York: Oxford University Press.

Parker, Robert. 2005. *Polytheism and society at Athens*. Oxford and New York: Oxford University Press.

Parker, Robert. 2011. *On Greek religion*. Ithaca and London: Cornell University Press.

Patera, Ioanna. 2011. Changes and arrangements in a traditional cult: The case of the Eleusinian rituals. In *Ritual dynamics*, ed. Chaniotis, 119–37.

Paul, Stéphanie. 2013. *Cultes et sanctuaires de l'île de Cos*. Liège: Centre International d'Étude de la Religion Grecque Antique.

Pellegrini, Ann. 2007. Signaling through the flames: Hell House performance and structures of religious feeling. *American Quarterly* 59 (3): 911–35.

Pfaff, Christopher. 2013. Artemis and a hero at the Argive Heraion. *Hesperia* 82: 277–99.

Pirenne-Delforge, Vinciane and Emilio Suárez de la Torre, eds. 2000. *Héros et héroïnes dans les mythes et les cultes grecs*. Liège: Centre International d'Étude de la Religion Grecque Antique.

Porta, Fred R. 1999. *Greek ritual utterances and the liturgical style*. Dissertation, Harvard University.

Purvis, Andrea. 2003. *Singular dedications: Founders and innovators of private cults in Classical Greece*. New York and London: Routledge.

Richardson, N. J. 1985. Early Greek views about life after death. In *Greek religion and society*, ed. Easterling and Muir, 50–66.

Riedweg, Christoph. 1987. *Mysterienterminologie bei Platon, Philon und Klemens von Alexandrien*. Berlin: de Gruyter.

Rohde, Erwin. 1987 [1925]. *Psyche: The cult of souls and belief in immortality among the ancient Greeks*. Tr. W. B. Hillis. Reprint. Chicago: Ares Publishers.

Roller, Lynn. 1999. *In search of god the mother: The cult of Anatolian Cybele*. Berkeley and Los Angeles: University of California Press.

Rosen, Ralph M. 1987. Hipponax Fr. 48 Dg. and the Eleusinian Kykeon. *AJPh* 108 (3): 416–26.

Rosen, Ralph M. and Joseph Farrell, eds. 1993. *Nomodeiktes: Greek Studies in Honor of Martin Ostwald*. Ann Arbor: University of Michigan Press.

Roussel, P. 1930. L'initiation préalable et le symbole eleusinien. *BCH* 54: 51–7.

Rusten, Jeffrey. 2014. Unlocking the Orphic doors: Interpretation of poetry in the Derveni Papyrus between Presocratics and Alexandrians. In *Poetry as initiation*, ed. Papadopolou and Muellner, 115–34.

Salapata, Gina. 2006. The tippling serpent in the art of Lakonia and beyond. *Hesperia* 75 (4): 541–60.

Scarpi, Paolo. 2002. *Le religione dei misteri*. 2 Vols. Milan: Mondadori.

Schmitt-Pantel, Pauline. 1982. Évergétisme et mémoire du mort. In *La mort, les morts dans les sociétés anciennes*, ed. Gnoli and Vernant, 177–88.

Seaford, Richard. 1994. *Reciprocity and ritual: Homer and tragedy in the developing city-state*. Oxford and New York: Clarendon Press and Oxford University Press.

Shear, T. Leslie. 1982. The demolished temple at Eleusis. *Hesperia Suppl.* 20: 128–40, 210–12.

Simms, Robert M. 1990. Myesis, telete and Mysteria. *GRBS* 31 (2): 183–95.

Simon, Erika. 1983. *Festivals of Attica: An archaeological commentary*. Madison: University of Wisconsin Press.

Snodgrass, Anthony. 1980. *Archaic Greece: The age of experiment*. Berkeley: University of California Press.

Snodgrass, Anthony. 1982. Les origines du culte des héros dans la Grèce antique. In *La mort, les morts dans les sociétés anciennes*, ed. Gnoli and Vernant, 107–19.

Sourvinou-Inwood, Christiane. 1995. *"Reading" Greek death: To the end of the Classical period*. New York and London: Oxford University Press.

Sourvinou-Inwood, Christiane. 1997. Reconstructing change: Ideology and the Eleusinian mysteries. In *Inventing ancient* culture, ed. Golden and Toohey, 132–64.

Sourvinou-Inwood, Christiane. 2003. Festival and mysteries: Aspects of the Eleusinian cult. In *Greek mysteries*, ed. Cosmopoulos (2003a), 25–49.

Spencer, Nigel, ed. 1995. *Time, tradition, and society in Greek archaeology: Bridging the "great divide."* London and New York: Routledge.

Stamatopolou, Maria and Marina Yeroulanou, eds. 2002. *Excavating Classical culture: Recent archaeological discoveries in Greece*. Oxford: Archaeopress.

Stehle, Eva. 2007. Thesmophoria and Eleusinian Mysteries. In *Finding Persephone*, ed. Parca and Tzanetou, 165–85.

Stucchi, Sandro. 1965. *L'agorà di Cirene I: I lati nord ed est della platea inferiore*. Rome: Bretschneider.

Thomas, Oliver R. H. 2007. Charting the Atlantic with Hesiod and Hellanicus. *ZPE* 160: 15–23.

Thönges-Stringaris, Rhea. 1965. Das griechische Totenmahlrelief. *MDAI(A)* 80: 1–99.

Tsagalis, Christos C. 2008. *Inscribing sorrow: Fourth century Attic funerary epigrams*. Berlin: Walter de Gruyter.

van Dongen, van Pieter W. J., and Akosua N.J.A. de Groot. 1995. History of ergot alkaloids from ergotism to ergometrine. *European Journal of Obstetrics & Gynecology and Reproductive Biology* 60 (2): 109–16.

Vermeule, Emily. 1979. *Aspects of death in early Greek art and poetry*. Berkeley and Los Angeles: University of California Press.

Visser, Margaret. 1982. Worship your enemy: Aspects of the cult of heroes in ancient Greece. *HThR* 75: 403–28.

West, M. L. 1983. *The Orphic poems*. Oxford: Clarendon Press.

Whitehouse, Harvey. 2013. Immortality, creation and regulation: Updating Durkheim's theory of the sacred. In *Mental culture*, ed. Xygalatas and McCorkle, 66–79.

Whitehouse, Harvey and James Laidlaw, eds. 2007. *Religion, anthropology and cognitive science*. Durham, NC: Carolina Academic Press.

Whitley, James. 1988. Early states and hero cults: A re-appraisal. *JHS* 108: 173–82.

Whitley, James. 1995. Tomb cult and hero cult. The uses of the past in archaic Greece. In *Time tradition and society in Greek archaeology*, ed. Spencer, 43–63.

Whitley, James. 2002. Too many ancestors. *Antiquity* 76: 119–26.

Wittenburg, Andreas. 1990. *Il testamento di Epikteta*. Trieste: Bernardi.

Wypustek, Andrzej. 2013. *Images of eternal beauty in funerary verse inscriptions of the Hellenistic and Greco-Roman periods*. Leiden and Boston: Brill.

Xygalatas, Dimitris and William W. McCorkle, Jr., eds. 2013. *Mental culture: Classical social theory and the cognitive science of religion*. Durham, UK, and Bristol, CT: Acumen.

Zuntz, Günther. 1971. *Persephone: Three essays on religion and thought in Magna Graecia*. Oxford: Clarendon Press.

# 6 Memory, continuity and change

*In this chapter, we consider environmental, cultural and cognitive constraints on the transmission of religious representations in the ancient Greek world. Although Greek religion is often described as "conservative," it was characterized by constant change, even as its intuitive foundations, including anthropomorphism and reciprocity, remained stable over centuries. The Greeks viewed themselves as faithful custodians of unchanging ancestral traditions, but many forms of change were invisible to them while others were welcomed because of the nature of polytheism as an open system. The chapter includes a brief outline of key developments from the Early Iron Age through the Hellenistic period. We conclude with an examination of the processes by which representations spread across cultures. "Syncretism" and "Hellenization" are contested terms, yet widely used by scholars describing various forms of cultural blending. The illustrative essays examine continuity in the cult association of the Molpoi at Miletos, the spread of cults of Herakles through the Mediterranean world, and the reasons for the growth of the Sarapis cult in early Ptolemaic Egypt.*

## Mechanisms of continuity and change

Greek religious concepts and norms were transmitted through multiple channels. The great theologians of early Greek civilization were the poets, who by tradition claimed divine inspiration. While the works they produced were not treated as scripture, these texts possessed significant authority in spite of their inconsistencies. At the end of the sixth century, public performance was still the primary method of dissemination for poetry, yet new genres like comedy and tragedy were dependent on writing. Visual theology also played a role, for Greek cities and sanctuaries were filled with images of the gods. In the absence of authoritative doctrine, public discourse about matters divine was fluid and freewheeling compared to that of the monotheistic religions. Yet as the Athenians' reception of Socrates' ideas demonstrates, deviations from certain shared norms were subject to comedic ridicule, social disapproval and, occasionally, harsh punishment.

In contrast to the ferment permitted in theology, conventional Greek piety required that rituals regarded as ancestral be observed continuously and without change. Isocrates, for example, speaks approvingly of Athenians in the days of Solon and Kleisthenes:

> For this alone was their concern, to destroy none of their fathers' traditions (*tōn patriōn*) and to add nothing to that which was customary, for they thought that piety was not to be found in extravagance, but in disturbing nothing which their ancestors had handed down to them.
>
> (Isoc. 7.30)

As we will see, these ancestral customs could be written or unwritten, but in the majority of cases there was no written manual to guide what people did and said in religious contexts. Yet accurate transmission of *ta patria* was considered vitally important. How did the Greeks accomplish it? The short answer is that they did not. It is safe to say, at least, that they did not maintain complex ritual traditions completely unchanged over centuries-long periods. As we will see, change was driven by a variety of factors: environmental, cultural and cognitive.

Local gods and forms of worship were vulnerable to localized disasters. If a settlement was destroyed and the majority of its people sold into slavery or killed, as happened to Corinth in 146, its unique rituals could not survive; any "revivals" by new settlers could be only approximations. Disasters such as droughts, plagues, floods and earthquakes similarly caused shifts in population and the abandonment of cult sites.[1] Thucydides' description of the impact of a virulent plague on religious practice in Athens during the second year of the Peloponnesian War helps us visualize how all social values, including those of religion, deteriorate in catastrophic circumstances where short-term survival is in question: "However often they supplicated at temples, consulted oracles, and the like, their efforts were useless; finally they ceased doing these things, overcome by the disaster" (Thuc. 2.47).

> The bodies of the dead lay piled on each other, and people rolled about in the streets half dead, and gathered round all the fountains in their desire for water. Also, the sanctuaries where they were camping were full of corpses of people who had died there. The disaster was so overwhelming that people had no idea what would happen to them, and they neglected standards both sacred (*hierōn*) and profane (*hosiōn*).
>
> (Thuc. 2.52)

Even though the most dire effects of the plague were temporary, and the Athenian polis survived this disaster, the high mortality rate made some damage to institutional memory inevitable. The effects of the plague were intensified by the deprivations of the Peloponnesian War and Athens' ultimate defeat. Keeping in mind that intermittent war was a fact of life throughout most of Greek antiquity, we begin to see just how serious were the obstacles to maintaining long continuity of belief and practice in any given cult.

As pessimistic as the foregoing picture seems, there are counterexamples, and "continuity" could take many forms. On the Aegean island of Andros, the town of Zagora maintained an open-air sanctuary during the Geometric period, with regular sacrifices of piglets and lambs. Around 700, the site of Zagora was abandoned, yet people did not cease honoring the god(s) of the place. Indeed, they went so far as to add a new temple to the sanctuary during the mid-sixth century. Presumably the population had moved to other settlements on the island, but the primary deity of Zagora was neither forgotten nor neglected.[2]

The transmission of cults, particularly those regarded as "ancestral," was profoundly affected by social structures and the contexts of worship. Some cults were maintained in the home. In Athens, for example, the male head of the household was responsible for offerings to Zeus of Property (Ktesios) and Zeus of the Fence (Herkeios), as well as maintenance of the family grave plot.[3] Some cults corresponded to broader kinship structures, while others were the responsibility of private associations, neighborhoods or local governments. Most important were the public cults supervised by the state. The survival of tradition at each of these levels was dependent on the continuity of the corresponding social structures. Throughout Greek history, dynamic processes of political change affected the organization of worship. For example, synoecism, the union of politically independent towns and villages into a single state, required religious reforms. After the unification of Kos in 366, the people of Halasarna and the other villages worshiped the gods of the new city-state (Zeus Polieus, Athena Polias, Aphrodite Pandamos and others) even as they maintained local traditions.[4] The tendency was always toward accretion, the adding of new cults rather than the abandonment of old ones, yet resources were not infinite. At the end of the fifth century, the Athenians assigned a commission the complex task of synthesizing the old Solonian festival calendar with the many sacrifices more recently ordained by the state. In 399, after several years of work, the commissioner Nichomachos was prosecuted for allegedly shortchanging the ancestral observances in favor of lavish newer ones voted by the people. Pious intentions had outstripped the budget.[5]

## Intuition, conservatism and change

The "rules" regarding acceptable and unacceptable change were rarely articulated, yet widely shared, which shows that they depended in part on intuitive inferences about what pleased or displeased the gods and heroes. Without the need to reason consciously, worshipers predicted how a god would react to certain forms of change by mentally putting themselves in the same situation. Whenever people's intuitions did not match and questions were raised about a proposed change, it was considered prudent to consult an oracle. For example, a proposal to alter the garments and jewelry worn by Athenian cult statues of Artemis, Demeter, Kore and other goddesses was worrisome enough to require a trip to Delphi, even though the intent was to make the items "larger and finer."[6]

Contrary to Isocrates' moralizing claim that "extravagance" was unwelcome to the gods, forms of change that simply added to the honor or material wealth of a god (e.g. gilding the horns of sacrificial animals) were felt to be unproblematic in all but the most sensitive ritual contexts (e.g. altering the jewelry of "the goddesses"). More lavish sacrifices, new sacrifices, the addition of festivals and games, the refurbishment of sanctuaries and temples, and the building of new temples were rarely controversial in and of themselves. By the same token, anything perceived as a reduction in divine honor or wealth was suspect. Omission of a specific gift promised in a vow and reduction of fixed and customary tithes were offenses violating the recognized rights of a god. Festivals were to be celebrated "in as fine a manner as possible," yet the mentality of gift exchange prevailed, so that the resources of the worshipers were taken into account.[7]

Many aspects of Greek rituals, particularly those pertaining to the status, responsibilities and privileges of the participants, were open to negotiation and change at the discretion of the organizing body (typically the state). Inscribed decrees regarding the conduct of cults show that cities felt free to dictate such variables as who walked first in a procession, who was to marshal and supervise, who received which cuts of meat, how the sacrifices and other expenses were to be financed and so forth – as long as such modifications did not conflict with ritual efficacy. No state, for example, was free to dictate that men instead of women celebrate the Thesmophoria for Demeter and Kore, because the gender of the performers was considered essential to the success of the ritual.[8]

Receptiveness to change was inversely correlated with the perceived age of a given tradition. For example, very old cults were typically administered by *genē* such as the Branchidai, who served Apollo at Didyma. When cities began to assign priestly duties by lot among all the citizens, this leveling innovation was applied only to newly established priesthoods, not imposed on the older ones.[9] The same was true for the use of writing as a mnemonic aid to ritual language and technique. Even during the Hellenistic period, when written instructions for ritual became much more common, elements regarded as *ta patria* (ancestral) or *nomizomena* (customary) were less likely to be recorded in writing and less tolerant of perceived deviation.[10] Newly established cults and rituals, on the other hand, lacked supporting oral traditions and experts devoted to their maintenance; therefore detailed written guidelines were both desirable and acceptable. Writing was also used to record the outcome of disputes about existing procedures.[11]

The material aspects of Greek religion presented special challenges to conservatism, as the passage of time and the accumulation of wealth made once-grand wooden temples seem small and mean. Thus a city's desire to honor the gods in the best style, and to display wealth and power by constructing impressive stone monuments, came into conflict with the requirements of piety. Generally, there was no objection to the demolition of an old altar or temple so that a fine new one could be built, but there was strong reluctance to move it from its original spot. Once the ground beneath an altar or the spot where a divine image stood was identified as the point of contact with a god, the space became sacred in its own right.

Because a cult statue could be perceived either as a representation of a deity or as the deity itself, an old image could not be replaced, even when its workmanship was crude in comparison to later artistic productions. Splendid new statues were commissioned for new temples, but they had to coexist with their predecessors, which typically retained their primacy in ritual. At the Heraion on Samos, for example, the base for the venerable old cult image was kept in its original position through several iterations of the temple. When the sixth-century "Rhoikos temple" was constructed, the old statue, still in its original spot, stood in the pronaos (front room) of the temple, while a new statue and base were placed in the cella. A fourth-century inventory (from a still later temple) refers to the old Hera as "the goddess" and the newer Hera in the cella as "the goddess behind."[12] The small size and portability of many Archaic cult images allowed them to be carried about during rituals, and then returned to their hallowed resting places. During the Classical period, larger and heavier statues were crafted to match the stone temples with their higher elevations, but the change in style meant that many newer images were immobile, and could not be manipulated in the same ways. Over time, then, changes in technology and aesthetics had important but unplanned consequences for ritual.

The wealth of the gods was vast, and sanctuaries were crammed with valuable objects, many of which were not kept under lock and key. The unilateral removal of any object from a sanctuary, even a cheap clay figurine left by another worshiper or a few sticks of firewood, was virtually always prohibited, and sanctuary administrators kept careful inventories of the resident gods' property, which they handed over to their successors with great ceremony. Extant inventories list a surprising number of worthless and damaged items.[13] Because they could not be removed from sanctuaries, huge numbers of small vases, figurines and other inexpensive objects were buried in pits to make room for newer offerings. Although *hierosulia*, or temple robbery, was considered one of the vilest crimes, public use of the gods' riches was contemplated under crisis conditions. During the Peloponnesian War, for example, Perikles assured the Athenians that they might avail themselves of the "uncoined gold and silver" of offerings to the gods, and even remove the gold from the Athena Parthenos statue in the Parthenon, provided that "having made use of it for their salvation," they restored the same amount of wealth to the gods afterwards.[14] (The gods, it seems, did not charge interest.)

Perikles' liberal attitude was exceptional. The recasting of damaged metal dedications into new cult utensils was generally permitted, yet elaborate measures were taken to ensure that the *substance* of a dedicated object, not merely its equivalent in value, remained in a sanctuary. A craftsman recasting coins dedicated to Asklepios, for example, could not receive dedicated coins as wages and make up the weight with others. Prior to dedication, however, tithed coins or goods in kind could be converted to purpose-made gifts, such as statues. Fines and fees increased the "liquid" wealth of a sanctuary, and sacred lands were often rented out to produce income. Land use, however, could be a ritually sensitive matter. An Athenian proposal to rent out sacred land, previously untouched by the plow, in order to finance a new portico for Demeter and Kore was controversial enough to require consultation at Delphi, and the project was not pursued.[15]

## Cognition, continuity and change

As Dan Sperber has noted, virtually everything we know about human memory argues against the likelihood that our mental representations will be preserved unchanged over time. Especially in the absence of writing, what requires explanation is not change but whether and by what means accurate transmission can ever take place.[16] Broadly speaking, the matter of Greek religion can be divided into that which was intuited (and thus did not need to be remembered); that which was easy to transmit; and that which was difficult to transmit. The first category includes the implicit concepts which we have examined throughout this book, such as "Zeus has emotions" or "The new temple must be built on the same spot." This chapter will focus on the other two categories.

Both the content itself and the circumstances under which it was transmitted affected the creation of accurate long-term memories. To illustrate this point, let us take the example of normative animal sacrifice. Adults, and particularly men, were expected to know how to competently perform a sacrifice. The common procedure in each locality was known to every resident, whether layperson or priest, who might be called upon to take responsibility for conducting a sacrifice: how to proceed to the altar, what kind of music to provide, what equipment and supplies to bring, how to build a fire, how to pray, how to slaughter an animal, how to direct the butchering (a specialty function which often involved hired assistants) and what to do with the parts thus obtained. People learned the proper technique and sequence of events through repeated observation from childhood onward, and in the case of boys, through participation as acolytes. By witnessing many instances of sacrifice, they learned what degree of variation was permissible, and which elements must not be omitted. The lessons were frequent: the sacrificial calendar of the Attic deme of Erchia includes twenty-five days of sacrifice per year. While an individual demesman might not attend all of these, the deme events were supplemented by domestic sacrifices and visits to the city for state festivals.[17]

Greeks, therefore, learned a mental schema or *script* of a standard sacrifice, just as we learn how to prepare a favorite meal by observing and helping more experienced family members in the kitchen.[18] As in the skill of cooking, this script could be broken down into a series of simpler tasks, many of which were familiar and supported by "commonsense" intuitive knowledge (e.g. you must kill a large mammal before you can butcher it, and you must butcher it before you can cook it). As we saw in Chapter 4, "ritual" is characterized by what seems to outsiders to be a lack of causal connections between actions and goals. Yet at the core of the scripts used in most Greek sacrificial procedures was a practical task involving clear goals in which each step led to the next (e.g. in normative sacrifice, slaughter of an animal led to cooking, which led to distribution and consumption). Frequent repetition ensured that many steps in rituals like sacrifice entered the procedural memory, the form of long-term memory in which we encode the knowledge of familiar skills, such as dressing, dancing or cooking.[19]

The corpus of Greek "sacred laws," regulations pertaining to religious matters, provides valuable testimony to what was considered general knowledge, on the one hand, and on the other, the kinds of details that did not conform to the script, and thus were more likely to be committed to writing.[20] For example, an early fifth-century regulation from the agora of Thasos forbids the offering of sheep or pig to Apollo Nymphagetes and the Nymphs, while goat and pig are prohibited on the altar of the Charites.[21] Instead of prescribing procedures, sacred laws noted the exceptions. Normally participants could take away their shares of meat to be eaten later or sold, but sometimes the rules specified that the meat must be consumed on the spot. The norm was to pour libations of wine on the altar, but the rules might specify that wine could not be used. Pregnant animals were not usually sacrificed, but certain goddesses required them.[22] Interestingly, however, inscriptions pertaining to sacrifice often functioned more to define priestly privileges and prevent disputes than to ensure the "correct" wording of prayers or a strict sequence of detailed ritual acts. Among the most common provisions were those stating who was to supply what equipment, what share of the animal was to be given to the priest or priestess as a perquisite and who was eligible (or ineligible) to participate in the banquet.

"Sacrifice," then, was mentally represented as a standard script plus individual variations pertaining to specific deities, cults and festival dates. Unless written, these details were liable to change during transmission. Another form of religious knowledge vulnerable to inaccurate transmission was the spoken or sung content of a ritual (as opposed to wordless acts). Verbal content included hymns, prayers and cult exegesis, all of which were potential vehicles for myth.[23] This type of content is stored in declarative long-term memory, and unlike the skills in procedural memory, it requires conscious effort to encode and reproduce. Furthermore, the verbal content of a civic ritual was likely to be repeated no more than once per year, the typical interval between specific sacrifices and festivals. An exception to this rule is the repertoire of hymns that Greek youngsters learned in the course of their education. For example, Xenophon describes how the Spartans on campaign, shaken by an earthquake, spontaneously began to sing a paean to Poseidon, one which they clearly all knew by heart.[24] Young people also learned the elements of prayer through frequent repetition as they assisted at sacrifices; at least some of this content was interchangeable among cults.

We are now in a position to see that in the absence of writing, the transmission of "ancestral custom" produced differential outcomes for ritual actions and ritual words.[25] Ritual procedures typical of civic cults (sacrifice, procession, traditional dances) were sustained by familiar scripts, they were oft-repeated over the course of a year, and they were encoded through a combination of procedural and declarative (semantic) memory. Their verbal accompaniments, including any myths and other exegesis pertinent to the cult, were repeated far less often and entered long-term memory solely through the more arduous semantic pathway.[26] Within local ritual contexts, traditional hymns offered virtually the only vehicle by which verbal information pertinent to a given cult could be transmitted in stable form over several generations. Unless it consisted of very brief formulaic utterances, the other verbal content was highly fluid. Indeed, without the application of a mnemonic technique, such as meter, melody or rhyme, content of more than a few dozen words cannot be transmitted verbatim between individuals in the absence of a written version. Nor can even the gist of a prose story be accurately transmitted over long periods of time unless it conforms to certain requirements of form, organization and content. In a culture that valued *ta patria*, meter and music were not ornamental; they were essential aids to memory.[27]

The advent of writing transformed the hymnic genre, giving poets greater scope for personal creativity, and allowing them to shape the mythic content of hymns in response to the immediate concerns of their clients.[28] Many paeans, dithyrambs and processional hymns (*prosōidia*), songs commissioned from the finest poets of the day for festival performance, have been preserved in whole or in part.[29] These songs capture myths formulated by individual artists at a specific moment in time and in a specific place. But the complex songs of Pindar, Bacchylides and the other choral masters are not necessarily representative of traditional hymns performed in less exalted ritual contexts.[30] Polybius, a Greek from Arkadia writing during the Hellenistic period, said of his countrymen's education:

> For it is well known to all that the Arkadians are virtually the only people whose boys from early childhood are accustomed by law to sing hymns and paeans, in which each singer celebrates according to ancestral custom (*kata ta patria*) his local heroes and gods. After these they learn the songs of Philoxenos and Timotheus (i.e. dithyrambic poets of the Classical period), dancing with great distinction each year to the pipers of the Dionysiac festivals in the theaters, the boys in the boys' competition, and the youths in what they call the men's competition.
>
> (Polyb. 4.20.8–9)

Polybius here distinguishes between "ancestral" hymns maintained orally and hymns belonging to a literary canon. He suggests that among the other Greeks of his day, musical education has declined. Already in Aristophanes' *Clouds* (968) we hear of a traditional hymn to Athena, "Awesome Pallas, City Sacker," which boys learned from the lyre-master in the good old days, but it is implied that such training is going out of fashion.

Inscriptions and other forms of writing served as mnemonic aids as early as the sixth century, but as we have seen, their use was often limited. Literacy itself was not widespread until the end of the fifth century, and even then, it was far from universal.[31] Ritual efficacy was also a factor. Rituals with strong magical or purity elements depended for their efficacy on adherence to prescribed sequences of actions or words. Not coincidentally, these ritual acts and words were committed to writing earlier and more often.[32] The Greek preference for "unwritten ritual" in the domain of civic religion meant that minor changes in the wording of prayers or in ritual technique went unnoticed, precisely because no "original version" existed with which to compare them. What mattered was the perception, not the reality, of fidelity to past performances.[33] The contrast with Rome, where writing was integrated into ritual procedures from earliest times, is striking. Livy, for example, mentions (41.16.1–2) a mistake made during the Latin festival at

Lanuvium: the magistrate failed to pray "for the Roman people of the Quirites" during the sacrifice of one of the animals. This error required the deliberation of the Senate and the college of priests called *pontifices*, who decided that the entire festival must be repeated.[34] Greek priestesses and priests working from memory did not perceive themselves as any less pious; they simply operated with a non-literate definition of what it meant to reproduce a ritual. Greek oracles offer an additional point of contrast. Because the interpretation of oracles often turned on their exact wording, both poetic meter and writing were used as memory aids, and oracle collections gained a quasi-scriptural status in some circles.[35]

With these conclusions in mind, we turn now to the question of strategies for the unwritten transmission of exceptions to familiar procedure, unique or complex rituals, and verbal content – all the information that was vulnerable to change or loss. The Greeks divided this labor and assigned it to priests, priestesses and other religious specialists connected with individual cults. In the absence of written manuals, the surest way to transmit ritual details was specialization, with certain families adopting the responsibility for individual cults and their procedures. The existence of hereditary priesthoods is often interpreted in relation to power and control, with aristocratic elites jealously maintaining their privileges, but it was also a necessity if complex ritual traditions were to be maintained. At Athens, for example, the noble *genos* of the Eteoboutadai always provided the priestess of Athena Polias, while the Hierophant of the Eleusinian Mysteries had to be a member of the Eumolpidai. Noble Athenian families also produced the "expounders" who advised citizens on the fine points of ritual. (Other forms of specialized knowledge, such as divination and the performance of epic poetry, were similarly passed down through families or through quasi-kinship systems of apprenticeship.)[36]

As they developed, Greek states assumed authority over a wide range of festivals and sacrifices, making written calendars desirable for financial and supervisory purposes even as most details were left to priests and other ritual performers. At Athens, Solon codified ancestral sacrifices on a series of wooden tablets, which were eventually revised and reinscribed on stone. This type of calendar typically listed little more than the date, deity and type of offering.[37] State control of public religion also had the effect of broadening access to priestly office (and its attendant status and privileges) in many cults. Annual priesthoods, in which individual men or women held office for only a year, were very common. Priesthoods chosen by lot were also unremarkable, even within the *genē* of Athens. By the Classical period, priesthoods were sometimes sold.[38] Therefore, most prospective priests and priestesses were not trained from childhood for the specialized parts of their ritual roles.

All this being the case, priests and priestesses tasked with conducting festivals often had to rely on reservoirs of collective memory or on experienced colleagues for anything not covered in writing. "Collective memory" could take many forms, but it was always contingent on the existence of a group with knowledge of the proper procedures. Therefore the number of witnesses or participants at a given ritual and the degree to which it was kept secret were important limiting factors.

At Athens, for example, the priestess of Athena Polias supervised a pair of young girls called *arrhēphoroi* who lived on the Akropolis for a year and performed a variety of tasks relating to the goddess, some of which were secret.[39] The priestess of Athena Polias served for life, and must have carefully trained the woman expected to serve as her successor, yet the potential for breaks in the transmission of her specialized knowledge is all too obvious. Priestly families could have compensated for this weakness by sharing information beyond the current holder of the office. The fact that until the Hellenistic period, the priestess of Athena Polias was always a woman from Bate, the native deme of the Eteoboutadai, makes such sharing at least plausible.[40] On the other hand, if secret rituals witnessed by only a few people were inaccurately transmitted, such errors probably went unrecognized.

In the case of rituals performed publicly before large groups of people, collective memory may have served less as a reservoir of knowledge than as a check on major deviations from tradition. Collective memory is likely to have played a significant role in situations where gender-segregated groups led by laypersons assembled to carry out traditional rituals (e.g. the Adonia and Thesmophoria). Annual renegotiation of ritual procedure among a few experienced elders, however, seems likely to have resulted in significant change over time.[41] In some contexts, cult associations like that of the Molpoi at Miletos (Essay 6.1) functioned to provide a pool of knowledgeable individuals who were not necessarily priests. Another potential source of mnemonic support for inexperienced priests and priestesses was the expert assistant or temple attendant, often called a *neokoros* or *zakoros*. For example, the *orgeōnes* of the Mother, a private cult association in the Peiraieus at Athens, stipulated that their priestess was to be chosen by lot, but that she was to appoint a former priestess from the group as *zakoros* to assist her during her year in office. Well-established sanctuaries with a large number of cult personnel could thus draw on a store of collective expert memory.[42]

Assuming that the social structures supporting a custom regarded as "ancestral" were continuous and robust, the most important factors otherwise affecting its transmission were cognitive. In many cases, what the Greeks perceived and represented as unbroken tradition was in fact the product of continuous incremental change. In the absence of written guidance, components of ritual optimized for memory (those which were frequently repeated, part of an intuitively supported script and/or encoded in procedural memory) were more likely to be transmitted accurately. Mnemonic tools, such as meter and melody, enhanced the memorability of some verbal content, but did not prevent incremental change. Everything else (including non-scripted procedures, exegesis of the ritual not handed down through song, and anything secret or exclusive) was highly vulnerable to change or loss. For example, the "sacred stories" (*hieroi logoi*) associated with secret rituals were likely to undergo significant change, as we saw in Essay 5.1.[43]

The history of Greek religion was very long. This fact alone requires us to approach it not as a fixed body of practices and beliefs but as a set of constantly evolving phenomena within Greek culture. "Evolution" does not imply movement toward a goal, but continuous change driven by human cognitive constraints, cultural selection and historical contingencies of social structure and environment. So far in this chapter, we have surveyed mechanisms of change at the "micro" level of the individual ritual. The next four sections provide a brief outline of observed trends at the "macro" level.

## After the collapse: The eleventh to ninth centuries

The collapse of Mycenaean civilization in mainland Greece ca. 1100, with its dramatic migrations and displacements in population, seemingly created such traumatic disruption that even at sites where cult activity is archaeologically visible in both the Bronze Age and the Early Iron Age, there is a substantial gap in the chronology. Eleusis, Olympia and Delphi, for example, were all Mycenaean sites, but the record does not support the hypothesis of continuity with the Archaic period. To judge from the vast majority of the material record, Greek religion sprang up quite suddenly in the eighth century, like a phoenix rising from the long-cooled ashes of Mycenaean culture. This is not, of course, how it happened. On the other side of the Aegean, Greeks maintained certain Mycenaean traditions, exporting ideas and copper from Cyprus back to Greece. Meanwhile large numbers of Greeks emigrated and found prosperity on the coast of Asia Minor in the Ionian, Aeolian and Dorian colonies. The so-called Dark Age (ca. 1100–800) of mainland Greece was a period of great ferment and innovation in religion, but it is not easily visible to the archaeologist because of the relative poverty and social disorganization of the time. Yet the number of archaeological sites with evidence of cult prior to 800 has been growing, slowly but steadily, over the past two decades.[44]

The collapse of Mycenaean power was more destructive of tradition in some places than others. On Crete, worshipers returned to the Idaian cave, Psychro cave and other such venerable sites very soon after the collapse.[45] On the Greek mainland, signs of continuity are fewer. In areas affected by depopulation, people met periodically at "neutral," sometimes quite remote spots to sacrifice and feast together in the open air and to deposit gifts for the gods. Olympia and Isthmia were early regional meeting places of this type; each had Bronze Age structures which could have attracted interest.[46] Periodic regional festivals also imply organization and planning by the participants, including a shared method of reckoning time. The existence of widely distributed Greek festivals (e.g. the Thesmophoria) and festivals shared by distant cousins (the Attic-Ionian Anthesteria and Thargelia), as well as "birthdays" of the gods widely celebrated on specific days of the month, point to a common origin in the Dark Age.[47]

The sanctuary at Kalapodi/Abai in Phokis (central Greece) was also a regional meeting and feasting place during the Dark Age, but activity at this rural site was continuous from the Bronze Age. Beneath the Archaic South temple are the remains of several predecessors, beginning with a fifteenth-century Mycenaean structure. This cult building possessed an associated altar and sacrificial table, and contained fragments of a sizable female figurine, comparable to those found in other Mycenaean shrines of the period.[48] As a remarkable and rare instance of archaeological continuity, Kalapodi raises many questions about ritual continuity.

As we have seen, in the absence of disruption, the locus associated with a superhuman agent will be maintained; this requires very little cognitive effort. But over seven or eight centuries, complex rituals and associated myths will change beyond recognition, dependent as they are on sociopolitical context and oral tradition. Even the names and genders of the resident gods may change through processes of accretion and obsolescence. Apollo was the principal deity of Archaic Abai. If he arrived at the sanctuary during the Dark Age, it is easy to see how he could have coexisted with and gradually supplanted an earlier resident goddess. During the ninth century, interest in male deities substantially increased, at the expense of the goddesses so prominent in Bronze Age religion.[49]

Dedications of bronze tripod cauldrons (first seen at Olympia; Figure 6.1) and other prestige objects of metal were an innovation at this time. Tripods, in particular, advertised the wealth of their dedicators. They were gifts of honor, awarded to the victors in aristocratic funeral games and exploited in networks of aristocratic gift exchange.

*Figure 6.1* Bronze tripod cauldron from Olympia, eighth century. Archaeological Museum, Olympia. Photo: Marie Mauzy/Art Resource

The novel appearance of purpose-made luxury objects in sanctuaries suggests that elite Greeks were treating the gods the same way they treated each other, as partners in reciprocal relationships of *charis*.[50] Still, the sparseness of the material culture belies the richness of the Greek religious imagination during the Dark Age. By the mid-eighth century, the familiar Panhellenic personas of the major Greek deities, together with a scheme organizing them into an Olympian family, had already been distilled in epic poetry from a plethora of local traditions. Apollo and Aphrodite, both absent from the Mycenaean Linear B tablets, became universally recognized Panhellenic gods. Shared ritual conventions and vocabulary developed as well. Homer assumes an audience conversant with temples, animal sacrifice, libations, vows, first-fruits offerings, priests and priestesses, choral dances, seers and oracles.[51]

## The birth of civic religion: The eighth and seventh centuries

After three hundred years of relatively slow economic and social recovery, the eighth century was transformative. Kings and chieftains gave way to a ruling class of aristocrats. Emergent states pooled resources, established laws and made decisions on behalf of the *dēmos*, defined as the body of citizen males. States assumed jurisdiction over important cults and established their own festival calendars. Populations grew, and pressure on land caused internal and external expansion. Greek religion was carried early to the coasts of Italy, Sicily and Libya, among other frontiers, where colonists blended indigenous traditions with their own and established the custom of cult honors for founders. At the same time, Greeks in general were highly receptive to Syro-Phoenician and Egyptian culture.[52] As the popularity of the Homeric and Hesiodic poems reveals, there was a growing interest in the heroic past and in Panhellenic representations of the gods.

Communal worship in cults restricted to citizens and their families was a hallmark of the newly formed Greek states. Sanctuaries and festivals rapidly proliferated. Many of the most prestigious sanctuaries, including Delphi, Eleusis and the Argive Heraion, were founded (or refounded over Mycenaean remains) around this time, while a few venerable sanctuaries, such as Olympia, Isthmia and Dodona, had already achieved wide renown. After 750, states had begun to direct vast resources toward the construction of temples, first in wood, then in stone. The social function of the temple as a form of civic display is well recognized, but the Archaic vogue for temples, which reached a peak ca. 550, also reveals a significant shift in ritual practice and in the representation of certain gods. Most temples housed an anthropomorphic statue of the resident deity, which received special treatment and veneration as the focus of worship (Chapter 2). The Greek convention of temple and cult statue crystallized from a complex brew of West Semitic and Anatolian influences together with Mycenaean, Minoan and homegrown Dark Age practices. As states invested more communal resources in sanctuaries, elite individuals followed the trend, bringing gifts to the gods instead of burying them in graves.[53] Many of these early votives were objects of daily life (jewelry, vases, tools, weapons, armor), but the number and variety of gifts quickly increased, with more purpose-made dedications. The spectrum of value also widened, revealing broader participation in worship.

## Oracles, mysteries and heroes: The sixth and fifth centuries

By the mid-sixth century, festivals at Olympia, Nemea, Isthmia, Delphi and Athens were occasions for major athletic, musical and dance competitions. Greek states conducted a kind of sacred diplomacy, sending ambassadors (*theoroi*) to witness each other's festivals. As the age of the polis reached its peak, myths and cults of heroes were ever more boldly employed as a means of expressing political relationships; thus in 508 the Thebans could request military assistance from the Aiginetans based on the sisterhood of the heroines Thebe and Aigina, both daughters of the river Asopos.[54] Vast amounts of wealth were presented to the gods, who received tithes and elaborate votive monuments, especially from war booty. Oracular sanctuaries proliferated and prospered. Although the Delphic oracle must have had a hand in many an early colonial venture, its period of greatest influence came during the sixth century, when even a fabulously wealthy and powerful foreign ruler like Kroisos of Lydia found it expedient to send lavish gifts to Pythian Apollo. He sent equivalent gifts to Apollo at Didyma, the second most influential oracular shrine of the Archaic period.[55] Yet the uncertainties of the Persian Wars tested the oracles, and Apollo could not prevent the destruction of Didyma.

In addition to consulting oracles, people sought blessed afterlives at Eleusis and in Bacchic-Orphic mysteries (Chapter 5). The popular ascendance of Dionysos during this period is especially visible in Athens, where his festivals were augmented with dramatic and dithyrambic competitions. Dionysos was even installed at Delphi, while strong Dionysiac influence was felt at Eleusis. The trance-inducing cult of Meter/Kybele spread widely and the goddess's affinity with Dionysos was recognized. Herakles too was newly dominant during this period (Essay 6.2). Even as the Greeks' greatest hero was transformed into a Pan-Mediterranean god, the distinctive Greek practice of worshiping the heroes and heroines of myth took form ca. 600 and continued to develop during the fifth century. Meanwhile a select few of the recently deceased were recognized as powerful dead.

## Multicultural religion: The fourth, third and second centuries

The cumulative impact of the Peloponnesian War (431–404) permanently reduced the vitality and prestige of Athens and Sparta, which had come to dominate mainland Greece and the Aegean. The rise of Macedonian power followed in the mid-fourth century, and during the third, Rome absorbed the western Greek poleis. Together with the loss of political independence, the upheavals and constant warfare of this period led to a widening gap between rich and poor. As had been the case in the period when the Greek states were nascent, a new aristocratic class arose, providing all-important funding for festivals, dominating priesthoods and leaving abundant evidence of its activities in inscriptions.[56] The wealthy and educated were attracted to Greek philosophy as an adjunct or alternative to traditional religion, and allegorizing reinterpretations of traditional myth and ritual achieved a wider distribution.[57] Starting in the fourth century, purity beliefs were increasingly subjected to reflective reinterpretation, as moralists insisted that in order to enter a sanctuary, one must be clean not only in the body but also in the soul.[58]

With Alexander's conquests and the establishment of the Hellenistic kingdoms, waves of Greeks settled abroad and engaged with the gods of their new homes: Atargatis, Osiris-Apis, Ba'al. These emigrants, uprooted from their ancestral, place-bound traditions, now had the ability to choose from a dizzying array of cults. Often they established private clubs through which to practice the worship of familiar Greek deities, especially Dionysos. The new multiculturalism affected long-established Greek cities to a lesser extent, though popular cults like those of Isis and Sarapis proliferated on the margins of traditional polis religion, and major ports like Delos reveal a "melting pot" of Syrian, Egyptian, Roman and Greek traditions.[59] In the past, scholars have detected in this period a breakdown of traditional civic religion, which supposedly gave way to atheism on the one hand, and on the other, "superstitious" and mystical "foreign" beliefs. Today the scholarly consensus holds that the system of civic religion suffered no widespread breakdown; in fact, traditional civic cults were maintained when circumstances allowed.[60] On the other hand, as we have seen, social disruption and depopulation inevitably produce breaks in the transmission of ritual knowledge. Across the Greek world, many thousands of minor and rural cults must have been abandoned or significantly changed during this period.[61]

The Hellenistic age saw increased interest in highly mobile deities whose international popularity was based on their appeal to the individual rather than the group. These gods were "special agents" (Chapter 3) who also manifested themselves outside ritual contexts through dreams and miracles. They traveled along trade routes through private initiative, and they thrived in large urban centers conducive to the formation of religious subcultures.[62] The worship of the universalizing goddess Isis, for example, approached henotheism and was qualitatively different from that of traditional civic or regional goddesses, such as Hera Argeia in the Argolid or Athena Polias at Athens. The healer Asklepios was an equally popular if less theologically ambitious "special agent."[63] New mysteries proliferated; in addition to those of Isis, the mysteries of Demeter and Kore at Andania, Despoina at Lykosoura, and Ephesian Artemis were introduced, while those of the Kabeiroi were widely propagated.[64]

From the late fourth century onward, the age-old symbiosis of state and religion was adapted to accommodate ruler worship, a development perhaps facilitated by the long-standing Greek tradition of hero cult. The adoption of ruler cult throughout the Greek world did not signify a devaluation of traditional belief.[65] Instead, it was a logical extension of civic religion, which was characterized by relations of reciprocity with superhuman beings able to bestow safety and prosperity. What Greek dynasts lacked in immortality, they made up for in power. Often they displayed both power and piety through the monumental elaboration of existing sanctuaries, as Philip II and others did at the sanctuary of the Samothracian gods.[66] A similar extension of traditional religion was the development of civic cults devoted to personified abstractions, such as Eirene (Peace), Homonoia (Concord) and Tyche (Luck).[67]

## The intercultural spread of religious representations

From the Mycenaean period through the Hellenistic, Greek worshipers borrowed ritual practices, iconography and myths from other cultural systems. In turn, Greek ideas were adopted by non-Greek peoples around the Mediterranean. The successful spread of religious representations between and within cultures depends on three conditions. First, there must be networks by which information and goods can travel. Second, groups encountering new religious representations (oral or visual) must be receptive in some degree. Third, the content itself must be cognitively compelling in order to motivate transmission, and it must lend itself to memory or be supported by aids like written scrolls or iconography.

The special role of the Mediterranean physical environment in shaping its cultures has long been a subject of interest to historians (Essay 6.2).[68] From earliest times, the sea was less a barrier than a road, one far faster (if occasionally more hazardous) to travel than any overland route. Therefore, islands and coasts had greater connectivity than hinterlands. Except for the interior of Greece itself, the "Greek world" was made up of a thin ribbon of coastal settlements ringing the Aegean, southern Italy and other parts of the Mediterranean and Black Sea. In modern terms, it was as though most people lived near an airport.

The cross-cultural spread of religious ideas and iconography was also facilitated by the similarity between Greek religion and other Mediterranean polytheisms. Their lack of fixed dogmas, scriptures and centrally policed doctrines made them receptive to changes in belief and practice, within the limits we have described earlier. As for "foreign" ideas, although we moderns speak of the Phoenicians, the Greeks, the Egyptians, the Romans and so on, such distinctions obscure the degree to which the identities of these groups overlapped. Indeed, before the sixth century, the Greeks do not seem to have considered themselves "Hellenes" at all, but, for example, Korinthians and Milesians, or Dorians and Ionians.[69] It may not have occurred to them to favor a new god from Athens over one from Tyre.

Polytheistic openness also served a vital social function in the multicultural environment of the Mediterranean. In Malkin's words, "Religion sometimes served as a common matrix by mediating between Greeks, Phoenicians, Etruscans and local populations."[70] The Etruscan city of Caere, with its port at Pyrgi, provides an example. During the late sixth century, a community of Ionian Greeks resided in Caere, a city which was also a major hub for trade in the Attic vases so prized by Etruscans. Around 500, the sanctuary at Pyrgi contained both a temple in the local "Tuscan" style and a Greek-style peripteral temple. The ruler of Caere made a bilingual dedication on gold tablets to the goddess of the peripteral temple, who bears two names: Etruscan Uni and Punic Astarte. The resident Greeks probably thought of her as Hera.[71]

Thus, the sanctuary at Pyrgi, like many sanctuaries in port towns, facilitated the meeting and blending of elements from Etruscan, Greek and Phoenician traditions. Cult (and perhaps myth) here functioned as a tool which allowed Caeretan residents and visitors of different ethnicities to find common ground. Throughout antiquity, such cosmopolitan environments facilitated the transfer of religious ideas and artifacts from Syro-Palestine, Anatolia, Egypt and local non-Greek populations to Greek worshipers and vice versa.

Finally, cognitive factors ensure that some types of content will be favored over others. Throughout this book, we have explored the mental systems involved in interpreting our physical environment, recognizing other minds, protecting ourselves from danger and functioning as social animals. Although religious ideas and images can be spread through proselytizing, imperialist and colonialist efforts, they will not take root unless they capture our attention by activating these intuitive mental systems, and unless they are presented in a memorable, transmissible format. Moreover, much ancient cultural transfer was unguided. There were no missionaries of Herakles, and no church. This is not to say that worship of Herakles was never introduced through military conquest, yet his worship was enthusiastically adopted by peoples, such as the Samnites of Italy, whose lands the Greeks never colonized. Within Greek culture, similarly blind selection processes seem to have facilitated the spread of popular deities like Meter/Kybele, Adonis, Asklepios, Sarapis and Isis.[72]

The equation of Etruscan Uni with Phoenician Astarte in the gold tablets from Pyrgi was a step toward the syncretism of the two goddesses. "Syncretism," the blending of elements from different cultures, is a potentially problematic word for a number of reasons. First, it originated as a pejorative term in Christian discourses that rejected creolized and blended forms of Christianity as doctrinally impure.[73] A second difficulty arises from the vagueness of the word, because there is no consensus on what degree of blending constitutes "syncretism." The most superficial level is the simple equation of two deities outside of a worship context. In his description of Egypt, Herodotus writes, "All the Egyptians worship no gods in common, except Isis and Osiris, who they say is Dionysos" (Hdt. 2.42.2). Of Meroë, the capital of Ethiopia, he says, "The people here worship Zeus and Dionysos alone of the gods, and honor them greatly, and they have an oracle of Zeus. They send out armies whenever and to whatever place his pronouncements command" (Hdt. 2.29.7).

We do not know whether it was Herodotus himself or his informants, the Egyptian priests, who assigned the equivalencies Zeus/Amun and Dionysos/Osiris, but the observation is almost purely theological; in Herodotus' day, the blending of these deities in actual ritual contexts at Meroë must have been limited or nonexistent. Lebrun suggests that this superficial stage be described as "assimilation." Therefore we might propose that at a minimum, "religious syncretism" must involve a blending of formerly distinct features from two or more cultures within a specific ritual context, as Zeus and a local form of Amun were blended through sustained Greek participation at a famous oracle in the Libyan oasis of Siwa.[74] Finally, application of the term "syncretism" may disguise significant variations in the phenomena under study: was the process of blending guided or spontaneous? Did it happen within a brief period, or require centuries to develop?[75] Scholars have suggested that the term "syncretism" be retired in favor of alternatives like "hybridity." But provided that we dispense with value judgments about the supposed purity or impurity of traditions, "syncretism" remains a useful general term to denote a family of related phenomena.

"Hellenization" is another word often applied to the blending of Greek and non-Greek traditions, and this term too can be problematic because it encourages the assumption that politically dominant Greeks were actively shaping the culture of passive non-Greeks (Essay 6.3), or, conversely, that non-Greeks naively imitated Greek customs because of their perceived superiority.[76] Such assumptions tend to break down whenever the specifics of cultural encounters are examined. One example is the popular oversimplification of the relationship between the Greek and Roman pantheons. Comparing lists of twelve major deities, we may be tempted to conclude that the "Hellenizing" Romans imported a ready-made pantheon for themselves, imposing the personas of the Greek gods on less distinctive Italian *numina*. Closer study reveals that Venus was quite distinct from Aphrodite, and Mars from Ares; Roman appropriation of Greek culture always happened in ways that served Roman needs and appealed to Roman tastes. Also, as we will see, syncretism could affect each of the participant cultures, for networks do not carry content in only one direction.

## ESSAY 6.1: MEMORY AND THE MOLPOI

The famous Molpoi Decree from Miletos reveals how the technology of writing aided continuity in cult practice through conditions of extreme disruption. We begin by sketching the history of Miletos and the social context of the decree.[77] Colonized during the Dark Age, Miletos was arguably the most prosperous and important Greek city of the seventh and sixth centuries. The settlers had brought with them the cult of Apollo Delphinios, a god much concerned with matters of citizenship and governance. In many Greek cities he presided over the enrollment of youths as citizens, and in his sanctuaries treaties and laws were "published" by inscription on stone at an early date. The walls of the Archaic Delphinion at Dreros in Crete, for example, were inscribed with some of the earliest known Greek laws. The strong connection between Apollo and political life, so evident in Archaic Crete, was also present at Miletos. Furthermore, because the gods were deeply concerned with the affairs of the city and vice versa, laws covered both religious and political matters.

From at least the eighth century, Miletos maintained an oracle of Apollo, located nearby at Didyma.[78] The Milesians were prolific founders of colonies, and they focused their efforts on the Propontis and Black Sea, establishing Olbia, Sinope, Tomis and dozens of other cities. Apollo Didymeus played a role in these efforts similar to the role which Pythian Apollo played for colonists from the Greek mainland, selecting the leaders of the expeditions and specifying their destinations.[79]

The first recognizable Delphinion at Miletos was built in the late sixth century (530–20). Once completed, its south wall was inscribed with a monumental version of the city's sacrificial calendar.[80] Around the same time, the city began to publish the names of its *aisumnetai* ("judges") on stone, and the citizens kept track of succeeding years by the names of these annual officials. Although the matter has been disputed, it seems quite likely that the *aisumnētēs*, together with his five *proshetairoi* ("companions"), governed the city during the periods when it was under oligarchic rule. This system of rule by a rotating group of wealthy aristocrats replaced the previous Dark Age system of kingship.

The *aisumnētes* together with his companions led a cult association devoted to Apollo Delphinios and known as the Molpoi ("Singer-Dancers").[81] The group was a very ancient one, and before the advent of writing, all its traditions must have been maintained through collective memory. Such a college or sodality could transmit information effectively provided that at least some of its members at any given time were expert. Thus the Molpoi operated in a fashion different from the Branchidai, the specialized *genos* who oversaw the oracular sanctuary of Didyma. Whereas the expert role of the Branchidai was hereditary, the annually selected *aisumnētēs* and *proshetairoi* could not be trained from youth to carry out their duties. Some members of the group needed to have served in previous years and learned the procedures through repetition. Both the hallowed nature of the institution and its role in governance are reflected in the fact that several Milesian colonies had their own Molpoi.[82]

Around 520, perhaps, at roughly the same period the names of *aisumnetai* began to be publicly recorded, the Molpoi wrote down a set of guidelines for their ritual duties, though it was not (as of yet) inscribed for public view. They may have stored records of such decisions in the Delphinion on papyri, or on wooden tablets. As we will see, much of the content is to do with the roles of participants in the festival for Apollo Delphinios, so the written document may have been motivated by a desire to clarify rights and responsibilities (this concern with finances and perquisites is typical of Greek cult regulations). But the text also explains the proper ritual for handing over power from the old *aisumnētēs* to the new, and it describes the essential elements of the annual procession from Miletos to the oracular sanctuary at Didyma. Therefore it attests an intent to ensure the preservation of these aspects of the ritual. Perhaps the written document was a response to political changes that threatened the continuity of the board's membership and therefore its ability to reproduce the procedures properly.

Whatever the reasons for the first drafting of the document, dramatic political change followed within a couple of decades. The Molpoi were stripped of their political power, and Miletos was governed by tyrants until 499. We do not know how the ritual duties of the Molpoi were carried out under these conditions. The Ionian cities, including Miletos, then joined a revolt against their Persian overlords, and in 494 the revolt was brutally put down. Miletos was destroyed, and the majority of its people killed, deported or scattered. In 478, immediately after Xerxes' defeat, the city was refounded.[83] One of the first structures to be rebuilt was the sanctuary of Apollo Delphinios. The new Delphinion was constructed directly over the foundations of the old, and inscribed blocks bearing remnants of the old calendar were incorporated by design, demonstrating that some of the citizens remembered the structure as it had been fifteen years before. The oligarchy, with its governing board and cult association of Molpoi, was restored.

Most fascinating of all is the fact that at least one of the perishable written records of the Molpoi survived. In 476/5, two years after the refounding of Miletos, the *aisumnētēs* Charopinos made an addition to the document, and other portions too are thought to be amendments, although the dates of those changes are not noted. Almost thirty years later (447/6), when Philtes was *aisumnētēs*, the Molpoi had their ritual prescriptions inscribed on stone: "The Molpoi decided to engrave the rites (*orgia*), to place them in the sanctuary [i.e. the Delphinion], and to act in accordance with them. And thus the following was engraved and placed."[84]

Again, we do not know the reasoning behind their decision to make a public, imperishable record of the text at a time when detailed cult inscriptions were still unusual, but once again change was in the air. Only a few years after Philtes' version of the text was set up, Athens flexed its imperial muscle, ending the oligarchic rule of Miletos and making it a subject city governed by a "democracy." The version of the decree that we possess today is a Hellenistic copy made around 200.[85] This late recopying may indicate that the rites had been revived after a long lapse, but it is also possible that they had survived more or less continuously during the intervening 240 years, with the fifth-century inscription available as a guide. As we will see, however, "continuous" does not mean "unchanged."

After the initial dating formula naming Philtes the *aisumnētēs* and his five *proshetairoi*, and noting the decision to have the rites recorded on stone, the decree continues with a description of the festival. (Note that headings and the text in parentheses are my explanatory additions, while words and phrases in bold indicate amendments by the Molpoi to the original written text.)

## The installation of the new *Aisumnētēs*

> At the Hebdomaia . . . (missing text). On the eighth day the *aisumnētēs* of the Molpoi provides to the persons pouring libations the holy things or *splanchna*. The *aisumnētēs* chooses the companions, when all the kraters have been poured and they have sung the paean.

The Hebdomaia was an annual Apolline festival held on the seventh day of the month, a day sacred to the god.[86] On the first "Apollo's day" of the first month of the year (Taureon, April/May in our reckoning), the new *aisumnētēs* took over from the old, and chose his co-governors. The activities for the Hebdomaia are missing, but later in the inscription we learn that the city has provided two full-grown animals to the Molpoi for sacrifice. The text pertaining to the eighth is difficult to interpret and perhaps corrupt, but the mention of *splanchna*, the viscera of a sacrificed animal, indicates that another animal has been sacrificed. The *splanchna* were the first parts of the animal to be eaten, consumed by the participants in a sacrifice. Here perhaps they are distributed among the candidates for office ("the persons pouring libations"?).[87] A highlight of the ritual was the pouring of libations from four kraters, vessels similar in function to punch bowls. (That the Molpoi used four is mentioned later in the inscription.) The libations to Apollo were accompanied by a type of hymn characteristic of his worship, the paean. Not all paeans were sung to Apollo, but the genre may have originated in his cults or those of a Bronze Age predecessor, Paiawon.[88] In the *Iliad* (1.472–4), Greek youths sang a paean to Apollo, praying for release from the plague, and the Homeric *Hymn to Apollo* (3.514–19) includes a performance of the paean, led by the god himself. Although paeans varied in form and topic, requests for aid and salvation, or thanks (if such aid had been supplied) were common themes. Therefore the paean was appropriate for the celebration of a civic festival inaugurating a new year and new leadership. In an omission typical of cult inscriptions, especially those of the Archaic and Classical periods, the Molpoi recorded neither the prayers likely spoken on this occasion nor the words of the paean they customarily sang. The oral transmission of this content was taken for granted.

> On the ninth day, the new *aisumnētēs* gets an equal share first, both from the loin meat and from the fifth part which the crown-wearers receive. They begin to sacrifice the victims to Apollo Delphinios by starting (?) to sacrifice from these. And the kraters are mixed just as in the Molpon, and there is a paean. And the outgoing *aisumnētēs* sacrifices to Hestia from the halves. **Let him pour a libation from the kraters himself, and sing the paean**.

On the ninth, the Molpoi reconvened for another round of sacrifice and drinking. The status of the new *aisumnētēs* was emphasized through his right to be served first from the choicest portion of the meat, and through his right to a share of what the "crown-wearers" got. This is the first we hear of the crown-wearers (*stephanēphoroi*), who are mentioned several times in the document (a garland or *stephanos* was worn on the head for special occasions, and was a privilege accorded to athletic victors as well as others thought to be especially deserving of honor). There is debate over who the crown-wearers were and how this group overlapped with the Molpoi; Alexander Herda, who most recently studied the text, thinks that the term refers to the pair of incoming and outgoing *aisumnetai*.[89] The "Molpon" appears to be the meeting hall of the Molpoi, which must have been located in the Delphinion; it was where the Molpoi regularly met to dine, drink and discuss the affairs of the city.[90] At this time, the outgoing *aisumnētēs* marked the completion of his term with offerings to Hestia, the goddess of the civic hearth. His high status was further emphasized by the pouring of a libation and a solo (?) rendition of the final paean for Apollo – elements of the ritual which are added (or clarified) in the earliest amendment to the text.[91]

> On the tenth day are the Competitions (*Hamillētēria*), and two full grown victims are given by the Molpoi to the crown-wearers and sacrificed to Apollo Delphinios. And the crown-wearers compete, both the new ones and the

> priest, and they drink the wine of the Molpoi, and they pour libations just as in the Molpon. The outgoing *aisumnētēs* provides what the Onitadai provide, and he has as his perquisites what the Onitadai have.

The nature of the "Competitions" performed by the crown-wearers is unknown. They may have been choral songs for Apollo or athletic events, and those "competing" may have done so directly, or as sponsors of teams. On the tenth day, attention focuses on the crown-wearers, for whom the Molpoi supply wine and two adult sacrificial animals. The identity of the "new ones" is disputed; Herda translates "the crown wearers and the young men (*neoi*) and the priest compete," understanding the *neoi* as the age-class of youths who are admitted to citizenship.[92] Regardless of whether this interpretation is correct, it is clear that in many Archaic Greek cities, Apollo presided over the admission of young men to citizen status. (In earliest times, this status was marked by the privilege of dining and drinking wine in a "men's house" off-limits to women and other non-citizens. The "Molpon" may be the remnant of such an institution, which is attested for the historical period in Crete and at Sparta.) The priest mentioned here is surely the priest of Apollo Delphinios. It is not the case, as is often assumed, that the Molpoi themselves are priests of Apollo, although they have authority to sacrifice on behalf of the polis by virtue of their office.[93]

At this point, no fewer than seven animals, four of them full-grown, have been slaughtered over the course of four days. Even assuming the victims from days eight and nine were immature, the amount of meat produced was substantial, enough for hundreds of servings. This gives us a clue to the size of the group of Molpoi and crown-wearers. (They must have feasted in the Delphinion, which possessed two halls, each with a capacity of about sixty.)[94] A new group, the Onitadai, is mentioned in the last line of this section. The Onitadai, who receive detailed treatment later in the inscription, were a hereditary association of ritual experts specializing in sacrificial logistics, the equipment and techniques for butchering and cooking animals.[95]

## Public funding of the Molpoi and associated rites

> When the crown-wearers go to Didyma, the city gives as a hecatomb three full grown victims, one of which is to be female and another with testicles. And the city gives a full-grown victim to the Molpon at the festival of Targelia, and a full grown victim at the festival of Metageitnia, and two full-grown victims at the Hebdomaia, and at each festival an old *chous* (liquid measure) of wine. The king is present at these sacrifices, but he receives no more than the other Molpoi. And the crown-wearers begin in the month of Taureon to sacrifice to Apollo Delphinios, making first offerings from the left-side parts, and he (the new *aisumnētēs*?) pours libations from the four kraters.

This part of the text covers the financial responsibility of the Milesian public with regard to the activities of the Molpoi throughout the year, including the procession to Didyma led by the crown-wearers. A "hecatomb" was an offering of sacrificial animals as a group; the hecatomb of three victims here may have been destined for Apollo, Artemis and their mother Leto, on the occasion of the great procession. Metageitnia and T(h)argelia were festivals with Apolline associations, also celebrated at Athens.[96] The mention of the Hebdomaia and the month of Taureon seem to refer back to the procedures of day seven at the beginning of the document. Like Athens, Miletos had a magistrate called the "king" (*basileus*) who may have inherited some ritual duties of the original kings.[97] Because the sacrifices listed in this section are publicly funded, the king is expected to be present, but he is not to be privileged over the other Molpoi when it comes to dividing the meat. As was so often the case in Greek sacrificial rituals, access to meat functioned as a sign of honor and prestige.

## The procession to Didyma

> Two sacred stones (*gulloi*) are brought. One is placed beside Hekate in front of the gates (of Miletos); it is garlanded and a libation of unmixed wine is poured. The other is placed at the doors of Didyma. And after doing these things, they march the broad road as far as the Heights, and from the Heights through the woods.

Based on an ancient lexicographer who defines *gullos* as "a cubic or four-sided stone," the *gulloi* of the decree are thought to be sacred stones. To garland the stones and pour a libation over them was to treat them like portable altars, though it is possible that they possessed counterintuitive properties (e.g. having fallen from heaven) in their own right. The Archaic Milesian calendar mentions that two *gulloi* were garlanded in another festival, perhaps for Dionysos, during the month of Artemision.[98] In the Decree, the function of the twin *gulloi* is to mark the start and endpoints of a state procession, magically binding the city to Apollo's sanctuary at Didyma. Led by the crown-bearers, the procession leaves from the gates (*pulai*) of the city, which are guarded by the civic goddess Hekate, and makes its way to the "doors" (*thurai*) of Didyma.[99]

> And paeans are sung, first beside Hekate in front of the gates, beside Power, then in the meadow on the Heights beside the Nymphs, then beside Hermes in (the shrine of) Kelados, beside Phylios opposite the Horned One, beside Chares' statues. **In the year of all offerings**, a skinned victim is offered beside the Horned One, and beside Phylios cakes are offered **every year.**

The procession stops at a series of landmarks on the Sacred Way to sing paeans for Apollo, binding Miletos to Didyma through song in a fashion analogous to the binding by means of the *gulloi*.[100] The stops along the way "connect the dots" between the two *gulloi*, focusing on places of special interest to the Molpoi.[101] The personification of Dynamis ("Power") as a god finds a possible parallel in Classical Teos, where a curse against subversive citizens was recited "beside Memory and Power."[102] Both the nymphs and the river god Kelados would have been deities concerned with the nurture of boys, which allies them with Apollo. Phylios ("He of the Tribe") appears to be a local hero whose altar or statue is situated in the sanctuary of (Apollo) Keraïïtes, "the Horned One."[103] Phylios is an appropriate name for a hero associated with Apollo's patronage of family lines and hereditary citizenship. As for "Chares' statues," an Archaic statue (ca. 570–550) dedicated to Apollo by a local ruler named Chares was recovered in the excavation of Didyma (Figure 6.2). With it were nine other fragmentary statues of people, as well as two lion sculptures. Because all the other stops mentioned in the text are sacred places, scholars usually assume that Chares was heroized, perhaps together with others in the same statue group. However, there is no other evidence for this. It is also possible that "Chares' statues" simply constituted a landmark of interest to the Molpoi for reasons unclear to us.

Why was this list of stops included in the decree when so many other pieces of information were omitted? The procession did not simply pause at every landmark it encountered along the Sacred Way, since it skipped at least one located on the Heights.[104] Therefore some principle of selection was at work; we have hypothesized that the stops had special significance either for Apollo in his role as patron of youths or for the Molpoi as his cult association. Yet as the Molpoi followed the Sacred Way and encountered the landmarks, it would not have been especially difficult to remember which ones had been singled out. They included the list, then, less as a mnemonic for remembering the landmarks themselves than as a way of ensuring that their successors did not change the stops. Furthermore, the Molpoi were careful to specify the exact place where each paean was to be sung (e.g. not merely in the shrine of Kelados, but beside the statue of Hermes there).

As we have seen, one of the key ritual duties of the Molpoi was to sing paeans for Apollo. Their name is related to the verb *melpō*, "I celebrate with song and dance," and therefore it was they who performed the paeans at the stops on the procession to Didyma (especially in the early period, they may have danced as well). The extant portions of the decree mention a minimum of eight paeans, six of which (in my reading) belong to the procession. The most important memory task of the Molpoi was therefore verbal and musical. Of the content of these paeans, the decree tells us nothing. That is, the Molpoi were simply expected to learn and remember them, and to pass them on to their successors. Given the venerable office they held, the core repertoire probably consisted of traditional hymns connected with Apollo.[105] The specific stops on the route could have functioned as memory aids, each associated with a different hymn and procedure. Such techniques of memorization were known to the Archaic Greeks. Cicero and others attributed the device of linking content with places to the lyric poet Simonides (fl. ca. 500):

> [According to the poet], those who wish to train this faculty [memory] must select places and form mental images of the things they wish to remember, and store the images in these places, so that the order of the places will preserve the order of the things, and the images of the things will denote the things themselves. The places will serve us as wax writing tablets, and the images as the letters written upon them.[106]

*Figure 6.2* "I am Chares, son of Kleisias, ruler of Teichoussa. The statue belongs to Apollo." Marble seated statue of Chares from the Sacred Way between Miletos and Didyma, ca. 560. Photo: The Trustees of The British Museum/Art Resource

Of course, the decree makes none of this explicit, and the Molpoi may not have had a formal mnemonic technique in mind, but regardless of whether they did, taking care always to pause at the same spots, and to sing the hymns in the same order, would have eased their task. The ritualization of the musical program, with songs sung according to ancestral custom, may also have been considered important for the efficacy of the annual performance in securing Apollo's blessings. The stop at "Chares' statues" was added (at the earliest) only 20–30 years before the original text of the regulation was committed to writing, representing a modification to an older itinerary. If the stops were tied to a set of hymns in the way I have suggested, any additions would have had to be made at the *end* of the sequence, in order to avoid disrupting the memorized order.

## The duties and perquisites of the Onitadai

> The Onitadai are to provide the equipment of pottery, of iron, of bronze, of wood, of water, of round plates, of pinewood chips, of wicker for cutting the meat, of wooden blocks and of fetters for the sacrificial animals. **At (?) the crown-wearers, lamp and oil.** (The Onitadai are also responsible for) the roasting of the entrails, the boiling of the meat, the haunch and the fifth part which the crown-wearers receive, the boiling, cutting and distribution of the portion. **The flat cakes for Apollo are to be cooked from half a *medimnos* (of grain) and the ones for Hekate separately.** All the haunches go to the Onitadai from the Molpoi, apart from those that the crown-wearers receive, and all skins, three *thualēmata* from every victim, **the remaining *thua*, and the wine that is left in the krater,** a fifth every day. **In case the Onitadai do not supply whatever (is needed) of these things, the Molpoi decided in the year of Charopinos that the crown-wearers should supply them from Hestia's funds. And whatever the Onitadai claim, the Molpoi have decided to entrust it to the crown-wearers.**

The Onitadai were responsible for the specialized task of butchering, cooking and distributing the meat from the sacrifices performed once the procession reached Didyma. They also had to bake the cakes for Apollo and Hekate (a substantial job, considering that half a *medimnos* of grain or flour was 20.5 liters). In return, they received many perquisites, including prime cuts of meat and leftovers. The *thualēmata* were either pieces of meat or balls of kneaded barley used during the sacrifice; the *thua* ("sacrificed things") were probably cakes.[107] This part of the decree includes several later additions, the most important of which is the decision made by the Molpoi in the year of Charopinos (476/5) to use public funds for the supplies in case the Onitadai did not carry out their duties. The addition was made soon after the refounding of Miletos, and it may indicate that the *genos* of the Onitadai had declined as a result of the Persian destruction of Miletos, losing the personnel and resources to participate.

## Other matters concerning the expenses

> **For the herald, (there is) an exemption from all expenses in the Molpon, and (he has) the (duty of) dividing the entrails of each of the sacrifices, and transporting the wine to the cooler at his own expense, but the wine is provided by the Molpoi. And the priest (of Apollo Delphinios) provides the feast to the singer, and the *aisumnētēs* provides the lunch.**

According to Herda, these provisions date to the Classical or late Classical period (as do most of the additions to the original written text). Like the earlier section on the duties and privileges of the Onitadai, these additions clarify which persons are to undertake which tasks and expenses, and what each is to receive in return.[108]

Multiple changes to the original text accrued over time, and they show that whenever a question of precedence, duties or expenses arose, clarifications to the procedure were recorded. For example, a question arose about how much flour was to be used for the cakes, and whether the allotments of cakes for Apollo and Hekate were separate. What we almost completely lack is instructions for the use of the cakes in the ritual, because knowledge of these aspects was assumed. Continuity in the elements of the ritual most pertinent to efficacy depended on the unbroken service of the Molpoi over the years, and their collective memories. We can only wonder how many former Molpoi survived the destruction of Miletos in order to return and reestablish the ritual, and what losses and reconstructions occurred as a result of the probable gap in performance.[109] What the Molpoi Decree tells us is that despite the use of writing, many aspects of ritual procedure must have changed over time. The hymns too were transmitted from one man to the next over the generations, almost certainly without the aid of writing. Their musical and rhythmic format helped to preserve them in memory, and as we have seen, the maintenance of a strict performance order could have been a mnemonic tool as well.

There is, however, a hint that some part of the age-old duty of memory and performance was eventually handed over to professionals. In this section of the decree, dated to the fourth century, we learn that the Molpoi have begun to require the services of a singer (*ōidos*), who is to be fed by the priest of Apollo Delphinios and the *aisumnētēs*. Like temple architecture and sculptural styles, musical fashions changed, and the role of the singer may have been to delight Apollo with exquisite new songs, in addition to the hymns deemed essential to ancestral custom.[110]

## ESSAY 6.2: HERACLES AS A PAN-MEDITERRANEAN DEITY

Uniquely among Greek heroes, Herakles was known and worshiped throughout the Mediterranean world and beyond, by both Greeks and non-Greeks.[111] But how did knowledge of Herakles spread so broadly and thoroughly, and what was its appeal? To investigate this question, we will first consider intercultural and cross-cultural networks, which allowed information to be disseminated within and beyond the Greek world. Map 6.1 illustrates a simple network, constructed from data in Pindar's victory odes, of athletes attending the Olympic games at the Panhellenic sanctuary of Olympia between 476 and 456. This is the period when the Temple of Zeus, with its twelve metopes representing the Labors of Herakles, was under construction. It was at Olympia, scholars have suggested, that the set of labors later canonized as the Twelve were first depicted as a group.[112] From the map we can see (on a strictly hypothetical basis) how this idea of a fixed canon of Twelve Labors, rather than an indefinite number, could become widely distributed in a relatively short time. Assuming that the network operated consistently, with athletes traveling back and forth from the same cities, information originating in any city could easily spread to all the others. Alternatively, we might construct networks based on religious ambassadorship and pilgrimage (*theoria*), the visits of itinerant craftsmen and merchants to Olympia for the games and so on.[113]

The diffusion of religious culture in the Mediterranean and Black Sea was facilitated by the unique physical environment of the region, with its extensive coastlines and numerous islands. Imagine a far more detailed map marked with dots ("nodes") representing Greek cities in the fifth century. As in Map 6.1, the fact of connectivity between two nodes is represented by a line between them, and content (goods and information) moves back and forth along these lines. If we mark up the map with dots and lines, what emerges is a decentralized network characterized by "clusters" (groups of nodes which all link to a highly connective node, such as a mother-city, an interstate trade depot or a Panhellenic sanctuary). Clusters in turn are not self-contained, but connect with each other, sometimes from one central node to another, and sometimes less directly. Crucially, these clusters or regional networks may possess only indirect or weak ties with each other, but as long as a few such ties exist, the larger network maintains an unimpeded ability to circulate goods or information. This is what network theorists call a "small world."[114] In a small world, distance is not measured geographically, but by the number of nodes between two points (in Map 6.1, for example, all the cities of the athletic victors are "equidistant" from each other). In the ancient Mediterranean, connectivity was achieved primarily through sea travel, so that geographically distant cities often had more interaction than closer ones separated by land.

Our map could also be expanded to include connections with non-Greek maritime networks and with both Greeks and non-Greeks in the hinterlands. The latter two possibilities are especially pertinent to the creation of a Pan-Mediterranean deity like Herakles. Network theory thus offers us productive new ways to think about cultural change and exchange in the Greek world. Irad Malkin has theorized, for example, that during the early Archaic period, strong connectivity among far-flung coastal Greek cities was responsible for the emergence of a Hellenic cultural identity. This means that, in contrast to our Olympia example, ideas from the "periphery" fundamentally changed the way Greeks in the homeland thought of themselves. Network theory challenges traditional notions of center and periphery, since a "center" is defined not by cultural prestige but by high connectivity, and a network may have more than one highly connective node.[115]

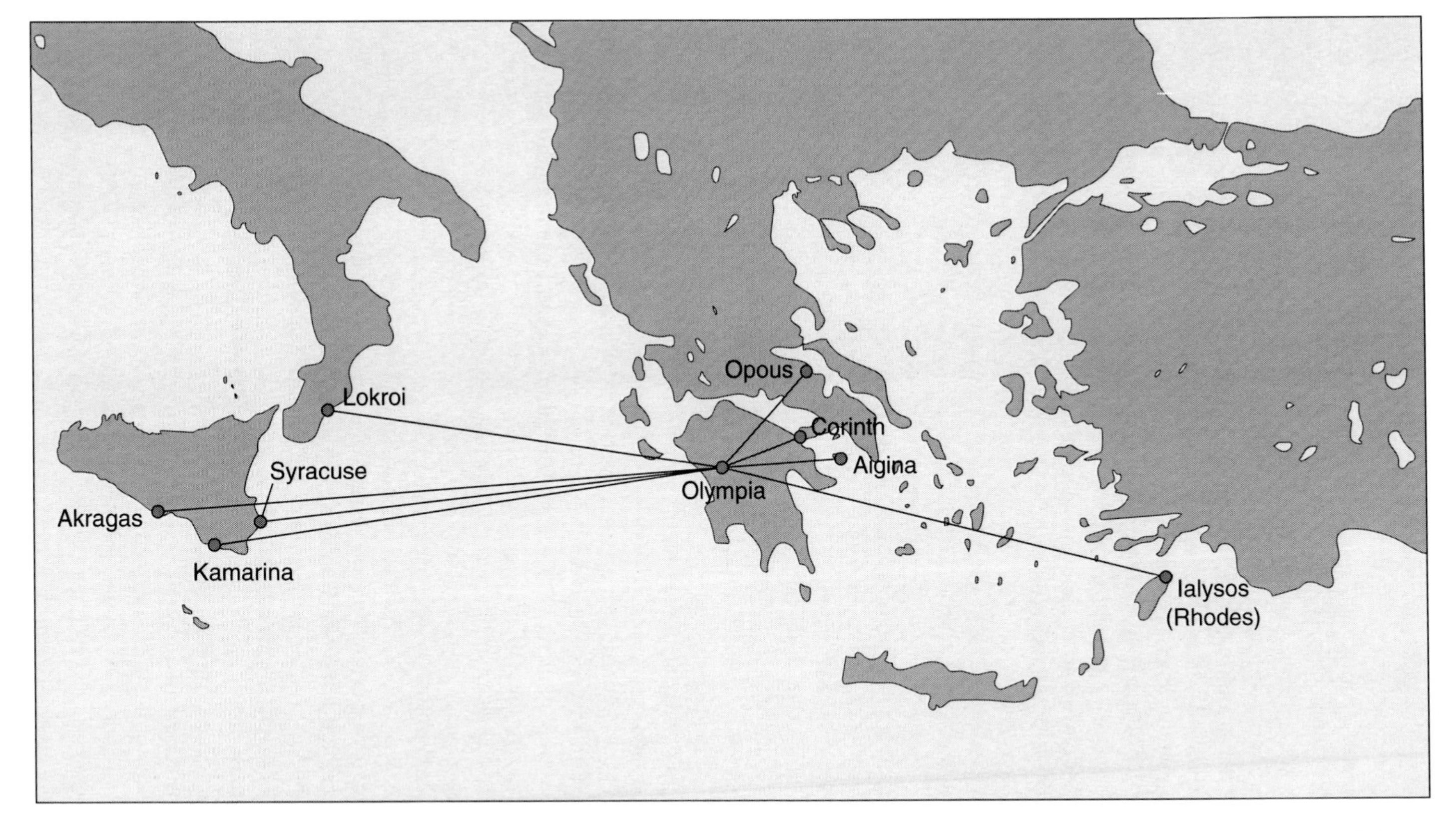


*Map 6.1* A simple network: athletes attending the Olympic games at the Panhellenic sanctuary of Olympia between 476 and 456, who commissioned victory odes by Pindar.

Network theory helps us see how a given representation (e.g. Herakles wrestling the Nemean Lion), whether spoken, written or crafted, could be rapidly disseminated, especially in a polytheistic context favorable to cultural blending. Yet we still need to explain why it was Herakles, rather than some other hero or god, who became so widely known. According to the principles laid out in previous chapters, we should expect wider cross-cultural dissemination of Herakles as a superhuman *agent* than as an inert, dead man, no matter how impressive his past exploits. Herakles the god was more salient and compelling to non-Greek peoples than Herakles the man because they could expect to interact with him or to benefit from his magical potency (on which more below).

Dan Sperber and Deirdre Wilson have proposed that the process of cultural transmission exerts pressure in the direction of representations that are *relevant*.[116] Relevance in this technical sense means, first, that a given representation (e.g. a mental image of Herakles with his club raised to strike, or fighting a monster for his cattle) requires *less cognitive effort* to grasp and remember than others which are available for transmission (e.g. Herakles' dual identity as man and god, which was a complex piece of theology). Second, it means that a given representation produces *more cognitive effects* than others. That is, the representation is cognitively salient (strongman battles monster being an ever-popular concept), or activates mental tools (Is the strongman a god?), or is emotionally compelling (Could the strongman help me?), or is richly evocative, reminding an individual of multiple things already known to him or her (I herd cattle too) or all of these things.

Theoretically, Herakles could evoke an infinite number of associations, but in practice we find that certain themes were recurrent because they resonated with the recipient peoples. The Phoenicians, active colonizers like the Greeks, emphasized the motif of Herakles as founder, while trade, cattle herding, general warding off of evils and healing were important to the Italian peoples. Some of these themes were grounded in Herakles' myths and were dependent on bilingual interaction, while others could have been shaped purely by local responses to iconography or very simple kernels of translated narrative. In each case, the concepts selected for elaboration were relatively simple compared to their Greek counterparts, and closely matched the needs and interests of the receptive individuals and cultures. Transmission occurred both visually and linguistically, as we see from iconography, from shared myths and from the retention of Herakles' name (Hercules in Latin, Hercle in Etruscan).

## Herakles among the Greeks

As one of the oldest Greek heroes, Herakles may have been known to the Mycenaeans. Already in the eighth century, his fame was Panhellenic. The *Iliad* alludes to the hero's conception and birth at Thebes, his servitude to Eurystheus, his attack on Pylos and his sack of Troy. Despite his divine parentage, Herakles was doomed to share the common fate of mortals (Hom. *Il.* 18.117–19): "For not even the mighty Herakles escaped death, he who was dearest to Lord Zeus son of Kronos, but Fate and the grievous anger of Hera overpowered him." In the *Odyssey* (11.601–26), however, only Herakles' simulacrum (*eidōlon*) is said to reside in Hades, whereas he himself feasts on Olympos and has Hebe as his bride. Hesiod's *Theogony* too recognizes Herakles' apotheosis, and does not seek consistency with the *Iliad*:

> The mighty son of lovely-ankled Alkmene, Herakles,
> When his groaning ordeals were ended, wed Hebe,
> The child of great Zeus and gold-sandaled Hera,
> And made her his reverend wife on snowy Olympos.
> That blessed one (*olbios*), his great work complete, dwells
> With the immortals, carefree and ageless all his days.
> (Hes. *Theog.* 950–55)

Both passages likely result from early sixth-century additions to these prestigious texts, revealing how quickly and thoroughly the novel concept of Herakles' divinity had penetrated Greek culture. His transformation into a god heralded the sixth-century interest in afterlife rewards and the universalizing eschatologies of mystery cults. Herakles the Blessed was unique, yet blessedness was soon to become accessible to other mortals.[117]

The first firmly attested cults of Herakles did not appear until the seventh century, when the Greek city-state had already emerged. Only Thasos, itself founded in the seventh century, and a few other colonial cities claimed Herakles as a principal civic god. Yet his cults required no special efforts to ensure their propagation. By the sixth century, both the worship of Herakles and the doctrine of his apotheosis were ubiquitous; already ca. 600, a vase depicting his introduction to Olympos was produced in Corinth and exported to Etruria.[118] That Herakles was widely worshiped in Archaic and Classical Attica, even though none of his early myths are set there, illustrates his broad appeal. The Athenians boasted that they were the first to worship Herakles as a god, and eagerly created new myths of his reception in Athens: he was the first foreigner admitted to the Eleusinian Mysteries, and good king Theseus gave aid to Herakles and his children.[119]

Pindar calls Herakles a hero-god (*hērōs theos*), and this term sums up the conundrum faced by the Greeks when constructing rituals for him. Should they treat him as a god or as a hero? While both modes of worship involved animal sacrifice, hero cult was partly adapted from the rites for the dead and had a different set of conventions for the handling of the victim's blood and meat. Cults of Herakles tended to resemble those of the Olympian gods more than those of the heroes, but the great geographical scope of Herakles' worship ensured variety in his rituals. Herodotus approvingly states that some communities established a dual rite according to which Herakles received two sacrifices, one heroic and one divine. Often there was an emphasis on meat consumption (beef was a preferred food) and male commensality, which might involve the exclusion of women from the ritual.[120]

The unsurpassed prestige of Zeus' favorite son made him a desirable ancestor. Apollodorus lists sixty-seven children of Herakles, all sons. Among these offspring were the progenitors of aristocratic and royal families in Thebes, Thessaly, Sparta, Macedonia, Epeiros and Lydia.[121] Although Herakles was not in origin a Dorian hero, the Dorian people who entered the Peloponnese during the Early Iron Age appropriated him as an ancestor and promulgated the myth called the Return of the Herakleidai, which helped to establish their territorial claims. According to this account, Herakles was the rightful ruler of all the districts in the Peloponnese either by birth or by conquest, having overcome Neleus of Pylos, Augeias of Elis and Hippokoön, the usurper who temporarily wrested Sparta from Tyndareos. When Herakles died, his sons (known as the Herakleidai) were persecuted by his old enemy Eurystheus and driven away to the district of Doris in northern Greece. In the third generation, they returned as conquerors, and their people were the Dorians.

As a powerful hero-god, Herakles fulfilled many roles for the Greeks, but the most important are correlated with his mythic exploits. Before he could walk, Herakles strangled two serpents sent by Hera to attack him and his twin brother Iphikles in their crib. This popular story of his childhood points to Herakles' cultic role as a protector of the household. Just as Herakles fought monstrous beasts, cruel highwaymen and other adversaries during his lifetime, the hero-god protected his worshipers and their homes from all dangers material and metaphysical, including disease and misfortunes caused by malevolent spirits. People wore rings and other jewelry with Herakles' image in order to avail themselves of the god's magical protection, and painted verses with his name over their doorways. This Herakles, often called Kallinikos (Fair Conqueror) or Alexikakos (Averter of Evil), was depicted wielding both club and bow simultaneously.[122]

The rapid diffusion of Greek Herakles cults was motivated by perceptions of his powerful agency within ritual contexts and, often, outside of them. He was both "special patient" and "special agent," in the latter role presiding over cults of healing. Many legends tell of his agency on the battlefield, especially when armies encamped at or near his shrines. He appeared in dreams and effected miracles, such as the disappearance of his armor from his temple at Thebes before the Battle of Leuktra. The widespread magical use of Herakles' image and name in amulets depended on the belief that he was ever-active and potent against evils. Several of these agentive and magical features recur in his non-Greek cults.[123]

The transmission of representations about Herakles proceeded in stages, the earliest of which involved encounters between Greeks and the Phoenicians, especially the Tyrians, who colonized Carthage, Malta, Sardinia and Gadir (modern-day Cádiz). Melqart was a city god of Tyre, a dynastic founder-figure claimed as ancestor by the king. So important was he that the colonists of Gadir built a sanctuary for Melqart before they constructed the city itself. Like Herakles, Melqart combined the characteristics of god and hero.[124] In the Greek imagination, it was Herakles who first traveled to the far West, the ends of the earth, in the course of his Labors. Hesiod (*Theog*. 287–95, 979–83) speaks vaguely of Herakles' triumph over Geryon "in sea-girt Erythea," where there existed a "murky farmstead beyond glorious Ocean."

When Greek explorers, traders and colonists of the eighth century reached Sicily and the western shores of the Mediterranean, they found these lands already occupied not only by indigenes but also by the Phoenicians, whose seagoing and mercantile habits resembled their own. Through the process of evocation, which involves comparison with one's existing knowledge, individual Greeks "recognized" Herakles in the god Melqart, and Phoenicians recognized Melqart in the Greek hero-god. Like Melqart, Herakles was an ancestor of kings and a founder of dynasties, and like Melqart, he had staked a claim at the ends of the earth. Greek Herakles and Phoenician Melqart both evoked the concepts of territorial rights and land possession. In Herakles' case, as we saw, the myth of his great-great grandsons, the warlike Dorian Herakleidai, justified Spartan domination of the Peloponnese.[125] The detailed and extensive nature of these correspondences suggests a high degree of bilingual interaction and exchange of myths over centuries.

For his part, Melqart had much to do with colonization and the founding of cities. Herakles absorbed this property from his counterpart, and he became something of a patron saint for the Western Greek colonists. They had gained a foothold in Italy beginning in the eighth century, and over the next hundred years they went on to colonize the coastal lands of southern Italy and Sicily. New geographical knowledge was applied to the myth of Geryon, and the hero's journey with Geryon's cattle was traced through the West in great detail, providing a charter for Greek colonization. Many a Greek city in the West boasted some landmark or monument connected with Herakles. By the Classical period, Herakles himself was regarded as a founder of colonies.[126] A bilingual inscription from Hellenistic Malta illustrates a syncretism with much older roots: two brothers identifying themselves as Tyrians made a dedication to "Our Lord Melqart Baal of Tyre," who is rendered in Greek as "Herakles Archegetes."[127] The Greek title *archēgetēs* has the combined meaning of founder and ancestor, and is very close indeed to the Tyrian concept of Melqart.

The West was not the only point of repeated contact between Greeks and Phoenicians. The multicultural island of Cyprus, settled by Greeks as early as the second millennium, hosted Phoenician colonies by the eighth century, and its geographical location made it a natural point of dissemination for both Greek and Phoenician culture. By the fifth century, the workshops of Kition had developed a hybrid iconography of a youthful, unbearded deity wearing the lionskin and raising his hand to strike with a club.[128] The Greek settlers on Thasos in the mid-seventh century encountered a preexisting Tyrian colony and a thriving cult of Melqart, in whom they, like their counterparts in the West, recognized Herakles. The Thasian cult was unusual in that Herakles functioned as the city god, and it was noted in antiquity for its distinctive dual sacrifice to Herakles as both hero and god. In fact, the early syncretism with Melqart, reinforced in multiple locations throughout the Mediterranean, may have been responsible for the growing emphasis on the concept of "immortality achieved" in representations of Herakles. Interaction between Herakles and Melqart was thus a cumulative and reciprocal phenomenon.[129] Melqart contributed the *archēgetēs* element to the persona of Herakles, yet the lion attributes of Herakles were used in depictions of Melqart at Tyre itself as early as the sixth century, and in Cyprus.[130]

Among the peoples of Italy, it was the Etruscans who first worshiped Herakles, probably beginning ca. 600, when he began to be represented in their art. (Significantly, one of the earliest images shows Hercle with the cattle of Geryon.) The cultural impact of the Greeks, whose Italian colony of Cumae was already thriving in the eighth century, is illustrated by the Etruscans' use of a Greek-derived alphabet. Like most non-Greek peoples who encountered Herakles, the Etruscans seem to have considered him a god from the start. Hercle's rapid rise to popularity may also have been facilitated by syncretism with a preexisting deity, whom some scholars have recognized in an older god with attributes of bow and animal skin. The fact that several artistic depictions of myths about Hercle appear to have no Greek counterparts points in this direction.[131] Alternatively, representations of Herakles may simply have been compelling enough to generate new mythmaking within the Etruscan cultural context.

In Archaic Rome and its environs, local leaders were quick to adopt representations of Herakles, apparently hiring emigrant Ionian craftsmen for the purpose. Architectural sculptures of the late sixth and early fifth century from the roofs of temples at Rome, Veii, Caere, Satricum and Pyrgi share the iconography of Herakles' apotheosis. Introduced at Athens some thirty years previously, this "apotheosis" imagery of Herakles accompanied by a helmeted Athena was used, surprisingly, to decorate the temples of local goddesses connected with light and birth, such as Mater Matuta. Puzzled by this seeming mismatch, some scholars have characterized the sculptures as meaningless decorations, in spite of the fact that there is a clear pattern in their use, while others subscribe to the theory that local rulers were casting themselves (like the Athenian Peisistratos) in the role of Herakles, elevated to power under the care of the goddess. It seems most likely that the representations were not interpreted primarily in Greek cultural terms, but in the context of local religion, where such a pair could be understood as a ruler with a divine advisor, or as god and consort goddess.[132]

Dominated by Oscan and Umbrian-speaking peoples, the Eastern half of central Italy enthusiastically adopted representations of Herakles (from the Etruscans, Greeks or both) prior to Romanization. The first diffusion of the cult is traceable during the fifth and early fourth centuries through the production of bronze statuettes, intended as votive gifts, of the god in "smiting" pose with upraised arm (Figure 6.3).[133] Here the pertinent network has been identified as the *calles publicae*. These well-traveled routes for trade and seasonal movement of livestock held chains of sanctuaries containing dedications to Hercules. In many, he appears to have been the principal or sole recipient of worship. The fact that the sanctuaries were given monumental elaboration demonstrates that not only herdsmen but also local moneyed elites took an interest in the god and his protective powers. Several such sanctuaries were located in cattle markets, as at Superaequum, Alba Fucens and Rome itself, where the mythic link to cattle herding was again Hercules' labor in driving the Cattle of Geryon. His (non-Greek) adventure with Cacus illustrates the dangers herdsmen faced from cattle-raiders. From the evidence of anatomical ex-votos, he seems to have also functioned as a healing deity, particularly at sanctuaries associated with springs.[134]

*Figure 6.3* Bronze votive statuette of Hercules, from the sanctuary at Villa Cassarini in Bologna, Italy, ca. 400. Soprintendenza Archaeologica Emilia Romagna. Photo: Alfredo Dagli Orti/Art Resource

Thus, Herakles became a Pan-Mediterranean deity over the course of several centuries and by means of multiple networks: seagoing Greek colonists carried oral representations east and west, bringing them to the attention of their inland neighbors, while trade in objects bearing images of Herakles also stimulated interest. The extended encounters of Greeks and Phoenicians throughout the Mediterranean affected cultural perceptions of Herakles/Melqart on both sides, while Italian peoples reshaped Herakles for their own purposes. In order to achieve "relevance" in Sperber's sense, complex Greek versions of his myths were simplified or transformed, and certain themes were selected for elaboration because of their cognitive impact and cultural resonance. These included Herakles the cattle herder, the potent divine protector and the founder. As a superhuman agent, Herakles possessed strong appeal because of his potential to confer tangible benefits, such as successful trade and protection from disease. Vase paintings and figurines of Herakles wielding his bow, raising his club or battling monsters were easy to interpret as images of a powerful god. By comparison, the worship of an Achilles or Oedipus would have had to travel more slowly, with the spread of Greek language and culture among non-Greeks. But the same factors that allowed Herakles to move so rapidly beyond the boundaries of Greek culture also permitted recipient individuals and cultures to freely adapt representations of the hero-god to their own needs.

In later centuries, Alexander's conquests witnessed a different modality of diffusion for representations of Herakles, which were deliberately implanted in the Near East as signs of triumphant and politically dominant Hellenism. In royal iconography, Alexander wore the lionskin of the hero he had claimed as his ancestor, and the conqueror's successors adopted images of Herakles for their own use.[135] The diffusion in this case took place from a series of capital city "nodes" where the new ruling class had installed itself. Herakles was carried far afield to Palmyra, Parthia, Iran and the borderland of India; in each of these regions some degree of assimilation with local deities took place. Herakles evoked immortality, divine protection/healing, military victory and other concepts of broad appeal. So productive was Herakles as a syncretic deity that Cicero could list six distinct Herculeses who belonged to differing ages and lands; this list, including a Hercules of Egypt, of Tyre and of India, was certainly only a fraction of the total.[136]

## ESSAY 6.3: THE ORIGINS OF SARAPIS

> The early Ptolemies, kings of Egypt, Macedonians themselves, wished to blend the traditions of the native Egyptians, their Macedonian soldiers and the many Greek settlers, and they transformed and Hellenized Osiris, renamed him Sarapis and made him into the patron of their dynasty. Ptolemy I Soter had an Egyptian priest, Manetho, and two Athenians, the Eumolpid Timotheus and Demetrios of Phaleron, develop mythology, liturgy and ritual hymns for Sarapis, and his cult statue was Greek, not Egyptian, in form.[137]

This recent description of the god Sarapis reflects a conventional wisdom which continues to hold sway among many Classicists. Yet most elements of this scholarly construct have been questioned.[138] It is helpful to shift our perspective and to reexamine the common assumption that the story of Sarapis illustrates the political use of syncretism and Hellenization in order to unite a populace. We may ask instead – or in addition – to what degree the Ptolemies and their Greek subjects were being Egyptianized by the environment in which they found themselves, and we may question the claim that the robust Ptolemaic Sarapis cult was a product engineered by a committee of court experts rather than the result of more organic and spontaneous processes arising from the intersection of popular piety and royal patronage. Finally, the degree and pace of "Hellenization" in the first century of the cult need to be considered. Let us examine in detail four pieces of received wisdom about the origin of Sarapis.

## Sarapis did not exist before the reign of Ptolemy I Soter

In 1927, Ulrich Wilcken demonstrated that the name Sarapis and the origins of the god are to be attributed to the cult of the Apis bull in the ancient Pharaonic capital of Memphis. Upon its death, each Apis bull was divinized, joined with the godhead of Osiris and referred to as *Wsir-Ḥp* ("Osiris-Apis").[139] Among other papyrus materials adduced by Wilcken is a curse from Memphis, commissioned by a Greek-speaking woman, Artemisia, in the mid-fourth century. It appeals to "Oserapis" as an underworld deity able to carry out the curse. Although Artemisia's is the earliest known use of the name transcribed into Greek, archaeological evidence shows that Greek residents in Memphis were "going native" by worshiping this deity as early as the fifth century.[140] Artemisia's curse demonstrates that she regarded Oserapis as an underworld god similar to Hades/Plouton, to whom Greek magical curses were often addressed.[141]

That the name "Sarapis" is unattested before the time of Ptolemy I has often been cited in order to prove that Sarapis was a "new" god, yet both "Sarapis" and "Oserapis" must have originated as attempted transcriptions of *Wsir-Ḥp* or, alternatively, the form *Sr-Ḥp* ("Omen-Apis"), referring to *Wsir-Ḥp's* oracular powers.[142] By the middle of the long reign of Ptolemy I Soter as satrap and king (323–283), the name "Sarapis" had already become widely disseminated. In the late fourth century, Nymphodoros of Syracuse proposed an etymology for the name Sarapis based on the god's origins in the Apis cult. Nikokreon, a king of Cyprus who died in 312/11, received an oracle identifying Sarapis with the cosmos. In a fragment of the Athenian comic poet Menander (died 290), a character exclaims, "How holy is the god Sarapis!"[143]

Was Ptolemy I responsible for the expanded Greek interest in this deity? None of these early sources connects him with Sarapis. Nor do they associate Sarapis with Alexandria; rather, they speak of Memphis. Scholars have confidently attributed the "creation" of Sarapis to Ptolemy I Soter because it is clear that the name was known during the reign of Soter, and because Plutarch and Tacitus name Soter as the innovator. But as we will see, these two accounts partake more of myth than of history.

## Sarapis was the "creation" of Ptolemy I, who formed a strategic plan to Hellenize an indigenous god

In 1972, John Stambaugh deplored the common claim that the Ptolemies had "created" Sarapis, given archaeological evidence that the cult of Osiris-Apis predated the reign of Ptolemy I, and had become popular among Greeks living in Memphis by the time of his accession.[144] No ancient witness says that a Ptolemy deliberately set out to create a new deity, much less that he did so for political reasons. The creation theory as well as the milder formulation that the Ptolemies "transformed and Hellenized" Osiris is based primarily on a pair of related first-century CE narratives by Plutarch and Tacitus. According to Plutarch,

> Ptolemy Soter saw in a dream the colossal statue of Plouton in Sinope, although he had never seen it and did not know what it looked like. In his dream the statue commanded him to bring it immediately to Alexandria. He had no information and no way of knowing where the statue had been set up, but when he related the vision to his friends, they located for him a man named Sosibios, who had traveled much. He said that he had viewed in Sinope just such a colossal statue as the king thought he saw. Ptolemy, therefore, sent Soteles and Dionysios, who, after a long time, barely managed to steal the statue and bring it away, with the help of divine providence. When it had been brought to Egypt and displayed, Timotheus the Exegete and Manetho of Sebennytos, together with their associates, concluded that it was the statue of Plouton because of the Kerberos and the serpent with it, and they convinced Ptolemy that it was none other of the gods but Sarapis. It did not come from Sinope with this name, but, after it had been brought to Alexandria, it acquired the name which Plouton bears among the Egyptians, Sarapis.
>
> (Plut. *De Is. et Os.* 361f–362a)

Notice that Plutarch's account is narrowly focused on the advent of a distinctive statue. Tacitus' version differs in several details, but likewise is concerned exclusively with the origin of "the god" (i.e. the statue in Alexandria):

> The origin of this god has not yet been made generally known by our writers. The Egyptian priests give the following account. When Ptolemy, the first of the Macedonians to consolidate the power of Egypt, was providing the newly-built city of Alexandria with fortifications, temples, and rites of worship, there appeared to him in his sleep a young man of extraordinary beauty and more than human stature, who advised the monarch to send his most faithful friends to Pontos, and bring back his statue. He said that this would be a happy thing for the kingdom, and that the city which received it would be great and famous. As soon as these words were spoken, the young man seemed to ascend to heaven in a great flame. Roused by this ominous and wondrous event, Ptolemy disclosed his night vision to the Egyptian priests, whose business it is to understand such things. But they knew little of Pontos or of foreign countries, so he questioned the Athenian Timotheus (a man of the Eumolpid clan whom he had invited from Eleusis as an overseer of the sacred rites) about this worship, and who the deity was. By asking people who had been to Pontos, Timotheus learned that a city Sinope was there, and nearby a temple of Jupiter Dis [i.e. Hades/Plouton], long famous among the locals, for beside him sat a female figure, which most called Proserpina [i.e. Kore/Persephone]. But although

> Ptolemy was prone to alarm, as is the nature of kings, once a feeling of security returned he grew more intent on pleasures than on religious matters. Gradually he began to neglect the matter, turning his mind to other concerns, until the same vision, now more terrible and insistent, threatened ruin to king and realm alike unless his orders were carried out.
>
> [Ptolemy dispatches a delegation to Sinope with gifts for King Scydrothemis. The ambassadors receive an oracle from Pythian Apollo instructing them to "fetch the statue of his father but to leave that of his sister." Scydrothemis hesitates and procrastinates for three years in the face of increasingly dire divine omens, finally putting the matter to the people, who reject Ptolemy's request.]
>
> The story becomes more strange at this point: the god of his own accord came on board the fleet, which was lying onshore, and miraculously they crossed the wide expanse of sea, arriving at Alexandria on the second day. A temple, proportioned to the grandeur of the city, was erected in a place called Rhakotis. On that spot there had been in ancient times a chapel dedicated to Sarapis and Isis. Such is the most popular account of the origin and arrival of the god Sarapis. Yet I am aware that there are some who say that he was brought from Seleukia, a city of Syria, in the reign of Ptolemy III, while others claim that it was the act of the same king, but that the place from which he was brought was Memphis, once a famous city and the strength of ancient Egypt.
>
> (Tac. *Hist*. 4.83–4)

Far from being the mastermind of a new religious policy, Ptolemy I is portrayed by Tacitus as neglectful of divine mandates, and by Plutarch as a rather hapless but pious king who requires multiple friends and advisors to interpret his dream experience. These characterizations are compounded from folklore motifs which recur in Greek, Near Eastern and Egyptian accounts of dream epiphanies. (The most familiar version of the tale is Genesis 41, in which Pharaoh sends for "all the magicians and the wise men of Egypt" to interpret his dream.) The variation among the three witnesses to the story and the miraculous nature of the accounts demonstrate that this is a highly embellished cult legend rather than a straightforward narrative of historical events.[145] A far less elaborate version of the story, this time pertaining to Ptolemy II, is preserved by Clement of Alexandria:

> They dare to speak of Egyptian Sarapis as having been made without the work of hands, but some relate that he was sent as a gift of thanks by the people of Sinope to Ptolemy [II] Philadelphos, king of the Egyptians, who gained their friendship by sending them grain from Egypt when they were dying in a famine; and that this carved image was a statue of Plouton; and Ptolemy, having received the figure, placed it on the height which is now called Rhakotis . . .
>
> (Clement of Alexandria *Protreptikos* 4)

The common thread in all three accounts is that a statue was brought (from Sinope or Seleukia or Memphis) to Alexandria during the reign of one of the Lagid kings (Ptolemy I according to Plutarch and Tacitus, Ptolemy II according to Clement, and Ptolemy III according to other versions known to Tacitus).[146] This statue was thought to represent Plouton/Sarapis, and was installed in a shrine on the hill of Rhakotis in Alexandria (for a Roman copy, see Figure 6.4).

The sources say nothing of a plan to create a new god. Instead, they record pious legends developed to explain how a fully anthropomorphic, Greek-style statue was introduced to a preexisting Egyptian cult. Native Egyptian cult images of Apis depicted a bull with the sun disk between its horns, and *Wsir-Ḥp* was regularly shown as a seated male figure with a bull's head.[147] To Greek eyes, this form of his cult image would have suggested the Cretan Minotaur, a circumstance which made an alternative iconography desirable – particularly as *Wsir-Ḥp* was to receive royal patronage as a dynastic god, closely associated with the king. In this capacity, his Osiris aspect came to the fore and he was (as in Pharaonic tradition) constantly paired with his consort Isis. Thus Sarapis and Isis became divine counterparts of Ptolemy II and his queen Arsinoë.[148]

Tacitus and others speak of an ancient shrine on Rhakotis; unfortunately the earliest rock-cut foundation trenches at the site cannot be dated. Dedications suggest that the site was first used as a sanctuary between 300 and 275, which is compatible with initial construction at the end of the long reign of Ptolemy I Soter, or the beginning of the reign of Ptolemy II Philadelphos. The oldest architectural remains consist of a T-shaped building enclosing a staircase with an underground passage to the "South Building." Both of these structures, as well as an unidentified foundation wall, predate the enclosure of the sanctuary and the lavish temple built by Ptolemy III Euergetes (246–221). In this temple, Euergetes left native-style foundation plaques of gold, silver, bronze, mud and other materials, bilingually recording his dedication of the structure to *Wsir-Ḥp*/Sarapis.[149] His successor, Ptolemy IV Philopator (221–205), used similar plaques of multiple materials, including six different colors of glass, when he added a temple for Harpokrates to the complex. These plaques show that, far from being represented as a new god, Alexandrian Sarapis was, in the minds of the early Ptolemies and their allied priests, the same god as the venerable *Wsir-Ḥp*.[150]

In the Alexandrian Serapeion, the Ptolemies created a hybrid cultural environment for the god. The Serapeion was built not on low ground in Egyptian style but in Greek fashion on the highest hill of the city: Sarapis was to be the patron god of Alexandria. The architecture of the sanctuary was uniformly "Classical" Greek in appearance. Several identifiable conventions pertaining to ritual, however, were distinctively Egyptian, including the foundation plaques, a Nilometer, a birth house and an underground passage which may have been related to a native-style oracle. These circumstances point to an Egyptian priesthood.[151] The ethnicity of Sarapis' priests during the early Ptolemaic period is difficult to determine because of a lack of evidence and the fact that Egyptians often took Greek names. The earliest documented priest of Sarapis is the Egyptian Phemmenas, mentioned as *hiereus* of Isis and Sarapis at Philadelphia in a papyrus of the mid-third century.[152] Another Egyptian priest (with the Greek name Apollonios) brought the cult from Memphis to Delos in the third century. By 166, the priest on Delos was a Greek,

*Figure 6.4* Statue of Sarapis, seated with Kerberos. Roman copy of the famous cult statue in Alexandria. Hermitage, St. Petersburg. Photo: HIP/Art Resource

but he required the assistance of an Egyptian.[153] Taken together, this evidence suggests that during the first hundred years of Ptolemaic rule, Egyptian priests remained important in Sarapis' cults.

The Alexandrian branch of the cult did not involve the tending and burial of the physical Apis bull, which could take place in only one location, and which was firmly entrenched in Memphis. Inevitably, the shift of the capital from Memphis to Alexandria, which happened early in the reign of Ptolemy I, left the *Wsir-Ḥp* cult open to change. Once it arrived in the new capital, it seems to have developed a function as a precursor to full dynastic cult (so that dedications to Sarapis were made "for" or "on behalf of" the king). It may also have reproduced features of the Memphis cult pertaining to healing, dreams and oracles.[154] These "special agent" aspects of Sarapis, rather than the "special patient" elements of his dynastic cult, allowed the god to capture the imagination of his Greek worshipers.

Whether we deem a *Wsir-Ḥp* in Greek dress to be a "new god" is a matter of perspective. Egyptians generally did not consider Sarapis a new god; at most he was, like Osiris, merely another aspect of *Wsir-Ḥp*, but one with limited appeal because of his Greek cultural trappings.[155] Most Greeks must likewise have perceived Sarapis as an old Egyptian god while simultaneously identifying him with Plouton, and later with other Greek deities, including Asklepios and Dionysos. There is no evidence that worshipers perceived Sarapis as a previously unknown god who had suddenly begun to manifest himself. Sarapis' Alexandrian sanctuary appears to have combined Greek architecture and a Greek cult statue with preexisting Egyptian ritual procedures. The real question at issue is whether this syncretism was planned as a strategic measure.

At the end of his reign, Ptolemy I (or more likely, Ptolemy II) attempted to strengthen his legitimacy in Egyptian eyes by following the Pharaonic tradition of treating Osiris-Apis as a dynastic deity.[156] The new location of the capital in Alexandria, however, required the establishment of a branch sanctuary for the god. That Greek rulers desired Greek architecture for the "akropolis" of their new capital is not surprising. Even the famous cult statue, the source of the "new god" myth, seems less innovative when viewed as part of a building program; it was normal Greek practice to provide a new cult statue for a new temple.[157] Each of these innovations flowed naturally from the decision to adopt *Wsir-Ḥp* as a dynastic deity. In other words, the novel aspects of Sarapis in Alexandria resulted from the need for the Ptolemies to meet Egyptian expectations about the relationship between the ruler and the gods. They illustrate a process of mutual accommodation by both the Ptolemies and the Egyptian priests of *Wsir-Ḥp*. Above all, they can be explained without recourse to the idea that Ptolemy I Soter developed a sophisticated religious policy in furtherance of strategic goals.

## Ptolemy I convened a council of experts, including the Greeks Timotheus and Demetrios, and the Egyptian Manetho, who created the god and elaborated his rituals

Although often presented as historical fact, the "council of experts" is a hypothesis based primarily on the account by Plutarch, who mentions Timotheus, Manetho and "their associates." Tacitus speaks of Egyptian priests who fail to interpret the dream, causing the king to turn to Timotheus for help, while Clement has nothing to say of experts. None of the three names Demetrios of Phaleron, an exiled Athenian statesman who was resident at the court of Ptolemy I. He was added to the "council" because he is known to have penned hymns to the god, apparently after he himself was cured of eye problems, and to have compiled an extensive collection of dream epiphanies of Sarapis.[158]

Timotheus was a Eumolpid, a member of the Athenian *genos* responsible for administering the Eleusinian Mysteries. According to Tacitus, Ptolemy I had "invited him from Eleusis, as an overseer of the sacred rites." Timotheus has therefore been assigned a role in establishing the offshoot of the Attic Demeter cult which was situated in an Alexandrian suburb named after Eleusis.[159] Timotheus is sometimes said also to have established mysteries for Isis and/or Sarapis, but this is only a guess based on his presence at court and a hymn of the second century CE which links Eleusinian and Isaic rites.[160] Mysteries involving Sarapis are not actually attested until the Roman period. As for the Egyptian priest Manetho, doubts have been raised about his role, and even his presence, at the Ptolemaic court.[161]

New work by Giles Gorre indicates that contact between the priestly class and the Macedonian court was limited during the reign of Ptolemy I, and that coordination and cooperation were lacking. Due to the conditions under which he became the ruler of Egypt, Ptolemy I did not enjoy close relations with the old priestly families. The impact of his military occupation on the temples is made clear in private priestly inscriptions which do not recognize him as a king or as a pharaoh (and it is doubtful whether he underwent coronation as a pharaoh).[162] Thus it is unlikely that a sophisticated political strategy to harness religion for political purposes, particularly one involving close cooperation with Egyptian priests and dynastic cult, could have been developed until late in his reign.

Ptolemy II, on the other hand, is known to have formulated a religious policy. He funded temples and appointed priests on the condition that they install statues of himself and his queen. Ptolemy II seems a better fit for the push to transform Sarapis into a true dynastic deity; indeed only with the co-regency of Ptolemy II was a Ptolemaic "dynasty" actually established. According to Gorre, his reign inaugurated a new period of contact between the Macedonian court and Egyptian priests, whereby temples began to grow financially dependent on the sovereign, and a new group of Egyptian priests, unrelated to the older priestly families, administered cults closely associated with the royal house.[163] This scenario is a good fit for the archaeological evidence from the Alexandrian Serapeion, both chronologically and with respect to the role of Egyptian priests. Crucially, however, Sarapis cannot have been "created" by Ptolemy II, because as we have seen, the god's name was already widely known in the late fourth century. That Demetrios of Phaleron was able to gather enough dream epiphanies of Sarapis to fill five books between ca. 297 and his death ca. 283 points to a strong popular element in the growth of the cult under Ptolemy I. Perhaps the Macedonian court was reacting to Greek interest in Sarapis rather than creating it.

## Ptolemy I Soter promoted the cult of Sarapis in order to unite his Egyptian and Greek subjects

Sarapis clearly had a political function as a patron god of Alexandria associated with the Ptolemaic dynasty, yet no ancient source supports the hypothesis of a plan by the Ptolemies to unify Greeks and Egyptians through religion.[164] Had the Ptolemies specifically wished to attract Egyptians to the Alexandrian Serapeion, they would hardly have constructed a distinctively Greek-appearing sanctuary and installed a Greek statue. At least until the second century, most dedications to Sarapis under that name in Egypt were (not surprisingly) made by Greeks, while Egyptians continued to focus their attentions on the native version of the *Wsir-Ḥp* cult.[165] From the time they began to settle in Memphis, the Greek population had "Egyptianized" through their participation in this foreign cult, and even if the god now possessed a comfortingly familiar Greek-style cult statue and temple in Alexandria, many of Sarapis' ritual procedures remained Egyptian in flavor. The prominence of Egyptian elements in the ritual, however, was not due to strategic planning, but rather to the fact that the *Wsir-Ḥp* cult required them. Initially, Greeks lacked the expertise to perform the rituals, and Egyptian ethnicity may even have been perceived as necessary for ritual efficacy. Hybridization followed, but it must have proceeded at different rates in different places.

Both in Egypt and abroad, the cult of Sarapis spread not through the efforts of the Ptolemies but through the piety and curiosity of individual Greeks experiencing the god.[166] Sarapis' agency regularly involved highly motivating dream epiphanies and healing miracles, which occurred when people were visiting his sanctuaries, either spontaneously or as the result of formal incubation. Within Egypt, we have the evidence of a papyrus letter sent in 257 to Apollonios, an official in the court of Ptolemy II. The sender, Zoïlos, relates that Sarapis appeared to him in a dream "while I was paying worship on behalf of your health and success with King Ptolemy." If Kent Rigsby is correct that the letter refers to Memphis, this likely means that Zoïlos had his dream at the great *Wsir-Ḥp* sanctuary outside the city at Saqqara. The god commanded the construction of a branch altar and shrine "in the Greek quarter, near the port." Zoïlos reported that his initial failure to obey the oracle (*chrēmatismon*) resulted in a near-mortal illness, from which he recovered only by vowing to carry out the divine instructions. Zoïlos therefore was a Greek devotee of *Wsir-Ḥp*/Sarapis who hoped to establish a shrine in his own neighborhood, with financial assistance from Apollonios. It would be interesting to know what blend of Greek and Egyptian features Zoïlos planned, and whether he envisioned a Greek or Egyptian priest.[167]

Two instances of the cult's early dissemination abroad further illustrate the role of individual worshipers. In Greece, Sarapis appeared to a man named Xenainetos, directing him to go to Opous and there announce to one Eurynomos that he must receive Sarapis and Isis; the story was recorded in an inscription placed in the sanctuary founded there.[168] On Delos, Sarapis was introduced from Memphis (not from Alexandria) by an Egyptian named Apollonios, who brought sacred objects to the island and handed down his priesthood to his son and grandson. The grandson was instructed in a dream to build a sanctuary, and succeeded in doing so, battling a lawsuit over the project with the miraculous help of Sarapis. He too recorded his experience in an inscription.[169]

As Ian Moyer notes, the word "syncretism" often carries an unacknowledged baggage of cultural assumptions about who is guiding the process and for what purposes. In the nineteenth century, Classicists uncritically assumed imperialist planning by wise Greeks, and considered "Hellenization" a signal benefit to benighted "Oriental" peoples.[170] During the twentieth century, the religious skepticism of many scholars was projected into the past, exaggerating the powers of the Ptolemies to manufacture religious fervor according to a predetermined script, and in service to political goals. Reexamination of the fourth and third centuries yields a picture of growing Greek interest, manifested at both the popular and elite levels, in an indigenous god who fortuitously combined "special agent" features with an important political function.

## Notes

1 Corinth: see Spaeth 2011.63–5n.5; I thank Barbette Spaeth for allowing me to read a portion of her book in progress on cultic discontinuity at Corinth. See also Mackil 2004.70.
2 Zagora: Cambitoglou *et al.* 1988.171, 242.
3 Zeus and domestic worship: Mikalson 2010.124–6; Dowden 2006.80–4.
4 Kos: Paul 2013.217–8.
5 Nichomachos: Lys. 30.19; Parker 1996.152–3, 218–20; Stavrianopoulou 2011.86–96. For the remains of this calendar see Lambert 2002.
6 Delphi: Fontenrose 1978.255 (H33), mid-fourth century.
7 For neglected tithes see Suk Fong Jim 2014.83–4, 120, 235. Fine: e.g. the *pannuchis* at the Panathenaia is to be conducted "in the finest way for the goddess": *IG* II$^2$ 334 B 32–4 (mid-fourth century).
8 Ritual efficacy: see Essay 4.3 and Chaniotis 2007.96–7.
9 Priesthoods: Ostwald 1986.138 describes the particulars for democratic Athens; cf. Jameson 2014.248, 251.
10 *Ta patria*: Chaniotis 2007.102. Deviation certainly took place, but it was not necessarily perceived.
11 New cults: for example, the cult foundation of Epikteta (Essay 5.3) includes minute details, such as the size and type of cakes to be offered. Dispute: e.g. the decree of the Salaminioi (*RO* no. 37, dated 363/2), recording the arbitration of a dispute between two branches of the family. The use of inscriptions as mnemonic aids for cult practice increased substantially during the fourth century and after. On writing and religious authority see Henrichs 2003b.54–8.
12 Samian Heraion: Ohly 1953; Romano 1980.250–71.
13 Removal of votives forbidden: van Straten 1992.272. For inventories see Linders 1972; Aleshire 1989; Harris 1995; Hamilton 2000. For sanctuaries, treasuries and looting see Arafat 2009, esp. 587–8.
14 Perikles: Thuc. 2.13.4–5. Compare the outrage at the Phokians' conversion of dedications from Delphi into coin for their war effort (which was also, however, an appropriation of gifts made by others): Diod. Sic. 16.27.1–30.1; Paus. 10.2.3–4; Arafat 2009.587.
15 Coins for Asklepios: Linders 1987.116–17. Tithes converted to monuments and cult fees: Suk Fong Jim 2014.177–81, 250–66. Delphi: Fontenrose 1978. 251 (H21); for the oracular method used see Essay 2.2.

16 Change: Sperber 1996.58, 65–6. As textual critics know, even writing is subject to plenty of changes in transmission.

17 On learning ritual procedures see Rudhardt 1988.42–7; Bremmer 1995; Auffarth 2005. Basic knowledge of entrail-reading seems to have been passed from father to son: Flower 2008.53–58 (vase paintings with three generations). Compare Isae. 8.15–6 (sons learning sacrifice and domestic ritual); Xen. *Cyr.* 1.6.2–8 (instruction in divination). For a recent review of the debate over women's roles in sacrifice see Foxhall 2013.137–40. For the Erchia deme calendar see Essay 1.1.

18 For narrative mental schemata (scripts) as an organizing principle of long-term memory see Czachesz 2013.50–54. On scripts and religious ritual see McCauley and Lawson 2002.49.

19 On procedural memory, see the discussion of Whitehouse's modes theory in Chapter 4. On the role of emotion in remembering festivals, see Chaniotis 2006.

20 Details that did not conform: Lupu 2005.56.

21 Thasos: *LSCG* 114.

22 On the spot: Scullion 1994.99–101; Ekroth 2002.313–25. Pregnant animals: Lupu 2005.68; Bremmer 2005.

23 I use "exegesis" as a broad term encompassing both traditional content (myth, lore, procedural matters) and idiosyncratic content contributed by individual performers. Although verbal content was a normal part of Greek ritual, it has rarely been preserved and thus is downplayed in scholarly discussions: Pilz 2011.154–5.

24 Paean: Xen. *Hell.* 4.7.4. Compare Hom. *Il.* 1.472–4 (Achaian warriors sing the paean to Apollo); Thuc. 2.91.2, 7.75.7. On traditional hymns see Furley and Bremer 2001.1.14–28. With procedural and semantic memory, compare the "mechanical" and "deliberate" forms of memorization proposed by Borgeaud (Borgeaud ed. 1988.10) and discussed by Prescendi 2010.

25 Differential outcomes: my conclusions here agree with those of Whitehouse (2004.84n.21, 87–104), who emphasizes the disconnect between procedural and "exegetical" knowledge, citing experimental evidence that people are able to remember a sequence of ritual actions far more accurately than a statement about the meaning of the acts.

26 Verbal accompaniments: Naerebout (1997.201, 2006.53) is overoptimistic about the ability of people in oral cultures to memorize and transmit verbal elements of new choral performances seen once or even multiple times. Dance steps may have been a different matter, because they were stored by dancers in procedural memory, but see Naerebout's cautions (2006.55–8) against assuming that folk dances do not change in transmission.

27 A few dozen words: for discussion see McCauley and Lawson 2002.52 with bibliography. Gist: Rubin 1995.28 (e.g. stories consisting of causal chains, where the occurrence of each event is dependent on the previous one, are characteristic of stable oral traditions). Thomas 1989.123–31 demonstrates that family tradition among the Classical Athenians rarely showed accuracy beyond seventy years or three generations. On the essential role of metrical forms in the memorization of verbal content see Havelock 1982.186–7 and on the instability of oral tradition Vansina 1985.14–21. Porta 1999 collects and discusses the corpus of surviving Greek ritual utterances, which are characterized by simplicity, repetition, assonance, alliteration and rhyme.

28 On the use of choral song to reflect circumstances specific to time and place, see Kowalzig 2007.21, 29 and *passim*. Kowalzig's analysis of the interaction between myth and ritual is best applied to situations where writing was in play. It is not that new hymns were never composed orally, but that oral composition was subject to much greater constraints of form and content.

29 On the expense and "special occasion" nature of cult songs commissioned from poets see Kowalzig 2007.7. On the question of reperformance, see Herington 1985.48–50, 207–10 (primary sources); Naerebout 2006.52 with n. 49.

30 Traditional hymns: almost all have been lost because of the near-exclusive use of oral transmission. In the extant corpus of hymns, Furley and Bremer (2001, Vol. 1) identify as traditional the Palaikstro hymn to Zeus (1.1), the Erythraian paean to Asklepios (6.1) and the Elean women's invocation of Dionysos (12.1).

31 Literacy: Havelock 1982.187–8, 262; Harris 1989; Thomas 1992. "Literacy" in many cases consisted of very elementary skills, such as the ability to write one's name.

32 Ritual efficacy: Chaniotis 2012.124 distinguishes between "dedications and prayers" and "magical rituals and rituals of purification," with the latter more likely to be written. (See e.g. the level of detail in the Kyrene cathartic law, Essay 3.3.)

33 Perceived and actual variation: McCauley and Lawson 2002.52–3, 84. On perceptions of continuous tradition in ritual see Bell 2009.118–24.

34 Rome: Hahn 2007.236. On the importance of writing in early Roman religion and its close association with priestly duties see Beard, North and Price 1998.1.9–20. See also Auffarth 2005.15–16 (on Greeks vs. Romans).

35 On written oracles, in use from the late seventh century, see Bremmer 2010.14–16. In the case of curse tablets and amulets, the magical efficacy attributed to the words themselves required that an exemplar be reproduced as accurately as possible.

36 On hereditary priesthoods and ritual expertise see Chaniotis 2008.21–2, 31; Parker 2011.43–4; Jameson 2014.240, 248. On the oral transmission of aristocratic family tradition see Thomas 1989.95–195. For "expounders" (*exegētai*) at Athens and elsewhere see Kearns 2010.170–1; Parker 2011.45, and for "rememberers" (*mnēmones*, *hieromnēmones*) of ritual, financial and legal matters see Parker 1996.52; Carawan 2008. Cole 2008.61–2 points out that hereditary status was no guarantee of expertise.

37 Solonian calendar of the sixth century: Parker 1996.43–55, esp. 51–2: "it is clear that traditional usage remains unexpressed in the early calendars, and must have been left to the collective memory of the memory of priests."

38 Methods for allocation of priesthoods: Lupu 2005.44–53 with bibliography. The earliest attested sale of a priesthood is from fifth-century Miletos, and the custom was common only in parts of Asia Minor (Ionia, Karia and Kos). Allocation by lot within *genē*: Parker 1996.58, 292n. 21.

39 *Arrhēphoroi* ("carriers of [x]"; the etymology of the second element is debated): Parker 2005.220–23. Priestess of Athena Polias: Connelly 2007.59–64.

40 Bate and the Eteoboutadai: Connelly 2007.59. The secret procedures for the washing of Athena's statue at the Athenian Plynteria, performed by members of the *genos* Praxiergidai, are another example: Xen. *Hell.* 1.4.12; Plut. *Alc.* 34.1; Parker 2005.478. On secrecy as a memory enhancer for individuals see McCauley and Lawson 2002.76.

41 Renegotiation: for this process in illiterate cultures see McCauley and Lawson 2002.68–9.

42 *Zakoros*: e.g. *LSCG* 48 B (second century); Lupu 2005.53. For other examples of assistance from experienced priests, see Parker 2011.43–4 with n.11.

43 On secrecy, writing and *hieroi logoi* see Henrichs 2003a. Interest in written versions of mystery texts gradually increased during and after the fifth century.

44 For the key role of Cyprus see Burkert 1985.47–53 and for Asia Minor, see Vanschoonwinkel 2006. Chronologically, the "Dark Age" is roughly equivalent to what archaeologists call the Early Iron Age, and art historians the Protogeometric. Cults prior to 800: Schnapp-Gourbeillon 2002.183–253.

45 On continuity in Crete see Wallace 2003.263; Prent 2005.579–80 (Kato Symi); Haysom 2011.101.

46 Cult activity at Olympia in the Submycenaean period: Kyrieleis 2002b.216; at Isthmia only slightly later: Morgan 2002.252.

47 Festivals: Burkert 1985.226–7; Dietrich 1986.50–51 (usually overoptimistic in his assessments of continuity). Birthdays: Mikalson 1975.13–24.

48 Kalapodi/Abai: Deutsches Archäologisches Institut 2012. Other sites used continuously from the Bronze Age include the sanctuary of Apollo Maleatas at Epidauros,

the sanctuary of Aphaia on Aigina, the sanctuary of Agia Irini on Keos, and on Crete, Psychro cave, the Ida cave and Kato Symi: Schnapp-Gourbeillon 2002.191–205.

49 Interest in male deities: e.g. the appearance of "Zeus" figurines at Olympia (for debate over their identity see Barringer 2010.158–62). See Langdon 1987.108 (switch away from Mycenaean female clay figurines).

50 Reciprocity and *charis*: see Essay 1.3. Metal sculptures an "invention of the Geometric period": Langdon 1987.107. Tripods: Himmelman 2002.93–4; Papalexandrou and Papalexandrou 2005.27–34.

51 Homer: e.g. *Il.* 1.23 (priest), 1.39 (temple), 1.68–9 (seers), 6.300 (priestess), 7.81–6 (vow), 9.177 (libation before drinking), 9.534 (festival), 16.183 (chorus), 16.233–5 (oracles); *Od.* 14.414 ("first fruits" offering), 22.481–94 (purification after bloodshed).

52 Syro-Phoenician and Egyptian: for introductions see Burkert 1992; Morris 1995.

53 Temple and cult statue: Burkert 1985.88; Mazarakis Ainian 1997.270–4. Widespread development of temples between 800 and 700: Snodgrass 2006.213. Wealth: measured by the amounts of metal deposited (Snodgrass 1980.52–4); Morgan (1998.89) notes that this was variable by place.

54 Thebans: Hdt. 5.80–1, Pind. *Isthm.* 8.17. Discussion: Polinskaya 2013.136–9.

55 Kroisos: Hdt. 1.46.2, 1.92.2, 5.36.3.

56 Inscriptions: the "epigraphic habit" grew for most parts of the Hellenistic world, in religion and all other aspects of public life. See Gauthier 1985.13–14, 118–9.

57 Philosophers: Parker 1996.279–80 (Athens). Allegorizing: Obbink (2003.180) places the start of a new appetite for "extended forms of metonymical explanation" of myth and ritual in the fifth century, with the Derveni papyrus an early example.

58 Clean not only in the body: Chaniotis 2012.125–6.

59 Delos: Mikalson 2010.186–7, 192–3.

60 A concise summary for the Hellenistic period: Mikalson 2006. Change within an overall context of continuity: Shipley 2000.155; Mikalson 2010.187–8, 194.

61 Parker 1996.264–5 (impact on rural cults in Attica), 270 (possible loss of traditional festivals after ca. 300), 275–6 (possible loss of hero cults).

62 Subcultures: Hegedus 1998.

63 Isis and henotheism: Versnel 1990.39–95. On the powers and miracles of Asklepios: Versnel 2011.400–19.

64 Mysteries: Blakely 2006 (Kabeiroi and similar figures); Gawlinski 2012 (Andania); Rogers 2012 (Ephesian Artemis).

65 Ruler worship and hero cult: Currie 2005.158–200. Rulers, however, were typically afforded divine honors. For the older scholarly view that ruler cult was a sign of "degeneration" of Greek religion and lacked "truly religious content" see Nilsson 1967.2.182. Resistance in Athens: Parker 1996.256–64.

66 Samothracian gods: Burkert 1993.185–6.

67 Personifications: Stafford 2000.173–97 (Eirene), 2007.81–4.

68 For Mediterranean studies see Horden and Purcell 2000; Harris ed. 2005; Malkin ed. 2005a.

69 Hellenes: Hall 2002.226.

70 Common matrix: Malkin 2011.8. This function of religion has a long history stretching back to the Bronze Age: Assmann 2008.140–1 (religion as a promoter of "cultural translatability").

71 Pyrgi temples: Colonna 2006.143–4, 155–6. Tablets: *CIE* 6314–16. On the politics of syncretism at Pyrgi: Bloch 1981 (arguing that the Greeks knew the goddess as Eleithyia, with reply by Colonna); Jannot 2005.88–92.

72 For syncretism, cognition and selection processes see Sperber 1996.101–2, 108; Martin 2001; Martin and Leopold 2008.100–1.

73 On syncretism as a pejorative term see Martin 2001; Leopold 2004.105–6. For definitions of syncretism and further discussion see Shaw and Stewart eds. 1994; Leopold and Jensen eds. 2005.

74 Assimilation: Lebrun 1999. Specific context: more broadly, we can speak of syncretic systems, but in the Mediterranean polytheistic context, it is often more useful to speak of individual cults. For Zeus Ammon at Siwa, see Parke 1967; Kuhlmann 1988.
75 On lack of specificity in the term "syncretism" see Motte 1999.38.
76 On Hellenization and the more general term "acculturation" see Malkin 2002.153.
77 The Molpoi Decree: *LSAM* 50; *Milet* 1.3.133 (cf. 6.1.134). On the decree see Herda 2006, 2011 (summary in English with updated content). Despite my occasional departures from Herda's interpretations in what follows, my debt to his detailed and expert analysis of the decree will be obvious. Graf (2009.110–16) provides an accessible discussion of the Molpoi and their broader cultural context.
78 Didyma: Fontenrose 1988; Morgan 1985 (on its differences from Delphi). Apollo Didymeus as cult partner of Delphinios: Herda 2008.20–4, 35–9.
79 Milesian colonization: Gorman 2001.50–85; Herda 2008.24–35, 2011.74–81.
80 Calendar: *LSAM* 41; *Milet* 1.3, no. 31 and 6.3, no. 1215; Herda 2005.265–72, 2011.70. Parker 1996.43–55 discusses the Solonian calendar at Athens. Early monumental calendars were inscribed on temple walls in Gortyn (*LSCG* 146–7) and Corinth (*IG* IV 1597, ca. 600; Lupu 2005.65–6).
81 For the double meaning of *molpē* as "song/dance" see Georgoudi 2001.153–5.
82 Molpoi in colonies: Herda 2008.35–6.
83 On the survival of parts of the population: Erhardt 2003.18. Compare Hdt. 6.19.3: "most (*pleunes*) of their men were killed."
84 My translation is adapted from the text and translation in Herda 2011.82–5. For *orgia* in the cult of Apollo Delphinios see *Hymn. Hom. Ap.* 389 (with mention of *orgiones*) and Herda 2006.35–7.
85 Hellenistic copy: according to Herda (2006.28). Others have dated it about a hundred years later.
86 Hebdomaia: Herda 2006.38–48, 247.
87 Alternatively, Herda (2006.52–3) interprets the handling of *splanchna* as part of an oath ceremony for those chosen.
88 On paeans see Furley and Bremer 2001.84–91; Rutherford 2001.3–136 (with 14–16 on the god Paiawon); Herda 2006.105–18.
89 Crown-wearers: Herda 2006.58–61.
90 Molpon: Herda 2005.263–73, 2006.78–81. Herda (2011.70–1) argues that it was identical to the *prutaneion* or city hall of Miletos, which contained the civic hearth sacred to Hestia.
91 Earliest (line 13): Herda 2006.57, 82–3; 2011.84.
92 *Neoi*: Herda 2006.86–112, esp. 89 with n. 562. *Contra*: Chaniotis 2010.378.
93 Not priests: Herda 2006.63–76. The Molpoi were likely not subject to the ritual stipulations typically required of a priest (e.g. wholeness of body); presumably the priest's presence at their activities increased ritual efficacy. See Essay 4.3.
94 Size of the halls in the Delphinion and their use for dining: Herda 2005.261–8.
95 Onitadai: Herda 2006.124–3, 433–4 (connecting them with the cult of Herakles at Miletos and Didyma).
96 Metageitnia: Herda 2006.225–6. T(h)argelia (on the seventh of the month Thargelion at Athens and Delos): Herda 2006.220–5.
97 King: Herda 2006.229–37; compare the *archōn basileus* at Athens (Parker 1996.7–8).
98 *Gulloi*: Hsch. s.v. *gullos*; Herda 2006.249–56.
99 Sacred Way: Greaves 2010.180–93 (similar processional roads in other Ionian cities). Hekate: Herda 2006.282–9, 397–9.
100 For Apollo: it is also possible to read the inscription as specifying paeans for each of the deities or heroes on the list (e.g. Herda 2006.279). Herda (2006.265–8) argues that some of the paeans were sung in passing, while others were performed as the procession paused at altars.

101 Each of the stops is discussed in detail by Herda (2006.282–350).

102 Teos: *SEG* 31.985, D, lines 17–9 (cf. the similar text *ML* no. 30, line 31). Whether "Memory and Power" were regarded as divinities is debated: see Georgoudi 2001.166; Carawan 2008.169–71.

103 Herda (2006.266, 279–80) counts seven stations, reading Phylios and the Horned One as separate shrines of Apollo, with the paean sung "toward" (*kata*) Keraïtes from the road except in years when the skinned victim is offered. (Depending on how one punctuates the inscription and interprets the prepositions, one can produce anywhere from four to seven stops.) In my reading, however, the preposition *para* with the dative case (translated here as "beside") marks each of the official stations.

104 Skipped cult place: Herda (2006.343–9) identifies both it and the site of "Chares' statues" as cult places tied to specific *genē*.

105 Content of the hymns: Herda 2006.448–9 (content relating the shrines in the Sacred Way to Apollo and the history of Miletos).

106 Cicero *De Oratore* 2.86.354. Cf. Arist. *Top.* 163b; [Cic.] *Rhet. Her.* 3.16–24; Quint. *Inst.* 3.3.4; Yates 1966.1–39; Barrett 2011.59–61. For serial recall, imagery and cuing in oral traditions see Rubin 1995.59–60, 175–93.

107 Duties of the Onitadai: Herda 2006.353–4, 385–404. *Thualēmata* as kneaded barley: van Straten 1995.141–3; as meat: Herda 2006.401–4. *Thua* as cakes: Herda 2006.315–7.

108 Herald and Singer: Herda 2006.414–24.

109 Ehrhardt (2003.18) argues that a pro-Persian remnant survived the destruction and remained in Miletos, allowing some continuity of tradition.

110 Herda (2006.422, pers. comm.) suggests that the singer did not change the content of the hymns but their musical style.

111 For overviews of Herakles see Larson 2007.183–95, 2009; Stafford 2010, 2012.

112 Canonization of the Labors: Stafford 2012.24–30.

113 Theoric networks: Rutherford 2009.

114 My explanation of network theory is drawn from Malkin 2011.3–64. For networks and the Classical world see also the essays in Malkin, Contantakopoulou and Panagopoulou eds. 2009; Eidinow 2011. For the crucial role of weak ties in "small worlds" see Watts 1999.14–15.

115 Malkin 2005b.71, 2011.24–5.

116 On the concept of relevance and "the epidemiology of representations," see Sperber 1985, 1994, 1996.53 (definition of relevance), 56–97. Cf. Sperber and Wilson 1995.118–32 (relevance in verbal communication).

117 Older strata of the *Theogony* mention Herakles and Prometheus (526–31), Geryon (289–94) and the Hydra (314–18). Like the *Odyssey*, the sixth-century *Catalogue of Women* (fr. 25 M-W), attributed to Hesiod, mentions both Hades and Olympos. Apotheosis: Holt 1992. For the eschatological potential of Herakles see Burkert 1985.211; Stafford 2012.172.

118 Corinthian vase: Stafford 2012.173 fig. 6.1.

119 On Herakles in Attica see Woodford 1971; Kearns 1989.35–6, 166; Shapiro 1989. 157–63, Stafford 2012.176–80.

120 *Hērōs theos*: Pind. *Nem.* 3.22. Dual rite: Hdt. 2.44. Cult practices: Larson 2007.183–7; Stafford 2012.171–97. Women: Stafford 2012.176, 184, 190.

121 Children: Apollod. *Bibl.* 2.7.8. Herakles' daughter is a unnamed character in Euripides' *Heraclidae*; Pausanias (1.32.6) calls her Makaria. Families: Volkommer 1988.88.

122 Doorway: Diog. Laert. 6.50 "Herakles of Beautiful Victory, son of Zeus, lives here; let nothing evil enter." Amulets: Diod. Sic. 5.64.6–7. Alexikakos: Woodford 1976; Stafford 2012.177 fig. 6.2. Herakles is Kallinikos already in the seventh century: Archil. fr. 324 West (a ritual song); Stafford 2012.176. See also Paul 2013.99–108 (Kos).

123 For "special patient" and "special agent" patterns of cult see Chapter 4. Healing: in Attica, Herakles Menytes (Stafford 2012.178, with legend of Sophocles' dream);

Paus. 9.24.3 (Hyettos), Ath. 12.6 (512f) (connection with hot springs). Battles: Hdt. 6.108 (Marathon); Thuc. 5.64–6 (Mantineia); Xen. *Hell.* 6.4.7 (Leuktra, with miracle of armor). Even an oracle is attested: Paus. 7.25.10.

124 Sanctuary: Aubet 2001.150. Most recently on Herakles and Melqart: Malkin 2011.119–42; Stafford 2012.187–93. God and hero: Bonnet 1988.76, 108–9.

125 For the myth of the Herakleidai see Thuc. 1.12; Apollod. *Bibl.* 2.8.2–4; Malkin 1994.15–45; Luraghi 2008.46–67.

126 Colonization: Malkin 2011.123–8. Landmarks: Diod. Sic. 4.17.1–4.24.7. The Sicilian poet Stesichorus composed an influential *Song of Geryon* in the sixth century. On Herakles and Geryon see Jourdain-Annequin 1989.478–88.

127 Bonnet 1988.244–7; Jourdain-Annequin 1992.276–8; Malkin 2011.128–9. Herakles and western colonization: Jourdain-Annequin 1989.221–92; cf. the papers in Mastrocinque ed. 1993.

128 Kition: Yon 1992.151. On Cyprus, the Phoenicians and Herakles, cf. Jourdain-Annequin 1989.167–9.

129 Melqart and Thasos: Jourdain-Annequin (1989.158–61) is more cautious, emphasizing the Greek aspects of Thasian Herakles. The Thasian sanctuary itself did not have a Phoenician prehistory; however, the motifs of Herakles' burning on the pyre and his apotheosis may have been borrowed from Melqart and/or the Hittite god Sandon: Stafford 2012.187–98. Reciprocal: Bonnet 1988.401.

130 Lion attributes: Bonnet 1988.409–12, 1992.175–6.

131 Etruscans: Bradley 2005.131; Jannot 2005.165–6.

132 Athenian art: Shapiro 1989.157–63. Issues of interpretation: Cornell 1995.146–8, 162; Lulof 2000 (with bibliography on Etrusco-Roman kings and goddesses); Bradley 2005.130–1. On Roman Hercules cf. Stafford 2012.194–7.

133 First diffusion: van Wonterghem 1992.320. Discussion: Bradley 2005.131–4. Woodford 1976.293, Pl. 55 fig. 4 illustrates examples of the "Alexikakos" type from Abbruzo.

134 Van Wonterghem 1998.242–53 with plate 26 (principal routes of transhumance on the Adriatic coast). Cf. van Wonterghem 1992.322 (possible transmission by mercenaries). Cacus: Verg. *Aen.* 8.184–279. On Herakles and cattle, cf. Jourdain-Annequin 1998; McInerney 2010.102–12.

135 Lionskin: Bonnet 1992.169.

136 Six Herculeses: Cic. *Nat. D.* 3.16.

137 Mikalson 2010.188.

138 New deity: Fraser (1972.252) repeatedly asserts that Sarapis was "created" by Ptolemy I Soter, but also says that he could be presented as a Greek version of "the old Memphian god." Bommas 2005.23–4 dismisses the "creation" narrative as scholarly myth. The allied theory that the Ptolemies deliberately exported the cult of Sarapis as part of an imperial policy (e.g. Brady 1935.17–23) has, with good reason, been challenged (already in Fraser 1960.47).

139 Wilcken 1927.25–9. In Wilcken's day the debate over the origins of Sarapis was already long-standing (e.g. Bouché-Leclercq 1902.10). On the cult of Apis see Thompson 2012.177–92.

140 Artemisia: Wilcken 1927.97–104. On the "Hellenomemphites" and their worship of Apis see Świderek 1975; Moyer 2011.148; Thompson 2012.89–90, 188. The early spelling "Sarapis" was overtaken by "Serapis" during the Roman period: Vidman 1970.24.

141 For Greek curses addressing Hades/Plouton see Gager 1992.12. An alternative Greek reading of *Wsir-Ḥp* as Dionysos is notable in the decoration of the temple complex of *Wsir-Ḥp* at Memphis: Fraser 1972.1.255–6; Thompson 2012.25, 188. Compare Hdt. 2.42.2 (interpreting Osiris as Dionysos).

142 Omen-Apis: Kessler 2000.189–90; Bommas 2005.24–5. On the likelihood that the name Sarapis was already in use among the Greek residents of Memphis: Wilcken

1927.85–6; Świderek 1975.674–5. Heyob (1975.1–9) discusses more of the voluminous older bibliography on the debate over Sarapis' origins.

143 Etymology: Nymphodorus of Syracuse (= Clement of Alexandria *Stromata* 1.21.106; cf. Phylarchos *FGrH* 81 F 78 = Plut. *De Is. et Os.* 362c). Nikokreon: Macrob. *Sat.* 1.20.16; Borgeaud and Volokhine 2000.55–6. Menander (fr. 139 Körte-Thierfelder).

144 Stambaugh (1972.12) echoed even earlier complaints, such as that by Welles (1962), whose arguments for Alexander's role in fostering the cult have been largely dismissed (e.g. Fraser 1967). The evidence connecting Alexander and Sarapis can (with effort) be explained away, yet it is surprisingly voluminous.

145 Cult legend: Borgeaud and Volokhine 2000.42–6.

146 The place name Sinope can itself be traced to Memphis: Wilcken 1927.78–9; Schmidt 2005.294.

147 Stambaugh 1972.8–13, 62. On the Alexandrian cult image, cf. Schmidt 2005.295–302.

148 Isis was regularly paired with Sarapis in cult inscriptions by the reign of Ptolemy II in the early third century: Fraser 1960.5–7; Vidman 1969 nos. 269–70; Vidman 1970.32–3.

149 The plaques were inscribed in hieroglyphs and Greek: Bernand 2001 no. 13; McKenzie, Gibson and Reyes 2004.81–85, 101.

150 Bernand 2001 no. 21; McKenzie, Gibson and Reyes 2004.81. Ptolemy IV also placed foundation plaques in the large Greek temple he built for Sarapis and Isis northeast of the Serapeion. A few of these survived: Tod 1942; Bernand 2001 no. 18. Cf. Kessler 2000.195.

151 Greek appearance: McKenzie, Gibson and Reyes 2004.111, 115–120. In the light of their work, Kessler's argument (2000.208–13, 224) that the Alexandrian Serapeion was a fully Egyptian cult place with a separate interior shrine for the Greek god Sarapis cannot stand, but he makes important observations (192–214) about its Egyptian features (cf. McKenzie, Gibson and Reyes 2004.90). The Harpokrates temple is thought to have functioned as a birth house, used in the dynastic cult to celebrate the birth of a young god (heir). For native Egyptian oracular and incubation practices see Frankfurter 1998.145–97.

152 *PSI* 5.539 (in the Zenon archive).

153 On the Egyptian origins of Apollonios, see Moyer 2011.161. On the Delian priest Demetrios see Dignas 2008.76n.12. After 166, the Delian priesthoods, including that of Sarapis, were taken over by Athenians: Dignas 2008.78. At Priene ca. 200, the public cult of Sarapis required an Egyptian expert (not the official priest) to perform the sacrifices: *LSAM* no. 36.20, Dignas 2008.83. Renberg and Bubelis 2011.184–5n.25 mention two priests with Greek names, one dating to 224 (regarding a *nakoros* or temple assistant named Achilles) and one undated but probably late (regarding a priest named Syron).

154 Healing and oracles in the Apis cult at Memphis: Wilcken 1927.31–5, 88–9. Cf. Stambaugh 1972.61; Frankfurter 1998.148; Thompson 2012.183, 193. The Sarapis and Isis cult at Canopus similarly involved incubation and oracles: Strabo 17.1.17; Frankfurter 1998.162–5. There is debate over whether incubation and dream oracles in Egypt had an Egyptian origin or were adopted from Greek practice during the Late Period (664–323); see the literature cited in von Ehrenheim 2011.157–9. However, spontaneous oracular dreams and dream epiphanies were well recognized already in the New Kingdom: Szpakowska 2003.

155 On Sarapis from an Egyptian perspective see Kessler 2000.175–92.

156 Alexander: Arrian *Anab.* 3.1.3–4 (sacrifice to Apis and other gods with competitions). Donation by Ptolemy I to the Apis bull's funeral: Diod. Sic. 1.84.8. On Apis as a royal god and his relationship to the pharaohs see Pfeiffer 2008.389.

157 Subsequent Ptolemaic temples were more strongly Egyptianizing, but the gods concerned were also less intimately tied to the rulers. For the "kingly" pose of the Alexandrian statue, see Stambaugh 1972.24–5.

158 Demetrios: Diog. Laert. 5.5.76; Artem. 2.44. Fraser (1972.1.257) attributes to Demetrios an attempt to "popularize the new god." On the career of Demetrios in relation to religion see Mikalson 1998.46–74 and on Sarapis, 229n.39.

159 Timotheus: For debate over the hypothesis of Alexandrian mysteries modeled on those in Athens see Clinton 1974.8–9; Stephens 2010.58. The scholiast on Callim. *Hymn* 6 (Pfeiffer ed. 1949.2.77) says that it was Ptolemy II who "established some customs of the Athenians" in Alexandria. Fraser (1972.1.251) attributes to Timotheus "an influential part in the development of cults in the reign of Soter." The persistence of the "council of experts" theory may be due to its inclusion in two influential articles in *RE* (s.v. Manetho [W. Kroll], Timotheus [O. Weinrich]).

160 So Bremmer (2012.385) citing Mesomedes Hymn 5 (Heitsch) and Burkert 1983 [1972].291n79, 1987.160n.116. Mysteries not attested until Roman period: Fraser 1960.4n1, 1972.1.199–202; Hopkinson 1984.32–9.

161 In a careful study of Egyptians at the Ptolemies' court, Legras (2002.975–77) finds too many problems with the sources to permit even the certainty that Manetho was at court under Ptolemy I. On Egyptian experts and the early Ptolemies see further Thompson 2012.107.

162 Gorre 2009.489–91, 507–12.

163 Gorre 2013.100–106, 112. For priests closely allied with the Ptolemies see Gorre 2009.567–8, 579, 623–6. Gorre does not directly address the problem of Sarapis.

164 This persistent view ("now widely rejected" according to Schmidt 2005.295) is still expressed e.g. by Pfeiffer 2008.388: "to offer the subjects of various ethnic origins a common focus for their religiosity."

165 Egyptians: Fraser 1960.9; Stambaugh 1972.96; Moyer 2011.148. Fraser (1972.1.252) argues that Ptolemy I wished to provide a patron god specifically for his Greek subjects, who were a diverse group of immigrants.

166 Individual Greeks: Fraser 1960.49.

167 Zoïlos: *PSI* 4.435; Borgeaud and Volokhine 2000.46–8; Rigsby 2001.21; Renberg and Bubelis 2011 (with new Greek text).

168 *IG* X 2.1.255; Borgeaud and Volokhine 2000.48. The text is a set of aretologies of imperial date but is thought to preserve an original of the third century from the Sarapeion of Opous.

169 Moyer (2011.153–207) provides summary, analysis and bibliography as well as a text and translation of the inscription *IG* XI.4 1299 (282–6); see also Borgeaud and Volokhine 2000.48–9.

170 Syncretism: Moyer 2011.151–2. For Orientalism and Hellenism in the historiography of Egypt see Moyer 2011.2–36.

## References

Albersmeier, Sabine, ed. 2009. *Heroes: Mortals and myths in ancient Greece*. Baltimore and New Haven: The Walters Art Museum and Yale University Press.

Aleshire, Sara B. 1989. *The Athenian Asklepieion: The people, their dedications, and the inventories*. Amsterdam: J. C. Gieben.

Antes, Peter, Armin W. Geertz and Randi R. Warne, eds. 2008. *New approaches to the study of religion*. 2 Vols. Berlin and New York: Walter de Gruyter.

Arafat, K. W. 2009. Treasure, treasuries and value in Pausanias. *CQ* 59 (2): 578–92.

Assmann, Jan. 2008. Translating gods: Religion as a factor of cultural (un)translatability. In *Religion: Beyond a concept*, ed. de Vries, 139–49.

Aubet, María Eugenia. 2001. *The Phoenicians and the West: Politics, colonies and trade*. Tr. M. Turton. New York: Cambridge University Press.

Auffarth, Christoph. 2005. How to sacrifice correctly – Without a manual? In *Greek sacrificial ritual*, ed. Hägg and Alroth, 11–21.

Barrett, Justin L. 2011. *Cognitive science, religion and theology: From human minds to divine minds*. West Conshohocken, PA: Templeton Press.

Barringer, Judith. 2010. Zeus at Olympia. In *The gods of ancient Greece*, ed. Bremmer and Erskine, 155–77.

Beard, Mary, John North and Simon Price. 1998. *Religions of Rome*. 2 Vols. Cambridge: Cambridge University Press.

Beck, Herbert, Peter C. Bol and Maraike Bückling, eds. 2005. *Ägypten, Griechenland, Rom: Abwehr und Berührung; Städelsches Kunstinstitut und Städtische Galerie, 26*. Frankfurt am Main: Liebighaus.

Bell, Catherine. 2009. *Ritual theory, ritual practice*. New York and London: Oxford University Press.

Bernand, Étienne. 2001. *Inscriptions grecques d'Alexandrie ptolémaïque*. Cairo: Institut français d'archéologie orientale.

Bingen, Jean, Guy Cambier and Georges Nachtergael, eds. 1975. *Le monde grec: Pensée, littérature, histoire, documents. Hommages à Claire Préaux*. Brussels: Éditions de l'Université de Bruxelles.

Blakely, Sandra. 2006. *Myth, ritual, and metallurgy in ancient Greece and recent Africa*. Cambridge and New York: Cambridge University Press.

Bloch, Raymond. 1981. Le culte etrusco-punique de Pyrgi vers 500 avant J.C. In [n. a.] *Die Göttin von Pyrgi: Archäologische, linguistische und religionsgeschichtliche Aspekte*, 123–35.

Bol, Renate, Ursula Höckmann and Patrick Schollmeyer, eds. 2008. *Kult(ur)kontakte: Apollon in Milet/Didyma, Histria, Myus, Naukratis und auf Zypern*. Rahden/Westphalia: Verlag Marie Leidorf.

Bommas, Martin. 2005. *Heiligtum und Mysterium: Griechenland und seine ägyptischen Gottheiten*. Mainz: Phillip Von Zabern.

Bonnet, Corinne. 1988. *Melqart: Cultes et mythes de l'Héraclès tyrien en Méditerranée*. Namur: Presses Universitaires; Leuven: Peeters.

Bonnet, Corinne. 1992. Héraclès en Orient: Interprétations et syncrétismes. In *Héraclès d'une rive à l'autre*, ed. Bonnet and Jourdain-Annequin, 165–98.

Bonnet, Corinne and Colette Jourdain-Annequin, eds. 1992. *Héraclès d'une rive à l'autre de la Méditerranée Bilan et perspectives*. Brussels: Institut belge de Rome; Rome: Academia Belgica.

Bonnet, Corinne, Colette Jourdain-Annequin and Vinciane Pirenne-Delforge, eds. 1998. *Le bestiaire d'Héraclès: IIIe rencontre héracléenne*. Liège: Centre International d'Étude de la Religion Grecque Antique.

Bonnet, Corinne and André Motte, eds. 1999. *Les syncrétismes religieux dans le monde méditerranéen antique*. Brussels: Institut Historique Belge de Rome.

Borgeaud, Philippe, ed. 1988. *La mémoire des religions*. Geneva: Labor et Fides.

Borgeaud, Philippe and Youri Volokhine. 2000. La formation de la légende de Sarapis: Une approche transculturelle. *ARG* 2 (1): 37–76.

Bouché-Leclercq, Auguste. 1902. Le politique religieuse de Ptolémée Soter et le culte de Sérapis. *RHR* 46:1–30.

Boys-Stones, G. R., ed. 2003. *Metaphor, allegory and the Classical tradition: Ancient thought and modern revisions*. Oxford: Oxford University Press.

Bradley, Guy. 2005. Aspects of the cult of Hercules in central Italy. In *Herakles and Hercules*, ed. Rawlings and Bowden, 129–51.

Brady, Thomas A. 1935. *The reception of Egyptian cults by the Greeks (330–30 BC)*. Columbia: University of Missouri.

Bremmer, Jan. 1995. The family and other centres of learning in antiquity. In *Centres of learning*, ed. Drijvers and MacDonald, 29–38.

Bremmer, Jan. 2005. The sacrifice of pregnant animals. In *Greek sacrificial ritual*, ed. Hägg and Alroth, 155–65.

Bremmer, Jan. 2010. Manteis, magic, mysteries and mythography: Messy margins of polis religion? *Kernos* 23: 13–35.

Bremmer, Jan. 2012. Initiation into the Eleusinian Mysteries: A "thin" description. In *Mystery and secrecy in the Nag Hammadi collection*, ed. Bull, Lied and Turner, 375–98.

Bremmer, Jan and Andrew Erskine, eds. 2010. *The gods of ancient Greece: Identities and transformations*. Edinburgh: Edinburgh University Press.

Brulé, Pierre, ed. 2007. *La norme en matière religieuse en Grèce ancienne*. Liège: Centre International d'Étude de la Religion Grecque Antique.

Brulé, Pierre and Christophe Vendries, eds. 2001. *Chanter les dieux: Musique et religion dans l'antiquité grecque et romaine*. Rennes: Presses Universitaires.

Bugh, Glenn R., ed. 2006. *The Cambridge companion to the Hellenistic world*. Cambridge and London: Cambridge University Press.

Bull, Christian, Liv Ingeborg Lied and John D. Turner, eds. 2012. *Mystery and secrecy in the Nag Hammadi collection and other ancient literature: Ideas and practices. Studies for Einar Thomassen at sixty*. Leiden: Brill.

Burkert, Walter. 1983 [1972]. *Homo Necans: The anthropology of ancient Greek sacrificial ritual and myth*. Tr. Peter Bing. Berkeley, Los Angeles and London. University of California Press.

Burkert, Walter. 1985. *Greek religion*. Cambridge, MA: Harvard University Press.

Burkert, Walter. 1987. *Ancient mystery cults*. Cambridge, MA: Harvard University Press.

Burkert, Walter. 1992. *The Orientalizing revolution: Near Eastern influence on Greek culture in the early Archaic age*. Cambridge, MA, and London: Harvard University Press.

Burkert, Walter. 1993. Concordia discors: The literary and the archaeological evidence on the sanctuary of Samothrace. In *Greek sanctuaries*, ed. Marinatos and Hägg, 178–91.

Cambitoglou, Alexander, A. Birchall, J. J. Coulton and J. R. Green. 1988. *Zagora 2: Excavation of a Geometric town on the island of Andros*. 2 Vols. Athens: Athens Archaeological Society.

Carawan, Edwin. 2008. What the *MNEMONES* know. In *Orality, literacy, memory*, ed. Mackay, 163–84.

Chaniotis, Angelos. 2006. Rituals between norms and emotions: Rituals as shared experience and memory. In *Ritual and communication*, ed. Stavrianapoulou, 211–38.

Chaniotis, Angelos. 2007. The dynamics of ritual norms in Greek cult. In *La norme en matière religieuse*, ed. Brulé, 91–105.

Chaniotis, Angelos. 2008. Priests as ritual experts in the Greek world. In *Practitioners of the divine*, ed. Dignas and Trampedach, 17–34.

Chaniotis, Angelos. 2010. The Molpoi inscription: Ritual prescription or riddle? *Kernos* 23: 375–9.

Chaniotis, Angelos, ed. 2011. *Ritual dynamics in the ancient Mediterranean*. Dresden: Franz Steiner Verlag.

Chaniotis, Angelos. 2012. Greek ritual purity from automatisms to moral distinctions. In *How purity is made*, ed. Rösch and Simon, 123–39.

Clauss, James J. and Martine Cuypers, eds. 2014. *A companion to Hellenistic literature*. Chichester, UK, and Malden, MA: Wiley-Blackwell.

Clinton, Kevin. 1974. *The sacred officials of the Eleusinian mysteries*. Philadelphia: American Philosophical Society.

Cole, Susan G. 2008. Professionals, volunteers and amateurs: Serving the gods kata ta patria. In *Practitioners of the divine*, ed. Dignas and Trampedach, 55–72.

Colonna, Giovanni. 2006. Sacred architecture and the religion of the Etruscans. In *The religion of the Etruscans*, ed. de Grummond, 132–64.

Connelly, Joan B. 2007. *Portrait of a priestess: Women and ritual in ancient Greece*. Princeton and Oxford: Princeton University Press.

Cornell, Tim. 1995. *The beginnings of Rome: Italy and Rome from the Bronze Age to the Punic Wars (c.1000–264 BC)*. Abingdon, UK: Routledge.

Currie, Bruno. 2005. *Pindar and the cult of heroes*. Oxford and New York: Oxford University Press.

Czachesz, István. 2013. Rethinking Biblical transmission: Insights from the cognitive neuroscience of memory. In *Mind, morality and magic*, ed. Czachesz and Uro, 43–61.

Czachesz, István and Risto Uro, eds. 2013. *Mind, morality and magic: Cognitive science approaches in Biblical studies*. Durham: Acumen.

Dasen, Véronique and Thomas Späth, eds. 2010. *Children, memory and family identity in Roman culture*. Oxford and New York: Oxford University Press.

de Grummond, Nancy, ed. 2006. *The religion of the Etruscans*. Austin: University of Texas Press.

Deutsches Archäologisches Institut. 2012. Kalapodi. *BCH Chronique des fouilles en ligne* 3056. http://chronique.efa.gr/index.php/fiches/voir/3056/. Accessed 8/15/2015.

de Vries, Hent, ed. 2008. *Religion: Beyond a concept*. New York: Fordham University Press.

Dietrich, Bernard C. 1986. *Tradition in Greek religion*. Berlin and New York: Walter de Gruyter.

Dignas, Beate. 2008. Greek priests of Sarapis? In *Practitioners of the divine*, ed. Dignas and Trampedach, 73–88.

Dignas, Beate and Kai Trampedach, eds. 2008. *Practitioners of the divine: Greek priests and religious officials from Homer to Heliodorus*. Cambridge, MA: Harvard University Press.

Dowden, Ken. 2006. *Zeus*. Abingdon and New York: Routledge.

Drijvers, Hendrik Jan Willem and Alasdair A. MacDonald, eds. 1995. *Centres of learning: Learning and location in pre-modern Europe and the Near East*. Leiden: Brill.

Ehrhardt, Norbert. 2003. Milet nach den Perserkriegen: ein Neubeginn? In *Stadt und Stadtentwicklung in Kleinasien*, ed. Schwertheim and Winter, 1–19.

Eidinow, Esther. 2011. Networks and narratives: A model for ancient Greek religion. *Kernos* 24: 9–38.

Ekroth, Gunnel. 2002. *The sacrificial rituals of Greek hero cults*. Liège: Centre International d'Étude de la Religion Grecque Antique.

Flower, Michael. 2008. *The seer in ancient Greece*. Berkeley: University of California Press.

Fontenrose, Joseph. 1978. *The Delphic oracle: Its responses and operations with a catalogue of responses*. Berkeley and Los Angeles: University of California Press.

Fontenrose, Joseph. 1988. *Didyma: Apollo's oracle, cult and companions*. Berkeley: University of California Press.

Foxhall, Lin. 2013. *Studying gender in Classical antiquity*. Cambridge and New York: Cambridge University Press.

Frankfurter, David. 1998. *Religion in Roman Egypt: Assimilation and resistance*. Princeton: Princeton University Press.

Fraser, P. M. 1960. Two studies on the cult of Sarapis in the Hellenistic world. *OpAth* 3: 1–54.

Fraser, P. M. 1967. Current problems concerning the early history of the cult of Sarapis. *OpAth* 7: 23–45.

Fraser, P. M. 1972. *Ptolemaic Alexandria*. 3 Vols. Oxford: Clarendon Press.

Furley, William D. and Jan Maarten Bremer. 2001. *Greek hymns*. 2 Vols. Tübingen: Mohr Siebeck.

Gager, John. 1992. *Curse tablets and binding spells from the ancient world*. New York: Oxford University Press.

Gauthier, Philippe. 1985. *Les cités grecques et leurs bienfaiteurs*. Athens: École Française d'Athènes.

Gawlinski, Laura. 2012. *The sacred law of Andania: A new text with commentary*. Berlin and Boston: Walter de Gruyter.

Georgoudi, Stella. 2001. La procession chantante des Molpes de Milet. In *Chanter les dieux*, ed. Brulé and Vendries, 153–71.

Görg, Manfred and Günther Hölbl, eds. 2000. *Ägypten under der östliche Mittelmeerraum im 1: Jahrtausend v. Chr*. Wiesbaden: Harrassowitz.

Gorman, Vanessa B. 2001. *Miletos: The ornament of Ionia*. Ann Arbor: University of Michigan Press.

Gorre, Gilles. 2009. *Les relations du clergé Égyptien et des lagides d'après les sources privées*. Leuven: Peeters.

Gorre, Gilles. 2013. A religious continuity between the dynastic and Ptolemaic periods? Self-representation and identity of Egyptian priests in the Ptolemaic period (332–30 BCE). In *Shifting social imaginaries in the Hellenistic period*, ed. Stavrianapoulou, 99–114.

Graf, Fritz. 2009. *Apollo*. London and New York: Routledge.

Greaves, Alan M. 2010. *The land of Ionia: Society and economy in the Archaic period*. Chichester, UK, and Malden, MA: Wiley-Blackwell.

Hägg, Robin, ed. 1998. *Ancient Greek cult practice from the archaeological evidence*. Stockholm: P. Åströms Förlag.

Hägg, Robin and Brita Alroth, eds. 2005. *Greek sacrificial ritual, Olympian and chthonian*. Stockholm: P. Åströms Förlag.

Hahn, Frances Hickson. 2007. Performing the sacred: Prayers and hymns. In *A companion to Roman religion*, ed. Rüpke, 235–48.

Hall, Jonathan M. 2002. *Hellenicity: Between ethnicity and culture*. Chicago and London: University of Chicago Press.

Hamilton, Richard. 2000. *Treasure map: A guide to the Delian inventories*. Ann Arbor, MI: University of Michigan Press.

Harris, Diane. 1995. *The treasures of the Parthenon and Erechtheion*. Oxford: Clarendon Press.

Harris, William V. 1989. *Ancient literacy*. Cambridge, MA: Harvard University Press.

Harris, William V., ed. 2005. *Rethinking the Mediterranean*. Oxford and New York: Oxford University Press.

Havelock, Eric. 1982. *The literate revolution in Greece and its cultural consequences*. Princeton, NJ: Princeton University Press.

Haysom, Matthew. 2011. The strangeness of Crete: Problems for the protohistory of Greek religion. In *Current approaches to religion in ancient Greece*, ed. Haysom and Wallensten, 95–109.

Haysom, Matthew and Jenny Wallensten, eds. 2011. *Current approaches to religion in ancient Greece*. Stockholm: Swedish Institute at Athens.

Hegedus, Tim. 1998. The urban expansion of the Isis cult: A quantitative approach. *Studies in Religion/Sciences Religieuses* 27 (2): 161–78.

Henrichs, Albert 2003a. Hieroi logoi and hieroi bibloi: The (un)written margins of the sacred in ancient Greece. *HSPh* 101: 207–66.

Henrichs, Albert. 2003b. Writing religion: Inscribed texts, ritual authority, and the religious discourse of the polis. In *Written texts and the rise of literate culture in ancient Greece*, ed. Yunis, 38–58.

Herda, Alexander. 2005. Apollon Delphinios, das Prytaneion und die Agora von Milet. *AA* 243–94.

Herda, Alexander. 2006. *Der Apollon-Delphinios-Kult in Milet unde die Neujahrsprozession nach Didyma: Ein neuer Kommentar der sog. Molpoi-Satzung*. Mainz am Rhein: Philipp von Zabern.

Herda, Alexander. 2008. Apollon Delphinios—Apollon Didymeus: Zwei Gesichter eines milesischen Gottes und ihr Bezug zur Kolonisation Milets in archaischer Zeit. In *Kult(ur) kontakte*, ed. Bol, Höckmann and Schollmeyer, 13–75.

Herda, Alexander. 2011. How to run a state cult: The organization of the cult of Apollo Delphinios in Miletos. In *Current approaches to religion in ancient Greece,* ed. Haysom and Wallensten, 57–93.

Herington, John. 1985. *Poetry into drama: Early tragedy and the Greek poetic tradition*. Berkeley and Los Angeles: University of California Press.

Heyob, Sharon Kelly. 1975. *The cult of Isis among women in the Graeco-Roman world*. Leiden: Brill.

Himmelman, Nikolaus. 2002. Frühe Weihgeschenke in Olympia. In *Olympia 1875–2000*, ed. Kyrieleis, 91–107.

Hirschfeld, Lawrence A. and Susan Gelman, eds. 1994. *Mapping the mind: Domain specificity in cognition and culture*. Cambridge: Cambridge University Press.

Holt, Philip. 1992. Herakles' apotheosis in lost Greek literature and art. *AC* 61: 38–59.

Hopkinson, Neil, ed. 1984. *Callimachus: Hymn to Demeter*. Cambridge: Cambridge University Press.

Horden, Peregrine and Nicholas Purcell. 2000. *The corrupting sea: A study of Mediterranean history*. Oxford and Malden MA: Blackwell.

Jameson, Michael H. 2014. *Cults and rites in ancient Greece: Essays on religion and society*. Cambridge: Cambridge University Press.

Jannot, Jean-René. 2005. *Religion in ancient Etruria*. Tr. J. Whitehead. Madison: University of Wisconsin Press.

Jourdain-Annequin, Colette. 1989. *Héraclès aux portes du soir: Mythe et histoire*. Paris: Belles Lettres.

Jourdain-Annequin, Colette. 1992. Héraclès en occident. In *Héraclès d'une rive à l'autre*, ed. Bonnet and Jourdain-Annequin, 263–91.

Jourdain-Annequin, Colette. 1998. Héraclès et le boeuf. In *Le bestiaire d'Héraclès*, ed. Bonnet, Jourdain-Annequin and Pirenne-Delforge, 285–300.

Kearns, Emily. 1989. *The heroes of Attica*. *BICS* Supplement 57. London: Institute of Classical Studies.

Kearns, Emily. 2010. *Ancient Greek religion: A sourcebook*. Malden, MA, and Oxford: Wiley-Blackwell.

Kessler, D. 2000. Das hellenistische Serapeum in Alexandria und Ägypten in ägyptologischer Sicht. In *Ägypten under der östliche Mittelmeerraum*, ed. Görg and Hölbl, 163–230.

Kowalzig, Barbara. 2007. *Singing for the gods: Performances of myth and ritual in Archaic and Classical Greece*. Oxford and New York: Oxford University Press.

Kuhlmann, Klaus P. 1988. *Das Ammoneion, Archäologie, Geschichte, und Kultpraxis des Orakels von Siwa*. Mainz: Philipp von Zabern.

Kyrieleis, Helmut, ed. 2002a. *Olympia 1875–2000: 125 Jahre deutsche Ausgrabungen: Internationales Symposion, Berlin. 9–11 November 2000*. Mainz am Rhein: Philipp von Zabern.

Kyrieleis, Helmut. 2002b. Zu den Anfängen des Heiligtums von Olympia. In *Olympia 1875–2000*, ed. Kyrieleis (2002a), 213–20.

Lambert, Stephen D. 2002. The sacrificial calendar of Athens. *ABSA* 97: 353–99.

Langdon, Susan. 1987. Gift exchange in the Geometric sanctuaries. In *Gifts to the gods*, ed. Linders and Nordquist, 107–13.

Larson, Jennifer. 2007. *Ancient Greek cults: A guide*. New York and London: Routledge.

Larson, Jennifer. 2009. The Singularity of Herakles. In *Heroes: Mortals and myths in ancient Greece*, ed. Albersmeier, 31–8.

Lebrun, René. 1999. Observations concernant des syncrétismes d'Anatolie centrale et méridionale aux second et premier millénaires avant notre ère. In *Les syncrétismes religieux*, ed. Bonnet and Motte, 179–89.

Legras, Bernard. 2002. Les experts égyptiens à la cour des Ptolémées. *RH* 4: 963–91.

Leopold, Anita M. 2004. Syncretism and the interaction of modes of religiosity: A formative perspective on Gnostic-Christian movements in late antiquity. In *Theorizing religions past*, ed. Whitehouse and Martin, 105–21.

Leopold, Anita M. and Jeppe S. Jensen, eds. 2005. *Syncretism in religion: A reader*. London and New York: Routledge.

Linders, Tullia. 1972. *Studies in the treasure records of Artemis Brauronia found in Athens*. Stockholm: Swedish Institute at Athens.

Linders, Tullia. 1987. Gods, gifts, society. In *Gifts to the gods*, ed. Linders and Nordquist, 115–22.

Linders, Tullia and Gullög Nordquist, eds. 1987. *Gifts to the gods: Proceedings of the Uppsala Symposium 1985*. Uppsala: Almqvist and Wiksell.

Lulof, Patricia S. 2000. Archaic terracotta akroteria representing Athena and Heracles: manifestations of power in central Italy. *JRA* 13: 207–19.

Lupu, Eran. 2005. *Greek sacred law: A collection of new documents*. Leiden and Boston: Brill.

Luraghi, Nino. 2008. *The ancient Messenians: Constructions of ethnicity and memory*. New York: Cambridge University Press.

Lyons, Claire and John Papadopoulos, eds. 2002. *The archaeology of colonialism*. Los Angeles: Getty Research Institute.

Mackay, Anne, ed. 2008. *Orality, literacy, memory in the ancient Greek and Roman world*. Leiden and Boston: Brill.

Mackil, Emily. 2004. Wandering cities: Alternatives to catastrophe in the Greek polis. *AJA* 108 (4): 493–516.

Malkin, Irad. 1994. *Myth and territory in the Spartan Mediterranean*. Cambridge and London: Cambridge University Press.

Malkin, Irad. 2002. A colonial middle ground: Greek, Etruscan, and local elites in the Bay of Naples. In *The archaeology of colonialism*, ed. Lyons and Papadopoulos, 151–81.

Malkin, Irad, ed. 2005a. *Mediterranean paradigms and Classical antiquity*. London and New York: Routledge.

Malkin, Irad. 2005b. Networks and the emergence of Greek identity. In *Mediterranean paradigms and Classical antiquity*, ed. Malkin (2005a), 56–74.

Malkin, Irad. 2011. *A small Greek world: Networks in the ancient Mediterranean*. Oxford and New York: Oxford University Press.

Malkin, Irad, Christy Contantakopoulou and Katerina Panagopoulou, eds. 2009. *Greek and Roman networks in the Mediterranean*. London and New York: Routledge.

Marinatos, Nanno and Robin Hägg, eds. 1993. *Greek sanctuaries: New approaches*. London and New York: Routledge.

Martin, Luther H. 2001. To use "syncretism" or not to use "syncretism": That is the question. *Historical Reflections/Réflections Historiques* 27: 389–400.

Martin, Luther H. and Anita Maria Leopold. 2008. New approaches to the study of syncretism. In *New approaches to the study of religion*, ed. Antes, Geertz and Warne. 93–107.

Mastrocinque, Attilio, ed. 1993. *Ercole in occidente*. Trento: Dipartimento di scienze filologiche e storiche.

Mazarakis Ainian, Alexander. 1997. *From rulers' dwellings to temples: Architecture, religion and society in Early Iron Age Greece (1100–700 B.C.)*. Jonsered: P. Åströms Förlag.

McCauley, Robert N. and E. Thomas Lawson. 2002. *Bringing ritual to mind: Psychological foundations of cultural forms*. Cambridge and New York: Cambridge University Press.

McInerney, Jay. 2010. *The cattle of the sun: Cows and culture in the world of the ancient Greeks*. Princeton: Princeton University Press.

McKechnie, Paul and Philippe Guillaume, eds. 2008. *Ptolemy II Philadelphus and his world*. Leiden and Boston: Brill.

McKenzie, Judith S., Sheila Gibson and A. T. Reyes. 2004. Reconstructing the Serapeum in Alexandria from the archaeological evidence. *JRS* 94: 73–121.

Mikalson, Jon. 1975. *The sacred and civil calendar of the Athenian year*. Princeton: Princeton University Press.

Mikalson, Jon. 1998. *Religion in Hellenistic Athens*. Berkeley: University of California Press.

Mikalson, Jon. 2006. Greek religion: Continuity and change in the Hellenistic period. In *The Cambridge companion to the Hellenistic world*, ed. Bugh, 208–22.

Mikalson, Jon. 2010. *Ancient Greek religion*. Second edition. Chichester, UK, and Malden, MA: Wiley-Blackwell.

Mitten, David G., John G. Pedley and Jane A. Scott, eds. 1971. *Studies presented to George M. A. Hanfmann*. Cambridge, MA: Fogg Art Museum.

Morgan, Catherine. 1985. Divination and society at Delphi and Didyma. *Hermathena* 147: 17–42.

Morgan, Catherine. 1998. Ritual and society in Early Iron Age Corinthia. In *Ancient Greek cult practice*, ed. Hägg, 73–90.

Morgan, Catherine. 2002. The origins of the Isthmian festival. In *Olympia 1875–2000*, ed. Kyrieleis (2002a), 251–71.

Morris, Sarah P. 1995. *Daidalos and the origins of Greek art*. Princeton: Princeton University Press.

Motte, André. 1999. La notion de syncrétisme dans l'oeuvre de Franz Cumont. In *Les syncrétismes religieux*, ed. Bonnet and Motte, 21–58.

Moyer, Ian S. 2011. *Egypt and the limits of Hellenism*. Cambridge and New York: Cambridge University Press.

Naerebout, Frederick G. 1997. *Attractive performances. Ancient Greek dance: Three preliminary studies*. Amsterdam: J. C. Gieben.

Naerebout, Frederick G. 2006. Moving events. Dance at public events in the ancient Greek world: Thinking through its implications. In *Ritual and communication*, ed. Stavrianopoulou, 37–67.

Nilsson, Martin Persson. 1967. *Geschichte der griechischen Religion.* Third edition. 2 Vols. Munich: Beck.

Noegel, Scott, Joel Walker and Brannon Wheeler, eds. 2003. *Prayer, magic and the stars in the ancient and late antique world.* University Park, PA: University of Pennsylvania Press.

Obbink, Dirk. 2003. Allegory and exegesis in the Derveni Papyrus: The origins of Greek scholarship. In *Metaphor, allegory and the Classical tradition*, ed. Boys-Stones, 178–88.

Ogden, Daniel, ed. 2007. *A companion to Greek religion.* Oxford and New York: Oxford University Press.

Ohly, Dieter. 1953. Die Göttin und ihre Basis. *MDAI(A)* 68: 25–50.

Ostwald, Martin. 1986. *From popular sovereignty to the sovereignty of law: Law, society, and politics in fifth-century Athens.* Berkeley and Los Angeles: University of California Press.

Papalexandrou, Nassos and Athanasius Christou Papalexandrou. 2005. *The visual poetics of power: Warriors, youths, and tripods in Early Greece.* Lanham, MD: Lexington Books.

Parke, H. W. 1967. *The oracles of Zeus: Dodona, Olympia, Ammon.* Cambridge: Harvard University Press.

Parker, Robert. 1996. *Athenian religion: A history.* Oxford and New York: Oxford University Press.

Parker, Robert. 2005. *Polytheism and society at Athens.* Oxford and New York: Oxford University Press.

Parker, Robert. 2011. *On Greek religion.* Ithaca and London: Cornell University Press.

Paul, Stéphanie. 2013. *Cultes et sanctuaires de l'île de Cos.* Liège: Centre International d'Étude de la Religion Grecque Antique.

Pfeiffer, Rudolph, ed. 1949. *Callimachus.* 2 Vols. Oxford: Clarendon Press.

Pfeiffer, Stefan. 2008. The god Serapis, his cult and the beginnings of ruler cult in Ptolemaic Egypt. In *Ptolemy II Philadelphus and his world*, ed. McKechnie and Guillaume, 387–408.

Pilz, Oliver. 2011. The performative aspect of Greek ritual. In *Current approaches to religion in ancient Greece*, ed. Haysom and Wallensten, 151–67.

Polinskaya, Irene. 2013. *A local history of Greek polytheism: Gods, people and the land of Aigina, 800–400 BCE.* Leiden and Boston: Brill.

Porta, Fred R. 1999. *Greek ritual utterances and the liturgical style.* Dissertation, Harvard University.

Prent, Mieke. 2005. *Cretan sanctuaries and cults: Continuity and change from Late Minoan IIIC to the Archaic period.* Boston and Leiden: Brill.

Prescendi, Francesca. 2010. Children and the transmission of religious knowledge. In *Children, memory and family identity in Roman culture*, ed. Dasen and Späth, 73–93.

Rawlings, Louis and Hugh Bowden, eds. 2005. *Herakles and Hercules: Exploring a Graeco-Roman divinity.* Swansea and Oakville, CT: The Classical Press of Wales.

Reed, Jonathan and Joseph Brodd, eds. 2011. *Rome and religion: A cross-disciplinary dialogue on the imperial cult.* Atlanta, GA: Society of Biblical Literature.

Renberg, Gil and William S. Bubelis. 2011. The epistolary rhetoric of Zoilos of Aspendos and the early cult of Sarapis: Re-reading P. Cair.Zen. I 59034. *ZPE* 177: 169–200.

Rigsby, Kent J. 2001. Founding a Sarapeum. *GRBS* 42 (1): 117–24.

Rogers, Guy Maclean. 2012. *The mysteries of Artemis of Ephesus: Cult, polis and change in the Graeco-Roman world.* New Haven: Yale University Press.

Romano, Irene B. 1980. *Early Greek cult images.* Dissertation, University of Pennsylvania.

Rösch, Petra and Udo Simon, eds. 2012. *How purity is made*. Wiesbaden: Harrassowitz Verlag.

Rubin, David C. 1995. *Memory in oral traditions: The cognitive psychology of epic, ballads, and counting-out rhymes*. Oxford and New York: Oxford University Press.

Rudhardt, Jean. 1988. Mnémosyne et les Muses. In *La mémoire des religions*, ed. Borgeaud, 37–62.

Rüpke, Jörg, ed. 2007. *A companion to Roman religion*. Malden, MA, and Oxford: Blackwell.

Rutherford, Ian. 2001. *Pindar's paeans: A reading of the fragments with a survey of the genre*. Oxford: Oxford University Press.

Rutherford, Ian. 2009. Network theory and theoric networks. In *Greek and Roman networks*, ed. Malkin, Constantakopoulou and Panagopoulou, 24–38.

Schachter, Albert, ed. 1992. *Le sanctuaire grec*. Geneva: Fondation Hardt.

Schmidt, Stefan. 2005. Serapis – ein neuer Gott für die Griechen in Ägypten. In *Ägypten, Griechenland, Rom*, ed. Beck, Bol and Bückling, 291–304.

Schnapp-Gourbeillon, Annie. 2002. *Aux origines de la Grèce : XIIIe–VIIIe siècles avant notre ère, la genèse du politique*. Paris: Les Belles Lettres.

Schwertheim, Elmar and Engelbert Winter, eds. 2003. *Stadt und Stadtentwicklung in Kleinasien*. Bonn: Dr. Rudolf Habelt GMBH.

Scullion, Scott. 1994. Olympian and chthonian. *ClAnt* 13 (1): 75–119.

Shapiro, H. A. 1989. *Art and cult under the tyrants in Athens*. Mainz: Von Zabern.

Shaw, Rosalind and Charles Stewart, eds. 1994. *Syncretism/Anti-syncretism: The politics of religious synthesis*. New York and London: Routledge.

Shipley, Graham. 2000. *The Greek world after Alexander, 323–30 B.C.* London and New York: Routledge.

Snodgrass, Anthony. 1980. *Archaic Greece: The age of experiment*. Berkeley: University of California Press.

Snodgrass, Anthony. 2006. *Archaeology and the emergence of Greece: Collected papers on early Greece and related topics*. Edinburgh: Edinburgh University Press.

Spaeth, Barbette. 2011. Imperial cult in Roman Corinth: A response to "The cult of the Roman emperor: Uniter or divider" by Karl Galinsky. In *Rome and Religion*, ed. Reed and Brodd, 61–82.

Sperber, Dan. 1985. Anthropology and psychology: Towards an epidemiology of representations. *Man* (New Series) 20 (1): 73–89.

Sperber, Dan. 1994. The modularity of thought and the epidemiology of representations. In *Mapping the mind*, ed. Hirschfeld and Gelman, 39–67.

Sperber, Dan. 1996. *Explaining culture: A naturalistic approach*. Oxford: Blackwell.

Sperber, Dan and Deirdre Wilson. 1995. *Relevance: Communication and cognition*. Second edition. Cambridge, MA: Blackwell.

Stafford, Emma. 2000. *Worshipping virtues: Personification and the divine in ancient Greece*. London and Swansea: Duckworth and The Classical Press of Wales.

Stafford, Emma. 2007. Personification in Greek religious thought and practice. In *A companion to Greek religion*, ed. Ogden, 71–85.

Stafford, Emma. 2010. Herakles between gods and heroes. In *The gods of ancient Greece*, ed. Bremmer and Erskine, 228–69.

Stafford, Emma. 2012. *Herakles*. Abingdon and New York: Routledge.

Stambaugh, John. 1972. *Sarapis under the early Ptolemies*. Leiden: Brill.

Stavrianapoulou, Eftychia, ed. 2006. *Ritual and communication in the Graeco-Roman world*. Liège: Centre International d'Étude de la Religion Grecque Antique.

Stavrianopoulou, Eftychia. 2011. The role of tradition in the forming of rituals in ancient Greece. In *Ritual dynamics*, ed. Chaniotis, 85–103.

Stavrianapoulou, Eftychia, ed. 2013. *Shifting social imaginaries in the Hellenistic period: Narrations, practices and images*. Leiden and Boston: Brill.

Stephens, Susan. 2010. Ptolemaic Alexandria. In *A companion to Hellenistic literature*, ed. Clauss and Cuypers, 46–61.

Suk Fong Jim, Theodora. 2014. *Sharing with the gods: Aparchai and dekatai in ancient Greece*. Oxford: Oxford University Press.

Świderek, A. 1975. Sarapis et les Hellénomemphites. In *Le monde grec*, ed. Bingen, 670–75.

Szpakowska, Kasia. 2003. The open portal: Dreams and divine power in Pharaonic Egypt. In *Prayer, magic and the stars*, ed. Noegel, Walker and Wheeler, 111–24.

Thomas, Rosalind. 1989. *Oral tradition and written record in Classical Athens*. Cambridge and New York: Cambridge University Press.

Thomas, Rosalind. 1992. *Literacy and orality in ancient Greece*. Cambridge and New York: Cambridge University Press.

Thompson, Dorothy J. 2012. *Memphis under the Ptolemies*. Second edition. Princeton, NJ: Princeton University Press.

Tod, Marcus N. 1942. A bilingual dedication from Alexandria. *The Journal of Egyptian Archaeology* 28: 53–6.

Tsetskhladze, Gocha R., ed. 2006. *Greek colonisation: An account of Greek colonies and other settlements overseas*. 2 Vols. Leiden and Boston: Brill.

Vanschoonwinkel, Jacques. 2006. Greek migrations to Aegean Anatolia in the early Dark Age. In *Greek colonisation*, ed. Tsetskhladze, 115–41.

Vansina, Jan. 1985. *Oral tradition as history*. Madison and Oxford: University of Wisconsin Press.

van Straten, Folkert T. 1992. Votives and votaries in Greek sanctuaries. In *Le sanctuaire grec*, ed. Schachter, 247–90.

van Straten, Folkert T. 1995. *Hiera kala: Images of animal sacrifice in archaic and classical Greece*. Leiden and New York: Brill.

van Wonterghem, Frank. 1992. Il culto di Ercole fra i popoli osco-sabellici. In *Héraclès d'une rive à l'autre*, ed. Bonnet and Jourdain-Annequin, 319–51.

van Wonterghem, Frank. 1998. Hercule et les troupeaux en Italie centrale: Une nouvelle mise au point. In *Le bestiaire d'Héraclès*, ed. Bonnet, Jourdain-Annequin and Pirenne-Delforge, 241–55, plates 26–33.

Versnel, Henk S. 1990. *Inconsistencies in Greek and Roman religion I. Ter unus: Isis, Dionysos, Hermes. Three studies in henotheism*. Leiden and New York: Brill.

Versnel, Henk S. 2011. *Coping with the gods: Wayward readings in Greek theology*. Leiden: Brill.

Vidman, L. 1969. *Sylloge inscriptionum religionis isiacae et sarapiacae*. Berlin: de Gruyter.

Vidman, L. 1970. *Isis und Sarapis bei den Griechen und Römern: Epigraphische Studie zur Verbreitung und zu den Trägern des ägyptischen Kultes*. Berlin: de Gruyter.

Volkommer, Rainer. 1988. *Herakles in the art of Classical Greece*. Oxford: Oxford University Committee for Archaeology.

von Ehrenheim, Hedvig. 2011. *Greek incubation rituals in Classical and Hellenistic times*. Dissertation, Stockholm University.

Wallace, Saro. 2003. The perpetuated past: Re-use or continuity in material culture and the structuring of identity in Early Iron Age Crete. *ABSA* 98: 251–77.

Watts, Duncan J. 1999. *Small worlds: The dynamics of network between order and randomness*. Princeton: Princeton University Press.

Welles, C. B. 1962. The discovery of Sarapis and the foundation of Alexandria. *Historia* 11: 271–98.

Whitehouse, Harvey. 2004. *Modes of religiosity: A cognitive theory of religious transmission*. Walnut Creek, CA, Lanham, MD and New York: Altamira Press.

Whitehouse, Harvey and Luther H. Martin, eds. 2004. *Theorizing religions past: Archaeology, history, and cognition*. Walnut Creek, CA: Altamira Press.

Wilcken, Ulrich. 1927. *Urkunden der Ptolemäerzeit (ältere Funde)*. Volume 1. Berlin: de Gruyter.

Woodford, Susan. 1971. Some cults of Herakles in Attica. In *Studies presented to George M. A. Hanfmann*, ed. Mitten, Pedley and Scott, 211–25.

Woodford, Susan. 1976. Herakles Alexikakos reviewed. *AJA* 80 (3): 291–4, Pl. 55.

Yates, Francis. 1966. *The art of memory*. Chicago: University of Chicago Press.

Yon, Marguerite. 1992. Héraclès à Chypre. In *Héraclès d'une rive à l'autre*, ed. Bonnet and Jourdain-Annequin, 145–63.

Yunis, Harvey, ed. 2003. *Written texts and the rise of literate culture in ancient Greece*. Cambridge and New York: Cambridge University Press.

# Glossary of terms used in the cognitive science of religion

I hope that this glossary will assist readers not only with this book but also in approaching the works on CSR cited in the bibliography. Note, however, that there is terminological variation in the literature. For example, in this book I use the term "mental tool" while other authors may speak of mental "modules" or "systems."

**Action representation system** A mental tool which functions to permit awareness of one's own agency (e.g. that my physical movement results from my intent to move) and that of other beings. Closely related to theory of mind.

**Agency** Ability to act in the world, on people or things. In this book the term is almost always shorthand for intentional agency (either human or superhuman), though agents may also include nonhuman animals with varying degrees of humanlike intent.

**Agency detection** The inference that changes in one's environment result from an intentional agent other than oneself. See also hyperactive agency detection.

**Cognitive architecture** The aggregate of mental tools in an individual mind-brain.

**Cognitive science** The interdisciplinary study of the mind and thought.

**Compelling** Producing consequences, such as emotional or physiological arousal, that exceed the mere focusing of attention. Some authors also use "compelling" to describe beliefs which are resistant to change. See also salient.

**Confirmation bias** The selection, recall or interpreting of evidence in ways that favor existing beliefs. For example, people tend to "test" a hypothesis they favor by searching for evidence supporting it, not evidence against it.

**Constraints, cognitive** Limits on the content and manner of human thought that arise from the properties of our mental tools. For example, there are limits on how much information we can memorize in a brief period, and how many tasks we can attend to at once.

**Counterintuitive concept** A concept which violates intuitive beliefs, particularly those pertaining to intuitive ontological categories (e.g. an invisible person). See also minimally counterintuitive concept.

**Declarative memory** See memory.

**Disposition** A cognitive tendency or bias, such as the tendency toward hyperactive agency detection, which has been positively selected for in the process of biological evolution. See also susceptibility.

**Dual-process theory** A theoretical model widely used in cognitive and other branches of psychology to distinguish between fast, automatic, emotive, verbally implicit mental processes/beliefs and slow, effortful, more easily changed, verbally explicit ones. In this book I use the terms "intuitive" and "reflective" to refer to these mental processes and the resulting beliefs.

**Episodic memory** See memory.

**Evocation** According to Dan Sperber, the process of memory searching which supports symbolic thought. See also symbolic thought.

**Folk biology** A domain-specific mental tool which generates intuitive inferences about living kinds – for example, the belief that a cat belongs to a different ontological category from a tulip, or the belief that a mother cat will give birth to kittens rather than puppies.

**Folk physics** A domain-specific mental tool which generates inferences about the physical properties of the environment – for example, the belief that an arrow hitting a wall will not pass through the wall, or the belief that water will spill from a glass if it is knocked over.

**HAD** See hyperactive agency detection.

**Hazard-precaution system** A mental tool which functions to help people avoid threats in the environment, including predators, pathogens and contaminants.

**Hyperactive agency detection (HAD)** The cognitive disposition to over-attribute intentional agency when evaluating stimuli. A "hyperactive agency detection device" (HADD) has been proposed as a mental tool. See also agency, agency detection.

**Inference** A conclusion reached on the basis of an individual's existing knowledge and perceptions. Inferences may be intuitive or reflective.

**Inferential potential** The likelihood that a given concept will activate mental tools and generate inferences. Agentive concepts tend to have more inferential potential than non-agentive ones (e.g. ghosts who cause illness vs. ghosts who are green).

**Intuitive belief** (1) A belief, usually implicit and unspoken, which is automatically generated by domain-specific mental tools. Examples of domains include ontological categorization (e.g. artifact, living thing, animal, person), folk physics and biology, and theory of mind. "Natural" intuitive beliefs develop spontaneously; that is, they are not acquired through teaching or cultural osmosis. (2) An initially reflective belief which becomes so ingrained that it seems self-evident (feels like "second nature") and operates in the same way as beliefs described under (1). Some intuitive beliefs are unconscious while others are accessible to the mind (typically as "common sense"). See Chapter 1.

**Intuitive cognition** Thought characterized by automaticity, speed and implicitness. Sometimes called nonreflective thought. Intuitive cognition is unconscious in that we are not aware of its operation, as we are aware of reflective cognition. Intuitive cognition may result (1) from the functioning of "first-order" mental tools, such as face recognition or folk biology, or (2) from acquired expertise, as in a skilled musical performance, or automatically knowing that switch A on the wall controls light B.

**MCI** See minimally counterintuitive concept.

**Memory** The process of mentally storing and retrieving information. Human long-term memory may be divided into two principal types. (1) Procedural memory (for skills such as riding a bicycle) is an implicit form of memory, meaning that it is not consciously recalled. (2) Declarative memory (for mental representations such as the appearance of a specific bicycle) is an explicit form of memory, meaning that it is consciously recalled. Declarative memory may be further divided into the episodic (memory for events one has experienced, such as a bicycle accident) and the semantic (memory for knowledge about the world, such as the brand of bicycle one owns). See Chapters 4 and 6.

**Mental tool** A module (or system of modules) in the mind which enables a specific cognitive ability, such as agency detection, episodic memory, theory of mind or metarepresentation. Like structures in the body, mental tools are the result of natural selection. "First-order" mental tools are those concerned with perceptual input, the representation of basic concepts and categories and many other fundamentals of survival. "Second-order" mental tools (e.g. metarepresentation and theory of mind) manipulate the basic concepts generated by "first-order" tools.

**Metarepresentation** A thought about another thought. The ability to metarepresent is the mental tool that enables reflective cognition. For example, "The dog is friendly" involves not only the concept DOG but also a representation about it. Metarepresentational tasks vary in difficulty; for example, "Henry is afraid that his parents believe that his dog is vicious" involves three levels of metarepresentation. Some researchers prefer to limit the term "metarepresentation" to cases of awareness that one's representations are representations, and that *mis*representation is therefore possible. This includes the ability to attribute mistaken beliefs to others ("Jean is wrong to think *that the keys are in the car*").

**Minimally counterintuitive concept (MCI)** A concept which violates one or more intuitive beliefs (e.g. a pig that flies) without overloading conceptual or memory capacities. Minimal counterintuitiveness makes concepts memorable, while too many violations render a concept excessively (rather than minimally) counterintuitive and less easy to remember. Other properties of a concept, such as its inferential potential and its epistemic value (apparent falseness or truth), may also be factors in memorability.

**Modes of religiosity theory** The theory, proposed by Harvey Whitehouse, that religious systems are drawn toward two principal "attractor" positions distinguished by differing levels of ritual frequency and emotional intensity, and encoded in different systems of memory. See Chapter 4.

**Pattern recognition** The mental tool that permits us to recognize patterns even if they are incomplete (e.g. in a puzzle requiring a child to "connect the dots").

**Procedural memory** See memory.

**Reflective belief** A belief, usually explicit and amenable to verbalization, that is generated through metarepresentation. Most beliefs which we are aware of holding are reflective.

**Reflective cognition** Thought characterized by slowness, effort and explicitness (all relative to intuitive cognition). Reflective cognition functions via metarepresentation. Compared to nonhuman animals, humans are "massive users" of metarepresentation and reflective cognition, though there is evidence that the great apes possess limited reflective abilities.

**Relevance** With respect to representations, the property of simultaneously producing the greatest cognitive effect at the lowest cognitive cost (mental effort). The process of transmission exerts selective pressure in favor of relevant representations. Factors contributing to relevance will be near-universal in some respects (e.g. the low relevance of a random string of ten digits) and in others unique to the individual (e.g. the high relevance of a winning lottery number). See Essay 6.2.

**Representation** (1) A simple mental object (thought, idea, concept) which stands for something else (e.g. the idea of an apple). (2) A simple public object or sound pattern which stands for something else (e.g. a picture of an apple, the word "apple" either written or spoken). (3) A complex object, mental or public, constructed from (1) or (2) through metarepresentation.

**Ritual form theory** The theory, proposed by McCauley and Lawson, that properties of rituals (e.g. frequency of performance and emotionality) are determined by the action roles of the superhuman agent(s) and human participant(s) in the ritual. See Chapter 4.

**Salient** Attention-capturing. Cognitively salient phenomena and concepts are those that activate mental tools such as facial recognition or pattern recognition, with the result that we focus on them instead of the myriad other stimuli in the environment. See also compelling.

**Semantic memory** See memory.

**Simulation hypothesis** The suggestion that we attribute mental states to others by representing how we would react under the same conditions. This is one of the explanations of the mechanism underlying theory of mind. A version of the simulation hypothesis was applied by Jesse Bering in his studies of afterlife beliefs (Chapter 5).

**Susceptibility** A cognitive tendency or bias which is a side effect of a disposition. We are *disposed* to prefer sweet foods as a result of natural selection, and have a *susceptibility* to overconsumption of sugar as a result. See also disposition.

**Symbolic thought** According to Dan Sperber, a type of metarepresentation based on incomplete understanding of one or more of the concepts involved. Symbolic thought is rational and is essential to learning. See Chapter 2.

**Theological correctness** The tendency for people to use more difficult and abstract religious concepts when in situations that permit time and space to reflect (e.g. "God is omniscient"), and to fall back on more concrete and intuitive religious concepts in situations where their attention is divided and/or they need to perform a task quickly (e.g. "God thinks about one thing at a time"). Related to this is the finding that people's explicit statements about their beliefs often do not match their implicit theoretical knowledge.

**Theory of mind** The mental tool that permits us to attribute mental states (e.g. beliefs, desires, emotions, intentions and memories) to other beings. Sometimes abbreviated as TOM, theory of mind requires at least a minimal ability to metarepresent ("James feels sad") and may function intuitively or reflectively, depending on the difficulty of the task. More advanced TOM permits several orders of metarepresentation ("Louise noticed that Terry suspects that James feels guilty") as well as the attribution of false beliefs to others.

# The cognitive science of religion

## A bibliographical essay

CSR is an emergent, interdisciplinary field drawing upon cognitive psychology, evolutionary theory, anthropology, philosophy and religion studies. General introductions abound; those I have found most useful include Boyer 1994, 2001; Pyysiäinnen 2003; Barrett 2004 and 2011b; and Tremlin 2006. The groundwork for CSR was laid in the 1970s and 1980s by Stewart Guthrie and Dan Sperber, both anthropologists. Guthrie's article "A Cognitive Theory of Religion" (1980) focused on anthropomorphism, defining religion as "the systematic application of human-like models to non-human, in addition to human, phenomena," while Sperber outlined a cognitive approach to symbolic thought (1974, 1982, 1985b) and established a philosophical basis for a "naturalistic" theory of religion compatible with evolutionary biology (1985a). Both men shared the fundamental insight that religious beliefs arise in connection with the normal operation of human cognitive structures shaped by natural selection. Meanwhile, the rapid development of computing and artificial intelligence offered new metaphors, models and experimental avenues for the investigation of cognition. During the 1980s, cognitive psychologists developed and fine-tuned many of the building blocks of CSR: dual-process theory (Evans 1984), a detailed account of the way human memory works (e.g. Tulving 1983) and the key concept of "theory of mind" (e.g. Baron-Cohen, Leslie and Frith 1985). Finally, cognitivists challenged the prevailing idea that humans are equipped with a general set of reasoning abilities which we apply to any task. Instead, many aspects of human cognition, such as the use of language, appear to be modular and domain-specific (Chomsky 1988).

CSR was born during the early 1990s with a critical mass of books applying various aspects of cognitive theory to religion. In 1990, Robert McCauley and E. Thomas Lawson published *Rethinking Religion: Connecting Cognition and Culture*. The year 1993 saw Stewart Guthrie's *Faces in the Clouds: A New Theory of Religion*, followed in 1994 by Pascal Boyer's *The Naturalness of Religious Ideas: A Cognitive Theory of Religion*. Harvey Whitehouse's *Inside the Cult: Religious Innovation and Transmission in Papua New Guinea* appeared in 1995. The next year, a conference on "Cognition, Culture and Religion" took place at Western Michigan University, with attendees including Boyer, Lawson, McCauley and Whitehouse. Boyer would go on to write an important synthesis of CSR with the ambitious title *Religion Explained: The Evolutionary Origins of Religious*

*Thought* (2001), while the latter three formulated theories of ritual discussed in my Chapter 4 (McCauley and Lawson 2002; Whitehouse 2000, 2004). Also in attendance was Justin Barrett, who has acted as midwife to and chronicler of the infant discipline. For this essay, I have drawn liberally upon his account of the birth of CSR (Barrett 2011a), which I highly recommend as a summary of its fundamentals. In addition to generating a substantial body of experimental research specific to CSR, Barrett has set an agenda for the field by identifying testable hypotheses in colleagues' theories, and by pointing the way to future studies (e.g. Barrett and Lawson 2001; Malley and Barret 2003). He introduced the useful term "theological correctness" (Barrett 1999); I have also adopted his coinage "mental tools" to describe the varied, extracultural systems which make up the "software" of the human mind-brain (Barrett 2004).

Important in CSR is the idea that within the "massively modular mind," domain-specific mental tools generate content which is relatively invariable across cultures. That is, people the world over possess an extracultural, intuitive grasp of language, folk psychology (theory of mind), folk biology (properties of living kinds), folk physics (properties of midsize objects, the states of matter, etc.) and social interaction, including intuitive moral concepts (for summaries with bibliography see Sperber and Hirschfeld 2004.41; Barrett 2011b.58–95). These mental tools contribute in various ways to religious beliefs and behaviors (as when minimally counterintuitive concepts disproportionately attract and hold our attention). Additionally, we possess tools which function as safeguards in dangerous environments. Examples include hyperactive agency detection (Guthrie 1993; Barrett 2000), which seems to play a key role in the establishment of new cults, and the hazard-precaution system (Liénard and Boyer 2006), which is deeply implicated in ritual behavior. Most religious rituals possess structural properties shaped by the mental tools we use to represent agency (Lisdorf 2007; McCauley and Lawson 2002), but many rituals also include magical components, which arise from intuitions (as in the "law of contamination/contagion") about non-agentive causes and effects (Rozin, Millman and Nemeroff 1986; Rozin, Haidt and McCauley 1999; Nemeroff and Rozin 2000; etc.). A mental tool underlying the magical "law of similarity" has not yet been clearly identified, but the pervasive, worldwide existence of belief in the law's efficacy points to a causal explanation in extracultural, intuitive cognition.

The existence of these mental tools helps to explain cross-cultural patterns in religion (and the recurrence of similar beliefs and behaviors separated by many centuries and cultural upheavals). CSR does not explain the variables that occur within the parameters set up by our mental tools; these are the result of the historical contingencies of culture, physical environment and individual agency. On the other hand, the impact of the constraints, the canals into which variables of culture and history are poured, may extend beyond general patterns to illuminate certain details, something I have attempted to demonstrate in this book. In order to give an adequate account of any religion, we must study both the patterns and the variables. Despite a certain amount of polemic in the rejection of what has come to be called "the standard social science model" there is general agreement among the pioneers of CSR that both humanistic and scientific investigations are essential to the study of religion, and that only when these interact do we increase our knowledge (McCauley and Lawson 1990.2; Whitehouse 2007).

Memory and transmission are central concerns of CSR. One of Boyer's important contributions has been the theory that minimally counterintuitive concepts (MCIs) are more memorable than others and therefore more likely to be transmitted. Since he first formulated this theory (Boyer 1994), it has been tested and modified. For example, experimental evidence suggests that the inferential potential of MCIs is an important factor in transmission. Take the example of "a potato that eats people" (high inferential potential) versus "a potato with no spatial location" (low inferential potential). Both are minimally counterintuitive concepts, but the former is presumably more likely to be transmitted than the latter because it generates more thoughts in people's heads. Other factors may include the epistemic incongruity of a given concept (whether it strikes us as false or true) and, interestingly enough, the age of the individual exposed to the concept (Gregory and Barrett 2009). The question of "cognitive optima" for transmission will continue to be debated, and will be especially important for the study of orally transmitted content.

More detailed investigations focusing on cultural specifics are essential if we ever hope to see how Sperber's "epidemiology of representations" works in practice (Sperber 1985a, 1994, 1996). Together with contingencies of the environment, properties of human minds, such as the mechanics of memory, have important roles to play in determining which representations are passed on and in what form. Memory aids like inscriptions and books complicate the picture, but they do not erase the selective effects of our cognitive susceptibilities; some texts are read and reproduced far more than others in part because they "activate" intuitive systems – even as they generate emotions or engage our capacity for reflective reasoning. Central to the understanding of cultural transmission is Sperber and Wilson's (1995) concept of "relevance," the idea that the representations most likely to be selected for transmission are those which offer higher inferential potential at a lower cognitive cost. Despite the problems created by gaps in our sources, the ancient Mediterranean offers a rare opportunity to investigate the transmission of representations both horizontally across divergent cultures, and vertically through multiple centuries.

According to Barrett (2011a), the chief impetus for CSR came from religion scholars who wanted to "science up" the study of religion. Like those of any scientific enterprise, the theoretical assumptions of CSR will require modification in coming years as hypotheses are tested and ethnographic and historical data are applied. Although basic cognitivist theories, such as the existence of "folk biology," are supported by robust layers of developmental, neurocognitive and cross-cultural evidence, the same is not yet true for many hypotheses specific to CSR. In many cases, the experimental data are still limited to developmental studies with children or involve only subjects from Western cultures. Emma Cohen (2007) and Rita Astuti (2001, 2007a, 2007b), however, have both conducted fieldwork with non-Western people, and Astuti's work is particularly important because she applied experimental methods in an ethnographic context. Anthropologists disagree on the future scope of CSR within their discipline. An evenhanded presentation of the debate is the introduction to *Religion, Anthropology and Cognitive Science* (Whitehouse and Laidlaw eds. 2007), in which Laidlaw suggests that while CSR can shed light on many aspects of religion, such as ghosts, gods and magic, it will never be able to explain the particularities of religious practices in their cultural contexts, and has little to offer concerning the self-conscious and reflective aspects of religion. Whitehouse, on the other hand, expects that CSR will ultimately generate methods for studying cultural variation as the product of interaction between minds and highly complex environments, and that awareness of the dynamic between explicit and implicit cognition in the transmission of religious systems will be essential in future investigations of religion.

As I write, CSR continues to generate interest across disciplines, and a number of new journals have been founded in order to provide forums for cognitivist scholarship. The *Journal for the Cognitive Science of Religion* is the official publication of the International Association for the Cognitive Science of Religion, established in 2006. The *Journal of Cognition and Culture*, edited by E. Thomas Lawson and Pascal Boyer since 2001, accepts papers devoted to "the mental foundations of culture and the cultural foundations of mental life." The *Journal of Cognitive Historiography*, edited by Classicist Esther Eidinow and historian Luther H. Martin, was established in 2014. Several scholarly centers have also been founded, including the Institute of Cognition and Culture at Queen's University, Belfast; the Religion, Cognition and Culture unit in the Religion Department at Aarhus University, and the Centre for Anthropology and Mind at the University of Oxford.

## References


Astuti, Rita. 2001. Are we all natural dualists? A cognitive developmental approach. *Journal of the Royal Anthropological Institute* 7 (3): 429–47.

Astuti, Rita. 2007a. Ancestors and the afterlife. In *Religion, anthropology and cognitive science*, ed. Whitehouse and Laidlaw, 161–78.

Astuti, Rita. 2007b. What happens after death? In *Questions of anthropology*, ed. Astuti, Parry and Stafford, 227–48.

Astuti, Rita, J. P. Parry and C. Stafford, eds. 2007. *Questions of anthropology*. New York: Berg.

Baron-Cohen, Simon, Alan M. Leslie and Uta Frith. 1985. Does the autistic child have a theory of mind? *Cognition* 21: 37–46.

Barrett, Justin L. 1999. Theological correctness: Cognitive constraint and the study of religion. *Method and Theory in the Study of Religion*. 11: 325–39.

Barrett, Justin L. 2000. Exploring the natural foundations of religion. *Trends in Cognitive Sciences* 4 (1): 29–34.

Barrett, Justin L. 2004. *Why would anyone believe in God?* Walnut Creek, CA: Altamira Press.

Barrett, Justin L. 2011a. Cognitive science of religion: Looking back, looking forward. *Journal for the Scientific Study of Religion* 50 (2): 229–39.

Barrett, Justin L. 2011b. *Cognitive science, religion and theology: From human minds to divine minds*. West Conshohocken, PA: Templeton Press.

Barrett, Justin L. and E. Thomas Lawson. 2001. Ritual intuitions: Cognitive contributions to judgments of ritual efficacy. *Journal of Cognition and Culture*. 1 (2): 183–201.

Boyer, Pascal. 1994. *The naturalness of religious ideas: A cognitive theory of religion*. Berkeley and Los Angeles: University of California Press.

Boyer, Pascal. 2001. *Religion explained: The evolutionary origins of religious thought*. New York: Basic Books.

Chomsky, Noam. 1988. *Language and problems of knowledge*. Cambridge, MA: MIT Press.

Cohen, Emma. 2007. *The mind possessed: The cognition of spirit possession in an Afro-Brazilian religious tradition*. Oxford and New York: Oxford University Press.

Evans, Jonathan. 1984. Heuristic and analytic processes in reasoning. *British Journal of Psychology* 75: 451–68.

Gregory, Justin P. and Justin L. Barrett. 2009. Epistemology and counterintuitiveness: Role and relationship in epidemiology of cultural representations. *Journal of Cognition and Culture* 9 (3): 289–314.

Guthrie, Stewart E. 1980. A cognitive theory of religion. *Current Anthropology* 21 (2): 181–203.

Guthrie, Stewart E. 1993. *Faces in the clouds: A new theory of religion*. Oxford: Oxford University Press.

Liénard, Pierre and Pascal Boyer. 2006. Whence collective rituals? A cultural selection model of ritualized behavior. *American Anthropologist* 108 (4): 814–27.

Lisdorf, Anders. 2007. *The dissemination of divination in Roman Republican times – A cognitive approach*. PhD Dissertation, University of Copenhagen.

Malley, Brian and Justin Barrett. 2003. Can ritual form be predicted from religious belief? A test of the Lawson-McCauley hypotheses. *Journal of Ritual Studies*. 17 (2): 1–14.

McCauley, Robert N. and E. Thomas Lawson. 1990. *Rethinking religion: Connecting cognition and culture*. Cambridge and New York: Cambridge University Press.

McCauley, Robert N. and E. Thomas Lawson. 2002. *Bringing ritual to mind: Psychological foundations of cultural forms*. Cambridge and New York: Cambridge University Press.

Nemeroff, Carol and Paul Rozin. 2000. The makings of the magical mind: The nature and function of sympathetic magical thinking. In *Imagining the impossible*, ed. Rosengren, Johnson and Harris, 1–34.

Pyysiäinen, Illka. 2003. *How religion works: Toward a new cognitive science of religion*. Leiden: Brill.

Rosengren, Karl S., Carl N. Johnson and Paul L. Harris, eds. 2000. *Imagining the impossible: Magical, scientific and religious thinking in children*. Cambridge and New York: Cambridge University Press.

Rozin, Paul, Jonathan Haidt and Clark R. McCauley. 1999. Disgust: The body and soul emotion. In *Handbook of cognition and emotion*, ed. Dalgleish and Power, 429–45.

Rozin, Paul, L. Millman and Carol Nemeroff. 1986. Operation of the laws of sympathetic magic in disgust and other domains. *Journal of personality and social psychology* 50: 703–12.

Sperber, Dan. 1974. *Rethinking symbolism*. Tr. Alice L. Morton. Cambridge: Cambridge University Press.

Sperber, Dan. 1982. Is symbolic thought prerational? In *Between belief and transgression*, ed. Izard and Smith, 245–64.

Sperber, Dan. 1985a. Anthropology and psychology: Towards an epidemiology of representations. *Man* (New Series) 20 (1): 73–89.

Sperber, Dan. 1985b. *On anthropological knowledge: Three essays*. Cambridge and London: Cambridge University Press.

Sperber, Dan. 1994. The modularity of thought and the epidemiology of representations. In *Mapping the mind*, ed. Hirschfeld and Gelman, 39–67.

Sperber, Dan. 1996. *Explaining culture: A naturalistic approach*. Oxford: Blackwell.

Sperber, Dan and Lawrence A. Hirschfeld. 2004. The cognitive foundations of cultural stability and diversity. *Trends in Cognitive Sciences* 8 (1): 40–6.

Sperber, Dan and Deirdre Wilson. 1995. *Relevance: Communication and cognition*. Second edition. Cambridge, MA: Blackwell.

Tremlin, Todd. 2006. *Minds and gods: The cognitive foundation of religion*. Oxford and New York: Oxford University Press.

Tulving, Endel. 1983. *Elements of episodic memory*. Oxford: Clarendon Press.

Whitehouse, Harvey. 1995. *Inside the cult: Religious innovation and transmission in Papua New Guinea*. Oxford: Clarendon Press.

Whitehouse, Harvey. 2000. *Arguments and icons: Divergent modes of religiosity*. Oxford: Clarendon Press.

Whitehouse, Harvey. 2004. *Modes of religiosity: A cognitive theory of religious transmission*. Walnut Creek, CA, Lanham, MD and New York: Altamira Press.

Whitehouse, Harvey. 2007. Towards an integration of ethnography, history and the cognitive science of religion. In *Religion, anthropology and cognitive science*, ed. Whitehouse and Laidlaw, 247–80.

Whitehouse, Harvey and James Laidlaw, eds. 2007. *Religion, anthropology and cognitive science*. Durham, NC: Carolina Academic Press.

# Index

*Note:* References to illustrations are given in italics; references to tables are given in bold.